DRUG ADDICTION
AND ITS TREATMENT

NEXUS OF NEUROSCIENCE
AND BEHAVIOR

Drug Addiction and its Treatment

Nexus of Neuroscience and Behavior

Editors

Bankole A. Johnson, M.D., Ph.D.

and

John D. Roache, Ph.D.

Department of Psychiatry and Behavioral Sciences
University of Texas Mental Sciences Institute
University of Texas-Houston Health Science Center
Houston, Texas

Lippincott - Raven
PUBLISHERS
Philadelphia • New York

Acquisitions Editor: Mark Placito
Developmental Editor: Mattie Bialer
Manufacturing Manager: Dennis Teston
Production Manager: Lawrence Bernstein
Production Editor: Mary Antoniette V. Manaois
Cover Designer: Ed Schultheiz
Indexer: Jayne Percy
Compositor: Lippincott-Raven Electronic Production
Printer: Maple Press

Printed in the United States of America

9 8 7 6 5 4 3 2 1

Library of Congress Cataloging-in-Publication Data

Drug addiction and its treatment : nexus of neuroscience and behavior
  / editors, Bankole A. Johnson and John D. Roache.
    p.   cm.
  Includes bibliographical references and index.
  ISBN 0-397-51764-5
  1. Drug abuse—Treatment. 2. Drug abuse—Physiological aspects.
I. Johnson, Bankole A. II. Roache, John D.
  [DNLM: 1. Substance Dependence—therapy. 2. Behavior, Addictive.
3. Neuroscience—methods.   WM 270 D793447 1997]
RC564.D778   1997
616.86′06—dc20
DNLM/DLC
For Library of Congress

For Lyn and Efun Johnson

For Ann, Daniel, and David Roache
and
Thanking God for the lives of Russell F. Roache,
Hilda and Babatunde Johnson,
and Joseph E. Zabik

Contents

IV. Treatment Applications

Contributors

John P. Allen, Ph.D.
Treatment Research Branch, National Institute on Alcohol Abuse and Alcoholism, 6000 Executive Boulevard, Rockville, Maryland 20892-7003

Raymond F. Anton, M.D.
Department of Psychiatry and Behavioral Sciences, Medical University of South Carolina, 171 Ashley Avenue, Charleston, South Carolina 29425

Peter L. Bonate, Ph.D.
Department of Pharmaceutical Sciences, School of Pharmacy, University of Pittsburgh, 904 Salk Hall, Pittsburgh, Pennsylvania 15261

Jing-Yu Chang, Ph.D.
Department of Physiology and Pharmacology, Bowman Gray School of Medicine, Medical Center Boulevard, Winston-Salem, North Carolina 27157-1083

James B. Daunais, Ph.D.
Department of Physiology and Pharmacology, Bowman Gray School of Medicine, Medical Center Boulevard, Winston-Salem, North Carolina 27157-1083

Steven I. Dworkin, Ph.D.
Department of Physiology and Pharmacology, Bowman Gray School of Medicine, Medical Center Boulvard, Winston-Salem, North Carolina 27157-1083

Frank R. George, Ph.D.
Amethyst Technologies, Inc., 1435 North Hayden Road, Scottsdale, Arizona 85257-3773

Errol M. Gould, Ph.D.
Medical College of Pennsylvania, Broad & Vine Streets, Mail Stop 409, Philadelphia, Pennsylvania 19102-1192

Scott E. Hemby, Ph.D.
Department of Pharmacology, University of Pennsylvania School of Medicine, 36th and Hamilton Walk, Philadelphia, Pennsylvania 19104-6055

Steven T. Higgins, Ph.D.
Department of Psychiatry, Human Behavioral Pharmacology Laboratory, University of Vermont, Ira Allen School, 38 Fletcher Place, Burlington, Vermont 05401

Martin A. Javors, Ph.D.
Departments of Psychiatry and Pharmacology, University of Texas Health Science Center at San Antonio San Antonio, Texas 78284-7792

Bankole A. Johnson, M.D., Ph.D.
Department of Psychiatry and Behavioral Sciences, University of Texas-Houston Health Science Center, Mental Sciences Institute, 1300 Moursund Street, Houston, Texas 77030-3406

Thomas S. King, Ph.D.
Departments of Cellular and Structural Biology and Obstetrics and Gynecology, University of Texas Health Science Center at San Antonio, San Antonio, Texas 78284

Kimberly C. Kirby, Ph.D.
Division of Addiction Research and Treatment, Department of Mental Health Sciences, Hahnemann University School of Medicine, Mailstop 984, Broad & Vine Streets, Philadelphia, Pennsylvania 19102-1192

Thomas R. Kosten, M.D.
Department of Psychiatry, Yale University School of Medicine; Veterans Administration Connecticut Healthcare Systems, 950 Campbell Avenue, West Haven, Connecticut 06516

Sharon R. Letchworth, Ph.D.
Department of Physiology and Pharmacology, Bowman Gray School of Medicine , Medical Center Boulevard, Winston-Salem, North Carolina 27151-1083

Raye Z. Litten, Ph.D.
Treatment Research Branch, National Institute on Alcohol Abuse and Alcoholism, 6000 Executive Boulevard, MSC 7003 Bethesda, Maryland 20892-7003

Scott E. Lukas, Ph.D.
Alcohol and Drug Abuse Research Center, McLean Hospital, 115 Mill Street, Belmont, Massachusetts 02178

David J. Lyons, Ph.D.
Department of Physiology and Pharmacology, Bowman Gray School of Medicine , Medical Center Bouelvard, Winston-Salem, North Carolina 27157-1083

Adande J. Mattox, Ph.D.
Department of Psychiatry, University of Minnesota Medical School, Box 392, Mayo Memorial Building, 420 Delaware Street, S.E. Minneapolis, Minnesota 55455-0392

David J. Nutt, M.D., Ph.D.
Department of Mental Health, University of Bristol, Bristol School of Medical Sciences, University Walk, BS8 ITD United Kingdom

Joseph M. Paris, M.D.
Department of Physiology and Pharmacology, Bowman Gray School of Medicine, Medical Center Boulevard, Winston-Salem, North Carolina 27157-1083

Ismene L. Petrakis, M.D.
Department of Psychiatry, Yale University School of Medicine; Veterans Administration Medical Center, 950 Campbell Avenue, West Haven, Connecticut 06516

John T. Pichot, M.D.
Addiction Psychiatry Residency Program, The University of Texas Health Science Center; Substance Abuse Treatment Unit, Audie Murphy Veterans Administration Hospital, San Antonio, Texas 78284-7792

Linda J. Porrino, Ph.D.
Department of Physiology and Pharmacology, Bowman Gray School of Medicine, Medical Center Boulevard, Winston-Salem, North Carolina 27157-1083

Kenzie L. Preston, Ph.D.
Clinical Trials Section, Treatment Branch, Division of Intramural Research, National Institute on Drug Abuse, P.O. Box 5180, 5500 Nathan Shock Drive, Baltimore, Maryland 21224

John D. Roache, Ph.D.
Department of Psychiatry and Behavioral Sciences, University of Texas-Houston Health Science Center, Mental Sciences Institute, 1300 Moursund Street, Houston, Texas 77030-3406

John M. Rutter, Ph.D.
Medical College of Pennsylvania-Hahnemann University School of Medicine, Allegheny University of the Health Sciences, Broad & Vine Streets, Mail Stop 408, Philadelphia, Pennsylvania 19102-1192

Christine A. Sannerud, Ph.D.
Drug and Chemical Evaluation Section ODE, Drug Enforcement Administration, Washington, D.C. 20537

Joy M. Schmitz, Ph.D.
Department of Psychiatry and Behavioral Sciences, University of Texas-Houston Health Science Center, Mental Sciences Institute, 1300 Moursund Street, Houston, Texas 77030-3406

Charles R. Schuster, Ph.D.
Department of Psychiatry and Behavioral Neurosciences, Wayne State University School of Medicine, University Psychiatric Center, 2761 East Jefferson, Detroit, Michigan 48207

Peter B. Silverman, Ph.D.
Department of Psychiatry and Behavioral Sciences, University of Texas-Houston Health Science Center, Mental Sciences Institute, 1300 Moursund Street, Houston, Texas 77030-3406

Linda Patia Spear, Ph.D.
Department of Psychology, Center of Developmental Psychobiology, Binghamton University, Binghamton, New York 13902-6000

Ralph Spiga, Ph.D.
*Department of Psychiatry and Behavioral Sciences,
University of Texas-Houston Health Science
Center, Mental Sciences Institute, 1300
Moursund Street, Houston, Texas 77030-3406*

Maxine L. Stitzer, Ph.D.
*Department of Psychiatry, Division of Behavioral
Biology, The Johns Hopkins University School of
Medicine, Baltimore, Maryland 21205*

Christopher K. Surratt, Ph.D.
*Molecular Neurobiology Section, Division of
Intramural Research, National Institute on Drug
Abuse, P.O. Box 5180, 5500 Nathan Shock Drive,
Baltimore, Maryland 21224*

Sheila L. Vrana, Ph.D.
*Department of Physiology and Pharmacology,
Bowman Gray School of Medicine, Medical
Center Boulevard, Winston-Salem, North
Carolina 27157-1083*

Kent E. Vrana, Ph.D.
*Department of Physiology and Pharmacology,
Bowman Gray School of Medicine, Medical
Center Boulevard, Winston-Salem, North
Carolina 27157-1083*

Rudy E. Vuchinich, Ph.D.
*Department of Psychology, Auburn University, 226
Thach Street, Auburn, Alabama 36849*

Sharon L. Walsh, Ph.D.
*National Institute on Drug Abuse, Division of
Intramural Research, P.O. Box 5180, 5500
Nathan Shock Drive, Baltimore, Maryland
21224*

Jia Bei Wang, M.D., Ph.D.
*University of Maryland at Baltimore, Department
of Pharmaceutical Sciences, School of
Pharmacy, 20 North Pine St., Baltimore,
Maryland 21201*

Barry D. Waterhouse, Ph.D.
*Medical College of Pennsylvania, Mail Stop 409,
Broad & Vine Streets, Philadelphia, Pennsylvania
19102-1192*

Donald J. Woodward, Ph.D.
*Department of Physiology and Pharmacology,
Bowman Gray School of Medicine, Medical
Center Boulevard, Winston-Salem, North
Carolina 27157-1083*

Foreword

This volume is broad in its coverage of the scientific literature on the etiology, consequences, and treatment of drug abuse/dependence. The title of this volume reflects the editors conception of the problem(s) of addiction as being an interaction between environmental and genetic variables shaping behavior, pharmacology, and the molecular and neurobiological mechanisms underlying drug action. I applaud the editors' marshalling of contributors who represent the very best in scholarship across this range of topics.

This volume begins with five excellent chapters that review the scientific literature on the behavioral aspects of drug abuse. These chapters serve to emphasize the fact that the propensity for humans to self-administer certain drugs because of their positive reinforcing properties is shared by many other animal species. The fact that other animals self-administer many of the drugs that get people into trouble allows rigorous laboratory studies in animal models of addiction that could not be carried out in humans for practical and ethical reasons. On the other hand, great progress has been made in the development of procedures allowing the study of drugs of abuse in humans under controlled laboratory conditions. Studies in both animals and humans have shown the importance of behavioral variables such as cost and conditioned stimuli associated with drugs in the maintenance of drug-seeking and drug-taking behaviors.

Great progress has been made in determining the neurobiological correlates of drug reinforcement, tolerance, and physical dependence. The accomplishments in this area are well summarized in the second section on neurobiological processes. This section reviews some of the latest research regarding the role of genetics in vulnerability to addiction using both inbred animal strains as well as biological markers of addiction vulnerability in humans. Finally, this section reviews what is known regarding the developmental consequences of *in utero* exposure to drugs of abuse. This area of research is of the utmost importance because policies regarding the treatment of women who use drugs during pregnancy often are based upon emotion, rather than facts.

A variety of new electrophysiological and imaging procedures are emerging which allow the assessment of brain activity in the intact animal or human under the influence of various drugs of abuse. This allows for the simultaneous assessment of behavioral and neuropharmacological function which can suggest the mechanisms mediating the behavioral effects of drugs. This, of course has great implications for the development of pharmacological therapies for drug abuse/dependence. Similarly, progress in molecular biological research has allowed the precise characterization of the receptors mediating the actions of almost all drugs of abuse. This information allows studies of changes in receptor expression associated with tolerance to the actions of drugs of abuse as well as a more rational development of specific antagonists which might be useful therapeutically. One of the most exciting new fields of drug abuse research is the area dealing with how abused drugs modify gene expression. It is here that we may find the biological correlates of drug dependence. All of these topics are authoritatively reviewed and chapters present both the techniques as well as summarize the major conclusions of research employing them.

The final section of this volume deals with treatment implications. Nowhere in the volume is it more clear why it is essential to view the problem(s) of drug abuse/dependence as resulting from an interaction of genetic, behavioral, and pharmacological variables. Such a complex multi-determined problem demands treatment approaches which involve interventions at the neuropharmacological, behavioral, and psychosocial levels. The strengths and weaknesses of the currently available behavioral, psychosocial, and pharmacological treatments, and their use in combination, are well described in the final chapters of this book. I believe this section is of vital importance to the field in demonstrating that drug abuse/dependence treatment can work. This book has clearly proved that improvements in drug abuse treatment are needed and can be achieved through continued research.

I believe that the editors and authors of this book deserve great credit for summarizing the most important highlights of research in the field of drug abuse/dependence in a manner which makes it of value to those working in the area of substance abuse research/treatment as well as to the non-specialist. This is of increasing importance in this era of health care reform where primary care physicians are being called upon to both treat and refer people with drug problems. This volume should prove invaluable to those who wish to go beyond simple *cookbook* guidelines and seek out the scientific basis for their clinical practices.

Charles R. Schuster, Ph.D.
Department of Psychiatry and Behavioral Neurosciences
Wayne State University School of Medicine
Detroit, Michigan

Preface

The idea to compile this book arose out of collegial interactions between the editors. Following his training in the neuroscience of drug addiction at Oxford, England, Dr. Johnson joined a largely behavior-orientated group of researchers in Houston, Texas. There, Dr. Johnson's idea for this book was developed with Dr. Roache as they learned to speak the same language, and sought to understand the nexus between the behavioral and neuroscience disciplines. Soon, it became obvious that the two disciplines had developed independently for the most part and that each could benefit from understanding the other's technology. We believe that it is essential that these two disciplines should become more entwined and that the field needs a vehicle to promote this nexus. In our quest to understand, develop, and apply the knowledge base that resides in this nexus, we came to the conclusion that a book such as this one could help fulfill the need.

Given the increasing evidence for a bio-psycho-social model for understanding drug abuse and addiction, it is important that biomedical neuroscientists work together with behavioral psychologists for a more integrated approach to the pervasive problem of alcohol and drug abuse. Neuroscientists need to understand the behavioral plasticity of drug effects. Behaviorists need to understand that environmental factors affect the biological brain, and that this modulates the behavioral process. Treatment practitioners need to integrate pharmacological, behavioral, and social work technologies into a comprehensive treatment plan.

The nexus of neuroscience and behavior deals with material that lies between the two disciplines and that is on the cutting edge of current technology. For instance, there has been an explosion of knowledge concerning molecular aspects of neurotransmitter system function and a concomitant increase in understanding the process of drug reinforcement and behavior modification. However, it is striking that, until recently, few experiments have sought to simultaneously assess the impact of brain function on behavior and vice versa. Medications development research has all too often focused on the molecular brain without understanding the behavioral mechanisms involved. Likewise, little psychological research focuses on how behavioral processes may alter brain function. This produces a philosophical dichotomy in much the same way as earlier efforts in the psychological and medical sciences resulted in a mind-body dualism. Presumably, the mind-body dichotomy has evolved into a more holistic approach in the pursuit of the mental health sciences, but at times, we appear to be less holistic than we would like to believe of ourselves.

We have organized this book in such a way as to provide a basic understanding of the behavioral and biological processes involved in drug addiction. We requested that our authors review and illustrate the procedures, results, and significance of research in their field and to do so in a way that would be educational and could be understood by a non-expert. We have assembled an impressive group of authors, all of whom have responded admirably to the challenge. As much as possible, chapters are organized around the theme of stressing the commonality of actions between drugs of abuse, thus breaking away from the traditional practice of grouping addictive substances by drug class. Unusual for a book like this is the unified format we employed. Each chapter concludes with sections in which authors specify their view of the future and summarize the material and conclusions contained in the chapter. Also, all chapters have undergone a peer review process by specialists to aid the editors in assuring an accurate and comprehensible presentation of material. We are grateful to the reviewers who assisted in this effort and we commend our authors for boldly charting this nexus and remaining true to the mission of the book.

This book is written for a wide audience of M.D., Ph.D., and other scientifically-oriented professionals interested in drug addiction. High caliber chapters are written to satisfy both experts and non-experts in the area under consideration. Since none of us are experts in all areas, it should benefit everyone who wants to keep abreast of science and technology in other fields as applied to a common problem. The chapters range from basic science to clinical treatment in scope. The first section of the book starts with behavioral concepts that are considered to be central to the process of drug addiction. We have emphasized drug reinforcement, not because it is the only determinant of drug-seeking behavior, but because it is, arguably, the most important. Behaviorists should find this information a valuable and critical review of the field and non-experts in behavioral analysis should be able to learn more about the complex processes involved in determining the behavioral pathology of addiction. The second section of the book focuses on the biological processes involved in reinforcement, addiction, and dependence phenomena. The nexus concept is well developed in this section which includes integration of behavior with genetic, biological, molecular, and pharmacological variables important to substance abuse phenomenology. The third section of the book highlights some of the state-of-the-art techniques in neuroscience. Several of these are excellent examples of a nexus as they pioneer the integration of neuroscience and behavior. The fourth and final section of the book concentrates on treatment applications and is the most conventional, but most important part of this book. The emphasis here remains on drawing commonalties of treatment and integrating pharmacological and behavioral treatments. We did not seek to cover every conceivable topic related to either neuroscience or behavior. This does not suggest that what has been left out is not important, but that it was necessary for us to ensure that the topics contained in this book melded together in a way that counterbalanced the issues raised by discussions of both disciplines. Also, we resisted the additional temptation of straying into areas which are, simply, beyond our own expertise as editors.

In reviewing the material contained in this book, the reader will see that its concept is not so much a creative work of the editors as it is a natural outcome of the fascinating interplay between drugs, the environment, and the brain. The phenomenon of drug addiction it seems, is forcing us to learn more about each of these factors to solve the puzzle that is the wonder of human life and behavior.

Bankole A. Johnson
John D. Roache
Department of Psychiatry and Behavioral Sciences
University of Texas-Houston Health Science Center
Mental Sciences Institute
1300 Moursund Street
Houston, Texas, 77030-3406

Reference

1. Johnson BA. Computers in Psychiatry: On artificial intelligence—Is there a ghost in the machine? Psychiatric Bulletin 17 (2): 100–103, 1993.

Acknowledgments of Reviewers

We especially acknowledge the contributions of Richard Meisch, M.D., Ph.D. and Ralph Spiga, Ph.D. who served as both content advisors and manuscript reviewers.

We also gratefully acknowledge the following colleagues who served as peer reviewers for chapter manuscripts:

Susan Amara, Ph.D.
Vollum Institute, Oregon Health Science Center, Portland, Oregon

Warren Bickel, Ph.D.
Human Behavioral Pharmacology Laboratory, Department of Psychiatry, University of Vermont, Burlington, Vermont

Paul Buckland, Ph.D.
Department of Psychological Medicine, University of Wales College of Medicine, Heath Park, Cardiff, Wales

Carlo DiClementi, Ph.D.
Department of Psychiatry, University of Maryland Baltimore County, Baltimore, Maryland

Seamus Fanning, Ph.D.
Medical Science Section, Cork Regional Technical College, Bishopstown, Cork, Ireland

Zehava Gottesfeld, Ph.D.
Department of Neurobiology and Anatomy, The University of Texas-Houston Health Science Center, Houston, Texas

Steve Heischman, Ph.D.
National Institute on Drug Abuse, Division of Intramural Research, Baltimore, Maryland

Alane Kimes, Ph.D.
Neuroimaging and Drug Action Section, National Institute on Drug Abuse, Division Intramural Research, Baltimore, Maryland

Rick Lamb, Ph.D.
Department of Mental Health Sciences, Division of Addiction Research and Treatment, Hahnemann University School of Medicine, Philadelphia, Pennsylvania

Richard A. Meisch, M.D., Ph.D.
Department of Psychiatry and Behavioral Sciences, Universtiy of Texas-Houston Health Science Center, Mental Sciences Institute, Houston, Texas

Edward L. Reilly, M.D.
Department of Psychiatry and Behavioral Sciences, University of Texas-Houston Health Science Center, Mental Sciences Institute, Houston, Texas

Kenneth Silverman, Ph.D.
Behavioral Pharmacology Research Unit, Behavioral Biology Research Center, John Hopkins University School of Medicine, Baltimore, Maryland

Ralph Spiga, Ph.D.
Department of Psychiatry and Behavioral Sciences, University of Texas-Houston Health Science Center, Mental Sciences Institute, Houston, Texas

Robert Stewart, Ph.D.
Department of Psychology, Purdue School of Science, Indiana University/Purdue University at Indianapolis, Indianapolis, Indiana

PART I

Behavioral Processes

Drug Addiction and its Treatment: Nexus of Neuroscience and Behavior, edited by Bankole A. Johnson and John D. Roache. Lippincott–Raven Publishers, Philadelphia, © 1997.

1

Drug Reinforcement in Animals

Marilyn E. Carroll and Adande J. Mattox

Department of Psychiatry, University of Minnesota, Minneapolis, Minnesota 55455

Drug addiction is a major health concern worldwide. Many resources are devoted to preventing and treating addiction, and the study of the etiology, prevention, and treatment of drug-seeking and drug-taking behavior of individuals. The use of animal models that mimic the different phases of addiction has been essential to the development and evaluation of behavioral, pharmacologic, and social interventions for drug abuse. There are several advantages to using animal models. First, it is clear from biomedical research in many areas that the mechanisms of many behavioral and biologic processes are similar in nonhuman animals and humans. Thus, the data generated by animals can provide important information about processes of drug addiction in humans. A second advantage is the ability to control environmental variables and isolate certain factors for study. In animals, variables of interest can be studied alone or in combination; the drug and behavioral history and current circumstances can be carefully controlled. The complexity of human behavior does not allow for this degree of environmental control. A third advantage of using animal models is that screening of new pharmacologic agents can be more effectively accomplished before drugs are tested in clinical settings. Lastly, animal models have been useful in conceptualizing the process of drug addiction from acquisition to maintenance and recovery, from drug-seeking to drug-taking to relapse behavior.

Before we can discuss the reinforcement of behavior by drugs, we must first define reinforcement. A reinforcement occurs when the consequence of a response increases the future probability of the response. There is a body of literature from animal operant conditioning studies that demonstrates that positive reinforcement results from ingestive behaviors. For instance, animals that have been food-deprived engage in operant behaviors such as lever-pressing for the presentation of food pellets. Similarly, animals that have been water deprived engage in behaviors such as licking a spout to obtain access to water. In these instances, the delivery of food and water increase the responding that results in these deliveries and, as such, represent positive reinforcement. The concept of drugs delivery as positive reinforcement in animals is an extension of the operant conditioning principles that govern the functioning of food- and water-reinforced behavior.

This chapter describes methods for establishing drug reinforcement by different routes of administration in animals. Animal models have been developed that allow for examination of several aspects of the addiction process including acquisition, withdrawal, craving, and relapse. Criteria for the demonstration of drug reinforcement are discussed, and methods used to assess reinforcing efficacy (strength) are presented. Finally, organismic and environmental variables that influence and modify drug reinforcement in animals are illustrated. Emphasis is placed on newly developed methods and areas of research that have not been extensively reviewed elsewhere. If recent review articles exist in an area, these alternative sources of information are cited, and a brief overview is presented.

CRITERIA FOR DEMONSTRATING DRUG REINFORCEMENT IN ANIMALS

Animals will perform operant responses for drug deliveries for a variety of reasons including thirst, exploratory behavior, and generalized increases in behavior produced by the drug. However, the self-administration of a drug under these conditions should not be taken as evidence that the drug is reinforcing. To demonstrate the reinforcing effects of a drug, there are several lines of evidence that should be gathered, and these are described below.

Vehicle Substitution

The first and most important criterion is that higher rates of responding for drug delivery versus vehicle delivery should occur. Implicit in this criterion is that the drug is what is reinforcing the behavior, and not other aspects of the administration of the vehicle containing the drug. Thus, responding should decrease when the drug reinforcement is absent. Vehicle substitution effects can be best demonstrated using the ABA experimental design. According to this design, a baseline of drug-reinforced responding is established (A), the vehicle is substituted for the active drug (B), and then the drug is reinstated (A). Using this design, responding in the presence of the drug can be compared with responding in the absence of the drug. A study by Carroll et al. (1989) illustrates the importance of both vehicle substitution and the ABA design. In this study, rats were trained to self-administer 0.2 mg/kg/infusion of cocaine via the intravenous route. The infusions were delivered under a fixed-ratio (FR 1) schedule of rein-

forcement, whereby each infusion was contingent upon one lever press. The rats readily acquired self-administration, receiving a mean of 500 cocaine infusions per day. When cocaine was replaced by its saline vehicle, responding decreased dramatically. After 5 days of saline infusions, cocaine was reintroduced and the number of infusions returned to previous baseline levels. The increased responding during cocaine availability suggests that the responding was reinforced by the drug itself. The repetition of the effects in the second "A" condition suggests that behavior did not change due to nonspecific changes that could occur over time, but because of the presence of drug. Thus, vehicle substitution and the ABA experimental design can provide strong evidence of drug reinforcement. A variation of this method is the concurrent choice method in which drug and vehicle are concurrently available under identical reinforcement schedules. Significantly greater responding for the drug versus the vehicle is an indication of drug reinforcement. With the intravenous (i.v.) drug self-administration procedure, concurrent choice methods require double-lumen catheters so that drug and vehicle may be delivered from separate pumps. When the oral route of self-administration is used, two liquids, drug and vehicle, are concurrently available from two separate drinking spouts.

Pattern of Responding

The second criterion is that responding should be maintained under intermittent schedules of reinforcement, and patterns of responding maintained by drug should be similar to those produced by traditional forms of reinforcement such as food. A schedule of reinforcement is the contingency, or relationship, between responding and the delivery of a reinforcement. There are two basic types of intermittent schedules: the first is based on the number of responses and the second is based in the timing of responding. A ratio schedule of reinforcement is one that requires a certain number of responses for the delivery of the reinforcement. The number of responses can be set, called a fixed ratio (FR) schedule, or the number of responses can vary around an average, called a variable ratio (VR) schedule. Under interval schedules of reinforcement, the first response emitted after a certain amount of time has elapsed results in the presentation of the reinforcement. Just as there are FR and VR ratio schedules, there are fixed (FI) and variable (VI) interval schedules.

For both ratio and interval schedules, there are characteristic patterns of responding. With ratio schedules, there is a stable rate of responding and a pause after reinforcement delivery, called the postreinforcement pause. There is also a positive correlation between the response rate and the number of reinforcements delivered such that increases in response rate result in increases in reinforcement delivery. If a drug is functioning as a reinforcement, these relationships should be demonstrated. A different pattern of responding is generated by interval schedules of reinforcement. Very little responding occurs at the start of the interval, and progressively more responding occurs toward the end of the interval. This pattern is referred to as the "scallop." When VR or VI schedules are used, the rates are usually higher and more steady than under the fixed schedules; thus, variable schedules are used when a high baseline rate of behavior is needed. One advantage of interval schedules is that the number of infusions delivered is independent of the rate at which the animal responds. Several studies have used interval schedules in the drug–self-administration procedure. Rhesus monkeys will self-administer codeine and ethanol under a VI 2-min schedule of reinforcement (Carney et al., 1976) and cocaine and pentobarbital under a FI 5-min schedule of reinforcement (Johanson, 1982). However, ratio schedules are most often used to determine the reinforcing effects of drugs.

In general, drug and nondrug reinforcements generate similar patterns of responding, and drugs generate characteristic patterns of responding under a wide variety of behavioral schedules. For example, Winsauer and Thompson (1991) reported a study in which pigeons were implanted with intravenous catheters and were trained to peck an illuminated key. The key pecking was reinforced under a FR 50 schedule of reinforcement such that every 50th response resulted in the delivery of either a cocaine infusion or food. The pigeons key pecked for both cocaine and for food, and the patterning of responding for both of these reinforcements was similar to that seen with non-drug reinforcements under an FR schedule (i.e., high constant rates of responding followed by pauses after the delivery of the reinforcement).

Lever Reversal

Lever reversal refers to switching the contingency such that responding on a previously inactive lever results in drug delivery, and the lever that was previously associated with drug delivery now has no consequences. For instance, the animal is trained to respond on a certain lever for drug delivery. This lever is the active lever. When the contingencies change such that responding on a different lever is now reinforced by drug delivery, the animals should decrease its responding on the previously active lever and increase its responding on the currently active lever. Reinforcement is demonstrated by this reallocation of responding. Olds (1962, 1979) tested this hypothesis by training rats to self-administer morphine directly into the hypothalamus, a brain region that is important for the reinforcing effects of drugs. When responses on the left lever resulted in the delivery of drug and responses in the right lever had no consequence, the rats allocated more of their responses on the left lever. However, when the contingencies were switched, and responding on the right lever now resulted in drug delivery, responding switched to the right lever.

Dose-Response Functions

The last criterion concerns the demonstration of an orderly dose-response function.

This criterion is not necessary or sufficient for demonstrating drug reinforcement, but it is an important step in extending the generality of an initial finding that a given dose of a drug functions as a reinforcement. Dose-response functions are derived by giving increasing doses of the drug and measuring the amount of responding for each dose. As the dose or concentration of the drug increases, responses typically follow an inverted U-shaped function. Decreased responding at the higher doses may be explained by satiation, aversive effects, generalized behavioral disruption, or a combination of effects. In a study conducted by Winger et al. (1992) rhesus monkeys were trained to press a lever under an FR 30 schedule of drug delivery. With this schedule, i.v. drug infusion was delivered after the 30th response by the animal. After the infusion, there was a 45-sec timeout when responding did not produce an infusion. Low doses of heroin and cocaine produced little responding for infusions. However, as the dose of each drug increased, the number of responses produced for drug infusions increased. At the highest drug doses, response rates for drug delivery decreased. These data demonstrate the classical inverted-U–shaped function that characterizes dose-response functions. Thus, the amount of behavior maintained by the drug is highly influenced by the dose of drug available and this interaction between dose and responding occurs in a predictable fashion.

METHODS FOR ESTABLISHING DRUG REINFORCEMENT

The following sections briefly discuss the methods used to study drug self-administration in animals. More detailed discussions of these techniques may be found in the recent methodologic review of Meisch and Lemaire (1993).

Intravenous (I.V.)

The route of administration that has been most commonly used for establishing drug re-inforcement in animals is the intravenous route. This method was developed to model i.v. heroin use in human addicts. It is an efficient method to use in animals because it rapidly delivers drug via the blood to the brain and bypasses taste and olfactory input factors that may be aversive. This type of experiment is usually conducted in rats or monkeys, and the techniques have been described in detail by a number of investigators (e.g., Carroll et al., 1981; Koob et al., 1987, Roberts et al., 1980; Winger and Woods 1973). These procedures involve placing an intravenous catheter in a major vein (e.g., jugular or femoral) of an animal (usually a rat or a monkey). This procedure has as its major advantages rapid and consistent drug delivery, similarity to many forms of human drug abuse, and reliability.

Initially, i.v. infusions are contingent upon one lever-press response, but later response requirements may be raised gradually to 10 to 30 in rats and much higher in monkeys. Acquisition of the lever-press response may be accelerated by previously training the animal to lever press for a food reward, by priming the animal with an injection at the beginning of the session, or by baiting the lever with food. Acquisition is usually accomplished in at least 5 to 10 days, and behavior is allowed to stabilize according to various criteria before experimental manipulations are made. A method used for testing whether or not the i.v. cannula has been properly placed is to inject sodium methohexital, a short-acting barbiturate, through the cannula system. If the animal immediately loses consciousness, it is assumed that the drug solution was delivered i.v. If i.v. self-administration sessions are short, and drug is not flowing through the cannula system throughout the day, often heparin is added to the drug or saline solution that resides in the cannula to prevent blood from clotting, and this extends catheter life.

Intracerebroventricular (I.C.V.)

This route of administration is similar to the i.v. route except that the cannula exits into the cerebral ventricles, which are located with a stereotaxic instrument. The method has been successfully used to demonstrate opioid (Belluzzi and Stein, 1977; Smith et al., 1982), amphetamine (Gustafson and Pickens, 1975), and acetaldehyde (Brown et al., 1979) self-administration; however, ethanol was not self-administered via this route. There is a longer recovery time with the i.c.v. route than with i.v., and the preparation lasts only a few weeks before the cannula becomes clogged or dislodged. Placement is histologically verified by injecting dye into the ventricle and examining brain slices postmortem. Thus, the i.c.v. method is difficult, short-term, and labor intensive, and it has not been frequently used. Its advantage is that only small amounts of drug are used, it can be used with drugs that do not cross the blood-brain barrier, and it separates peripheral from CNS effects. It does not offer many advantages over the intracranial methods that identify discrete sites of action (Goeders and Smith, 1987).

Intracranial

Although intravenous drug self-administration experiments are useful for identifying neuronal pathways and circuits involved in drug reward, a direct self-administration method is needed to identify specific brain regions that mediate the reinforcing effects of specific types of drugs. Intracranial self-administration is a variation on the i.v. and i.c.v. methods by which the cannula is directed to a specific brain region. The details of this procedure have been described by a number of investigators (e.g., Bozarth and Wise, 1981; Goeders and Smith, 1983; Koob and Goeders 1989; Hoebel et al., 1983; Olds, 1962). The cannula is typically made of small-gauge elastic tubing. It is placed in the specific brain region by stereotaxic techniques. The infusions are contingent upon an operant response as they are in the i.v. and i.c.v. procedures. There are more technological demands with the intracranial self-administration paradigm

compared with the i.v. method. For instance, selection of the proper control solution, infusion pressure, and infusion volume parameters is crucial because verification of the injection site requires histologic analysis. Electrolytic drug delivery systems have also been used for intracranial self-administration (cf. Koob and Goeders, 1989) and they produce less movement artifact.

Studies have mainly been conducted with opioids and psychomotor stimulants. Studies using these procedures in rats have reported cocaine self-administration in the medial prefrontal cortex not the nucleus accumbens (Goeders and Smith, 1983). Amphetamine is self-administered into the nucleus accumbens (Hoebel et al., 1983). Morphine has been self-administered into the ventral tegmental area (VTA) (Bozarth and Wise, 1981) and nucleus accumbens (Olds, 1962). Methionine enkephalin was also self-administered in the VTA (Goeders and Smith, 1985). Dopamine (Dworkin et al., 1985) and putative neurotransmitters such as neurotensin (Glimcher et al., 1983) and cholecystokinin (Hoebel and Aulisi, 1984) have been self-administered in the VTA (neurotensin) or nucleus accumbens (cholerystokinin). These studies emphasize the importance of the VTA-NA system for the reinforcing effects of opioids and psychomotor stimulants.

Oral

The oral route of drug self-administration is highly relevant to human drug abuse because most human drug abuse problems occur through this route. For instance, alcohol ingestion, amphetamine and caffeine use all occur orally. There are several factors regarding this route that enhance drug-reinforced behavior such as the ease of use, ability to titrate dose, and taste factors that may function as discriminative stimuli or conditioned reinforcing stimuli. There are also special conditions associated with the oral route that may impede oral drug self-administration, such as the long delay between ingestion and central nervous system effects, and aversive taste. Another limitation to the oral procedure is that drug reinforcement can be established with only a few drugs (e.g., cocaine, ethanol, etonitazene) in rats and mice when the drugs are ingested orally . It is thought that monkeys are less resistant than rats to sampling novel bitter tastes, because their physiology allows them to vomit poisonous materials. This species difference is due to the bait-shyness of rodents and the bitter taste of most drugs. The oral procedures are more successful and versatile in monkeys, but a negative aspect is that monkeys are more expensive than rats. Factors that facilitate or impair oral self-administration have been taken into account in developing animal models of oral drug abuse.

The earlier methods of oral self-administration were two-bottle tests. Typically, drug was available from one bottle and vehicle from the other. Reinforcing effects were implied by a preference for drug over vehicle. However, this method does not closely parallel oral drug abuse in humans. Instead, an operant procedure is used in which more effort and specific response requirements are met before drug is obtained. Operant procedures allow for elaborate sequences of behavior leading up to drug seeking and drug taking, which is more similar to the human drug-seeking behavior. Operant oral procedures have been extensively reviewed (e.g., Meisch and Carroll, 1987), and they will be briefly described here. The oral route has the advantage of allowing for long-term, interlocking within-subject studies. Some monkeys, for example, have been used for 10 to 20 years in repeated oral experiments. Drug history has some effect on acquisition of drug self-administration, but once steady-state levels of intake have been achieved, intersubject differences that were present during acquisition disappear. A major disadvantage of the oral route is the elaborate and time-consuming training methods that are needed in some cases to achieve oral self-administration. These methods are detailed in the following sections.

Schedule-Induced Polydipsia

The first acquisition procedure that was used was schedule-induced polydipsia (SIP). When small amounts of food are delivered to food-deprived rats at fixed or variable time periods (e.g., 1 min) excessive drinking occurs between food deliveries (Falk, 1961). Water is replaced by low drug concentrations that are gradually increased after responding stabilizes. When the SIP schedule is discontinued, and all food is given at the end of the session, oral drug self-administration often persists and then tests for reinforcing effects may be done. This may be accomplished with a pre-SIP component (e.g., 1 hr) to the session where drug is available without the food or the SIP schedule (Meisch and Thompson, 1971). When drug-reinforced responding begins to occur during this component, it is usually an indication of drug reinforcement. This method initially was used to establish ethanol reinforcement (Meisch and Thompson, 1971), and it was later extended to other drugs (e.g., etonitazene) and rhesus monkeys (Carroll and Meisch 1978). The use of this method with drugs other than ethanol that do not have calories illustrated that acquisition of oral drug intake is not based on caloric substitution.

Food-Induced Drinking

This method is similar to SIP except that an intermittent schedule of food delivery is not used. Instead, the animal is given the entire daily food ration during the time that the drug is available. Postprandial drinking results and liquid intake can be substantial, although not as high as with SIP. Similar methods of gradually increasing drug concentration are used and there may be an initial session component during which drug but not food is available. After maximal drug intake is achieved, food availability is moved to after the drug session. This procedure can be accelerated by maintaining the animals at reduced body weights (Carroll, 1982b). This procedure has been used with mice (Elmer et al., 1987 a, b), rats

(Meisch and Kliner, 1979), and monkeys (Meisch et al., 1981), and with a number of drugs such as cocaine, etonitazene, ethanol, pentobarbital, and phencyclidine.

Drug Access

This is the simplest procedure since it involves no induction methods. The drug is made available for a fixed period of time (e.g., 3 hr) each day, and during this time water is not available. Eventually many animals consume the drug, and concentrations are gradually increased. Reducing body weight increases the probability and rate of drug consumption.

Fading Method

Drinking is initially sustained by a drug (e.g., ethanol) or nondrug substance (e.g., sucrose). The drug to be tested for its reinforcing effects is then added to the established solution first at low concentrations, then gradually increased to higher concentrations. When behaviorally active concentrations and intakes of the test drug are achieved, the concentration of the initial solution is reduced in steps until the test drug is mixed in water. Thus, the test drug is gradually faded in, and the background drug or substance is gradually faded out. This method has been successfully used to establish ethanol self-administration in rats (Samson, 1986), pentobarbital (Lemaire and Meisch, 1985) and cocaine (Meisch et al., 1990) self-administration in monkeys, and cocaine self-administration in mice (George et al., 1991).

Substitution Method

This is a simple variation of the fading method for substituting a new drug for a drug for which reinforcement has been established. The new drug replaces the initial drug at a low but behaviorally active concentration, and the concentration may then be further increased if responding is maintained. This method has

been used to establish d-amphetamine and ketamine (Carroll and Stotz, 1983), as well as methohexital (Carroll et al., 1984) and phencyclidine analogue (Carroll, 1982a) reinforcement for rhesus monkeys. The method is not as reliable as the fading procedure, but may be used as a first step to save time. Substitution has been commonly used and is more successful with i.v. drug self-administration.

Concurrent Access to Established Drug Reinforcement and Test Drug

This method is another variant on the substitution procedure, but it involves concurrent access to two drug solutions. The animals are initially trained to self-administer a familiar drug with concurrent water. The water is replaced with gradually increasing concentrations of a second drug. When the new drug is self-administered at a stable rate, the familiar drug is replaced by water. This method has been used to establish ethanol reinforcement in monkeys that had only had experience with phencyclidine self-administration (Carroll, 1987b; Carroll et al., 1990b). It has been used only on a limited basis, and may work best with drugs that share discriminative stimulus effects.

Drug-Admixed Food

This method developed in rats by Suzuki (1990) involves mixing drug powder in ground food. For the first 2 days the animals are restricted to the drug-admixed food, but on the third day they are given a choice between the mixture and the food vehicle. The 3-day cycle is repeated, and eventually the rats prefer drug-admixed food to plain food. When rats are required to pull a weight to reach food, they will also pull a heavier weight to reach the food-drug mixture. These tests are both indications of reinforcement. This method has been adapted to procedures in which food (45-mg pellets) was delivered by operant methods. By using responding maintained by food, food and drug pellets were compared, and higher response rates were maintained by pellets containing morphine, codeine (Suzuki, 1990), or pentobarbital (Suzuki et al., 1989) than by standard unadulterated pellets.

Inhalation of Volatile Substances

This section discusses self-administration by inhalation of substances that are volatile at room temperature. Smoking is described in the next section as inhalation of substances that must be heated to volatilize. Inhalation experiments require an inhalation chamber or helmet (e.g., Wood et al., 1977), a nasal catheter (e.g., Yanagita et al., 1970), or a face mask for the subject and some type of air flow regulator system (e.g., respirator, vaporizer, aerosol spray) to deliver a quantifiable amount of volatilized substance. This method is technologically demanding and there are concerns about side effects such as burning the eyes. However, there have been several attempts to produce animal models of inhalant abuse. Jaffe and coworkers (1989) trained rats to lever press for exposure to an aerosol containing sufentanil. Yanagita et al. (1970) obtained self-administration of several volatile solvents (chloroform, lacquer thinner) and anesthetics (e.g., ether) using the nasal catheter in monkeys. Nitrous oxide self-administration has been reported in squirrel monkeys (Wood et al. 1977) and in rhesus monkeys (Grubman and Woods, 1982; Nemeth and Woods, 1982) using the helmet technique. While this is a feasible animal model, it has not been widely used in recent years, probably due to technical complexities. Animal models of inhalant abuse are needed because it is a significant problem in humans, especially teens and young adults (Balster, 1987; Carroll and Comer, 1993).

Inhalation by Smoking

An animal model of smoking would also be extremely valuable, as it is a common route of drug abuse in humans. However, many attempts to produce such a model have failed (cf. Wood, 1990). In some studies it was possible to obtain smoking behavior by rewarding smoking with food or water (e.g., Jarvik, 1967; Ando and Yanagita 1981; Rogers 1985). Recently, cocaine base smoking has been established in rhesus monkeys (Carroll et al., 1990a; Comer et al., 1994a, 1995b), and the same procedure has also been used to establish heroin smoking in monkeys. There are two factors that contribute to the success of this method. First, training is easier in younger monkeys (3–4 years) who are very active and still have an innate sucking response or older monkeys who have experienced either oral or i.v. drug self-administration. Second, the monkeys received smoke from a device that is very similar to a brass spout they use to obtain orally delivered drugs, water, or sweetened liquids (e.g., saccharin). Thus, they tend to automatically direct their licking and sucking behavior to the smoking spout.

The protocol that is used to obtain smoking behavior is a chained FR-FR schedule. Monkeys are required to make a fixed number of lever press responses, ranging from 1 to 4,096, and they are subsequently required to make five inhalation responses on the smoking spout to receive a smoke delivery. The apparatus used for smoking has been described in detail (Carroll et al., 1990a). Briefly, it consists of a coil of nichrome wire that is inserted through the back of a stainless steel tube that extends into the monkey cage. The wire coil is coated with a fixed dose of drug (e.g., cocaine base or heroin) dissolved in 95% ethanol. When the ethanol evaporates, drug remains on the coil and the coil is weighed before and after being coated with the drug to verify dose. Inhalation responses are detected by a vacuum sensor switch. After the appropriate number of responses a heater fixture is activated, and it vaporizes the drug without pyrolizing it. A number of experimental manipulations have indicated that in vaporized cocaine base and heroin reinforcement (1) there are orderly dose-response curves, (2) progressive-ratio performance is maintained,

(3) substitution of drugs with similar peripheral effects and fewer CNS effects (e.g., lidocaine, loperamide) extinguished behavior, (4) naloxone pretreatment produced dose-dependent reductions in heroin self-administration, and (5) behavior was maintained under high FR (e.g., FR 2,048, 4,096) values. Furthermore, intake of cocaine was verified by analysis of blood samples in one monkey, and the pharmacokinetic profile was very similar to that obtained in human subjects (Hatsukami et al., 1990). A disadvantage of this method is that it is very labor intensive. Each coil (10 per monkey) is hand loaded, weighed, and inserted into the smoking apparatus.

Intragastric (I.G.)

This route is similar to the i.v. route except that the cannula exits in the stomach of the animal rather than the jugular vein. Several different surgical procedures have been used, such as entering directly into the stomach (e.g., Altshuler and Phillips, 1978), through the esophagus (Smith et al., 1975), and through the nasal cavity to the esophagus and stomach (Yanagita, 1968). The surgery recovery time is slightly longer than with the i.v. route, but the catheter life may be slightly longer than with the i.v. route. Behavioral training is longer with the i.g. route than with the i.v. route, presumably due to the delay between responding and postingestional effects. The process can be accelerated by adding palatable tastes (e.g., Waller et al., 1984) or other cues as discriminative stimuli. Advantages of this method are that it allows for self-administration of suspensions of water-insoluble drugs (e.g., benzodiazepines), and drugs that have aversive tastes may be self-administered. The i.g. procedure has been used extensively with a wide variety of drugs in rats and monkeys (cf. Meisch and Lemaire, 1993); however, it has not been used in the last 10 years. Lack of interest in this method may be due to the technical complexity and extensive behavioral training. Furthermore, oral and inhalation methods developed in the last decade more rapidly produce a more durable model of oral drug abuse.

Intramuscular (I.M.)

This is a method that has not been frequently used, but i.m. morphine (Goldberg et al., 1976) and cocaine (Goldberg et al., 1976; Katz 1979, 1980; Nader and Barrett, 1990; Valentine et al., 1983) self-administration has been reliably produced in rhesus and squirrel monkeys. A disadvantage of this method is that only one drug injection is given at the end of the session; thus, complex second-order schedules have been used to maximize the behavioral output. Under a second-order schedule, completion of one schedule (e.g., FR, FI) is counted as a unitary response toward completion of the other schedule. A brief stimulus usually accompanies completion of each component schedule, and presentation of the primary reinforcer (i.m. drug injection) occurs when all schedule requirements are completed). The i.m. model offers the advantages that long sequences of complex behavior are similar to human behavioral patterns, and since drug delivery occurs at the end of the session, the behavior is not influenced by the direct rate-altering effects of the drug. Disadvantages of this method are the longer training time required than with other methods, the labor involved with i.m. injections, and that the feasibility of this method has not yet been demonstrated in rats.

MODELING PHASES OF DRUG ADDICTION

Acquisition

Acquisition of drug-reinforced behavior is a gradual process that may vary widely across individual animals. The rate of acquisition of drug-reinforced behavior may also vary considerably with the type of drug, the dose that is available, and the route of administration. Drug reinforcement is established rapidly with drugs that are absorbed quickly (e.g., smoked cocaine), and they will yield faster acquisition rates than drugs that are absorbed more gradually and have less intense effects (e.g., caffeine). There have been only a few studies that have focused on animal models of acquisition. Most laboratory investigations of drug self-administration have required well-trained behavior with steady baselines upon which variables controlling the drug-taking behavior have been examined. However, increased interest in developing strategies for preventing drug abuse has led investigators to devote more attention to the acquisition process and to the study of variables that may impede or enhance the process.

The most simple method of evaluating acquisition is to allow animals access to a drug contingent upon an operant response (e.g., lever press) for a period of time each day. A separate group of animals would have access only to saline or the drug vehicle. When the amount of drug is greater than the amount of vehicle consumed, acquisition is completed. The dependent variable of interest is usually the number of days or drug sessions until criterion acquisition performance is achieved.

The advantage of using acquisition methods such as this is that they simulate the naturalistic environment. All of the animals are used in the analysis, and the proportion of responders and nonresponders is typically reported. Often in studies involving steady-state behavior, nonresponders are screened out, the impression is given that all of the animals readily acquire drug self-administration. Finally, since acquisition data have not yet reached a ceiling, it is possible to examine treatments that both increase and decrease drug-reinforced behavior (acquisition, response rate). A disadvantage of using acquisition methods is that they require more expensive, time-consuming group designs, since acquisition can occur only once in each animal (cf. Sidman, 1960). It is also necessary to use a large number of subjects per group because there is considerable variability between subjects. For this reason, rats are the species most commonly used.

Methods have been developed to reduce the variability between subjects. For instance, if a lever-press response is required for drug delivery, there are often large differences in the time it takes to come into contact with the lever. This difference can be reduced by first training the rats to press a lever for food and then making drug available. Another method that has been used in an effort to reduce variability is autoshaping, a method that was previously developed to automatically train rats and pigeons to respond on a lever or lighted key for food reward (Brown and Jenkins, 1968). When autoshaping is used, a retractable lever is extended into the test chamber for 15 seconds and then retracted. After it is retracted, the animal automatically receives an infusion of cocaine. Eventually the animal associates the lever retraction with the effects of a drug such as cocaine. When the animal touches the extended lever, it immediately retracts and cocaine is delivered. During another part of the day the lever remains extended, and each lever press results in a cocaine infusion. Using these acquisition models, investigators have explored a number of organismic, environmental, and drug history variables that influence acquisition rates.

Organismic

Organismic variables may range from innate differences in locomotor activity or dietary preferences to genetic strain, gender, and age. For example, Piazza and coworkers (1989) placed naive rats in a novel environment and selected two groups: one with high locomotor activity and the other with low activity. They tested acquisition of i.v. amphetamine self-administration, and found that the high-activity group acquired amphetamine-maintained behavior more rapidly. In another series of experiments Gosnell and Krahn (1992) and Bell and coworkers (1994) selected rats for high and low saccharin preference. The high preferrers acquired higher levels of oral ethanol self-administration. Others have shown that fat preference predicts morphine (Marks-Kaufman and Lipeles, 1982) and ethanol (Krahn and Gosnell, 1991) intake. Sweets preference was not related to the rate at which the rats acquired i.v. cocaine self-administration, but the same rats consumed greater amounts of ethanol when they were food-satiated (Gahtan et al., 1995).

Genetic differences in the acquisition of opiate- and ethanol-reinforced behavior have been demonstrated in selective breeding experiments and in comparisons of inbred lines of rats. The results of these studies are discussed in other reviews (George, 1987; George and Goldberg, 1989; see also Chapter 8). Age and gender differences in rates of acquisition are often noted anecdotally, but few studies have controlled these variables while quantitatively assessing acquisition.

Environmental

Environmental conditions that have been examined with acquisition paradigms include stress, social factors, feeding conditions, and the availability of alternative nondrug reinforcement. Several studies have shown that stress affects the acquisition of drug self-administration in rats, and the results depend on the drug used and type of stressful event. For instance, Piazza and coworkers (1989) found that tail pinch increased acquisition of amphetamine self-administration. Ramsey and van Ree (1990) reported no effect of extensive handling, hot plate stress, or repeated foot shock stress on acquisition of i.v. cocaine self-administration. However, a group of rats that received emotional stress by observing other rats receive foot shock did show a higher acquisition rate than controls. Shaham (1993) reported increased oral opioid self-administration in rats exposed to restraint stress, and these findings have recently been extended to ethanol self-administration (Rawleigh et al., 1995).

Feeding conditions markedly alter the rate of acquisition of drug self-administration (Carroll, 1996). In initial studies, food was withheld to increase activity near the drug lever or the lever was baited with food. In re-

cent studies acquisition of cocaine self-administration was quantitatively evaluated by the autoshaping method and food-deprived and food-satiated groups of rats (Comer et al., 1995a). Only 71.4% of the rats in the food-satiated group acquired cocaine-maintained behavior within the 30-day allotted time limit, while 100% of the food-deprived group acquired cocaine-maintained behavior. Of the rats whose behavior was ultimately maintained by cocaine, the rate of acquisition was significantly slower in the food-satiated group.

In an extension of this study, Specker and colleagues (1994) compared cocaine acquisition in a group of rats that had a food-deprivation history to controls that had remained on free access to food. The food-deprived group received three brief intervals of restricted feeding when they were 30, 90, and 140 days old, according to a procedure described by Hagan and Moss (1991). This exposure resulted in longer eating intervals and greater food intake than free-fed controls when the animals were challenged with butorphanol (a drug that stimulates feeding) several months after free access to food had been restored. The group that had a history of food deprivation and an elevated feeding response with butorphanol acquired i.v. cocaine acquisition at a faster rate with 86% (vs 69% of controls) of the rats meeting the acquisition criteria within 30 days.

Similar findings were reported in a study of rhesus monkeys acquiring oral self-administration of phencyclidine (Carroll, 1982b). Monkeys that were food deprived to 85% of their free-feeding weights resulted in more rapid acquisition and greater intakes of the orally delivered drug. Food deprivation also changed the patterning of self-administration such that responding began immediately and continued at a high rate throughout the first hour of the 3-hr session. During food satiation the onset of responding was slower, more variable, and responding occurred sporadically throughout the 3-hr session.

Palatable dietary substances that have little or no caloric content also have been shown to affect the rate of acquisition of drug self-administration in a way that is very similar to food satiation. In a study of the acquisition of i.v. cocaine self-administration in rats, four groups of rats were compared (Carroll and Lac, 1993). One had a three-week history of exposure to a palatable solution of glucose and saccharin (G-S), and the rats had access to the G-S throughout cocaine autoshaping. A second group had the history of G-S but no current access during autoshaping. A third group had no history but did have current access, and the fourth group had no exposure to G-S. All groups had unlimited access to water, and 20 g of food each day. The groups with no G-S exposure or a G-S history only were the fastest to acquire, with 100% of the rats meeting the acquisition criterion. Thus, a history of exposure to a palatable substance had little effect on current behavior. The group with the G-S history and current exposure was the slowest to acquire, and only 50% of the rats met the acquisition criteria in 30 days. The group with current G-S exposure also showed slower acquisition, with only 83% meeting criteria. Thus, the alternative source of reinforcement prevented or slowed acquisition in most rats. Further, the extended exposure (history plus current) resulted in higher G-S intakes, which had the greatest suppressant effect on cocaine acquisition. Since the question remained whether the previous results could be attributed to caloric content or palatability of G-S, a subsequent study compared three levels of feeding—10 g, 20 g, or ad libitum with or without a palatable noncaloric substance, saccharin (0.2% wt vol), added to the food (Lac et al., 1994). Cocaine acquisition was delayed and reduced by saccharin at all feeding conditions, and the speed of acquisition varied directly with the level of food deprivation. This study shows that the amount of food and palatability of food are factors that may separately and additively interfere with the acquisition of cocaine self-administration.

Drug History

Most of the drug acquisition studies that have been conducted to date have examined pharmacologic variables. For example, several studies have shown that drug pretreatment facilitates acquisition of drug self-administration. For example, rats pretreated with naltrexone, an opiate antagonist, for 12 days acquired cocaine self-administration more rapidly than those treated with saline (Ramsey and van Ree, 1990). The effect of naltrexone on acquisition agrees with data showing that naltrexone increases levels of cocaine self-administration in rats once it is already acquired (Carroll et al., 1986). In both studies naltrexone had a greater facilitating effect at moderate (vs. high) cocaine doses. Horger and colleagues (1991) exposed rats to intraperitoneal (i.p.) injections of caffeine for 9 days before cocaine self-administration access began, and found a significant increase in the rate at which cocaine self-administration was acquired (compared with saline controls) at a cocaine dose of 0.25 mg/kg but not 0.125 mg/kg. There also has been a study of the effects of prenatal exposure to morphine from gestational day 7 to parturition and its effect on saline, cocaine, or heroin self-administration. Acquisition of cocaine and heroin self-administration was enhanced by prenatal exposure to morphine (Ramsey and van Ree, 1990).

In summary, acquisition is sensitive to a number of internal and external factors. These variables can be experimentally combined and manipulated to provide an animal model of prevention. A final note about acquisition procedures is that regardless of the acquisition methods used, the ultimate steady-state performance that is achieved appears to be the same regardless of the type of acquisition procedure that was used (Meisch, 1975; Winger and Woods, 1973).

Withdrawal

There have been two basic methods used to assess drug withdrawal effects in animals. The first is an observational approach. A checklist of withdrawal signs is constructed with levels of severity indicated for each. Ideally, observers who are blind to the experimental conditions rate the animals on the signs at several intervals after drug access is terminated. With some drug withdrawal states it is also possible to quantify physiological signs of withdrawal such as number and duration of audiogenic seizures (alcohol) or number of fecal boli (opioids). These types of measures strengthen the more subjective observational measures.

A second way of examining withdrawal effects is by the use of operant behavior. Animals are trained to respond under a relatively demanding schedule (e.g., high FR) for food while they are receiving experimenter- or self-administered drug. When drug access terminates, the drug withdrawal effect is expressed as a suppression in food-maintained responding. This measure of withdrawal has been used with drugs that also produce observable withdrawal signs during drug abstinence, such as morphine (Ford and Balster, 1976; Holtzman and Villarreal, 1973; Thompson and Schuster, 1964), ethanol (Ahlenius and Engel, 1974), chlordiazepoxide (McMillan and Leander, 1978), PCP (Beardsley and Balster, 1987; Slifer et al., 1984), and ketamine (Beardsley and Balster, 1987). The time course of the most severe behavioral disruptions closely parallels that of the observable physical signs; however, milder behavioral disruptions may persist for several weeks after drug access is terminated. While monkeys will not work for food at rates as high as pre-withdrawal baselines, they will readily accept food from the experimenter. This suggests that drug withdrawal is associated with a long-term motivational deficit. The method is sensitive enough to detect withdrawal of those drugs when the dose used was too low to produce observable withdrawal signs. Furthermore, withdrawal disruptions in operant behavior occur with drugs that produce no observable signs of withdrawal such as caffeine (Carney, 1982), cocaine (Carroll and Lac, 1987; Woolverton and Kleven, 1988), and Δ^9-tetrahydrocannabinol (THC) (Branch et al., 1980).

Studies using the operant measures of withdrawal have identified several variables that modulate the severity of the withdrawal effect. For instance, the longer the duration of access to the drug (e.g., Carroll, 1987a) or the higher the dose (Wessinger and Owens, 1991), the more severe and long-lasting the withdrawal disruption. Cross-dependence has been demonstrated by reversal of withdrawal disruptions when a similar drug is substituted (Carroll, 1988, Carroll et al., 1994).

A recent study indicated that the severity of withdrawal-induced disruptions in operant behavior is determined by the schedule of reinforcement (Carroll and Carmona, 1991). Self-administration of orally delivered PCP was established in six rhesus monkeys, and drug was then periodically replaced with water for 8-day periods. Withdrawal effects were compared as the food FR was increased (in nonsystematic order) across a range of values (e.g., 64, 128, 256, 512, and 1,024). As the FR increased from 64 to 256 the severity of withdrawal increased, but at the two highest FRs it decreased. In a second part of the experiment feeding conditions were manipulated to examine the effect on withdrawal. The food FR was held constant at FR 1,024 for some time, and body weights began to slightly decrease. When the withdrawal test was repeated, the monkeys did not show a disruption in food-maintained responding (i.e., a withdrawal effect). Next, they were given 100 g of hand-fed food in addition to the food earned under the FR 1,024. A marked withdrawal effect occurred. When the initial FR 1,024 unsupplemented conditions was repeated, the withdrawal disruption again could not be demonstrated. These results suggest that the price (FR) of food and whether or not the animal earns all of its food or is supplemented are environmental conditions that can affect the severity of drug withdrawal using operant measures. Again these results suggest that drug withdrawal produces motivational deficits that last beyond the period (e.g., 24 – 48 hr) when withdrawal signs and symptoms can be detected.

Craving

Craving is a term that has presented difficulties for the clinical and experimental analysis of drug abuse, and in 1955 a committee of the World Health Organization suggested that it be excluded from scientific use.

There had not been a clear operational definition of craving, so studies that have attempted to measure or demonstrate craving may have been describing several different behaviors. For many years there were very few experimental attempts to directly address the concept of craving; it existed as one of many dependent measures in studies with other goals. Further, the term *craving* has such extensive common usage, the lay use of the word became confused with its use in scientific language. Finally and importantly, craving is a condition that is sometimes related to drug self-administration behavior, but it is not a necessary or sufficient condition to explain drug use. For example, it does not explain first-time use.

In recent years the term *craving* has been addressed by the scientific community at the theoretical level (e.g., Markou et al., 1993; Pickens and Johanson 1992; Tiffany 1990), in clinical research (Childress et al., 1986), and in the development of animal models (Markou et al., 1993). In 1992 the United Nations and World Health Organization defined drug craving as "The desire to experience the effect(s) of a previously experienced psychoactive substance" (UNDCP and WHO, 1992). In a recent review Markou and coworkers (1993) have provided a discussion of drug craving as an incentive motivation for drugs. They also defined criteria for evaluating animal models of craving and gave several examples of animal models of craving that meet the criteria. Since their review is recent and extensive, only a brief summary of animal models of craving will be included here.

In humans, intense craving has been reported within minutes after a drug is consumed (e.g., Jaffe et al., 1989), during the drug withdrawal period (e.g., Gawin and Kleber, 1986), and after an extended period beyond withdrawal (Childress et al., 1988). Thus, it may be useful to develop animal models of craving when the drug is present as well as when the drug is absent. The animal models of craving that have been suggested by Markou and coworkers (1993) for the condition in which drug is present are the progressive-ratio and

choice paradigms. An additional measure of reinforcing efficacy, behavioral economic analyses of demand, may also serve as an index of drug craving. These terms are also discussed in another section as measures of reinforcing efficacy; thus, the question remains whether craving (in the presence of the drug) is a useful independent concept or just another word for reinforcing efficacy (see Pickens and Johanson, 1992). Others have postulated that separate neural systems mediate drug "liking" or euphoria and drug "wanting" or craving (Robinson and Berridge, 1993).

Other models of drug craving operationalize this concept as the persistence of drug seeking behavior in drug-experienced animals when the drug is no longer present. Three paradigms have been shown to have reliability and predictive validity for this purpose (cf. Markou et al., 1993). The first is an extinction test in which primary reinforcement is removed, yet responding continues to be measured. It provides three measures of resistance to extinction: (1) duration that responding persists after drug access is terminated, (2) total number of responses that are emitted during that time, and (3) reinstatement of responding after behavior has extinguished. Reinstatement is also used as a model of relapse and is discussed in greater detail in the next section. Self-administration behavior that has been extinguished can be precipitated by priming the animal with an interoceptive (e.g., drug injection) or exteroceptive (e.g., sound, light) stimulus that was previously associated with drug self-administration (Davis and Smith, 1976).

The second method is the conditioned reinforcement paradigm (Davis and Smith, 1976). According to this method, drug delivery is repeatedly paired with an external neutral stimulus. Drug is then replaced by saline and behavior is allowed to extinguish in the absence of the stimulus. When the stimulus is then reintroduced on a response-contingent basis, the rate and duration of responding is compared with baseline (before drug) and/or responding on an inactive lever. A higher rate of stimulus-maintained responding serves as an indicator of conditioned reinforcement. The rate of responding maintained by conditioned reinforcement varies directly with the dose of drug that was previously self-administered. A stronger test of conditioned reinforcement is the new response procedure (Davis and Smith, 1987). This requires the animal to acquire a new response that is rewarded by the stimulus previously associated with the drug. For example, rats previously trained to press a lever for drug and a paired stimulus may be trained to enter a maze arm or chamber in which the stimulus is presented. The conditioned place preference paradigm may be considered a variant of this technique (Mucha et al., 1982). A drawback of this approach for studying craving is that extinction does not provide a stable or long-lasting baseline to repeatedly test behavioral or pharmacologic interventions for craving.

The third model used to assess craving in the absence of drug is the second-order schedule. According to this method completion of a schedule contingency is treated as a unitary response governed by another, overall schedule (Goldberg et al., 1976). The primary reinforcement (drug) is delivered upon completion of the overall schedule, while a brief external stimulus occurs upon completion of each unit schedule and thereby becomes associated with drug. For instance, in a second-order FR 100 (FR 20:S) schedule a brief stimulus (S) would occur after every 20 responses; then after 100 brief stimuli were delivered, drug reinforcement would occur. Thus, 2000 responses would be emitted before the drug was available. This type of schedule maintains high rates of behavior for long periods of time and often uses elaborate sequences of behavior that are analogous to human drug-seeking behavior and often terminate in drug self-administration. The strength of the second-order schedule responding is increased by increasing drug dose (Goldberg and Gardner, 1981) and by food deprivation (Carroll, 1985b).

Relapse

Relapse is one of the most tenacious problems in treating drug abuse. Between 70% and 80% of all patients that are treated for drug abuse relapse within 6 months of treatment (e.g., Higgins et al. 1994b). Relapse is defined here as a reinstatement of regular drug use, and it occurs after treatment for tobacco smoking and abuse of a wide range of drugs (e.g., alcohol, cocaine, and heroin). Both external (e.g., drug-using peers, money, places) and internal (e.g., brief exposure to the drug itself, hunger, or mood states) cues may trigger relapse in humans. Thus, animal models have paralleled these conditions so that relapse can be reproduced and experimentally modified in the laboratory. Often the external stimulus prompts the reinitiation of drug use, which leads to more drug use. Craving is not always coexistent with drug use, but some studies have reported that craving in human drug users is actually highest shortly after drug intake compared with right before (Jaffe et al., 1988; Meyer and Mirin, 1979).

The role of external stimuli has been examined in only a few animal studies. Davis and Smith (1976) trained rats to self-administer i.v. morphine. They then replaced morphine with the saline vehicle. When a buzzer that had previously been associated with morphine injections was sounded, responding was reinitiated, although it only resulted in saline infusions. The effect of the buzzer in sustaining responding increased with higher morphine doses. It was not necessary for the morphine to have been delivered contingently upon lever pressing. The buzzer controlled lever pressing even when morphine had been administered only in the presence of the buzzer. Finally, an important observation of Davis and Smith (1976) was that if the external stimulus (buzzer) was present during saline substitution (extinction) it did not later generate relapse responding. This strategy of cue exposure during abstinence has been applied to the clinical management of drug abuse and prevention of relapse (Childress et al., 1993).

In the laboratory, more attention has been given to the role of internal stimuli. In one of the early studies, Stretch and Gerber (1973) trained monkeys to self-administer i.v. amphetamine, and then saline was substituted for the drug. After responding extinguished, saline remained in the infusion pumps, and a single amphetamine injection was given, and responding was reinstated as if the monkeys were injecting amphetamine. This method was later modified and used with rats (e.g., de Wit and Stewart, 1981, 1983). According to the basic procedure, i.v. self-administration is established. Saline is then substituted, and after responding has extinguished, a priming injection is delivered either i.v. or i.m., and responding on the lever (that now yields only saline infusions) is monitored. When the self-administered drug is given as the priming injection responding is reinstated. A saline prime results in very little responding. Priming injections can be given every few days, and drug-induced reinstatement of responding is produced reliably. It is important to give occasional saline primes to extinguish the conditioned responding that can occur with infusion-related stimuli (e.g., pump sounds and vibrations, light stimuli). The reinstatement of responding that occurs with priming injections of drug is presumed to be due to the interoceptive stimulus effects of the drug.

This reinstatement or relapse model has made it possible to examine variables that may enhance or impede relapse (See Carroll and Comer, 1995). The priming effect has been demonstrated in rats self-administering opioids, ethanol, psychomotor stimulants, and barbiturates. An even greater number of drugs have been tested as priming stimuli. Dose of the self-administered drug does not seem to be systematically related to the magnitude of the priming effect; however, the priming dose is directly related. Another finding is that often it takes a priming dose much higher than the self-administered dose to produce a sizable priming effect. Generally, drugs from the same pharmacologic class as the self-administered drugs function best as primes. In human studies of cue exposure and drug craving, drugs from the same pharmacologic class were also more effective at eliciting craving than other drugs or neutral stimuli (Ehrman et al., 1992). Another general finding is that

only drugs that had been established in drug reinforcement paradigms for animals and/or humans function as primes.

Several other parameters of the relapse model have been explored, such as the temporal and schedule aspects. De Wit and Stewart (1981) examined the time interval between the last self-administered drug injection and the priming injection. They found that as the interval increased, reinstatement of responding decreased. It was recently reported that a priming injection reinstated responding 3 to 4 days after self-administration had extinguished (Shaham et al., 1994). Several studies indicate that priming injections can be given repeatedly with no diminution in the magnitude of the response, although occasionally rats exhibit their greatest responding after the first prime. In most of the priming studies the schedule that is used is a fixed ratio (FR) 1 during the self-administration and priming period. However, in a recent study, the schedule was varied from 2 to 4 and 8 (Rawleigh, *personal communication*). Rats self-administering cocaine during hours 1 and 2 increased their responding such that the number of infusions remained constant, but extinction responding and reinstatement of responding after the cocaine prime decreased as FR increased.

The value of producing a reliable animal model of relapse is to test potential treatment strategies. Several initial attempts have been made to examine pharmacologic and behavioral treatments. One use of the model is to determine whether drugs that are used in the treatment of current and abstinent drug users may themselves promote relapse behavior. For instance, desipramine is an antidepressant that was used to relieve post-cocaine anhedonia and craving (e.g., Gawin and Kleber, 1984; Kosten et al., 1987), yet others have reported that desipramine may stimulate relapse by producing an interoceptive state (jitteriness) that is similar to the effects of cocaine (Weiss, 1988). In the laboratory desipramine did not function as a prime for cocaine-trained rats (Comer, *personal communication*, 1994). Bromocriptine, a dopamine D_2 receptor agonist with low abuse potential, has been used to treat cocaine craving in humans (Dackis and Gold, 1985). In the rat relapse paradigm Wise et al. (1990) found that bromocriptine reinstated responding that had previously been reinforced by cocaine or heroin. Buprenorphine, a partial agonist at the mu opioid receptor, also is used for treatment of heroin and cocaine abusers (Kosten et al., 1989); however, it did not have a priming effect in cocaine-trained rats (Comer et al., 1994b; Stewart and Wise, 1992).

Another approach to studying treatment drugs with the relapse model has been to pre-treat the cocaine-trained animals with the treatment drug of interest before administering the cocaine prime. In an initial study of this type, cocaine-trained rats were pretreated with buprenorphine and a dose-related suppression in responding elicited by a 3.2 mg/kg cocaine prime resulted (Comer et al., 1994b). The purpose of this test was to determine whether buprenorphine would block the cocaine-priming effect. The highest dose of buprenorphine (0.4 mg/kg) suppressed the effects of a cocaine prime given on the second day, while it did not interfere with cocaine self-administration on day 2. This study was replicated with etonitazene, a full mu agonist, and naltrexone, an opioid antagonist, to determine whether the agonist or antagonist effects of buprenorphine were responsible for blocking the cocaine priming effect. Etonitazene had effects similar to buprenorphine, while naltrexone had no effect, indicating it was the mu agonist activity.

Another method of reducing drug self-administration in animals (e.g., Carroll et al., 1989, Carroll and Rodefer, 1993; Nader and Woolverton, 1992a,b) and humans (e.g., Higgins et al., 1993, 1994a,b) is to enrich the environment with alternative nondrug reinforcement. This method also prevents or reduces the rate of acquisition of drug self-administration (Carroll and Lac, 1993). This approach was applied to the relapse model in one laboratory study. In the first, food was used as alternative reinforcement, and rats had access to 8 to 12 g, 20 g, or ad libitum amounts of food each day (Comer et al., 1995a). The differing feeding conditions had no effect on number of infusions during a 2-hr cocaine self-administration period, but as the amount of food availability increased, there was a systematic decrease in extinction and relapse responding, indicating that alternative reinforcement suppressed the relapse response.

In summary, animal models of relapse have been useful for identifying pharmacologic and behavioral conditions that may suppress relapse tendencies in humans. Discussions regarding mechanisms of the priming effect can be found in reviews of this topic (e.g., Carroll and Comer, 1995). Briefly, one theory that has been advanced recently is that the relapse model is similar to drug discrimination training (e.g., Bickel and Kelly, 1988). Another interpretation is advanced in the incentive-motivation theory (e.g., Stewart, 1984; Stewart and de Wit, 1987; Stewart and Wise, 1992). This hypothesis assumes that drugs that function as priming stimuli have strong motivational-appetitive effects. They are reinforcing, and they increase locomotion and exploration of the environment. Other stimuli such as electrical brain stimulation and ethologically relevant stimuli activate the same neural reward pathways, and priming effects have been demonstrated with these stimuli as well as food.

ASSESSING REINFORCING EFFICACY OF DRUGS

Essential to the evaluation of the drug reinforcement in animals is the measurement of the reinforcing efficacy of drugs. Reinforcing efficacy is the degree to which a drug or any other reinforcement maintains behavior. It is not useful to discuss reinforcing efficacy as an absolute value; rather, reinforcement is discussed in terms of their relative reinforcing efficacy when compared with reinforcement established by other stimuli, different amounts of the same substance, or the same substance under different conditions.

There are several methods for estimating the reinforcing efficacy of drugs in animals.

Two of these methods, choice and progressive ratio (PR), have been previously reviewed (Katz, 1990; Woolverton and Nader, 1990), and they will be briefly summarized here. Another method of evaluating reinforcing efficacy is derived from the recent application of behavioral economic principles to drug-reinforced behavior (e.g., Hursh, 1991). A behavioral economic analysis of drug self-administration data can determine several parameters of reinforcing efficacy, such as the elasticity of responding to increases in price or response requirement. These methods are described in more detail below.

Choice

In choice procedures, the animal is allowed to select, by the allocation of its response, whether to self-administer drug or vehicle or a high versus low drug dose or some other event such as food presentation. Animals will choose to self-administer a reinforcing drug over its vehicle. Johanson and Schuster (1975) trained rhesus monkeys to self-administer cocaine intravenously under an FR 5 schedule. For each sampling trial, only responses on one lever resulted in the drug infusions, and the active lever alternated between the two sampling trials. Each animal was allowed to self-administer five infusions during the sampling trials. During the choice trials, the animal could respond on either lever to receive the infusions associated with that lever. The results showed that the animals chose to self-administer cocaine over saline. The drug maintained higher rates of responding for its delivery than the saline vehicle, suggesting that cocaine was more reinforcing or had a greater reinforcing efficacy than saline.

Different doses of drug can vary in reinforcing efficacy. Iglauer and Woods (1974) used a concurrent VI-VI procedure with rhesus monkeys trained to lever press for i.v. administration of cocaine. Responding on one lever resulted in the delivery of a fixed dose of cocaine, whereas responding on the other lever resulted in the delivery of variable doses of cocaine. They found that responding was always greater on the lever associated with the highest dose of cocaine. When given a choice, the monkeys selected the larger cocaine dose. This procedure demonstrated that higher doses of drug have greater relative reinforcing efficacy.

Progressive Ratio Schedule

The progressive ratio (PR) schedule is another measure that is frequently used in studying drug reinforcement in animals. Under a PR schedule, the number of responses required for drug delivery (i.e. the ratio) is systematically increased until responding for the drug decreases. Presumably, the amount of effort (i.e., work) that an animal will perform for the drug is a measure of that drug's reinforcing efficacy. This amount of effort is referred to as the break point, i.e., the last completed ratio for drug delivery before responding stopped for a predetermined amount of time. Drugs with greater reinforcing efficacy maintain more behavior than drugs with less reinforcing efficacy and higher drug doses maintain more behavior than lower drug doses. Griffiths et al. (1979) and Woolverton (1995) studied various doses of i.v. cocaine in baboons and rhesus monkeys, respectively, and responding under PR schedules that ranged from 160 to 7,200 (Griffiths et al. 1979) or 120 to 1,920 (Woolverton, 1995) responses. They reported that lower doses of cocaine maintained lower break points and higher cocaine doses maintained higher break points in these animals. These studies also showed that higher break points are achieved when the intertrial interval (ITI) is increased, and the inverted-U–shaped dose-effect function becomes a steadily increasing function of dose as ITI increases. Thus, while the progressive-ratio schedule reduces the direct-response rate-decreasing effects of drugs that can complicate interpretations of reinforcing efficacy by scheduling fewer drug injections than an FR schedule, drug-reinforced behavior may still be suppressed if injections are too closely spaced. These data support the idea that higher drug doses are more efficacious reinforcement than lower drug doses under a PR schedule of reinforcement.

Behavioral Economic Analysis of Demand for Drug

Reinforcing efficacy can also be evaluated using a behavioral economic analysis. Behavioral economics is the concept of applying microeconomic theories to the study of response-reinforcement interactions (see Chapter 3). A fundamental aspect of behavioral economics is the demand function, or curve. This function defines the relationship between the consumption and the cost of drug reinforcement. It has shown that demand is usually a positively decelerating function, with the consumption of drug reinforcement decreasing as its cost increases. In the self-administration procedure, cost is defined as responses/mg, and it can be changed by altering either number of required (FR) responses or dose. Thus, the demand function is derived by varying the ratio required or the dose and measuring the amount of drug self-administered under each FR. Elasticity is represented by the slope of the demand curve, and it provides information about the value of the drug. Elastic demand occurs when increases in the cost of the drug result in proportionally greater decreases in its consumption. In this case a demand curve would have a slope < -1. Elastic demand is typically seen with commodities that are not considered to be essential items and can be eliminated if their cost is too high. In contrast, when increases in the cost of the commodity result in relatively small decreases in its consumption (slope > -1), the demand for the commodity is said to be inelastic and the commodities can be thought of as essential items like food and water. Many studies have demonstrated that the demand for drugs is inelastic. The goal of the treatment programs would be to make the demand for drugs more elastic.

A related concept is the P-max value, or the drug price at which maximum responding occurs. While elasticity/inelasticity is concerned with the amount of drug administered relative to price, the P-max value is the maximum amount of effort expended for the delivery of drug. It is very important to note, however, that the demand for reinforcement is not inherent to that substance or event. For instance, P-max values are altered differently by behavioral (Carroll, 1993; Comer et al., 1994a), pharmacologic (Carroll et al., 1994; Carroll et al., 1992), and combinations of behavioral and pharmacologic (Rawleigh et al., 1995) interventions. For example, behavioral interventions such as concurrent availability of reinforcement and pharmacologic treatments such as buprenorphine injections shift P-max to the left. However, when both treatments are given, overall responding is so markedly suppressed the demand curves are flattened and there is a smaller shift to the left in P-max. A better way to compare shifts in P-max across different interventions would be to use normalized demand curves (see Hursh and Winger, 1995). A goal of drug abuse treatment would be to decrease P-max by increasing the elasticity of demand for drug.

VARIABLES THAT MODIFY DRUG REINFORCEMENT

Pharmacologic Variables

Type of Drug

Reinforcement occurs with animal models and psychoactive drugs from several pharmacologic classes. Reinforcing effects have been demonstrated with (1) sedative hypnotics such as ethanol, benzodiazepines (e.g., diazepam, midazolam, triazolam), and barbiturates (e.g., pentobarbital, methohexital, secobarbital), (2) opioids (e.g., morphine, heroin, fentanyl, etonitazene, and methadone), (3) psychomotor stimulants (e.g., cocaine, methamphetamine, and amphetamine), and (4) dissociative anesthetics/N-methyl-D-aspartate (NMDA) receptor antagonists (e.g., ketamine, phencyclidine, dizocilpine). Almost every drug that humans abuse is self-administered by animals.

The notable exceptions are LSD and THC. It is not yet clear whether these are true species differences or whether procedural or technical problems have prevented the development of an animal model. For instance, LSD is not used regularly by humans, and the number of users is very low (Monitoring the Future Study, 1994). Most animal models are designed for frequent administration and a high percentage of animals are expected to acquire self-administration. A problem with THC is that it is not soluble in water, which would rule out i.v. or oral methods. A reliable method for drug smoking has only recently been developed with cocaine (Carroll et al., 1990a) and extended to heroin (Mattox et al., 1995). This method may prove useful in developing an animal model for THC smoking.

While nicotine and caffeine are the most commonly used drugs in humans, they have not been widely studied in animals. Nicotine self-administration has been demonstrated with i.v. methods in animals (e.g., Corrigal, 1992; Henningfield and Goldberg, 1985), but it has not been easily established and occurs under a limited range of experimental conditions. Caffeine self-administration occurs under even more limited conditions (e.g., Griffiths and Woodson, 1988; Heppner et al., 1986). Again, this discrepancy may be a result of the delivery method and the temporal parameters used in most self-administration studies. For instance, nicotine self-administration in the form of cigarette smoking has been maintained in nonhuman primates only when the behavior is reinforced by a sweetened liquid or other nondrug substances (e.g., Ando and Yanagita, 1981). Another approach that may be successful is to initiate smoking behavior with a drug that is smoked (e.g., cocaine or heroin) and substitute or fade in nicotine. Dose also may be critical with drugs such as nicotine and caffeine where high doses may be aversive. For example, the discriminative stimulus effects of caffeine appear to be different at low and high doses (Mumford and Holtzman, 1991). Another inconsistency is that there are a few drugs self-administered by animals (e.g., lidocaine,

mazindol, procaine) that are rarely abused by humans. However, overall there is a consistent pattern that drugs self-administered by animals are also abused by humans, and drugs not abused by humans are not self-administered by animals.

Dose

Dose or the amount of drug delivered at the completion of each response requirement may be varied by changing the volume or the drug concentration. Another term for dose is *reinforcement magnitude*. With all routes of administration, the dose (mg/kg) of drug per delivery or unit dose is set by the experimenter and serves as an independent variable; however, the animal controls the total amount of drug intake per session; thus, total drug intake (mg/kg) is a dependent variable. The dose-response function for most self-administered drugs resembles an inverted-U shape. There is a gradual increase in response rate as dose increases followed by a plateau and a decline at higher doses. The descending limb of the dose-response function could be due to several factors or a combination thereof. For instance, high doses could (1) impair the motor performance needed to obtain more drug; (2) produce an aversive or punishing effect; (3) result in satiation; and (4) with oral self-administration and smoking, strong taste may be a limiting factor at high doses/concentrations. Despite the decrease in responding that occurs at higher drug doses or concentrations, it is usually the case that drug intake (mg/kg) continues to increase at higher doses and that higher doses have greater reinforcing efficacy (e.g., Meisch et al., 1981). Higher doses sustain behavior at higher FRs, and higher doses are chosen over lower doses in concurrent choice studies.

The factors that control the descending limb may vary with drug type. A control that would identify motor impairment would be to have a concurrent or multiple schedule that would also offer access to nondrug reinforcement (e.g., food, sweetened liquid). It would be important to ensure that low doses of the drug and the nondrug alternative reinforcement generated comparable rates and patterns of behavior under the same schedule of delivery for both events before comparisons could be made. If performance maintained by both drug and nondrug reinforcement was disrupted, it would be assumed that the higher doses of the drug produced a general rate-decreasing effect. If drug intake selectively decreased, it might be interpreted as a satiation effect. When this type of control was used in an oral phencyclidine self-administration study in monkeys, it was found that at higher drug concentrations, drug self-administration declined, but self-administration of a concurrently available nondrug reinforcement, saccharin, continued at a high and steady rate (Carroll, 1985a). However, this comparison does not rule out the possibility that the drug may be aversive or suppressive for all operant behavior. To examine this possibility, the drug could be used in a negative reinforcement paradigm to determine whether the animal would increase the response to turn off administration of the drug.

There are a number of factors that alter the shape of a dose-response function. Dose-response functions are generally the same inverted-U shape for i.v., i.g., and oral routes of self-administration; however, the smoking route has produced relatively flat curves (e.g., Carroll et al., 1990a; Mattox et al., 1995). This may be due to different smoking topographies at high concentrations. Some drugs have a very narrow range over which responding occurs, such as dissociative anesthetics like phencyclidine (Carroll and Stotz, 1984) and ketamine (Carroll and Stotz, 1983). Another factor that results in a deviation from the inverted U is adding a timeout after each drug delivery (e.g., Balster and Schuster 1973, Griffiths et al., 1980; Woolverton and Virus, 1989). In this case, responding steadily increases with increases in dose. Furthermore, certain types of schedules, such as the second-order schedules in which drug is delivered at the end of the session and/or only a single injection is delivered per day, yield rel-

atively flat dose-response curves (Goldberg, 1973). Even with simple schedules (e.g., FR, FI) there is an interaction between the schedule values used and the dose-response function. Young and Herling (1986), in their review of the literature noted that the maximum response rate increases with dose.

Infusion Duration

There is some evidence suggesting that the speed at which an infusion occurs will determine the strength of the reinforcing effect. Specifically, Balster and Schuster (1973) and Kato et al., (1987) showed that in monkeys the longer the duration of a cocaine or pentobarbital infusion, (with dose held constant) the less the reinforcing effect. In fact, reinforcing efficacy is negatively correlated with infusion duration assuming dose is held constant. These laboratory data are consistent with reports from the human literature. That rate of onset is an important determinant of the abuse potential of drugs (e.g., de Wit et al. 1993; Jaffe 1990). The rush created by rapid onset of a drug's subjective effects is reported to be more euphorigenic than drugs that have a gradual onset of action. Rate of onset has been considered a determinant of abuse liability among drugs within the same pharmacologic class (e.g., psychomotor stimulants, sedative-hypnotics) and when comparing different routes of administration (i.v. or smoking vs oral).

Drug History

Studies comparing drug history are limited by the expense of drug-naive monkeys and by the lack of adequate methods for quantifying acquisition. However, several examples in the literature from different species, routes of self-administration, and drug classes indicate that drug history will determine the probability that an animal will self-administer a drug and the rate at which it will occur. With the oral route, monkeys that had a history of pentobarbital self-administration acquired methohexital self-administration more readily than monkeys that had experience with phencyclidine (Carroll et al., 1984). Young and Woods (1981) found that the antitussive drug dextrorphan maintained responding in ketamine-trained animals but not in codeine trained animals. Beardsley et al. (1990) studied rhesus monkeys and PCP or cocaine reinforcement. Initially, the animals were self-administering either PCP or cocaine. They were then tested for the self-administration of dizocilpine (MK 801), a drug that has pharmacological effects similar to PCP. In the animals that were self-administering cocaine, dizocilpine was not self-administered; however, monkeys that had a PCP self-administration history readily self-administered dizocilpine. Schlichting et al. (1971) reported higher rates of amphetamine self-administration in monkeys with a cocaine self-administration history than in those with a codeine or pentobarbital history. They suggested that responding is more likely to be maintained when the first and second drug have similar discriminative stimulus effects. This is usually determined by training the animal to make one response after a drug injection and another response after the vehicle injection. If drug-appropriate responding occurs after a second drug is substituted for the initial drug, then it is assumed both drugs have similar discriminative stimulus effects. Shared discriminative stimulus effects (Grant et al., 1991) may explain the rapid establishment of ethanol reinforcement in monkeys trained to self-administer orally delivered phencyclidine (Carroll, 1987b). There is also evidence that contradicts this hypothesis. For instance, Woolverton and coworkers (1980) reported higher rates of self-administration of amphetamine analogues in pentobarbital than cocaine-trained monkeys. In studies of opioid self-administration, drug history also carries with it the variable of physical dependence. Opioid partial agonist (e.g., pentazocine, buprenorphine) reinforcement was established in nondependent but not in dependent animals (Hoffmeister, 1979). Other examples of drug history are given in the section on acquisition.

Organismic Variables

The following sections describe variables that are innately determined. Although organisms may be irreversibly altered by surgery, neurochemical treatments, drug history, and other variables, those factors are considered to be environmentally determined.

Species

Drug-reinforced behavior has been demonstrated in baboons, cats, dogs, mice, rhesus and squirrel monkeys, pigeons, rats, and humans. The use of a particular species is limited by the amount of training required, the expense, and the requirements of the operant apparatus. For example, the apparatus for mice is very small and custom made, and total drug intake is low; however, they are inexpensive and offer an opportunity for genetic studies. In contrast, the apparatus for monkeys is larger and commonly available, and monkeys take a wide range of drugs; however, they are expensive and genetic variables are difficult to study. Rodents and cats are less likely to consume drugs orally than rhesus monkeys (Carroll and Meisch, 1984). For dogs, a special apparatus is used so that the response is a foot pedal. Overall, most of the work has been done with rats and monkeys, and with only a few exceptions the data produced have been similar in rats, monkeys, and humans. The use of baboons and rhesus and squirrel monkeys has been more successful than the use of rodent species in extending drug self-administration models to many types of drugs. For example, there are few drugs that rats will self-administer orally (e.g., ethanol, etonitazene), and drug reinforcement does not readily occur when some drugs are delivered intravenously (e.g., ethanol, phencyclidine) in rats. This generality across many species suggests, as discussed by Macenski and Meisch (1994), that drug self-administration is a variant of a normal process that exists to assist the animal to find food, mates, and other natural rewards necessary for survival.

Genetics

This variable has been thoroughly reviewed previously (George, 1987; George and Meisch, 1984), and in other sections of this volume (see Chapter 8). Much of the work investigating genetic variables has been done with alcohol. There are two commonly used rat lines, one from Indiana University (P and NP) and one from Finland (AA and ANA), that have been selectively bred for high alcohol and low alcohol intake, respectively. In an intragastric ethanol self-administration procedure P rats self-injected 9.4 g/kg per day while NP rats self-administered only 0.7 g/kg (Waller et al. 1984). Similarly, AA rats consistently maintained higher rates of lever pressing for ethanol and exceeded vehicle (water) levels, compared with ANA rats (Ritz et al., 1986).

Another method used to examine genetic variables is the comparison of inbred rat and mouse strains. For instance, both Lewis and Fischer 344 rat strains consume ethanol in volumes greater than the water vehicle, and blood ethanol concentrations in both strains reflected increases in concentration. However, Lewis rats showed more evidence of reinforcing effects. They consumed more ethanol, responding increased in proportion to increased FR values, and an inverted-U–shaped concentration-response function was obtained (Ritz et al., 1986). Similar results were obtained in studies of inbred mice. Reinforcing effects of ethanol were demonstrated for C57BL/6J mice but not for BALB/6J mice, although both strains had comparable amounts of food-induced drinking (Elmer et al., 1987a,b, 1988).

Gender

Epidemiologic studies of drug abuse indicate that with the exception of tranquilizers and cigarettes (in teenagers), males abuse drugs more often than females (Monitoring the Future Study, 1994). It is not clear whether these differences, which are striking with some drugs, are due to true gender differences or societal pressures. This is an instance where animal studies would be invaluable; however, gender is a variable that has received little attention in animal research. With most drugs and species self-administration has been demonstrated in both males and females; direct within-experiment comparisons are limited. In one study, male monkeys acquired oral ethanol self-administration more readily than female monkeys (Grant and Johanson, 1988). A recent report indicated that a higher percentage of males than females acquired self-administration of orally delivered phencyclidine (Pakarinen and Woods, 1994). A number of earlier ethanol studies conducted with rats generally indicate that once acquisition has occurred, female rats self-administer more drug than male rats, and they are more sensitive to drug effects. For instance, female rats drink more ethanol than male rats, and this has been attributed to a higher rate of metabolism in female rats (Ericksson, 1969, 1971). Female rats also consumed more caffeine (Heppner et al., 1986) and morphine (Alexander et al., 1978; Hill, 1978) and a morphine-sucrose solution (Hadaway et al., 1979) than male rats. It is important to include female subjects not only because they appear to be more sensitive to reinforcing effects of drugs, but also because research needs to determine whether this may vary as a function of hormonal cycles.

ENVIRONMENTAL VARIABLES IN DRUG-REINFORCED BEHAVIOR

As in humans, drug-reinforced behavior in animals involves a complicated interaction of the pharmacology of the drug, several different organismic variables, and the environmental context in which drug-taking occurs. Although much research has been conducted to determine the role of the first two variables, it is also clear that the environment plays a very important role in drug-reinforced behavior. There are several environmental variables that influence this process. Some of the more studied variables are access to drug, feeding conditions, the availability of alternative reinforcement in the environment, drug and behavioral reinforcement history, stress, and social factors.

Drug Access

Whether the animal has limited or unlimited access to the drug is a critical element in determining drug reinforcement. Generally, animals with limited access to the drug self-administer more of the drug and exhibit more regular rates of self-administration than when drug access is unlimited. However, the patterning of intake can depend on the drug that is being self-administered. In a classic study, Bozarth and Wise (1985) demonstrated that in rats self-administering cocaine, there was a cyclic patterning of administration with periods of high rates of self-administration followed by periods of no drug administration. In contrast, rats self-administering heroin showed a more invariable rate of self-administration. The results suggest that the patterning of drug self-administration is influenced by the drug itself.

Unlimited access to drugs in the self-administration paradigm can result in toxicity and death. Johanson et al. (1976) illustrated that in rhesus monkeys given unlimited opportunity to self-administer several psychomotor stimulant drugs, 11 of the 15 subjects died of drug overdose. Others have shown that continuous access to ethanol led to patterns of high and low intakes periodically characterized by withdrawal signs (Woods et al., 1971). Thus, unlimited drug access leads to different toxic effects depending on type of drug and route of administration.

Feeding Condition

Another important variable is the feeding condition. It has been shown consistently that food-deprived animals self-administer greater amounts of drugs than animals that are food satiated. There are several reviews of this finding that discuss the interaction between feeding conditions and drug self-administration (e.g., Carroll and Meisch, 1984; Carroll, 1996). In a study published by Comer et al. (1995b), rhesus monkeys were trained to self-administer smoked cocaine base under a chained FR-FR schedule of reinforcement. The animals were tested in both a food-satiated condition in which they were maintained at 100% of their free-feeding weight (no food restrictions) and also under a food-restricted condition, at 90% of their free-feeding weight. Under the food-restricted condition, the number of drug deliveries increased, as did the number of responses emitted for the drug delivery. This finding also has been reported with oral PCP self-administration (Rodefer et al., 1996). An economic analysis of the feeding effects showed that food satiation decreased the intensity of demand for PCP and ethanol and shifted the P-max value to the left. Intensity is defined as a parallel shift up or down in the demand curve. Figure 1 illustrates the change in intensity and shift in P-max. These results demonstrate that food deprivation increases the reinforcing efficacy of drugs.

Alternative Nondrug Reinforcement

The availability and magnitude of alternative nondrug reinforcement is another environmental variable that alters drug-reinforced behavior. Nader and Woolverton (1991) allowed rhesus monkeys to choose between i.v. cocaine deliveries and differing numbers of food pellets. The experimental design was such that two colored lights were present during the session. Each color was paired with either food or reinforcement. Thirty presses on the lever in the presence of the food stimulus light resulted in the delivery of food pellets, whereas 30 presses on the lever in the presence of the cocaine stimulus light resulted in an infusion of cocaine. The results demonstrated that when the choice was one food pellet versus various doses of cocaine, the animals chose to respond for the cocaine. However, as the number of food pellets increased, the number of cocaine choices decreased. These results suggest that the reinforcing efficacy of a drug can be altered by varying the magnitude of an alternative nondrug reinforcement.

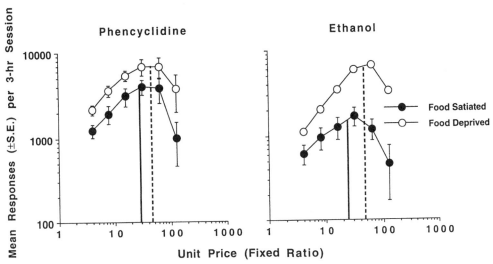

FIG. 1. Mean (I.S.E.) responses for phencyclidine (left) and ethanol (right) are presented for six or seven rhesus monkeys, respectively, over a range of fixed ratio (FR) values (4, 8, 16, 32, 64, and 128) under food deprivation (filled circles) and food satiation (open circles) conditions. Each liquid delivery (0.6 ml) was contingent upon completion of the FR schedule; water-maintained responding was low and is not presented. Vertical lines represent P-max values or an estimate of the unit price at which maximum responding occurred. The solid lines refer to the food satiation condition, and broken lines indicate food deprivation. Each point represents a mean of the last 5 days of stable behavior. (From Rodefer et al.)

Data from our laboratory also indicate that the availability of alternative reinforcement alters drug-reinforced behavior. For example, rats given concurrent access to a solution of glucose plus saccharin in addition to cocaine will self-administer less cocaine than rats that have access to water (Carroll et al., 1989; Comer et al., 1994). Similarly, the self-administration of phencyclidine (PCP) is decreased in rhesus monkeys with concurrent access to saccharin (Rawleigh et al., 1996). It is possible that nondrug reinforcement is competing with drug reinforcement. This hypothesis was tested by Comer et al. (1995b). Rhesus monkeys were trained to self-administer smoked cocaine base and tested with several behavioral and pharmacologic manipulations. As the FR required for cocaine deliveries increased, the number of cocaine deliveries decreased. Simultaneously, the amount of saccharin consumed increased. The authors suggested that under

these conditions, saccharin was substituting for cocaine reinforcement. Thus, the availability of alternative reinforcement can decrease drug self-administration in many species of animals and under a variety of experimental conditions.

Stress

There have been relatively few studies done evaluating stress in drug-reinforced behavior. The combination of different types of stressors and different drugs makes it difficult to determine a clear-cut role for stress. Physical immobilization is one of the more frequently used stressors in animals. Shaham et al. (1992) studied the role of this stressor on the self-administration of the opioids morphine and fentanyl. Rats were immobilized before the start of the self-administration period and their preference, as defined by the amount of drug that they drank, was measured daily. The rats that had been stressed preferred to drink the opioids over water significantly more than rats that had not undergone the stress. Another study (Ramsey and van Ree, 1992) examined the effects of two very different types of stressors on the self-administration of cocaine. Different groups of rats were exposed either to the physical stress induced by hot plate exposure or repeated foot shocks or to the emotional stress of watching another rat undergoing these stressors. The rats that were physically stressed did not increase cocaine self-administration. In contrast, the rats that were emotionally stressed did increase their self-administration of cocaine. These authors suggest that physical stress does not alter drug reinforcement whereas emotional stress does.

A set of interesting studies by Piazza and coworkers (1989, 1993) has provided evidence for an interaction between stress, dopamine, and drug reinforcement. As discussed earlier, tail-pinch induced stress increases the acquisition of amphetamine self-administration. Additionally, the stress hormone, corticosterone, is self-administered by rats via the i.v. (Piazza et al., 1993) and the oral (Deroche et al., 1993) routes of administration in doses that are within the range that is released during stressful situations. Lastly, this stressor also appears to increase the release of dopamine, a neurotransmitter thought to be critical for reinforcement (Rouge-Pont et al., 1993). All of these lines of evidence support the hypothesis that stress plays some role in drug reinforcement and may serve to enhance the reinforcing effects of other drugs.

Social Isolation

Although equivocal, the data appear to suggest an influence of social isolation on the development of the self-administration of drugs. Schenk et al. (1987) tested the self-administration of cocaine in rats that were either housed alone or in groups. The rats that were housed alone self-administered cocaine, whereas the group-housed animals did not. In contrast, Boyle et al. (1990) reported no differences between groups of isolated rats and group-housed rats in the self-administration of cocaine. Another study conducted by Zimmerberg and Brett (1992) evaluated the effects of social isolation and gender on the self-administration of drugs. Male and female rats were either group housed or isolated. When given a choice between drinking a stimulant or a depressant, male isolated rats chose the stimulant, but female isolated rats chose the depressant. Rats that had been group housed did not demonstrate a preference for either drug, suggesting an interaction between gender and social isolation. Further study is necessary to determine the role of isolation in drug reinforcement.

Behavioral History

It is clear that the behavioral history of the organism plays a major role in the drug effects observed. Barrett and colleagues have written several excellent reviews on the importance of environmental variables, especially behavioral and drug history, on behavior maintained by food, shock, and drugs (Barrett, 1987; Barrett and Witkin, 1986; Nader et al., 1992). The influence of behavioral and drug history in drug-reinforced behavior is an extension of the operant conditioning rules that govern behavior maintained by other events. For example, in the Nader et al. (1992) review, data on two monkeys that were self-administering cocaine under an FI 15-min schedule for reinforcement was reported. One monkey had previous operant experience under only FI schedules of reinforcement, whereas the other monkey had previous operant experience only under FR schedules of reinforcement. When both monkeys were started on the FI 15-min schedule for cocaine delivery, the monkey with the experience on the FR schedules produced more responding than the monkey with no such behavioral history. Two other monkeys were trained to self-administer cocaine under an FR 100 or 90 schedule for reinforcement. Again, one monkey had a history of responding under FI schedules, whereas the other monkey had no experience with FI schedules. The monkey with the FI experience exhibited the classic "scalloped" pattern of responding seen with FI schedules, even though his responding was being reinforced under the FR schedule. These data suggest that previous experience with different schedules of reinforcement alter both the rate of responding and the patterning of responding for drug delivery.

Drug-reinforcement history is also a very important determinant of drug reinforcement. Hypothetically, if an animal has demonstrated a history of self-administering a certain drug, it is possible that the animal will differentially self-administer other drugs.

CONCLUSION

This review of drug reinforcement in animals discussed methods of establishing drug reinforcement via several routes of administration, including smoking, and models for different phases of the addiction process were presented. Methods for quantifying the reinforcing efficacy of self-administered drugs were examined, and the influence of organismic, pharmacologic, and historical variables as well as current conditions on the reinforcing efficacy of drugs was shown to be substantial. Overall, there are many similarities between animal and human drug-taking behavior. For example, they both use a variety of routes of administration and they find the same drugs to be reinforcing; patterns of drug intake are similar, but they vary with class of drug and drug availability; and access to alternative nondrug reinforcement reduces drug self-administration. In both animals and humans, drug-rewarded behavior appears to have commonalities and interactions with behavior rewarded by other events. For example, in animals drug self-administration interacts with behavior rewarded by food or intracranial self-stimulation (e.g., Hubner and Kornetsky, 1991; Katz et al., 1978; Kornetsky and Espos-

ito, 1979). In humans interactions also occur between feeding and drug abuse, and parallels have been drawn between drug addiction and gambling and compulsive eating. These may all be pathologic conditions of a reward system that exists for adaptive purposes. A number of behavioral principles have been identified that apply to animals and humans. For instance, the more drug that is available, the more drug will be taken, and more work will be done for a higher dose of drug.

Important differences exist between animal and human drug taking. For instance, most animals given the opportunity to self-administer a drug such as cocaine, codeine, heroin, pentobarbital, or phencyclidine will do so; however, only a small fraction of humans abuse these drugs. Obviously, there are cultural factors and environmental enrichments that prevent drug abuse in most humans; however, more research is needed to identify these factors and incorporate them into prevention and treatment strategies. Drug treatment studies have investigated a variety of treatment drugs based on positive results of animal research, but a major difference between animal and human drug-taking behavior is that the treatment drugs are much more effective in the animal laboratory than in the clinical setting. These differences are not necessarily weaknesses of the animal models; they may ultimately be the key to a better understanding of factors controlling human drug abuse.

FUTURE DIRECTIONS

Studies of drug reinforcement in animals have focused primarily on the steady-state phase of self-administration behavior. A great deal has been learned about experimental, environmental, pharmacologic, and organismic variables that control drug reinforcement. Future work is needed to better understand the transition states, acquisition, withdrawal, long-term craving, and relapse of reinstatement of drug self-administration. These are the critical stages for prevention or treatment attempts in humans. Thus, animal models that have excellent reliability and validity in stimulating human behavior would be desirable. Another suggestion would be to standardize methods of measuring reinforcing efficacy so that comparisons can be more easily made across laboratories and with different drugs and behavioral and/or pharmacologic treatments. Additionally, it is important to direct future attention to the type of drug that is studied. Epidemiologic reports indicate that the use of drugs such as THC may serve as a gateway for more serious (e.g., cocaine, opiates) drug use (Pagliaro and Pagliaro, 1993), and animal data suggest that seemingly benign agents such as caffeine may accelerate cocaine self-administration. Studies of drug reinforcement in animals have paid little attention to drugs such as nicotine, THC, and caffeine that are widely used by children and young adults, and may have an important role as gateway drugs. This is likely due to methodologic difficulties that could be overcome. Finally, a theme that ran through this chapter is the interaction between feeding and drug-taking behavior that is robust and occurs throughout all phases of the addiction process. Animal studies of this interaction need to be more closely tied to normal and pathologic human behavior.

SUMMARY

- Methods for establishing drug self-administration in animals and criteria for demonstrating drug reinforcement have been developed.
- Using these procedures, it is possible to examine animal models of several phases of drug addiction.
- Studies of the acquisition of drug reinforcement have shown the importance of several variables including a history of drug exposure, feeding conditions, and organismic factors such as activity level. Knowledge of these variables may aid in the study of prevention approaches; for example, animal data indicate that an increased amount and/or palatability of food prevents or delays acquisition of behavior maintained by cocaine reinforcement.

- Animal models of withdrawal suggest that feeding condition may modify withdrawal severity and that protracted withdrawal effects may be due to motivational deficits.
- Animal models of relapse may be useful in identifying factors that lead to craving and reinitiation of drug use in abstinent individuals. Both internal and external cues reinitiate extinguished responding that was previously maintained by drug reinforcement. Priming injections of the drug are the most effective method of reinstating responding and higher priming doses, lower response requirements, stress, and restricted feeding, which are all factors that enhance reinstatement. Interestingly, drugs that are not easily established as reinforcers in rats (e.g., caffeine, bromocriptine) are effective as priming stimuli to reinstate cocaine-maintained responding that has been extinguished.

REFERENCES

Ahlenius, S., and Engel, J. (1974) Behavioral stimulation induced by ethanol withdrawal. *Pharmacol. Biochem. Behav.* 2: 847–850.

Alexander, B.K., Coambs, R.B. and Hadaway, P.F. (1978) The effect of housing and gender on morphine self-administration in rats. *Psychopharmacology* 58: 175–179.

Altshuler, H.L. and Phillips, P.E. (1978) Intragastric self-administration of drugs by the primate. In: Ho, B.T., Richards, D.W., III and Chute, D.L. (eds.) *Drug discrimination and state dependent learning.* New York: Academic Press, pp. 263–282.

Ando, K. and Yanagita, T. (1981) Cigarette smoking in rhesus monkeys. *Psychopharmacology* 17: 117–127.

Balster, R.L. (1987) Abuse potential evaluation of inhalants. *Drug Alcohol Depend.* 49: 7–15.

Balster, R.L. and Schuster, C.R. (1973) Fixed-interval schedule of cocaine reinforcement: effect of dose and infusion duration. *J. Exp. Anal. Behav.* 20: 119–129.

Barrett, J.E. (1987) Nonpharmacologic factors determining the behavioral effects of drugs. In: Melzer, H.Y. (ed.) *Psychopharmacology, the third generation.* New York: Raven Press.

Barrett, J.E. and Witkin, J.M. (1986) The role of behavioral and pharmacological history in determining the effects of abused drugs. In: Goldberg, S.R. and Stolerman, I.P. (eds.), *Behavioral analysis of drug dependence.* New York: Academic Press, 1986.

Beardsley, P.M. and Balster, R.L. (1987) Behavioral dependence upon phencyclidine and ketamine in the rat. *J. Pharmacol. Exp. Ther.* 242: 203–211.

Beardsley, P.M., Hayes, B.A. and Balster, R.L. (1990) The self-administration of MK-801 can depend upon drug reinforcement history, and its discriminative stimulus properties are phencyclidine-like in rhesus monkeys. *J. Pharmacol. Exp. Ther.* 252: 953–959.

Bell, S.M., Gosnell, B.A., Krah, D.D. and Meisch, R.A. (1994) Ethanol reinforcement and its relationship to saccharin preference in Wistar rats. *Alcohol*, in press.

Belluzzi, J. and Stein, L. (1977) Enkephalin- and morphine-induced facilitation of long-term memory. *Neurosci. Abstr.* 3: 230.

Bickel, W.K. and Kelly, T.H. (1988) The relationship of stimulus control to the treatment of substance abuse. In: Ray, B.A. (Ed.) *Learning factors in substance abuse.* Washington, DC: U.S. Government Printing Office, pp.122–140.

Boyle, A.E., Gill, K., Smith, B.R. and Amit, Z. (1990) Differential effects of an early housing manipulation on cocaine-induced activity and self-administration in laboratory rats. *Pharmacol Biochem. Behav.* 39: 269–274.

Bozarth, M.A. and Wise, R.A. (1981) Intracranial self-administration of morphine into the ventral tegmental area in rats. *Life Sci.* 28: 551–555.

Bozarth, M.A., Wise, R.A. (1985) Toxicity associated with long-term intravenous heroin and cocaine self-administration in the rat. *J. Am. Med. Assoc.* 254: 81–83.

Branch, M.N., Dearing, M.E. and Lee, D.M. (1980) Acute and chronic effects of D⁹-tetrahydrocannabinol on complex behavior of the squirrel monkeys. *Psychopharmacology* 71: 247–256.

Brown, P.L. and Jenkins, H.M. (1968) Auto-shaping of the pigeon's key-peck. *J. Exp. Anal. Behav.* 11: 1–8.

Brown, Z.W., Amit, Z. and Rockman, G.E. (1979) Intraventricular self-administration of acetaldehyde, but not ethanol, in naive laboratory rats. *Psychopharmacology* 64: 271–276.

Carney, J.M. (1982) Effects of caffeine, theophylline and theobromine on schedule controlled responding in rats. *Br. J. Pharmacol.* 75: 451–454.

Carney, J.M., Llewellyn, M.E. and Woods, J.H. (1976) Variable interval responding maintained by intravenous codeine and ethanol injections in the rhesus monkey. *Pharmacol. Biochem. Behav.* 5: 577–582.

Carroll, M.E. (1982a) Oral self-administration of phencyclidine analogs by rhesus monkeys. *Psychopharmacology* 78: 116–120.

Carroll, M.E. (1982b) Rapid acquisition of oral phencyclidine self-administration in food-deprived and food-satiated rhesus monkeys: concurrent phencyclidine and water choice. *Pharmacol. Biochem. Behav.* 17: 341–346.

Carroll, M.E. (1985a) Concurrent phencyclidine and saccharin access: presentation of an alternative reinforcer reduces drug intake. *J. Exp. Anal. Behav.* 43: 131–144.

Carroll, M.E. (1985b) Performance maintained by orally-delivered phencyclidine under second-order, tandem and fixed interval schedules in food-satiated and food-deprived rhesus monkeys. *J. Pharmacol. Exp. Ther.* 232: 351–359.

Carroll, M.E. (1987a) A quantitative assessment of phencyclidine dependence produced by oral self-administration in rhesus monkeys. *J. Pharmacol. Exp. Ther.* 242: 405–412.

Carroll, M.E. (1987b) Self-administration of orally-delivered phencyclidine and ethanol under concurrent fixed-ratio schedules in rhesus monkeys. *Psychopharmacology* 93: 1–7.

Carroll, M.E. (1988) Self-administration of orally-delivered N-allylnormetazocine (SKF-10,047) in the rhesus monkey. *Pharmacol. Biochem. Behav.* 30: 493–500.

Carroll, M.E. (1993) The economic context of drug and nondrug reinforcers affects acquisition and maintenance of drug-reinforced behavior and withdrawal effects. *Drug Alcohol Depend.* 33: 201–210.

Carroll, M.E. (1996) Interactions between food and addiction. In: Niesink, R.J.M. and Kornet, M.L.M.W. (eds.) *Behavioral toxicology and addiction:* food, drugs and environment. The Netherlands: Open University Press.

Carroll, M.E. and Carmona, G. (1991) Effects of food FR and food deprivation on disruptions in food-maintained performance of monkeys during phencyclidine withdrawal. *Psychopharmacology* 104: 143–149.

Carroll, M.E., Carmona, G.N., May, S., Buzalsky, S. and Larson, C. (1992) Buprenorphine's effects on self-administration of smoked cocaine base and orally delivered phencyclidine, ethanol and saccharin in rhesus monkeys. *J. Pharmacol. Exp. Ther.* 261: 26–37.

Carroll, M.E., Carmona, G.N. and Rodefer, J.S. (1994) Phencyclidine (PCP) self-administration and withdrawal in rhesus monkeys: effects of buprenorphine and dizocilpine (MK-801) pretreatment. *Pharmacol. Biochem. Behav.* 48: 723–732.

Carroll, M.E. and Comer, S.D. (1993) Inhalants. In: *The National Institute on Drug Abuse Fourth Triennial Report to Congress on Drug Abuse and Drug Abuse Research.* Washington, DC: U.S. Government Printing Office.

Carroll, M.E. and Comer S.D. (1996) Animal models of relapse. *Exp. Clin. Psychopharmacol.* 4: 11–18.

Carroll, M.E., France, C.P. and Meisch, R.A. (1981) Intravenous self-administration of etonitazene, cocaine and phencyclidine in rats during food deprivation and satiation. *J. Pharmacol. Exp. Ther.* 217: 241–247.

Carroll, M.E., Krattiger, K.L., Gieske, D. and Sadoff, D.A. (1990a) Cocaine-base smoking in rhesus monkeys: reinforcing and physiological effects. *Psychopharmacology* 102: 443–450.

Carroll, M.E. and Lac, S.T. (1987) Cocaine withdrawal produces behavioral disruptions in rats. *Life Sci.* 40: 2183–2190.

Carroll, M.E. and Lac, S.T. (1993) Autoshaping i.v. cocaine self-administration in rats: effects of nondrug alternative reinforcers on acquisition. *Psychopharmacology* 110: 5–12.

Carroll, M.E., Lac, S.T. and Nygaard, S.L. (1989) A concurrently available nondrug reinforcer prevents the acquisition or decreases the maintenance of cocaine-reinforced behavior. *Psychopharmacology* 97: 23–29

Carroll, M.E., Lac, S.T., Walker, M., Kragh, R. and Newman, T. (1986) The effects of naltrexone on intravenous cocaine self-administration in rats during food satiation and deprivation. *J. Pharmacol. Exp. Ther.* 238: 1–7.

Carroll, M.E. and Meisch, R.A. (1978) Etonitazene as a reinforcer: oral intake of etonitazene by rhesus monkeys. *Psychopharmacology* 59: 225–229.

Carroll, M.E. and Meisch, R.A. (1984) Increased drug reinforced behavior due to food deprivation. In: Thompson, T., Dews, P.B. and Barrett, J.E. (Eds.) *Advances in Behavioral Pharmacology,* vol 4.L. New York: Academic Press, pp. 47–88.

Carroll, M.E. and Rodefer, J.S. (1993) The effects of income on choice between drug and an alternative nondrug reinforcer in monkeys. *Exp. Clin. Psychopharmacol.* 1: 110–120.

Carroll, M.E., Stitzer, M.L., Strain, E. and Meisch, R.A. (1990b) The behavioral pharmacology of alcohol and other drugs. In: Galanter, M. *(Ed.) Recent developments in alcoholism,* vol. 8. New York: Plenum, pp. 5–46.

Carroll, M.E. and Stotz, D.C. (1983) Oral d-amphetamine and ketamine self-administration by rhesus monkeys: effects of food deprivation. *J. Pharmacol. Exp. Ther.* 227: 28–e4.

Carroll, M.E. and Stotz, D.C. (1984) Increased phencyclidine self-administration due to food deprivation: interaction with concentration and training conditions. *Psychopharmacology* 84: 299–303.

Carroll, M.E., Stotz, D.C., Kliner, D.J. and Meisch, R.A. (1984) Self-administration of orally-delivered methohexital in rhesus monkeys: effects of food deprivation and satiation. *Pharmacol. Biochem. Behav.* 20: 145–151.

Childress, A.R., Hole, A.V., Ehrman, R., Robbins, S.J., McLellan, A.T. and O'Brien, C.P. (1993) Cue reactivity and cue reactivity interventions in drug dependence. In: Onken, L.S., Blaine, J.D. and Boren, J.J. (Eds.) *Behavioral treatments for drug abuse and dependence.* NIDA Research Monograph 137. Washington, DC: U.S. Government Printing Office, pp. 73–96.

Childress, A.R., McLellan, A.T., Ehrman, R. and O'Brien, C.P. (1988) Classically conditioned responses in opioid and cocaine dependence: A role in relapse? In: Ray, B.A. (ed.) *Learning factors in substance abuse.* NIDA Research Monograph. Washington, DC: U.S. Government Printing Office, pp. 44–61.

Childress, A.R., McLellan, A.T. and O'Brien, C.P. (1986) Abstinent opiate abusers exhibit conditioned craving, conditioned withdrawal and reductions in both through extinction. *Br. J. Addict.* 81: 655–660.

Comer, S.D., Hunt, V.R. and Carroll, M.E. (1994a) Effects of concurrent saccharin availability and buprenorphine pretreatment on demand for smoked cocaine base in rhesus monkeys. *Psychopharmacology* 115: 15–23.

Comer, S.D., Lac, S.T., Curtis, L.K. and Carroll, M.E. (1994b) Effects of buprenorphine and naltrexone in a model of cocaine relapse in rats. *J. Pharmacol. Exp. Ther.* 267: 1470–1477.

Comer, S.D., Lac, S.T., Wyvell, C.L., Curtis, L.K. and Carroll, M.E. (1995a) Food deprivation affects extinction and reinstatement of responding in rats. *Psychopharmacology.* 121:150–157.

Comer, S.D., Turner, D.M. and Carroll, M.E. (1995b) Effects of food deprivation on cocaine base smoking in rhesus monkeys. *Psychopharmacology* 119: 127–132.

Corrigal, W.A. (1992) A rodent model for nicotine self-administration. In: Boulton, A.A. and Baker, G.B. (eds.) *Animal models of drug addiction, neuromethods,* Vol. 21. Totowa, NJ: Humana Press, pp. 315–344.

Dackis, C.A. and Gold, M.S. (1985) Bromocriptine as treatment of cocaine abuse. *Lancet* 1: 1151–1152.

Davis, W. M. and Smith, S.G. (1987) Conditioned reinforcement as a measure of the rewarding properties of drugs.

In: Bozarth, M.A. (Ed.) *Methods of assessing the reinforcing properties of abused drugs.* New York: Springer-Verlag, pp. 199–210.

Davis, W.M. and Smith S.G. (1976) Role of conditioned reinforcers in the initiation, maintenance and extinction of drug-seeking behavior. *Pavlov. J. Biol. Sci.* 11: 222–236.

Deroche, V., Piazza, P.V., Deminiere, J.M., LeMoal, M. and Simon, H. (1993) Rats orally self-administer corticosterone. *Brain Res.* 622: 315–320.

de Wit, H., Dudish, S. and Ambre, J. (1993) Subjective and behavioral effects of diazepan depend on its rate of onset. *Psychopharmocology.* 112: 324–330.

de Wit, H. and Stewart, J. (1981) Reinstatement of cocaine-reinforced responding in the rat. *Psychopharmacology* 75: 134–143.

de Wit, H. and Stewart, J. (1983) Reinstatement of heroin-reinforced responding in the rat. *Psychopharmacology* 79: 29–31.

Dworkin, S. I., Goeders, N.E. and Smith, J.E. (1985) The reinforcing and rate effects of intracranial dopamine administration. In: Harris, L.S. (ed.) *Problems of drug dependence.* NIDA Research Monograph, pp. 242–248.

Ehrman, R.N., Robbins, S.J., Childress, A.R. and O'Brien, C.P. (1992) Conditioned responses to cocaine-related stimuli in cocaine abuse patients. *Psychopharmacology* 107: 523–529.

Elmer, G.I., Meisch, R.A. and George, F.R. (1987a) Differential concentration-response curves for oral ethanol self-administration in C57BL/6J and BALB/cJ mice. *Alcohol* 4: 63–68.

Elmer, G.I., Meisch, R.A. and George, F.R. (1987b) Mouse strain differences in operant self-administration of ethanol. *Behav. Genet.* 17: 439–451.

Elmer, G.I., Meisch, R.A., Goldberg, S.R. and George, F.R. (1988) Fixed-ratio schedules of oral ethanol self-administration in inbred mouse strains. *Psychopharmacology (Berl)* 96: 431–436.

Eriksson, K. (1969) Factors affecting voluntary alcohol consumption in the albino rat. *Ann. Zool. Fennici* 6: 227.

Eriksson, K. (1971) Inheritance of behavior towards alcohol in normal and motivated choice situations in mice. *Ann. Zool. Fennici* 8: 400–405.

Falk, J.L. (1961) Production of polydipsia in normal rats by an intermittent food schedule. *Science* 133: 195–196.

Fitch, T.E. and Roberts, D.C.S. (1993) The effects of dose and access restrictions on the periodicity of cocaine self-administration in the rat. *Drug Alcohol Depend.* 33: 119–128.

Ford, R.D., and Balster, R.L. (1976) Schedule-controlled behavior in the morphine dependent rat. *Pharmacol. Biochem. Behav.* 4: 569–573.

Gahtan, E., LaBounty, L., Wyvell, C. and Carroll, M.E. (1995) The relationship between saccharin consumption, oral ethanol and i.v. cocaine self-administration. *Pharmacol. Biochem. Behav.* 53: 919–925.

Gawin, F.H. and Kleber, H.D. (1986) Abstinence symptomatology and psychiatric diagnosis in cocaine abusers. *Arch. Gen. Psychiatry* 43:107–113.

Gawin, F.H. and Kleber, H.D. (1984) Open pilot trial with desipramine and lithium carbonate. *Arch. Gen. Psychiatry* 41: 903–910.

George, F.R. (1987) Genetic and environmental factors in ethanol self-administration. *Pharmacol. Biochem. Behav.* 27: 379.

George, F.R., Elmer, G.I., Meisch, R.A. and Goldberg, S.R. (1991) Orally delivered cocaine functions as a positive reinforcer in C57BL/6J mice. *Pharmacol. Biochem. Behav.* 38: 897–903.

George, F.R. and Goldberg, S.R. (1989) Genetic approaches to the analysis of addiction processes. *Trends Pharmacol. Sci.* 10, 78-83.

George, F.R. and Meisch, R.A. (1984) Oral narcotic intake as a reinforcer: genotype and environmental interactions. *Behavioral Genetics.* 14: 603 (abstract).

Glimcher, P.W., Giovino, A.A. and Hoebel, B.G. (1983) Self-injection of neurotensin into the ventral tegmental area (VTA). *Neurosci. Abstr.* 9: 120.

Goeders, N.E. and Smith, J.E. (1983) Cortical dopaminergic involvement in cocaine reinforcement. *Science* 221: 773–775.

Goeders, N.E. and Smith, J.E. (1985) Parameters of intracranial self-administration of cocaine into the medial prefrontal cortex. In: Harris, L.S. (ed.) *Problems of drug dependence,* 1984. pp. 132–137. Washington D.C: U.S. Government Printing Office. DHHS Publication Number (ADM) 85–1393.

Goeders, N.E. and Smith, J.E. (1987) Intracranial self-administration methodologies. *Neurosci. Biobehav. Rev.* 11: 319–329.

Goldberg, S.R. (1973) Comparable behavior maintained under fixed-ratio and second-order schedules of food presentation, cocaine injection or d-amphetamine injection in the squirrel monkey. *J. Pharmacol. Exp. Ther.* 18618–30

Goldberg, S.R. and Gardner, M.L. (1981) Second-order schedules: extended sequences of behavior controlled by brief environmental stimuli associated with drug-administration. In: Thompson, T. and Johanson, C.E. (eds.) *Behavioral pharmacology of human drug dependence.* NIDA Research Monograph No. 37. Washington, DC: U.S. Government Printing Office, pp. 241–270.

Goldberg, S.R. and Kelleher, R.T. (1976) Behavior controlled by scheduled injections of cocaine in squirrel and rhesus monkeys. *J. Exp. Anal. Behav.* 25: 93–104.

Goldberg, S.R., Morse, W.H. and Goldberg, D.M. (1976) Behavior maintained under a second-order schedule of intramuscular injections of morphine or codeine in rhesus monkeys. *J. Pharmacol. Exp. Ther.* 199: 278–286.

Gosnell, B.A. and Krahn, D.D. (1992) The relationship between saccharin and alcohol intake in rats. *Alcohol* 9: 203–206.

Grant, K.A. and Johanson, C.E. (1988) Oral ethanol self-administration in free-feeding rhesus monkeys. *Alcohol Clin. Exp. Res.* 12: 780–784.

Grant, K.A., Knisley, J.S., Tabakoff, B., Barrett, J.E. and Balster, R.L. (1991) Ethanol-like discriminative stimulus effects of noncompetitive n-methyl-d-aspartate antagonists. *Behav. Pharmacol.* 2: 87–95.

Griffiths, R.R., Bigelow, G.E. and Henningfield, J.E. (1980) Similarities in animal and human drug taking behavior. In: Mello, N.K. (Ed.) *Advances in substance abuse,* vol. 1. Greenwich, CT: JAI Press, pp. 1–90.

Griffiths, R.R., Bradford, L.D. and Brady, J.V. (1979) Progressive ratio and fixed ratio schedules of cocaine-maintained responding in baboons. *Psychopharmacology* 65: 125–126.

Griffiths, R.R. and Woodson, P.P. (1988) Reinforcing properties of caffeine: studies in humans and animals. *Pharmacol. Biochem. Behav.* 29: 419.

Grubman, J. and Woods, J.H. (1982) Schedule-controlled behavior maintained by nitrous oxide delivery in rhesus monkeys. In: Saito, S. and Yanagita, T. (eds). *Learning and memory:* drugs as reinforcer. Amsterdam: Excerpta Medica, pp. 259–274.

Gustafson, L.K. and Pickens, R. (1975) Intraventricular amphetamine self-administration in rats. *Fed. Proc.* 34: 780.

Hadaway, P.F., Alexander, B.K., Coombs, R.B. and Beyerstein, B. (1979) The effect of housing and gender on preference for morphine-sucrose solutions in rats. *Psychopharmacology* 66: 87–91.

Hagan, M.M. and Moss, D.E. (1991) An animal model of bulimia nervosa: opioid sensitivity to fasting episodes. *Pharmacol. Biochem. Behav.* 39(2): 421–422.

Hatsukami, D., Keenan, R., Carroll, M.E., Colon, E., Gieske, D., Wilson, B. and Huber, M. (1990) A method of delivery of precise doses of cocaine base to humans for smoking. *Pharmacol. Biochem. Behav.* 36: 1–7.

Henningfield, J.E. and Goldberg, S.R. (1985) Stimulus properties of nicotine in animals and human volunteers: a review. In: Seiden, L.S. and Balster, R.L. (eds.) *Behavioral pharmacology:* the current status. New York: Alan R. Liss, pp. 433–450.

Henningfield, J.E., Lukas, S. F., and Bigelow, G.E. (1986). Human studies of drugs as reinforcers. In: Goldberg, S.R. and Stolerman, I.P. (eds.) *Behavioral analysis of drug dependence.* Orlando, FL: Academic Press, pp. 69–113.

Heppner, C.C., Kemble, E.D. and Cox, W.M. (1986) Effects of food deprivation on caffeine consumption in male and female rats. *Pharmacol. Biochem. Behav.* 24: 1555–1559.

Higgins, S.T., Bickel, W.K. and Hughes, J.R. (1994a) Influence of an alternative reinforcer on human cocaine self-administration. *Life Sci.* 55(3): 179–187.

Higgins, S.T., Budney, A.J., Bickel, W.K., Foerg, F.E., Donham, R. and Badger, G.J. (1994b) Incentives improve outcome in outpatient behavioral treatment of cocaine dependence. *Arch. Gen. Psychiatry* 51: 568–576.

Higgins, S.T., Budney, A.J., Bickel W.K., Hughes, J.R., Foerg, F. and Badger, G. (1993) Achieving cocaine abstinence with a behavioral approach. *Am. J. Psychiatry* 150: 763–769.

Hill, S.Y. (1978) Addiction liability of tryon rats: independent transmission of morphine and alcohol consumption. *Pharmacol. Biochem. Behav.* 9: 107–110.

Hoebel, B.G. and Aulisi, E. (1984) Cholecystokinin self-injection in the nucleus accumbens and block with proglumide. *Neurosci. Abstr.* 10: 694.

Hoebel, B.G., Monaco, A.P., Hernandez, L., Aulisi, E.F., Stanley, B.G. and Lenard, L. (1983) Self-injection of amphetamine directly into the brain. *Psychopharmacology* 81: 158–163.

Hoffmeister, F. (1979) Preclinical evaluation of reinforcing and aversive properties of analgesics. In: Beers, R.F. and Bassett, E.G. (eds.) *Mechanisms of pain and analgesic compounds.* New York: Raven Press, pp. 447–466.

Holtzman, S.G. and Villarreal, J. (1973) Operant behavior in the morphine dependent rhesus monkey. *J. Pharmacol. Exp. Ther.* 184: 528–541.

Horger, B.A., Wellman, P.J., Morien, A., Davies, B.T. and

Schenk, S. (1991) Caffeine exposure sensitizes rats to the reinforcing effects of cocaine. *Neuroreport* 2: 53–56.

Hursh, S.R. and Winger, G. (1995) Normalized demand for drugs and other reinforcers. *J. Exp. Anal. Behav.* 64: 373–384.

Iglauer, C. and Woods, J.H. (1974) Concurrent performances: reinforcement by different doses of intravenous cocaine in rhesus monkeys. *J. Exp. Anal. Behav.* 22: 179–196.

Jaffe, J.H. (1990) Drug addiction and drug abuse. In: Gilman, A.G., Rall, T.W., Nies, A.S. and Taylor, P. (eds.). Goodman and Gillman's The Pharmacological Basis of Therapeutics. New York: Pergamon. pp. 522–573.

Jaffe, J.H., Cascella, N.G., Kumor, K.M. and Sherer, M.A. (1988) Cocaine-induced cocaine craving. *Psychopharmacology* 97: 59–64.

Jaffe, A.B. Sharpe, L.G. and Jaffe, J.H. (1989) Rats self-administer sufentanil in aerosol form. *Psychopharmacology* 99: 289–293.

Jarvik, M.E. (1967) Tobacco smoking in monkeys. *Ann. NY Acad. Sci.* 142: 280–294.

Johanson, C.E. (1982) Behavior maintained under fixed-interval and second-order schedules of cocaine or pentobarbital in rhesus monkeys. *J. Pharmacol. Exp. Ther.* 221: 384–393.

Johanson, C.E., Balster, R.L. and Bonese, K. (1976) Self-administration of psychomotor stimulant drugs: the effects of unlimited access. *Pharmacol. Biochem. Behav* 4: 45–51.

Johanson, C.E. and Schuster, C.R. (1975) A choice procedure for drug reinforcers: cocaine and methylphenidate in the rhesus monkeys. *J. Pharmacol. Exp. Ther.* 193: 676–688.

Kato, S., Wakasa, Y. and Yanagita, T. (1987) Relationship between minimum reinforcing doses and injection speed in cocaine and pentobarbital self-administration in crab-eating monkeys. *Pharmacol. Biochem. Behav.* 28: 407–410.

Katz, J.H., Baldrighi, G., and Roth, K. (1978) Appetitive determinants of self-stimulation. *Behav. Biol.* 23: 500–508.

Katz, J.L. (1979) A comparison of responding maintained under second-order schedules of intramuscular cocaine injection or food presentation in squirrel monkeys. *J. Exp. Anal. Behav.* 32: 419–431.

Katz, J.L. (1980) Second-order schedules of intramuscular cocaine injection in the squirrel monkey: comparisons with food presentation and effects of d-amphetamine and promazine. *J. Pharmacol. Exp. Ther.* 212: 405–411.

Katz, J.L. (1990) Models of relative reinforcing efficacy of drugs and their predictive utility. *Behav. Pharmacol.* 1: 283–301.

Koob, G.F., Goeders, N.E. (1989) Neuroanatomical substrates of drug self-administration. In: Liebman, J.M., Cooper, S.J. (eds.) *The neuropharmacological basis of reward.* New York: Oxford University Press, pp. 214–263.

Koob, G.F., Vaccarino, F.J., Amalric, M. and Bloom, F.E. (1987) Positive reinforcement properties of drugs: search for neural substrates. In: Engel J., Oreland L. (eds.) *Brain reward systems and abuse.* New York: Raven Press, pp. 35–50.

Kornetsky, C. and Esposito, R.U. (1979) Euphorogenic drugs: effects on reward pathways of the brain. *Fed. Proc.* 38: 2473–2476.

Kosten, T.R., Kleber, H.D. and Morgen, C. (1989) Role of opioid antagonists in treating intravenous cocaine abuse. *Life Sci.* 44: 887–892.

Kosten, T.R., Schumann, B., Wright, D., Carney, M.K. and Gawin, F.H. (1987) A preliminary study of desipramine in the treatment of cocaine abuse in methadone maintenance patients. *J. Clin. Psychiatry* 48: 442–444.

Krahn, D.D. and Gosnell, B.A. (1991) Fat-preferring rats consumer more alcohol than carbohydrate-preferring rats. *Alcohol* 8: 313–316.

Lac, S.T., Wyvell, C.L. and Carroll, M.E. (1994) Cocaine acquisition in rats: effect of feeding conditions and palatability (abstract). *Pharmacol. Biochem. Behav* 48: 836.

Lemaire, G.A. and Meisch, R.A. (1985) Oral drug self-administration in rhesus monkeys: interactions between drug amount and fixed-ratio size. *J. Exp. Anal. Behav.* 44: 377–389.

Macenski, M.J. and Meisch, R.A. (1984) Oral drug reinforcement studies with laboratory animals: applications and implications for understanding drug-reinforced behavior. *Curr. Dir. Psy. Sci.* 3: 22–27.

Markou, A., Weiss, F., Gold, L.H., Caine, S.B., Schulteis, G. and Koob, G.F. (1993) Animal models of drug craving. *Psychopharmacology* 112: 163–182.

Marks-Kaufman, R. and Lipeles, B.J. (1982) Patterns of nutrient selection in rats orally self-administering morphine. *Nutr. Behav.* 1: 33–26.

Mattox, A.J., Rodefer, J.S. and Carroll, M.E. (1995) Heroin smoking in rhesus monkeys. In: *Proceedings of the College on Problems of Drug Dependence, 1995.* NIDA Research Monograph. Washington, DC: U.S. Government Printing Office.

McMillan, D.E. and Leander, J.D. (1978) Chronic chlordiazepoxide and pentobarbital interactions on punished and unpunished behavior. *J. Pharmacol. Exp. Ther.* 207: 515–520.

Meisch, R.A. (1975) The function of schedule-induced polydipsia in establishing ethanol as a positive reinforcer. *Pharmacol. Rev.* 27: 465–473.

Meisch, R.A. and Carroll, M.E. (1987) Oral drug self-administration: drugs as reinforcers. In: Bozarth, M.A. (ed.) *Methods of assessing the reinforcing properties of abused drugs.* New York: Springer-Verlag, pp. 143–160.

Meisch, R.A., George, F.R. and Lemaire, G.A. (1990) Orally delivered cocaine as a reinforcer for rhesus monkeys. *Pharmacol. Biochem. Behav.* 35: 245–249.

Meisch, R.A. and Kliner, D.J. (1979) Etonitazene as a reinforcer for rats: increased etonitazene-reinforced behavior due to food deprivation. *Psychopharmacology* 63: 97–98.

Meisch, R.A., Kliner, D.J. and Henningfield, J.E. (1981) Pentobarbital drinking by rhesus monkeys: establishment and maintenance of pentobarbital-reinforced behavior. *J. Pharmcol. Exp. Ther.* 217: 114–120.

Meisch, R.A. and Lemaire, G.A. (1993) Drug self-administration. In: van Haaren, F. (ed.) *Methods in behavioral pharmacology.* New York: Elsevier Science, pp. 257–300.

Meisch, R.A. and Thompson, T. (1971) Ethanol intake in the absence of concurrent food reinforcement. *Psychophar-*

macologia 22:72–79.

Meyer, R. and Mirin, S. (1979) *The heroin stimulus: implications for a theory of addiction.* Plenum Press, New York.

Monitoring the future study, NIDA Notes, February/March, 1994.

Mucha, R.F. van der Kooy, D., O Shaughnessy, M., and Bucenieks, P. (1982). Drug reinforcement studied by the use of place conditioning in rat. *Brain Res.* 243: 91–105.

Mumford, G.K. and Holtzman, S.G. (1991) Qualitative differences in the discriminative stimulus effects of low and high doses of caffeine in the rat. *J. Pharmacol. Exp. Ther.* 258: 857–865.

Nader, M.A. and Barrett, J.E. (1990) Effects of chlordiazepoxide, buspirone and serotonin receptor agonists and antagonists on responses of squirrel monkeys maintained under second-order schedules of intramuscular cocaine injection or food presentation. *Drug Dev. Res.* 20: 5–17.

Nader, M.A., Tatham, T.A. and Barrett, J.E. (1992) Behavioral and pharmacological determinants of drug abuse. *Ann. NY Acad. Sci.* 654: 368–385.

Nader, M.A. and Woolverton, W.L. (1991) Effects of increasing the magnitude of an alternative reinforcer on drug choice in a discrete-trials choice procedure. *Psychopharmacology* 105: 169–174.

Nader, M.A. and Woolverton, W.L. (1992a) Choice between cocaine and food by rhesus monkeys: effects of conditions of food availability. *Behav. Pharmacol.* 3: 635–638.

Nader, M.A. and Woolverton, W.L. (1992b) Effects of increasing response requirement on choice between cocaine and food in rhesus monkeys. *Psychopharmacology* 108: 295–300.

Nemeth, M.A. and Woods, J.H. (1982) Effects of morphine and cocaine on responding under a multiple schedule of food or nitrous oxide presentation. In: Saito, S. and Yanagita, T. (Eds), *Learning and memory: drugs as reinforcers.* Amsterdam: Excerpta Medica, pp. 275–285.

Olds, J. (1962) Hypothalamic substrates of reward. *Physiol. Rev.* 42: 554–604.

Olds, M.E. (1979) Hypothalamic substrate for the positive reinforcing properties of morphine in the rat. *Brain Res.* 168: 351–360.

Pagliaro, L.A. and Pagliaro, A.M. (1993) The phenomenon of abusable psychotropic use among North American youth. *J. Clin. Pharmacol.* 33: 676–690.

Pakarinen, E.D. and Woods, J.H. (1994) Oral discriminative and reinforcing effects of etonitazene in rhesus monkeys. *Soc. Neurosci. Abstr.* 20: 1231.

Piazza, P.V., Deminiere, J.M., LeMoal, M. and Simon, H. (1989) Factors that predict individual vulnerability to amphetamine self-administration. *Science.* 245: 1511–1513.

Piazza, P.V., Deroche, V., Deminiere, J.M., Maccari, S., Le Moal, M and Simon, H. (1993) Corticosterone in the range of stress-induced levels possess reinforcing properties: implications for sensation-seeking behaviors. *Proc. Natl. Acad. Sci. U.S.A.* 90: 11738–11742.

Pickens, R.W. and Johanson, C.E. (1992) Craving: consensus of status and agenda for future research. *Drug Alcohol Depend.* 30: 127–131.

Ramsey, N.F. and van Ree, J.M. (1990) Chronic pretreatment with naltrexone facilitates acquisition of intra-

venous cocaine self-administration in rats. *Eur. Neuropsychopharmacol.* 1: 55–61.

Ramsey, N.F. and van Ree, J.H. (1992) Emotional but not physical stress enhances intravenous cocaine self-administration in drug-naive rats. *Brain Res.* 608: 216–222.

Rawleigh, J.M., Rodefer, J.S., Hansen, J.J. and Carroll, M.E. (1996) Combined effects of buprenorphine and an alternative nondrug reinforcer on phencyclidine self-administration in rhesus monkeys. *Exp. Clin. Psychopharmacol.* 4: 68–76.

Ritz, M.C., George, F.R., deFiebre, C.M. and Meisch, R.A. (1986) Genetic differences in the establishment of ethanol as a reinforcer. *Pharmacol. Biochem. Behav.* 24: 1089–1094.

Roberts, D.C.S., Koob, G.F., Klonoff, P. and Fibiger, H.C. (1980) Extinction and recovery of cocaine self-administration following 6-hydroxydopamine lesions of the nucleus accumbens. *Pharmacol. Biochem. Behav.* 12: 781–787.

Robinson, T.E. and Berridge, K.C. (1993) The neural basis of drug craving: an incentive-sensitization theory of addiction. *Brain Res. Rev.* 18: 247–291.

Rodeter, J.S., De Roche, K.K., Lynch, W.A., and Carroll, M.E. (1996) Feeding conditions after the demand for phencyclidine and ethanol: a behavioral economic analysis. *Exp. Clin. Psychopharmacol.* 4:61–67.

Rogers, W.R. (1985) Effects of cigarette nicotine content on smoking behavior of baboons. *Addict. Behav.* 10: 225–233.

Rouge-Pont, F., Piazza, P.V., Kharouby, M., Le Moal, M. and Simon, H. (1993) Higher and longer stress-induced increase in dopamine concentrations in the nucleus accumbens of animals predisposed to amphetamine self-administration: a microdialysis study. *Brain Res.* 602: 169–174.

Samson, H.H. (1986) Initiation of ethanol reinforcement using a sucrose-substitution procedure in food- and water-satiated rats. *Alcohol Clin. Exp. Res.* 10: 436–442.

Schenk, S., Lacelle, G., Gorman, K and Amit, Z. (1987) Cocaine self-administration in rats influenced by environmental conditions: implications for etiology of drug abuse. *Neurosci. Lett.* 81: 227–231.

Schlichting, U.U., Goldberg, S.R., Wuttke, W. and Hoffmeister, F. (1971) d-Amphetamine self-administration by rhesus monkeys with different self-administration histories. *Excerpta Med. Int. Cong. Ser.* 220: 62–69.

Shaham, Y. (1993) Immobilization stress-induced oral opioid self-administration and withdrawal in rats: role of conditioning factors and the effects of stress on "relapse" to opioid drugs. *Psychopharmacology* 111: 447–485.

Shaham, Y., Alvares, K., Nespor, S.M. and Grunberg, N.E. (1992) Effect of stress on oral morphine and fentanyl self-administration in rats. *Pharmacol. Biochem. Behav.* 41: 615–619.

Shaham, Y., Rodaros, D. and Stewart J. (1994) Reinstatement of heroin-reinforced behavior following long-term extinction. Implications of the treatment of relapse to drug-taking behavior. *Behav. Pharmacol.* 5: 360–364.

Sidman M. (1960) *Tactics of scientific research:* evaluating experimental data in psychology. Boston, MA: Authors' Cooperative.

Slifer, B. Balster, R. Woolverton, W. (1984) Behavioral dependence produced by continuous phencyclidine infusion in rhesus monkeys. *J. Pharmacol. Exp. Ther.* 230: 399–406.

Smith, J.E., Co, C., Freeman, M.E. and Lane, J.D. (1982) Brain neurotransmitter turnover correlated with morphine-seeking behavior of rats. *Pharmacol. Biochem. Behav.* 16: 509–519.

Smith, S.G., Werner, T.E. and Davis, W.M. (1975) Technique for intragastric delivery of solutions: application for self-administration of morphine and alcohol by rats. *Physiol. Psychol.* 3: 220–224.

Specker, S.M., Lac, S.T. and Carroll, M.E. (1994) Food deprivation history and cocaine self-administration: an animal model of binge eating. *Pharmacol. Biochem. Behav.* 48: 1025–1029.

Stewart, J. (1984) Reinstatement of heroin and cocaine self-administration in the rat by intracebral application of morphine in the ventral tegmental area. *Pharmacol. Biochem. Behav.* 20: 917–923.

Stewart, J. and deWit, H. (1987) Reinstatement of drug-taking behavior as a method of assessing incentive motivational properties of drugs. In: Bozarth, M.A. (ed.) *Methods of assessing the reinforcing properties of abused drugs.* New York: Springer-Verlag, pp. 211–227.

Stewart, J. and Wise, R.A. (1992) Reinstatement of heroin self-administration habits: morphine prompts and naltrexone discourages renewed responding after extinction. *Psychopharmacology* 108: 79–84.

Stretch, R. and Gerber, G.J. (1973) Drug-induced reinstatement of amphetamine self-administration behavior in monkeys. *Can. J. Psychol.* 27: 168–177.

Suzuki, T. (1990) Pharmacological studies on drug dependence in rodents: dependence on opioids and CNS depressants. *Jpn. J. Pharmacol.* 52: 1–10.

Suzuki, T., Tanaka, C., Yoshii, T., Misawa, M. and Meisch, R.A. (1989) Oral self-administration of pentobarbital and pentobarbital-induced sleep time in Lewis and Fischer 344 inbred rats. *Jpn. J. Psychopharmacol.* 9: 95.

Thompson, T. and Schuster, C. (1964) Morphine self-administration, food reinforced and avoidance behaviors in rhesus monkeys. *Psychopharmacology* 5: 87–94.

Tiffany, S.T. (1990) A cognitive model of drug urges and drug-use behavior: role of automatic and nonautomatic processes. *Psychol. Rev.* 97: 147–168.

UNDCP and WHO Informal Expert Committee on the Craving Mechanism: Report. (1992) United Nations International Drug Control Programme and World Health Organization technical report series (No. V. 92-54439T).

Valentine, J.O., Katz, J.L., Kandel, D.A. and Barrett, J.E. (1983) Effects of cocaine, chlordiazepoxide, and chlorpromazine on responding of squirrel monkeys under second-order schedules of IM cocaine injection or food presentation. *Psychopharmacology* 81: 164–169.

Waller, M.B., McBride, W.J., Gatto, G.L., Lumeng, L. and Li, T.-K. (1984) Intragastric self-infusion of ethanol by ethanol-preferring and non-preferring lines of rats. *Science* 225: 78–80.

Weiss, R.D. (1988) Relapse to cocaine abuse after initiating desipramine treatment. *JAMA* 260: 2545–2546.

Weissenborn, R., Yackey, M., Koob, G.F. and Weiss, F. (1995) Measures of cocaine-seeking behavior using a multiple schedule of food and drug self-administration in rats. *Drug Alcohol Depend.* 38: 237–246.

Wessinger, W.D. and Owens, S.M. (1991) Phencyclidine dependence: the relationship of dose and serum concentrations to operant behavioral effects. *J. Pharmacol. Exp. Ther.* 258: 207–215.

Winger, G., Skjodager, P. and Woods, J.H. (1992) Effects of buprenorphine and other opioid agonists and antagonists on alfentanil- and cocaine-reinforced responding in rhesus monkeys. *J. Pharmacol. Exp. Ther.* 261: 311–317.

Winger, G.D. and Woods, J.H. (1973) The reinforcing property of ethanol in the rhesus monkey: I. Initiation, maintenance and termination of intravenous ethanol-reinforced responding. *Ann. N.Y. Acad. Sci.* 215: 162–175.

Winsauer, P.J. and Thompson, D.M. (1991) Cocaine self-administration in pigeons. *Pharmacol. Biochem. Behav.* 40: 41–52.

Wise, R.A., Murray, A. and Bozarth, M.A. (1990) Bromocriptine self-administration and bromocriptine-reinstatement of cocaine-trained and heroin-trained lever pressing in rats. *Psychopharmacology* 100: 355–360.

Wood, R.W. (1990) Animal models of drug self-administration by smoking. In: Chiang, C.N. and Hawks, R.L. (eds.) *Research findings on smoking of abused substances.* Rockville, MD: National Institute on Drug Abuse, Research Monograph 99, DHHS Publication No. (ADM) 90-1690, pp. 159–171.

Wood, R.W., Grubman, J. and Weiss, B. (1977) Nitrous oxide self-administration by the squirrel monkey. *J. Pharmacol. Exp. Ther.* 202: 491–499.

Woods, J.H. Ikomi, F.I., and Winger, G. (1971) The reinforcing properties of ethanol. In: Roach, M.K., McIsaac, W.M. and Creaven, P.J. (eds.) *Biologic aspects of alcoholism.* Austin: University of Texas Press, pp. 371–388.

Woolverton, W.L. (1995) Comparison of the reinforcing efficacy of cocaine and procaine in rhesus monkeys responding under a progressive-ratio schedule. *Psychopharmacology* 120:296–302.

Woolverton, W. and Kleven, M. (1988) Evidence for cocaine dependence in monkeys following a prolonged period of exposure. *Psychopharmacology* 94: 288–291.

Woolverton, W.L. and Nader, M.A. (1990) Experimental evaluation of the reinforcing effects of drugs. In: Adler, M.W. and Cowan, A. (eds.). Modern methods in pharmacology, vol. 6. Testing and evaluation of drugs of abuse. New York: Wiley-Liss, pp. 165–192.

Woolverton, W.L., Shybut, G. and Johanson, C.E. (1980) Structure-activity relationships among some d-N-alkylated amphetamines. *Pharmacol. Biochem. Behav.* 13: 869–876.

Woolverton, W.L. and Virus, R.M. (1989) The effects of a D1 and a D2 dopamine antagonist on behavior maintained by cocaine or food. *Pharmacol. Biochem. Behav.* 32: 691–697.

WHO Expert Committees on Mental Health and on Alcohol (1955). The "craving" for alcohol. *Q. J. Stud. Alcohol* 16: 33–66.

Yanagita, T. (1968) Self-administration studies of water-insoluble drugs to monkeys by means of chronically implanted stomach catheter. *Community Probl. Drug Depend.* 30: 5631–5635.

Yanagita, T., Takahashi, S., Ishida, K. and H. Funamoto (1970) Voluntary inhalation of volatile anesthetics and organic solvents by monkeys. *Jpn. J. Clin. Pharmacol.* 1: 13–16.

Young, A.M. and Herling, S. (1986) Drugs as reinforcers: studies in laboratory animals. In: Goldberg, S.R. and

Stolerman, I.P. (eds.), *Behavioral analysis of drug dependence*. New York: Academic Press, pp. 9–67.

Young, A.M. and Woods, J.H. (1981) Maintenance of behavior by ketamine and related compounds in rhesus monkeys with different self-administration histories. *J.*

Pharmacol. Exp. Ther. 218: 720–727.

Zimmerberg, B. and Brett, M.B. (1992) Effects of early environmental experience on self-administration of amphetamine and barbital. *Psychopharmacology* 106: 474–478.

Drug Addiction and its Treatment: Nexus of Neuroscience and Behavior, edited by Bankole A. Johnson and John D. Roache. Lippincott–Raven Publishers, Philadelphia, © 1997.

2

Human Drug Self-Administration: A Review and Methodological Critique

Ralph Spiga and John D. Roache

Department of Psychiatry and Behavioral Sciences, University of Texas-Houston Health Science Center, Houston, Texas 77030

Human drug dependence may be defined broadly as persistent drug-taking behavior. Over the past 30 years a variety of human drug self-administration paradigms have demonstrated that the apparently complex human behavior of drug taking is amenable to a scientific analysis. Orderly relationships have been observed between pharmacologic (e.g., drug dose) and behavioral (e.g., responses required to gain access to drug) variables (Bigelow et al., 1976; Pickens et al., 1977). Despite methodologic differences between human and animal studies, in either case when a contingent relationship between a behavioral response and drug administration is arranged, the pattern of drug-taking behavior is similar (Griffiths, et al., 1980).

HUMAN DRUG-TAKING BEHAVIOR AS AN OPERANT

In a pioneering study, Wikler (1952) demonstrated the feasibility of experimentally examining drug self-administration in humans. In this study a research volunteer with a history of heroin dependence was confined to a research ward. The subject's verbal request for heroin (the behavioral response) resulted in the administration of a small dose of heroin. Thus, a contingent relationship was established between the subject's verbal response and drug access. This contingency produced a stable pattern of heroin self-administration during this period. Many studies subsequent to this adopted the assumptions, methods, and strategies of investigation (see the Operant Behavior: Assumptions and Strategies of Investigation section), which characterize the field of *operant behavioral analysis*. Operant behavior is a class of responses that "operates" on the environment, altering the environment and thus producing consequent events that shape, maintain, or extinguish the response over time. This approach refines the law of effect and the concept of instrumental behavior originally proposed by E. L. Thorndike (Skinner, 1953).

The conceptual foundation for a laboratory analysis of drug taking as an operant was first exemplified in a study of morphine self-administration (Weeks, 1962). Rats implanted with an intravenous catheter received an injection of morphine as a consequence when they pressed a lever. Manipulation of the morphine dose and the number of responses required for injection of morphine served to establish that morphine injections were maintaining the drug-taking responses (i.e., morphine functioned as a positive reinforcer). Application of this approach to the design and interpretation of human drug-taking behavior is clearly exemplified by the work of (Mello and Mendelson, 1966). In that study, subjects sat in front of a response panel consisting of buttons and a drug delivery system.

By pressing a response key, subjects could obtain delivery of either small (10 ml) volumes of alcohol or points that were exchangeable for money. Alcohol consumption maintained responding to a greater extent than did the point presentation. In historical perspective, the results of these studies demonstrate the value of viewing drug-taking behavior as an operant behavior. According to Skinner (1953), *operant behavior* is a class of responses that are emitted and that are increased or decreased by the response-contingent consequences. *Positive reinforcers* are consequences that increase the future likelihood of the response. For example, in the Wikler (1952) study, the request was the operant response, and the administration of the small dose of heroin by the research ward staff and the pharmacologic effects of the accumulated doses can be conceptualized as the reinforcing consequence maintaining the drug-seeking request.

The operant approach is the basis for an *experimental analysis of behavior*. The analysis is not restricted to a determination of response-consequence relations, but includes examination of the role of antecedent stimuli. These antecedent stimuli can come to control operant responding and thereby function as *discriminative stimuli*. Verbal instructions given to subjects prior to a drug self-administration trial are a particularly important example of an antecedent stimulus exerting discriminative control of responding. A body of behavioral research has demonstrated that preexperimental verbal instructions alter responding maintained by identical response-consequence contingencies (Baron and Galizio, 1983; Wearden, 1988). Other events that occur prior to the self-administration trial may also influence experimental performance. These events may be viewed as an instance of discriminative and/or instructional stimulus control (Rosenthal, 1978, 1994). These stimuli may include subtle hints of expected performance communicated during the process of obtaining informed consent or even cues derived from the dress and demeanor of the experimenter. A recent study by Chait and Perry (1992) exemplifies the discriminative effects of instructions. In their study, subjects with a history of marijuana use were permitted an opportunity to smoke placebo marijuana from which the Δ^9-tetrahydrocannabinol (THC) had been chemically extracted. One group of subjects was instructed that they would be allowed to self-administer active marijuana when, in fact, only placebo was available. This group was the deceptive administration group. A second group was told that they might receive inactive marijuana and then were permitted to self-administer the placebo. This group was the placebo double-blind group. Compared to the double-blind group, subjects in the deceptive administration group self-administered more placebo marijuana and reported greater marijuana-induced subjective effects such as drug liking. These instructional effects on self-administration and subjective ratings presumably resulted from the historical association of the word *marijuana* (the antecedent) and the actual administration of THC-containing marijuana (the reinforcer). Thus, a human subject's history of antecedent-reinforcer relationships can affect current behavior. The result of such a history is that at any one time, the subject's behavior includes (1) responses engendered by behavioral history, (2) responses engendered by the experimental instructions, and (3) responses evoked by the current response-consequence relationship (Baron and Galizio, 1983).

The relationship between antecedent, behavior, and consequence are the constituent elements of the three-term operant contingency: the basic unit of the experimental analysis of behavior. Fig. 1 illustrates the three-term contingency as applies to human drug self-administration paradigms. We have included genetic and historical variables and setting events (current environment) as important elements that may modulate the ongoing relationship between antecedent, behavior, and consequence (Skinner, 1969). This figure illustrates that behavior (e.g., drinking) emitted in the presence of specific antecedent stimuli (e.g., a beer advertisement) is rein-

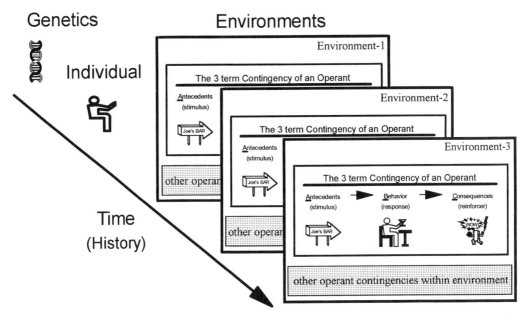

FIG. 1. An illustration of the factors determining drug reinforcement. Principal among these are the three-term operant contingency describing antecedent stimuli, behavior, and reinforcing consequence. Other factors influence and modulate this process, including the genetic and biologic composition of the individual, the behavioral history of the individual, and the surrounding environment that provides the setting circumstances and alternative opportunities. Thus, reinforcing effects of drugs are a complex interplay of genetics, history, environment, and the operant schedule described by the three-term contingency.

forced by the consequent drug effects. Genetic and behavioral history variables may act alone or in combination to influence drug-taking behavior. For instance, individuals may drink excessively as a result of a behavioral history of reinforcement by alcohol drinking (e.g., experience with drug). Additionally, sons of alcoholics may be at greater risk for alcoholism due to genetic factors (McGue et al.; 1992) than are men without a family history of alcoholism. Ambient temperature, the physical and social surroundings in which the contingency occurs, and alternative response-consequence relationships are all examples of setting factors. Setting factors can be broadly defined as environmental events that are not differentially related to the ongoing contingency maintaining the target response but that may enhance or suppress behavior. By abstracting the essential features of drug taking in the natural environment, the use of the three-term contingency simplifies the re-

searcher's task of manipulating and measuring the effects of environmental and pharmacologic variables that alone, and in combination, influence human drug self-administration. Furthermore, this analytic approach provides a common vocabulary and a standard set of procedures for communicating and replicating drug self-administration procedures across drugs, routes of administration, species, and laboratories (Henningfield, et al., 1991).

OPERANT BEHAVIOR: ASSUMPTIONS AND STRATEGIES OF INVESTIGATION

The experimental analysis of operant behavior has provided the conceptual and methodologic framework for the laboratory study of nonhuman and human drug self-administration. Table 1 lists the assumptions,

TABLE 1. *Assumptions, principles, and strategies of the operant approach*

PRINCIPLES	EXEMPLARS
Assumptions	
1. Behavior is lawful; it stands in orderly relation to environment events.	1. Bigelow et al. (1976) demonstrated that increasing the number of tokens required to purchase diazepam or pentobarbital decreased amount of drug purchased. Each token was earned by pedaling a bike for 2 min.
2. Because behavior is lawful, the purpose of behavior analysis is to predict and control behavior.	2. DeGrandpre et al.'s (1992) reanalysis of nicotine regulation suggests that smokers who switch to low-nicotine cigarettes will in fact smoke more so as to maintain desired nicotine levels. Furthermore, in so doing they increase their exposure to other harmful agents.
Basic principles	
1. Operant behavior is emitted and changes the environment producing consequences. This implies that "selection by consequences" is the mechanism of behavioral evolution.	1. Griffiths et al. (1974b) demonstrated that social isolation contingent on drinking alcohol suppressed alcohol self-administration. Thus, "social time-out" was a punisher.
2. Operant behavior can be brought under the control of antecedent events.	2. Chait and Perry (1992) demonstrated that subjects informed that placebo marijuana was in fact active marijuana smoked more placebo marijuana and reported greater subjective responses associated with abuse liability that those subjects informed that they might receive inactive placebo marijuana.
3. The basic unit of analysis is the three-term contingency: antecedent, behavior and consequence.	3. Foltin and Fischman (1992) provided subjects concurrent access to smoked or intravenously injected cocaine. Choice, signaled by the presence of two squares, one on the right the other on the left of the computer monitor, was defined as a directional movement of a computer joystick and drug seeking response on a button. The location of the square was associated with either smoked or intravenous cocaine.
Strategies of investigation	
1. Behavior is objectively described and defined. Responses are often machine-defined.	1. Henningfield et al. (1983) used pocket-held puff monitors to record cigarette intake and smoking behavior.
2. Absolute-unit based scales are the measures of choice.	2. Sobell et al. (1972) used measurements of time between sips and volume of each sip to differentiate the behavior of alcoholics and social drinkers.
3. Prediction and control of behavior by independent variables is established by an experimental analysis.	3. de Wit and Chutuape (1993) demonstrated that preloads of ethanol (0, 0.25 and 0.50 g/kg) 1 hour before sessions increased choice for ethanol relative to money.
4. The goal of the experimental analysis is a statement of functional relationships.	4. Silverman et al. (1994b) controlled caffeine self-administration by manipulating the behavioral requirements of tasks following caffeine self-administration. When the task required vigilance, caffeine self-administration increased relative to that span with a task requiring only relaxation.

principles, and strategies of investigation that distinguish the operant approach. Each assumption, principle, or strategy is illustrated by an example taken from the research literature. For instance, a fundamental assumption of the operant approach is that behavior is lawful. This implies that orderly relationships can be found between human drug-taking behavior, drug administration factors, and environmental variables. An example of this principle is a study demonstrating an orderly relationship between drug cost and amount of drug consumed (Bigelow et al., 1976). Once orderly relationships have been described, behavior can be predicted and potentially controlled. For example, behavior analysis predicts that smokers may increase their smoking when they switch from high to low nicotine concentration cigarettes (DeGrandpre et al., 1992). Due to the increased exposure to other toxic by-products of smoke, this may not be a desirable way to control smoking and health.

The experimental analysis of behavior also (1) emphasizes the objective description of behavior without reference to hypothetical agencies, (2) relies on absolute unit-based measurement systems, (3) requires that experimental control be demonstrated by the systematic and repeated manipulation of the events presumed to affect the target behavior, and (4) requires statements of the relationships between behavior and environmental determinants in the form of a functional relationship (Johnston and Pennypacker, 1980). This objective description of behavior has resulted in the use of automated machinery to define behavioral responses. Henningfield et al. (1983), for example, used a pocket-held puff monitor to record nicotine intake. The strategies listed and described in Table 1 constitute the standards for evaluating the adequacy of a study's design. Adherence to these standards permits easy comparison of the results of human drug self-administration to the substantial body of literature examining operant behavior maintained by reinforcers other than drugs. These comparisons enhance the interpretability of the results of human drug self-administration research.

Several issues involved in the study of human drug self-administration can be illustrated by close examination of a study conducted by Foltin and Fischman (1992). They examined whether smoked or intravenous (iv) administration of cocaine was preferred by subjects with a history of intravenous and smoked cocaine use. On a research ward, subjects were seated in a lounge chair before a computer monitor. A joystick attached to the computer was used to record choice and subject reports of psychoactive effects induced by the cocaine. One measurement scale, the Addiction Research Center Inventory (ARCI), assessed whether the subject's reports of drug effects corresponded to effects measured by empirically-derived stimulant, sedative, opiate, and hallucinogen scales. Subject ratings were also obtained on visual analog scales (VAS) which require subjects to mark a 100 mm line to indicate the magnitude of drug effect on a variety of commonly-reported drug effects. Such verbal self-reports of subjective drug effects are commonly employed in behavioral pharmacologic studies of drug effects in humans (Fischman and Foltin, 1991).

During the laboratory session, subjects were limited to five choices between cocaine administered i.v. (0, 16, and 32 mg of cocaine) or smoked (25 and 50 mg of cocaine). Choice trials were signaled by the appearance of two boxes on the computer monitor screen: one on the left and the other on the right. Each box was associated with delivery of either smoked cocaine or i.v. cocaine. Subjects selected the preferred option by moving the joystick left or right and then pressing the button 200 times. After subjects completed the response requirement, cocaine was administered by the indicated route, if and only if the subject's heart rate and blood pressure were within specified safety limits. This study illustrates several important methodologic features of human drug self-administration research: (1) the use of validated and standardized paper-and-pencil self-report instruments to measure drug-induced subjective effects; (2) the use of operant response procedures to measure drug-taking behavior; (3) ethical and safety constraints limiting the selection of subjects to individuals with a history of cocaine use; and (4) potential adverse cardiovascular effects of cocaine that limited the dosage range that could be safely examined, and determined whether or not subjects actually received the consequence of their choice behavior.

ASSESSING DRUG REINFORCING EFFECTS WITH CHOICE PROCEDURES

A notable methodological feature of the Foltin and Fischman (1992) study is the use of a two-choice drug preference procedure to quantify the reinforcing effects of drug. Measures of drug preference are used widely and are particularly well suited for examining the reinforcing effects of drugs (Johanson and de Wit, 1989). In various species, choice behavior has been examined as a relationship between response allocation and relative reinforcement rate; this has been formalized as the matching law (Herrnstein, 1970). An important implication derived from the matching law is that sources of reinforcement extraneous to the reinforcer maintaining the target response may modulate the effectiveness of the target reinforcer. An extensive body of literature and recent clinical research has clearly demonstrated this principle (Davison and Mc-Carthy, 1988; de Villiers, 1977; Noll, 1995). Most importantly, the matching law implies that reinforcing effects of conventional, nondrug reinforcers (e.g., money, status, or food) and *drug reinforcers only can be established relative to the effects of other reinforcers*. That is, a given reinforcer does not have a fixed intrinsic magnitude but rather reinforcing effects depend on the alternative choices available. Drug choice or preference procedures operationalize this fundamental principle and therefore are preferred. Whether or not the various response-consequence options for nondrug reinforcers are well defined and specified, these relationships certainly may influence the reinforcing effects of the drug. Thus, choice procedures permit only statements of relative re-

inforcing effects (Herrnstein, 1970; Davison and McCarthy, 1988).

We should note that the study of relative reinforcing effects has not been limited solely to reinforcers from the same class. Indeed, studies have compared the relative reinforcing effects of distinct and qualitatively different reinforcers when both are concurrently available. In human drug self-administration research, alternative reinforcers have included placebo, different doses, different drugs, different activities, or money. Stitzer and her colleagues (1983) observed that supplemental doses of methadone were more effective reinforcers than small amounts of concurrently available money in methadone-maintained patients. Opiate users maintained on 50 mg of methadone were provided an opportunity to self-administer 0, 1, 5, 10, 25, or 50 mg of methadone in addition to their 50-mg methadone maintenance dose. Instead of the supplemental methadone, subjects also could select to receive as an alternative either $1 or $5 per dose. Subjects selected the methadone dose more frequently when the alternative was $1 than when the alternative was $5. Methadone doses exceeding 10 mg were selected more frequently than the money. This pattern of methadone self-administration demonstrates that relative to $1, higher doses of supplemental methadone were more effective reinforcers than a small amount of money.

Viewing substance abuse as occurring in the context of alternative nondrug reinforcers has clinical implications. Following a comprehensive review of studies examining ethanol consumption, Vuchinich and Tucker (1988) concluded that consumption of alcohol (1) decreases with direct constraints on access to alcohol, (2) decreases with the availability of alternative reinforcers, and (3) increases with constraints on access to the alternative reinforcers. In two interview studies, one retrospective (Tucker et al., 1995) and the other a prospective longitudinal study (Vuchinich and Tucker, 1996), it was found that drinking in recovering alcoholics was related to events occurring in the social environment. Decreases in participation in positive social activities and relationships increased risk for drinking relapse. Thus, concurrent access to valuable activities other than drinking reduced the risk of relapse. These findings support the argument that the frequently observed relationship between life circumstance (e.g., marriage and employment) and alcohol consumption can be explained as an inverse relationship between ethanol consumption and alternative reinforcers. In this view, marriage, employment, and other social activities are conceptualized as important alternative reinforcers that need to be strengthened and maximized to reduce the risk of relapse.

A more direct link between laboratory self-administration research and clinical practice has been demonstrated in the area of cocaine abuse and dependence. In a two-phase laboratory study (Higgins et al., 1994a), cocaine users were permitted to receive either 10 mg of cocaine intranasally or concurrently available money on 10 occasions during a daily session. During the first sampling phase, subjects received only cocaine on one day and placebo on the other day. During subsequent choice sessions, subjects could self-administer either cocaine, placebo, or money on each of 10 occasions. Subjects self-administered cocaine when placebo was the alternative. However, cocaine self-administration decreased as a function of increasing the value of the monetary alternative (Higgins et al., 1994a). These laboratory results are consistent with data from clinical treatment studies from the same group (Higgins et al., 1994b), in which monetary payments for cocaine-free urine samples reduced the frequency of cocaine-positive urine samples in dependent patients. The clinical results illustrate the benefit of viewing substance abuse as an instance of operant behavior, and the clinical utility of considering drug reinforcement in the context of alternative nondrug reinforcers. Other studies taking the same approach to understanding human substance abuse and discussing policy implications have appeared and deserve the attention of the interested reader (Bickel et al., 1993; Hursh, 1991).

THE ROLE OF SUBJECTIVE DRUG EFFECTS

This chapter focuses on the procedures for evaluating the reinforcing effects drugs in humans. As identified above, reinforcement is an operant process involving drug self-administration. Subjective effects assessment does not measure reinforcing effects of drugs but rather measures the psychoactive effects subjects experience when they consume drugs of abuse. Because psychoactive drug effects are subjectively experienced, private events, we rely almost entirely on questionnaires through which subjects quantitatively rate their experience on various dimensions. It is then assumed that these ratings are an accurate self-report of the subjective effects experienced. Approaches to subjective effects assessment have been reviewed elsewhere (Fischman and Foltin, 1991; Jaffe and Jaffe, 1989). Much of the human research conducted on the subjective effects of drugs of abuse has been reviewed in assessments of the abuse liability of sedatives (de Wit and Griffiths, 1991; Roache and Griffiths, 1989b), stimulants (Foltin and Fischman, 1991), and opioids (Preston and Jasinski, 1991). Abuse liability studies have shown that drugs of abuse generally produce a characteristic profile of subjective drug effects in subjects with experience using those drugs. Although the specific profile of effects varies for different drug classes (e.g., sedatives, stimulants, etc.), there are certain general effects that reasonably are associated with drug abuse. These include ratings of drug liking, estimates of the monetary value of drugs, ratings of intent or desire to use the substance again, and other measures indicating euphoric mood or positive subjective drug effects or mood states.

There is a great deal of face validity to the idea that a drug would have a potential for abuse if it produces euphoria, subject ratings of drug liking, or ratings indicating an intent to use the drug in persons who have abused other drugs. There also is a great deal of consistency between drugs producing such subjective effects and those drugs that actually are abused (Fischman and Foltin, 1991; Jasinski et al., 1984). However, one needs to recognize that subjective effects do not measure reinforcing effects—a point discussed by Preston and colleagues (Chapter 4). Although subjective effects are sometimes considered as causative in determining drug-taking behavior, we suggest that they are two different classes of responses that appear to be correlated. The strength of that correlation has been the subject of several studies.

Relationship Between Subjective Effects and Drug Reinforcement

Some of the earliest human laboratory studies suggested that subjective drug effects may differ in various subject populations (Beecher, 1959). These studies examined the effects of sedatives, stimulants, and opioids in patient populations, normal volunteers, and subjects with histories of opioid abuse or dependence. One of the most significant findings was that addictive drugs such as morphine produced euphoric and positive mood changes only in the subjects with histories of abuse, not in the normal subjects or patient populations. Although these data have been questioned (McAuliffe, 1975), they laid the foundation for the idea that subjective drug effects may vary in different individuals or as a function of drug history and experience. Using double-blind self-administration procedures wherein subjects are given a choice between drug and placebo, Johanson and colleagues frequently have reported differential subjective effects in those subjects who reliably chose to self-administer drug as compared to those who chose mostly placebo. In their initial studies, Johanson and Uhlenhuth (1980a,b) reported that the majority of normal volunteer subjects preferred amphetamine over placebo but preferred placebo over diazepam. Consistent with this choice behavior, they noted that amphetamine produced positive mood changes including increases in vigor and arousal, whereas diazepam produced mainly sedative effects including de-

creased vigor and arousal and increased fatigue and confusion. A later study by these investigators (de Wit et al., 1986a) divided the subjective drug-effect data into groups of subjects to compare those who preferred drug and those who preferred placebo. Subjects preferring amphetamine reported increased positive mood, euphoria, and drug liking, while those subjects preferring placebo showed amphetamine-induced depression, anxiety, and no drug liking. When the same individuals were tested with diazepam, the majority, who preferred placebo over diazepam, reported greater placebo liking and more sedative effects of diazepam than did the minority of subjects who preferred diazepam over placebo. The authors concluded that there are orderly relationships between subjective mood and drug preference. More recent reports conducting similar data analyses from choice experiments (Chait, 1993; Chutuape and de Wit, 1994; de Wit et al., 1989b; Dohrn et al. 1992;) have drawn similar conclusions supporting logical relationships between drug choice and subjective mood response. However, the specific subjective effects that differentiate the drug choosers and nonchoosers seem to vary across drugs and across experiments. Furthermore, whether positive effects are associated with drug choice or negative effects are associated with drug avoidance seems to vary with different drugs. In part this may be a consequence of the forced-choice paradigm where subjects may either (1) choose to take one of the choice alternatives or (2) may be forced to avoid the other choice alternative.

In human studies assessing the abuse liability of drugs, subject ratings of drug liking have become one of the subjective effects most commonly used to predict drug-taking behavior (Jasinski et al., 1984). Perhaps this is because it is a more general measure of positive subjective response than are more specific measures of mood state (e.g., anxiety, sedation, vigor); thus it is more commonly detected for different drugs. Furthermore, studies have more often found associations between drug liking and self-administration. In normal volunteers given repeated opportunities to choose between amphetamine and placebo, amphetamine continued to produce stimulant-like subjective effects despite the fact that both choice behavior and ratings of drug liking declined over time (Johanson and Uhlenhuth, 1981). However, drug liking and drug-taking behaviors are not perfectly correlated. One study (Roache and Griffiths, 1989a) showed that sedative abusers repeatedly self-administering diazepam and triazolam exhibited decreased drug liking in the presence of continued drug-taking behavior. Furthermore, Lamb and colleagues (1991) reported reinforcing effects of morphine in former addicts at low doses that did not produce significant increases in drug liking. Nonetheless, drug-liking ratings obtained following experimenter-administered doses have been shown to predict subsequent benzodiazepine self-administration behavior in sedative abusers (Roache and Griffiths, 1989b; Roache et al., 1995). It is important to note that a recent study of triazolam self-administration showed that drug-liking ratings obtained on the next day following dosing predicted self-administration behavior better than drug-liking ratings obtained while subjects were under the influence (Roache et al., 1995). While the generality of this finding to other drugs remains to be determined, it is logical to conclude that how one subsequently feels about a previous drug experience might predict future behavior better than how one felt at the moment of drug intoxication.

Verbal Reports of Choice or Preference

Besides ratings of positive mood or drug liking, abuse liability studies increasingly have employed rating scales on which subjects express their willingness to take the drug again if given a chance or report how much money they or others may be willing to pay for the drug (Roache and Griffiths, 1989b). Again these are face valid ratings of self-administration potential for subject populations who have histories of purchasing and using

drugs. Recently, Griffiths and colleagues (1993) have reported the use of a multiple-choice questionnaire to investigate the reinforcing effects of pentobarbital. In this procedure, subjects completed a questionnaire following the experience of experimenter-administered doses of a letter-coded drug. On the questionnaire, subjects recorded their preference of obtaining the drug again or receiving various amounts of money. There were dozens of such choices between drug and progressively increasing amounts of money. The assumption of this procedure is that reinforcing drugs will be preferred over small amounts of money but that large amounts of money will be preferred over drug. The dollar value at which subjects stopped recording a drug preference and begin choosing the money alternative was the crossover point, which presumably reflects the point at which the larger amounts of money are considered more reinforcing than drug. Conceptually, this procedure is related to progressive ratio procedures where more reinforcing drugs maintain behavior at higher response requirements than do less reinforcing drugs. The data showed that higher pentobarbital doses resulted in greater monetary value crossover points. However, there are questions as to whether this procedure measures reinforcing effects because the subject is not necessarily receiving the consequence of his/her behavior. Subjects are instructed that each of their responses will be entered into a lottery-type drawing and they will receive, at some later time, the choice option they rated for the particular response that was selected in the lottery drawing. In this situation there are two variables that may affect the subject's response. The first is the time delay between choice ratings and the actual delivery of the consequence. The second is the probability that any particular response will receive its consequence (only one out of many is selected in the lottery drawing). Each of these variables (delayed reinforcement and reduced probabilities of reinforcement) are known to diminish the strength of the reinforcement process.

A recent study by Griffiths and colleagues (1996) sought to validate the multiple-choice questionnaire procedure by demonstrating that choice ratings were sensitive to manipulations known to affect operant behavior. The study examined choices between money and cigarettes in cigarette smokers. The experimental manipulations were extinction, satiation, and a comparison of single and multiple-choice procedures. However, this study incorporated two important modifications of the original procedure. First, they trained subjects on the multiple-choice questionnaire with repeated trials so that subjects repeatedly experienced the lottery selection process and the consequence of their randomly selected choice. This certainly would enhance the validity of the procedure by firmly establishing a relationship between the choice and consequence. Furthermore, experimenter instructions directed subjects to respond in a pattern to produce only one crossover point; i.e., subjects should select cigarettes over small amounts of money but should select large amounts of money over cigarettes. Subjects who did not produce ratings following this pattern were excluded from the study. Whereas these instructions and study inclusion criteria bias the pattern of responding, the specific crossover point or monetary value that subjects placed on the cigarettes was unrestricted. The second important procedural modification involved the immediate delivery of consequences. During the training and experimental phases of the study, the lottery drawing and consequence delivery occurred immediately after subjects completed the questionnaire. This modification would be more likely to establish reinforced behavior than the original procedure involving long time delays between choice behavior and consequence.

The results of three experiments (Griffiths et al., 1996) showed that subject ratings of choice on the questionnaire were sensitive to experimental manipulation. When the experimenter ceased to deliver cigarettes on repeated choice trials but continued giving money consequences, subjects chose the money option rather than cigarettes (extinction). When subjects were tobacco deprived, they rated a higher

crossover point indicating increased value of the cigarettes as compared to when they had just been permitted to smoke (deprivation vs satiation). The last experiment compared the choices of subjects using an abbreviated form of the multiple-choice questionnaire as compared with single discrete choices of cigarettes vs an amount of money. The results showed similar monetary crossover points for both procedures. Whereas there are a number of procedural differences between this modified procedure and the one reported previously, the recent data do support the validity of the modified procedure. Hence, choices made under conditions of immediate consequences scheduled on a probabilistic basis (it is still a lottery drawing that determines which choice gets reinforced) do appear to be a form of operant behavior.

A CRITIQUE OF HUMAN DRUG SELF-ADMINISTRATION STUDIES

An experimental scientist is interested in two basic and practical questions: First, does the manipulated variable, the independent variable, reliably alter some measurable aspect of behavior? Second, how general are the relationships observed between the experimental manipulation and behavior? These are questions of *internal* and *external validity*, respectively. In this section we examine, from the perspective of internal and external validity, examples of human drug self-administration research. Within each of these broad categories, we examine those elements of a human drug self-administration study that may enhance or jeopardize internal or external validity. Table 2 lists prototypic methodologic elements of human drug self-administration research that may affect external validity. The titles of each of the sections correspond with the column titles of the table. Entries in the table indicate the methodologic elements observed in a particular study.

Internal Validity

We believe that without the strategies of investigation previously described (see Table 1) and the methodologic standards described in this section, the results of any experiment may be difficult to interpret. Adherence to these standards permits the investigator to answer the question: Do the experimental arrangements justify the conclusion that the drug has functioned as a reinforcer, and how reinforcing is it? The question of interpretability is one of internal validity (Campbell and Stanley, 1966). In the following subsection we discuss those experimental procedures that, if implemented, would enhance the internal validity of the self-administration procedure. Without the use of these procedures, the validity and interpretability of the results may be jeopardized.

Procedure Response Options

As we have discussed earlier, choice procedures dominate human drug self-administration research. If properly arranged, choice procedures permit unambiguous statements of the relative reinforcing effects of a drug, thereby assuring internal validity. Then the researcher can determine whether the self-administered drug functions as a reinforcer. In the following discussion we describe the choice procedures most frequently found in human drug self-administration research and evaluate the methodologic soundness of these procedures. To assist the reader we have devised a taxonomy of choice procedures as illustrated in Fig. 2.

Early studies arranged two options: subjects could choose to use or not use a drug. An early study of human self-administration of sedatives illustrates the *single drug free-choice (A or none) procedure* (Bigelow et al. 1976). Hospitalized male volunteers with a history of sedative abuse were given the opportunity to self-administer up to 20 oral doses per day of diazepam or pentobarbital. Doses could be purchased with tokens earned by riding an exercise bicycle. Subjects had the option of riding the bicycle to earn tokens for drug purchase or not. The results showed that increasing the number of tokens required to purchase a single dose decreased the amount of drug consumed. While repeated choice of the drug may indicate drug reinforcing effects, the procedure does not permit rejection of the alternative explanation that baseline responding may be controlled by a bias to "take drugs" rather than the pharmacological effects of the drug.

Another self-administration procedure is the *multiple drug forced-choice (A vs B) procedure* (Fig. 2). Arranging an alternative response-consequence relation, for instance a placebo or another drug, permits a statement about the relative reinforcing effects of the drug compared with the alternatives (i.e., placebo or other drug). Thus, a choice between two distinct, well-defined, response-consequence relationships (i.e., A vs B) allows statements about the ordinal ranking of the relative reinforcing effects of the two response consequences. When one option is a placebo, a preference for drug suggests drug reinforcement. The multiple drug forced-choice (A vs B) procedure is illustrated by an early study of amphetamine self-administration in normal volunteers (Johanson and Uhlenhuth, 1980a). The two drug conditions were 5 mg amphetamine and placebo administered under double-blind conditions. On two of four sampling sessions, subjects received a capsule containing amphetamine; on the remaining sessions they received placebo. The color of the placebo and amphetamine capsules differed and were constant throughout the experiment so that subjects could discriminate between the two. On each of five choice-sessions, subjects were required to choose either a placebo or amphetamine capsule. The results showed that amphetamine functioned as a reinforcer in that 77% of subjects chose it on four or more occasions. The procedure is illustrated in Fig. 3: and is characterized by the following features. First, a drug sampling phase precedes a choice phase to permit subjects to "experience" the effects of drugs that will become available in the choice phase. Second, drugs are administered as single bolus doses. Third, the drug-taking behavior is a verbal choice of a color-coded capsule, and

TABLE 2. *Free-choice procedures for drug and nondrug reinforcers*

		Internal validity		
Study	Procedure response options	>Placebo?	Schedule response requirement	Sensitive to manipulations?
Wikler (1952)	Free choice: A or none	Not tested	Verbal request	Not tested
Jick, et al. (1966)	Self-stated preference (not self-administration): A vs. B	Yes	Stated preference	Not tested
Mendelson and Mello (1966)	Free choice: alcohol vs. money	Not tested	Complex task performance, multiple schedule	Not tested
Sobell et al. (1972)	Free choice: A or none	Not tested	Verbal request	Not tested
Griffiths et al. (1974b)	Free choice: A or none	Not tested	Verbal request, 40-min intervals	Social time-out ⇒ ↓ consumption
Bigelow et al. (1976)	Free choice: A or other or none (multiple reinforcers)	Not tested	Bike riding response Token purchase	↑ cost ⇒ ↓ consumption
Mendelson et al. (1976)	Free choice: A or money	Not tested	FR 1800:F.I. 1 s point earnings, point exchange	Not tested
Pickens et al. (1977)	Free choice: A or B or none	Not tested	F. I. 30-min button press	Dose response
Babor et al. (1978)	Free choice: A or none	Not tested	F.I. 1 s point earnings point exchange 24 hr/day	↓ cost ⇒ ↑ consumption
Griffiths et al. (1979)	Free choice: A or None	Yes PTB > DZ > Placebo	15-min bike ride	Dose response
Stitzer et al. (1979)	Free choice: A or none	Not tested	Verbal choice	Methadone dose or take home contingent on diazepam use
Johanson and Uhlenhuth (1980a)	Forced choice: A vs. B	Yes	Verbal choice	Not tested
Mello et al. (1981)	Free choice: A or none	Not tested	FR 300:F.I. 1 s Point exchange 6-hr interval	Naltrexone antagonized
Henningfield et al. (1983)	Free choice: A or none	Yes	FR 10	Dose response
McLeod and Griffiths (1983)	Free choice: A or none	Yes	Progressive ratio, button press or bike ride	Dose response
Griffiths et al. (1984)	Forced choice: A vs. B	Yes	Verbal choice	Diazepam dose response
Mendelson and Mello (1984)	Free choice: A or B or C or D or None	Yes Smoked marijuana > placebo	FR 3600:F.I 1 s point earnings, point exchange	Not tested

	External validity		
Subject population	Route/drugs	Duration (# days)	Reinforcement opportunities (per day)

M
  opiate user
	i.v.
	  Morphine
	  dose unlimited
		112	Unlimited

Therapeutic patient populations	Many hypnotic, analgesic, and arthritic drugs	N/A	N/A

M
  alcoholics
	Oral
	  alcohol (86 proof)
	  (bourbon, ethanol)
		14	Unlimited

M
  normal drinkers and alcoholics
	Oral
	  alcohol beverages
	  (beer, wine, liquor)
		1?	Up to 16 drink equivalents

M
  alcoholics
	Oral
	  ethanol in juice
		3–11	17

M
  sedative abusers
	Oral
	  pentobarbital (30 mg)
	  diazepam (10 mg)
		2	20

M
  marijuana users
	Inhalation
	  marijuana cigarette
	  (1.8–2.3% Δ^9 THC)
		21	Multiple unlimited?

M, F
  sedative patients in detoxification
	Oral
	  pentobarbital (30–200 mg)
		Up to 3 weeks	Multiple unlimited

M
  casual and heavy drinkers
	Oral
	  alcohol beverages
	  (beer, wine, liquor)
		20	Unlimited

M
  sedative abusers
	Oral
	  pentobarbital (30, 90 mg)
	  diazepam (10, 20 mg)
	  chlorpromazine (25, 50 mg)
		10	Up to 10

Sex unspecified
  methadone patients–
  benzodiazepine users
	Oral
	  diazepam (10 mg)
		42	2

M, F
  normals
	Oral
	  d-amphetamine (5 mg)
		5	Single

M
  treatment-resistant heroin addicts
	i.v. (10 mg)
	  Heroin
		10	4

M
  smokers
	i.v. (0.75, 1.5, 3 mg)
	  Nicotine
		7	Multiple unspecified (>49)

M
  sedative abusers
	Oral
	  pentobarbital
	  (200, 400, 600 mg)
		1	Single

M
  sedative abusers
	Oral
	  diazepam (40–160)
	  oxazepam (480 mg)
		1	1

M
  marijuana users
	Oral
	  Δ^9 THC (17.5 mg)
	  nabilone (2 mg)
	  smoked marijuana
	  (1.83% THC)
		1	Single

TABLE 2. *Continued*

		Internal validity		
Study	Procedure response options	>Placebo?	Schedule response requirement	Sensitive to manipulations?
Preston et al. (1985)	Forced choice: A vs. B and free choice additional	Yes Hydromorphone > others	Verbal choice	Not tested
de Wit et al. (1986b)	Forced choice: A vs. B	No	Verbal choice	Not tested
Chait et al. (1987)	Forced choice: A vs. B	Yes (some were)	Verbal choice	Not tested
de Wit and McCracken (1990)	Forced choice: A vs. B and free choice additional	Yes	Verbal choice 15-min F.I.	Not tested
Bickel et al. (1991)	Free Choice: A or none	Not tested	FR 200–FR1600	↑ FR ⇒ ↓ consumption
Hughes et al. (1991)	Forced choice: A vs. B (4 coffee minimum)	Yes	Coffee drinking	Not tested
Lamb et al. (1991)	Free choice: A or None	Yes	FR 30 (FR 100:s)	Not dose related
Chait and Perry (1992b)	Free choice: A or None	Only placebo	Cigarette smoking	Not tested
Chait and Zacny (1992)	Forced choice: A vs. B	Yes	Verbal choice	Not tested
Dohrn et al. (1992)	Forced choice: A vs. B	No	Verbal choice	Not tested
Foltin and Fischman (1992)	Forced choice: A vs. B	Yes	FR 200 14-min interval	Not tested
Oliveto et. al. (1992)	Forced choice and free choice comparison	No	Coffee drinking	Not tested
Chait (1993)	Free choice: A or B or none independent trials	Some	Verbal choice	Not tested
Griffiths et al. (1993)	Multiple choice questionnaire: drug vs. money dose vs. dose	Yes	Questionnaire: money vs. drug choice	Dose response
Evans et al. (1994)	Forced choice: A vs. B and free choice additional	Yes	Verbal choice Signaled F. I. 1 hr	Not sensitive to dose changes
Higgins et al (1994)	Free choice: A or money	Yes	Signaled F. I. 2 min:FR10	↑ $ ⇒ ↓ cocaine
Mitchell et al. (1994)	Free choice: Money or cigarettes	Not tested	Random ratio task performance to earn $ and cigarettes	↑ # of "free" cigarettes ⇒ ↓ # worked for

	External validity		
Subject population	Route/drugs	Duration (# days)	Reinforcement opportunities (per day)
M methadone detoxification patients	Oral hydromorphone (1 mg) clonidine (0.1 mg) oxazepam (10 mg)	2	3
M, F anxious volunteers	Oral diazepam (5, 10 mg)	5	Single
M, F normals	Oral mazindol (0.5, 1, 2 mg) benzphetamine (25, 50 mg) phenmetrazine (25, 50 mg) phenylpropanolamine (12.5, 25, 50 mg)	5	Single
M social drinkers w/ & w/o family history of alcoholism	Oral ethanol (0.5g / kg)	3	Up to 11
M, F smokers	Inhalation tobacco cigarettes (1, 2, 4 puffs)	??	Multiple unspecified (40?)
M, F coffee users	Oral caffeine (100 mg) in coffee	12	Multiple (#?)
M opiate post-addicts	i.m. (7.5, 15, 30 mg) Morphine	5	Single
M, F marijuana users	Inhalation placebo marijuana (1/2 cigarette)	4	Up to 10
M, F marijuana users	Oral Δ^9 THC and smoked marijuana	2	Vary dose or 1–8 puffs
M, F normals	Inhalation nitrous oxide (30, 40%)	3	Single opportunity
M cocaine abusers	i.v. Cocaine (16, 32 mg) or smoked cocaine (25, 50 mg)	1	5
M, F coffee drinkers	Oral caffeine (100mg) in coffee	6 days	Up to 10
M, F normals	Oral amphetamine (7.5–10 mg)	3	Single
M, F sedative abusers	Oral pentobarbital (200, 400 mg)	5	Probabilistic consequence
M, F caffeine users	Oral caffeine (50, 100 mg)	3 days/week × 24 weeks	1–7
M, F cocaine users	Intranasal cocaine (10 mg)	1	10
M smokers	Inhalation tobacco cigarettes	1	Approx. 9 cigarettes

TABLE 2. *Continued*

		Internal validity		
Study	Procedure response options	>Placebo?	Schedule response requirement	Sensitive to manipulations?
Silverman et al. (1994a)	Forced choice: A vs. B vs. C	Yes	Questionnaire (on evening before)	Amp. TZ choice depended on environmental context
Roache et al. (1995)	Free choice: A or B or none	Yes	Verbal request 10 min F.I.	Dose Response (two subjects)
Roache et al. (1996a)	Free choice: A or B or none	Yes	PRN self-medication pill use	Color-reversal in one patient
Spiga et al. (1996)	Free choice: A or B or none	Yes	FR 32–128	↑ FR ⇒ ↓ methadone Dose response

then the capsule is administered. Finally, the choice trials are not independent. This last point is important in that the repeated choice trials are not independent expressions of preference but rather are the basis for a measure of preference.

Inspection of Table 2 demonstrates that the drug vs placebo (A vs B) forced-choice procedure has been one of the most frequently employed methods for the study of human drug self-administration. In its earliest form, Jick et al. (1966) used it to assess verbal statements of preference. There, experimenters administered placebo and a variety of psychotropic medications to subjects under double-blind conditions and asked them to state, verbally, their preference for drug A vs drug B. The study by Johanson and Uhlenhuth (1980a) was the first to use the paradigm to study actual drug-taking behavior. Since that

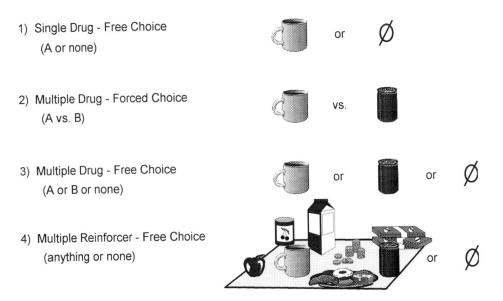

1) Single Drug - Free Choice
   (A or none)

   or   Ø

2) Multiple Drug - Forced Choice
   (A vs. B)

   vs.

3) Multiple Drug - Free Choice
   (A or B or none)

   or   or   Ø

4) Multiple Reinforcer - Free Choice
   (anything or none)

   or   Ø

FIG. 2. A taxonomy of human drug self-administration procedures with graphic illustrations of each.

		External validity	
Subject population	Route/drugs	Duration (# days)	Reinforcement opportunities (per day)
M mixed substance abusers	Oral amphetamine (15 mg) triazolam (0.25 mg)	1	Single
M sedative abusers	Oral triazolam (0.125, 0.25 mg)	10 +	Up to 18
F anxious patients	Oral diazepam (4 mg)	28	8
M methadone maintenance patients	Oral methadone (0.27–1.08 mg)	3	50–200

time, the procedure described in Fig. 3 has been widely used to study the reinforcing effects of sedatives and stimulants in normal volunteers (de Wit, 1991a; Johanson and de Wit, 1989). More recently, the procedure was modified to include only three forced-choice sessions but to permit subjects an opportunity to self-administer additional doses of the drug (A vs B) they selected (de Wit et al., 1989a,b).

The potential advantages of using a choice procedure are diminished by requiring subjects to choose one or the other of the alternatives; i.e., it is a forced choice. When a forced-choice procedure is used, it does not permit an

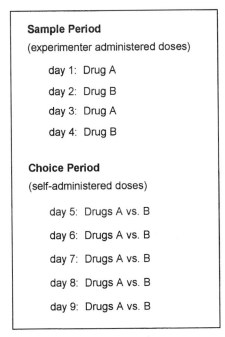

Sample Period
(experimenter administered doses)

    day 1: Drug A

    day 2: Drug B

    day 3: Drug A

    day 4: Drug B

Choice Period
(self-administered doses)

    day 5: Drugs A vs. B

    day 6: Drugs A vs. B

    day 7: Drugs A vs. B

    day 8: Drugs A vs. B

    day 9: Drugs A vs. B

Features

1) Subjects "sample" drugs

2) Single bolus doses are administered

3) Drugs are coded by letter or color

4) Subjects must verbally choose one

5) Multiple choice trials are not independent

FIG. 3. A summary of the multiple drug forced-choice (A vs B) procedure first used by Johanson and Uhlenhuth (1980a).

unambiguous conclusion that A is more rein-forcing than B when A is selected more fre-quently than B. An alternative explanation not eliminated by the forced-choice procedure is that the response alternative B was avoided rather than that A was selected. This situation is illustrated by a study (Johanson and Uhlen-huth 1980b) that reported that placebo was preferred over diazepam, presumably because the sedative effects of diazepam were being avoided. Using a choice procedure that pro-vides a third option of choosing "neither A nor B" (in addition to the two drug options) allows a more unambiguous statement about the rein-forcing effects of A and B. Thus, a *multiple drug free-choice* (Fig. 2) procedure eliminates alternative explanations that threaten the inter-nal validity of the experiment.

A study by Oliveto and colleagues (1992) utilized the basic choice paradigm illustrated in Fig. 3 to compare *forced-choice* and *free-choice* procedures. In this study, subjects in the forced-choice condition were required to drink four cups of coffee each day. The two drug conditions were established by providing a choice between caffeine-containing and caf-feine-free (decaffeinated) coffee. However, under the free-choice conditions, there was no minimum coffee drinking requirement so that subjects could drink as few or as many of ei-ther coffee (caffeinated and/or decaffeinated) as they wished. In this study, neither proce-dure demonstrated reinforcing effects of caf-feine since only one of nine subjects showed a clear preference for the caffeine-containing coffee. However, subjects in the free-choice condition consumed a lot less coffee indicat-ing that the forced-procedure was, indeed, forcing consumption. As is typical for studies of human drug self-administration, subjects were required to rate drug effects including the strength of the coffee administered, how well they liked the coffee, and their intent to consume caffeine if given the opportunity. The subject ratings and the amount of caf-feine self-administered were significantly re-lated using the free-choice procedure but not the forced-choice procedure. Thus, the free-choice procedure quantified more sensitively

the relationship between subjective effects and reinforcing effects of caffeine.

Another illustration of the free-choice pro-cedure comes from a study of amphetamine and placebo preference by Chait (1993). That study involved three independent choice trials where two sampling sessions preceded each of three choice sessions (i.e., successive choices were A or B, C or D, E or F). Color-coded amphetamine capsules were adminis-tered during one sampling session and color-coded placebo capsules were administered in the other. During the choice session, subjects chose between the color-coded capsules or chose a no-drug ("neither") option. The most significant finding of this study was that the majority of subjects did not prefer amphetam-ine and the neither drug option was chosen by subjects on 52% of the choice opportuni-ties. This represents a substantially lower rate of amphetamine preference than had previ-ously been reported using the forced-choice procedure (de Wit et al., 1986a; Johanson and de Wit, 1989; Johanson and Uhlenhuth, 1980a). The use of free-choice procedures, however, permitted a conclusion that those 11 of 29 subjects who did choose amphetamine on at least two occasions were truly selecting the drug and not just choosing the greater (or lesser) of two (forced) alternatives. The free-choice procedure also detected differences in subject characteristics. Cigarette smokers re-ported more unpleasant effects of amphetam-ine during sampling sessions and chose am-phetamine less often than their nonsmoking counterparts (Chait, 1993). Recent studies have reported that multiple drug (drug or placebo) free-choice procedures involving multiple reinforcer deliveries are sensitive enough to demonstrate robust reinforcing ef-fects in individual subjects (Roache et al., 1995; 1996a,b; Spiga et al., 1996).

The range of conclusions permitted by *free-choice* procedures can be increased by includ-ing nondrug consequences (i.e., money) as an alternative to the drug. With drug and nondrug alternatives this becomes the *multiple rein-forcer free-choice* procedure (Fig. 2). There are examples of free-choice procedures providing both drug and nondrug reinforcers (see Table 2). In one example of this, marijuana users were allowed to work to earn tokens exchangeable for money or marijuana (Mendelson et al., 1976). On average, casual users purchased three marijuana cigarettes per day and heavy users bought six marijuana cigarettes per day. Subjects in both groups exchanged points for money more frequently than for marijuana and saved more money than was spent on marijuana. This indicates that money was more reinforcing (i.e., was selected more frequently) than marijuana, at least under the exchange rate employed in this study. The advantage of providing money as an alternative to drug is that ordinal statements of the reinforcing effects of drug are made relative to the familiar standard— money. To our knowledge, there is only one example of a human study permitting a two-drug choice in the context of a third nondrug reinforcer. In that study (Foltin and Fischman, 1994), subjects with histories of i.v. cocaine use lived in a residential research environment and had three choices available to them under free-choice conditions. They could choose between two different doses of cocaine and tokens exchangeable for food snacks, cigarettes, and audio or video tapes. The study examined various combinations of cocaine dose (4, 8, 16, and 32 mg) and the number of tokens (one, two, and four tokens) available. The results showed that the high cocaine dose or the token options were selected equally often but that the lower cocaine dose was rarely selected. This study demonstrates that the lower doses of cocaine were not as reinforcing as the higher doses or the nondrug (token) reinforcer.

Comparison to Placebo

The use of placebo is considered an essential control condition to demonstrate reinforcing effects (Roache and Meisch, 1991). One can conclude that the drug's pharmacologic effects are reinforcing only when drugs are self-administered more frequently than either placebo or no drug at all. As the reader may

recall, the study by Olivetto et al. (1992) reported that only one of ten subjects selected caffeine more frequently than expected by chance. Thus, it appears that caffeine functioned as a reinforcer only for that one subject. Most subjects drank similar amounts of caffeinated and decaffeinated coffee in the free-choice condition, suggesting that nonpharmacologic factors of coffee drinking maintained consumption, but it was not the pharmacologic effects of caffeine. These results demonstrate clearly the importance of the placebo condition (i.e., the decaffeinated coffee) to control for nonspecific effects that are unrelated to the stimulus effects of the drug. The absence of a placebo makes statements about reinforcing effects of the drug difficult and therefore threaten the internal validity. Table 2 shows that a number of studies did not include a placebo control. This mainly involved early studies using single-drug free-choice procedures. For these studies, reinforcing effects only can be assumed when response requirement or other variables were manipulated to demonstrate that behavior was under the control of the drug stimulus.

A study of placebo marijuana self-administration illustrates clearly the possibility that drug self-administration may be controlled by variables other than the reinforcing effects of drug (Chait and Perry, 1992). One group of subjects (the deceptively instructed group) were told that the marijuana they would receive was active; a second group was told that marijuana cigarettes might be inactive. Deceived subjects smoked more placebo marijuana and showed greater marijuana-like subjective responses than subjects in the second group. More extensive drug histories were associated with more placebo self-administration and subjective responses were greater for persons who had novelty-seeking personalities. These observations suggest that nonpharmacologic factors such as behavioral history and temperament may influence drug-taking behavior. Such factors may be especially important in the initiation of drug use. In summary, the inclusion of a placebo control in studies of drug self-administration is imperative because drug taking may be controlled by factors other than the reinforcing effects of the drug.

Schedule Response Requirement

In nonhuman research, the operant approach to the study of drug reinforcement has been characterized by a precise specification of the operant schedule. A schedule of reinforcement specifies the probability of drug delivery contingent upon responses occurring in some scheduled temporal or numeric pattern. For example, *ratio schedules* of reinforcement deliver a reinforcer after a specified number of responses have been emitted, and *interval schedules* deliver reinforcers when a response occurs after a specified interval of time has elapsed (Ferster and Skinner, 1957). Unfortunately, the human self-administration literature often has not specified clearly the reinforcement schedule and experimental manipulation of the reinforcement schedule has been rare. Inspection of Table 2 shows that most studies delivered drug contingent upon a verbal request only. Several studies have employed procedures where there was a specified relationship between an instrumental response and drug delivery. Responses have included button or lever pressing (e.g., Bickel et al., 1991; Mendelson et al., 1976) or bicycle riding (Bigelow et al., 1976). Some researchers have employed token economies where instrumental responses earned points or tokens that were exchangeable for either money or drugs (e.g., Mello et al., 1981; Mendelson et al., 1976). Only a few studies have manipulated the cost per dose by varying response requirements (e.g., Babor et al., 1978; Bickel et al., 1991; Spiga et al., 1996).

One study by McLeod and Griffiths (1983) manipulated the response requirement using a progressive ratio schedule to examine the reinforcing effects of pentobarbital. Subjects were required to complete a specified work requirement (either a number of button presses or a time period of exercise bicycle riding) to obtain access to placebo, or to 200,

400, or 600 mg sodium pentobarbital. The work required to gain access to the dose was increased systematically each day. This method (a progressive ratio schedule) was used to assess the relative reinforcing effects of different drugs or doses. Each drug dose was administered in a letter-coded capsule. Each day before the work session, subjects were informed which letter-coded dose was available and the work requirement that was in effect; subjects had a free-choice option of working or not working to obtain drug. Higher pentobarbital doses maintained more responding at greater ratio work requirements than did lower doses. These results suggest that the progressive ratio procedure is a sensitive method for examining the relative reinforcing effects of drugs. Manipulation of response requirement permits construction of a quantifiable scale of ordinal differences in the reinforcing effects. Parameter manipulation also helps to define the range of conditions under which a drug will function as a reinforcer. The relative resistance to disruption of responses maintained by a reinforcer is an important metric for ranking the reinforcing effects of differing stimuli (e.g., Nevin, 1974, 1979, 1988). In the McLeod and Griffiths (1983) study, increasing the work requirement did not decrease (i.e., disrupt) responding when large doses were available but did suppress responses maintained by smaller drug doses. Because large doses maintained behavior at greater work requirements than smaller doses, the investigator can conclude that the larger doses were more reinforcing.

A recent study employed a multiple drug (A or B or none) free-choice procedure to examine the reinforcing effects of methadone in methadone maintenance patients (Spiga et al., 1996). Subjects were permitted to press a button on a fixed-ratio schedule to gain access to small unit doses of methadone or concurrently available water. The number of responses was varied systematically by requiring that subjects press a button 32, 64, or 128 times to obtain 10 ml of methadone or water. Subjects also had the option to sit and do nothing. Figure 4 shows that increasing the re-

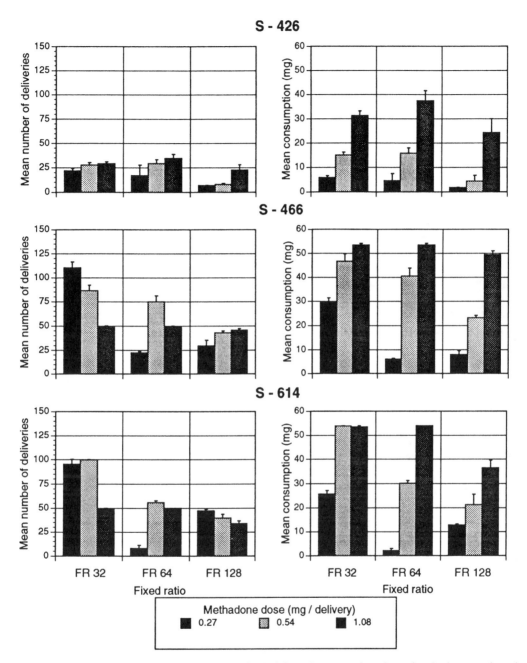

FIG. 4. This graph illustrates methadone self-administration as a function of unit dose and work (fixed ratio) requirement. The lines extending upward from each bar indicate ±1 SEM. These graphs illustrate that as work requirement is increased the frequency of deliveries and consumption is decreased as a function of ratio requirement. Replotted from original data (Spiga et al., 1996).

sponse requirement decreased methadone self-administration at the lower but not the higher doses. Thus, relative to lower doses, higher doses more effectively maintained responding and may be considered to be more effective reinforcers.

Sensitivity to Manipulation

Table 2 illustrates a number of studies that have examined the effects of several environmental, pharmacologic, and schedule variables on human drug self-administration. Pharmacologic variables include dose and antagonist pretreatment; environmental variables include the postingestional environment and required tasks and schedule variables include response requirement. When drug-taking behavior is an orderly function of variables known to affect operant behavior, we can more confidently assert that drug reinforcement is demonstrated. For example, demonstrating that the reinforcing effect of a drug varies as a function of dose shows that the drug stimulus is of primary importance in maintaining behavior (Henningfield et al., 1983; McLeod and Griffiths, 1983; Pickens et al., 1977; Spiga et al., 1996). An operant behavioral process also is demonstrated when variations in schedule parameters result in orderly changes in drug self-administration behavior. For instance, increases in the fixed ratio (Bickel et al., 1991; Spiga et al., 1996) or the time interval between doses (Griffiths et al., 1976) have been shown to decrease self-administration. Also, manipulations of consequence should affect behavior, as in a study reporting decreased alcohol consumption (Griffiths et al., 1974b) when the consequence of drinking was that subjects were prevented from social interaction (i.e., a social time-out). Demonstration that behavior is modifiable by experimental manipulation of operant parameters is most important for those studies that do not include a placebo control (Griffiths et al., 1980), because without such evidence it is difficult to conclude that the drug is functioning as a re-

inforcer (Roache and Meisch, 1991). However, such experimental manipulation is valuable even for studies including a placebo because they help to quantify the conditions under which the drug is reinforcing.

Another approach to manipulation of operant variables includes pharmacologic alteration of the reinforcing consequence or the drug stimulus. Mello and Mendelson and colleagues have reported effects of pharmacologic pretreatments on heroin self-administration in treatment-resistant opiate addicts. They employed a free-choice procedure in which hospitalized subjects responded on manipulanda to accumulate points that were exchangeable for either heroin injections (i.v.) or money. Initially, they reported that 10 days of maintenance on the partial agonist, buprenorphine, suppressed heroin self-administration (Mello and Mendelson, 1980; Mello et al., 1982). A second study reported that acute doses of the antagonist naltrexone decreased heroin self-administration in opiate users (Mello et al., 1981). More recently, Fischman and Foltin and colleagues have conducted similar experiments in cocaine abusers. In the first study (Fischman et al., 1990), chronic dosing with the tricyclic antidepressant desipramine failed to alter the preference for cocaine over placebo in a free-choice procedure. In the second study (Foltin and Fischman, 1994), subjects had a multiple-drug free-choice option to choose between two different cocaine doses and a token exchangeable for money. Under conditions of placebo pretreatment, subjects chose the high cocaine dose or money equally often but rarely chose the low cocaine dose. Compared to placebo, acute doses of buprenorphine pretreatment (4 mg) increased the money preference. These studies suggest that the human drug self-administration paradigm may be useful to evaluate possible pharmacologic adjuncts to treatment. But they also demonstrate that pharmacologic manipulation of the reinforcing stimulus alters behavior in predictable ways.

Recent research utilizing a behavioral economic approach to understanding the relationship between reinforcer magnitude and response cost has demonstrated the theoretical necessity of parametric manipulation (see Chapter 3). For example, Bickel and colleagues (1991) tested human cigarette smokers and made available varying magnitudes of the reinforcer (i.e., one, two, and eight cigarette puffs) under varying fixed ratio requirements (200, 400, and 1,600 responses per reinforcer delivery). They reported that the number of ratios completed by subjects when one puff was delivered after 200 responses was roughly equivalent to 400 responses for two puffs or 1,600 responses for eight puffs. These data support the concept of a unit price analysis where a constant price per puff (i.e., 1,600 responses for eight puffs = 200 responses per puff) yields similar amounts of behavioral output. Behavioral economic principles of cost seem to explain a lot of variations in consummatory behavior for many different drugs (cf. Bickel et al., 1993; Chapter 3).

External Validity

Experimental studies examining drug self-administration in humans clearly have established that drugs acting as reinforcers in laboratory animals also do so for human subjects under experimental conditions. However, reviews of human methods of drug self-administration only rarely have discussed (Henningfield et al., 1991a) how the methodologic features typical of human drug self-administration studies can limit the generalizability and representativeness of the results. The basic question is one of *external validity* (Campbell and Stanley, 1966). It asks, to what populations, settings, range of doses, and routes of administration can the results of laboratory research be extended? The answer depends on the range of conditions that have been tested and their ability to serve as valid predictors of natural behavior that occurs beyond the confines of the experimental setting. The following sections discuss issues of external validity.

Subject Population

It can be seen in Table 2 that many different populations of drug users have been employed in drug self-administration studies. For most drugs or experiments, ethical and safety considerations require that human studies of self-administration not expose subjects to substances in amounts or patterns exceeding those of the subject's own experience. Consequently, opiate studies have employed opiate users, marijuana studies employed marijuana users, etc. Unfortunately, the consequence of these restrictions is that the results may not generalize to more broadly defined populations. Several studies have employed normal non–drug-using volunteers who did not have specified histories of drug use. Self-administration studies in non–drug users were ethically justified given their focus on over-the-counter or prescription drugs that may be used medically in such populations.

An example of the way that results from one population may or may not generalize to another population comes from studies of benzodiazepine self-administration. Laboratory research has shown repeatedly that benzodiazepines function as reinforcers for subjects with sedative abuse histories but do not do so for normal volunteers without such histories (de Wit et al., 1986a; Roache and Meisch, 1995; Roache et al., 1995). On one level, it adds to the external validity of laboratory self-administration procedures to find that benzodiazepines are reinforcers only to people who use and/or abuse sedatives. However, on the other hand, one can question the general significance of the finding that benzodiazepines are reinforcing. Specifically, there have been questions regarding the reinforcing effects of these drugs and the extent to which this may contribute to addiction in anxious patient populations receiving prescription medication (Roache and Meisch, 1995). Using the basic forced-choice procedure illustrated in Fig. 3, studies have shown that normal volunteers prefer placebo over diazepam (de Wit et al., 1986a;

Johanson and Uhlenhuth, 1980b). When subjects with generalized anxiety disorder were tested with this procedure, again the majority preferred placebo (de Wit et al., 1986b; McCracken et al., 1990), although diazepam was preferred in a few patients. However, the low level of diazepam preference in those studies may be due to the use of the laboratory forced-choice procedure. Recently, a small study of four patients with generalized anxiety disorder used a free-choice procedure to measure self-medication behavior on an outpatient basis and reported clear preference for diazepam over placebo in three of the four patients (Roache et al., 1996a). The finding that benzodiazepines do function as reinforcers in anxious outpatients has been extended to alprazolam as well (Roache et al., 1996b).

Another approach to understanding differences in reinforcing effects of drugs among individuals is to examine subgroups within the category of users to determine whether reinforcing effects differ between the subgroups. Sobell and colleagues (1972) compared the drinking topography of social drinkers and alcoholics in a simulated barroom environment. Both groups drank alcohol; however, the drinking topography of social drinkers and alcoholics differed. Compared with normal social drinkers, alcoholics consumed more drinks, took larger sips, drank more rapidly, waited longer between sips, and showed greater preference for straight shots of hard liquor. Although this study did not include a placebo control to infer reinforcing effects, it seems reasonable to suggest that alcohol was reinforcing drinking behavior in both subject groups. The observed topographical differences in drinking behavior do not necessarily indicate that alcohol was more reinforcing in alcoholics than in social drinkers because measures of response rate are not good indices of reinforcement (Roache and Meisch, 1991). These differences in drinking topography may be due to other factors including acquired or innate tolerance and drinking history or experience.

More recent work has examined drug reinforcement in subgroups of normal social drinkers participating in a group recreational environment. The self-administration procedure was a combination of *forced-choice/ free-choice* procedures wherein subjects were forced to choose between drug vs placebo alternatives but then were permitted to freely self-administer additional doses if they so desired. In the first of these studies, it was reported that diazepam was reinforcing and that moderate drinkers self-administered more diazepam than light drinkers (de Wit et al., 1989a). Using the same procedure, two studies compared drug use in male subjects with a family history of alcoholism to subjects without such a family history. In these studies, subjects with a family history of alcoholism showed no differences in the patterns of alcohol (de Wit and McCracken, 1990) or diazepam (de Wit, 1991) self-administration as compared to subjects without family histories of alcoholism. Given the limitations of the laboratory techniques used to assess drug reinforcement in these studies, it would be premature to rule out a role for family history and possible genetic factors as determinants of drug use. However, the fact that diazepam self-administration did vary as a function of drinking history but did not vary as a function of family history variables suggests that recent history of drug use is a better predictor of laboratory self-administration behavior.

An alternative approach for addressing population issues in drug abuse is the evaluation of individual differences. Typically, this approach involves a post hoc analysis of data wherein subjects are divided into groups based on their response to the experimental manipulation. Differences among the high responders and the low (or no) responders are reported. Several self-administration studies have reported differences among choosers and nonchoosers of drug in their subjective responses to drugs (Chutuape and de Wit, 1994; de Wit et al., 1986a). More importantly, however, subjects self-reporting greater patterns of drug use also tend to self-administer more drug in the laboratory. This effect has been shown for marijuana (Mendelson et al., 1976), alcohol (Sobell et al., 1972), and diazepam (de Wit et al., 1989a). The finding that human laboratory self-administration behavior is positively correlated with previous histories of drug use greatly supports the external validity of the laboratory studies and is consistent with animal studies suggesting the importance of historical variables as determinants of drug reinforcement (Griffiths et al., 1980; Roache and Meisch, 1991). However, the likelihood that observed laboratory behavior will be related to the drug experience of subjects makes the issue of population selection all the more important. Given the small sample size and nonrandom selection process for enrolling subjects in human self-administration research studies, strong selection biases can influence outcome.

Drugs/Route

Examination of Table 2 shows that a variety of drugs of abuse and dependence have been self-administered by humans in controlled laboratory settings. These drugs include alcohol, barbiturates, and benzodiazepines; caffeine, cocaine, and other stimulants; heroin, morphine, and other opiates; tobacco and nicotine; marijuana and cannabinoids; and volatile inhalants. With only a few exceptions, these same drugs maintain drug-taking responses in nonhuman species (Griffiths et al., 1980; Meisch and Stewart, 1994; Young and Herling, 1986). To our knowledge, human self-administration of hallucinogens has not been examined experimentally. Evidence from nonhuman studies suggest that hallucinogens of the LSD or indolamine types are aversive and are avoided (Roache and Meisch, 1991; Young and Herling, 1986). The concordance of findings in human and animal subjects strongly supports the validity of animal studies of drug reinforcement and their applicability to human populations (Griffiths et al., 1980).

The fact that such pharmacologically diverse drugs all are behaviorally reinforcing supports the hypothesis that the operant reinforcement process is one of the most fundamental variables establishing or maintaining drug abuse and addiction (Roache and Meisch, 1991). A little-studied issue of validity for human studies of drug reinforcement is the use of negative controls. The issue here is whether a drug user subject population, such as is commonly employed in human studies, would have a bias or tendency to self-administer almost any drug. To answer this question, it is noteworthy that some studies have reported negative results in attempts to measure drug reinforcement in drug users (Preston et al., 1985). The importance of a placebo control cannot be over-emphasized, especially given the finding by Chait and Perry (1992) that marijuana users readily self-administered placebo marijuana. There is one study by Griffiths et al. (1979) that well demonstrated that human drug self-administration paradigms could discriminate between pharmacologically active positive and negative control drugs. This study employed a single drug, free-choice procedure in subjects with histories of sedative abuse or dependence. The results showed that pentobarbital, and to a lesser extent diazepam, was self-administered but chlorpromazine and placebo were not. Animal studies also have shown that antipsychotics like chlorpromazine are not good reinforcers (Griffiths et al., 1980; Roache and Meisch, 1991; Young and Herling, 1986).

Examination of Table 2 shows that the routes of drug administration used in humans have included oral (opiates, sedatives, stimulants, cannabinoids), inhalation (tobacco, marijuana, cocaine, and nitrous oxide), intranasal (cocaine), intravenous (opiates, cocaine, and nicotine), and intramuscular (opiates). The route selected for drug administration in human drug studies most often reflects the primary way that the drug is used in the natural environment. To our knowledge, only one self-administration study (Foltin and Fischman 1992) has directly compared two different routes of drug administration. They examined the reinforcing effects of smoked and intravenously delivered cocaine in cocaine users having experience with both routes, and gave subjects an opportunity to choose between them. Experimentally, subjects preferred the inhalation route even though 80% of the subjects reported a bias in favor of the intravenous route. However, the inhalation doses (25 and 50 mg) were higher than the intravenous doses (16 and 32 mg) and could account for an inhalation preference despite the fact that previous research showed that these doses produced comparable blood levels.

The self-administration of nicotine and tobacco is an interesting example of issues related to the route of administration in demonstrating a cross-species generality of drug reinforcement. Although humans normally consume nicotine by smoking, chewing, and insufflation (intranasal) of tobacco products, research in tobacco addiction has been hampered by the difficulties of getting animals to ingest tobacco or nicotine by these routes. Behavioral analyses of human cigarette smoking have suggested that tobacco smoking is reinforcing to cigarette smokers (Bickel et al., 1991; Griffiths and Henningfield, 1982), but these studies did not use placebo controls or other procedures to control for the biases of cigarette users to smoke. Early animal research had great difficulty trying to get laboratory animals to smoke cigarettes, although nicotine had been shown to be a modest reinforcer by the intravenous route (c.f., Henningfield, 1984 for review). Even though nicotine is not normally consumed by the intravenous route of administration, it is this route that clearly demonstrated the generality of nicotine as a reinforcer and as an addictive substance. First, it was reported that tobacco dependent smokers pressed levers to self-administer nicotine intravenously (Henningfield et al., 1983). Subsequently, the same intravenous nicotine injection procedure was used (Goldberg and Henningfield, 1988) to demonstrate similar dose response functions in humans and monkeys. The authors made the

point that nicotine reinforcement was robust only under a limited range of conditions. The conditions that increased nicotine self-administration included the following: (1) intermittent availability of nicotine, (2) intermittent presentation of stimuli paired with nicotine delivery, and (3) concurrent access to food reinforcement. It was noted that cigarettes, the typical vehicles used to deliver nicotine, provide paired stimuli in the form of tobacco smoke and odor and intermittent dosing in the form of puffs on multiple cigarettes. Whereas nicotine also is administered through bucal (i.e., gum or chew) and transdermal (i.e., nicotine patch) absorption, the reinforcing effects of these routes have not been examined to our knowledge.

Reinforcement Opportunities

Many human studies of drug reinforcement (Table 2) have provided only a few limited opportunities to self-administer the drug. Frequently, the drug is available as a single bolus dose that subjects may choose or reject in an all-or-none fashion. While it is true that the oral abuse of prescription sedatives or stimulants generally occurs in single bolus doses, most drug abuse or dependence does not. For example, smokers of crack, marijuana, or tobacco consume numerous small puffs from multiple cigarettes or pipes; drinkers of alcohol or coffee ingest several drinks spaced over time with many small sips per drink; and intravenous users of opiates or stimulants may use only once per day, but frequently inject drugs on multiple occasions per day.

One of the most basic principles of operant behavioral analysis is to provide the reinforcer in multiple small units so as to more precisely observe and quantify the operant behavior maintained by the reinforcer (Ferster and Skinner, 1957). Animal research has shown that compared with sessions limiting the number of drug deliveries, procedures permitting more self-administrations per session result in an increased sensitivity to measure reinforcing effects at lower doses of drug (Young and Herling, 1986). Statistically, it makes sense that the limited range of variation resulting from an all-or-none procedure (i.e., 0 or 1) would be less sensitive than procedures allowing greater quantitative variation (i.e., 0, 1, 2, 3 deliveries, etc.). Furthermore, behavioral studies have documented that small behavioral response requirements may be maintained by the immediate delivery of small magnitude reinforcers. However, it requires larger magnitudes of reinforcement (i.e., larger doses of drug) to maintain behavior with higher response requirements or longer time delays between response and reinforcement (Meisch and Lemaire, 1993).

Certainly it is possible to demonstrate reinforcement using procedures in which the drug is given in single bolus doses after the subject completes the response requirement. Due to the limited range of responses (i.e., 0 or 1), the data are commonly analyzed as the percentage of subjects selecting drug over placebo. Examples of this type of analysis (Table 2) can be seen for the single-drug free-choice (Griffiths et al., 1984; Mendelson and Mello, 1984), the multiple-drug forced-choice (Johanson and Uhlenhuth, 1980a,b), and the multiple-drug free-choice (Chait, 1993) procedures. However, the availability of multiple reinforcer deliveries increases the quantitative sensitivity of the procedure and enables conclusions regarding reinforcing effects for individual subjects. Examples of this procedure and analysis also are found in Table 2 (Bickel et al., 1991; Henningfield et al., 1983; Roache et al., 1995, 1996a). Studies using forced-choice procedures recently have begun to permit several drug deliveries following an initial forced-choice between drug and placebo (e.g., de Wit and McCracken, 1990; Evans et al., 1994). One advantage is that this allows subjects to titrate their own total dose. However, another important aspect of this modification is the increased quantitative information obtained (i.e., amount of drug consumed). For example, light vs moderate

drinkers were differentiated by the number of deliveries of diazepam (de Wit et al., 1989a) or ethanol (de Wit et al., 1989b) they self-administered.

Duration

Human drug self-administration procedures typically involve very short periods of time in which drugs were available for self-administration. Few studies have gone beyond 5 days of repeated opportunity to self-administer a particular drug/dose condition. Thus, we are limited in the statements that can be made concerning the stability of a drug's reinforcing effects over time. There are few data on transitional states or final stabilization baselines. The reasons for the use of short-term observations are varied and may be as simple as the study was not interested in issues of stability. However, another factor for human studies is the limited time period that one can expect to keep a volunteer subject under protocol restrictions. Several studies have examined drug intake for longer periods but most of those have been accomplished by the hospitalization of subjects (e.g., Griffiths et al., 1979; Mendelson et al., 1976; Wikler, 1952). Outpatient procedures employing longer periods of observation have been few but there are several examples. Stitzer and colleagues (1979) examined diazepam use in methadone maintenance patients over 42 days; Hughes et al. (1991) observed coffee drinking over a 12-day time period; and Roache et al. (1996a) reported diazepam self-administration in anxious patients over a time period as long as 10 weeks.

The long-term stability of drug self-administration is an important issue for several reasons. First is the issue of test-retest reliability. Studies that assess reinforcing effects on only one day have no data on the reliability of their observations. Second, drugs may be self-administered at one time, and not the next, due to a variety of factors unrelated to the pharmacology or reinforcing effects of the drug including uncontrolled psychosocial event changes in the subject's life or uncontrolled changes in the subject's environment (most important for outpatient studies). Third, there are important reasons to examine long-term stability related to pharmacology and reinforcing effectiveness. For example, there have been questions regarding the reinforcing strength of benzodiazepines in part because self-administration behavior may decrease over time (Roache and Griffiths, 1989a). However, more recent studies have reported conditions under which self-administration behavior did persist over time (Roache et al., 1995, 1996a,b). Another example is a pharmacologic issue. The first human study of opiate self-administration (Wikler, 1952) showed a regular but increasing pattern of morphine self-administration. Combined with animal self-administration data, there has been a conclusion that opiates maintain stable patterns of behavior but cocaine self-administration is erratic presumably due to stimulant-induced toxicity (Young and Herling, 1986). In the human literature, an early study by (Mello and Mendelson, 1970) showed that alcoholics tended to drink in irregular binge patterns where periods of heavy drinking are followed by periods of less or no drinking. A final reason for studying drug self-administration over time is the issue of evaluating potential pharmacotherapies in the context of chronic drug abuse. While short-term or acute studies may suggest a treatment, we need to determine the effects of chronic pharmacotherapy or what the effects of treatment are on chronic drug use.

FUTURE DIRECTIONS

This review of human drug self-administration research focused on two basic questions: To what extent do the experimental arrangements typically found in the research literature justify the conclusion that the drug functions as a reinforcer (internal validity)? How generalizable or representative are the results (external validity)? In considering these issues, we have tried to provide a critique of methods with the view of highlighting strengths or weaknesses of different approaches. The review has shown that functional relationships between response and drug consequence have been systematically replicated across different settings and methods. Thus, the generality of the interpretation that human drug-taking behavior is an instance of operant behavior is well established. Furthermore, we have identified the range of conditions (populations, drug doses, situations, etc.) under which drugs will reinforce self-administration behavior. Even though animal studies of drug reinforcement may be better able to examine systematically the behavioral and pharmacologic variables influencing drug reinforcement, human studies are essential in the final determination of parameters and conditions under which drugs will function as reinforcers in human populations. The consistency of findings among experimental studies and their correspondence with clinical findings supports the utility of conclusions coming from human experimental studies of drug-taking behavior.

Early experimental arrangements approximated both the natural environment and animal operant procedures by providing frequent and sustained opportunities for self-administration of drug in a controlled environment. Many of these studies demonstrated reinforcement through experimental manipulation of variables known to affect operant behavior or by the use of nondrug alternatives. More recent procedures have better utilized placebo controls but have tried to simplify the paradigm by reducing the number of self-administration opportunities and studying self-administration without confining subjects to hospital environments. All together, research has established that most major classes of drugs of abuse function as reinforcers for humans. The methods have differed within and across studies with regard to subject population, self-administration procedure, drugs and doses, reinforcement schedule and schedule parameters, and the availability of alternative reinforcers. Now that validity has been established and experimental parameters are known, it is important for human drug self-administration research to address clinically relevant details about individual risk factors and potential treatments. Until now, only a few studies have examined potential behavioral or pharmacologic treatment approaches. Similarly, only a few studies have focused on the influence of risk factors including drug history, genetic or family history, personality, and personal expectations about drug effects. However, these potential risk factors may play only a modulating role in the basic phenomena of drug reinforcement, and thus we need to utilize procedures that will be sensitive to quantitative variations in reinforcing effectiveness.

Our review of the literature leads us to suggest that free-choice procedures involving placebo controls and multiple reinforcer deliveries provide the most powerful techniques to unequivocally establish drug reinforcement. Studies relying upon single bolus doses with only a few opportunities for self-administration often (but not always) are sufficient to demonstrate self-administration and therefore are a convenient approach to suggest reinforcing effects and abuse potential. However, these procedures do not necessarily provide a sufficient range of variability to provide a baseline that would be sensitive to change or modulatory influences. We encourage the current trend in human research procedures that give subjects more control over dosing in a more chronic procedure. We believe this approach takes better advantage of current technology in the experimental analysis of behavior. Thus, procedures involving multiple deliveries of multiple reinforcers should provide a more sensitive baseline to rank relative reinforcing effects of different drugs, evaluate population and individual differences, and examine the potential efficacy of pretreatment medications. To take the greatest advantage of current technology, drug reinforcement needs to be interpreted in the context of the behavioral economics of drug consumption. This usually will necessitate the experimental manipulation of drug dose and response cost variables as part of the experiment.

A final topic for future research is the critically understudied area of the effects of experimental instructions and subject expectations on self-administration behavior. Whereas the use of placebos may control for nonspecific biases, it is important to understand how these biases and expectations affect drug-taking behavior. It is these sorts of variables that are the target of drug abuse prevention strategies. It is bias and expectation that best seem to predict the potential for abuse, and these variables may turn out to be among the greatest predictors of individual risk.

SUMMARY

- Most of the major classes of drugs of abuse have been evaluated in human laboratory studies directly examining self-administration behavior.

- Many studies have established that drugs of abuse function as reinforcers in humans as they do also for nonhuman subjects in operant studies of drug reinforcement. However, many human studies have not utilized the best procedures to unequivocally demonstrate a reinforcement process.

- Self-administration procedures that allow subjects to choose between drug and placebo (and/or other possible reinforcers) on multiple occasions provides one of the most sensitive procedures for measuring changes as a function of the experimental manipulation of other variables.

- Studies of drug self-administration have been utilized to examine:

  1. the species generality of drug reinforcement as a process;
  2. the relationship between drug-taking behavior and subjectively perceived drug effects;
  3. population or personality predictors of drug use;
  4. the effects of drug treatment/pretreatment on subsequent drug use behavior; and
  5. the effects on consumption of environmental costs and consequences.

- Future research needs to more carefully address possible influences of instructions and subject expectations on self-administration behavior.

- Studies of drug self-administration remain the most valid predictors of naturalistic drug-taking behavior. The species generality of drug reinforcement supports the validity of nonhuman studies of self-administration. However, human studies are better able to achieve the complexity and ecologic validity of real-world environments and can better identify individual and population predictors of abuse or addictive behavior.

REFERENCES

Babor, T.F., Mendelson, J.H., Greenberg, I. and Kuehnle, J. (1978) Experimental analysis of the "happy hour": effects of purchase price on alcohol consumption. *Psychopharmacology* 58: 35–41. Baron, A. and Galizio, M. (1983) Instructional control of human operant behavior. Psychol. Rec. 33: 495–520.

Beecher, H.K. (1959) *Measurement of subjective responses: quantitative effects of drugs*. New York: Oxford University Press.

Bickel, W.K., DeGrandpre, R.J., and Higgins, S.T. (1993) Behavioral economics: a novel experimental approach to the study of drug dependence. *Drug Alcohol Depend.* 33: 173–192.

Bickel, W.K., DeGrandpre, R.J., Hughes, J.R. and Higgins, S.T. (1991) Behavioral economics of drug self-administration: II. A unit-price analysis of cigarette smoking. *J. Exp. Anal. Behav.* 55: 145–154.

Bigelow, G.E, Griffiths, R.R. and Liebson, I.A. (1976) Effects of response requirement upon human sedative self-administration and drug-seeking behavior. *Pharmacol. Biochem. Behav.* 5: 681–685.

Bradshaw, C.M. and Szabadi, E. (1988) Quantitative analysis of human operant behavior. In: Davey, G. and Cullen, C. (eds.) *Human operant conditioning and behavior modification*. Chichester, England: John Wiley, pp. 225–259.

Campbell, D.T. and Stanley J.C. (1966) Experimental and quasi-experimental designs for research. In: *Handbook of research on teaching*. Chicago: Rand McNally, 1963.

Chait, L.D. (1993) Factors influencing the reinforcing and subjective effects of d-amphetamine in humans. *Behav. Pharmacol.* 4: 191–199.

Chait, L.D. and Perry, J.L. (1992) Factors influencing self-administration of, and subjective response to, placebo marijuana. *Behav. Pharmacol.* 3: 545–552.

Chait, L.D., Uhlenhuth, E.H. and Johanson, C.E. (1987) Reinforcing and subjective effects of several anorectics in normal human volunteers. *J. Pharmacol. Exp. Ther.* 242: 777–783.

Chait, L.D. and Zacny, J.P. (1992a) Reinforcing and subjective effects of oral delta 9-THC and smoked marijuana in humans. *Psychopharmacology* 107: 255–262.

Chutuape, M.A. and de Wit, H. (1994) Relationship between subjective effects and drug preferences: ethanol and diazepam. *Drug Alcohol Depend.* 34: 243–251.

Davison, M. and McCarthy, D. (1988) *The matching law: a research review*. Hillsdale, NJ: Lawrence Erlbaum.

DeGrandpre, R.J., Bickel, W.K., Higgins, S.T. and Hughes, J.R. (1994) A behavioral economic analysis of concurrently available money and cigarettes. *J. Exp. Anal. Behav.* 61: 191–201.

DeGrandpre, R.J., Bickel, W.K., Hughes, J.R. and Higgins, S.T. (1992) Behavioral economics of drug self-administration: III. A reanalysis of the nicotine regulation hypothesis. *Psychopharmacology* 108: 1–10.

de Villiers, P. (1977) Choice in concurrent schedules and a quantitative formulation of the law of effects. In: Honig, W.K. and Staddon, J.E.R. (eds.) *Handbook of operant behavior*. Englewood Cliffs, NJ: Prentice-Hall, pp. 233–287.

de Wit, H. (1991) Diazepam preference in males with and without an alcoholic first-degree relative. *Alc. Clin. Exp. Res.* 15: 593–600.

de Wit, H. and Chutuape, M.A. (1993) Increased ethanol choice in social drinkers following ethanol preload. *Behav. Pharmacol.* 4: 29–36.

de Wit, H. and Griffiths, R.R. (1991) Testing the abuse liability of anxiolytic and hypnotic drugs in humans. *Drug and Alc. Depend.* 28: 83–111.

de Wit, H. and McCracken, S.G. (1990) Ethanol self-administration in males with and without an alcoholic first-degree relative. *Alcohol Clin. Exp. Res.* 14: 63–69.

de Wit, H., Pierri, J. and Johanson, C.E. (1989a) Reinforcing and subjective effects of diazepam in nondrug-abusing volunteers. *Pharmacol. Biochem. Behav.* 33: 205–213.

de Wit, H., Pierri, J. and Johanson, C.E. (1989b) Assessing individual differences in ethanol preference using a cumulative dosing procedure. *Psychopharmacology* 98: 113–119.

de Wit, H., Uhlenhuth E.H. and Hedeker, D. (1986b) Lack of preference for diazepam in anxious volunteers. *Arch. Gen. Psychiatry* 43: 533–541.

de Wit, H., Uhlenhuth E.H. and Johanson, C.E. (1986a) Individual differences in the reinforcing and subjective effects of amphetamine and diazepam. *Drug Alcohol Depend.* 16: 341–360.

Dohrn, C.S., Lichtor, J.L., Coalson, D.W., Uitvlugt, A., de Wit, H. and Zacny, J.P. (1993) Reinforcing effects of extended inhalation of nitrous oxide in humans. *Drug Alcohol Depend.* 31: 265–280.

Evans, S.M., Critchfield, T.S. and Griffiths, R.R. (1994) Caffeine reinforcement demonstrated in a majority of moderate caffeine users. *Behav. Pharmacol.* 5: 231–238.

Ferster, C.B. and Skinner, B.F. (1957) *Schedules of reinforcement*. Englewood Cliffs, NJ: Prentice-Hall.

Fischman, M.W. and Foltin, R.W. (1991) Utility of subjective-effects measurements in assessing abuse liability of drugs in humans. *Br. J. Addict.* 86: 1563–1570.

Fischman, M.W., Foltin, R.W., Nestadt, G., and Pearlson, G.D. (1990) Effects of desipramine maintenance on cocaine self-administration by humans. *J. Pharmacol. Exp. Ther.* 253: 760–770.

Foltin, R.W. and Fischman, M.W. (1991) Assessment of abuse liability of stimulant drugs in humans: a methodological survey. *Drug Alcohol Depend.* 28: 3–48.

Foltin, R.W. and Fischman, M.W. (1992) Self-administration of cocaine by humans: choice between smoked and intravenous cocaine. *J. Pharmacol. Exp. Ther.* 261: 841–849.

Foltin, R.W. and Fischman, M.W. (1994) Effects of buprenorphine on the self-administration of cocaine by humans. *Behav. Pharmacol.* 5: 79–89.

Goldberg, S.R. and Henningfield, J.E. (1988) Reinforcing effects of nicotine in humans and experimental animals responding under intermittent schedules of i.v. drug infection. *Pharmacol. Biochem. Behav.* 30: 227–234.

Griffiths, R.R., Bigelow, G.E. and Henningfield, J.E. (1980) Similarities in animal and human drug-taking behavior. In: Mello, N.K. (ed.) *Advances in substance abuse,* vol. 1. Greenwich, CT: JAI Press, pp. 1–90.

Griffiths, R., Bigelow, G. and Liebson, I. (1974a) Assessment of effects of ethanol self-administration on social interactions in alcoholics. *Psychopharmacologia* 38: 105–110.

Griffiths, R., Bigelow, G. and Liebson, I. (1974b) Suppression of ethanol self-administration in alcoholics by contingent time-out from social interactions. *Behav. Res. Ther.* 12: 327–334.

Griffiths, R.R., Bigelow, G.E. and Liebson, I. (1976) Human sedative self-administration: effects of interingestion interval and dose. *J. Pharmacol. Exp. Ther.* 197: 488–494.

Griffiths, R.R., Bigelow, G.E. and Liebson, I. (1979) Human drug self-administration: double-blind comparison of pentobarbital, diazepam, chlorpromazine and placebo. *J. Pharmacol. Exp. Ther.* 210: 301–310.

Griffiths, R.R. and Henningfield, J.E. (1982) Experimental analysis of human cigarette smoking behavior. *Fed. Proc.* 41: 234–240.

Griffiths, R.R., McLeod, D.R., Bigelow, G.E., Liebson, I.A., Roache, J.D. and Nowoieski, P. (1984) Comparison of diazepam and oxazepam: preference, liking, and extent of abuse. *J. Pharmacol. Exp. Ther.* 229: 501–508.

Griffiths, R.R., Rush, C.R. and Puhala, K.A. (1996) Validation of the multiple-choice procedure for investigating drug reinforcement in humans. *Exp. Clin. Psychopharmacol.* 4: 97–106.

Griffiths, R.R., Troisi, J.R. II, Silverman K. and Mumford, G.K. (1993) Multiple-choice procedure: an efficient approach for investigating drug reinforcement in humans. *Behav. Pharmacol.* 4: 3–13.

Henningfield, J.E. (1984) Behavioral pharmacology of cigarette smoking. In: Thompson, T., Dews, P.B. and Barrett J.E. (eds.) *Advances in behavioral pharmacology,* vol. 4. Orlando, FL: Academic Press, pp.131–210.

Henningfield, J.E., Cohen, C. and Heishman, S.J. (1991a) Drug self-administration methods in abuse liability evaluation. *Br. J. Addict.* 86: 1571–1577.

Henningfield, J.E., Miyasato, K. and Jasinski, D.R. (1983) Cigarette smokers self-administer intravenous nicotine. *Pharmacol. Biochem. Behav.* 19: 887–890.

Herrnstein, R.J. (1970) On the law of effect. *J. Exp. Anal. Behav.* 13: 243–266.

Higgins, S.T., Bickel, W.K. and Hughes, J.R. (1994a) Influence of an alternative reinforcer on human cocaine self-administration. *Life Sci.* 55: 179–187.

Higgins, S.T., Budney, A.J. and Bickel, W.K. (1994b) Review article: applying behavioral concepts and principles to the treatment of cocaine dependence. *Drug Alcohol Depend.* 34: 87–97.

Hughes, J.R., Higgins, S.T., Bickel, W.K., Hunt. W.K., Fenwick, J.W., Gulliver, S.B. and Mireault, G.C. (1991) *Caffeine self-administration, withdrawal, and adverse effects among coffee drinkers.* Arch. Gen. Psychiatry 48: 611–617.

Hursh, S.R. (1991) Behavioral economics of drug self-administration and drug abuse policy. *J. Exp. Anal. Behav.* 56: 377–393.

Jaffe, J.H. and Jaffe, F.K. (1989) Historical perspectives on the use of subjective effects measures in assessing the abuse potential of drugs. In: Fischman, M.W. and Mello, N.K. (eds). *Testing for abuse liability of drugs in humans.* NIDA Research Monograph No. 92. Washington, DC: U.S. Government Printing Office, pp. 43–72.

Jasinski, D.R., Johnson, R.E., and Henningfield, J.E. (1984) Abuse liability assessment in human subjects. *Trends Pharmacol. Sci.* 5: 196–200.

Jick, H., Slone, D., Dinan, B. and Muench, H. (1966) Evaluation of drug efficacy by a preference technic. *N. Engl. J. Med.* 275: 1399–1403.

Johanson, C.E. and de Wit, H. (1989) The use of choice procedures for assessing the reinforcing properties of drugs in humans. In: Fischman, M.W. and Mello, N.K. (eds.) *Testing for abuse liability of drugs in humans.* NIDA Research Monograph No. 92. Washington, DC: U.S. Government Printing Office, pp. 171–209.

Johanson, C.E. and Uhlenhuth, E.H. (1978) Drug self-administration in humans. In: Krasnegor, N.A. (ed.) *Self-administration of abused substances: methods for study.* NIDA Research Monograph No. 20. Washington, DC: U.S. Government Printing Office, pp. 68–85.

Johanson, C.E. and Uhlenhuth, E.H. (1980a) Drug preference and mood in humans: d-Amphetamine. *Psychopharmacology* 71: 275–279.

Johanson, C.E. and Uhlenhuth, E.H. (1980b) Drug preference and mood in humans: diazepam. *Psychopharmacology* 71: 269–273.

Johanson, C.E. and Uhlenhuth, E.H. (1981) Drug preference and mood in humans: repeated assessment of d-amphetamine. *Pharmacol. Biochem. Behav.* 14: 159–163.

Johnston, J.M. and Pennypacker, H.S. (1980) *Strategies and tactics of human behavioral research.* Hillsdale, NJ: Lawrence Erlbaum.

Lamb, R.J., Preston, K.L., Schindler, C.W., Meisch, R.A., Davis, F., Katz, J.L., Henningfield, J.E. and Goldberg, S.R. (1991) The reinforcing and subjective effects of morphine in post-addicts: a dose-response study. *J. Pharmacol. Exp. Ther.* 259: 1165–1173.

McAuliffe, W.E. (1975) A second look at first effects: the subjective effects of opiates on nonaddicts. *J. Drug Issues* 5: 369–399.

McCracken, S.G., de Wit, H., Uhlenhuth, E.H., and Johanson, C.E. (1990) Preference for diazepam in anxious adults. *J. Clin. Psychopharmacol.* 10: 190–196.

McGue, M., Pickens, R.W. and Svikis, D.S. (1992) Sex and age effects on the inheritance of alcohol problems: a twin study. *J. Abnormal Psychol.* 101: 3–17.

McLeod, D.R. and Griffiths, R.R. (1983) Human progressive-ratio performance: maintenance by pentobarbital. *Psychopharmacology* 79: 4–9.

Meisch, R.A. and Lemaire, G.A. (1993) Drug self-administration. In: van Haaren, F. (ed.) *Methods in behavioral pharmacology.* New York, Elsevier Science Publishers B.V., pp. 257–300.

Meisch, R.A. and Stewart, R.B (1994) Ethanol as a rein-forcer: a review of laboratory studies of non-human primates. *Behav. Pharmacol.* 5: 425–440.

Mello, N.K., and Mendelson, J.H. (1970) Experimentally induced intoxication in alcoholics: A comparison between programmed and spontaneous drinking. *J. Pharmacol. Exp. Ther.* 173: 101–116.

Mello, N.K., and Mendelson, J.H. (1980) Buprenorphine suppresses heroin use by heroin addicts. *Science* 207: 657–659.

Mello, N.K., Mendelson, J.H. and Kuehnle, J.C. (1982) Buprenorphine effects on human heroin self-administration: an operant analysis. *J. Pharmacol. Exp. Ther.* 223: 30–39.

Mello, N.K., Mendelson, J.H., Kuehnle, J.C. and Sellers, M.S. (1981) Operant analysis of human heroin self-administration and the effects of naltrexone. *J. Pharmacol. Exp. Ther.* 216: 45–54.

Mendelson, J.H., Kuehnle, J.C., Greenberg, I. and Mello, N.K. (1976) Operant acquisition of marijuana in man. *J. Pharmacol. Exp. Ther.* 198: 42–53.

Mendelson, J.H. and Mello, N.K. (1966) Experimental analysis of drinking behavior of chronic alcoholics. *Ann. N.Y. Acad. Sci.* 133: 828–845.

Mendelson, J.H. and Mello, N.K. (1984) Reinforcing properties of oral delta 9-tetrahydrocannabinol, smoked marijuana, and nabilone: influence of previous marijuana use. *Psychopharmacology* 83: 351–356.

Mitchell, S.H., de Wit, H. and Zancy, J.P. (1994) Effects of varying the "openness" of an economy on responding for cigarettes. *Behav. Pharmacol.* 5: 159–166.

Nevin, J. (1974) Response strength in multiple schedules. *J. Exp. Anal. Behav.* 21: 389–408.

Nevin, J. (1979) Reinforcement schedules and response strength. In: Zeiler, M.D. and Harzem, P. (eds.) *Advances in the analysis of behavior: vol. 1: Reinforcement and the organization of behavior*. Chicester: John Wiley, pp. 117–158.

Nevin, J. (1988) Behavioral momentum and the partial reinforcement effect. *Psychol. Bull.* 103: 44–56.

Noll, J.P. (1995) The matching law as a theory of choice in behavior therapy. O'Dononhue, W. and Drasner, L. (eds.) In: *Theories of behavior therapy: Exploring behavior change*. Washington, DC: American Psychological Association Press, pp. 129–144.

Oliveto, A.H., Hughes, J.R., Higgins, S.T., Bickel, W.K., Pepper, S.L., Shea, P.J. and Fenwick, J.W. (1992) Forced-choice versus free-choice procedures: caffeine self-administration in humans. *Psychopharmacology* 109: 85–91.

Pickens, R. Cunningham, M.R., Heston, L.L., Eckert, E. and Gustafason, L.K. (1977) Dose preference during pentobarbital self-administration by humans. *J. Pharmacol. Exp. Ther.* 203: 310–318.

Preston, K.L., Bigelow, G.E. and Liebson, I.A. (1985) Self-administration of clonidine, oxazepam, and hydromorphone by patients undergoing methadone detoxification. *Clin. Pharmacol. Ther.* 38: 219–227.

Preston, K.L. and Jasinski, D.R. (1991) Abuse liability studies of opioid agonist-antagonists in humans. *Drug Alcohol Depend.* 28: 49–82.

Roache, J.D. and Griffiths, R.R. (1989a) Diazepam and triazolam self-administration in sedative abusers: concordance of subject ratings, performance and drug self-administration. *Psychopharmacology* 99: 309–315.

Roache, J.D. and Griffiths, R.R. (1989b) Abuse liability of anxiolytics and sedative/hypnotics: methods assessing the likelihood of abuse. In: Fischman, M.W. and Mello, N.K.

(eds.) *Testing for abuse liability of drugs in humans.* NIDA Research Monograph No. 92. Washington, DC: U.S. Government Printing Office, pp. 123–146.

Roache, J.D. and Meisch, R.A. (1991) Drug self-administration research in drug and alcohol addiction. In: Miller, N.S. (ed.) *Comprehensive handbook of drug and alcohol addiction.* New York: Marcel Dekker, pp. 625–638.

Roache, J.D. and Meisch, R.A. (1995) Findings from self-administration research on the addiction potential of benzodiazepines. *Psychiatr. Ann.* 25: 153–157.

Roache, J.D., Meisch, R.A., Henningfield, J.E., Jaffe, J.H., Klein, S. and Sampson, A. (1995) Reinforcing effects of triazolam in sedative abusers: correlation of drug liking and self-administration measures. *Pharmacol. Biochem. Behav.* 50: 171–179.

Roache, J.D., Stanley, M.A., Creson, D.L., Meisch, R.A. and Shah, N.N. (1996a) Diazepam reinforcement in anxious patients. *Exp. Clin. Psychopharmacol.* 4: 308–314.

Roache, J.D., Stanley, M.A., Creson, D.L., and Schmitz, J.M. (1996b) Alprazolam self-medication in anxious patients: demonstration of reinforcing effects. In: Harris, L.S. (ed.) *Problems of drug dependence 1995: Proceedings of the 57th Annual Scientific Meeting. The College on Problems of Drug Dependence.* NIDA Research Monograph No. 162. Washington, DC: U.S. Government Printing Office, pp. 247.

Rosenthal, R. (1994) Interpersonal expectancy effects: a 30-year perspective. *Curr. Dir. Psychol.* Sci. 3: 176–179.

Rosenthal, R. and Rubin, D.B. (1978) Interpersonal expectancy effects: the first 345 studies. *Behav. Brain Sci.* 3: 377–386.

Silverman, K., Kirby, K.C. and Griffiths, R.R. (1994a) Modulation of drug reinforcement by behavioral requirements following drug ingestion. *Psychopharmacology* 114: 243–247.

Silverman, K., Mumford, G.K. and Griffiths, R.R. (1994b) Enhancing caffeine reinforcement by behavioral requirements following drug ingestion. *Psychopharmacology* 114: 424–432.

Skinner B.F. (1969) *Contingencies of reinforcement: a theoretical analysis.* New York: Appleton-Century-Crofts.

Skinner, B.F. (1953) *Science and human behavior.* New York: Macmillan.

Sobell, M.B., Schaefer, H.H. and Mills, K.C. (1972) Differences in baseline drinking behavior between alcoholics and normal drinkers. *Behav. Res. Ther.* 10: 257–267.

Spiga, R., Grabowski, J., Silverman, P.B. and Meisch, R.A. (1996) Human methadone self-administration: effects of dose ratio requirement. *Behav. Pharmacol.* 7(2): 1–8.

Stitzer, M.L., Bigelow, G.E. and Liebson, I. (1979) Reducing benzodiazepine self-administration with contingent reinforcement. *Addict. Behav.* 4: 245–252.

Stitzer, M.L., McCaul, M.E., Bigelow, G.E. and Liebson, I.A. (1983) Oral methadone self-administration: effects of dose and alternative reinforcers. *Clin. Pharmacol. Ther.* 34: 29–35.

Tucker, J.A., Vuchinich, R.E., and Pukish, M.M. (1995) Molar environments contexts surrounding recovery from alcohol problems by treated and untreated problem drinkers. *Exp. Clin. Psychopharmacol.* 3: 195–204.

Vuchinich, R.E. and Tucker, J.A. (1988) Contributions from behavioral theories of choice to an analysis of alcohol abuse. *J. Abnorm. Psychol.* 97: 181–195.

Vuchinich, R.E. and Tucker, J.A. (1996) Alcoholic relapse, life events, and behavioral theories of choice: a prospective analysis. *Exp. Clin. Psychopharmacol.* 4: 19–28.

Wearden, J.H. (1988) Some neglected problems in the analysis of human operant behavior. In: Davey, G. and Cullen, C. (eds.) *Human operant conditioning and behavior modification.* Chichester, England: John Wiley, pp. 197–224.

Weeks, J.R. (1962) Experimental morphine addiction: Method for automatic intravenous injections in unrestrained rats. *Science.* 138: 143–144.

Wikler, A. (1952) A psychodynamic study of a patient during experimental self-regulated re-addiction to morphine. *Psychiatr. Q.* 26: 270–293.

Young, A.M. and Herling, S. (1986) Drugs as reinforcers: studies in laboratory animals. In: Goldberg, S.R. and Stolerman, I.P. *(eds) Behavioral analysis of drug dependence.* Orlando, FL: Academic Press, pp. 9–67.

Drug Addiction and its Treatment: Nexus of Neuroscience
and Behavior, edited by Bankole A. Johnson and John D. Roache.
Lippincott–Raven Publishers, Philadelphia, © 1997.

3

Behavioral Economics of Drug Consumption

Rudy E. Vuchinich

Department of Psychology, Auburn University, Auburn, Alabama 36849

This chapter summarizes research on the behavioral economics of drug consumption (the term *drug* is used generically to refer to all abused substances, including alcohol). After a brief description of the historical development of behavioral economics, rudimentary behavioral economic concepts are defined and selective examples of analyses of drug consumption based on those concepts are discussed.

ORIGIN OF BEHAVIORAL ECONOMICS

Understanding the allocation of behavior (choice) among available activities is a longstanding and fundamental problem in behavior theory. The control of behavior by its consequences has been unquestioned in most of this century (cf. Williams, 1988), but about three decades ago Premack (1965) and Herrnstein (1970) dramatically changed the basic orientation to studying the problem. Prior to that time, traditional reinforcement theory had focused on the strength of either individual operants (Skinner, 1938) or individual stimulus-response connections (e.g., Hull, 1943).

But Premack showed that the likelihood of engaging in any activity depends on what other activities are also available and on those activities. Herrnstein showed that the frequency of any given operant is a function of its reinforcement *relative* to the reinforcement obtained from other possible operants.

Thus, Premack's and Herrnstein's work revealed the inadequacy of focusing on individual responses in accounts of choice, and demonstrated that behavioral allocation is critically affected by the more general context of environmental conditions that surrounds individual responses.

That insight spawned a large and lively literature aimed at describing how the specific consequences of alternative responses and the more general contextual conditions control behavioral allocation (reviewed by Williams, 1988). It was recognized fairly early in the development of this choice literature that the problem of understanding the behavioral allocation of animals in the laboratory was similar to the problems addressed by consumer demand theory in economics (Allison, 1979; Hursh, 1980; Lea, 1978; Rachlin and Burkhard, 1978; Rachlin et al., 1976; Staddon, 1979). That is, both animal subjects and human consumers allocate limited resources (e.g., time, behavior, money) to obtain access to activities of varying value (eating, drinking, leisure) under various conditions of environmental constraint. Recognizing this connection led to some behavioral psychologists' using economic concepts and to some economists' using behavioral methods. This merger of the behavioral analysis of choice and of microeconomic theory, now known as *behavioral economics*, has been mutually beneficial.

Economic concepts have successfully organized data from behavioral experiments (e.g., Rachlin et al., 1981) and behavioral methods have allowed critical experimental tests of postulates in economic theory (e.g., Kagel et al., 1975). A thorough description of behavioral economics is beyond the scope of this chapter and can be found in Green and Kagel (1987), Hursh (1980, 1984), Kagel et al. (1995), and Staddon (1980).

BEHAVIORAL ECONOMICS APPLIED TO DRUG CONSUMPTION

The potential relevance of behavioral economics for studying drug abuse was recognized soon after its inception (Allison, 1979; Elsmore et al., 1980; Vuchinich, 1982; Vuchinich and Tucker, 1983) and has since grown into an active research area (e.g., Green and Kagel, 1996; Vuchinich, 1995). The remainder of this chapter presents the high points of this research. Specifically, the behavioral economic concepts of the demand curve, demand elasticity, unit price, commodity substitutability, and income will be described and applications to drug consumption summarized.

DEMAND CURVE ANALYSIS

The Demand Curve

Demand is the primary dependent variable in microeconomics and simply refers to the amount of a commodity that is purchased (and presumably consumed). Given that the primary concern in drug abuse is excessive drug consumption, the focus of behavioral economics on consumption renders the framework especially applicable to drug abuse research (Hursh, 1993). This may seem trivial and obvious, but behavioral research traditionally has used behavioral output as the primary dependent variable, and the relation between responding and consumption depends on the economic context (Hursh and Bauman, 1987).

The basic *demand curve* plots consumption of a commodity as a function of its price. The general economic law of demand states simply that there is an inverse relation between consumption of a commodity and its price. Figure 1 (Hursh, 1993) illustrates typical demand and expenditure curves for an animal subject, which in this case was a rhesus monkey responding to gain access to either saccharin or food under fixed ratio (FR) response requirements. In behavioral economic experiments, price is typically defined as the number of responses that must be emitted in order to gain access to a unit of the commodity. In this instance, the FRs varied from 10 to 372 responses per reinforcer, which means the subject had to press a lever the number of times specified by the FR in order to receive the specified amount of food or saccharin. The left and right panels show consumption (demand) and response output (expenditures), respectively, as a function of FR requirement (price). These data are plotted in log-log coordinates, which is conventional in economics.

Elasticity of Demand

The basic parameters of demand curves are *intensity* and *elasticity* of demand, which are the height and slope of the curve, respectively. Thus, intensity of demand refers to the amount of consumption at a given point and the dynamic concept of elasticity of demand refers to how consumption changes as a function of price. The left panel of Fig. 1 illustrates the importance of the distinction between intensity and elasticity of demand. At low prices (FRs), food and saccharin showed similar intensity of demand, but as price increased food consumption tended to be maintained (inelastic demand) while saccharin consumption dropped precipitously (elastic demand).

Own-price elasticity of demand is defined as the ratio of proportional changes in consumption to proportional changes in price. When a demand curve is plotted in log-log coordinates, the slope directly represents elasticity. Figure 2 (Hursh and Bauman, 1987) shows demand curves (in both arithmetic and

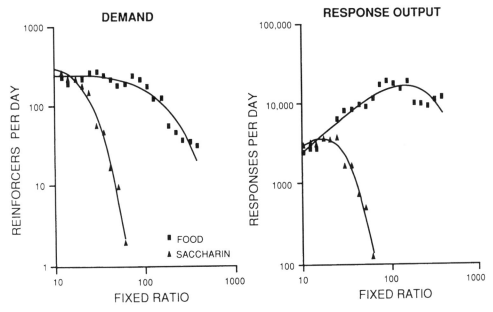

FIG. 1. Consumption (*left panel*) and behavioral *output* (*right panel*) data from a rhesus monkey responding for either food (*squares*) or saccharin solution (*triangles*). The reinforcers were available under fixed-ratio (FR) schedules that ranged from FR 10 to FR 372. (From Hursh, 1993.)

log-log coordinates) and expenditure curves (in arithmetic coordinates) for hypothetical commodities that represent the range of elasticities. Unit elasticity (slope = -1 in log-log coordinates) denotes proportional consumption decreases that equal proportional price increases; total expenditures remain constant while absolute consumption decreases. Inelastic demand (slope > -1 in log-log coordinates) denotes proportional consumption decreases that are less than proportional price increases; total expenditures increase even though absolute consumption may decrease. Elastic demand (slope < -1 in log-log coordinates) denotes proportional consumption decreases that are greater than proportional price increases; total expenditures and absolute consumption both decrease. These are idealized curves to illustrate the concept, and it is rare for elasticity to remain constant along the demand curve. The bottom row of Fig. 2 shows the more typical finding of mixed elasticity. In this case, demand is inelastic (expenditures increase) in the portion of the curve at low prices, but is elastic (expenditures decrease) in the portion of the curve at higher prices.

Unit Price

Two central issues for an application of behavioral economics to drug consumption are (1) whether abused substances obey the law of demand, and (2) whether the quantitative properties of the demand curve aid in the description and analysis of drug consumption. Recent work on the concept of unit price has yielded a positive answer on both counts. The economic notion of *unit price* was introduced into behavioral research by Hursh et al. (1988) in the context of animals responding for food under various constraints; they defined unit price generally as a cost-benefit ratio that reflects the amount of behavioral output required to obtain a unit of food value. In their experiment, the behavioral output required was manipulated by varying the fixed-ratio schedule and the weight of the lever, and food value was manipulated by varying the number of food

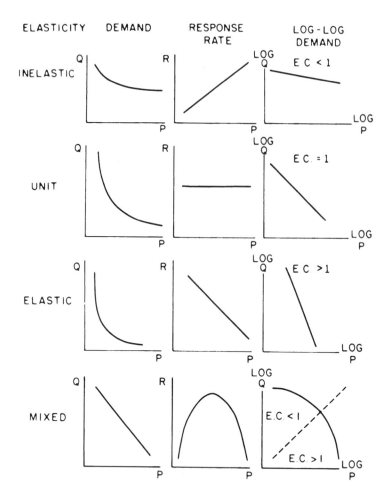

FIG. 2. Demand and expenditure curves for hypothetical commodities that illustrate the range of own-price elasticities of demand. The first and second columns plot demand and expenditures, respectively, as a function of price in arithmetic coordinates. The third column plots demand as a function of price in log-log coordinates. Each row represents a different type of demand elasticity. (From Hursh and Bauman, 1987.)

pellets per reinforcement and the probability of reinforcement. Thus, in this study unit price was defined specifically as (Fixed Ratio x Lever Weight) / (Pellets x Probability).

Figure 3 (Hursh et al., 1988) shows the main results of the Hursh et al. (1988) study. These data provide strong support for the unit price concept by showing that all of the experimental manipulations produced patterns of consumption that converged on the same demand curve. The positively decelerating curve in Fig. 3 was fitted by Equation 1,

$$\log Q = \log L + b(\log P) - aP, \qquad (1)$$

where Q is consumption, P is unit price (as defined above), L approximates consumption at a unit price of 1.0, b is the slope of the demand curve at low prices, and a is the accel-

eration of that slope as price increases. The b and a parameters are derived from regression analyses of the consumption data and unit price values. When this equation was applied to the data from each of their 108 subjects individually, Hursh et al. (1988) found that it accounted for a median of 93% of the variance. Thus, this equation, based on the unit price concept, provided a precise quantitative description of demand for food of individual subjects. Moreover, Hursh et al. showed how such demand curves can provide a "template" for understanding the effects of biologic variables (e.g., brain lesions) on demand for food and behavioral output.

The utility of the unit price concept for studying demand for drugs has been explored extensively by Bickel, DeGrandpre, and col-

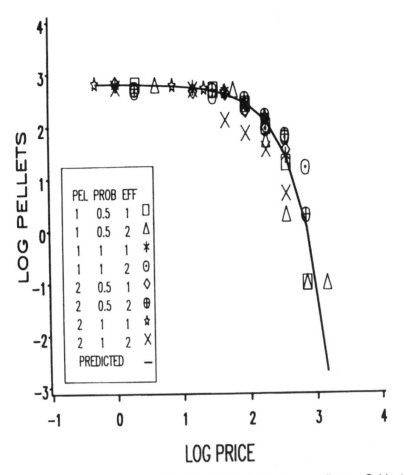

FIG. 3. Demand for food plotted as a function of unit price in log-log coordinates. Subjects were rats responding for food reinforcement according to fixed-ratio (FR) schedules of reinforcement. The legend shows for each symbol the number of food pellets per reinforcer (PEL), the probability of receiving food after completing the FR schedule (PROB), and weight of the lever (EFF). See text for details. (From Hursh et al., 1988.)

leagues (e.g., Bickel et al., 1990, 1991; De-Grandpre et al., 1992, 1993a). Numerous studies have found that response requirement (number of responses required to obtain a drug ingestion) and drug dose (amount of drug received per ingestion) have important effects on drug self-administration (Griffiths et al., 1980). In general, there is an inverse relation between response requirement and drug ingestions, and an inverted-U–shaped function between drug dose and drug ingestions such that drug ingestions first increase and then decrease as drug dose increases (e.g., Lemaire and Meisch, 1984). Although response requirement and drug dose typically have been seen as having separate and independent effects on drug consumption, the unit price concept suggests that these effects are the result of the same basic process (Bickel et al., 1990). For example, if an animal obtained 0.01 mg/kg cocaine for every 10 responses, or 0.10 mg/kg cocaine for every 100 responses, in both cases the unit price would be 1,000 (response requirement divided by drug dose), which should produce the same demand. Thus, the same unit price can be comprised of a large number of combinations of different response requirements and drug doses, and the same response requirement or the same drug dose can be a constituent of a large number of different unit prices. Even though response requirement and drug dose have different effects on self-administration, the unit price concept holds that those effects are a common expression of the same underlying demand curve that relates consumption to unit price. Bickel et al. (1991) conducted a direct experimental evaluation of the unit price concept with five human cigarette smokers. Subjects participated in multiple sessions in which different combinations of response requirement (FRs of 200, 400, or 1,600 responses) and reinforcer magnitude (one, two, or four cigarette puffs) were arranged to produce six unit prices ranging from 50 to 1,600. Results showed that smoke consumption was a positively decelerating function of unit price (see Equation 1), regardless of the response requirement and dose constituents of that price. Data from one subject are shown in Fig. 4 (Bickel et al., 1993) as an example of the typical demand curve.

The utility of the unit price concept also has been evaluated by three studies that reanalyzed data from earlier experiments that did not employ a demand curve analysis but that did manipulate relevant variables. First, Bickel et al. (1990) reanalyzed data from 10 studies of animal drug self-administration (including cocaine, ethanol, ketamine, methohexital, pentobarbital, and phencyclidine) that had manipulated FR values and drug dose. In 8 of the 10 studies, the reanalyzed data converged on a single, positively decelerating demand curve highly similar to the demand curve Hursh et al. (1988) found for food.

Second, DeGrandpre et al. (1992) applied the unit price concept to the popular nicotine regulation hypothesis in the smoking literature. This hypothesis maintains that when smokers consume cigarettes with different nicotine yields (dose), they will modify their smoking behavior to hold their nicotine intake constant. Such regulation requires an inverse linear relation between nicotine dose and cigarette consumption, which is different from

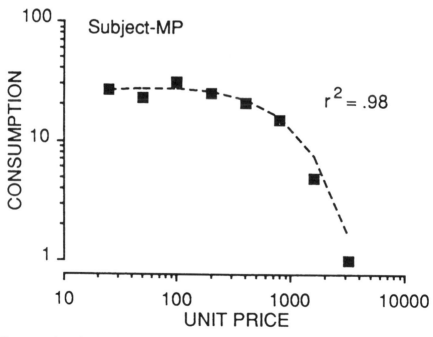

FIG. 4. Consumption of cigarette puffs as a function of unit price for one human subject. See text for a description of the line of best fit and variance accounted for. (From Bickel et al., 1993.)

the positively decelerating demand curve that relates consumption to unit price. DeGrandpre et al. (1992) reanalyzed 17 studies that had manipulated nicotine dose and had measured the cigarette consumption of smokers. In general, the reanalyzed data showed typical demand curves with mixed elasticity of demand rather than a linear relation between dose and consumption. Third, the generality of this finding was strengthened considerably by De-Grandpre et al. (1993a; also see Bickel et al., 1993). They reanalyzed data from 38 experiments that had manipulated magnitude of reinforcement; 16 studies used food reinforcement and 22 studies used drug reinforcement (including cocaine, *d*-amphetamine, procaine, codeine, morphine, methohexital, and pentobarbital). Their consistent finding was that the consumption of both food and drugs was accurately described by positively decelerating demand as a function of unit price.

Implications of Demand Curve Analyses

Research to date on demand curve analyses of drug consumption is important for several reasons. First, manipulations that vary behavioral output requirements (e.g., FR value) and reinforcer magnitude (e.g., drug dose) appear to have functionally equivalent effects on drug consumption by altering unit price (Bickel et al., 1990; DeGrandpre et al., 1993a). The concept of unit price therefore unifies the effects of these variables on drug self-administration (Bickel et al., 1993).

Second, these analyses of demand as a function of unit price indicate that the consumption of a wide variety of reinforcers, including drugs, can be accurately described by the same general positively decelerating demand curve (see Equation 1). This suggests that the demand for drugs is but one instance of a "ubiquitous behavioral process" (Bickel et al., 1993, p. 181), and that drugs of abuse do not constitute a special class of commodities that requires unique concepts for effective analysis and understanding.

Third, the quantification of elasticity of demand for different drugs, or of the same drug

under different conditions, may be especially useful in providing a common metric for evaluating the abuse liability of drugs (Hursh, 1993). For example, Bickel et al. (1992) reanalyzed some of the data from a study by Goldberg et al. (1971) in which monkeys self-administered pentobarbital and cocaine in separate sessions under variable FR requirements. Self-administration of the two drugs was identical at FR 1 (i.e., equal intensity of demand), but pentobarbital consumption decreased much more than cocaine consumption as price increased (i.e., different elasticity of demand). Specifically, the own-price elasticity coefficients for pentobarbital and cocaine were -.64 and -.05, respectively. Thus, although demand for both drugs was inelastic (elasticity > -1), demand for pentobarbital was over 12 times more responsive to price increases than was cocaine, which implies that pentobarbital has less abuse potential than cocaine. Elasticity coefficients derived from demand curve analyses therefore may provide a common metric to compare and contrast the motivational properties of different drugs.

Fourth, the distinction between intensity and elasticity of demand and the quantitative properties of demand curve analyses may be useful in the development of pharmacotherapies for drug abuse (Bickel et al., 1993). The most common pharmacotherapies for drug abuse are agonists and antagonists (Jaffe, 1990; cited in Bickel et al. 1993); agonists mimic and antagonists block drug effects (e.g., methadone and naltrexone are an agonist and an antagonist of heroin, respectively). As a demonstration of the utility of behavioral economics in this area, Bickel et al. (1993) reanalyzed data from a study by Harrigan and Downs (1980) that had investigated the effects of methadone and naltrexone on heroin self-administration. This reanalysis showed that methadone did not change intensity of demand for heroin at low unit prices, but it increased the elasticity of demand for heroin as unit price increased. Naltrexone, on the other hand, both increased intensity of demand at low unit prices and increased elasticity of demand as unit price increased. These findings imply that if the price of heroin is low, methadone may have minimal effects on heroin demand and that naltrexone may actually increase it (a countertherapeutic effect). As the price of heroin increases, however, the presence of either methadone or naltrexone would produce greater heroin consumption decreases, which would be a therapeutic effect.

REINFORCEMENT CONTEXT AND DEMAND FOR DRUGS

As mentioned earlier, since the early 1970s research on behavioral allocation has explicitly recognized that engaging in a particular activity depends critically on the surrounding context of other activities and environmental constraints. Most behavioral analyses of choice, however, have employed situations where the programmed response alternatives produced qualitatively identical reinforcers that varied along some quantitative dimension, such as amount, rate, or delay (reviewed by Williams, 1988). But as Hursh and Bauman (1987) have noted, studying choice between qualitatively identical reinforcers is "a bit like studying consumer behavior in a store with only one product on the shelves" (pp. 129–130). Intuitively it would seem that directly addressing the issue of choice among qualitatively different activities is central to understanding how drug consumption develops and changes in the natural environment. The research discussed above studied demand for drugs in situations devoid of opportunities for consuming other commodities. Although it is important to understand drug consumption in such circumstances, it also is true that those settings lack a potentially critical feature of the contexts in which drug abuse typically develops. That is, strong preferences for drugs arise in contexts that presumably contain opportunities to engage in a wide variety of other activities. Thus, understanding the conditions under which drug consumption emerges as a highly preferred activity from a large array of qualitatively different activities

is a basic problem for drug abuse research (Vuchinich and Tucker, 1988).

Alternative Reinforcers Reduce Drug Consumption

In general, the behavioral economic perspective suggests that demand for drugs should vary inversely with the availability of alternative activities and directly with constraints on access to those alternatives. In an early study that investigated this issue, Vuchinich and Tucker (1983) studied human normal drinkers in a choice situation involving access to an alcoholic beverage or money. They found that subjects' preference for alcohol varied inversely with the amount of money available and directly with the delay of receipt of the money. Similar findings were obtained with animal subjects by Nader and Woolverton (1991, 1992). They gave rhesus monkeys discrete trial choices between intravenous injections of cocaine (doses ranged from 0.01 to 1.0 mg/kg/injection) and food (either one or four pellets), and found that cocaine consumption decreased when the amount of food available increased. As the reviews by Vuchinich and Tucker (1988) and Carroll (1996) have shown, this general inverse relation between drug consumption and alternative reinforcers has been found in a number of studies with human and animal subjects with a variety of different drugs.

The following two studies (Bickel, et al., 1995b; Carroll et al., 1991) provided a more detailed analysis of this relationship by manipulating the price of drugs along a broad range and measuring drug demand in the presence and absence of an alternative reinforcer. Carroll et al. (1991) studied how the availability of saccharin affected phencyclidine (PCP) consumption in rhesus monkeys. Subjects first were exposed to a choice situation in which orally delivered PCP (0.25 mg/ml) and water were available according to FR schedules. The water FR remained constant at 16 while the PCP FR was varied in a range from 4 to 128. These FR manipulations were then repeated with a saccharin solution (0.03% wt/vol) available instead of water, and a third condition used a lower dose of PCP (0.125 mg/ml). The main results of this study are shown in Fig. 5 (Carroll, 1993). The left and right panels are demand and expenditure curves, respectively, for PCP. The top and bottom panels are data from the PCP-water choice and the PCP-saccharin choice, respectively. As Fig. 5 shows, the availability of saccharin reduced the intensity of demand for PCP and increased the elasticity of demand for PCP, and these effects did not vary with dose of PCP. Also, the effect of saccharin availability on PCP consumption depended on the price (FR requirement) of PCP. Compared

to PCP consumption during the PCP-water condition, PCP consumption during the PCP-saccharin condition was reduced by 21.1% when the PCP FR was 4 and by 87.5% when the PCP FR was 128.

Bickel et al. (1995b) conducted an analogous study with human subjects that investigated the availability of money (Experiment 1) or "recreational activities" (Experiment 2) on demand for cigarettes. In both experiments, subjects responded for cigarette puffs on FR schedules (that varied from 50 to 6,400) when the alternative activity both was and was not available. The results were similar to those of Carroll et al. (1991) in that the intensity of demand for cigarettes was sub-

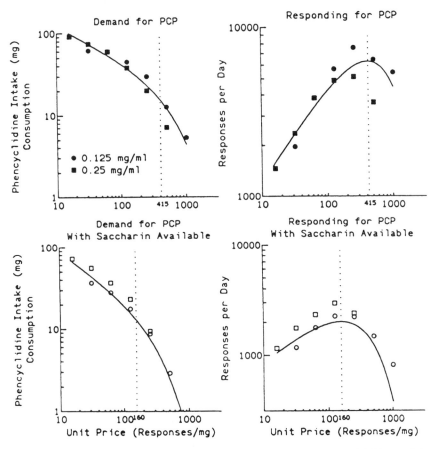

FIG. 5. Monkeys' consumption of PCP (*left panels*) and behavioral output (*right panels*) as a function of unit price when saccharin was (*bottom panels*) and was not (*top panels*) available. The vertical dotted lines intersect the x-axis at the unit price value at which the most total responses would occur. (From Carroll, 1993.)

stantially reduced by the availability of an alternative activity, and the effect of the alternative activity on drug consumption was the greatest at the highest drug prices. The above research studied the effects of alternative reinforcers on drug demand after the behavior of drug self-administration had been well established. Recent research by Carroll and colleagues (e.g., Carroll et al., 1989; Carroll and Lac, 1992) has added an interesting and potentially important dimension to this general area by investigating how the availability of alternative reinforcers affects the acquisition of the behavior of drug self-administration. For example, Carroll and Lac (1992) studied the acquisition of cocaine self-administration in rats over a 30-day period. They manipulated access to a glucose and saccharin (G+S) solution before and during the acquisition phase. They found that 100% of the rats that had access to water before and during the cocaine acquisition phase developed cocaine self-administration. On the other hand, only 50% of the rats that had access to G+S both before and during the cocaine acquisition phase met the acquisition criteria. The acquisition of cocaine self-administration also was prevented or delayed in the group of rats that had access to water before and had access to G+S during the cocaine acquisition phase. Thus, not only can the availability of alternative reinforcers reduce the demand for drugs, it also can decrease the likelihood of the development of drug self-administration.

Economic Commodity Substitutability

The above research demonstrates clearly that there are important qualitative relations between demand for drugs and the availability of alternative reinforcers. However, the framework of behavioral economics offers concepts that can move this research beyond the qualitative level and provide a quantitatively precise description of how drug demand interacts with the availability of and demand for other reinforcers. These concepts concern substitutability relations between commodities (e.g., Green

and Freed, 1993). In general, *substitutability* relations categorize and quantify how consumption of one commodity changes as a function of price-induced changes in the consumption of another commodity. These relations lie along a continuum, with *substitutable* commodities and *complementary* commodities at opposite ends of the continuum, and *independent* commodities at the center. The consumption of substitutable commodities varies inversely (e.g., coffee and tea), that of complementary commodities varies directly (e.g., flour and baking powder), and that of independent commodities does not covary (e.g., textbooks and soft drinks).

Demand curves for hypothetical substitutable and complementary commodities are shown in Fig. 6 (Hursh, 1993). In this figure, the consumption of one commodity (B) is plotted as a function of the price of another commodity (A). Commodities A and B would be substitutes if an increase in the price of A leads to the consumption of less A and more B (the squares in Fig. 6). Commodities A and B would be complements if an increase in the price of A leads to the consumption of less A and less B (the triangles in Fig. 6). Independent commodities are not shown in the figure, but would be manifested as a flat demand curve for B as the price of A varied.

Cross-price elasticity of demand quantifies these relations between commodities, and is defined as the ratio of proportional changes in consumption of one commodity to proportional changes in the price of another commodity. As with own-price elasticity (discussed earlier), when the demand curve is plotted in log-log coordinates (as in Fig. 6), its slope directly represents cross-price elasticity. Cross-price elasticity coefficients greater than zero indicate that the commodities are substitutes, those less than zero indicate that the commodities are complements, and coefficients of zero indicate that the commodities are independents.

Bickel et al. (1995a) conducted a reanalysis of 16 drug self-administration studies that permitted an evaluation of substitutability relations between drug consumption (including

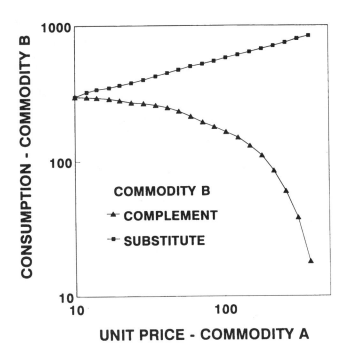

FIG. 6. Demand curves for hypothetical commodities that illustrate economic complements (*triangles*) and substitutes (*squares*). (From Hursh, 1993.)

caffeine, nicotine, cocaine, etonitazene, ethanol, heroin, methadone, morphine, pentobarbital, and PCP) and alternative drug and nondrug reinforcers. This study showed that these drugs can enter into substitutability relations with other reinforcers at all points along the substitutability continuum, and that these behavioral economic concepts are useful for understanding how drug consumption interacts with demand for other commodities.

For example, several experiments (Samson et al., 1982, 1983; Samson and Lindberg, 1984) have studied demand for ethanol by rats in situations with ethanol and sucrose available according to concurrent FR schedules. These rats typically show a strong preference for sucrose when the FR requirements for ethanol and sucrose are equal and low (e.g., FR 8), but show a large increase in consumption of ethanol when the FR requirement for sucrose is increased (e.g., to FR 64). This suggests qualitatively that ethanol is an economic substitute for sucrose, but computing the cross-price elasticity of demand coefficient can quantify the relation. That is, Bickel et al. (1995a; also see Bickel et al., 1992) reanalyzed the data from these studies and found

that the cross-price elasticity of demand for ethanol (when the price of sucrose was increased) ranged from .26 to .50, depending on the individual subject and experiment. These coefficients are well within the substitution range of the continuum and provide a precise metric for comparison with other data.

It is critical to note that substitutability relations are not always symmetrical. Even though commodity A may be a substitute (or complement) for commodity B if the price of B is increased, commodity B may not be a substitute (or complement) for commodity A if the price of A is increased. An example of asymmetrical economic substitutes is provided by a study by Carroll (1987). In two experiments, rhesus monkeys responded to gain access to PCP and ethanol according to concurrent FR schedules, and the unit price of one of the drugs was manipulated in each experiment by altering drug dose. The unit price of PCP was manipulated in Experiment 1, and the unit price of ethanol was manipulated in Experiment 2. In both experiments, price increases reduced demand for the drug that had its price manipulated (PCP in Experiment 1 and ethanol in Experiment 2). However, consumption of the drug that did not have its price manipulated differed in the two experiments. In Experiment 1, ethanol consumption increased as the price of PCP increased (cross-price elasticity coefficient of .22; Bickel et al., 1995a). On the other hand, in Experiment 2 PCP consumption did not increase as the price of ethanol increased (cross-price elasticity coefficient of .01; Bickel et al., 1995a). Thus, ethanol served as a substitute for PCP in Experiment 1, but PCP did not serve as a substitute for ethanol in Experiment 2.

A study by Bickel et al. (1992) provides an example of asymmetrical economic complements. They gave seven human cigarette smokers and coffee drinkers access to cigarettes and coffee according to concurrent FR schedules. In one condition, they increased the price of cigarettes and held the price of coffee constant, and, in a second condition, they raised the price of coffee and held the price of cigarettes constant. The consumption of each commodity decreased in a similar manner in the condition in which its price was increased (i.e., coffee and cigarettes had nearly identical own-price elasticities of demand). However, there were asymmetrical changes in the consumption of the unmanipulated commodity when the price of the other commodity was manipulated. That is, when the price of cigarettes was increased (and the price of coffee was held constant), cigarette consumption and coffee consumption both decreased. On the other hand, when the price of coffee was increased (and the price of cigarettes was held constant), coffee consumption decreased but cigarette consumption did not change. Thus, when the price of cigarettes was increased, coffee served as a complement to cigarettes, but when the price of coffee was manipulated, cigarettes and coffee were independents.

A final example illustrates symmetrical economic independents. DeGrandpre et al. (1994) employed basically the same design and experimental manipulations as Bickel et al. (1992), except that subjects responded to gain access to cigarettes and money, instead of cigarettes and coffee, according to concurrent schedules. Like Bickel et al. (1992), DeGrandpre et al. (1994) found that price in-creases reduced demand for each commodity in the condition in which its price was increased (although the demand for money was much more elastic than the demand for cigarettes). However, unlike the Bickel et al. (1992) results, DeGrandpre et al. (1994) found no interactions between demand for the commodities. That is, price induced decreases in the demand for cigarettes did not alter the demand for money, and price induced decreases in the demand for money did not alter the demand for cigarettes.

Implications of Reinforcement Context

The behavioral economic perspective on drug abuse research has focused attention on the importance of the molar context (Vuchinich and Tucker, 1996) of drug consumption. Clearly, the variety and availability of reinforcing activities other than drugs can have a critical influence on drug consumption, and these relations have considerable relevance to prevention, assessment, and treatment applications. For example, epidemiologic studies indicate that the vast majority of drug users establish patterns of drug self-administration in a several-year period in late adolescence (Kandel and Logan, 1984). The work by Carroll and Lac (1992) discussed above suggests that a useful prevention strategy may be to attempt to engage youth in nondrug activities prior to and during this potentially critical period of initial exposure to drugs. Of course, it is a large leap from an animal experiment to preventing human drug abuse, and the types of activities that will effectively engage the behavior of adolescents and compete with drug use are not likely to involve consumption. Nevertheless, the behavioral economic perspective and the preliminary data suggest that this is a worthwhile approach to prevention.

It also has been found that reductions in access to valued activities (e.g., intimate and family relationships) are correlated with relapse in alcoholics after treatment (Vuchinich and Tucker, 1996) and increases in access to such activities are correlated with treatment-assisted and natural recovery from alcohol problems (Tucker et al., 1995). These studies emphasize the importance of explicitly assessing these relations in clinical populations for purposes of treatment planning (Vuchinich et al., 1988). Moreover, drug abuse treatment interventions that increase clients' access to nondrug reinforcers in the natural environment are highly effective (e.g., Higgins et al., 1991).

Studying relations between drug consumption and alternative reinforcers also has important implications for more basic research. The quantification of commodity substitutability relations through cross-price elasticity of demand coefficients may be a metric useful in the identification of the neurochemical substrates of reinforcement and incentive systems, including drugs (e.g., Green and Rachlin, 1991; Hursh, 1991; Rachlin et al., 1980). This, in turn, may be critical information in the development of pharmacotherapies for drug abuse (e.g., George and Ritz, 1993).

INCOME

Bickel et al. (1993) noted that behavioral economics has introduced income as a new and potentially important variable in analyses of behavioral allocation. In microeconomic theory, *income* is defined as the total amount of services, goods, or funds received over a given period (Pearce, 1986), and economists have long known that changes in income can produce changes in consumption patterns (cf., Silberberg et al., 1987). The primary categories of commodities for describing income-induced changes in consumption are *normal* and *inferior* goods, which vary directly and inversely, respectively, with income.

As an example of an investigation of the effects of income on drug consumption, Elsmore et al. (1980) gave two baboons discrete trial choices between receiving food (3.0 g) or an injection of heroin (0.1 mg/kg). Income was manipulated by varying the intertrial interval (ITI) in the range from 2 to 12 minutes. Thus,

ITI length was inversely related to the number of commodity consumption opportunities that were available. With high income (2-minute ITI), both subjects made an approximately equal number of food and heroin choices. With low income (12-minute ITI), both subjects dramatically reduced their heroin choices (by about 75%) but maintained food choices approximately constant. Although both food and heroin were normal goods, the income manipulation had a stronger effect on the consumption of heroin than food (i.e., demand for heroin was more elastic in this context than demand for food).

As another example, Carroll and Rodefer (1993) had six rhesus monkeys respond to gain access to PCP and saccharin according to concurrent FR schedules. The FR for saccharin remained constant at 32 while the FR for PCP was varied in the range of 4 to 128. Income was manipulated by varying the length of the daily experimental sessions (20, 60, or 180 minutes). The decrease in income from 180 to 20 minutes produced reductions in the consumption of saccharin and PCP of 90% and 54%, respectively. Both saccharin and PCP were normal goods, but the income manipulation had a stronger effect on the consumption of saccharin than PCP (i.e., demand for saccharin was more elastic in this context than demand for PCP).

Although both of these studies found that drugs were normal goods, the Elsmore et al. (1980) study found that consumption of the drug (heroin) was more responsive to changes in income than consumption of the alternative reinforcer (food), but the Carroll and Rodefer (1993) study found that consumption of the drug (PCP) was less responsive to the income manipulation than consumption of the alternative reinforcer (saccharin). The many differences between the two studies (e.g., subjects, methods, definition of income, reinforcers) preclude identifying one or more critical variables that could account for these somewhat different relations between drug and alternative reinforcer consumption and income. A likely possibility, however, is the large difference between the economic contexts in the two studies. Elsmore et al.'s subjects received all of their food in the experimental sessions. Under these conditions, demand for heroin will almost certainly be more elastic than demand for food, because the latter is necessary for survival while the former is not. In contrast, Carroll and Rodefer's subjects received food between sessions, and neither of the reinforcers studied (PCP and saccharin) was necessary for survival. Moreover, an earlier study by Carroll et al. (1991) had found that demand for saccharin was more elastic than demand for PCP. Thus, even though Elsmore et al. and Carroll and Rodefer found somewhat different effects of income on demand for drugs in relation to alternative reinforcers, these effects were consistent in terms of the relative demand elasticities of the reinforcers used. In both cases, income had a larger effect on demand for the more elastic commodity.

A third study of income effects (DeGrandpre et al., 1993b) gave six human cigarette smokers access to their preferred ("own") brand and to a less preferred ("other") brand of cigarettes of equal nicotine content. Income was manipulated across sessions by varying the amount of money available, in the range of $1 to $36, to purchase cigarette puffs. The price of cigarette puffs was held constant across sessions, with the price of "other" ($.10) being 20% of the price of "own" ($.50). The main results of this study showed that as income increased, consumption of "own" puffs increased and consumption of "other" puffs decreased. Thus, "own" puffs was a normal good, and "other" puffs was an inferior good. DeGrandpre et al. (1993b) also included an additional condition in which income was held constant and the price of "other" puffs was raised to $.25. The purpose of this condition was to determine if a price increase would be functionally equivalent to an income decrease, in which case increasing the price of "other" puffs would increase demand for them. Three of the six subjects showed increased relative consumption of "other" puffs at the higher price, while the other three subjects demanded fewer "other" puffs.

Implications of Income

These three studies of income effects on drug consumption do not permit any firm statements regarding their basic research or applied implications. The definition of income varied across studies, and it is not at all clear what relation these manipulations might have to the money income of humans in the natural environment, which is inversely related to drug abuse (Anthony et al., 1994). The DeGrandpre et al. (1993b) study is particularly interesting because it demonstrated a *Giffen-good* effect in human drug consumption for two subjects. Giffen-goods are defined by increased consumption at higher prices; they therefore are paradoxical and are the only logical exception to the law of demand (DeGrandpre et al., 1993b). Moreover, the incorporation of Giffen-good effects into a general behavioral theory of choice may require fundamental revisions in existing models (Degrandpre et al., 1993b; Silberberg et al., 1987). Although they have a long history in economic theory, the actual existence of Giffen goods has been empirically demonstrated only recently in the behavioral economic literature (Silberberg et al., 1987).

Giffen-good effects apparently are only possible if a large proportion of income is spent on an essential good that also is an inferior good (Degrandpre et al., 1993b; Lea et al., 1987), which would be indicative of a severely constrained environmental context. It is possible that the motivational systems that underlie drug consumption may be most clearly understood by studying such severely constrained environments, and the manipulation of income may be an important element of such studies.

FUTURE DIRECTIONS

Given the positive contributions of the early phase of behavioral economic research on drug consumption, there are many avenues to pursue in future research. The following suggestions are merely a selective sampling of those numerous possibilities. Much of the evidence that supports behavioral economic analyses of drug consumption is derived from reanalyzed data from earlier studies that manipulated relevant variables. Although most of the experiments that have been explicitly designed in light of behavioral economic concepts have produced consistent data, there obviously is a need for more of these studies with both animals and humans with a variety of drugs.

An interesting example of this point concerns the concept of unit price. Some recent studies with drug (Nader et al., 1993; Winger, 1993) and food (Foltin, 1994) reinforcement have reported exceptions to the unit price notion that all manipulations that affect behavioral output or reinforcer magnitude produce consumption that converges on the same demand curve. It is not clear if these exceptions represent boundary conditions of the unit price concept or if they represent phenomena that will necessitate a more fundamental revision of the concept. This is an important topic for future research.

Another possible future direction concerns the fact that virtually all of the experiments that have studied demand for drugs as a function of the availability of alternative reinforcers have employed situations in which the drug and alternative were concurrently available. These are important investigations, but it may be relevant to study situations in which the drug and alternative are available in a repeating sequential cycle rather than concurrently. For example, McSweeney et al. (1988) studied choice between food and ethanol in rats in two situations. In one situation, food and ethanol were available concurrently. Under these conditions, increases in the price of food produced increases in ethanol consumption, consistent with economic substitution. In a second situation, food and ethanol were available sequentially (i.e., multiple schedules of reinforcement). Under these conditions, increases in the price of food produced no changes in ethanol consumption, consistent with economic independence. Exploring the generality of these

different consumption patterns in these two situations is a potentially important area for the further development of behavioral economic concepts.

Studying intertemporal choice (Kagel et al., 1995; Williams, 1988) situations involving drug and nondrug reinforcers is a related area for future work. Preparations that involve choice between an immediate, small reinforcer and a large, delayed reinforcer have produced a fruitful behavioral model of self-control and impulsiveness (Ainslie, 1975). These psychological concepts figure prominently in most approaches to studying drug abuse, but, with few exceptions (e.g., Vuchinich and Tucker, 1983) these laboratory preparations for studying intertemporal choice have not been applied in research on drug consumption. These issues probably are critical for understanding how drug abuse develops and changes in the natural environment, and adequately studying them from a behavioral economic perspective will require the development of appropriate methods (Vuchinich and Tucker, 1996).

SUMMARY

Despite its relatively recent origin, behavioral economic research on drug consumption already has made substantial contributions. These may be summarized as follows:

- It is well grounded in the basic behavioral science of choice.
- It directs attention to the environmental context of drug availability.
- It provides a coherent set of concepts for the analysis of drug consumption.
- Its concepts and methods permit quantitative precision in the analysis of relationships, which may be useful in understanding reinforcing and incentive properties of drugs and the neurochemical events that underlie drug consumption.
- It provides a more parsimonious account of the effects of some independent variables on drug consumption (e.g., response re-

quirement and drug dose operate by altering unit price).

- It suggests practical applications for drug abuse prevention (e.g., engaging youth in alternative, nondrug activities).
- It measures and/or manipulates access to alternative reinforcement, which has improved understanding of clinically significant phenomena (e.g., relapse and natural recovery) and improved the effectiveness of treatment.

REFERENCES

Ainslie, G. (1975). Specious reward: a behavioral theory of impulsiveness and impulse control. *Psychol. Bull.* 82: 463–496.

Allison, J. (1979). Demand economics and experimental psychology. Behavioral Science, 24: 403–415.

Anthony, J. C., Warner, L. A. and Kessler, R. C. (1994). Comparative epidemiology of dependence on tobacco, alcohol, controlled substances, and inhalants: basic findings from the National Comorbidity Study. *Exp. Clin. Psychopharmacol.* 2: 244–268.

Bickel, W. K., DeGrandpre, R. J. and Higgins, S. T. (1993). Behavioral economics: a novel experimental approach to the study of drug dependence. *Drug Alcohol Depend.* 33: 173–192.

Bickel, W. K., DeGrandpre, R. J. and Higgins, S. T. (1995a). The behavioral economics of concurrent drug reinforcers: a review and reanalysis of drug self-administration research. *Psychopharmacology* 118: 250–259.

Bickel, W. K., DeGrandpre, R. J., Higgins, S. T. and Hughes, J. R. (1990). Behavioral economics of drug self-administration: I. Functional equivalence of response requirement and drug dose. *Life Sci.* 47: 1501–1510.

Bickel, W. K., DeGrandpre, R. J., Higgins, S. T., Hughes, J. R. and Badger, G. J. (1995b). Effects of simulated employment and recreation on human drug taking: a behavioral economic analysis. *Exp. Clin. Psychopharmacol.* 3: 467–476.

Bickel, W. K., DeGrandpre, R. J., Hughes, J. R. and Higgins, S. T. (1991). Behavioral economics of drug self-administration: II. A unit-price analysis of cigarette smoking. *J. Exp. Anal. Behav.* 55: 145–154.

Bickel, W. K., Hughes, J. R., DeGrandpre, R. J., Higgins, S. T. and Rizzuto, P. (1992). Behavioral economics of drug self-administration: IV. The effects of response requirement on the consumption of and interaction between concurrently available coffee and cigarettes. *Psychopharmacology* 107: 211–216.

Carroll, M. E. (1987). Self-administration of orally-delivered phencyclidine and ethanol under concurrent fixed-ratio schedules in rhesus monkeys. *Psychopharmacology* 93: 1–7.

Carroll, M. E. (1993). The economic context of drug and non-drug reinforcers affects acquisition and maintenance of drug-reinforced behavior and withdrawal effects. *Drug and Alcohol Depend.* 33: 201–210.

Carroll, M. E. (1996). Reducing drug abuse by enriching the environment with alternative nondrug reinforcers. In: Green, L. and Kagel, J. (eds.) *Advances in behavioral economics*, vol. 3. pp. 37–68. Norwood, NJ: Ablex.

Carroll, M. E., Carmona, G. G. and May, S. A. (1991). Modifying drug-reinforced behavior by altering the economic conditions of the drug and the non-drug reinforcer. *J. Exp. Anal. Behav.* 56: 361–376.

Carroll, M. E. and Lac, S. T. (1992). Autoshaping i.v. cocaine self-administration in rats: effects of non-drug alternative reinforcers on acquisition. *Psychopharmacology* 110: 5–12.

Carroll, M. E., Lac, S. T. and Nygaard, S. L. (1989). A concurrently available non-drug reinforcer prevents the acquisition or decreases the maintenance of cocaine-reinforced behavior. *Psychopharmacology* 97: 23–29.

Carroll, M. E. and Rodefer, J. S. (1993). Income alters choice between drug and an alternative nondrug reinforcer in monkeys. *Exp. Clin. Psychopharmacol.* 1: 110–120.

DeGrandpre, R. J., Bickel, W. K., Higgins, S. T. and Hughes, J. R. (1994). A behavioral economic analysis of concurrently available money and cigarettes. *J. Exp. Anal. Behav.* 61: 191–201.

DeGrandpre, R. J., Bickel, W. K., Hughes, J. R. and Higgins, S. T. (1992). Behavioral economics of drug self-administration: III. A reanalysis of the nicotine regulation hypothesis. *Psychopharmacology* 108: 1–10.

DeGrandpre, R. J., Bickel, W. K., Hughes, J. R., Layng, M. P. and Badger, G. (1993a). Unit price as a useful metric in analyzing effects of reinforcer magnitude. *J. Exp. Anal. Behav.* 60: 641–666.

DeGrandpre, R. J., Bickel, W. K., Rizvi, S. A. T. and Hughes, J. R. (1993b). Effects of income on drug choice in humans. *J. Exp. Anal. Behav.* 59: 483–500.

Elsmore, T. F., Fletcher, D. V., Conrad, D. G. and Sodetz, F. J. (1980). Reduction in heroin intake in baboons by an economic constraint. *Pharmacol. Biochem. Behav.* 13: 729–731.

Foltin, R. W. (1994). Does package size matter? A unit-price analysis of "demand" for food in baboons. *J. Exp. Anal. Behav.* 62: 393–306.

George, F. R. and Ritz, M. C. (1993). A psychopharmacology of motivation and reward related to substance abuse treatment. *Exp. Clin. Psychopharmacol.* 1: 7–26.

Goldberg, S. R., Hoffeister, F., Shlichting, U. U. and Wuttke, W. (1971). A comparison of pentobarbital and cocaine self-administration in rhesus monkeys: effect of dose and fixed-ratio parameter. *J. Pharmacol. Exp. Ther.* 179: 277–283.

Green, L. and Freed, D. E. (1993). The substitutability of reinforcers. *J. Exp. Anal. Behav.* 60: 141–158.

Green, L. and Kagel, J. H. (eds.) (1987). *Advances in behavioral economics*, vol. 1. Norwood, NJ: Ablex.

Green, L. and Kagel, J. H. (eds.) (1996). *Advances in behavioral economics*, vol. 3. Norwood, NJ: Ablex.

Green, L. and Rachlin, H. (1991). Economic substitutability of electrical brain stimulation, food, and water. *J. Exp. Anal. Behav.* 55: 133–143.

Griffiths, R. R., Bigelow, G. E. and Henningfield, J. E. (1980). Similarities in human and animal drug-taking behavior. In: Mello, N.K. (ed.) *Advances in substance abuse: behavioral. and biological research*, vol. 1, pp. 1–90. Greenwich, CT: JAI Press.

Harrigan, S. E. and Downs, D. A. (1980). Pharmacologic evaluation of narcotic delivery systems in rhesus monkeys. In: Willette, R.E. and Barnett, G. (eds.) *Naltrexone:*

research monograph 28, pp. 77–92. Washington, DC: National Institute of Drug Abuse.

Herrnstein, R. J. (1970). On the law of effect. *J. Exp. Anal. Behav.* 13: 243–266.

Higgins, S. T., Delaney, D. D., Budney, A. J., Bickel, W. K., Hughes, J. R., Foerg, F. and Fenwick, J. W. (1991). A behavioral approach to achieving initial cocaine abstinence. *Am. J. Psychiatry* 148: 1218–1224.

Hull, C. L. (1943). *Principles of behavior*. New York: Appleton-Century.

Hursh, S. R. (1980). Economic concepts for the Anal. Behav.. *J. Exp. Anal. Behav.* 34: 219–238.

Hursh, S. R. (1984). Behavioral economics. *J. Exp. Anal. Behav.* 42: 435–452.

Hursh, S. R. (1991). Behavioral economics of drug self-administration and drug abuse policy. *J. Exp. Anal. Behav.* 56: 377–393.

Hursh, S. R. (1993). Behavioral economics of drug self-administration: an introduction. *Drug Alcohol Depend.* 33: 165–172.

Hursh, S. R. and Bauman, R. A. (1987). The behavioral analysis of demand. In: Green, L. and Kagel, J. (eds.) *Advances in behavioral economics*, vol. 1. Norwood, NJ: Ablex.

Hursh, S. R., Raslear, T. G., Shurtleff, D., Bauman, R. and Simmons, L. (1988). A cost-benefit analysis of demand for food. *J. Exp. Anal. Behav.* 50: 419–440.

Jaffe, J. H. (1990). Drug addiction and abuse. In: Goodman, A.G., Rall, T.W., Nies, A.S. and Taylor, P. (eds.) *The pharmacological basis of therapeutics*, 8th ed., pp. 522–573. New York: Pergamon Press.

Kagel, J. H., Battalio, R. C. and Green, L. (1995). *Economic choice theory: an experimental analysis of animal behavior*. New York: Cambridge University Press.

Kagel, J. H., Battalio, R. C., Rachlin, H., Green, L., Basmann, R. L. and Klemm, W. R. (1975). Experimental studies of consumer demand behavior using laboratory animals. *Econ. Inq.* 13: 22–38.

Kandel, D. B. and Logan, J. A. (1984). Patterns of drug use from adolescence to young adulthood: periods of risk for initiation, continued use, and discontinuation. *Am. J. Public Health* 74: 660–666.

Lea, S. E. G. (1978). The psychology and economics of demand. *Psychol. Bull.* 85: 132–157.

Lea, S. E. G., Tarpy, R. M. and Webley, P. (1987). *The individual in the economy*. Cambridge: Cambridge University Press.

Lemaire, G. A. and Meisch, R. A. (1984). Pentobarbital self-administration in rhesus monkeys: drug concentration of fixed-interval size interactions. *J. Exp. Anal. Behav.* 42: 37–49.

McSweeney, F. K., Melville, C. L. and Higa, J. (1988). Positive behavioral contrast across food and alcohol reinforcers. *J. Exp. Anal. Behav.* 50: 469–481.

Nader, M. A., Hedeker, D. and Woolverton, W. L. (1993). Behavioral economics and drug choice: effects of unit price on cocaine self-administration by monkeys. *Drug Alcohol Depend.* 33: 193–199.

Nader, M. A. and Woolverton, W. L. (1991). Effects of increasing the magnitude of an alternative reinforcer on drug choice in a discrete-trials choice procedure. *Psychopharmacology* 105: 169–174.

Nader, M. A. and Woolverton, W. L. (1992). Effects of increasing response requirement on choice between cocaine and food in rhesus monkeys. *Psychopharmacology* 108: 295–300.

Pearce, D. W. (ed.) (1986). *The MIT dictionary of modern economics*, 3rd ed. Cambridge: MIT Press.

Premack, D. (1965). Reinforcement theory. In: Levine, D. (ed.) *Nebraska Symposium on Motivation,* pp. 123–180. Lincoln: University of Nebraska Press.

Rachlin, H., Battalio, R., Kagel, J. and Green, L. (1981). Maximization theory in behavioral psychology. *Behav. Brain Sci.* 4: 371–417.

Rachlin, H. and Burkhard, B. (1978). The temporal triangle: response substitution in instrumental conditioning. *Psychol. Rev.* 85: 22–47.

Rachlin, H., Green, L., Kagel, J. and Battalio, R. (1976). Economic demand theory and psychological studies of choice. In: Bower, G. (ed.) *The psychology of learning and motivation*. New York: Academic Press.

Rachlin, H., Kagel, J. H. and Battalio, R. C. (1980). Substitutability in time allocation. *Psychol. Rev.* 87: 355–374.

Samson, H. H. and Lindberg, K. (1984). Comparison of sucrose-sucrose to sucrose-ethanol concurrent responding in the rat: reinforcement schedule and fluid concentration effects. *Pharmacol. Biochem. Behav.* 20: 973–977.

Samson, H. H., Roehrs, T. A. and Tolliver, G. A. (1982). Ethanol reinforced responding in the rat: a concurrent analysis using sucrose as the alternate choice. *Pharmacol. Biochem. Behav.* 17: 333–339.

Samson, H. H., Tolliver, G. A. and Roehrs, T. A. (1983). Ethanol reinforced responding in the rat: relation of ethanol introduction to later ethanol responding. *Pharmacol. Biochem. Behav.* 18: 895–900.

Silberberg, A., Warren-Boulton, F. R. and Asano, T. (1987). Inferior-good and Giffen-good effects in monkey choice behavior. *J. Exp. Psychol. Anim. Behav. Process.* 13: 292–301.

Skinner, B. F. (1938). *The behavior of organisms: an experimental analysis*. Englewood Cliffs, NJ: Prentice-Hall.

Staddon, J. E. R. (1979). Operant behavior as adaptation to constraint. *J. Exp. Psychol. Gen.* 108: 48–67.

Staddon, J. E. R. (ed.) (1980). *Limits to action: the allocation of individual behavior*. New York: Academic Press.

Tucker, J. A., Vuchinich, R. E. and Pukish, M. A. (1995). Molar environmental contexts surrounding recovery from alcohol problems by treated and untreated problem drinkers. *Exp. Clin. Psychopharmacol.* 3: 195–204.

Vuchinich, R. E. (1982). Have behavioral theories of alcohol abuse focused too much on alcohol consumption? *Bull. Soc. Psychol. Substance Abuse* 1: 151–154.

Vuchinich, R. E. (1995). Alcohol abuse as molar choice: an update of a 1982 proposal. *Psychol. Addict. Behav.* 9: 223–235.

Vuchinich, R. E. and Tucker, J. A. (1983). Behavioral theories of choice as a framework for studying drinking behavior. *J. Abnorm. Psychol.* 92: 408–416.

Vuchinich, R. E. and Tucker, J. A. (1988). Contributions from behavioral theories of choice to an analysis of alcohol abuse. *J. Abnorm. Psychol.* 97: 181–195.

Vuchinich, R. E. and Tucker, J. A. (1996). Alcoholic relapse, life events, and behavioral theories of choice: a prospective analysis. *Exp. Clin. Psychopharmacol.* 4: 19–28.

Vuchinich, R. E. and Tucker, J. A. (1996). The molar context of alcohol abuse. In: Green, L. and Kagel, J. (eds.) *Advances in behavioral economics*, vol. 3. pp. 133–162. Norwood, NJ: Ablex Press.

Vuchinich, R. E., Tucker, J. A. and Harllee, L. (1988). Behavioral assessment (of alcohol dependence). In: Donovan, D. and Marlatt, A.G. (eds.) *Assessment of addictive behaviors*, pp. 51–93. New York: Plenum Press.

Williams, B. A. (1988). Reinforcement, choice, and response strength. In: Atkinson, R.C., Herrnstein, R.J., Lindzey, G. and Luce, R.D. (eds.) *S. S. Stevens' handbook of experimental psychology*, vol. 2, pp. 167–244. New York: Wiley.

Winger, G. (1993). Fixed-ratio and time-out changes on behavior maintained by cocaine or methohexital in rhesus monkeys: 2. Behavioral economic analysis. *Exp. Clin. Psychopharmacol.* 1: 154–161.

Drug Addiction and its Treatment: Nexus of Neuroscience and Behavior, edited by Bankole A. Johnson and John D. Roache. Lippincott–Raven Publishers, Philadelphia, © 1997.

4

Measures of Interoceptive Stimulus Effects: Relationship to Drug Reinforcement

*†Kenzie L. Preston, *Sharon L. Walsh, and *§Christine A. Sannerud

*Department of Psychiatry and Behavioral Sciences, Johns Hopkins University School of Medicine, Baltimore, Maryland 21205
†National Institute on Drug Abuse, Division of Intramural Research, Addiction Research Center, Baltimore, Maryland 21224
§Drug and Chemical Evaluation Section, Drug Enforcement Administration, Washington, D.C. 20537

Drugs from a wide array of pharmacologic classes with distinct stimulus profiles are self-administered by laboratory animals and abused by humans. These abused drugs are considered similar because they reinforce drug-taking behavior; however, the pharmacodynamic profiles of these drugs are quite diverse and can range, for example, from sedation to stimulation. Direct measures of reinforcing efficacy (e.g., self-administration and epidemiologic data) are sensitive measures of abuse potential, but do not readily detect the pharmacologic differences among abused drugs. Because all psychoactive drugs produce interoceptive stimulus effects, but not all are abused, it is believed that only a subset of these drug stimuli are related to abuse liability. The quest to understand the similarities and differences in interoceptive stimulus effects and their predictive value for identifying compounds with abuse potential have led to interest in other laboratory paradigms for testing nonhuman and human subjects.

The laboratory paradigms most frequently used to characterize interoceptive stimuli are the conditioned place preference paradigm, the drug discrimination paradigm, and subjective effect measures. The conditioned place preference paradigm is a widely used procedure that relies on classical conditioning to provide an index of a drug's capacity to produce either drug-seeking or drug-avoidance behavior (Bardo et al., 1995). Typically, the method involves pairing administration of a test drug with a particular set of exteroceptive stimuli and pairing administration of vehicle with a distinctly different set of exteroceptive stimuli during separate trials. Visual stimuli are the most frequently used exteroceptive stimuli and can include, for example, two different patterns, colors, or textures on the walls of a two-sided chamber. Once a specified number of conditioning trials are completed, the subject is tested for conditioning by giving it free access to both the drug-paired and vehicle-paired sides of the chamber in the absence of the drug. If the subject spends significantly more time in the drug-paired environment, the drug is said to have induced a conditioned place preference. In contrast, if the subject spends significantly more time in the vehicle-paired environment, the drug is said to have induced a conditioned place avoidance. This information is used to infer whether the interoceptive stimuli produced by the drug are rewarding or aversive.

Drug discrimination procedures have been widely used to characterize the stimulus effects of drugs in rodents, pigeons, and nonhuman primates over the past three decades. More recently these techniques have been applied to the study of discriminative stimulus effects of drugs in humans. The drug discrimination paradigm is based on the ability of psychoactive drugs to produce interoceptive stimuli, and the ability of nonhuman and human subjects to learn to identify the presence of these stimuli and to differentiate among the constellations of stimuli produced by different drug classes. In drug discrimination studies, the drug stimuli function as a cue for the subject to make an operant response in order to receive a reinforcer (for example, food or money). Repeated coupling of a reinforcer with only drug-appropriate responses (for example, pressing the correct lever) can engender reliable discrimination between drug and no-drug or among several drugs. Because some interoceptive stimuli are believed to be associated with the reinforcing effects of drugs, the drug discrimination paradigm can be used to evaluate abuse potential of new drugs and to screen medications for potential therapeutic efficacy in the treatment of substance abuse.

The drug discrimination procedure enables researchers to assess the nature of drug-induced interoceptive stimuli perceived by nonhumans, which have long been considered to be analogous to subjective drug effects in humans (Schuster and Johanson, 1988). Subjective effects in humans are defined as personal experiences of an individual subject that cannot be observed by others for public validation. Because subjective phenomena are not accessible to observers, it is difficult to reach objective or consensual agreement about the nature of the subjective experience. The drug discrimination paradigm can be used to quantify subjective drug experiences in humans as well, although this method has been employed in human studies only in recent years. Historically, the standard procedure for testing whether a drug effect was perceived by human subjects has been to collect verbal or written subjective reports, typically in the form of structured self-report questionnaires.

Subjective effect measures can be designed to measure the presence or absence of interoceptive stimuli, and, because of the unique ability of humans to communicate verbally, descriptive information characterizing the qualitative nature of the subjective drug experience can also be collected.

Described below are procedures and general findings from conditioned place preference studies in nonhuman subjects, drug discrimination studies conducted in both nonhuman and human subjects, and methods for collecting subjective effect measures in humans. The similarities and differences among drug classes on these various measures are reviewed. For the purpose of this chapter, drug classes are defined by the predominating pharmacodynamic action (i.e., sedatives, stimulants, opiates, and hallucinogens) and not by mechanism of action or chemical structure. In addition, the relationships among conditioned place preference results, discriminative stimulus effects, subjective effect profiles, and reinforcing effects are discussed. Finally, the utility of these methods in screening new medications for abuse potential and for potential efficacy as pharmacotherapies for substance abuse are described.

CONDITIONED PLACE PREFERENCE

The conditioned place paradigm uses classical conditioning to assess the interoceptive stimuli produced by drugs. This behavioral paradigm has been used to assess the abuse potential of drugs, to evaluate mechanisms of drug action, and to elucidate reward substrates in the brain. Detailed descriptions of procedures and a comprehensive review of the literature have recently been published (Bardo et al., 1995; Schechter and Calcagnetti, 1993) and will be reviewed only briefly here.

Experimental Procedures

In a standard conditioned place paradigm, a test drug and its vehicle (no drug) are separately paired with distinct environmental stimuli during multiple training trials. In addition to visual stimuli, auditory, tactile, and olfactory cues have been used to produce distinct environments. Unlike drug self-administration, drug administration is passive (i.e., experimenter controlled) and occurs before the start of the trial. The differential pairing of drug (the unconditioned stimulus) and environment (the conditioned stimulus) can lead to a conditioned response that occurs in the absence of the drug. The basic principle in the conditioned place paradigm is that drugs that produce positive stimuli increase time spent in a drug-paired environment (place preference), while drugs that produce negative stimuli decrease time spent in a drug-paired environment (place aversion).

While all studies ultimately compare the amount of time spent in an environment associated with drug administration to that spent in an environment associated with no drug or vehicle administration, the procedure for measuring drug-induced conditioning may vary. One common method involves testing animals prior to any drug or vehicle administration for a preference at baseline. This is accomplished by measuring the amount of time spent in each side of the test chamber when the subject has free access to both environments. Typically, the least-preferred side for each subject is then assigned to be paired with the drug. During the test procedure, the amounts of time spent in that environment before and after conditioning are compared, and significant increases in time spent in the drug-paired context after conditioning is interpreted as evidence of a conditioned place preference. In a variation of this procedure, no preconditioning preferences are determined, and assignments of contextual stimuli to drug and vehicle are made randomly. Another method involves using a group design, in which one group is conditioned as described above and a second group receives vehicle paired with both environments. The amounts of time spent in the drug-paired environment are then compared between the experimental and control groups.

Synopsis—Conditioned Place Preference

Drugs with high abuse potential generally produce conditioned place preference, while drugs with little or no abuse potential produce either no place preference or a place aversion. Conditioned place preference has been demonstrated for each of the major drug classes including sedatives (primarily benzodiazepines), psychomotor stimulants (amphetamine, cocaine, methylphenidate), and opiate agonists (heroin and morphine) (for review see Bardo et al., 1995; Schechter and Calcagnetti, 1993). In the sedative drug class, the prototypic benzodiazepines (e.g., diazepam) reliably produce a conditioned place preference. However, only one study was found that evaluated a barbiturate; surprisingly, this study of phenobarbital reported a conditioned place aversion in rats (Wilks and File, 1988). More research is needed to determine whether this is characteristic of other barbiturates; it would certainly be inconsistent with preclinical self-administration studies and epidemiologic data, which indicate that barbiturates have a high abuse potential. Within the class of psychomotor stimulants, cocaine and amphetamine consistently produce a conditioned place preference (e.g., Brown et al., 1991; Spyraki et al., 1988). Opioids with prominent mu receptor activity also reliably produce a conditioned place preference. The number of studies that have assessed the effects of opioids acting at other opiate receptor subtypes (i.e., kappa or delta) are quite limited. Similarly, relatively little work has been done with the hallucinogens. There are, however, a number of reports that PCP produces a conditioned place aversion (e.g., Acquas et al., 1989; Barr et al., 1985; Iwato, 1986), although a conditioned place preference has been reported in at least one study in which a low dose of PCP was tested (Marglin et al., 1989). One study has shown that Δ^9-tetrahydrocannabinol (THC), the primary active constituent in marijuana, can also produce a conditioned place preference (Lepore et al., 1995). No studies were found that evaluated the effects of LSD or mescaline in this paradigm.

DRUG DISCRIMINATION IN NONHUMANS

Drug self-administration research has revealed a high degree of concordance in the reinforcing effects of a wide range of drugs between laboratory animals and human drug abusers. In addition, drug discrimination procedures have been used extensively to characterize the behavioral profile of these drugs and to provide behavioral indices of central mechanisms of drug action. Since there are generally high correlations between the reinforcing and discriminative stimulus effects of drugs, the use of drug discrimination procedures has provided a means to predict abuse potential.

History

In the 1950s and early 1960s several groups of investigators independently demonstrated that drugs of different classes, including sedatives and alcohol, functioned as discriminative stimuli (cf. Overton, 1984, 1987; Schuster and Balster, 1977). These studies showed that animals could be trained to perform a response when the drug was present and to withhold the response or perform an alternate response when the drug was absent. Drug discrimination studies conducted in the 1960s primarily focused on demonstrating the basic phenomenon and defining the fundamental parameters of discrimination behavior. The number of drug discrimination studies published in each year after 1970 increased rapidly to the peak rates of 160 and 168 per year in 1990 and 1992, respectively (Samele et al., 1992, 1994). As different methods were evaluated, some degree of procedural standardization was established during the 1970s. About the same time, studies of receptor pharmacology began to elucidate mechanisms of drug action in the central nervous system, and drug discrimination studies were used to evaluate specific neuropharmacologic mechanisms of psychoactive compounds. More recently, drug discrimination techniques have been widely applied (1) to study mechanisms of tolerance and dependence to drug stimuli, (2) to differentiate among pharmacologically similar drugs, (3) to evaluate the activity of novel drugs, and (4) to evaluate correlates of the reinforcing effects or abuse potential of drugs.

Drug discrimination research has contributed extensively to the study of psychoactive drugs and their ability to serve as discriminative stimuli to guide choice behavior. Taken together, over 1,500 studies have been conducted to date that have examined the stimulus effects of drugs across a variety of experimental conditions, including subject species (rodents, monkeys, cats, baboons, pigeons), reinforcing events (food presentation or shock avoidance), task (operant or t-maze), specificity of the training conditions (training dose, two- or three-choice), schedules of reinforcement (fixed ratio, fixed interval, variable interval, differential reinforcement of low rate, second order), and acute versus multiple trials. Drugs from numerous classes (e.g., sedative-hypnotics, anxiolytics, antipsychotics, opioids, stimulants, hallucinogens, antidepressants, antihistamines) can serve as discriminative stimuli, generalize within drug classes across a variety of training conditions, and be differentiated across drug classes. The ability of drugs to serve as discriminative stimuli, despite disparate experimental conditions, attests to the robust nature and generality of this phenomenon.

Experimental Procedures

Several recent review chapters have detailed the behavioral procedures used in drug discrimination and the types of data that are generated (cf. Overton, 1987; Stolerman, 1991; Young, 1991). In experimental studies of drug discrimination, conditions are arranged so that the presence or absence of the drug are the only cues that co-vary with different behavioral responses. The procedures for establishing discriminative control by drugs most commonly employ a two- (or more recently three-) choice design within an operant conditioning paradigm. Stimulus control is achieved using a differential reinforcement procedure. During training sessions, reinforcer delivery is dependent on performing the particular response that has been associated with either the presence or absence of the drug stimulus. That is, following an injection of a drug dose administered before the experimental session (presession), responses on one of two (or more) levers produce reinforcer delivery. Following no drug administration or a presession injection of vehicle, responses on an alternate lever result in reinforcer delivery. All other environmental conditions (e.g., lights, sounds, handling, time of day, etc.) remain identical.

Successful acquisition of stimulus control is defined by the subject meeting several criteria identified a priori by the experimenter. Although the specific criteria may vary across experiments, they are typically designed to ensure highly accurate stimulus control by the drug. The experimental criteria are important because the relevant behavior (e.g., lever choice) can be altered by the reinforcer itself. One criterion often used is that the subject must not complete a response requirement on the incorrect lever before earning a reinforcer on the correct lever. This criterion may be employed to prevent subjects from adopting a "win/stay—lose/shift" strategy. That is, if completion of a response requirement on a lever results in the delivery of a reinforcer, they "win" and continue to respond ("stay") on that same lever. If they respond on the incorrect lever and fail to obtain a reinforcer, they "lose" and switch ("shift") to the alternate lever. When subjects use this strategy, it is likely that the delivery (or lack of delivery) of the reinforcer, rather than the discriminative stimulus effects of the drug, is guiding lever selection. To prevent the interpretation of this strategy as successful training, the total number of responses emitted on both levers prior to the first reinforcer is recorded and used to evaluate the degree of stimulus control over performance; fewer responses prior to the first reinforcer indicate greater accuracy. A second procedure commonly used to enhance stimulus control is to require that

the number of responses on the correct lever exceed a predetermined percent of the total responses emitted on both levers (typically > 90% on the stimulus-appropriate lever). In general, a strict criterion for discriminative control guarantees a well-trained subject with a discrimination based on the stimulus effects of the drug.

Once stimulus control is established, generalization or substitution testing with novel drug stimuli can begin. There are two basic reinforcement procedures used in generalization testing: (1) completion of the response on either lever produces reinforcer delivery, or (2) no reinforcer delivery follows completion of the response on either lever (that is, under extinction conditions). Both procedures have been widely used in generalization testing to determine the dose-response curve for the training drugs and to determine whether other drugs will generalize to or substitute for the training drug stimuli. Despite differences in reinforcing contingencies, these testing conditions generally produce similar generalization profiles for test drugs. Because there is the possibility that either method of testing can disrupt the baseline accuracy of the discrimination, it is important to have intervening training sessions during testing to maintain stimulus control.

Specificity of Stimulus Effects

Specificity of stimulus effects can be assessed through generalization testing with novel drugs or with different doses of the training drug. Generalization testing in drug discrimination can result in either (1) responding on the drug-appropriate lever, suggesting that the novel drug/dose substitutes for the training drug; (2) responding on the vehicle-appropriate lever, suggesting that the novel drug/dose does not share effects similar to the training drug stimulus; or (3) responding on both levers, suggesting that the novel drug/dose is similar, but not identical, to the training drug. Drugs within the same pharmacologic class as the training drug typically produce dose-related responding on the drug lever. Class specificity has been reported for all of the major classes of drugs of abuse, including sedatives, opiates, and stimulants (e.g., Ator and Griffiths, 1989a,b; Evans and Johanson, 1987; Shannon and Holtzman, 1976; Young, 1991) (Table 1). Conversely, when drugs from pharmacologic classes different from that of the training drug are tested, responses are typically made on the vehicle lever (i.e., it is a training-drug versus not–training-drug discrimination). When drugs are tested that share only a portion of the stimulus profile of the training drug, responses are often distributed among the vehicle and drug response options; a consensus on how to interpret this partial (or incomplete) generalization has not yet been resolved (cf. Stolerman, 1991). Discrimination studies can also be designed to differentiate among drugs within a major pharmacologic class (Overton, 1987; Sannerud and Ator, 1995a,b; Young, 1991). This can be accomplished by training a two-choice (drug versus drug) discrimination or a three-choice drug discrimination. For example, studies have trained low-dose versus high-dose training conditions to differentiate among a series of benzodiazepine agonists using midazolam as the training stimuli (Sannerud and Ator, 1995a,b) or among several opiates using morphine as the training drug (Young et al., 1992).

There are a number of variables that significantly can affect stimulus control, and thus alter the results obtained in generalization testing. One important variable is the dose of the training drug (Shannon and Holtzman, 1979) that can alter the pharmacologic specificity of the discriminative stimulus. In general, a low training dose produces a less pharmacologically specific stimulus indicated by a flattening of the generalization gradient, a lower median effective dose (ED_{50}) (i.e., generalization to lower doses), and cross-generalization to novel drugs outside the class that produce overlapping stimulus effects (cf. Colpaert et al., 1980). In contrast, a high training dose produces a highly specific stimulus, resulting in steep generalization gradients,

higher ED_{50}s, and cross-generalization only to drugs within a class that share very similar pharmacologic effects. Thus, an increase in sensitivity is accompanied by a decrease in specificity (and vice versa). In studies of sedative discriminations, for example, dose-response curves for drugs that fully substitute for the training drug typically shift to the right as the dose of the training drug increases (DeVry and Slangen, 1986; Shannon and Herling, 1983; Tang and Franklin, 1991; Sannerud et al., 1991). In addition to these quantitative differences, some studies have found qualitative differences in generalization profiles obtained under different training dose conditions. That is, test drugs that did not substitute at one dose of training drug fully substituted at a different training drug dose (Sannerud and Ator, 1995a,b; Shannon and Holtzman, 1979; Stolerman and D'Mello, 1981; Tang and Franklin, 1991). The training dose can also influence results of studies assessing antagonism of discriminative stimuli. For instance, the ability of the benzodiazepine-receptor antagonist flumazenil to block the discriminative stimulus effects of chlordiazepoxide was related to the training dose of chlordiazepoxide (DeVry and Slangen, 1986).

Another important variable that can significantly affect stimulus control is the selection of training conditions, particularly when more than one active drug or more than one dose of a drug is used. For example, in three-choice drug discrimination tasks that use a drug versus drug versus placebo or low-dose versus high-dose versus placebo discrimination, subjects must attend to subtle quantitative or qualitative differences between drug/doses to make appropriate responses. This can result in a more specific pharmacologic assay. Drug A versus drug B versus placebo three-choice discriminations can sometimes be trained, even when drug A and drug B substitute fully or partially for one another in two-choice procedures. Testing other drugs in subjects trained to discriminate between drug A and drug B permits further differentiation of their discriminative stimulus effects. In studies of

TABLE 1. *Drug discrimination findings in non-human and human subjects*

| | Sedative training drug | | | Stimulant training drug | | | Opiate training drug | |
| | Barbiturates | Benzodiazepines | | Cocaine | Amphetamine | | Mu Agonists | |
Test drug	Nonhuman	Nonhuman	Human	Nonhuman	Nonhuman	Human	Nonhuman	Human
Sedatives								
Barbiturates	+++ 1,2	+++ 1,2,8,9,10	++ 13	- 6	- 5	- 28,29	- 32	- 40
Benzodiazepines	+++ 1,2	+/- 1,2,8,9	+++ 13,14,15	- 16,17		- 27	- 33,34,35	- 40
Methocarbamol	- 3,4	- 4,11			- 3			
Antihistamines	- 5	- 12			+++ 5			
Meprobamate	+++ 1,2	++/- 1,2,10	- 15		+++ 5			
Tripelenamine		- 12						
Buspirone	- 1	- 1,8,10	++ 15					
Stimulants								
Amphetamine	- 6	- 11		+++ 6,18	+++ 23	+++ 29,30,31	- 33,35	- 40
Cocaine		- 11		+++ 18	+++ 23			
Methylphenidate				+++ 17,19	+++ 5	+++ 28		
Phenametrazine				+++ 19	+++ 5	+ 31		
Mazindol		- 10		+++ 6,20	+++ 5	++ 30		
Caffeine		- 11,12			+ 24,25	- 14		
Phenylpropanolamine					+ 5	++ 30		
Fenfluramine				+ 19	+ 5	- 31		
Benzphetamine					- 5	- 14		
Nicotine				+ 16,21	+ 26			
Opiates								
Morphine/heroin/hydromorphone	- 7	- 10,11		- 18,22	- 5	- 30	+++ 35,36	+++ 40,41
Codeine							+++ 33,36	
Propoxyphene	- 7						+++ 36	
Dextromethorphan							++ 36	
Pentazocine							+++ 33,35	+/- 41,42
Nalbuphine							+++ 35	+/- 41,42
Buprenorphine				- 18,22			+++ 34,37	++ 41,42
Butorphanol							+++ 38	+/- 41,42
Hallucinogens								
LSD					- 25		- 39	
Phencyclidine		- 9			- 5		- 32	
Marijuana/THC					- 25		- 36	

This compilation of literature citations is illustrative and is not exhaustive: (1) Ator and Griffiths, 1989b; (2) Nierenberg and Ator, 1990; (3) Leberer and Fowler, 1977; (4) Sannerud et al., 1991; (5) Evans and Johanson, 1987; (6) Witkin et al., 1980; (7) Herling et al., 1980; (8) Woudenberg and Slangen, 1989; (9) Shannon and Herling, 1983; (10) Evans and Johanson, 1989; (11) Sannerud and Ator, 1995a; (12) Spealman, 1985; (13) Johanson, 1991a; (14) Chait and Johanson, 1988; (15) Johanson, 1991b; (16) de la Garza and Johanson, 1985; (17) Emmett–Oglesby et al., 1983; (18) Dykstra et al., 1992; (19) Wood and Emmett–Oglesby, 1988; (20) Kleven et al., 1990; (21) de la Garza and Johanson, 1983; (22) Spealman and Bergman, 1992; (23) Kilbey and Ellinwood, 1979; (24) Holloway et al., 1985; (25)Kuhn et al., 1974; (26) Druhan et al., 1991; (27) Chait et al., 1985; (28) Heishman and Henningfield, 1991; (29) Lamb and Henningfield, 1994; (30) Chait et al., 1986a; (31) Chait et al., 1986b; (32) Holtzman, 1983; (33) Shannon and Holtzman, 1976; (34) France et al., 1984; (35) Young et al., 1992; (36) Overton and Batta, 1979; (37) Shannon et al., 1984; (38) Young et al.,1984; (39) Jarbe, 1978; (40) Bickel et al.,1989; (41) Preston et al., 1992; (42) Preston et al., 1989.

opioids and benzodiazepines, generalization profiles obtained when the response options were limited to drug versus placebo were significantly different from those obtained under a three-choice (placebo and two active doses or placebo versus two training drugs) procedure (Holtzman, 1983; Sannerud and Ator, 1995a,b).

Synopsis—Preclinical Drug Discrimination

A major advantage of using drug discrimination techniques is that they provide a substantial degree of pharmacologic specificity. As noted above, laboratory animals can be trained to discriminate a psychoactive drug from its vehicle and, thus, learn specifically to detect the presence or absence of the training drug. By testing with novel drugs within and across pharmacologic classes, the similarities to and differences from the stimulus profile of the training drug can be determined (cf. Glennon, 1991). For the majority of drug classes, cross-generalization occurs between drugs within the same class, although there are some exceptions (Ator and Griffiths, 1989b). Since stimulus control by drugs within a pharmacologic class (including opioids, benzodiazepines, and stimulants) appears to be mediated by the same biologic mechanisms that underlie some of their other behavioral effects (Colpaert, 1988; Glennon, 1991), the drug discrimination paradigm has helped to determine the neurochemical mechanisms through which prototypic and novel drugs exert their effects. Furthermore, similarity of interoceptive stimuli serves as the basis for inferences about similarity of abuse potential or reinforcing effects. Table 1 summarizes selected drug discrimination studies and illustrates the pharmacologic class specificity of the paradigm.

DRUG DISCRIMINATION IN HUMANS

Drug discrimination research has been conducted for more than three decades; however, it is only in the past 10 to 15 years that this technique has been applied to human sub-jects. The scope of published human drug discrimination research is more limited than preclinical drug discrimination research. This is due primarily to the fact that the use of these procedures in humans is relatively recent, and because of regulations regarding administration of experimental drugs in humans and safety considerations that limit the available test drugs and dose ranges. Nevertheless, there is a growing body of literature that has contributed significantly to our understanding of drug discrimination behavior. Human drug discrimination studies provide a unique opportunity to directly investigate the relationship between subjective effects and discrimination behavior (cf. Schuster and Johanson, 1988; Preston and Bigelow, 1991).

Experimental Procedures

Human drug discrimination studies are typically conducted in two phases: a training phase and a testing phase. In the discrimination training phase, subjects receive each training drug during separate sessions and are instructed to learn to recognize differences between the training drugs. During early training, the drugs are identified to the subject prior to drug administration by a label. Labels assigned by the investigator can either be arbitrary, as in a letter or number code (Chait et al., 1985), or can provide experimental information, such as "drug" or "placebo" (Griffiths et al., 1990). In later training sessions, acquisition of the discrimination is determined by re-exposing the subject to the training drugs and assessing whether the subject can identify the correct drug label. To provide continued training, the subject may be informed of the correct code at the end of the session after the discrimination responses have been made. In some studies, a testing (or generalization) phase is conducted after the training phase in which responses to a range of doses of one or more test drugs are assessed.

Most human and nonhuman drug discrimination studies have trained two-choice discriminations (e.g., drug vs. placebo or drug vs. drug) (Preston and Bigelow, 1991; Young,

1991). Use of more than two training conditions in preclinical studies has been uncommon, although the frequency of training these complex discriminations has increased in recent years. In contrast, a significant proportion of human studies has successfully employed three-choice discriminations. In addition, the training of human drug discrimination performance can be accomplished in fewer experimental sessions than are required for training nonhumans. Both the speed of acquisition and the ease of training complex discriminations may be attributable, in part, to the ability of the investigator to provide verbal instructions and feedback to the subjects.

Although there are variations in the methodologic approaches used to conduct human drug discrimination studies, there are a number of key elements that are common across laboratories. The training and test drugs are always administered under double-blind conditions using procedures that prevent identification of the drug by appearance or volume. An extrinsic reinforcer (typically money) is usually given for correct discrimination responses to enhance the accuracy of performance. During generalization testing when drugs other than the training drug/doses are given (i.e., when there is no "correct" response), subjects typically receive a predetermined amount of money that is independent of their discrimination responses. The schedule for study payment can vary with payment given immediately at the end of each session (Chait et al., 1988a; Kallman et al., 1982), or delayed until the next day (Chait et al., 1985) or until the end of the study (Bickel et al., 1989).

Discrimination performance measures may be collected using several methods that can vary in both physical mode and response format. Common modes of data collection include verbal reports, paper and pencil forms, and operant responses made on a computer keypad or other manipulanda. Response formats are usually binomial (e.g., drug vs. placebo, drug A vs. drug B), but can also be graded. For instance, subjects can be given a fixed number of points to distribute among their response options; this procedure can be used to gain quantitative information on the degree of stimulus similarity between the test drug and the training drug (Bickel et al., 1989; Preston et al., 1987, 1989). When binomial responses are collected as the primary discrimination measure, a point distribution procedure or analogue questionnaire can be used to collect quantitative information about the subjects' confidence in their discrimination response (Chait et al., 1985).

Synopsis—Human Drug Discrimination

The drug discrimination procedure has not yet been studied as extensively in humans as it has in nonhumans. However, a number of different drug classes and routes of administration have been tested. Successful discriminations have been trained with smoked nicotine (Kallman et al., 1982) and marijuana cigarettes (Chait et al., 1988a), oral caffeine (Griffiths et al., 1990; Oliveto et al., 1992), amphetamine (Chait et al., 1984, 1985, 1986a, 1986b; Chait and Johanson, 1988), cocaine (Oliveto et al., 1995), benzodiazepines (Johanson, 1991a; Bickel et al., 1993; Mumford et al., 1995), nonbenzodiazepine antianxiety agents (Johanson, 1993), and parenteral opiates (Bickel et al., 1989; Preston et al., 1987, 1989, 1990, 1994). The generality of drug discrimination findings in nonhuman subjects has been found to extend to studies using human subjects. Comparisons of results generated from nonhuman and human studies reveal qualitative, as well as quantitative, similarities between substitution profiles and potency relationships of drugs from several pharmacologic classes, including opioids, benzodiazepines, and psychomotor stimulants (for review see Kamien et al., 1993; Preston and Bigelow, 1991). An illustrative, but not exhaustive, summary of drug discrimination findings in humans and nonhumans is shown in Table 1.

SUBJECTIVE EFFECT MEASURES IN HUMANS

Subjective effects are feelings, perceptions, and moods that are the personal experiences of an individual. Because these subjective experiences are internal, they are not generally accessible to observers. Researchers have developed self-report instruments to assess the presence or absence of a drug effect and to determine the quantitative and qualitative characteristics of the subjective experience. Narrative descriptions of drug effects can be obtained through either interview or spontaneous reports. While this type of report is often informative, the format of narrative reports does not readily lend itself to quantification and may introduce experimenter bias. Narrative reports are probably most useful when the effects of the test drug are unknown. The development of standardized questionnaires has revolutionized the experimental approach to measurement of subjective drug effects. Results from these questionnaires can provide data that are reliable and replicable, that can be combined across subjects, and that can be analyzed to determine statistical and/or clinical significance. Subjective effect data can be used for the determination of pharmacologic properties, including time course, potency, abuse potential, side effects, and the therapeutic utility of drugs.

History

Illicit drug abuse and the misuse of medications have led to the adoption of increasing numbers of laws restricting the possession and sale of existing drugs throughout this century. In response to increased regulation, there was a movement in the pharmaceutical industry to develop efficacious medications with lower abuse liabilities. The pressing need to regulate drugs that could potentially be misused prompted the United States to sponsor research for the development of scientific methodologies that would be useful for assessing the abuse potential of new medications. Thus, the need to decrease the availability of drugs with significant abuse potential was one of the driving forces behind the development of standardized methods for assessing subjective drug effects.

The Addiction Research Center (ARC), a federal government laboratory in Lexington, Kentucky, and Henry Beecher and his colleagues at Harvard made major contributions to the development of subjective effect measures. Researchers at the ARC played a primary role in the government's quest to develop methods for abuse potential screening and application of those methods to evaluate new medications. Seminal studies on the acute and chronic effects of various abused drugs, as well as studies on physical dependence and withdrawal symptoms, have been conducted at the ARC since the 1930s (for review see Martin and Isbell, 1978). Many questionnaires and procedures currently used to study the subjective effects of drugs were developed there, including the Addiction Research Center Inventory (Haertzen, 1966) and the Single Dose Questionnaire (Fraser et al., 1961). Beecher and his colleagues conducted a lengthy series of well-designed studies that compared the subjective effects of various drugs, including opiates, sedatives, and stimulants (Lasagna et al., 1955; Smith and Beecher, 1962). These studies were conducted in a variety of subject populations including patients, substance abusers, and normal volunteers, and highlighted the importance of studying the appropriate patient population (Lasagna et al., 1955). In addition, this group laid the foundation for conducting studies with controlled experimental designs including double-blind and placebo controls, randomized dosing, and characterization of dose-response relationships. Although many of the tools and methods developed at these laboratories are still in use, many have since been modified and the subjective effect measures and their applications have been expanded.

Experimental Procedures

The subjective effects of psychoactive drugs have been extensively studied using a wide array of structured and unstructured self-report questionnaires further described below. Because assessment of abuse potential has been a major research focus, these studies typically have used subjects with histories of illicit drug use (de Wit and Griffiths, 1991; Jasinski et al., 1984). However, a growing number of studies have been conducted in healthy volunteers without histories of drug abuse (cf. de Wit et al., 1989; Johanson, 1993; Zacny et al., 1994). The experimental designs used to evaluate subjective drug effects typically employ a number of control procedures. Drugs are usually administered under double-blind conditions such that the subject and study staff are unaware of the test drug/dose in order to avoid the introduction of bias into subjects' reports. Most studies will evaluate a range of test doses that include therapeutic doses, supratherapeutic doses, and placebo. When the safety of supratherapeutic doses is unknown, doses are often administered in ascending order. Otherwise, administration of doses in randomized or counterbalanced order is preferred in order to minimize carryover and other order/sequence effects on the study outcome. Novel drugs are frequently compared with an active control drug that produces a known profile of subjective effects. Drugs can be evaluated following acute and chronic administration to measure various pharmacodynamic properties including abuse potential, physical dependence capacity, and withdrawal symptoms (Jasinski, 1977).

Subjective effects questionnaires can be designed to measure responses on scales using a variety of formats including visual analogue, ordinal, binomial (e.g., true/false), and nominal. These scales can be used to rate the magnitude of global (e.g., strength, liking) and specific (e.g., dizziness, dry mouth) drug effects. A visual analogue scale is a continuous scale presented as a line with or without tick marks that give some indication of gradation. The subject places a mark along the line to indicate his/her response. Lines are usually anchored at the ends with labels such as "none" and "maximum possible" to provide reference points. Visual analogue scales are frequently unipolar (example: "Excited" rated from "Not At All" to "Extremely"), or they may be bipolar (exam-

ple: "Sedated/Alert," with "Extremely Sedated" at one end, "Normal" in the center, and "Extremely Alert" at the other end). Ordinal scales are comprised of ranked values that are assigned based on the magnitude of the effect. Although these scales can have any number of fixed values, a commonly used scale is the 5-point scale where 0 = not at all, 1 = a little, 2 = moderately, 3 = quite a bit, and 4 = extremely. Another frequently used format is the binomial scale that is usually in the form of yes/no or true/false responses. Nominal scales are categorical in nature, and the response choices are mutually exclusive. A commonly used nominal scale is the drug class questionnaire on which subjects identify the type of drug that they received from a list such as opiate, barbiturate, cocaine, etc.

Some subjective effect questionnaires have been standardized and used extensively, such as the Profile of Mood States (POMS; McNair et al., 1971) and certain subscales of the Addiction Research Center Inventory (ARCI; Haertzen, 1966). Other questionnaires have been designed by investigators to detect specific drug effects (e.g., unusual side effects) or to address particular experimental needs (e.g., extremely brief duration of action). Investigator-generated questionnaires have the advantage of capturing drug effects that might otherwise be missed by the sole use of standardized questionnaires that were originally devised for other purposes. However, the uniqueness of these questionnaires can make it difficult to directly compare findings across studies.

The questionnaires used in drug studies often contain elements designed to measure global drug effects, drug-related changes in mood, and/or specific physical symptoms. Some questionnaires are designed to detect effects in only one of these categories (e.g., the POMS), while others measure combinations of these elements (e.g., the Single Dose Questionnaire). Adjective rating scales have been used to measure effects in all of these categories with adjectives describing global drug effects (e.g., high, strength of drug effect), mood effects (e.g., anxious, depressed), and physical symptoms (e.g., itchy, nausea). Subjects rate lists of symptoms, presented as either visual analog, binomial, or ordinal scales, to describe how they feel in response to drug administration. Items can be used singly or grouped into subscales, such as in the POMS. The specific adjectives used in a given questionnaire may depend on the class of drugs being studied and their expected effects. In addition to measuring the acute effects of drug administration, these questionnaires can also be used to study the chronic effects of drug administration including withdrawal symptoms and tolerance.

The Single Dose Questionnaire was originally developed to quantify the subjective effects of opioids (Fraser et al., 1961). It has been used extensively and, although it has been modified over time, the results have been remarkably consistent over three decades (Preston and Jasinski, 1991). This questionnaire consists of four sections: a binomial question in which subjects are asked whether or not they feel a drug effect; a nominal question in which subjects are asked to indicate which among a list of drugs or drug classes is most similar to the test drug such as placebo, opiate, stimulant, marijuana, and sedative; a list of symptoms such as relaxed, sleepy, and drunken (checked yes or no); and a question asking subjects to rate how much they liked the drug effects using an ordinal scale.

The ARCI was developed empirically to assess a range of physical, emotive, and subjective effects of drugs from several pharmacologic classes (Haertzen, 1966). The ARCI is a true/false questionnaire that, in its entirety, contains more than 550 items that are divided into various subscales. The subscales were designed to detect the acute effects of specific drugs and/or drug classes [e.g., Morphine-Benzedrine Group (MBG) for opiates and amphetamines], specific mood states (e.g., tired, excited), the effects of chronic drug administration (e.g., Chronic Opiate Scale), and drug withdrawal (e.g., the Weak Opiate Withdrawal, the Alcohol Withdrawal Scale). Only a subset of the ARCI scales is typically ad-

ministered within a given study. The scales that are most frequently used in studies of acute drug effects are the MBG (an index of euphoria), the Pentobarbital-Chlorpromazine-Alcohol Group (PCAG; an index of apathetic sedation), and the Lysergic Acid Diethylamide Group (LSD; an index of dysphoria or somatic discomfort). The use of these three scales has remained standard in most studies of abuse potential.

There are several experimental factors related to the use of questionnaires that require consideration when conducting studies of subjective drug effects. It is critical that the subjects are able to comprehend and respond appropriately to questionnaires. If questionnaires are presented in written form, subjects must be able to read them. In all cases, the language used in the questionnaires must be familiar to the subjects. If questionnaires are presented by way of computer, subjects must be adequately trained to enter responses on the manipulanda. Subjects must also be familiarized with the relevant dimensions of the scales (e.g., unipolar versus bipolar visual analogue scales). Questionnaires selected for use should have demonstrated sensitivity to the effects of the test drug. Finally, the intervals of questionnaire presentation and the duration of assessment need to correspond with the expected time course of drug effects. Drug effects can be assessed either as they occur (e.g., "How much drug do you feel now?") or after they have dissipated (e.g., "How much drug did you feel yesterday?") with properly phrased questions.

Synopsis—Subject Effect Measures

Subjective effect measures have been used extensively to characterize the dynamic effects of a number of different drug classes and routes of administration. Table 2 lists the three major pharmacologic classes of abused drugs (sedatives, stimulants, and opiates) and their typical effects on various subjective effect instruments. Prototypic drugs of these three classes are distinguishable from placebo as indicated by increased ratings on scales mea-

TABLE 2. *Typical response profiles for sedatives, stimulants, and opiates on selected subjective effect measures*

	Global effects*	ARCI	POMS	Adjectives
Sedatives	Drug effects Liking High	PCAG	Fatigue Vigor ↓	Tired Sleepy Relaxed Drunk
Stimulants	Drug effect Liking High	MBG	Vigor Fatigue ↓	Stimulated Nervous Thirsty Jittery
Opiates	Drug effect Liking High	MBG PCAG		Nausea Itching Nodding Energetic

*Direction of effects is increased unless otherwise noted
ARCI, Addiction Research Center Inventory; MBG, Morphine–Benzedrine Group; PCAG, Pentobarbital–Chlorpromazine–Alcohol Group; POMS, Profile of Mood States.

suring "any drug effect." This measure is widely used as an index of strength of drug effect and does not specify the qualitative nature of the subjective experience. Similarly, drugs of abuse in different classes increase ratings of "liking" and "high." These scales are frequently used as indirect measures of reinforcing efficacy and are particularly useful in abuse liability studies.

Subjective effect measures with greater specificity than the global measures, such as the POMS, ARCI, and adjective checklists, can be used successfully to detect differences between different pharmacologic classes. For example, sedatives and stimulants produce opposite effects on the fatigue and vigor scales of the POMS. Other measures associated with abuse liability can also exhibit some specificity for drug classes. For instance, the MBG scale of the ARCI, an index of "euphoria," is sensitive to stimulant and opiate effects but is usually insensitive to the positive mood effects of sedatives (de Wit and Griffiths, 1991; Haertzen, 1966). Subjective effect measures can also be used to differentiate among drugs within the same pharmacologic class. For example, opioids with mixed activity at multiple opioid receptors produce increased ratings on distinct clusters of symptoms from adjective scales (Jasinski, 1977; Preston and Jasinski, 1991). Similarly, amphetamine and mazindol, both of which are classified as stimulants, produce different profiles of effects on the POMS, ARCI and adjective rating scales (Chait et al., 1986a). Drugs within the same pharmacologic class often differ in their degrees of abuse potential, which may be directly related to their subjective effects profiles. Among drugs with sedative effects, for example, the novel nonbenzodiazepine anxiolytic tandospirone produces psychomotor impairment and subjective effects that are similar in overall magnitude to alprazolam, a frequently abused benzodiazepine, but is not rated as being liked and has qualitatively different subjective effects (Evans et al., 1994). Unlike typical benzodiazepines, tandospirone is not self-administered by primates (Sannerud et al., 1993) and likely has a low potential for abuse. An illustrative list of the major drug classes with several examples are shown in Table 3 along with estimates of the degree to which they produced subjective effect associated with abuse liability.

RELATIONSHIPS BETWEEN DIRECT MEASURES OF DRUG REINFORCEMENT AND MEASURES OF INTEROCEPTIVE DRUG STIMULI

Table 3 summarizes information for representative drugs from studies assessing rein-

TABLE 3. *Relationships between indirect and direct measures of reinforcing efficacy in nonhuman subjects*

	Preclinical: shares stimulus effects w/prototype[c]	Clinical: positive mood effects (liking, ARCI-MBG)	Preclinical: laboratory self-administration	Preclinical[a]: conditioned place preference	Clinical: epidemiologic evidence of abuse	Federal regulatory[b] status
Sedatives						
Barbiturates[c]						
Barbiturates	+++ 1	+++ 15,16	+++ 26,27	A 44	+++	P/C-II & P/C-III
Benzodiazepines	++ 1	++ 15,16	++ 26,27	P 45,46,47,48	++	P/C-IV
Meprobamate	+++ 2	+++ 16	+ 28	P 45	+	P/C-IV
Methocarbamol	- 3	++ 16	- 2	NF	-	P/NC
Antihistamines	- 4	++ 16	+/- 29,30	NF	-	OTC
Stimulants						
Amphetamine[c]						
Cocaine	+++ 1	+++ 16	+++ 31,32,33,34	P 45,49	+++	P/C-II
Amphetamine	+++ 1	+++ 15	+++ 33,34	P 48, 50,51,52,53	+++	P/C-II
Methylphenidate	+++ 5	++ 17	+++ 33,34	P 53,54	++	P/C-II
Nicotine	- 4	++ 15	++ 35,36	P 53,54/A 55	++	P/NC & OTC
Caffeine	+ 6,7	+/- 18	+/- 37	P 50/A 50	+/-	OTC
Phenylpropanolamine	+ 4	+/- 19,20	+/- 38	NF	-	OTC
Mazindol	++ 4	- 19	+/- 31	NF	-	P/C-IV
Opiates						
Morphine[c]						
Morphine/heroin/ hydromorphone	+++ 1	+++ 15,21,22	+++ 39	P 47,48,50,56,57,58	+++	C-I & P/C-II
Codeine	+++ 1	+++ 22	+++ 40	NF	++	P/C-II
Propoxyphene	+++ 8	+++ 22	+++ 41	NF	++	P/C-II
Buprenorphine	+++ 9	+++ 15,21	+++ 39	P 49,58	++	P/C-V
Pentazocine	+++ 1	++ 15,21	+/- 39,41	P 58	+	P/C-IV
Butorphanol	+++ 1	++ 21	++ 39	NF	-	P/NC
Nalbuphine	+/- 1,8	+ 21	++ 39	P 58	-	P/NC
Dextromethorphan	- 8	- 23	+++ 41	NF	-	OTC
Hallucinogens						
No prototype[c]						
Marijuana/THC	+ 10	+++ 15	+/- 41,42	P 59	+++	C-I
Phencyclidine	+ 11,12	+/- 24	+ 43	P 47/A 47,56,60	++	C-I
LSD	+ 13,14	+/- 25	- 41	NF	+	C-I

TABLE 3. *Continued.*

[a] P, Conditioned Place Preference; A, Conditioned Place Aversion.

[b] Information on regulatory status is from the Physicians Desk Reference-49th edition (1995). P, available by prescription only; C-I,II,III,IV, or V, scheduling under the Controlled Substances Act; OTC, available over the counter; NF, not found in literature.

[c] Indicates prototype training drug for generalization testing. No prototype was selected for the hallucinogens because of pharmacological differences among drugs in this category. Ratings of (+) on this category indicate that the drug serves as a discriminative stimulus.

This compilation of literature citations is illustrative and is not exhaustive: (1) Young, 1991; (2) Ator and Griffiths, 1989b; (3) Sannerud et al., 1991; (4) Evans and Johanson, 1987; (5) Druhan et al., 1991; (6) Kuhn et al., 1974; (7) Holloway et al., 1985; (8) Holtzman, 1983; (9) Young et al., 1984; (10) Balster and Prescott, 1992; (11) Holtzman, 1980; (12) Willetts and Balster, 1988; (13) Nielsen, 1985; (14) Winter and Rabin, 1988; (15) Jasinski et al., 1984; (16) de Wit and Griffiths, 1991; (17) Martin et al., 1971; (18) Griffiths and Mumford, 1995; (19) Chait et al., 1987; (20) Chait et al., 1988b; (21) Preston and Jasinski, 1991; (22) Jasinski, 1977; (23) Jasinski et al., 1971; (24) Peterson and Stillman, 1978; (25) Jaffe, 1985; (26) Griffiths et al.,1981; (27) Griffiths et al.,1991; (28) Sannerud et al., 1995; (29) Beardsley and Balster, 1992; (30) Harris et al., 1968; (31) Wilson et al.,1971; (32) Bergman et al., 1989; (33) Risner and Jones, 1976; (34) Risner and Jones, 1975; (35) Goldberg et al., 1981; (36) Sannerud et al., 1994; (37) Griffiths and Woodson, 1988; (38) Lamb et al.,1987; (39) Woods et al.,1982; (40) Hoffmeister and Schlechting, 1972; (41) Johanson and Balster, 1978; (42) Harris et al ., 1974; (43) Balster et al., 1973; (44) Wilkes and File, 1988; (45) Spyraki et al., 1985; (46) Spyraki and Fibiger, 1988; (47) Acquas et al., 1989; (48) Spyraki et al., 1988; (49) Brown et al., 1991; (50) Carboni et al., 1989; (51) Bowling and Bardo, 1994; (52) Brockwell et al., 1991; (53) Clarke and Fibiger, 1987; (54) Martin-Iverson et al.,1985; (55) Jorenby et al., 1990; (56) Barr et al., 1985; (57) Marglin et al., 1989; (58) Shippenberg and Herz, 1986; (59) Lepore et al., 1995; (60) Iwato, 1986.

forcing efficacy and interoceptive drug stimuli, including drug discrimination, subjective effects, self-administration, conditioned place preference, and epidemiology. In addition, the current federal regulatory status for each drug is shown for comparison. Within each pharmacologic class, both the degree of discriminative stimulus similarity to the prototype and capacity to produce positive mood effects can range widely. In general, there is good correspondence between the findings of drug discrimination and subjective effect studies in rating the degree of similarity between test and prototypic drugs. For example, among the opioid agonist/antagonist compounds, those with subjective effect profiles most distinct from that of prototypic mu agonists are also most readily differentiated from a mu agonist training drug in discrimination studies (Preston and Bigelow, 1991; Preston et al., 1989, 1994).

The degree of a drug's similarity to the prototype, as determined by these indirect measures, can be used to predict relative abuse potential. Indeed, using the above example, those agonist/antagonists that are most similar to morphine in subjective effect and discrimination studies are also the most likely to be self-administered, can produce a conditioned place preference, and are used illicitly (Jasinski, 1977; Young et al., 1983, 1984). As shown in Table 3, there is good correspondence between the indirect and direct measures of reinforcing efficacy for sedatives, stimulants, and opiates, and the degree of abuse liability generally is reflected in the regulatory control of these compounds. Thus, discriminative stimulus effects and subjective effect measures can be useful in evaluating the dependence and abuse potential of new drugs by comparing their profiles of effects to those produced by known drugs of abuse, and these relationships hold across the major classes of abused drugs.

One major exception to the agreement among experimental models of reinforcement and epidemiologic data is the hallucinogenic drugs. Drugs in the hallucinogen class have diverse pharmacologic profiles, and their reinforcing effects have not been studied as extensively as the other classes of abused drugs. Hallucinogens, including phencyclidine, THC, and LSD, can function as discriminative stimuli in animals (Glennon, 1991; Jarbe and Mathis, 1991). Results of conditioned place preference studies of these hallucinogenic agents, however, are mixed; THC produces a preference (Lepore et al., 1995), PCP can produce a preference or aversion (Acquas et al., 1989; Barr et al., 1985; Marglin et al., 1989), and LSD has not been evaluated. It has been a general finding that many of these drugs do not maintain self-administration in animals (Johanson and Balster, 1978); however, hallucinogens are known to be abused by humans. Some of these discrepancies may be due to experimental variables (e.g., dose, route of administration, drug solubility, drug histories) rather than true species differences. Further work is needed to elucidate the mechanisms of action of this diverse group of drugs and to resolve the discrepancies between the preclinical and clinical findings.

ASSESSMENT OF ABUSE POTENTIAL

Abuse potential is considered the likelihood that a drug will be used illicitly for nonmedical purposes. The assessment of the abuse potential of a new drug has historically been studied by comparing the test drug to a known drug whose effects have been previously characterized. Drugs that produce euphoria are considered more likely to be abused than drugs that do not produce euphoria. For most classes of abused drugs, a prototypic compound with high abuse liability has been identified as the standard comparison in abuse liability testing. Examples of prototypic agents include the opiate morphine, the stimulant amphetamine, and the sedative pentobarbital. The standard laboratory method for assessing abuse liability in animals is the drug self-administration paradigm, and, to a lesser extent, the conditioned place paradigm. However, drug discrimination is also well suited for assessing abuse liability because this paradigm provides information on the similarity of a test drug to a prototypic drug of abuse

(Bigelow and Preston, 1989; Overton, 1987; Young, 1991). Subjects are usually trained to discriminate the prototype drug from placebo, and the extent to which the test drug substitutes for the prototype serves as an estimate of their similarity.

Subjective effect measures have been the primary method used for assessing abuse liability in human subjects. The profile of effects of a test drug on multiple subjective effect measures are compared with that of a prototype drug. Subjective effect measures of global drug effects, such as Drug Liking, High, and Good Effects, are elevated by known drugs of abuse. A review of abuse liability studies conducted at the Addiction Research Center revealed that scores for Drug Liking, rated as a subscale of the Single Dose Questionnaire, were significantly elevated by a wide range of drugs including opioids, cocaine, benzodiazepines, barbiturates, Δ^9-tetrahydrocannabinol, and nicotine (Jasinski et al., 1984). The MBG subscale of the Addiction Research Center Inventory is often used as an indirect measure of euphoria and abuse liability. Scores on this scale are typically elevated following administration of opioids and stimulants (Haertzen, 1966; Jasinski and Preston, 1986, 1987). When a great deal is known about the expected effects and abuse liability of a drug or drug class, other subjective effect measures that are sensitive to that drug, such as adjective rating scales constructed to assess a specific array of psychoactive effects, may serve as an indirect index of reinforcing efficacy and/or abuse liability. On the other hand, data generated from subjective effects studies can be more difficult to interpret than self-administration and drug discrimination studies because they usually involve integration of information across multiple dependent variables. Sometimes the effects of drugs on different questionnaires can appear to be inconsistent, such that scores on both desirable and undesirable effects are increased. For example, a drug might increase the MBG scale, while simultaneously producing increases on the LSD scale. The LSD scale is an index of dysphoric effects; scores on this measure are typically inversely related to abuse liability. This mixed profile could result from a test drug that produces positive mood effects, but also produces significant unpleasant side effects that might ultimately mitigate its misuse. In this regard, however, subjective effect measures can provide more information about other factors that are related to abuse potential than either the self-administration or drug discrimination studies. These include unpleasant side effects or dysphoria, time course (drug onset, time to maximal or peak effect, and duration of drug effect), and characterization of the qualitative differences between the prototype and test drug.

MEDICATIONS DEVELOPMENT

One of the new directions in which these measures of interoceptive drug stimulus effects will be useful is in the development of pharmacotherapies for substance abuse. Various pharmacologic approaches have been taken to medications development and are commonly aimed at reducing the reinforcing efficacy of the abused drug. The conditioned place preference paradigm, drug discrimination, and subjective effects assessment can all be used to screen potential pharmacotherapies. The conditioned place paradigm may be used to measure the conditioned response to an abused drug and any change in that response produced by pretreatment with a targeted pharmacotherapy. Changes could include a reduction of strength of a conditioned place preference (e.g., shifting the dose response curve) or changing the response from a preference to an aversion. Using the drug discrimination paradigm, subjects can be trained to discriminate the targeted abused drug from placebo, and medications can be screened to assess the ability of the treatment to alter the stimulus effects of the abused drug. Subjective effect measures can also be used to assess therapeutically relevant pharmacologic interactions. Subjective effect measures can be collected following administration of the illicit drug in the presence and absence of the test medication. The ability of the treatment agent to alter or block the subjective effects that are related to the abuse potential of the illicit drug can be assessed. Both drug discrimination and subjective effect studies can be conducted under acute and chronic dosing conditions and can provide additional safety information about drug interactions.

Two mechanisms by which the reinforcing efficacy of abused drugs may be decreased are (1) to administer chronically agonists that produce cross-tolerance or (2) to administer antagonists that directly block through competitive or noncompetitive mechanisms. The drug discrimination procedure can be readily used to assess both cross-tolerance and antagonist activity. This type of pharmacologic interaction would shift the discrimination generalization curve to the right or completely block the discriminative stimulus effects, resulting in more frequent, or even exclusive, identifications as placebo. Similarly, in subjective effect studies, antagonist treatment or cross-tolerance would reduce drug-induced increases on measures of positive mood/euphoria. Methadone, a long-acting opioid agonist that produces cross-tolerance, and naltrexone, a long-acting opioid antagonist, are prototypic examples of treatment agents that have been assessed using these methods (Martin et al., 1973; McCaul et al., 1983; Overton and Batta, 1979; Preston et al., 1990; Young et al., 1991).

Several other important considerations in medication development can be addressed using these procedures. One desirable characteristic of a pharmacotherapy is low abuse liability. As described above, drug discrimination and subjective effect studies can be used to screen potential medications to determine the extent to which the stimulus profile of the test medication is similar to the abused drug. This information could be used to prevent the development of medications with unacceptably high abuse potential or to establish procedures for controlling the availability of efficacious medications with some abuse potential (e.g., methadone, LAAM). In addition, it is important to rule out the possibility that a treatment medication would interact in an additive or synergistic fashion, thus potentiating

the effects of the abused drug. Finally, these measures can also be used in humans to identify adverse interactions between the medication and abused drug that could be countertherapeutic (e.g., dysphoria, sedation) or that could make a medication unsafe (e.g., psychological impairment, palpitations). In summary, these techniques can be widely applied to identify medications of therapeutic interest prior to testing in costly and time-consuming clinical trials.

FUTURE DIRECTIONS

One important application for which measures of interoceptive drug stimulus effects may prove useful is to further elucidate the neural mechanisms of drug action as they relate to abuse potential, drug dependence, and withdrawal. This may be accomplished through coupling these behavioral paradigms in animals and humans with advanced neuroscience techniques that can be used in vivo. Most recently, scientists have combined in vivo microdialysis with the self-administration paradigm in order to assess the neurochemical response before, during, and after drug administration (Hemby et al., 1995; Parsons et al., 1995). Similarly, studies have combined electrophysiologic methods with the self-administration paradigm to evaluate the response of individual neurons during drug self-administration behavior (Carelli et al., 1993; Chang et al., 1994). These studies are technically complex and, to date, there is a limited number of published studies; nevertheless, they have contributed importantly to the identification of the neuroanatomic and neurochemical substrates that underlie drug action. To our knowledge, these methods have not been used in combination with the drug discrimination nor the conditioned place preference paradigms.

One area where advanced neuroscience techniques have already been coupled with measures of interoceptive drug stimulus effects is with human neuroimaging. Neuroimaging technology, including positron emission tomography (PET), single-photon emission computer tomography (SPECT), and functional magnetic resonance imaging (MRI), has advanced phenomenally in the last decade. These methods can be used to measure global changes in brain activity (e.g., cerebral blood flow or glucose metabolism) or to measure the binding of selective ligands (e.g., receptor or transporter occupancy). These techniques have been applied to the study of drugs of abuse in humans and have evaluated the central response to acute drug administration (de Wit et al., 1990; London et al., 1990) and the response to chronic drug administration and withdrawal (van Dyck et al., 1994; Volkow et al., 1992; Volkow et al., 1993). By concurrently using subjective effect measures during neuroimaging, it is possible to correlate neurophysiologic changes to changes in subjective states. Although this is a relatively new area of investigation, the limited number of studies completed have already had an important impact on the field of drug abuse.

One final application that will undoubtedly aid in our understanding of neural mechanisms of drug action will be to utilize these behavioral paradigms in combination with advanced molecular neurobiology. Previous studies have employed various behavioral paradigms to assess functional differences in animals selectively bred for neuroanatomic differences. For example, self-administration of opioid compounds has been evaluated in mice selectively bred to have significantly increased or decreased densities of mu opioid receptors in the brain (Elmer et al., 1995). The latest molecular advances have enabled researchers to delete genes in embryonic cells and, thus, to selectively breed "knockout" strains that do not express a specific physiologic feature (e.g., a receptor or enzyme) (Aguzzi et al., 1994; Robbins, 1993). It will be valuable to utilize these behavioral paradigms to study the functional consequences of these selective gene deletions and to identify further the neural mechanisms of drug stimuli. It is certain that continued efforts and technologic advances in these areas of neuroscience will advance our understanding of the relationship between interoceptive drug stimuli and their neural substrates.

SUMMARY

- Abused drugs come from many pharmacologic classes but their primary psychoactive effects generally fall within one of four categories: sedatives, stimulants, opiates, and hallucinogens.
- The most common indirect measures of reinforcing efficacy are conditioned place preference, drug discrimination, and subjective effect measures.
- Abused drugs share some similar effects; they are self-administered, can produce a conditioned place preference, can be discriminated from placebo, and produce increases of global measures of subjective effects, such as "high" and "liking."
- Drugs within the same pharmacologic classes or drugs that produce similar pharmacodynamic effects are generally discriminated as being similar by nonhuman and human subjects and produce similar profiles of subjective effects in humans.
- Drug discrimination and subjective effect measures can also be used to differentiate among abused drugs.
- Nonhuman and human subjects can be trained to discriminate reliably among drugs of various pharmacologic classes.
- Drugs with different pharmacodynamic profiles do not generalize to one another in drug discrimination.
- Drugs from different categories can produce some shared subjective effects, but can be differentiated by drug-specific measures.
- There is a high concordance between the ability of a drug to produce a conditioned place preference, to produce discriminative stimulus effects that are similar to a prototype abused drug in humans and nonhumans, and its ability to produce positive subjective effects in humans.

REFERENCES

Acquas, E., Carboni, E., Leone, P. and Di Chiara, G. (1989) SCH 23390 blocks drug-conditioned place-preference and place-aversion: anhedonia (lack of reward) or apathy (lack of motivation) after dopamine-receptor blockade. *Psychopharmacology* 99: 151–155.

Aguzzi, A., Brandner, S., Sure, U., Ruedi, D., Isenmann, S. (1994) Transgenic and knock-out mice: models of neurological disease. *Brain Pathol.* 4: 3–20.

Ator, N.A. and Griffiths, R.R. (1989a) Differential generalization to pentobarbital in rats trained to discriminate lorazepam, chlordiazepoxide, diazepam or triazolam. *Psychopharmacology* 98: 20–30.

Ator, N.A. and Griffiths, R.R. (1989b) Asymmetrical cross-generalization in drug discrimination with lorazepam and pentobarbital training conditions. *Drug Dev. Res.* 16: 355–364.

Balster, R.L., Johanson, C.E., Harris, R.T. and Schuster, C.R. (1973) Phencyclidine self-administration in the rhesus monkey. *Pharmacol. Biochem. Behav.* 1: 167–173.

Balster, R.L. and Prescott, W.R. (1992) Δ⁹-Tetrahydrocannabinol discrimination in rats as a model for cannabis intoxication. *Neurosci. Biobehav. Rev.* 16: 55–62.

Bardo, M.T., Rowlett, J.K. and Harris M.J. (1995) Conditioned place preference using opiate and stimulant drugs: a meta-analysis. *Neurosci. Biobehav. Rev.* 19: 39–51.

Barr, G.A., Paredes, W. and Bridger, W.H. (1985) Place conditioning with morphine and phencyclidine: dose dependent effects. *Life Sci.* 36: 363–368.

Beardsley, P.M. and Balster, R.L. (1992) The intravenous self-administration of antihistamines by rhesus monkeys. *Drug Alcohol Depend.* 30: 117–126.

Bergman, J., Madras, B.K., Johnson, S.E. and Spealman, R.D. (1989) Effects of cocaine and related drugs in nonhuman primates. III. Self-administration by squirrel monkeys. *J. Pharmacol. Exp. Ther.* 251: 150–155.

Bickel, W.K., Bigelow, G.E., Preston, K.L. and Liebson, I.A. (1989) Opioid drug discrimination in humans: stability, specificity, and relation to self-reported drug effect. *J. Pharmacol. Exp. Ther.* 251: 1053–1063.

Bickel, W.K., Oliveto, A.H., Kamien, J.B., Higgins, S.T. and Hughes, J.R. (1993) A novel-response procedure enhances the selectivity and sensitivity of a triazolam discrimination in humans. *J. Pharmacol. Exp. Ther.* 264: 360–367.

Bigelow, G.E. and Preston, K.L. (1989) Drug discrimination: methods for drug characterization and classification. In: Fischman, M.W. and Mello, N.K.(eds.) *Testing for abuse liability of drugs in humans*. NIDA Research Monograph No. 92. Washington, DC: U.S. Government Printing Office, pp. 101–102.

Bowling, S.L. and Bardo, M.T. (1994) Locomotor and rewarding effects of amphetamine in enriched, social, and isolate reared rat. *Pharmacol. Biochem. Behav.* 48: 459–464.

Brockwell, N.T., Eikelboom, R. and Beninger, R.J. (1991) Caffeine-induced place and taste conditioning: production of dose-dependent preference and aversion. *Pharmacol. Biochem. Behav.* 38: 513–517.

Brown, E.E., Finlay, J.M., Wong, J.T.F., Damsma, G. and Fibiger, H.C. (1991) Behavioral and neurochemical interactions between cocaine and buprenorphine: implications for the pharmacotherapy of cocaine abuse. *J. Pharmacol. Exp. Ther.* 256: 119–126.

Carboni, E., Acquas, E., Lione, P. and Di Chiara, G. (1989) 5HT3 receptor antagonists block morphine- and nicotine-but not amphetamine-induced reward. *Psychopharmacology* 97: 175–178.

Carelli, R.M., King, V.C., Hampson, R.E. and Deadwyler, S.A. (1993) Firing patterns of nucleus accumbens neurons during cocaine self-administration. *Brain Res.* 626: 14–22.

Chait, L.D., Evans, S.M., Grant, K.A., Kamien, J.B., Johanson, C-E. and Schuster, C.R. (1988a) The discriminative stimulus and subjective effects of smoked marijuana in humans. *Psychopharmacology* 94: 206–212.

Chait, L.D. and Johanson, C-E. (1988) Discriminative stimulus effects of caffeine and benzphetamine in amphetamine-trained volunteers. *Psychopharmacology* 96: 302–308.

Chait, L.D., Uhlenhuth, E.H. and Johanson, C-E. (1984) An experimental paradigm for studying the discriminative stimulus properties of drugs in humans. *Psychopharmacology* 82: 272–274.

Chait, L.D., Uhlenhuth, E.H. and Johanson, C-E. (1985) The discriminative stimulus and subjective effects of d-amphetamine in humans. *Psychopharmacology* 86: 307–312.

Chait, L.D., Uhlenhuth, E.H. and Johanson, C-E. (1986a) The discriminative stimulus and subjective effects of phenylpropanolamine, mazindol and d-amphetamine in humans. *Pharmacol. Biochem. Behav.* 24: 1665–1672.

Chait, L.D., Uhlenhuth, E.H. and Johanson, C-E. (1986b) The discriminative stimulus and subjective effects of d-amphetamine, phenmetrazine and fenfluramine in humans. *Psychopharmacology* 89: 301–306.

Chait, L.D., Uhlenhuth, E.H. and Johanson, C-E. (1987) Reinforcing and subjective effects of several anorectics in normal human volunteers. *J. Pharmacol. Exp. Ther.* 242: 777–783.

Chait, L.D., Uhlenhuth, E.H. and Johanson, C-E. (1988b) Phenylpropanolamine: reinforcing and subjective effects in normal human volunteers. *Psychopharmacology* 96: 212–217.

Chang, J.Y., Sawyer, S.F., Lee, R.S. and Woodward, D.J. (1994) Electrophysiological and pharmacological evidence for the role of the nucleus accumbens in cocaine self-administration in freely moving rats. *J. Neurosci.* 14: 1224–1244.

Clarke, P.B.S. and Fibiger, H.C. (1987) Apparent absence of nicotine-induced conditioned place preference in rats. *Psychopharmacology* 92: 84–88.

Colpaert, F.C. (1988) Intrinsic activity and discriminative effects of drugs. In: Colpaert, F.C. and Balster, R.L. (eds.) *Psychopharmacology series, transduction mechanisms of drug stimuli*. Berlin, Heidelberg: Springer-Verlag, pp. 154–159.

Colpaert, F.C., Niemegeers, C.J.E. and Janssen, P.A.J. (1980) Factors regulating drug cue sensitivity: limits of discriminability and the role of progressively decreasing training dose in fentanyl-saline discrimination. *J. Pharmacol. Exp. Ther.* 212: 474–480.

de la Garza, R. and Johanson, C-E. (1983) The discriminative stimulus properties of cocaine in the rhesus monkey. *Pharmacol. Biochem. Behav.* 19: 145–148.

de la Garza, R. and Johanson, C-E. (1985) Discriminative stimulus properties of cocaine in pigeons. *Psychopharmacology* 85: 23–30.

DeVry, J. and Slangen, J.L. (1986) Effects of chlordiazepoxide training dose on the mixed agonist-antagonist properties of benzodiazepine receptor antagonist Ro15-1788, in a drug discrimination procedure. *Psychopharmacology* 88: 177–183.

de Wit, H. and Griffiths, R.R. (1991) Testing the abuse liability of anxiolytic and hypnotic drugs in humans. *Drug Alcohol Depend.* 28 (1): 83–111.

de Wit, H., Metz, J., Wagner, N. and Cooper M. (1990) Behavioral and subjective effects of ethanol: relationship to cerebral metabolism using PET. *Alcoholism Clin. Exp. Res.* 14: 482–489.

de Wit, H., Pierri, J. and Johanson, C-E. (1989) Reinforcing and subjective effects of diazepam in nondrug-abusing volunteers. *Pharmacol. Biochem. Behav.* 33: 205–213.

Druhan, J.P., Fibiger H.C. and Phillips, A.G. (1991) Influence of some drugs of abuse on the discriminative stimulus properties of amphetamine. *Behav. Pharmacol.* 2: 391–403.

Dykstra, L.A., Doty, P., Johnson, A.B. and Picker, M.J. (1992) Discriminative stimulus properties of cocaine, alone and in combination with buprenorphine, morphine and naltrexone. *Drug Alcohol Depend.* 30: 227–234.

Elmer, G.I., Pieper, J.O., Goldberg, S.R., George, F.R. (1995) Opioid operant self-administration, analgesia, stimulation and respiratory depression in mu-deficient mice. *Psychopharmacology* 117: 23–31.

Emmett-Oglesby, M.W., Wurst, M. and Lal, H. (1983) Discriminative stimulus properties of a small dose of cocaine. *Neuropharmacology* 22: 97–101.

Evans, S.M. and Johanson, C-E. (1987) Amphetamine-like effects of anorectics and related compounds in pigeons. *J. Pharmacol. Exp. Ther.* 241: 817–825.

Evans, S.M. and Johanson, C-E. (1989) Discriminative stimulus properties of midazolam in the pigeon. *J. Pharmacol. Exp. Ther.* 248: 29–38.

Evans, S.M., Troisi, J.R. and Griffiths, R.R. (1994) Tandospirone and alprazolam: comparison of behavioral effects and abuse liability in humans. *J. Pharmacol. Exp. Ther.* 271: 683–694.

France, C.P., Jacobson, A.E. and Woods, J.H. (1984) Discriminative stimulus effects of reversible and irreversible opiate agonists: morphine, oxymorphazone and buprenorphine. *J. Pharmacol. Exp. Ther.* 230: 652–657.

Fraser, H.F., Van Horn, G.D., Martin, W.R., Wolbach, A.B. and Isbell, H. (1961) Methods for evaluating addiction liability. (A) "Attitude" of opiate addicts toward opiate-like drugs, (B) A short-term "direct" addiction test. *J. Pharmacol. Exp. Ther.* 133: 371–387.

Glennon, R.A. (1991) Discriminative stimulus properties of hallucinogens and related designer drugs. In: Glennon, R.A., Jarbe, T.U.C. and Frankenheim, J. (eds.) *Drug discrimination: applications to drug abuse research.* NIDA Research Monograph No. 116. Washington, DC: U.S. Government Printing Office, pp. 25–44.

Goldberg, S.R., Spealman, R.D. and Goldberg, D.M. (1981) Persistent behavior at high rates maintained by intravenous nicotine. *Science* 214: 573–575.

Griffiths, R.R., Evans, S.M., Heishman, S.J., Preston, K.L., Sannerud, C.A., Wolf, B. and Woodson, P.P. (1990) Low-dose caffeine discrimination in humans. *J. Pharmacol. Exp. Ther.* 252: 970–978.

Griffiths, R.R., Lamb, R.J., Sannerud, C.A., Ator, N.A. and Brady, J.V. (1991) Self-injection of barbiturates, benzodiazepines and other sedative-anxiolytics in baboons. *Psychopharmacology* 103: 154–161.

Griffiths, R.R., Lukas, S.E., Bradford, L.D., Brady, J.V. and Snell, J.D. (1981) Self-injection of barbiturates and benzodiazepines in baboons. *Psychopharmacology* 75: 101–109.

Griffiths, R.R. and Mumford, G.K. (1995) Caffeine—a drug of abuse? . In: Bloom F.E. and Kupfer D. J. (eds.) *Psychopharmacology: the fourth generation of progress.* New York: Raven Press, pp. 1699–1713.

Griffiths R.R. and Woodson P.P. (1988) Reinforcing properties of caffeine: studies in humans and laboratory animals. *Pharmacol. Biochem. Behav.* 29: 419–427.

Haertzen, C.A. (1966) Development of scales based on patterns of drug effects, using the Addiction Research Center Inventory (ARCI). *Psychol. Rep.* 18: 163–194.

Harris, R.T., Claghorn, J.L. and Schoolar, J.C. (1968) Self administration of minor tranquilizers as a function of conditioning. *Psychopharmacologia* 313: 81–88.

Harris, R.T., Waters, W. and McLendon, D. (1974) Evaluation of reinforcing capability of delta-9-tetrahydrocannabinol in rhesus monkeys. *Psychopharmacologia* 37: 23–29.

Heishman, S.J. and Henningfield, J.E. (1991) Discriminative stimulus effects of d-amphetamine, methylphenidate, and diazepam in humans. *Psychopharmacology* 103: 436–442.

Hemby, S.E., Martin, T.J., Dworkin, S.I. and Smith J.E. (1995) The effects of intravenous heroin administration on extracellular nucleus accumbens dopamine concentrations as determined by in vivo microdialysis. *J. Pharmacol. Exp. Ther.* 273: 591–598.

Herling, S., Coale, E.H., Valentino, R.J., Hein, D.W. and Woods, J.H. (1980) Narcotic discrimination in pigeons. *J. Pharmacol. Exp. Ther.* 214: 139–146.

Hoffmeister, F. and Schlechting, U.U. (1972) Reinforcing properties of some opiates and opioids in rhesus monkeys with histories of cocaine and codeine self-administration. *Psychopharmacologia* 23: 55–74.

Holloway, F.A., Michaelis, R.C. and Huerta, P.L. (1985) Caffeine-phenylethylamine combinations mimic the amphetamine discriminative cue. *Life Sci.* 36: 723–730.

Holtzman, S.G. (1980) Phencyclidine-like discriminative effects of opioids in the rat. *J. Pharmacol. Exp. Ther.* 214: 614–619.

Holtzman, S.G. (1983) Discriminative stimulus properties of opioid agonists and antagonists. In: Cooper, S.J. (ed.) *Theory in psychopharmacology*, vol. 2. London: Academic Press, pp. 2–45.

Iwato, E.T. (1986) Place-aversion conditioned by phencyclidine in rats: development of tolerance and pharmacologic antagonism. *Alcohol Drug Res.* 6: 265–276.

Jaffe, J.H. (1985) Drug addiction and drug abuse. In: Gilman, A.G., Goodman, L.S., Rall, T.W., and Murad, F. (eds.) *The pharmacological basis of therapeutics,* 7th ed. New York: Macmillan, pp. 532–581.

Jarbe, T.U.C. (1978) Discriminative effects of morphine in the pigeon. Pharmacol. Biochem. Behav. 9: 411–416.

Jarbe T.U.C. and Mathis D.A. (1991) Discriminative stimulus functions of cannabinoids/cannabimimetics. In: Glennon, R.A., Jarbe, T.U.C. and Frankenheim, J. (eds.) *Drug discrimination: applications to drug abuse research.* NIDA Research Monograph No. 116. Washington, DC: U.S. Government Printing Office, pp. 75–100.

Jasinski, D.R. (1977) Assessment of the abuse potential of morphine-like drugs (methods used in man). In: Martin, W.R. (ed.) *Drug addiction I*, vol. 45. Heidelberg: Springer-Verlag, pp. 197–258.

Jasinski, D.R., Johnson, R.E. and Henningfield, J.E. (1984) Abuse liability assessment in human subjects. *Trends Pharmacol. Sci.* 5: 196–200.

Jasinski, D.R., Martin, W.R. and Mansky, P.A. (1971) Progress report on the assessment of the antagonists nalbuphine and GPA-2087 for abuse potential and studies of the effects of dextromethorphan in man. In: *Proceedings of the 33rd Annual Meeting of the Committee of Problems of Drug Dependence.* Washington, DC: National Research Council, U.S. Government Printing Office, pp. 143–178.

Jasinski, D.R. and Preston, K.L. (1986) Evaluation of mixtures of morphine and d-amphetamine for subjective and physiological effects. *Drug Alcohol Depend.* 17: 1–13.

Jasinski, D.R. and Preston, K.L. (1987) A comparative assay of nefopam, morphine and d-amphetamine. *Psychopharmacology* 91: 273–278.

Johanson, C-E. (1991a) Discriminative stimulus effects of diazepam in humans. *J. Pharmacol. Exp. Ther.* 257: 634–643.

Johanson, C-E. (1991b) Further studies on the discriminative stimulus effects of diazepam in humans. *Behav. Pharmacol.* 2: 357–367.

Johanson, C-E. (1993) Discriminative stimulus effects of buspirone in humans. *Exp. Clin. Psychopharmacol.* 1: 173–187.

Johanson, C-E. and Balster, R.L. (1978) A summary of results of a drug self-administration study using substitution procedures in rhesus monkeys. *Bull. Narcotics* 30: 43–54.

Jorenby, D.E., Steinpreis, R.E., Sherman, J.E. and Baker, T.B. (1990) Aversion instead of preference learning indicated by nicotine place preference in rats. *Psychopharmacology* 101: 533–538.

Kallman, W.M., Kallman, M.J., Harry, G.J., Woodson, P.P. and Rosecrans, J.A. (1982) Nicotine as a discriminative stimulus in human subjects. In: Colpaert, F. C. and Slangen, J. L. (eds.) *Drug discrimination: applications in CNS pharmacology.* Amsterdam: Elsevier Biomedical Press, pp. 211–218.

Kamien, J.B., Bickel, W.K., Hughes, J.R., Higgins, S.T. and Smith, B.J. (1993) Drug discrimination by humans compared to non-humans. *Psychopharmacology* 111: 259–270.

Kilbey, M.M. and Ellinwood, E.H. (1979) Discriminative stimulus properties of psychomotor stimulants in the cat. *Psychopharmacology* 63: 151–153.

Kleven, M.S., Anthony, E.W. and Woolverton, W.L. (1990) Pharmacological characterization of the discriminative stimulus effects of cocaine in rhesus monkeys. *J. Pharmacol. Exp. Ther.* 254: 312–317.

Kuhn, D.M., Appel, J.B. and Greenberg, I. (1974) An analysis of some discriminative properties of d-amphetamine. *Psychopharmacologia* (Berl) 39: 57–66.

Lamb, R.J. and Henningfield, J.E. (1994) Human d-amphetamine drug discrimination: methamphetamine and hydromorphone. *J. Exp. Anal. Behav.* 61: 169–180.

Lamb, R.J., Sannerud, C.A. and Griffiths, R.R. (1987) An examination of the intravenous self-administration of phenylpropanolamine using a cocaine substitution procedure in the baboon. *Pharmacol. Biochem. Behav.* 28: 389–392.

Lasagna, L., von Felsinger, J.M. and Beecher, H.K. (1955) Drug-induced mood changes in man. 1. Observations on healthy subjects, chronically ill patients, and "post-addicts." *JAMA* 157: 1006–1020.

Leberer, M.R. and Fowler, S.C. (1977) Drug discrimination and generalization in pigeons. *Pharmacol. Biochem. Behav.* 7: 483–486.

Lepore, M., Vorel, S.R., Lowinson, J. and Gardner, E.L. (1995) Conditioned place preference induced by Δ⁹-tetrahydrocannabinol: comparison with cocaine, morphine, and food reward. *Life Sci.* 56: 2073–2080.

London, E.D., Broussolle, E.P.M., Links, J.M., Wong, D.F., Cascella, N.G., Dannals, R.F., Sano, M., Herning, R., Snyder, F.R., Rippetoe, L.R., Toung, T.J.K., Jaffe, J.H. and Wagner, H.N. (1990) Morphine-induced metabolic changes in human brain. *Arch. Gen. Psychiatry* 47: 73–81.

Marglin, S.H., Milano, W.C., Mattie, M.E. and Reid, L.D. (1989) PCP and conditioned place preference. *Pharmacol. Biochem. Behav.* 33: 281–283.

Martin, W.R. and Isbell, H. (eds.) (1978) *Drug addiction and the U.S. Public Health Service—Proceedings of the symposium commemorating the 40th anniversary of the Addiction Research Center at Lexington, KY.* Washington, DC: Department of Health, Education and Welfare, U.S. Government Printing Office.

Martin, W.R., Jasinski, D.R., and Mansky, P.A. (1973) Nal-trexone, an antagonist for the treatment of heroin dependence—effects in man. *Arch. Gen. Psychiatry* 28: 784–791.

Martin, W.R., Sloan, J.W., Sapira, J.D. and Jasinski, D.R. (1971) Physiologic, subjective, and behavioral effects amphetamine, methamphetamine, ephedrine, phenmetrazine, and methylphenidate in man. *Clin. Pharmacol. Ther.* 12: 245–258.

Martin-Iverson, M.T., Ortmann, R. and Fibiger, H.C. (1985) Place preference conditioning with methylphenidate and nomifensine. *Brain Res.* 33: 59–67.

McCaul, M.E., Stitzer, M.L., Bigelow, G.E., and Liebson, I.A. (1983) Intravenous hydromorphone: effects in opiate-free and methadone maintenance subjects. In: Harris, L.S. (ed.) *Proceedings of the 44th Annual Scientific Meeting, The Committee on Problems of Drug Dependence, 1982.* NIDA Research Monograph No. 43. pp. 238–244.

McNair, D.M., Lorr, M. and Droppleman, L.F. (1971) *Manual for the profile of mood states.* San Diego: Educational and Industrial Testing Service.

Mumford, G.K., Rush, C.R. and Griffiths, R.R. (1995) Abecarnil and alprazolam in humans: behavioral, subjective, and reinforcing effects. *J. Pharmacol. Exp. Ther.* 272: 570–580.

Nielsen, E.B. (1985) Discriminative stimulus properties of lysergic acid diethylamide in the monkey. *J. Pharmacol. Exp. Ther.* 234: 244–249.

Nierenberg, J. and Ator, N.A. (1990) Drug discrimination in rats successively trained to discriminate diazepam and pentobarbital. *Pharmacol. Biochem. Behav.* 35: 405–412.

Oliveto, A.H., Bickel, W.K., Hughes, J.R., Shea, P.J., Higgins, S.T. and Fenwick, J.W. (1992) Caffeine drug-discrimination in humans: acquisition, specificity and correlation with self-reports. *J. Pharmacol. Exp. Ther.* 261: 885–894.

Oliveto, A.H., Rosen, M.I., Woods, S.W. and Kosten, T.R. (1995) Discriminative stimulus, self-reported and cardiovascular effects of orally-administered cocaine in humans. *J. Pharmacol. Exp. Ther.* 271: 48–60.

Overton, D.A. (1984) State dependent learning and drug discriminations. In: Iversen, S.D. and Snyder, S.H. (eds.) *Handbook of psychopharmacology*, vol. 18. New York: Plenum, pp. 59–127.

Overton, D.A. (1987) Applications and limitations of the drug discrimination method for the study of drug abuse. In: Bozarth, M.A. (ed.) *Methods for assessing the reinforcing properties of abused drugs.* New York: Springer-Verlag, pp. 91–340.

Overton, D.A. and Batta, S.K. (1979) Investigations of narcotics and antitussives using drug discrimination techniques. *J. Pharmacol. Exp. Ther.* 211: 401–408.

Parsons, L.H., Koob, G.F. and Weiss, F. (1995) Serotonin dysfunction in the nucleus accumbens of rats during withdrawal after unlimited access to intravenous cocaine. *J. Pharmacol. Exp. Ther.* 274: 1182–1191.

Petersen, R.C. and Stillman, R.C. (eds.) (1978) Phencyclidine: an overview. In: *PCP (phencyclidine) abuse: an appraisal.* Washington, DC: National Institute on Drug Abuse, U.S. Government Printing Office, pp. 1–17.

Physicians Desk Reference-49th Edition (1995) Montvale, NJ: Medical Economics Data.

Preston, K.L. and Bigelow, G.E. (1991) Subjective and discriminative effects of drugs. *Behav. Pharmacol.* 2: 293–313.

Preston, K.L., Bigelow, G.E., Bickel, W.K. and Liebson, I.A.

(1987) Three-choice drug discrimination in opioid-dependent humans: hydromorphone, naloxone and saline. *J. Pharmacol. Exp. Ther.* 243: 1002–1009.

Preston, K.L., Bigelow, G.E., Bickel, W.K. and Liebson, I.A. (1989) Drug discrimination in human post-addicts: agonist-antagonist opioids. *J. Pharmacol. Exp. Ther.* 250: 184–196.

Preston, K.L., Bigelow, G.E. and Liebson, I.A. (1990) Discrimination of butorphanol and nalbuphine in opioid-dependent humans. *Pharmacol. Biochem. Behav.* 37: 511–522.

Preston, K.L. and Jasinski, D.R. (1991) Abuse liability studies of opioid agonist-antagonists in humans. *Drug Alcohol Depend.* 28: 49–82 .

Preston, K.L., Liebson, I.A. and Bigelow, G.E. (1992) Discrimination of agonist-antagonist opioids in humans trained on a two-choice saline-hydromorphone discrimination. *J. Pharmacol. Exp. Ther.* 261: 62–71.

Preston, K.L., Liebson, I.A. and Bigelow, G.E. (1994) Drug discrimination assessment of agonist-antagonist opioids in humans: a three-choice saline-hydromorphone-butorphanol procedure. *J. Pharmacol. Exp. Ther.* 271: 48–60.

Risner, M.E. and Jones, B.E. (1975) Self administration of CNS stimulants by dogs. *Psychopharmacologia* 43: 207–213.

Risner, M.E. and Jones, B.E. (1976) Characteristics of unlimited access to self-administered stimulant infusions in dogs. *Biol. Psychiatry* 11: 625–634.

Robbins, J. (1993) Gene targeting: the precise manipulation of the mammalian genome. *Circ. Res.* 73: 3–9.

Samele, C., Shine, P.J. and Stolerman, I.P. (1992) Forty years of drug discrimination research: a bibliography for 1951–1991. In: *The drug discrimination database.* Rockville, MD: NIDA Administrative Document.

Samele, C., Shine, P.J. and Stolerman, I.P. (1994) A bibliography for of drug discrimination research, supplement for 1992–1993. In: *The drug discrimination database.* Rockville, MD: NIDA Administrative Document.

Sannerud, C.A. and Ator, N.A. (1995a) Drug discrimination analysis of midazolam under a three-lever procedure: I. Dose-dependent differences in generalization and antagonism. *J. Pharmacol. Exp. Ther.* 272: 100–111.

Sannerud, C.A. and Ator, N.A. (1995b) Drug discrimination analysis of midazolam under a three-lever procedure: II. Differential effects of benzodiazepine receptor agonists. *J. Pharmacol. Exp. Ther.* 275: 183–193.

Sannerud, C.A., Ator, N.A. and Griffiths, R.R. (1991) Methocarbamol: evaluation of reinforcing and discriminative stimulus effects. *Behav. Pharmacol.* 2: 143–150.

Sannerud, C.A., Ator, N.A. and Griffiths, R.R. (1993) Behavioral pharmacology of tandospirone in baboons: chronic administration and withdrawal, self-administration, and drug discrimination. *Drug Alcohol Depend.* 32: 195–208.

Sannerud, C.A., Kaminski, B.J. and Griffiths, R.R. (1995) Maintenance of H1 antagonist self-injection in baboons. *Exp. Clin. Psychopharmacol.* 3: 26–32.

Sannerud, C.A., Prada, J., Goldberg, D.M. and Goldberg, S.R. (1994) The effects of sertraline on nicotine self-administration and food-maintained responding in squirrel monkeys. *Eur. J. Pharmacol.* 271: 461–469.

Schechter, M.D. and Calcagnetti, D.J. (1993) Trends in place preference conditioning with a cross-indexed bibliography: 1957–1991. *Neurosci. Biobehav. Rev.* 17: 21–41.

Schuster, C.R. and Balster, R.L. (1977) The discriminative

stimulus properties of drugs. In: *Advances in behavioral pharmacology*, vol. 1. New York: Academic Press, pp. 85–138.

Schuster, C.R. and Johanson, C-E. (1988) Relationship between the discriminative stimulus properties and subjective effects of drugs. In: Colpaert, F. and Balster, R. (eds.) *Psychopharmacology, transduction mechanisms of drug stimuli*, no. 4. Berlin, Heidelberg: Springer-Verlag, pp. 161–175.

Shannon, H.E., Cone, E.J. and Gorodetzky, C.W. (1984) Morphine-like discriminative stimulus effects of buprenorphine and demethoxybuprenorphine in rats: quantitative antagonism by naloxone. *J. Pharmacol. Exp. Ther.* 229: 768–774.

Shannon, H.E. and Herling, S. (1983) Discriminative stimulus effects of diazepam in rats: evidence for a maximal effect. *J. Pharmacol. Exp. Ther.* 227: 160–166.

Shannon, H.E. and Holtzman, S.G. (1976) Evaluation of the discriminative effects of morphine in the rat. *J. Pharmacol. Exp. Ther.* 198: 54–65.

Shannon, H.E. and Holtzman, S.G. (1979) Morphine training dose: a determinant of stimulus generalization to narcotic antagonists in the rat. *Psychopharmacology* 61: 239–244.

Shippenberg, T.S. and Herz, A. (1986) Biphasic motivational properties of partial opioid agonists: role of u- and k-opioid receptors. *Psychopharmacology* 89: S33.

Smith, G.M. and Beecher, H.K. (1962) Subjective effects of heroin and morphine in normal subjects. *J. Pharmacol. Exp. Ther.* 136: 47–52.

Spealman, R.D. (1985) Discriminative-stimulus effects of midazolam in squirrel monkeys: comparison with other drugs and antagonism by RO 15-1788. *J. Pharmacol. Exp. Ther.* 235: 456–462.

Spealman, R.D. and Bergman, J. (1992) Modulation of the discriminative stimulus effects of cocaine by mu and kappa opioids. *J. Pharmacol. Exp. Ther.* 261: 607–615.

Spyraki, C. and Fibiger, H.C. (1988) A role for the mesolimbic dopamine system in the reinforcing properties of diazepam. *Psychopharmacology* 94: 133–137.

Spyraki, C., Kazandjian, A. and Varonos, D. (1985) Diazepam-induced place preference conditioning: appetitive and antiaversive properties. *Psychopharmacology* 87: 225–232.

Spyraki, C., Nomikos, G.G., Galanopoulou, P. and Daifotis, Z. (1988) Drug-induced place preference in rats with 5,7-dihydroxytryptamine lesions of the nucleus accumbens. *Behav. Brain Res.* 29: 127–134.

Stolerman, I.P. (1991) Measures of stimulus generalization in drug discrimination experiments. *Behav. Pharmacol.* 2: 265–282.

Stolerman, I.P. and D Mello, G.D. (1981) Role of training conditions in discrimination of central nervous system stimulants by rats. *Psychopharmacology* 73: 295–303.

Tang, A.H. and Franklin, S.R. (1991) The discriminative stimulus effects of diazepam in rats at two training doses. *J. Pharmacol. Exp. Ther.* 258: 926–931.

van Dyck, C.H., Rosen, M.I., Thomas, H.M., McMahon, T.J., Wallace, E.A., O'Connor, P.G., Sullivan, M., Krystal, J.H., Hoffer, P.B., Woods, S.W. and Kosten, T.R. (1994) SPECT regional cerebral blood flow alterations in naltrexone-precipitated withdrawal from buprenorphine. *Psychiatry Res. Neuroimaging* 55: 181–191.

Volkow, N.D., Hitzemann, R., Wang, G.-J., Wolf, A.P., Dewey, S.L. and Handelsman, L. (1992) Long-term frontal brain metabolic changes in cocaine abusers. *Synapse* 11: 184–190.

Volkow, N.D., Wang, G.-J., Hitzemann, R., Logan, J.,

Schlyer, D.J., Dewey, S.L. and Wolf, A.P. (1993) Decreased dopamine D_2 receptor availability is associated with reduced frontal metabolism in cocaine abusers. *Synapse* 14: 169–177.

Wilks, L.J. and File, S. (1988) Evidence for simultaneous anxiolytic and aversive effects several hours after administration of sodium phenobarbitone to the rat. *Neurobiology* 19: 86–89.

Willetts, J. and Balster, R.L. (1988) Phencyclidine-like discriminative stimulus properties of MK-801 in rats. *Eur. J. Pharmacol.* 146: 167–169.

Wilson, M.C., Hitomi, M. and Schuster, C.R. (1971) Psychomotor stimulant self-administration as a function of dosage per injection in the rhesus monkey. *Psychopharmacologia* 22: 271–281.

Winter, J.C. and Rabin, R.A. (1988) Interactions between serotonergic agonists and antagonists in rats trained with LSD as a discriminative stimulus. *Pharmacol. Biochem. Behav.* 30: 617–624.

Witkin, J.M., Carter, R.B. and Dykstra, L.A. (1980) Discriminative stimulus properties of d-amphetamine-pentobarbital combinations. *Psychopharmacology* 68: 269–276.

Wood, D.M. and Emmett-Oglesby, M.W. (1988) Substitution and cross-tolerance profiles of anorectic drugs in rats trained to detect the discriminative stimulus properties of cocaine. *Psychopharmacology* 95: 364–368.

Woods, J.H., Young, A.M. and Herling, S. (1982) Classification of narcotics on the basis of their reinforcing, discriminative, and antagonist effects in rhesus monkeys. *Fed. Proc.* 41: 221–227.

Woudenberg, F. and Slangen, J.L. (1989) Discriminative stimulus properties of midazolam: comparison with other benzodiazepines. *Psychopharmacology* 97: 466–470.

Young, A.M. (1991) *Discriminative stimulus profiles of psychoactive drugs.* In: Mello, N.K. (ed.) Advances in substance abuse, vol. 4. London: Jessica Kingsley, pp. 139–203.

Young, A.M., Masaki, M.A. and Geula, C. (1992) Discriminative stimulus effects of morphine: effects of training dose on agonist and antagonist effects of mu opioids. *J. Pharmacol. Exp. Ther.* 261: 246–257.

Young, A.M., Mattox, S.R. and Doty, M.D. (1991) Increased sensitivity to rate-altering and discriminative stimulus effects of morphine following continuous exposure to naltrexone. *Psychopharmacology* 103: 67–73.

Young, A.M., Stevens, K.R., Hein, D.W. and Woods, J.H. (1984) Reinforcing and discriminative stimulus properties of mixed agonist-antagonist opioids. *J. Pharmacol. Exp. Ther.* 229: 118–126.

Young, A.M., Woods, J.H., Herling, S. and Hein, D.W. (1983) Comparison of the reinforcing and discriminative stimulus properties of opioids and opioid peptides. In: Smith, J.E. and Lane, J.D. (eds.) *The neurobiology of opiate reward processes.* Amsterdam: Elsevier Biomedical Press, pp. 147–173.

Zacny, J.P., Lichtor, J.L., Flemming, D., Coalson, D.W., and Tompson, W.K. (1994) A dose-response analysis of the subjective, psychomotor and physiological effectives of intravenous morphine in healthy volunteers. *J. Pharmacol. Exp. Ther.* 268: 1–9.

Drug Addiction and its Treatment: Nexus of Neuroscience and Behavior, edited by Bankole A. Johnson and John D. Roache. Lippincott–Raven Publishers, Philadelphia, © 1997.

5

Role of Conditioned Stimuli in Addiction

*Peter B. Silverman and †Peter L. Bonate

Department of Psychiatry and Behavioral Sciences, University of Texas-Houston Health Science Center, Houston, Texas 77030; †Department of Pharmaceutical Sciences, School of Pharmacy, University of Pittsburgh, Pittsburgh, Pennsylvania 15261

It has been almost 50 years since Wikler (1948) proposed that the unconditional response to a drug may become conditioned to various situations or memories associated with taking the drug and that conditioning was one of the factors predisposing an individual to relapse long after withdrawal from opiates. In response to his questions about the circumstances under which they had relapsed, postaddicts told Wikler that they were doing fine after detoxification until returning home, or the anticipation of returning home, caused them to feel sick and crave drug. Perplexed colleagues related stories to Wikler of how long-detoxified postaddicts would become teary-eyed, runny-nosed, and yawn incessantly, as though experiencing a mild form of withdrawal, when the subject under discussion turned to dope (Wikler, 1977). Despite the fact that Wikler explicitly recognized that conditioning considerations applied to the human drug abuse situation, and the fact that Pavlov (1927) had described the rapid development of conditioned drug effects in dogs, general recognition of the importance of conditioning in drug addiction has been very slow in coming. Most standard pharmacology texts give scant, if any, consideration to the importance of conditioning. This chapter briefly reviews some of the essential features of classical conditioning and describes the basic research literature, which demonstrates the importance of such conditioning to substance abuse phenomena. Finally, the use of procedures intended to extinguish conditioned responses to drug-related stimuli as a means of preventing relapse is discussed.

CLASSICAL CONDITIONING

A great deal of research has been conducted utilizing and/or investigating the mechanisms involved in classical conditioning. Only the bare essentials of classical conditioning are presented here. A multitude of resources, including many of the references contained herein, describe classical conditioning, its history, and development in greater detail.

In the classical conditioning paradigm an unconditioned stimulus (US) produces an unconditioned response (UR) by means of "prewired" circuitry in the organism. The unconditioned response is one that does not have to be learned; it is the "natural" response to a stimulus. In fact, Pavlov called unconditioned responses unconditioned (or unconditional) "reflexes," which focuses attention on the automatic nature of the behaviors. For example, contact with a hot object (the US) results in a rapid withdrawal response (the UR). If the US is repeatedly paired with an initially neutral stimulus, say a tone of specified amplitude and frequency, the tone itself will come to elicit the response. The tone is referred to as the conditioned, or conditional, stimulus (CS). When the withdrawal response is elicited by the CS (after the response has been conditioned by repeated pairings of US and CS), it is considered to be a conditioned response (CR). Unconditioned stimuli may be simple, such as the hot object, or they may be more complex, such as the effects of a drug. Conditioned stimuli may also be as simple as a tone or a light, or they may be very complex, such as the sight, sound, and smells of a particular environment.

The classic examples of classical conditioning are provided by the work of Pavlov (1927). Indeed, classical conditioning is often referred to as Pavlovian conditioning, as well as associative learning. In the best known of his experiments, Pavlov paired food delivery (US) to dogs with the ticking of a metronome (CS). The unconditioned response to food was salivation. After repeated pairings, the sound of the metronome, unaccompanied by food delivery, produced the physiological response to food, i.e., salivation. In response to the metronome, the salivation is a conditioned response. Interestingly, Pavlov also termed the CR a conditioned (or conditional) "reflex," again calling attention to the automatic nature of the stimulus-response connection. Pavlov also observed and commented specifically on conditioned drug effects. Pavlov wrote (1927, p. 35) describing the experiments of his associate, Dr. Krylov:

"The first effect of a hypodermic injection of morphine [to dogs] is to produce nausea with profuse secretion of saliva, followed by vomiting, and then profound sleep....When the injections were repeated regularly, after 5 or 6 days the preliminaries of injection were in themselves sufficient to produce all these symptoms—nausea, secretion of saliva, vomiting, and sleep. Under these circumstances the symptoms are now the effect, not of the morphine acting through the blood stream...but of all the external stimuli which previously had preceded the injection of morphine....In the most striking cases all the symptoms could be produced by the dogs simply seeing the experimenter."

In this example the US was provided by morphine. Several unconditioned responses to morphine are included here: nausea, salivation, vomiting, and sleep. One CS that developed quickly was the preparations for injection, i.e., "the preliminaries." Eventually, the mere appearance of the experimenter served as an effective CS. This example suggests the wide diversity of conditioned stimuli and conditioned responses that can result from drug administration.

A discussion of the procedural details involved in classical conditioning is available in many introductory psychology textbooks. Consideration here is therefore quite abbreviated. The strength of the CR is dependent on many variables, some of which are intuitive, others of which may not be. The number of pairings of US with CS is of obvious importance. There is a positive correlation between the number of pairings and strength of the CR, and, typically, but not always as we shall see below, the US and CS must be presented in paired fashion a number of times to result in robust conditioned response to the CS.

Temporal considerations are important. In general, longer time intervals between conditioning trials will result in poor conditioning or no conditioning at all. The exact temporal arrangement of the pairings of US and CS is critical. Pavlov's conditioning procedure included presentation of the CS a few seconds prior to presentation of the US. The temporal arrangement can fall into one of three categories: presentation of the CS prior to the US (forward delayed and forward trace conditioning), presentation of the CS simultaneous to the US (simultaneous conditioning), and presentation of the CS after presentation of the US (backward conditioning). These are shown schematically in Fig. 1. Research has made clear that for optimal conditioning it is necessary that the CS begin prior to onset of the US. There is an optimal CS-US interval, with both shorter and longer intervals less effective, but the value of the optimal interval varies widely depending on the species and the nature of the US and the CS (Rescorla, 1988). Prolonged presentation of the CS prior to presentation of the US results in relatively poor conditioning. This phenomenon has come to be known as latent inhibition (Lubow, 1973). Presentation of the CS simul-

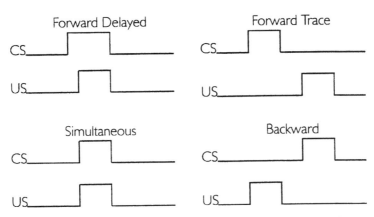

FIG. 1. Schemes for stimulus presentation. Upward deflection indicates stimulus onset and downward deflection indicates stimulus offset. The abscissa is time.

taneously with the US also has typically resulted in poor conditioning or no conditioning (e.g., Smith et al., 1969). Studies attempting backward conditioning (US-CS) have usually had negative results, although there have been a few reports of positive results. A review of the literature on backward conditioning (Hall, 1984) revealed that many of the studies that ostensibly demonstrated the phenomenon were poorly controlled. In those studies that were properly controlled, the backward conditioning trials actually resulted in retardation of subsequent CR acquisition, from which Hall infers that the backward conditioning trials result in inhibition. This conclusion is consistent with other findings that presentation of CS only or of US only prior to forward conditioning trials also results in retarded acquisition. Thus, just as preexposure to the CS results in poor conditioning (latent inhibition), preexposure to the US and preexposure to the US-CS (paired but backward) may also result in poor conditioning or no conditioning at all. It is easy (and correct) to conclude that conditioning can be a tricky business; many variables can affect the outcome of a conditioning experiment, some of which may be unidentifiable. Some of the conflicting results in what seem to be comparable drug conditioning experiments are almost certainly attributable to differences in procedural detail.

Studies of conditioning with drugs typically include an experimental group given conditioning sessions in which drug administration (the US) is paired with some other stimulus (the CS), which is often a distinctive environment. In subsequent test sessions this experimental group may be administered drug (if the test is of conditioned tolerance or sensitization) or vehicle (if the test is of a conditioned compensatory response or a placebo effect) and response to the CS is measured. Two control groups are typically used to ensure that a putative CR is in fact a CR to a CS associated with a drug US. The first control group is treated the same as the experimental group, except that vehicle administration is paired with the CS in training trials. The second control group is a pseudoconditioning control. This group is administered drug and is exposed to the CS, but in unpaired fashion.

Once a conditioned response has been established, repeated presentation of the CS in the absence of the US results in a decrement in the amplitude of the CR over time, a process known as extinction. The length of time or number of trials until a CR does not follow presentation of the CS alone is a measure of the robustness of the CR. Reintroduction of the US during the extinction period is often sufficient for the CR to recover to full strength and may result in a CR greater than previously observed.

Pavlov's description of the conditioned effects of morphine shows that associative learning allows for simultaneous development of diverse CRs. Through higher-order conditioning (Pavlov, 1927), greater complexity of stimulus-response relationships is made possible, and often, inevitable. Consider an organism with an established conditioned response to CS_1. If CS_1 is now repeatedly preceded by a new stimulus, the new stimulus comes to act as a conditioned stimulus, CS_2, which can, by itself, elicit the CR. Once established, the ability of CS_2 to elicit the conditioned response is retained, even if the CR to the initial conditioned stimulus, CS_1, is extinguished. (Holland and Rescorla, 1975; Rizley and Rescorla, 1972).

A second mechanism that extends the basic conditioning paradigm is stimulus generalization. An organism conditioned, for example, to salivate in response to a 1000-Hz tone will also salivate in response to tones near 1000 Hz. The further the tone deviates from the 1000-Hz training stimulus, the more attenuated the response. The generalization gradient thus established is a function of, among other things, the number of conditioning trials. In addition to exteroceptive stimuli, interoceptive stimuli are apparently generalized to similar interoceptive stimuli. That drugs can be classified by their interoceptive stimuli forms a key component of the conceptual framework for that area of research endeavor known as "drug discrimination" (e.g., Colpaert and Rosecrans, 1978; Glennon et al., 1991; Thompson and Pickens, 1971).

Conditioning mechanisms have been shown to play a role in producing two types of behavioral changes following drug administration (Cunningham, 1993). First, conditioning can be seen to modify the subjective and/or physiological effects of a drug when the drug is administered in the presence of stimuli associated with prior drug administration. These modifications of the unconditioned effects of drugs by stimuli previously associated with drug administration can reduce or enhance the effect of a given dose of drug, i.e., these effects comprise the classical conditioning components of the phenomena of tolerance and behavioral sensitization. Second, stimuli associated with drug administration can become conditional

stimuli that evoke behavioral or physiological response in the absence of drug. Such conditioned drug effects, which are discussed below, may be opposite to the observed effect of the drug (i.e., a conditioned compensatory response), or similar to the observed drug effect (i.e., a placebo effect).

CLASSICAL CONDITIONING AND TOLERANCE

Tolerance refers to a decreased response to a fixed dose of drug upon repeated administration. Tolerance is thus a shift to the right of the dose-response curve. While earlier definitions of drug dependence required a demonstration of tolerance (American Psychiatric Association, 1980), current definitions of drug dependence recognize that tolerance and withdrawal are neither necessary nor sufficient conditions for drug dependence (American Psychiatric Association, 1994). In other words it has been recognized that dependence can occur in the absence of clearly manifest tolerance or withdrawal.

Tolerance is a complex phenomenon involving multiple mechanisms through which the organism attempts to maintain homeostasis (Goudie and Emmett-Oglesby, 1989). Tolerance can result from both pharmacokinetic and pharmacodynamic adaptations. Pharmacokinetic or dispositional mechanisms of tolerance arise from alterations in absorption, distribution, metabolism, or excretion, which ultimately act to decrease the biophase drug concentration (Le and Khanna, 1989). In contrast, pharmacodynamic tolerance is due to alterations in sensitivity of the organism to a drug, either through biochemical or behavioral alterations. Associative or conditioning processes are certainly involved in the development of tolerance, most notably in tolerance to depressant and opioid drugs.

There is considerable evidence indicating a role for conditioning in the development of tolerance. For example, morphine-induced analgesia becomes attenuated with repeated administration of morphine. This tolerance to morphine analgesia is highly dependent on the repeated administrations occurring in the same environment, i.e., the tolerance is context-dependent (Siegel, 1975). This context-dependent tolerance is conceptualized to be a composite result of the unconditioned response to morphine, analgesia, and a conditioned compensatory response (Solomon, 1980) to the environment associated with morphine administration. The conditioned compensatory response increases with each pairing of drug and environment, such that the net effect is diminished response to drug administration. Tolerance to other unconditioned responses to opiates, hyperthermia and lethality, have also been demonstrated (Siegel, 1978; Siegel et al., 1982).

Similarly, when a high dose of ethanol is administered repeatedly in a distinctive environment, tolerance develops to the hypothermic effect of ethanol administered in that environment. Thus the CR to stimuli associated with ethanol administration is hyperthermia, an effect opposite the UR to ethanol (Crowell et al., 1981; Mansfield and Cunningham, 1980). As an example of the modulatory effect of environment on tolerance in a human

subjects experiment, Dafters and Anderson (1982) repeatedly administered ethanol to moderate social drinkers in a brightly illuminated room filled with mood music. Placebo was repeatedly administered on other occasions in a quiet, dimly lit room. For other subjects ethanol was paired with the quiet, dimly lit room and placebo with the bright, music-filled room. After the acquisition phase, subjects were administered ethanol in each of the environments. Subjects showed considerable tolerance to ethanol-induced tachycardia, but only when it was administered in the environment in which they were accustomed to receiving it. Thus, they showed significantly less tolerance to ethanol in the environment associated with placebo.

Eikelboom and Stewart (1982) proposed that conditioned compensatory responses are due to activation of a feedback regulatory system operative during the conditioning process (Fig. 2). In their model the CNS has two arms, afferent and efferent. The afferent arm has input from a sensor, which measures the overall activity of the system, and projects to the integrator, which summates all inputs. The efferent arm projects from the integrator to the

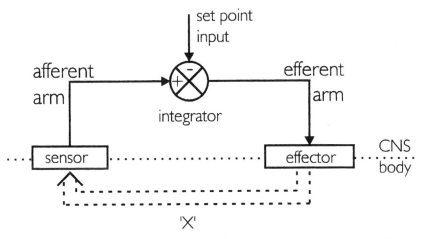

FIG. 2. Eikelboom and Stewart model of a regulatory feedback system. A drug acting on the afferent arm will result in a neural signal that is the unconditioned stimulus, and the observed drug effect is the unconditioned response. A drug acting on the efferent arm or on the effector organ is not an unconditioned stimulus. The observed effect of such a drug is the unconditioned stimulus, and the unconditioned response is the CNS mediated reaction. (From Eikelboom and Stewart, 1982, with permission.)

effector site. If the overall level of activity is different than the set-point activity, an error is produced and the integrator corrects the system activity to maintain homeostasis.

Eikelboom and Stewart (1982) have argued convincingly that it is wrong to assume that drug administration is always the US and the drug effect the UR. In their model, correct reference to the US and the UR is dependent on which arm of the system the drug acts on. Drugs acting on the afferent arm of the system are defined as the US, and observed drug effects that are CNS mediated are defined as the UR. This is consistent with the use common in the literature. But the effect of drugs acting on the efferent arm, including those drugs that act directly on effector organs themselves and drugs that act within the CNS at points distal to the integrator, are not due to direct changes in input to the integrator. Drugs that act on the efferent arm will activate, via a negative feedback system, other effectors that will attempt to counteract the direct drug effect. Therefore, Eikelboom and Stewart argue that the observed drug effect (rather than the drug) is the US and the effector-produced response attempting to counteract the drug effect should be labeled the UR.

Once the site of action is specified, the model predicts the direction of the CR. Drugs that act on the afferent arm act as the US producing a CR similar to the observed drug effect. Conversely, drugs that act on the efferent arm activate the negative feedback loop generating an opponent CR opposite to the observed drug effect. Whether an individual will develop tolerance or increased sensitivity to a repeatedly administered drug is then reduced to identifying the locus of drug action within the system. Eikelboom and Stewart propose that if the occurrence of the observed drug effect were prevented, conditioning should still occur for drugs with sites of action on the afferent arm, but not for drugs that act on the efferent arm.

The conditioned compensatory view of tolerance may be used to explain the development of withdrawal symptoms. If tolerance is indeed a conditioned compensatory mecha-

nism, the display of withdrawal symptoms should also be under the control of the CS, which, in the absence of drug, should elicit the opponent CR. For the opioids there is considerable evidence to suggest this may be the case (below). In addition to the previously described examples showing conditional tolerance to opiates and ethanol, conditional tolerance to a number of treatments including nicotine (Epstein et al., 1989), cigarette smoke (Epstein et al., 1991), and pentobarbital (Cappell et al., 1981) has been demonstrated.

Central to the theory that tolerance represents a conditioned process is that the relevant CS in a particular environment will elicit the opponent CR that mediates tolerance. Thus it should be possible not only to show that tolerance is under stimulus control (typically of a specific environment), but the conditioned compensatory response should be demonstrable in tests in which the subject is exposed to the environment in the absence of drug. In other words, the specific environment or other stimuli associated with drug should serve as CS for the compensatory CR. Conditioned compensatory responses have been demonstrated in a variety of circumstances (e.g., Ehrman et al., 1992; Krank, 1987; McCaul et al., 1989; Siegel, 1975). Nonetheless, a significant problem for opponent process theory is the not infrequent inability to demonstrate the compensatory CR that should be apparent when the subject is exposed to the environmental CS in the absence of drug (Goudie, 1990). Sometimes the inability to demonstrate the conditioned compensatory response may be due to insensitivity of the behavioral measure, including basement and ceiling effects. For example, there has been reported a failure to demonstrate hyperalgesia in the tail-flick test when rats made tolerant to morphine in a specific environment are tested with saline in that morphine-associated environment (Tiffany et al., 1983). This may be because the normal tail-flick response is so rapid that it is not possible for subjects to respond significantly more rapidly. Support for such an interpretation is found in the demonstration of a hyperalgesic response in the hot-plate test in the same rats that, when un-drugged, did not show a hyperalgesic response in the tail-flick assay (Krank, 1987).

Perhaps the most parsimonious explanation for the inability to consistently find a conditioned compensatory response is that the stimulus effect of the drug is determinative. Just as the environment may be controlling when it is the most salient stimulus, and the handling and injection procedures (Pavlov's "preliminaries") may overshadow the environmental stimuli when the test environment is not particularly distinctive (see Dafters and Bach, 1985), the interoceptive stimulus effect of the drug, and its absence in the test for a conditioned compensatory response, may be determinative. That many drugs of interest to the behavioral pharmacologist and to the drug abuser provide an interoceptive stimulus that may be critical in a variety of conditioning situations is an issue we will encounter again.

Behavioral mechanisms of tolerance do not operate alone; presumably physiological effectors must be called into play, at least where the dependent measure is physiological. Thus, conditioning may result in tolerance via surprising routes. For example, drug metabolism itself may be conditioned (Roffman and Lal, 1974) and the volume of distribution of ethanol has been shown to be under control of environmental stimuli (Melchior and Tabakoff, 1985).

CLASSICAL CONDITIONING AND SENSITIZATION

Behavioral sensitization is defined as an increased behavioral response to repeated administration of a fixed dose of drug, or a shift to the left of the dose-response curve. As such, it represents the opposite of tolerance, and is referred to as reverse tolerance in some of the literature. Just as the behavioral manifestation of tolerance may be the composite result of metabolic and learned factors, sensitization may represent the net consequence of more than one process. Sensitization has been observed as a consequence of treatment with a variety of drugs, most notably the psy-

chomotor stimulants, but also with ethanol, nicotine, MK-801, and morphine. The study of sensitization has been a real growth industry in behavioral pharmacology and has resulted in a number of recent reviews (Kalivas and Stewart, 1991; Robinson and Becker, 1986; Wise and Leeb, 1993).

A role for conditioning in behavioral sensitization is made quite clear by studies showing context dependence of the phenomenon. In these studies the response to drug is modulated by the presence or absence of stimuli external to the subject. An example of context dependent sensitization to cocaine is shown in Figure 3. Three groups of rats were tested. Rats in the first (paired) group were injected with 20 mg/kg cocaine and placed in the motor activity test box. They were subsequently injected with saline and returned to their home cages. Rats in the second (unpaired) group were injected with saline before being placed in the motor activity box, and subsequently with 20 mg/kg cocaine and returned to their home cages. The third group (saline control) was injected with saline before being placed in the motor activity box, and subsequently with saline and returned to their home cages. The next day, locomotor response to 5 mg/kg cocaine was tested in all three groups in the test boxes.

Significantly greater locomotor activity in response to the dose of cocaine was observed in the paired group compared with unpaired and no-drug control groups (Fig. 3). The only difference between treatment of the paired and unpaired groups was the environment associated with cocaine and saline injections. This experiment follows the so-called 2-day sensitization paradigm developed by Weiss et al. (1989). Note that it includes the two types of control groups described above. The results show the ability of the distinctive test environment to act as a conditioned stimulus and modify the response to cocaine. It is worth noting that in the sole study of context-dependent cocaine sensitization conducted in humans, no evidence of sensitization, context-dependent or otherwise, was found in any of several physiological measures, nor subjec-

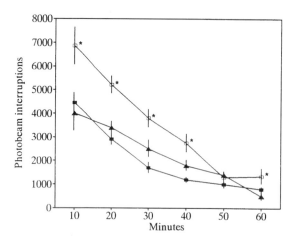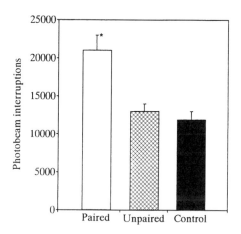

FIG. 3. Two-day sensitization. Locomotor activity in 10-minute bins *(left)* and total locomotor activity in a 60-minute session *(right)* after a 5-mg/kg injection of cocaine. The previous day rats had been treated with either 20 mg/kg cocaine in the test box and saline in their home cage (paired group, *open squares*), 20 mg/kg cocaine in their home cage and saline in the test box (unpaired group, *triangles*), or with saline in both places (control group, *filled squares*). Data are mean ± standard error for five rats per group. *Significantly different from both other groups.

tive report (Rothman et al., 1994). It should also be noted, however, that the human subjects were cocaine users who, having taken drug before, presumably in a variety of contexts, must be considered to be less than optimal subjects for such a conditioning study. It is unlikely that a similar study with drug naive subjects will be conducted any time soon.

Context-dependent sensitization has been reported with a variety of drugs, including amphetamine (Tilson and Rech, 1973), morphine (Mansfield et al., 1981; Mucha et al., 1981), cocaine (Hinson and Poulos, 1981; Post et al., 1981), apomorphine (Moller et al., 1987), and bromocriptine (Hoffman and Wise, 1992). Context-dependent cross-sensitization between amphetamine and morphine has also been reported (Stewart and Vezina, 1987).

Sometimes experiments involving repeated drug administration have been found to result in sensitization that is context-independent (Browne and Segal, 1977; Mattingly and Gotsick, 1989; Post and Rose; 1976; Robinson, 1984; Segal and Mandell, 1974). This has been taken by some as evidence that sensitization is not necessarily a conditioning phenomenon (Robinson and Becker, 1986). While the conclusion may be correct, the logic is not

compelling. Because an animal shows a sensitized response to a drug in an environment not previously associated with the drug does not mean the sensitized response is not a result of conditioning. In addition to whatever external stimuli may be associated with drug administration, centrally active drugs typically provide a discriminable stimulus. That this is the case is shown by the fact that most, if not all, drugs that induce behavioral sensitization serve as effective discriminative stimuli for differential operant behavior (i.e., serve as stimuli in drug discrimination experiments). This interoceptive stimulus is presented to the organism typically in perfect association with the US for locomotor activity. Thus, cocaine, for example, serves not only as the US for locomotor stimulation, but as an interoceptive stimulus that is a CS presented in perfect association with increased locomotion. Whether sensitization is found to be context-dependent in a given experiment then can be seen to depend on the salience of the interoceptive drug stimulus versus that of the context. If the drug stimulus overshadows the context stimulus, any sensitization observed would not be expected to be context-dependent. Support for this position is provided by the fact that sensitization to a given drug can be deemed context dependent or context independent depending on procedural detail. Experiments finding context dependence are likely to make use of lower doses of drug, and highly distinctive contexts, because this results in high relative context salience. Experiments in which higher doses of drug or less distinctive contexts are utilized would be more likely to find context-independent sensitization, because the interoceptive stimulus is made relatively more salient in such circumstances. Lack of sufficient difference between the conditioning environment and home environment, excessively high doses of drug administered, and latent inhibition have been offered as reasons for failure to find context dependency in some experiments (Pert et al., 1990). Such reasons are not inconsistent with the preceding logic. It should be clear that most, if not all, of the drugs that result in sensitization have central effects that are discriminable by the organism. That this is true is revealed by the ability of the drugs to serve effectively as discriminative stimuli (Colpaert and Rosecrans, 1978; Glennon et al., 1991; Thompson and Pickens, 1971). Thus, in every case the onset of the drug stimulus, predictive of hyperlocomotion, could be a CS for hyperlocomotion.

Segal (1975) asserted that conditioning could not account for behavioral sensitization because repeated administration of low doses of amphetamine, which at first resulted in increased locomotion, eventually resulted in stereotyped behavior (and little locomotor stimulation). The expectation seemingly is that a "new" behavior cannot be expected to emerge as a result of conditioning. But stereotyped behavior is the UR to higher doses of amphetamine and thus might not really be "new" behavior. Furthermore, there is at least some evidence (Schreiber et al., 1976) as well as a theoretical rationale (Eikelboom and Stewart, 1982) supporting the idea that a CR can be established, even if its performance is not observed during acquisition.

Robinson and Becker (1986) have suggested that conditioning cannot account for sensitization, because a single amphetamine injection results in a persistent enhancement of response to a subsequent administration of amphetamine, and, it is argued, conditioning requires repeated pairings. Robinson and Becker argue that it is difficult to imagine how conditioning would occur following a single drug exposure. But as described above, context-dependent sensitization can be demonstrated after a single pairing of drug and environment (Weiss et al.,1989). Further, as will be described below, an outright placebo effect can unambiguously be conditioned to the environment with a single drug administration.

Possible neurochemical mechanisms involved in behavioral sensitization have received much recent attention (Kalivas and Stewart, 1991; Robinson and Berridge, 1993; Wise and Leeb, 1993). An excellent case for important involvement of central dopamine systems has evolved, but the exact nature of the involvement is not established. The ventral tegmental area (VTA), but not the nucleus accumbens, may be crucial for the development of sensitization. Repeated administration of amphetamine in the ventral tegmental area results in sensitization, whereas repeated administration into the nucleus accumbens does not (Vezina and Stewart, 1990).

Beninger and Hahn (1983) demonstrated that development of context-dependent amphetamine sensitization could be blocked by pretreatment with the dopamine antagonist pimozide during the conditioning period. This should not be surprising, in that pimozide blocked the unconditioned locomotor response to amphetamine, and presumably the discriminable stimulus as well. Perhaps more surprisingly, pretreatment with pimozide did not block the expression of sensitization in rats in which it was already established. Pimozide pretreatment had a similar effect on cocaine sensitization, that is, it blocked the development but not the expression of the sensitized behavior (Beninger and Herz, 1986). Similar results were obtained using haloperidol (Weiss et al., 1989), raclopride (Post et al., 1992), and SCH-23390 (Post et al., 1992).

Early reviews of behavioral sensitization, in considering possible mechanisms, have given primary attention to changes within dopamine neurons and scant attention to the fact that repeated administration of direct-acting dopamine agonists may also result in the phenomenon. Results showing that direct-acting agonists can result in sensitization in animal preparations in which the dopamine neurons have been destroyed are particularly challenging to sensitization models relying on changes in those neurons (Klug and Norman, 1993; Silverman, 1991). Wise and Leeb (1993) recently reviewed the sensitization literature, paying attention to direct as well as indirect agonists, and reached the conclusion that it is very unlikely that a unitary theory of sensitization can satisfactorily account for all the data. While the conclusion may be correct, the logic is not compelling. One of the foundations of their argument is that drugs that result in sensitization may or may not result in cross-sensitization. This is not surprising, should not be unexpected, and does not preclude the possibility of a common mechanism. Consider the following simple hypothetical. A tone is presented to a dog and it is followed by meat powder. Initially, the tone elicits little or no salivation. With repeated paired presentations, the tone elicits an increasing volume of saliva until an asymptote is reached. A flash of light is presented to a second dog. It is followed by meat powder. Initially, the light elicits little or no salivation. With repeated paired presentations, the light elicits an increasing volume of saliva until an asymptote is reached. Both dogs are now sensitized to a stimulus and exhibit the same CR. Is the expectation that the light will elicit much salivation in dog 1, or the tone in dog 2? No, the CSs are different. Are the mechanisms involved in the conditioning the same? Not identical, they involve different sensory pathways, but the mechanisms involved in the conditioning are likely to have a great deal in common. If a rat shows a sensitized locomotor response to drug A, it can reasonably be expected to exhibit a sensitized locomotor response to drug B only if the drugs have similar interoceptive stimuli. The fact that both drugs are US for locomotion should not be taken to suggest that they should cross-sensitize.

In what follows, the term *conditioned drug effect* is used to describe a behavior that is elicited, in the absence of drug, by a stimulus or stimuli previously associated with drug administration. Thus, it is a placebo effect. While, as discussed above, tolerance and behavioral sensitization may be conditioned drug effects, the phenomena are technically different from what will be described because tolerance and sensitization can only be demonstrated in the presence of drug (by definition). An example of an outright conditioned drug effect is provided by the work of Schiff (1982). After being administered apomorphine or amphetamine on each of 10 consecutive days while placed in a distinct environment and exposed to a tone, rats were injected with saline and exposed to the environment and tone. The rats engaged in stereotyped behaviors to a significantly greater extent than did pseudoconditioned or saline-only controls. This placebo effect might be considered a maximal behavioral sensitization effect, i.e., a shift to the left of the dose-response curve such that the lowest possible dose of drug (zero) now has the effect a modest dose of stimulant might have in a naive rat. But in experiments described below, it is shown that development of sensitization does not necessarily result in a placebo effect, and a placebo effect can be shown under circumstances wherein sensitization technically cannot be demonstrated, because drug is only administered once.

A profound conditioned drug effect can be demonstrated in rats with a unilateral 6-hydroxydopamine lesion of one substantia nigra. The administration of dopamine agonists to such rats causes them to run in circles (Ungerstedt, 1971). Direct-acting dopamine agonists result in circling directed away from the lesioned side because, as a result of denervation supersensitivity, the direct agonists act with greater effect on the lesioned side. Indirect-acting dopamine agonists result in circling toward the lesioned side, by virtue of the fact that the indirect-acting agonists can promote release/block reuptake of dopamine only on the intact side.

A small dose (0.05 mg/kg) of apomorphine results not only in an acute episode of stereo-typed, contralaterally directed circling, but in conditioned circling in response to subsequent placement in the drug-associated environment (Silverman and Ho, 1981). Remarkably, this conditioned response to the drug-associated environment follows a single injection of apo-morphine, and, as shown in Fig. 4, can be demonstrated over a year after that single drug administration. Similarly lesioned rats treated with saline never exhibit the unconditioned cir-cling, and, of course, never exhibit the condi-tioned behavior. Not shown in the figure is that pseudoconditioned rats, placed in the rotation environment for the same period of time, then administered apomorphine and returned to their home cages, did not exhibit conditioned rotation upon subsequently being placed (un-drugged) into the rotation environment. But some rats in this pseudoconditioned group did exhibit a brief burst of contralateral circling *when returned to their home cage.* Thus, con-ditioned circling was established in some of the pseudoconditioned rats, although not to the same US as the experimental group. Other rats were also treated with apomorphine on each of 3 consecutive days and placed in one of two distinctive environments. They were later tested for conditioned circling, first in the un-paired environment, then in the paired environ-ment. They showed conditioned circling in the apomorphine-associated environment and lit-tle, if any, circling in the other environment.

Despite appropriate controls and consistent results, we were initially reluctant to accept conditioning as the entire explanation for the undrugged circling, for a number of reasons, three of which follow.

First was that the phenomenon resulted from a single drug administration and was re-markably robust. In short, it seemed too good to be true. But we have now replicated the es-sential features of our initial findings numer-

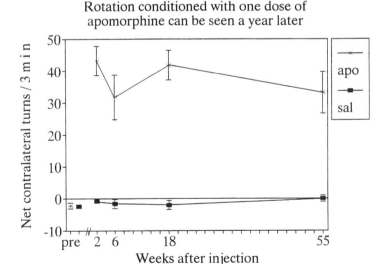

FIG. 4. Conditioned rotation. Rats with a unilateral 6-hydroxydopamine lesion of the substantia were administered 0.05 mg/kg apomorphine or saline one time, 2 to 3 weeks after they had been lesioned. Prior to injection (pre), rats made a few ipsilateral circles when placed in the test environment for a 3-min test. Immediately after injection (not shown) rats were left in the environment for 33 min, dur-ing which time apomorphine-treated rats circled contralaterally and saline treated rats did very little. After this single conditioning trial, rats were returned to the test environment periodically. The condi-tioned response to the environment following a single pairing with apomorphine was quite apparent over a year later.

ous times, as have others (Burunat et al., 1987; Casas et al., 1988). Additionally, we have now completed several experiments wherein the CS is, rather than the external environment, a drug coadministered with apomorphine in training sessions (Silverman, 1990; Silverman et al., 1992).

Second was the observation that we were unable to condition circling to the same environment using the indirect dopamine agonist amphetamine. At doses that resulted in comparable, but oppositely directed, unconditioned rotation, there was no sign of conditioning with amphetamine (Silverman and Ho, 1981). In subsequent experiments, several schedules of repeated administration of amphetamine (Silverman, 1988a) or cocaine (Silverman, 1992b) did not result in conditioned circling. Failure of weekly administrations of amphetamine to result in conditioned rotation was also reported by Robinson (1984). The possibility that differences in results are attributable to differences in the drug stimuli provided by apomorphine and amphetamine has been discussed (Silverman, 1993). Briefly, the issue is that, as a result of denervation, apomorphine serves as US for rotation at a dose that is probably not highly (perhaps not at all) discriminable, while amphetamine and cocaine induce circling only at doses that are established to serve as effective discriminative stimuli. Thus the most salient stimulus in an apomorphine session may be the environment, while in an amphetamine or cocaine session it may be drug. If that is the case, the CS for rotation (the test environment) is present in undrugged tests of previously apomorphine-treated rats, but for rats previously treated with either of the indirect agonists the CS (the drug) is missing in the tests. Contrary to this thinking, however, LSD, at doses that have unequivocal stimulus effects, results in conditioned contralateral circling (Silverman, 1988b). More recently we have found under circumstances wherein amphetamine acts with greater effect on the denervated side (results in contralateral rotation), it can result in conditioned rotation (Silverman and Lane, submitted). Thus, the alternative conclusion, that

conditioning is facilitated by denervation supersensitivity in this preparation, has considerable appeal. Whether such facilitation is a consequence of changes resultant from the lesion that facilitate postsynaptic transduction mechanisms or remove presynaptic inhibitory influences, or some combination, is open to speculation. In the lesioned rats D_1 and D_2 selective dopamine receptor agonists have the same unconditioned effect of inducing contralateral circling. Repeated administration of dopamine receptor agonists selective for either the D_1 or D_2 receptor subtypes results in increased circling with repeated administration, i.e., the response to either type of agonist becomes sensitized. Notably, however, the D_1 selective agonists result in circling conditioned to the environment while the D_2 agonists do not (Silverman, 1991, 1992a, 1993). Thus while the UR to a D_1 agonist looks very much like the UR to a D_2 agonist, and the response to either a D_1 or a D_2 agonist increases with repeated administration, the CRs are as completely different as possible (robust and absent, respectively). As, by definition (Kebabian and Calne, 1979), D_1 agonists activate adenyl cyclase, and D_2 agonists have no effect on, or inhibit, adenyl cyclase, a possible inference is that activation of this enzyme is importantly involved in the conditioned behavior. Alternatively, if the D_2 agonists at the doses used as US for rotation provide a salient interoceptive stimulus (more salient than is the rotation environment), the appropriate CS for rotation is not provided in their absence.

A final puzzling aspect of the phenomenon of rotation conditioned with apomorphine is the remarkably long average latency between conditioning trial(s) and appearance of the conditioned behavior. We showed that rats tested for conditioned rotation shortly (one day to one week) after a single apomorphine session more often than not did not exhibit the behavior, while rats tested 2 weeks or 4 weeks after the drug session invariably showed the conditioned response to the environment (Silverman and Ho, 1981). Again, our more recent results are consistent with this original observation. The fact that perhaps 1 rat in 10 shows fully developed conditioning a day after the conditioning trial shows that there is not an essential developmental process that requires 2 weeks. In the context of more recent findings (e.g., Paulson and Robinson, 1995) that stimulant-induced behavioral sensitization may become more robust as a function of time after the last drug treatment, our results are less conspicuously aberrant, but nonetheless unexplained.

EXTINCTION OF DRUG-CUED RESPONSES

There is no end of anecdotal evidence suggesting that external and internal stimuli associated with previous drug use, or previous drug withdrawal, may act to reinitiate drug-seeking behavior. Every ex-smoker and every ex-drinker has a tale to tell. O'Brien and colleagues have taken a leading role in attempts to identify, validate, and make therapeutic use of such conditioned responses to drug-associated stimuli. Initial experiments demonstrated conditioned opiate withdrawal (O'Brien, 1976; O'Brien et al., 1977). Patients on methadone maintenance were injected with a small dose of naloxone to precipitate withdrawal symptoms. Prior to naloxone injection a complex CS comprised of a tone and an odor was presented. The CS was terminated approximately 30 minutes after naloxone injection. After several conditioning trials, the establishment of a CR was evaluated. These test trials consisted of presentation of the tone and odor CS paired with a saline injection. All subjects in the latter study showed evidence of conditioned withdrawal on at least one of several physiological measures and in their subjective rating of the experience. These experiments provided good evidence that the objective and subjective elements of narcotic withdrawal syndrome in humans could be conditioned. Just as stimuli associated with drug withdrawal powerfully elicit a conditioned response, so do those associated with drug availability. Meyer and Mirin (1979) suggested that the most powerful stimulus for relapse was the

cue that drug was available. They reported that heroin-dependent subjects exhibited relatively little craving (a term discussed below) for drug when it was clear that drug was not available, for example, in a drug-free residential therapeutic community, or when drug efficacy was diminished by the presence of an antagonist, such as naltrexone. However, when drug became available for use or when subjects were placed in settings or situations in which drug procurement had previously occurred, subjective ratings for drug craving increased and remained elevated as long as the drug remained available. Craving decreased only minimally in response to drug injection, even when subjects were clearly intoxicated.

Of immediate relevance is the work of de Wit and Stewart (1981). In rats trained to self-administer cocaine, responding was extinguished by withholding drug. The rats were then (within the same session) given a single noncontingent "priming" injection of drug. The priming injection resulted in rapid reinstatement of responding. It was not necessary for the priming injection to be cocaine; responding was reinstated following noncontingent injection of amphetamine, apomorphine, or morphine, but not ethanol or heroin (perhaps because an inadequate dose of heroin was given). The same authors showed reinstatement of responding following a priming injection of morphine, and to a lesser extent amphetamine and apomorphine, but not cocaine or clonidine, in rats extinguished after being trained to self-administer heroin (de Wit and Stewart, 1983). The priming injections seemed to serve as indicators of drug availability. Not surprisingly, drugs with some similarity of interoceptive stimulus to that of the self-administered drug were most effective.

Thus, both stimuli associated with drug withdrawal and with drug availability may elicit conditioned responses that result in drug seeking. With this in mind the ability to control exposure to drug-related stimuli in the laboratory or clinic, and to extinguish responding to such stimuli in an effort ultimately to prevent relapse, is logically appealing. Opiate users have consistently been reported to exhibit subjective physiological signs of with-drawal in response to drug-related stimuli (Sideroff and Jarvik, 1980; Teasdale, 1973). Childress et al. (1986a) extended these find-ings by comparing reports of craving and withdrawal-like feelings in methadone-main-tained patients in a laboratory setting, clinic, and subjects' home. Subjects reported more such responses in their home than in the clinic, and in the clinic than in the laboratory. No-tably, craving and withdrawal symptoms were relatively independent. Subjects reported in-tense craving with no withdrawal symptoms, and vice versa.

Abstinent opiate abusers exposed to an in-tensive drug cue extinction regimen showed rapid and highly significant extinction in sub-jective craving and withdrawal ratings (Chil-dress et al., 1986b). While physiological mea-sures were taken, the physiological data were not presented, but were said to be poorly cor-related to one another and to subjective re-ports. Effect, if any, on subsequent drug use was not reported.

In methadone-maintained patients repeated drug stimulus exposure resulted in significant extinction of subjective craving, but not sub-jective withdrawal, and autonomic withdrawal symptoms were not significantly reduced (Childress et al., 1988).

The word *craving* has a long and con-tentious history that is succinctly reviewed by Bauer (1992). At one time the word was used specifically to refer to a loss of control by al-coholics following a drink that initiated a re-lapse. As such, it was deemed an unvalidated construct, and tautological as well (Mello, 1972). The word seems now to have lost all pretense at scientific meaning and specificity; its current meaning appears to have reverted to that of the layman, i.e., to have an intense desire or yearning. As a label, some find it more objectionable than most, probably be-cause its historical use has smacked of men-talism. Interestingly, only a very small pro-portion of relapsed alcoholics, crack addicts, or opiate addicts attribute their relapse to craving (Bauer, 1992). Nonetheless, subjects are able to report degrees of craving, and

changes in their verbal reports as a function of exposure to drug-related cues is a legitimate area of research endeavor.

In cocaine users, it is the subjective report of craving that seems to be the most consistent response to drug-related stimuli (Childress et al., 1988; Kranzler and Bauer, 1992; O'Brien et al., 1992). In cocaine abusers, craving in re-sponse to cocaine cues was extinguished by repeated exposure, but physiologic responses were not (Childress et al., 1988). It is interest-ing that reports of craving in response to drug-related stimuli correlate very poorly with physiological response to the same stimuli (McLellan et al., 1986).

By now the reader should appreciate the fact that stimuli associated with drug admin-istration may become conditional stimuli, and that repeated exposure to such stimuli in the absence of drug results in a greater or lesser degree of extinction of the conditioned re-sponse. The ultimate question so far as clini-cal application of this knowledge is con-cerned is whether extinction of conditioned responses to drug-related conditioned stimuli results in decreased relapse rates. There are few published studies that provide evaluation of the efficacy of extinction procedures in re-ducing relapse. Cue exposure was found no more effective in preventing relapse to ciga-rette smoking than rapid smoking or simple support at end of treatment or 1-year follow-up (Raw and Russell, 1980). Monti et al. (1993) reported that alcoholics receiving cue exposure and urge coping skills training had higher rates of abstinence in the second (but not the first) 3 months after treatment than did patients in a daily contact control group. As the treatments differed in, for example, time spent with a therapist, it is not possible to at-tribute the difference in outcome to cue expo-sure alone. Drummond and Glautier (1994) found that cue exposure treatment resulted in increased latency to relapse to heavy drinking and decreased total consumption when com-pared to relaxation control treatment in alco-holic subjects. They concluded that if the only acceptable outcome is abstinence, cue expo-sure showed no advantage over control treatment, but if outcomes less than abstinence are considered beneficial, cue exposure resulted in a measure of success.

Dawe et al. (1993) studied the effects of cue exposure on relapse in postwithdrawal opiate abusers. Cue exposure and control subjects did not differ in drug status at follow-ups averaging 7 and 32 weeks posttreatment. The most surprising finding of this study was that cue reactivity (craving and withdrawal-like scores) declined significantly in both cue exposure and control groups between the first and second assessment (3-week interval). The authors expressed reservations about the practical value of cue-exposure treatment given its time cost and the reluctant participation of clients.

The effectiveness of extinguishing responses to drug-related stimuli as a method of relapse prevention simply has not been adequately determined to allow one to reach even a tentative conclusion. But consideration of one characteristic of classically conditioned responses is sobering. We have seen that in the unilateral rat rotation experiment, a single administration of apomorphine results in the test environment serving as an effective conditioned stimulus for rotation for over a year, when the extinction tests are spaced weeks apart. Figure 5 shows results of daily extinction trials in a group of lesioned rats. These rats had been administered apomorphine a few (at most, four) times, the last administration being at least 2 weeks prior to the first extinction test. The conditioned response is extinguished very rapidly by daily undrugged exposure to the test environment. However, when tested again only a few weeks later, the conditioned response has recovered substantially. This spontaneous recovery is characteristic of classically conditioned responding and was, so far as clinical utility is concerned, ominously described by Pavlov (1927, p. 57): "We shall consider what happens to the conditioned reflexes after they have been subjected to experimental extinction and inquire whether they ever regain their original strength. . . . . All those conditioned reflexes which have been fully established invariably and spontaneously return sooner or later to their full strength."

FUTURE DIRECTIONS

Basic research directed at determining the conditions under which tolerance and sensitization to drug can be attributed to associative conditioning processes versus other processes will continue, as will intensive efforts to identify neurochemical correlates of the behavioral phenomena. Applied research to determine if extinction of reactivity to drug-related cues has therapeutic value will undoubtedly continue. Given that classically conditioned behaviors spontaneously recover after extinction, cue reactivity extinction protocols may ultimately prove not to be useful in reducing relapse rates. A recent clever demonstration of cue reactivity, extinction, and spontaneous recovery utilizing nondrug cues in human subjects (Corty and Coon, 1995) supports Pavlov's pessimistic prognostication as do the rotating rat data shown in Fig. 5. Measures of cue reactivity may well prove useful, however, as predictors of treatment outcome (Rohsenow et al., 1994) or as a means of screening for efficacy those pharmacologic agents proposed for use in treating drug dependence (Berger et al., 1996; Hersh et al., 1995; Kranzler and Bauer, 1992; Robbins et al., 1992).

SUMMARY

- The exact role of classical conditioning in critically important drug abuse phenomena such as tolerance, sensitization, and relapse is not always clear. But there is little doubt that classical conditioning is involved in each of these.
- The circumstances under which tolerance and/or sensitization develop in response to repeated drug administration continue to be elucidated. Difficulty in demonstrating (versus inferring) conditioned compensatory responses and conflicting findings regarding context-dependence of sensitization may be better reconciled when the interoceptive stimulus effects of

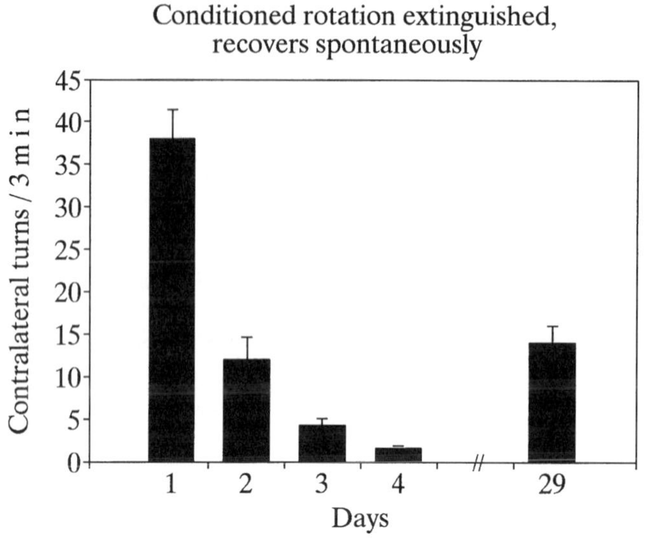

Conditioned rotation extinguished, recovers spontaneously

FIG. 5. Extinction of conditioned rotation. Lesioned rats that had been treated with apomorphine a few times circled rapidly when placed in the test environment on day 1 (which was at least 2 weeks after the last drug injection). This conditioned response extinguished quickly with daily undrugged exposure to the test environment, but recovered considerably after a few weeks without testing. Data shown are mean ± SEM for nine animals.

drugs are more fully taken into consideration.

- The extinction of reactivity to drug-related cues as a therapeutic approach is a logical outgrowth of both clinical impressions and basic research findings.
- The automatic nature of conditioned responding makes the established poor correspondence between autonomic and verbal reactivity and between relapse and verbalization of craving not unexpected.
- Outcome research evaluating effectiveness of treatment programs utilizing procedures intended to extinguish conditioned responses elicited by stimuli associated with drug use have not reached a level of maturity that allows any conclusions.
- The fact that, once extinguished, conditioned responses spontaneously recover, does not inspire confidence that efforts to reduce relapse via extinction of responses to drug stimuli are likely to be successful.
- Cue reactivity methods may be useful to predict treatment outcome and to evaluate drugs proposed to be useful in treating drug abuse.

REFERENCES

American Psychiatric Association. (1980) *Diagnostic and statistical manual of mental disorders,* 3rd ed. Washington, DC: American Psychiatric Association.

American Psychiatric Association. (1994) *Diagnostic and statistical manual of mental disorders,* 4th ed. Washington, DC: American Psychiatric Association.

Bauer, L.O. (1992) Psychobiology of craving. In: Lowinson, J., Ruiz, P. and Millman, P. (eds.) *Comprehensive textbook of substance abuse.* New York: Williams and Wilkins.

Beninger, R.J. and Hahn, B.L. (1983) Pimozide blocks establishment but not expression of amphetamine-produced environment-specific conditioning. *Science* 220: 1304–1306.

Beninger, R.J. and Herz, R.S. (1986) Pimozide blocks establishment but not expression of cocaine-produced environment-specific conditioning. *Life Sci.* 38: 1425–1431.

Berger, S.P., Hall, S., Mickalian, J.D., Reid, M.S., Crawford, C.A., Delucchi, K., Carr, K. and Hall, S. (1996) Haloperidol antagonism of cue-elicited cocaine craving. *Lancet* 347: 504–508.

Browne, R.G. and Segal, D.S. (1977) Metabolic and experiential factors in the behavioral response to repeated amphetamine. *Pharmacol. Biochem. Behav.* 6: 545–552.

Burunat, E., Diaz-Palarea, M.D., Castro, R. and Rodriguez, M. (1987) Undrugged rotational response in nigro-striatal system-lesioned rats is related to the previous early response to apomorphine when repeatedly administered. *Life Sci.* 41: 309–313.

Cappell, H., Roach, C. and Poulos, C.X. (1981) Pavlovian control of cross-tolerance between pentobarbital and ethanol. *Psychopharmacology* 74: 54–57.

Casas, M., Guix, T., Prat, G., Ferre, S., Cadafalsh, J. and Jane, F. (1988) Conditioning of rotational behavior after the administration of a single dose of apomorphine in rats with unilateral denervation of the dopaminergic nigrostriatal pathway: relevance to drug addiction. *Pharmacol. Biochem. Behav.* 31: 605–609.

Childress, A.R., McLellan, A.T., Ehrman, R. and O'Brien, C.P. (1988) Classically conditioned responses in opioid and cocaine dependence: a role in relapse? In: Ray, B.A. (ed.) *NIDA Research Monograph 84: Learning factors in substance abuse.* Washington, DC: U.S. Government Printing Office, pp. 25–43.

Childress, A.R., McLellan, A.T. and O'Brien, C.P. (1986a) Conditioned responses in a methadone population: a comparison of laboratory, clinic, and natural settings. *J. Subst. Abuse Treat.* 3: 173–179.

Childress, A.R., McLellan, A.T. and O'Brien, C.P. (1986b) Abstinent opiate abusers exhibit conditioned craving, conditioned withdrawal and reductions in both through extinction. *Br. J. Addict.* 81: 655–660.

Colpaert, F.C. and Rosecrans, J.A. (1978) *Discriminative stimulus properties of drugs: ten years of progress.* Amsterdam: Elsevier/North Holland.

Corty, E.W. and Coon, B. (1995): The extinction of naturally occurring conditioned reactions in psychoactive substance users—analog studies. *Addict. Behav.* 20: 605–618.

Crowell, C.R., Hinson, R.E. and Siegel, S. (1981) The role of conditional drug responses in tolerance to the hypothermic effects of ethanol. *Psychopharmacology* 73: 51–54.

Cunningham, C.L. (1993) Pavlovian drug conditioning. In: van Haaren, F. (ed) *Techniques in the behavioral and neural sciences, vol. 10: methods in behavioral pharmacology.* New York: Elsevier.

Dafters, R. and Anderson, G. (1982) Conditioned tolerance to the tachycardia effect of ethanol in humans. *Psychopharmacology* 78: 365–367.

Dafters, R. and Bach, L. (1985) Absence of environment-specificity in morphine tolerance acquired in non-distinctive environments: habituation or stimulus overshadowing? *Psychopharmacology* 87: 101–106.

Dawe, S., Powell, J., Richards, D., Gossop, M., Marks,I., Strang, J. and Gray, J.A. (1993) Does post-withdrawal cue exposure improve outcome in opiate addiction? A controlled trial. *Addiction* 88: 1233–1245.

de Wit, H. and Stewart, J. (1981) Reinstatement of cocaine-reinforced responding in the rat. *Psychopharmacology* 75: 134–143.

de Wit, H. and Stewart, J. (1983) Reinstatement of heroin-reinforced responding in the rat. *Psychopharmacology* 79: 29–31.

Drummond, D.C. and Glautier, S. (1994) A controlled trial of cue exposure treatment in alcohol dependence. *J. Consult. Clin. Psychol.* 62: 809–817.

Ehrman, R., Ternes, J., O'Brien, C.P. and McClellan, A.T. (1992) Conditioned tolerance in human opiate addicts. *Psychopharmacology* 108: 218–224.

Eikelboom, R. and Stewart, J. (1982) Conditioning of drug-induced physiological responses. *Psychol. Rev.* 89: 507–528.

Epstein, L.H., Caggiula, A.R., Perkins, K.A., McKenzie, S.J. and Smith, J.A. (1991) Conditioned tolerance to the heart rate effects of smoking. *Pharmacol. Biochem. Behav.* 39: 15–19.

Epstein, L.H., Caggiula, A.R., and Stiller, R. (1989) Environment-specific tolerance to nicotine. *Psychopharmacology* 97: 235–237.

Glennon, R.A., Jarbe, T.U.C. and Frankenheim, J. (1991)

NIDA Research Monograph 116: Drug discrimination: applications to drug abuse research. Washington, DC: U.S. Government Printing Office.

Goudie, A.J. (1990) Conditioned opponent processes in the development of tolerance to psychoactive drugs. *Prog. Neuropsychopharmacol. Biol. Psych.* 14: 675–688.

Goudie, A.J. and Emmett-Oglesby, M.W. (1989) *Psychoactive drugs: tolerance and sensitization.* Clifton, NJ: Humana Press.

Hall, J.F. (1984) Backward conditioning in Pavlovian type studies: reevaluation and present status. *Pavlov. J. Biol. Sci.* 19: 163–168.

Hersh, D., Bauer, L.O. and Kranzler (1995) Carbamazepine and cocaine-cue reactivity. *Drug Alcohol Depend.* 39: 213–221.

Hinson, R.E. and Poulos, C.X. (1981) Sensitization to the behavioral effects of cocaine: modification by Pavlovian conditioning. *Pharmacol. Biochem. Behav.* 15: 559–562.

Hoffman, D.C. and Wise, R.A. (1992) Locomotor-activating effects of the D2 agonist bromocriptine show environment-specific sensitization following repeated injections. *Psychopharmacology* 107: 277–284.

Holland, P.C. and Rescorla, R.A. (1975) Second-order conditioning with food unconditioned stimulus. *J. Comp. Physiol. Psychol.* 88: 459–467.

Kalivas, P.W. and Stewart, J. (1991) Dopamine transmission in the initiation and expression of drug- and stress-induced sensitization of motor activity. *Brain Res. Rev.* 16: 223–244.

Kebabian, J.W. and Calne, D.B. (1979) Multiple receptors for dopamine. *Nature* 277: 93–96.

Klug, J.M. and Norman, A.B. (1993) Long-term sensitization of apomorphine-induced rotation behavior in rats with dopamine deafferentation or excitotoxin lesions of the striatum. *Pharmacol. Biochem. Behav.* 46: 397–403.

Krank, M.D. (1987) Conditioned hyperalgesia depends on the pain sensitivity measure. *Behav. Neurosci.* 101: 854–857.

Kranzler, H.R. and Bauer, L.O. (1992) Bromocriptine and cocaine cue reactivity in cocaine-dependent patients. *Br. J. Addict.* 87: 1537–1548.

Le, A.D. and Khanna, J.M. (1989) Dispositional mechanisms in drug tolerance and sensitization. In: Goudie, A.J. and Emmett-Oglesby, M.W. (eds.) *Psychoactive drugs: tolerance and sensitization.* Clifton, NJ: Humana Press.

Lubow, R.E. (1973) Latent inhibition. *Psychol. Bull.* 79: 398–407.

Mansfield, J.G. and Cunningham, C.L. (1980) Conditioning and extinction of tolerance to the hypothermic effect of ethanol in rats. *J. Comp. Physiol. Psychol.* 94: 962–969.

Mansfield, J.G., Wenger, J.R., Benedict, R.S., Halter, J.B. and Woods, S.C. (1981) Sensitization to the hyperthermic and catecholamine-releasing effects of morphine. *Life Sci.* 29: 1697–1704.

Mattingly, B.A. and Gotsick, J.E. (1989) Conditioning and experiential factors affecting the development of sensitization to apomorphine. *Behav. Neurosci.* 103: 1311–1317.

McCaul, M., Turkkan, J.S. and Stitzer, M.L. (1989) Conditioned opponent responses: effects of placebo challenge in alcoholic subjects. *Alcohol. Clin. Exp. Res.* 13: 613–635.

McLellan, A.T., Childress, A.R., Ehrman, R., O'Brien, C.P. and Pashko, S. (1986) Extinguishing conditioned processes during opiate dependence treatment: turning laboratory findings into clinical procedures. *J. Subst. Abuse Treat.* 3: 33–40.

Melchior, C.L. and Tabakoff, B. (1985) Features of environment-dependent tolerance to ethanol. *Psychopharmacology* 87: 94–100.

Mello, N.K. (1972) Behavioral studies of alcoholism. In: Kissin, B. and Begleiter, H. (eds.) *The biology of alcoholism*, vol. 2. New York: Plenum Press.

Meyer, R.E. and Mirin, S.M. (1979) *The heroin stimulus: implications for a theory of addiction*. New York: Plenum Press.

Moller, H-G., Nowak, K. and Kuschinsky, K. (1987) Conditioning of pre- and post-synaptic behavioral responses to the dopamine receptor agonist apomorphine in rats. *Psychopharmacology* 91: 50–55.

Monti, P.M., Rohsenow, D.J., Rubonis, A.V., Niaura, R.S., Sirota, A.D., Colby, S.M., Goddard, P. and Abrams, D.B. (1993) Cue exposure with coping skills treatment for male alcoholics: a preliminary investigation. *J. Consult. Clin. Psychol.* 61: 1011–1019.

Mucha, R.F., Volkovskis, C. and Kalent, H. (1981) Conditioned increase in locomotor activity produced with morphine as the unconditioned stimulus and the relation of conditioning to acute morphine. *J. Comp. Physiol. Psychol.* 95: 351–362.

O'Brien, C.P. (1976) Experimental analysis of conditioning factors in human narcotic addiction. *Pharmacol. Rev.* 27: 533–543.

O'Brien, C.P., Childress, A.R. McLellan, A.T. and Ehrman, R. (1992) Classical conditioning in drug-dependent humans. *Ann. N.Y. Acad. Sci.* 654: 400–415.

O'Brien, C.P., Testa, T., O'Brien, T.J., Brady, J.P. and Wells, B. (1977) Conditioned narcotic withdrawal in humans. *Science* 195: 1000–1002.

Paulson, P.E. and Robinson, T.E. (1995) Amphetamine-induced time-dependent sensitization of dopamine neurotransmission in the dorsal and ventral striatum: a microdialysis study in behaving rats. *Synapse* 19: 56–65.

Pavlov, I.P. (1927) *Physiological reflexes*. (G.V. Anrep, trans.) New York: Dover, 1960.

Pert, A., Post, R., and Weiss, S.R.B. (1990) Conditioning as a critical determinant of sensitization induced by psychomotor stimulants. In: Erinoff, L. (ed.) *NIDA Research Monograph 97: neurobiology of drug abuse*. Washington, DC: U.S. Government Printing Office, pp. 208–241.

Post, R.M., Lockfeld, A., Squillace, K.M. and Contel, N.R. (1981) Drug-environment interaction: context-dependency of cocaine induced sensitization. *Life Sci.* 28: 755–760.

Post, R.M. and Rose, H. (1976) Increasing effects of repetitive cocaine administration in the rat. *Nature* 260: 731–732.

Post, R.M., Weiss, S.R.B., Fontana, D. and Pert, A. (1992) Conditioned sensitization to the psychomotor stimulant cocaine. *Ann. N.Y. Acad. Sci.* 654: 386–399.

Raw, M. and Russell, M.A.H. (1980) Rapid smoking, cue exposure and support in the modification of smoking. *Behav. Res. Ther.* 18: 363–372.

Rescorla, R.A. (1988) Behavioral studies of Pavlovian conditioning. *Annu. Rev. Neurosci.* 11: 329–52.

Rizley, R.C. and Rescorla, R.A. (1972) Associations in second-order conditioning and sensory preconditioning. *J. Comp. Physiol. Psychol.* 81: 1–11.

Robbins, S.J., Ehrman, R.N., Childress, A.R. and O'Brien, C.P. (1992) Using cue reactivity to screen medications for cocaine abuse: a test of amantadine hydrochloride. *Addict. Behav.* 17: 491–499.

Robinson, T.E. (1984) Behavioral sensitization: characterization of enduring changes in rotational behavior produced by intermittent injections of amphetamine in male and female rats. *Psychopharmacology* 84: 466–475.

Robinson, T.E. and Becker, J.B. (1986): Enduring changes in brain and behavior produced by chronic amphetamine administration: a review and evaluation of animal models of amphetamine psychosis. *Brain Res. Rev.* 11: 157–198.

Robinson, T.E. and Berridge, K.C. (1993) The neural basis of drug craving: an incentive-sensitization theory of addiction. *Brain Res. Rev.* 18: 247–291.

Roffman, M., and Lal, H. (1974) Stimulus control of hexobarbital narcosis and metabolism in mice. *J. Pharmacol. Exp. Ther.* 191: 358–369.

Rohsenow, D.J., Monti, P.M., Rubonis, A.V., Sirota, A.D., Niaura, R.S., Colby, S.M., Wunschel, S.M. and Abrams, D.B. (1994) Cue reactivity as a predictor of drinking among male alcoholics. *J. Consult. Clin. Psychol.* 62: 620–626.

Rothman, R.B., Gorelick, D.A., Baumann, M.H., Guo, X.Y., Herning, R.I., Pickworth, W.B., Gendron, T.M., Koeppl, B., Thomson, L.E.III and Henningfield, J.E. (1994) Lack of evidence for context-dependent cocaine-induced sensitization in humans: preliminary studies. *Pharmacol. Biochem. Behav.* 49: 583–588.

Schiff, S.R. (1982) Conditioned dopaminergic activity. *Biol. Psychol.* 17: 135–154.

Schreiber, H.L., Wood, W.G. and Carlson, R.H. (1976) The role of locomotion in conditioning methylphenidate-induced locomotor activity. *Pharmacol. Biochem. Behav.* 4: 393–395.

Segal, D.S. (1975) Behavioral and neurochemical correlates of repeated d-amphetamine administration. *Adv. Biochem. Psychopharmacol.* 13: 247–262.

Segal, D.S. and Mandell, A.J. (1974) Long-term administration of amphetamine: progressive augmentation of motor activity and stereotypy. *Pharmacol. Biochem. Behav.* 2: 249–255.

Sideroff, S.I. and Jarvik, M.E. (1980) Conditioned responses to a videotape showing heroin-related stimuli. *Int. J. Addict.* 15: 529–536.

Siegel, S. (1975) Evidence from rats that morphine tolerance is a learned response. *J. Comp. Physiol. Psychol.* 89: 498–506.

Siegel, S. (1978) Tolerance to the hyperthermic effect of morphine in the rat is a learned response. *J. Comp. Physiol. Psychol.* 92: 1137–1149.

Siegel, S., Hinson, R.E., Krank, M.D. and McCully, J. (1982) Heroin "overdose" death: the contribution of drug-associated environmental cues. *Science* 216: 436–437.

Silverman, P.B. (1988a) Apomorphine induces latent rotation in lesioned rats, amphetamine does not. *Life Sci.* 42: 2397–2401.

Silverman, P.B. (1988b) LSD: permanent behavioral effect in rats. *Eur. J. Pharmacol.* 147: 309–311.

Silverman, P.B. (1990) Direct dopamine agonist-like activity conditioned to cocaine. *Pharmacol. Biochem. Behav.* 37: 231–234.

Silverman, P.B. (1991) Sensitization and conditioned rotation: apomorphine, quinpirole, and SKF-38393 compared. *Neuroreport* 2: 669–672.

Silverman, P.B. (1992a) Sensitization, response fluctuation and long-term effect of SKF-82958 and bromocriptine in the hemi-parkinsonian rat. *Eur. J. Pharmacol.* 229: 235–240.

Silverman, P.B. (1992b) Classically conditioned rotation: tests with cocaine and l-dopa. In: Harris, L.S. (ed.) *NIDA*

Research Monograph 119: problems of drug dependence research. Washington, DC: U.S. Government Printing Office, p. 342.

Silverman, P.B. (1993) On-off effects of dopamine receptor agonists in the hemi-parkinsonian rat. *Eur. J. Pharmacol.* 242: 31–36.

Silverman, P.B., Grabowski, J. and Lane, K.E. (1992) Rotational behavior as a classically conditioned response to pentobarbital administration. *Eur. J. Pharmacol.* 212: 165–169.

Silverman, P.B. and Ho, B.T. (1981) Persistent behavioral effect of apomorphine in 6-hydroxydopamine-lesioned rats. *Nature* 294: 475–476.

Smith, M.C., Coleman, S.R. and Gormezano, I. (1969) Classical conditioning of the rabbit's nictitating membrane response at backward, simultaneous, and forward CS-US intervals. *J. Comp. Physiol. Psychol.* 69: 226–231.

Solomon, R.L. (1980) The opponent-process theory of acquired motivation: the costs of pleasure and the benefits of pain. *Am. Psychol.* 35: 691–712.

Stewart, J. and Vezina, P. (1987) Environment-specific enhancement of the hyperactivity induced by systemic or intra-VTA morphine injections in rats preexposed to amphetamine. *Psychobiology* 15: 144–153.

Teasdale, J. (1973) Conditioned abstinence in narcotic addicts. *Int. J. Addictions* 8: 273–292.

Thompson, T. and Pickens, R. (1971). *Stimulus properties of drugs*. New York: Plenum.

Tiffany, S.T., Petrie, E.C., Baker, T.B. and Dahl, J. (1983) Conditioned morphine tolerance in the rat: absence of a compensatory response and cross-tolerance with stress. *Behav. Neurosci.* 97: 335–353.

Tilson, H.A. and Rech, R.H. (1973) Conditioned drug effects and absence of tolerance to d-amphetamine induced motor activity. *Pharmacol. Biochem. Behav.* 1: 149–153.

Ungerstedt, U. (1971) Postsynaptic supersensitivity after 6-hydroxydopamine induced degeneration of the nigro-striatal dopamine system. *Acta Physiol. Scand. Suppl.* 367: 69–93.

Vezina, P. and Stewart, J. (1990) Amphetamine administered to the ventral tegmental area but not to the nucleus accumbens sensitizes rats to systemic morphine: lack of conditioned effects. *Brain. Res.* 516: 99–106.

Weiss, S.R.B., Post, R.M., Pert, A., Woodward, R. and Murman, D. (1989) Context-dependent cocaine sensitization: differential effects of haloperidol on development versus expression. *Pharmacol. Biochem. Behav.* 34: 655–661.

Wikler, A. (1948) Recent progress in research on the neurophysiologic basis of morphine addiction. *Am. J. Psychiatry* 105: 329–338.

Wikler, A. (1977) The search for the psyche in drug dependence: a 35-year retrospective survey. *J. Nerv. Ment. Dis.* 165: 29–40.

Wise, R.A. and Leeb, K. (1993) Psychomotor-stimulant sensitization: a unitary phenomenon? *Behav. Pharmacol.* 4: 339–349.

PART II

Neurobiological Processes

Drug Addiction and its Treatment: Nexus of Neuroscience and Behavior, edited by Bankole A. Johnson and John D. Roache. Lippincott–Raven Publishers, Philadelphia, © 1997.

6

Neurobiological Basis of Drug Reinforcement

*Scott E. Hemby, †Bankole A. Johnson, and ‡Steven I. Dworkin

*Department of Pharmacology, University of Pennsylvania School of Medicine,
Philadelphia, Pennsylvania 19104; †Department of Psychiatry, University of Texas Health Science Center-
Houston Mental Science Institute, Houston, Texas 77030; ‡Department of Physiology and Pharmacology,
Bowman Gray School of Medicine, Winston-Salem, North Carolina 27157*

Research related to the behavioral actions of abused drugs has established that these compounds can serve as reinforcers (i.e., increase the probability or frequency of a response that results in contingent drug presentation; Skinner, 1932). The relationship of this process with basic brain neurochemistry has been the objective of recent research. Although significant advances have occurred in identifying some of the basic neurobiological processes involved in the behavioral effects of abused drugs, this research field is still in its infancy. For example, while significant advances have been made in the technology used to assess neurotransmitter activity (e.g., neurotransmitter turnover and/or concentrations) during or following drug intake, it has not been as easy to discern how these observed changes are directly related to behaviors that are engendered and maintained by abused drugs. That is, few experiments have provided concurrent measures of reinforced behavior and neurotransmitter release or function. Studies evaluating the neurochemical effects of response-independent drug administration have provided data related to the pharmacologic actions of abused drugs. However, response-independent drug administration does not reliably produce reinforcing effects. Therefore, data obtained using such procedures may not reflect the magnitude or quality of neurotransmitter activity observed with response-dependent drug administration (i.e., reinforcement). Another difficulty in relating changes in neurotransmitter activity to behavior is the temporal resolution and neurochemical specificity of current analytical procedures, two parameters that appear to be sacrificed one on behalf of the other. For instance, under most conditions, microdialysis coupled with high-performance liquid chromatography (HPLC) provides adequate neurochemical specificity for relating neurochemistry with behavior. Nevertheless, it lacks the temporal resolution available with less specific neurochemical techniques (e.g., *in vivo* voltametry) or procedures without biochemical specificity (e.g., electrophysiology). Recent advances in bioanalytical technology may enable a more precise understanding of the interactions between neurochemistry and behavior.

The neurobiological basis of drug abuse requires an understanding of behavior, neurotransmitter systems, pharmacology, and neurochemistry. Therefore, this chapter is divided into several sections that will focus on these disciplines. The chapter begins with an overview of the behavioral and bioanalytical procedures used to discern the neuropharmacologic basis of drug reinforcement. Next, we review the theoretical basis of neurotransmitter involvement in drug reinforcement, with special attention on dopamine (DA). This is followed by a section on neurochemistry. The chapter concludes with a summary and the proposal of various criteria for establishing neurotransmitter involvement in drug reinforcement. The main species of focus in this chapter will be the rat inasmuch as the vast majority of research into the neuropharmacological/neurobiological underpinnings of drug reinforcement has been conducted in this species.

BEHAVIOR AND BIOANALYTICAL PROCEDURES

Two of the most widely used procedures in drug abuse research are the conditioned place preference (CPP) and self-administration procedures. Generally, CPP is considered to be a

reliable indicator of the abuse liability of drugs and is commonly used to approximate affective states associated with abused drugs. The basic premise with CPP is the ability of drugs to elicit approach responses and maintenance of contact (Carr et al., 1989). Generally, drug administration is paired with environmental stimuli distinctive from those paired with vehicle administration. Following training, subjects are tested for preference or aversion for the drug-paired environment, in the absence of the drug (Fig. 1).

Often-cited advantages of CPP include the ability to assess the rewarding or aversive effects of drugs, the ability to test subjects in a drug-free state (negating sensorimotor effects inherent with self-administration procedures), and the minimal number of drug exposures

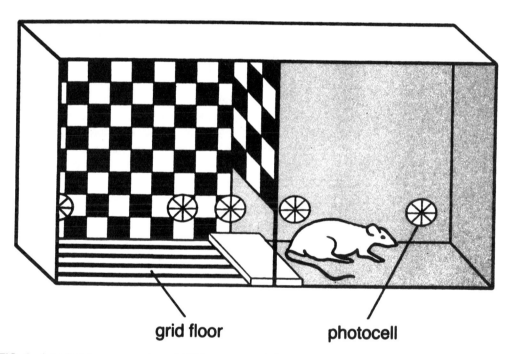

grid floor   **photocell**

FIG. 1. A typical two-compartment CPP apparatus. The compartments have distinct visual, tactile, and olfactory stimuli; one compartment has a grid floor and checked walls and the other compartment has a smooth floor and solid-colored walls. During conditioning trials, rats are allowed access to one compartment at a time. One compartment is paired with drug administration and the other is paired with vehicle administration, usually on alternate days. On the test day, rats are allowed access to the entire apparatus. Drug or vehicle is not administered on the test day. The amount of time the rat spends in each compartment is the dependent measure and can be assessed by photocell beams (see diagram) or recorded by an observer blind to experimental conditions. (Adapted from Stolerman, 1992.)

required to produce CPP. The utility of this procedure is also highlighted by the fact that there is general concordance between drugs that produce CPP, those drugs self-administered by laboratory animals, and those abused by humans. However, the utility of the CPP procedure is hindered by the lack of dose-dependent effects of tested drugs, and more importantly by the fact that drug administration in this paradigm is not dependent on a response emitted by the subject. Therefore, a strict interpretation of the definition of reinforcement indicates that CPP is simply not a measure of the reinforcing effects of drugs, but instead may yield insight into the conditioned stimulus effects of abused compounds.

Self-administration is a useful model for investigating the manner in which neurochemical and neuropharmacologic processes influence behaviors related to drug reinforcement. In general, a particular behavior or class of behaviors (lever press, alley running, nose poke) emitted by the experimental subject is maintained by drug administration (e.g., oral, intravenous, or intracranial; Fig. 2).

Skinner (1932) defined a reinforcing stimulus as a particular environmental event or set of events that follow a specific class of behaviors and increase the probability or frequency of the occurrence of the behavioral class. The presentation of the reinforcing stimulus maintains and controls behavior. Additionally, it engenders and maintains a classic pattern of responding such that the behavior(s) are emitted under specific stimulus conditions. Importantly, this definition deliberately avoids the association of positive reinforcement with increased hedonic tone or other emotion-related conditions, interpretations often made in CPP studies. Also, inherent in this definition of reinforcement is the contingent relationship between behavior and stimulus presentation (drug administration). Operant responding consists of a three-term contingency between environment stimuli that occasion responding, the response, and the contingent delivery of an environmental event that increases the probability or frequency of the response. Therefore, a taxonomy has been proposed to understand the role

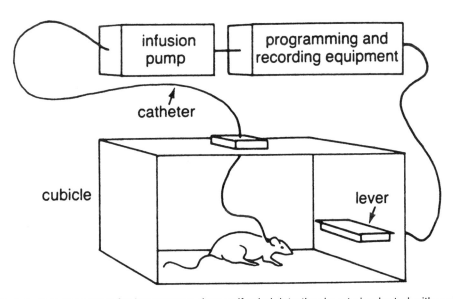

FIG. 2. A typical apparatus for intravenous drug self-administration in rats implanted with a chronic indwelling jugular catheter The catheter is connected to a syringe, containing a drug solution, mounted on a syringe infusion pump. In this case, lever pressing is maintained by delivery of a predetermined volume of the drug solution. Responses are recorded and drug delivery is controlled by programming and recording equipment (i.e., computer). (Adapted from Stolerman, 1992.)

of both contingent (i.e., the reinforcing effects) and noncontingent (i.e., direct effects including interoceptive state) stimuli in drug or stimulus-seeking behavior (Di Chiara, 1995; Katz, 1989). The concept of contingency represents an important difference between CPP and self-administration that is often ignored when comparing results from the two paradigms.

There are five principal advantages to the self-administration procedure. First, drugs abused by humans, such as cocaine, heroin, and alcohol can function as reinforcers (i.e., are self-administered) under laboratory conditions (reviewed in Katz, 1989). Second, there is general concordance between substances that are abused by humans and those that are self-administered by animals in the laboratory (Griffiths and Balster, 1979; Griffiths et al., 1980). Third, a variety of species have been shown to readily acquire and maintain behaviors by the delivery of drug injections under a variety of schedules (Pickens and Harris, 1968; Pickens and Thompson, 1968; Pickens et al., 1978; Yokel and Pickens, 1973). Fourth, clear dose-effect curves can be generated using the self-administration procedure. Dose-effect curves for response rate and/or the number of drug infusions are typically characterized by an inverted- U–shaped function. That is, low to moderate doses increase responding and higher doses result in dose-related decreases (Pickens et al., 1978; Wilson et al., 1971). The shape of the dose-response curve may reflect dose-dependent changes in the drug's reinforcing effects and/or the direct effects of the drug on responding (Katz, 1989). The shape of the dose-response function can be manipulated by altering the schedule employed or the behavioral or pharmacological history of the subject. Fifth, the self-administration procedure allows the study of both the primary and secondary reinforcing effects of drugs. For example, environmental stimuli that occasion responding are termed discriminative stimuli and signal when a particular response class is likely to result in the presentation of a reinforcing environmental event. Discriminative stimuli that maintain responding in a manner similar to the reinforcing environmental event are referred to as conditioned reinforcers. Procedures in which conditioned or secondary reinforcers are paired with drug self-administration and are presented following responses that ultimately result in the presentation of the drug are termed second-order schedules. The response to the secondary reinforcer can be so efficacious that it can maintain responding for extended periods of time in the absence of drug presentation (Goldberg et al., 1976, 1981; Goldberg and Tang, 1977). Contextual factors can alter profoundly the affective, behavioral, and neurophysiological effects of abused drugs (Goldberg and Schuster, 1967; Goldberg et al., 1969; O'Brien et al., 1992).

There are two main disadvantages of self-administration procedures. First, two of the most common routes of drug self-administration, intracranial and intravenous, require invasive surgical procedures. Second, direct effects of the self-administered drug may interfere with the dependent measure (rate of responding). While not a disadvantage of the self-administration procedure per se, overinterpretation of data is a common pitfall. Reinforcement does not explain drug addiction: simply, it allows for quantification of the initiation and maintenance of a response occurring in the presence of specific stimuli and resulting in the presentation of the reinforcing stimulus. Other factors such as learning, memory, and performance may alter both the acquisition and expression of reinforcement.

THEORETICAL CONSTRUCT

A driving hypothesis in drug abuse research has been the psychomotor stimulant theory of addiction; an attempt to provide a unifying theory of the mechanisms that mediate drug abuse (Wise and Bozarth, 1987). According to this theory, "all addictive drugs have psychomotor stimulant properties and...the biological mechanism of the psychomotor stimulant properties is the same as, or has common elements with, the biological mechanism of the reinforcing effects of these drugs." The authors further state that "opiates and psychomotor stimulants activate a common reinforcement mechanism" (Wise and Bozarth, 1987, p. 483). The proposed common mechanism of these effects is activation of dopaminergic neurons of the mesocorticolimbic system.

The mesocorticolimbic DA pathway has received considerable attention as a critical substrate for the reinforcing effects of a variety of events including feeding, drinking, sexual behavior, electrical brain stimulation, and drug self-administration (Damsma et al., 1992; Fibiger and Phillips, 1986; Fiorino et al., 1993; Koob and Bloom 1988; Wise and Bozarth, 1987). Results from several studies suggest that specific loci in the mesocorticolimbic pathway play an important role in the reinforcing effects of psychomotor stimulants, such as cocaine and amphetamine (Fig. 3, Table 1), and opiates, such as heroin and morphine (Fig. 4, Table 2).

NEUROTRANSMITTER SYSTEMS

Dopamine

Dopamine neurons of the ventral mesencephalon have been categorized into A8, A9, and A10 cell groups (Dahlström and Fuxe, 1965). The A9 group corresponds to the substantia nigra and the A10 region the ventral tegmental area (VTA). The A9 group contains the cell bodies of the nigrostriatal DA system that project predominantly, although not exclusively, to the caudate nucleus (striatum). Likewise, the cell bodies of the VTA project to several basal forebrain areas including the nucleus accumbens (NAcc/ventral anterior striatum), bed nucleus of the stria terminalis, diagonal band of Broca and olfactory tubercles, the prefrontal and anterior cingulate cortices, the hippocampus, and the amygdala) (Lindvall and Bjorklund, 1974, 1983; Ungerstedt, 1971). The term mesotelencephalic dopamine system is commonly used to refer to both pathways because of the close prox-

imity of the A9 and A10 cell bodies and the considerable overlap of the projection fields.

Like the other monoamine transmitters, DA in the synaptic cleft is deactivated by diffusion, metabolic degradation, and uptake into the presynaptic terminal. The enzymes responsible for monoamine metabolism are monoamine oxidase A and B, present primarily intraneuronally and extraneuronally respectively, and catechol-O-methyltransferase, which is primarily extraneuronal. DA is metabolized to dihydroxyphenylacetic acid (DOPAC) by monoamine oxidase and then to homovanillic acid (HVA) by catechol-O-methyltransferase (Cooper et al., 1986).

The termination of DA's actions in the synaptic cleft is accomplished by the aforementioned catabolic enzymes and to a greater degree by uptake into the presynaptic terminal via a voltage-dependent transporter. The uptake process is important in maintaining synaptic concentrations as well as limiting the extent and duration of DA's effects. Therefore, blockade of this process, by a drug such as cocaine, causes a significant increase in extracellular DA concentrations, an effect to which the principal behavioral effects of cocaine have been attributed (Bergman et al., 1989; Ritz et al., 1987). Initially, one or two sodium ions (Na^+) along with a chloride ion (Cl^-) bind to the transporter resulting in an outward orientation until DA binds (Bannon et al., 1995). The uptake process is voltage dependent with the sodium gradient providing the driving force for the cotransport of DA, Na^+ and Cl^-. During the depolarization phase of the action potential, voltage gated Na^+ channels are opened and Na^+ flows into the neuron, down its concentration gradient. Due to the dissipation of the gradient, the transporter is not activated. During repolarization, the sodium gradient is reestablished and the DA transporter is activated leading to the transport of dopamine into the presynaptic terminal. The net effect of this process is to allow maximal transmitter concentrations in the synaptic cleft during depolarization and rapid removal during repolarization (Bannon et al., 1995; Rudnick and Clark, 1993). Although the mechanism by which cocaine inhibits the uptake of DA is not completely understood, the synthesis of cocaine analogues have enabled further characterization of the binding site requirements for the potential treatment of drug abuse (Carroll et al. 1992a,b, Davies et al., 1993, 1994; Staley et al., 1994).

The effects of DA were originally considered to be mediated by activation of either D_1 or D_2 receptors (Kebabian and Calne, 1979). These receptors have been shown to be both pharmacologically and biochemically distinct. The antagonist SCH 23390 binds with high affinity to D_1 receptors and the antagonist spiperone binds selectively to D_2 receptors. While both receptors are coupled to G proteins, D_1 stimulates G_s protein activating adenylate cyclase and, in turn, stimulating cyclic adenosine monophosphate (cAMP) production. In contrast, the D_2 receptor interacts with G_i protein to inhibit adenylate cyclase activity. It should be noted that these effects may be dependent on neuroanatomical localization (Civelli, 1995). With the advent of recombinant deoxyribonucleic acid (DNA) technology, three variants of these receptors were cloned and dopamine receptors are now categorized into two subfamilies: D_1-like—D_1 and D_5 (D_{1b} in rats), and D_2-like—D_2, D_3, and D_4 (Sokoloff et al., 1990; Tiberi et al., 1991; see Civillei, 1995). Within the D_2-like subfamily, the receptors have been pharmacologically differentiated. The antagonists AJ76 and UH232 bind with greater affinity to D_3 versus D_2 receptors (Sokoloff et al., 1990) and clozapine is more highly selective for D_4 than D_2 or D_3 (Civelli, 1995). Additionally, the agonist 7-OHDPAT has greater affinity for D_3 than D_2 or D_4.

Localization of messenger ribonucleic acid (mRNA) for these receptors reveals considerable overlap with protein levels, although with varying specificity. Large amounts of D_1 and D_2 mRNA are present in the NAcc, caudate nucleus, and olfactory tubercles, and considerably less mRNA for these receptors is found in the hypothalamus and cortex. D_3 and D_4 mRNA appear to be restricted to limbic structures, whereas D_5 mRNA has been found in the hippocampus, hypothalamus, and thalamus (Civelli, 1995). In the VTA and substantia nigra there are larger amounts of D_2 mRNA than D_1, while the amygdala has D_1 mRNA but no measurable amounts of D_2 mRNA (Civelli, 1995).

Serotonin

It is important to stress that the mesolimbic dopamine system does not mediate reinforcement in isolation. Indeed, there is strong evidence that midbrain DA is itself modulated, primarily by γ-aminobutyric acid (GABA), serotonin (5-HT), endogenous opioids, and excitatory amino acids. In the last decade, there has been a dramatic increase in the understanding about 5-HT receptors and pathways and their involvement in the expression of numerous psychological and behavioral conditions including drug dependence. Of the nine 5-HT nuclei, the dorsal and median raphe and the centralis superior provide the most extensive 5-HT innervation of the midbrain and forebrain regions. For example, projections of the median raphe are coarse, thick, beaded, fibers with varicosed terminals and mainly innervate the hippocampus and septal areas, whereas the projections of the dorsal raphe mainly innervate the cortical and striatal areas terminate in several limbic regions including the NAcc (Audet et al., 1989; Dahlström and Fuxe, 1965). The organizational segregation of these ascending projections from 5-HT cell bodies is interesting in terms of the distinction in morphology and topographical distribution (Molliver, 1987).

These projections not only differ in morphology but in sensitivity and responsiveness to various neurochemicals, perhaps because they are associated with differential distribution of 5-HT receptor subtypes. In recent years the number of identified receptor subtypes has increased rapidly. In this chapter, the focus will therefore be on subtypes that have been investigated as having a role in drug-seeking behavior. The 5-HT₁ class (divided into an additional four subclasses, A–D), contains both presynaptic and postsynaptic receptors. The 5-HT$_{1a}$ receptor serves as an autoreceptor and also postsynaptic receptor. Receptors in the subclasses 5-HT$_2$ and 5-HT$_3$ are all postsynaptic receptors. There are, however, important functional differences among receptor subtypes. Of note, the 5-HT$_3$ receptor exerts its effects via the ligand-gated ion channel and has been shown to be a positive modulator of DA release, particularly in the NAcc. Recent studies indicate that 5-HT$_3$ receptors may augment the activities of GABA and cholecystokinin (CCK) in the central nervous system. The 5-HT$_2$ receptor manifests activity by increasing turnover of the second messenger, phosphatidyl inositol (PI). The 5-HT projections from the raphe have been shown to synapse on DA cells in the substantia nigra (SN) and VTA (Hervé et al., 1987; Nedergaard et al., 1988) and 5-HT$_2$ receptors have been shown to inversely modulate DA burst firing. Thus, 5-HT plays an important role as a modulator of DA function. While subclasses A, B, and D of the 5-HT$_1$ receptor exert their effects by increasing cAMP turnover, 5-HT$_{1c}$ (and 5-HT$_2$) receptors are linked to PI.

Opioids

Autoradiographic localization studies have shown a high density of μ opiate receptors in the VTA, and μ, δ, and κ receptors in several terminal projection fields including the NAcc (Dilts and Kalivas, 1989; Mansour et al., 1987; Tempel and Zukin, 1987). Morphine and endogenous opioid neuropeptides exert their effects by binding to distinct receptors generally classified as μ, δ, and κ (Gillan and Kosterlitz, 1982; Goldstein and Naidu, 1989; Paterson et al., 1983). Mu (μ) receptors have a high affinity for the agonists morphine, dihydromorphine, and oxymorphone and their effects are antagonized by naltrexone. Naloxonazine and naloxazone are antagonists that bind to the μ$_1$ receptor that exhibits high affinity for opiates and opioid peptides (Hahn et al., 1982; Pasternak and Hahn, 1980), while

the μ$_2$ subtype has lower affinity for opiates than the μ$_1$ receptor (Wolozin and Pasternak, 1981). Delta receptors exhibit greater affinity for met and leu enkephalin, [D-Pen^2-D-Pen^5]enkephalin (DPDPE) and [D-Ser^2-Leu^5]enkephalyl-Thr (DSLET) than morphine and their effects can be antagonized by ICI 154129 (Itzhak, 1988). Kappa receptors are highly selective for the agonists dynorphin, and U50488. The effects mediated by all of these receptors can be antagonized by naloxone. Over the past few years, the μ, δ, κ and opiate receptors have been cloned enabling further studies on regulation and distribution of these receptors (Evans et al., 1992; Kieffer et al., 1992; Wang et al., 1993; Yasuda et al., 1993).

Like D$_2$ receptors, opiate receptors are coupled to G proteins that inhibit adenylate cyclase activity and/or affect ion channel conductance (see Childers, 1991). The net result of opiate receptor activation is membrane hyperpolarization either by increased K$^-$ conductance (μ and δ) or inhibition of Ca^{2+} channels (κ; Wagner and Chavkin, 1995) resulting in inhibition of transmitter release (Heijna et al. 1990; Mulder et al., 1984; Schoffelmeer et al., 1988).

Opiate receptors are found throughout the central nervous system (Mansour et al., 1986, 1987). With regard to the mesocorticolimbic DA system, μ, δ, and κ receptors are found in high levels in the NAcc. Mu receptors exhibit patchy distribution and κ receptors are located more ventrally. In addition, all three are found in most cortical areas, the amygdala, parts of the hippocampus, olfactory tubercles, striatum septum, diagonal band of broca, and the stria terminalis. In the mesencephalon, high levels exist in the entopeduncular nucleus, while in the substantia nigra pars compacta only μ receptors are found. Low levels of all three opiate receptor subtypes are found in the pars reticulata. In the VTA, only μ and κ receptors are found at moderate and low levels, respectively (Mansour et al., 1986, 1987). The localization of opiate receptors in the regions of the cell bodies and terminal field projections of the mesocorticolimbic

DA pathway suggest considerable opportunity for interaction. Such interactions have been shown to exist both neurochemically (Di Chiara and Imperato, 1988b; Mulder et al., 1989; Wood, 1983) and behaviorally (reviewed in Cooper, 1991). The manner in which acute opiate administration increases NAcc extracellular DA concentrations ($[DA]_e$) occurs is by disinhibition of dopamine cell firing via inhibition of GABA in the VTA (Gysling and Wang, 1983; Johnson and North, 1992; Matthews and German, 1984). Activation of μ-opiate receptors on GABAergic interneurons results in their hyperpolarization and concomitant disinhibition of DA cell firing. Neurochemical studies have shown that direct application of opiate agonists into the VTA increases DA metabolism and $[DA]_e$ in the NAcc (Devine et al., 1993; Kalivas, 1985; Leone et al., 1991; Yoshida et al., 1993), as well as $[DA]_e$ and extracellular GABA concentrations in the VTA (Klitenick et al., 1992; Yoshida et al., 1993). In contrast to the opiate receptor influence in the VTA, it appears that κ receptors in the NAcc have an opposite effect to decrease DA release (Clow and Jhamandas, 1988; Di Chiara and Imperato, 1988b; Heijna et al., 1990; Spanagel et al., 1990a). Thus, the mesolimbic DA system is under tonic excitatory influence from the VTA and tonic inhibitory influence in the NAcc (Spanagel et al., 1992).

GABA

GABA is the most extensively distributed neurotransmitter in the central nervous system. GABA containing neurons are the main efferent pathway of the mesolimbic DA system. Importantly, GABA efferents innervate connections from the NAcc to the substantia innominate and ventral pallidum. GABA receptors are arranged in complexes, and the main subtypes are $GABA_A$ and $GABA_B$. $GABA_A$ receptors exert their effect via ion channels that result in increased chloride conductance while the $GABA_B$ receptors are coupled to G proteins (Bormann, 1988). Activity at the $GABA_A$ receptor is potentiated by seda-

tives such as barbiturates, benzodiazepines, and ethanol (Suzdak et al., 1986). Also, benzodiazepines and barbiturates have potent anxiolytic activity that might be related to their reinforcing effects and abuse liability; thus, in conflict paradigms, these drugs enhance anti-conflict effects (Sepinwall and Cook, 1978).

DRUG SELF-ADMINISTRATION

Pharmacology

Consistent with the psychostimulant theory of addiction (Wise and Bozarth, 1987) considerable attention has focused on both direct and indirect ways in which dopaminergic mechanisms mediate drug reinforcement. The most firmly established self-administration studies that demonstrate the neurotransmitter involvement remain those based on the effects of systemic and central administration of antagonists as well as lesions studies.

Dopamine Receptor Antagonists

Numerous studies have assessed the role of mesolimbic dopaminergic function on the reinforcing effects of abused drugs. Pharmacologic manipulations of monoaminergic transmitter function have indicated a critical role for DA in the reinforcement process. Specifically, the D_1 and D_2 dopamine receptor subtypes are clearly implicated in cocaine self-administration. Several studies have demonstrated that pretreatment with DA antagonists at low to moderate doses increase responding maintained by high unit doses of cocaine (i.e., doses on the descending limb of the dose-effect curve) under fixed-ratio schedules and decrease break points under progressive ratio schedules in rats (Table 3). The increase in the rate of self-administration is thought to be a compensation on the part of the animal for the decreased reinforcing efficacy of the drug, inasmuch as increases in responding are also seen by decreasing the dose (De Wit and Wise, 1977). Noradrenergic receptors do not appear to be in-

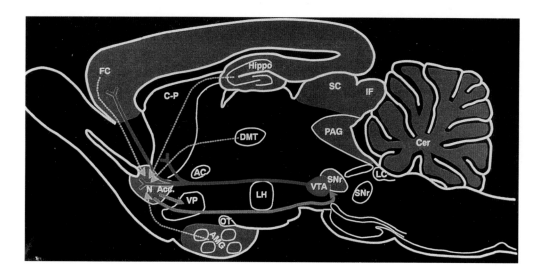

FIG. 3. Sagittal rat brain section illustrating a cocaine and amphetamine neural reward circuit that includes a limbic-extrapyramidal motor interface. Yellow indicates limbic afferents to the nucleus accumbens (NAcc) and orange represents efferents from the nucleus accumbens thought to be involved in psychomotor stimulant reward. Red indicates projections of the mesocorticolimbic dopamine system thought to be a critical substrate for psychomotor stimulant reward. This system originates in the A10 cell group of the ventral tegmental area (VTA) and projects to the NAcc olfactory tubercle and ventral striatal domains of the caudate-putamen (C-P). VP, ventral pallidum; LH, lateral hypothalamus; SNr, substantia nigra pars reticulata; DMT, dorsomedial thalamus; PAG, periaqueductal gray; OT, olfactory tract; AC, anterior commissure; LC, locus coeruleus; AMG, amygdala; Hippi, hippocampus; Cer, cerebellum. *Below:* effect of different experimental paradigms on cocaine and amphetamine reward in the rat.

Table 1. *Cocaine and amphetamine reinforcement*

Paradigm	Effect on reinforcement
Intracranial self-administration	
Medical Prefrontal Cortex (cocaine)	↑
Nucleus Accumbens (amphetamines)	↑
Intravenous self-administration	
Noradrenaline receptor antagonists	NE
5-HT receptor antagonists	NE, ↑
μ-Opioid receptor antagonists	NE
D_1 and D_2 dopamine receptor antagonists	↓
Noradrenaline denervation (6-hydroxydopamine)	NE
5-HT denervation (5.7-dihydroxytryptamine)	↑
Dopamine denervation (6-hydroxydopamine)	
Nucleus accumbens	↓
Ventral tegmental area	↓
Medial prefrontal area	NE, ↑

↑, facilitation; ↓, inhibition; NE, no effect.
Adapted, with courtesy, from George Koob (1992) and Elsevier publishers.

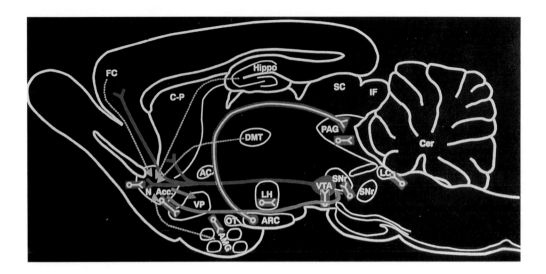

FIG. 4. Sagittal rat brain section illustrating opioid peptide-containing neurons (green), some of which may mediate opiate reward. These opioid peptide systems include the local enkephalin circuits (short segments) and the hypothalamic midbrain β-endorphin circuit (long segment). These opioid peptide systems are superimposed on the neural reward circuit shown in Fig. 3. FC, frontal cortex; VTA, ventral tegmental area; VP, ventral pallidum; LH, lateral hypothalamus; Snr, substantia nigra pars reticulata; DMT, dorsomedial thalamus; PAG, periaqueductal gray; OT, olfactory tract; AC, anterior commissure; LC, locus coeruleus; AMG, amygdala; Hippo, hippocampus; Cer, cerebellum; C-P, caudate-putamen; IF, inferior colliculus; SC, superior colliculus; ARC, arcuate nucleus. *Below:* effect of different paradigms on opiate reward in the rat.

Table 2. *Opiate reinforcement*

Paradigm	Effect on reinforcement
Intracranial self-administration	
Nucleus accumbens	↑
Lateral hypothalamus	↑
Ventral tegmental area	↑
Intravenous self-administration	
Opioid receptor antagonists	
μ-Receptor antagonists	↓
δ-Receptor antagonists	↑, NE
κ-Receptor antagonists	NE
Dopamine receptor antagonists	NE, ↓
Dopamine denervation (6-hydroxydopamine)	
Nucleus accumbens	NE

↑, facilitation; ↓, inhibition; NE, no effect.
Adapted, with courtesy, from George Koob (1992) and Elsevier publishers.

volved in the mediation of cocaine self-administration since the antagonists phentolamine and phenoxybenzamine do not alter cocaine-maintained responding (De Wit and Wise, 1977). While the majority of studies have examined the effects of DA antagonists on a single dose of the self-administered drug, the interpretation of data is more complex when considering the effects of various antagonist doses on multiple doses of the self-administered drug (Hemby et al., 1996a). Data from systemic DA antagonist administration are supported by studies examining the effects when the antagonists are administered centrally. For example, Caine et al. (1995) and Maldanado et al. (1993) have demonstrated that infusions of the D_1 antagonist SCH 23390 into the NAcc and amygdala, but not the striatum, increase rates of cocaine self-administration in rats. This provides further evidence that DA receptors in these regions are involved in cocaine reinforcement. More recently, the D_3 receptor has been implicated in cocaine reinforcement. The relatively selective D_3 receptor agonists 7-OHDPAT and quinelorane reduce cocaine self-administration under fixed ratio schedules resulting in a rightward shift in the cocaine dose-effect curves (Caine and Koob, 1993, 1995; Parsons et al., 1996a). These data are supported by the findings that the D_3 receptor antagonist (-) AJ-76 decreased break points for cocaine self-administration under progressive ratio schedules, suggesting a decrease in the reinforcing effects of cocaine (Richardson et al., 1993).

Doses of DA antagonists that alter cocaine self-administration do not alter heroin self-administration (Table 4; Ettenberg et al., 1982; Hemby et al., 1996a; Van Ree and Ramsey, 1987). Although high doses of DA antagonists can decrease heroin self-administration through a non-selective effect (Hemby et al., 1996a; Van Ree and Ramsey, 1987). In addition, DA antagonists do not block the acquisition of heroin self-administration in a consistent manner (Gerrits and Van Ree, 1996). These data suggest that opiate self-administration is mediated by dopamine-independent mechanisms (Koob and Bloom, 1988).

DA antagonists reduce ethanol consumption in a variety of paradigms including home cage drinking (Pfeffer and Samson, 1985). However, procedures that rely on a simple choice between ethanol and water have been criticized due to the confounding effects of water deprivation (Cunningham et al., 1992). Nonetheless, DA receptor antagonists administered either systemically (Pfeffer and Samson, 1985) or directly into the NAcc (Rassnick et al., 1992a; Samson et al., 1993) decrease ethanol self-administration in nondeprived rats.

The importance of DA pathways in the expression of nicotine reinforcement remains underexplored. Nicotine self-administration can be reduced by DA antagonists at low pharmacologic doses that also reduce responding maintained by food presentation (Corrigall and Coen, 1991c; Corrigall et al., 1992). At these low DA antagonist doses, performance impairment can be ruled out as the mechanism for these observations, although the specificity of the response is questionable since food intake also decreased.

Opiate Receptor Antagonists

In contrast to some nonspecific effects observed with dopamine antagonists on cocaine self-administration, opiate antagonists do not reliably alter cocaine self-administration. Decreases (Corrigall and Coen, 1991b; Ramsey and Van Ree, 1991), increases (Carroll et al., 1986), and no effect (Ettenberg et al., 1982) on responding maintained by high unit doses of cocaine have all been reported (Table 5). Recently, Hemby et al. (1996a) demonstrated that a range of naltrexone doses (1–30 mg/kg i.p.) failed to alter the cocaine dose-response curve (125–500 µg/infusion). In contrast, opiate receptor antagonists (µ and δ) increase responding maintained by high unit doses of heroin (Table 6; Ettenberg et al., 1982; Hemby et al., 1996a; Koob et al., 1984; Martin et al., 1995; Negus et al., 1993), suggesting a decrease in the reinforcing effects of heroin.

Opiate receptor systems have also been implicated in the reinforcing effects of alcohol (Ulm et al., 1995). For example, alcohol alters opiate binding to μ and δ receptors (Hiller et al., 1981; Tabakoff and Hoffman, 1983) and increases β-endorphin levels in alcohol-preferring (P) rats with a history of alcohol self-administration (de Waele and Gianoulakis, 1994). The nonspecific opiate antagonists naloxone and naltrexone decrease ethanol consumption in rodents (e.g., DeWitte, 1984; Froehlich et al., 1990; Hyytia and Sinclair, 1993; Volpicelli et al., 1986). More recently, Hyytia (1993) demonstrated that D-Phe-Cys-Try-D-Try-Orn-Thr-Pen-Thr-NH₂ (CTOP), a μ receptor antagonist, decreased alcohol consumption whereas the δ antagonist ICI 174, 864 had no effect on alcohol consumption in food- and water-sated rats during 30-min access periods to 10% w/v ethanol in the home cage. Additionally, morphine increases consumption of low doses of alcohol and decreases consumption of moderate to high doses (reviewed in Ulm et al., 1995). Consistent with these results, recent clinical trials have demonstrated that naltrexone treatment decreases alcohol drinking in dependent individuals (O'Malley et al., 1992; Volpicelli et al., 1995). These data suggest that opiate receptors may be involved in the reinforcing effects of alcohol.

Serotonin Receptor Antagonists

In the 1980s a series of papers were published by Lyness and colleagues concerning the role of serotonin in modulating intravenous amphetamine self-administration (Lecesse and Lyness, 1984; Lyness, et al., 1980; Lyness, 1983; Lyness and Moore, 1983). In general, factors that lead to increases in serotonin, such as increased tryptophan in the diet, resulted in decreases in amphetamine self-administration. In contrast, factors that decreased 5-HT, such as 5-hydroxytryptaminergic (5,7-DHT) lesions, result in increased amphetamine self-administration. As with amphetamine, some investigators found that factors that increase serotonin, such as increased tryptophan in the diet, decrease cocaine-reinforced behavior (Carroll et al., 1990; McGregor et al., 1993), whereas factors that decrease levels of 5-HT increase cocaine reinforced behavior. There are, however, some important inconsistencies. Carroll and colleagues (1990) observed that l-tryptophan had no effect on behavior maintained at the highest cocaine dose (0.4 mg/ml) in their experiments. Also, 5-HT antagonists do not appear to alter cocaine self-administration (Lacosta and Roberts, 1993; Porrino et al., 1989; Peltier and Schenk, 1991). However, the selective 5-HT₂ antagonist ritanserin reduced oral cocaine intake in rats that had developed a preference for cocaine following a period of forced exposure (Meert and Janssen, 1992; cf. Higgins et al., 1992). Ritanserin was not shown in recent clinical trials to be an efficacious treatment for either alcohol or cocaine dependence (Johnson et al., 1996a,b). The role of the 5-HT₃ receptor in amphetamine and cocaine-induced reinforcement also remains equally uncertain. Despite early results suggesting that 5-HT₃ antagonists may decrease cocaine-induced locomotion stimulation (Reith, 1990; Svingos and Hitzemann, 1992), they do not decrease cocaine self-administration (Lane et al., 1992; Peltier and Schenk, 1991).

More recent studies suggest the possibility of 5-HT involvement in cocaine self-administration. Parsons and colleagues (1996b) have demonstrated that the 5-HT₁ₐ/₁ᵦ agonist CGS-12066B increased self-administration of GBR-12909 but did not alter the self-administration of cocaine. However, administration of the more selective 5-HT₁ᵦ agonist RU 24969 altered self-administration of a low unit (0.0625 mg/kg/infusion) cocaine dose (Parsons, *personal communication*). Thus, cocaine self-administration may mask the excitatory effects of 5-HT₁ᵦ receptor stimulation by simultaneously activating other 5-HT receptor subtypes. Additional systematic examinations of serotonergic involvement in cocaine self-administration are warranted.

The 5-HT receptors may also be involved in ethanol reinforcement. Serotonergic 5-HT₁ᵦ,

TABLE 3. *Effects of dopamine receptor antagonists on cocaine self-administration in rats*

Antagonist	Dose	Cocaine dose	Schedule	Effect	References
Nonselective					
Flupenthixol	50–200 µg/kg; i.p.	0.25 mg/inf	FR1	INC	Ettenberg et al., 1982
	25–100 µg/kg; i.p.	0.25 mg/inf	FR1	INC	Roberts and Vickers, 1984
Chlorpromazine	50–200 µg/kg; i.p.	0.25 mg/inf	FR1	INC	Roberts and Vickers, 1984
Clozapine	2–12.5 mg/kg; i.p.	0.25 mg/inf	FR1	DEC	Roberts and Vickers, 1984
	10 mg/kg; i.p.	0.60 mg/inf	PR	INC BP	Loh et al., 1992
Haloperidol	50–200 µg/kg; i.p.	0.25 mg/inf	FR1	INC	Roberts and Vickers, 1984
Thioridazine	2.5–10 mg/kg; i.p.	0.25 mg/inf	FR1	INC	Roberts and Vickers, 1984
D1					
A69024	1.25 & 2.5 mg/kg; s.c.	0.25 mg/inf	FR5	INC	Caine and Koob, 1994
	0.625–2.5 mg/kg; s.c.	0.25 mg/inf	FR15 (2 min TO)	DEC	Caine and Koob, 1994
SCH23390	10 & 20 ,230>g/kg; s.c.	0.25 mg/inf	FR5	INC	Caine and Koob, 1994
	10 & 20 µg/kg; s.c.	0.25 mg/inf	FR15 (2 min TO)	DEC	Caine and Koob, 1994
	0.031–8 µg; i.c. (NAcc)	0.50 mg/inf	FR1	INC	Phillips et al. 1994
	2 µg; i.c. (NAcc)	0.25 mg/inf	FR5	INC	Maldonado et al., 1993
	10 µg/kg; i.p.	0.25 mg/inf	FR5	INC	Hubner and Moreton, 1991
	20 µg/kg; i.p.	0.25 mg/inf	FR5	DEC	Hubner and Moreton, 1991
	5–20 µg/kg; i.p.	0.25 mg/inf	PR	DEC BP	Hubner and Moreton, 1991
	3 µg/kg; i.p.	0.03–0.33 mg/inf	FR5	NE	Corrigall and Coen, 1991a
	30 µg/kg; i.p.	0.03–0.33 mg/inf	FR5	DEC	Corrigall and Coen, 1991a
	0.1–2.0 µg; i.c. (NAcc & Amyg)	0.5 mg/inf	FR1	INC	McGregor and Roberts, 1993
	0.1–2.0 µg; i.c. (NAcc & Amyg)	0.5 mg/inf	PR	DEC BP	McGregor and Roberts, 1993
	5–20 µg/kg; i.p.	0.25 mg/inf	FR5	INC	Koob et al., 1987
SCH39166	20 µg/kg; s.c.	0.25 mg/inf	FR5	INC	Caine and Koob, 1994
	20 & 40 µg/kg; s.c.	0.25 mg/inf	FR15 (2 min TO)	DEC	Caine and Koob, 1994
D2					
(+)-AJ 76	30.0 mg/kg; i.p.	0.6 mg/inf	PR	DEC BP	Richardson et al., 1993
Eticlopride	10 µg/kg; s.c.	0.25 mg/inf	FR5	INC	Caine and Koob, 1994
	20 & 40 µg/kg; s.c.	0.25 mg/inf	FR15 (2 min TO)	DEC	Caine and Koob, 1994
	0.03, 0.1, & 0.3 mg/kg; i.p.	0.125 mg/inf	FR10 (20 sec TO)	DEC	Hemby et al., 1996a
	0.03 & 0.1 mg/kg; i.p.	0.25 mg/inf	FR10 (20 sec TO)	INC	Hemby et al., 1996a
	0.3 mg/kg; i.p.	0.25 mg/inf	FR10 (20 sec TO)	DEC	Hemby et al., 1996a
	0.03, 0.1, & 0.3 mg/kg; i.p.	0.5 mg/inf	FR10 (20 sec TO)	INC	Hemby et al., 1996a
Pimozide	62.5–500 µg/kg; i.p.	1 mg/kg/inf	FR1	INC	de Wit and Wise, 1977
	25–100 µg/kg; i.p.	0.25 mg/inf	FR1	INC	Roberts and Vickers, 1984
Raclopride	0–400 µg/kg; s.c.	0.25 mg/inf	FR5	NE	Caine and Koob, 1994
	400 µg/kg; s.c.	0.25 mg/inf	FR15 (2 min TO)	DEC	Caine and Koob, 1994
Spiperone	20 µg/kg; s.c.	0.25 mg/inf	FR5	INC	Caine and Koob, 1994
	40 µg/kg; s.c.	0.25 mg/inf	FR5	DEC	Caine and Koob, 1994
	20 & 40 µg/kg; s.c.	0.25 mg/inf	FR15 (2 min TO)	DEC	Caine and Koob, 1994
	10 µg/kg; i.p.	0.25 mg/inf	FR5	INC	Hubner and Moreton, 1991
	20 & 40 µg/kg; i.p.	0.25 mg/inf	FR5	DEC	Hubner and Moreton, 1991
	10–40 µg/kg; i.p.	0.25 mg/inf	PR	DEC BP	Hubner and Moreton, 1991
	3–30 µg/kg; i.p.	0.03 & 0.1 mg/inf	FR5	NE	Corrigall and Coen, 1991a
	10 & 30 µg/kg; i.p.	0.33 mg/inf	FR5	INC	Corrigall and Coen, 1991a
	10 µg/kg; i.p.	0.25 mg/inf	FR5	INC	Koob et al., 1987
Sulpiride	5–20 mg/kg; i.p.	0.25 mg/inf	FR1	INC	Roberts and Vickers, 1984
	0.031–8 µg; i.c. (NAcc)	0.5 mg/inf	FR1	INC	Phillips et al., 1994
Autoreceptor					
(-)-DS 121	7.5 mg/kg; i.p.	0.072 mg/inf	PR	NE	Smith et al., 1995
	15 mg/kg; i.p.	0.072 mg/inf	PR	DEC BP	Smith et al., 1995
	7.5 & 15 mg/kg; i.p.	0.072 mg/inf	FR1	NE	Smith et al., 1995
(+)-UH-232	7.5 & 15 mg/kg; i.p.	0.072 mg/inf	PR	NE	Smith et al., 1995
	30 mg/kg; i.p.	0.072 mg/inf	PR	DEC BP	Smith et al., 1995

Cocaine doses are expressed as mg/inf for a 300g male rat.
Abbreviations: inf, infusions; FR, fixed ratio; PR, progressive ratio; TO, time out; INC, increase; DEC, decrease; NE, no effect; Amyg, amygdala; i. p., intraperitoneal; s.c., subcutaneous; i.c., intracranial.

TABLE 4. *Effects of dopamine receptor antagonists on heroin self-administration in rats*

Antagonist	Dose	Heroin dose	Schedule	Effect	References
Eticlopride	0.03 mg/kg; i.p.	5.4, 9.0 & 18.0 µg/inf	FR10 (20 sec TO)	NE	Hemby et al., 1996a
	0.1 & 0.3 mg/kg; i.p.	5.4, 9.0 & 18.0 µg/inf	FR10 (20 sec TO)	DEC	Hemby et al., 1996a
Flupenthixol	0.1 mg/kg; i.p.	18 µg/inf	FR1	NE	Ettenberg et al., 1982
	0.2 & 0.4 mg/kg; i.p.	18 µg/inf	FR1	DEC	Ettenberg et al., 1982
Haloperidol	0.125 mg/kg; s.c.	45 µg/inf	FR1	NE	Van Ree and Ramsey, 1987
	0.375 & 1.125 mg/kg; s.c.	45 µg/inf	FR1	DEC	Van Ree and Ramsey, 1987
	0.01–1 µg; i.c. (CP, NAcc, Amyg, Pyr Ctx)	45 µg/inf	FR1	NE	Van Ree and Ramsey, 1987
	0.1 µg; i.c. (mPFC)	45 µg/inf	FR1	INC	Van Ree and Ramsey, 1987

Heroin doses are expressed as mg/inf for a 300g rat.
Abbreviations: inf, infusions; FR, fixed ratio; PR, progressive ratio; TO, time out; INC, increase; DEC, decrease; NE, no effect; Pyr ctx, pyriform cortex; CP, caudate putamen; mPFC, medial prefrontal cortex.

but not serotonergic 5-HT$_{1A}$ receptors may selectively mediate discriminative cues (i.e., the ability to differentiate drug from nondrug conditions) associated with low doses of ethanol (Signs and Schecter, 1988). Haraguchi and colleagues (1990) showed that responding for ethanol decreased in a dose-related manner following same day pretreatments with fluoxetine. However, if pharmacologic inhibition of ethanol-reinforced responding is due to attenuation of the reinforcing effects of ethanol,

then it would exhibit classical extinction patterns of behavior associated with daily administration of such pharmacologic treatments. In one study, Murphy and colleagues (1988) showed that fluoxetine administered to rats in single daily injections produced a significant decrease in ethanol-reinforced responding beginning on the first day of treatment and increasing on subsequent days of the seven day treatment regimen. Responding for ethanol returned to pretreatment levels following cessa-

TABLE 5. *Effects of opiate receptor antagonists on cocaine self-administration in rats*

Antagonist	Dose	Cocaine dose	Schedule	Effect	References
Naloxone	1 & 10 mg/kg; s.c.	0.1 mg/inf	FR5	DEC	Corrigall and Coen, 1991b
Methyl naltrexone	1.0 µg; i.c. (PAG)	0.33 mg/inf	FR1	NE	Corrigall and Vaccarino, 1988
Naltrexone	0.1–10 mg/kg; i.p.	0.25 mg/inf	FR1	NE	Ettenberg et al., 1982
	10 mg/kg; s.c.	0.1 mg/inf	FR5	DEC	Corrigall and Coen, 1991b
	1–10 mg/kg; s.c.	0.03 & 0.33 mg/inf	FR5	NE	Corrigall and Coen, 1991b
	2 & 5 µg; i.c.v.	0.03 mg/inf	FR1	DEC	Ramsey and Van Ree, 1991
	1 & 2 mg/kg; i.v.	0.03 mg/inf	FR1	INC	Carroll et al. 1986
	1.0, 3.0 & 10.0 mg/kg; i.p.	0.125, 0.25 & 0.5 mg/inf	FR10 (20 sec TO)	NE	Hemby et al., 1996a

Cocaine doses are expressed as mg/inf for a 300g rat.
Abbreviations: inf, infusions; FR, fixed ratio; PR, progressive ratio; TO, time out; INC, increase; DEC, decrease; NE, no effect; i.c.v., intracerebroventricular; PAG, pinagueductal gray; i.v., intravenous.

TABLE 6. *Effects of opiate receptor antagonists on heroin self-administration in rats*

Antagonist	Dose	Heroin dose	Schedule	Effect	References
Nonselective					
Methyl naloxonium	0.05-30 mg/kg; i.p.	18 µg/inf	FR1	NE	Koob et al., 1984
	0.5–4.0 µg; i.c.v.	18 µg/inf	FR1	INC	Vaccarino et al., 1985b
	0.125–0.5 µg; i.c. (NAcc)	18 µg/inf	FR1	INC	Vaccarino et al., 1985a
	0.5–1.0 µg; i.c. (VTA)	18 µg/inf	FR1	NE	Vaccarino et al., 1985a
Naloxone	1.0 mg/kg; i.p.	18 µg/inf	FR1	INC	Koob et al., 1984
Methyl naltrexone	0.05–30 mg/kg; i.p.	18 µg/inf	FR1	NE	Koob et al., 1984
	1.0–3.0 µg; i.c. (NAcc & PAG)	18 µg/inf	FR1	INC	Corrigall and Vaccarino, 1988
	1.0 µg; i.c. (PAG)	9 µg/inf	FR1	INC	Corrigall and Vaccarino, 1988
	1.0 & 3.0 µg; i.c. (LH)	9 µg/inf	FR1	INC	Corrigall, 1987
	0.1–3.0 µg; i.c. (mPFC)	9 µg/inf	FR1	NE	Corrigall, 1987
Naltrexone	0.1–10 mg/kg; i.p.	9 µg/inf	FR1	NE	Ettenberg et al., 1982
	0.05–1.0 mg/kg; i.p.	9 µg/inf	FR1	NE	Koob et al., 1984
	0.1 mg/kg; i.v.	9 µg/inf	FR1	INC	Corrigall, 1987
	0.3 mg/kg; i.v.	18 µg/inf	FR1	INC	Corrigall and Vaccarino, 1988
	1.0, 3.0, & 10.0 mg/kg; i.p.	5.4 µg/inf	FR10 (20 sec TO)	DEC	Hemby et al., 1996a
	1.0 mg/kg; i.p.	9.0 µg/inf	FR10 (20 sec TO)	INC	Hemby et al., 1996a
	3.0 mg/kg; i.p.	9.0 µg/inf	FR10 (20 sec TO)	NE	Hemby et al., 1996a
	10.0 mg/kg; i.p.	9.0 µg/inf	FR10 (20 sec TO)	DEC	Hemby et al., 1996a
	1.0, 3.0, & 10.0 mg/kg; i.p.	18.0 µg/inf	FR10 (20 sec TO)	DEC	Hemby et al., 1996a
μ					
β-FNA	10 & 20 mg/kg; s.c.	18 µg/inf	FR5	INC	Negus et al., 1993
	40 nmol; i.c.v.	5.4 & 18 µg/inf	FR10	DEC	Martin et al., 1995
Naloxonazine	15 & 30 mg/kg; i.v.	18 µg/inf	FR5	INC	Negus et al., 1993
δ					
Naltrindole	10 & 17 mg/kg; s.c.	18 µg/inf	FR5	INC	Negus et al., 1993
κ					
Nor-BNI	5 & 10 mg/kg; s.c.	18 µg/inf	FR5	NE	Negus et al., 1993

Heroin doses are expressed as mg/inf for a 300-g rat.

Abbreviations: inf, infusions; FR, fixed ratio; PR, progressive ratio; TO, time out; INC, increase; DEC, decrease; NE, no effect; LH, lateral hypothalamus.

tion of fluoxetine treatment. Food intake, while somewhat suppressed initially, appeared to return to baseline levels on subsequent treatment days. These results are consistent with an initial fluoxetine-induced suppression, the further reduction in responding for ethanol, and an eventual return to baseline for food and water intake. These data suggest that fluoxetine reduces ethanol reinforcement by both specifically reducing its reinforcing effects and early nonspecific decreases in appetative behavior. Experimental data has shown that 5-HT$_3$ antagonists (e.g., ICS 205-930) block ethanol consumption and self-administration in rats (Fadda et al., 1991; Hodge et al., 1993; Knapp and Pohorecky, 1992; Oakley et al., 1988; cf. Beardsley et al., 1994). Extension of this work into humans has suggested that the 5-HT$_3$ antagonist ondansetron may decrease the urge to drink alcohol (Johnson et al., 1993; Johnson and Cowen, 1993, cf.; Swift et al., 1996; Doty et al., 1994) and alcohol consumption in dependent subjects (Sellers et al., 1994). In addition, 5-HT$_3$ antagonists (except zacopride) have been shown to attenuate alcohol-related behaviors in other paradigms such as drug discrimination, which may be critically involved in the expression of alcohol-seeking behavior (Grant and Barrett, 1991a, 1991b). Zacopride's inefficacy in this paradigm may be explained by non–site-specific effects, particularly actions at the 5-HT$_4$ receptor (Bockaert et al., 1990). Ondansetron may also have a bell-shaped dose-response characteristic in animals; however, the evidence for a similar effect in humans is uncertain. Further dose-response self-administration studies across animal species are needed to establish these promising preliminary results suggesting a role for the 5-HT$_3$ receptor in ethanol reinforcement.

The effects of 5-HT$_3$ antagonists on nicotine self-administration have also been investigated. Neither MDL 72222 nor ICS 205-930 produced significant alterations on nicotine self-administration. This suggests that the 5-HT$_3$ receptor is not involved in nicotine reinforcement (Corrigall and Coen, 1994). Nevertheless, it is intriguing to note that 5-HT$_3$ receptors do have indirect effects on acetylcholine (Ach) receptors, which lead to increases in cholinergic transmission, and some 5-HT$_3$ antagonists themselves such as MDL 72222 show affinity for the ACh receptor. Future studies should investigate the role of other 5-HT receptor subtypes on nicotine self-administration.

GABA Receptor Antagonists and Other Neuromodulators

The behavioral effects of several drugs of abuse have been associated with various other neurotransmitter systems including the inhibitory and excitatory amino acids. Also, GABA receptor function, particularly the benzodiazepine receptor site, is considered to be involved in the reinforcing effects of ethanol. Ethanol self-administration is attenuated by systemic administration of the benzodiazepine inverse agonist RO 15-4513 (June et al., 1994; Rassnick et al., 1992b, 1993a), the benzodiazepine antagonist RO 15-1788 (June et al., 1994; Rassnick et al., 1993a), and the picrotoxin ligand isopropylbicyclophosphate (Rassnick et al., 1992b, 1993a). In addition, the GABA$_A$ antagonist SR 95531 has been reported to decrease responding maintained by the presentation of 10% w/v ethanol in Wistar rats when administered directly into the central nucleus of the amygdala, bed nucleus of the stria terminalis or NAcc (Hyytia and Koob, 1995). N-methyl-d-aspartate (NMDA) and glutamate receptors also appear to be involved in drug reinforcement mechanisms. Intra-accumbens infusions of (±)-2-amino-5-phosphonopentanoic acid (AP-5), an NMDA receptor antagonist, decrease ethanol self-administration (Rassnick et al. 1992a,b), although another NMDA antagonist, acamprosate, failed to alter ethanol self-administration except at high doses (100 mg/kg i.p.) when administered systemically. Intra-accumbens infusions of the glutamate receptor antagonist APV altered cocaine self-administration but had no significant effect on heroin self-administration (Pulvirenti et al., 1992). A dose-dependent and site specific analysis of these effects on cocaine and opiate self-administration remain to be determined.

A growing area of current neuropharmacological research is the elucidation of stress in drug reinforcement. Stressful situations facilitate drug self-administration (Shaham et al., 1992), and reductions of negative feedback to corticosterone enhance the probability of amphetamine self-administration (Piazza et al., 1991). This effect is probably mediated by alterations in hippocampal corticosteroid receptor affinity. Furthermore, rats with higher and more exaggerated endocrine responses to novelty (HR rats) are more likely to self-administer amphetamine than low responding rats (LR rats). It has been suggested that these responses to corticosteroids may be mediated by DA since 6-OHDA lesions of the striatum and cortex lead to hypothalamic-pituitary-adrenal dysfunction (i.e., less output of corticosterone secretion to stressful or novel situations) (Piazza et al., 1991). Thus, the relationship between stress and drug-seeking behavior may provide information on individual differences or new strategies for the development of pharmaceuticals for the treatment of drug abuse.

New hypotheses are being proposed that challenge the now dominant role of midbrain DA as the mediator of reinforcement. For instance, there has recently been interest in drugs such as ibogaine (an alkaloid derivative of the West African Iboga plant). Nevertheless, the relative inconsistency of empirical studies (e.g., Dworkin et al., 1995; Glick et al., 1994) and toxicity (O'Hearn and Molliver, 1993) of ibogaine, have prevented even tentative scientific conclusions about efficacy. The role of neuropeptides in reinforcement is also under reevaluation. Neurotransmitters do not act in isolation, and there may yet be critical roles discovered for candidate neurotransmitters in reinforcement, particularly cholecystokinin, and neuropeptides due to their colocalization with midbrain DA neurons (Deutch and Bean, 1995; Elde et al., 1990; Iverfeldt et al., 1989; Wolfe and Beaudet, 1992).

While calcium channel antagonists decrease cocaine and opiate self-administration, arguments have been raised for the converse mechanism, that is, an increase in reinforcement (Kuzmin et al., 1992). The conventional hypothesis is that calcium channel blockers probably exert an inhibitory effect on midbrain DA, and this accounts for their ability to attenuate cocaine-induced locomotor stimulation (Pani et al., 1990). However, this effect is not produced by all members of this drug class. Also, in an important set of experiments, the calcium channel antagonist, *d-* but not *l*-isradipine, was shown to shift the nicotine self-administration dose-response curve to the right (i.e., lowering reinforcing value) (Martellotta et al., 1995). Calcium channel blockers also have been shown to decrease ethanol consumption in rats using a free-choice paradigm (Engel et al., 1988),

in alcohol-preferring rats (Pucilowski et al., 1992; Rezvani et al., 1993), and in monkeys (Rezvani et al., 1991). The role of calcium channel blockers in the reinforcing effects of other drugs of abuse such as nicotine is being assessed currently. It is important to point out that this renewed interest in the effects of calcium channel blockers on drug reinforcement may come to overshadow our previous understanding, in which the emphasis was on the development of tolerance and dependence.

Neurochemistry

Neurotoxic Lesions

In large part, the fundamental understanding of specific neurotransmitter involvement in drug reinforcement has been due to the use of neurotoxins injected into discrete brain regions. The relatively selective neurotoxins 6-OHDA and 5,7-DHT have been used to determine the roles of dopaminergic and noradrenergic (6-OHDA) and serotonergic (5,7-DHT) neuronal involvement, respectively. Pretreatment with selective monoamine uptake inhibitors (e.g., noradrenergic—desmethylimipramine; serotonergic—pargyline; dopaminergic—GBR 12909) enhances the selectivity of these neurotoxins. Factors that should be considered when interpreting the effects of neurotoxic lesions include the extent of the lesion, its neuroanatomical and neurochemical specificity of the lesion (i.e., fibers traversing through the lesioned brain region may be lesioned), and the amount of time between the onset of the lesion and the behavioral/neurochemical assessment. Excitotoxins (e.g., kainic acid and ibotenic acid) have also been used to determine the involvement of neurons both originating in and efferent from specific brain regions (e.g., GABA interneurons) in particular behaviors including drug self-administration.

The role of DA in drug reinforcement was extended by several studies examining the effects of 6-OHDA lesions. For example, 6-OHDA lesions of the NAcc decrease self-administration of cocaine (Caine and Koob,

1994a; Pettit et al., 1984; Roberts et al., 1977, 1980), amphetamine (Lecesse and Lyness, 1987; Lyness et al., 1979), nicotine (Corrigall et al., 1992), and ethanol (Rassnick et al., 1993b; cf. Myers and Melchoir, 1975; Quarfordt et al., 1991). Similar effects were reported for cocaine self-administration following 6-OHDA lesions of the VTA, which deplete DA in terminal regions of the mesolimbic system, including the NAcc and medial prefrontal cortex (mPFC; Roberts and Koob, 1982). Evidence that the VTA-NAcc projections are most important in drug reinforcement is supported by the fact that 6-OHDA lesions of the caudate nucleus (Koob et al., 1987) or amygdala (McGregor et al., 1994) do not alter cocaine self-administration. Additionally, 6-OHDA lesions of the mPFC do not attenuate amphetamine or cocaine self-administration (Martin-Iverson et al., 1986; cf. Schenk et al., 1991). Evidence implicating the NAcc in drug reinforcement is strengthened by the demonstration that kainic acid and ibotenic acid lesions of this region attenuate cocaine reinforcement (Hubner and Koob, 1987; Zito et al., 1985). This suggests the involvement of neurons, both originating in and efferent from the NAcc, and DA presynaptic terminals in drug reinforcement. In summary, these studies suggest that the functional integrity of the mesolimbic DA system is critical for the self-administration of most abused compounds and that projections from the NAcc to the ventral pallidum are of particular importance in the mediation of cocaine reinforcement. Future studies should explore the involvement of NAcc-ventral pallidal projections in the reinforcing effects of other abused drugs such as ethanol and nicotine.

Lesion studies do not support a role for DA in opiate self-administration. This is in agreement with pharmacologic and microdialysis studies. For example, heroin self-administration in non-opiate-tolerant rats is not disrupted by NAcc 6-OHDA lesions (Pettit et al., 1984). In rats rendered physically dependent to morphine, 6-OHDA lesions of the NAcc have been shown to reduce morphine self-administration when only one dose of morphine was self-administered (Smith et al., 1985). However, other studies revealed that 6-OHDA lesions of the NAcc did not alter morphine self-administration when responding was maintained by food, drug, and morphine on a multiple dosing schedule (Dworkin et al., 1988a). Kainic acid lesions of the NAcc have been shown to attenuate morphine self-administration in opiate-dependent rats (Dworkin et al., 1988b) and heroin self-administration in nondependent rats (Zito et al., 1985). These studies suggest that non-DA neuronal projections from the NAcc to the ventral pallidum are involved in the mediation of opiate reinforcement.

Serotonergic involvement in drug reinforcement processes has been proposed. Loh and Roberts (1990) reported that 5,7-DHT lesions of the medial forebrain bundle, which deplete forebrain 5-HT levels, increased the break point relative to the effects following sham lesions under a progressive ratio of cocaine reinforcement. This result was interpreted as an increase in the reinforcing effects of cocaine. However, both sham and 5,7-DHT lesions decreased break points relative to prelesion levels of responding, thus compromising the interpretation of the results. More recently, Roberts et al. (1994) reported that intracerebroventricular infusions of 5,7-DHT increased the break points of both cocaine and food reinforcement, indicating that the effects of 5-HT depletion produce nonspecific effects on responding. In contrast to the effects on cocaine self-administration, serotonergic innervations of the NAcc appear to be important in morphine self-administration in opiate-dependent rats. The 5,7-DHT lesions of the NAcc decrease morphine self-administration (Smith et al., 1987) and the effects appear to be specific to morphine as responding maintained by food and water are not disrupted (Dworkin et al., 1988c). Additional studies examining the effects of 5,7-DHT lesions of specific regions on the self-administration of cocaine, opiate, ethanol, and nicotine are warranted.

Intracranial Self-Administration (ICSA)

One way in which to more clearly identify the involvement of discrete neuroanatomical substrates in drug reinforcement is intracranial self-administration. In this procedure, drug self-administration is maintained by the direct application of the drug to discrete neuroanatomical loci (reviewed in Koob and Goeders, 1989). Interestingly, several positive neuroanatomical substrates for ICSA are located in the mesolimbic DA pathway.

ICSA of cocaine has been demonstrated in the mPFC, a terminal projection region of the VTA dopamine cell bodies, but not into the NAcc of rats (Goeders and Smith, 1983). This is attenuated by sulpiride, a D_2 antagonist, but not by SCH 23390 (D_1 antagonist), atropine (cholinergic antagonist), or propranolol (β-adrenergic antagonist; Goeders et al., 1986). In addition, selective lesions of DA terminals in this region using 6-OHDA attenuated cocaine ICSA (Goeders and Smith, 1986). These data suggest that cocaine ICSA into this region is a pharmacologically specific effect and results from direct interaction with DA receptors in this region. In contrast to the effects of cocaine, amphetamine is self-administered into the NAcc (Hoebel et al., 1983). However, the interpretation of these data are somewhat limited by the fact that responding was engendered with intracranial electrical self-stimulation at the site of subsequent amphetamine infusions. Furthermore, pharmacologic antagonism for amphetamine ICSA has not been demonstrated.

Opiate ICSA is supported by regions of the mesolimbic system also. Rats will self-administer morphine into the NAcc (Olds, 1982) and VTA (Bozarth and Wise, 1981a; Devine and Wise, 1994; Welzl et al., 1989). Furthermore, morphine injections into the VTA sustain second-order schedule responding (Hinson et al., 1986) and restore postextinction heroin self-administration (DeWit and Stewart, 1983). Additionally, Goeders et al. (1984) demonstrated that rats will self-administer the delta opiate receptor agonist met-enkephalin into the NAcc. This provides addi-tional support for the involvement of the NAcc in opiate reinforcement. Naloxone decreases the self-administration of morphine (Bozarth and Wise, 1981a; Olds, 1982) and met-enkephalin (Goeders et al. 1984). However, the effects of DA receptor antagonists on opiate ICSA have not been investigated.

Involvement of mesolimbic DA projections in the reinforcing effects of alcohol has been suggested. Recently, Gatto et al. (1994) demonstrated that alcohol preferring rats will self-administer alcohol (50–200 mg% ethanol) into the VTA. However, the pharmacologic and neuroanatomical specificity of these effects are unknown.

In Vivo *Microdialysis and Voltametry*

Recent advances in bioanalytical technology have permitted the *in vivo* sampling and subsequent analysis of neurochemical constituents in the extracellular space of subjects trained to perform behavioral tasks. Two of the more widely used techniques are *in vivo* microdialysis and *in vivo* voltametry. Although both techniques have provided important information into the neurochemical underpinnings of behavior, they differ in several respects. First, microdialysis is a sampling method, the basic principle of which is mass transport from the extracellular space into the internal space of the microdialysis probe. In most microdialysis procedures, the probe is perfused with artificial cerebrospinal fluid at a relatively low constant flow rate (0.2 to 1.0 μl/min). This maintains a concentration gradient between the inside and the outside of the probe; thus providing the means by which the aliquot is removed from the probe. The sample is analyzed for compounds of interest using chromatography coupled with appropriate detection methods. Microdialysis has been used to study the pharmacokinetics and pharmacodynamics of several compounds, and to examine the correlation of neurochemistry and behavior, including responding maintained by food (McCullough et al., 1993), sexual activity (Wenkstern et al., 1993), intracranial self-stimulation (Fiorino et al., 1993), cocaine (Pettit and Justice, 1989; Weiss et al., 1992), heroin (Hemby et al., 1995b), and alcohol (Weiss et al., 1993). Analysis of constituents in the aliquot is limited only by the available detection methods. Potentially, this allows detection of multiple constituents from the same sample. Although microdialysis is an invaluable bioanalytical procedure, there are several limitations of this technique. First, like all *in vivo* procedures, the relevance of microdialysis samples is based on the assumption that the neurotransmitter pool sampled is an accurate reflection of intrasynaptic neurochemical events. Under most circumstances, the sampled pool represents only a fraction of the actual intrasynaptic neurotransmitter concentration (Gonon, 1988). One factor that greatly affects sampling of this pool is the perfusion flow rate of the microdialysis probe. Methods such as no net flux (Lönnroth et al., 1989) and extrapolation to zero flow (Jacobson et al., 1985) control for such factors and provide alternatives to the conventional microdialysis methodologies. These methods are useful for the approximation of basal neurotransmitter concentrations but are of limited applicability for experiments designed to assess behavior and neurochemistry concurrently. Although dialysate neurotransmitter concentrations are dependent on several simultaneous synaptic processes (e.g., release, uptake, metabolic rate, and feedback mechanisms), neurotransmitters from the sampled pool have been shown to be both calcium-dependent and tetrodotoxin-sensitive, thus implying that such concentrations are neuronally derived (Moghaddam and Bunney, 1989; Osborne et al., 1991; Westerink et al., 1988).

In vivo voltametry also has been used to correlate changes in neurochemistry and behavior. The basic premise of voltametry is that electroactive chemicals in specific brain regions can be detected by their oxidation potential. The main advantage of voltametry is the outstanding temporal resolution (msec) compared with *in vivo* microdialysis (min). However, this advantage is generally gained at the expense of chemical selectivity, although current research into chemically specific electrodes as well as procedures such as cyclic voltametry have partially circumvented this problem. To date, only high-speed chronoamperometry with nafion-coated electrodes (to enhance neurochemical specificity) has been used in studies examining changes in neurotransmitter levels during drug self-administration sessions. Interpretation of data from these studies continue to be hampered by questions of chemical specificity. For example, the detected electrochemical signal attributable to DA may be confounded by the oxidation of 3-methoxytyramine, DOPAC, ascorbic acid, or other endogenous chemicals that can be oxidized at approximately the same potential. Another example is 5-HT, 5-hydroxyindoleacetic acid, and uric acid, all of which are oxidized at approximately the same potential. Similar confounds may exist between pharmacologic agents and neurotransmitters of interest. For example, morphine may contribute to a DA signal since it is known that heroin is metabolized to morphine and morphine is oxidized at a potential similar to DA (Pentney and Gratton, 1991). The use of *in vivo* microdialysis coupled with appropriate chromatographic procedures permits more selective identification of species with similar chemical properties (e.g., oxidation potentials). In summary, even though the number of studies employing *in vivo* neurochemical procedures is limited, the data obtained from such studies have made an important contribution to the understanding of the role of specific neurotransmitters in drug self-administration.

Due to the importance of mesolimbic DA function in drug reinforcement, most *in vivo* microdialysis and voltametry studies have focused on the role of NAcc DA. Numerous studies have demonstrated that experimenter-administered cocaine increases NAcc $[DA]_e$ in a dose-dependent manner (Carboni et al., 1989; Hemby et al., 1995a; Kalivas and Duffy, 1990; Kuczenski et al., 1991), and that cocaine concentrations ($[COC]$) in this region parallel the dose-dependent increase in $[DA]_e$ in this region (e.g., Hemby et al., 1995a). Similarly, several groups have reported increased [DA]$_e$ in the NAcc (300–500% above baseline concentrations) during cocaine self-administration sessions using *in vivo* microdialysis combined with HPLC (Meil et al., 1995; Parsons et al., 1995; Pettit and Justice, 1989, 1991; Weiss et al., 1992). Recently, these findings have been extended by demonstrating that increased NAcc [DA]$_e$ are paralleled by significant increases in cocaine concentration (from the same sample) in this region during the self-administration session (Fig. 5; Hemby et al., 1996b, 1996c).

In an interesting study, 1-min analysis of microdialysis samples during cocaine self-administration sessions revealed that [DA]$_e$ were phasically increased following each infusion followed by a phasic decrease preceding each infusion (Wise et al., 1995a). This suggests that [DA]$_e$ may be a critical stimulus for the subject to reinitiate responding for subsequent infusions. The phase-locked changes in [DA]$_e$ are contradicted by recent studies using high-speed chronoamperometry during cocaine self-administration sessions. Electrochemical signals reportedly indicative of [DA]$_e$ were shown to be time-locked with significant increases immediately preceding the infusion and abrupt decreases immediately following the infusion (Gratton and Wise, 1994; Kiyatkin and Stein, 1994, 1995). Explanations for this discrepancy remain unclear, although an obvious possibility may be the lack of chemical specificity of the voltametric procedure. Due to the qualitative similarities in the dopaminergic response to cocaine between studies employing response-independent and response-independent (self-administration) administration (Di Chiara and Imperato, 1988a), it is possible that the increases may be the result of direct effects of the drug and not related to the reinforcing effects. Recently, the relationship of NAcc [DA]$_e$ and cocaine self-administration was explored further using a yoked littermate design (Hemby et al., 1996b). In the first experiment, one rat from each litter was trained to self-administer (SA) cocaine intravenously (0.33 mg/infusion) under a fixed ratio 2 schedule, while a second rat received simultaneous infusions of cocaine yoked to the infusions of the SA (YC). NAcc

[DA]$_e$ and cocaine concentrations were assessed during the test sessions using *in vivo* microdialysis combined with microbore HPLC procedures. [DA]$_e$ and cocaine concentrations were significantly elevated in the SA and YC groups during the self-administration session. However, [DA]$_e$ was greater in the SA group compared to the YC group in the first hour of the session even though cocaine concentrations were not significantly different. On the following day, the rats previously allowed to self-administer cocaine were administered response-independent cocaine infusions yoked to the infusion pattern from the previous day. [DA]$_e$ was significantly elevated above baseline levels during the session but was significantly less than concentrations obtained when cocaine was self-administered by these subjects. Cocaine concentrations during the sessions were not significantly different between the two days. Baseline [DA]$_e$ was not significantly between the SA and YC groups or between day 1 and day 2. These results suggest that the context in which cocaine is administered significantly alters the neurochemical response to equivalent brain concentrations of cocaine. These findings are consistent with and extend previous findings by (1) assessing changes in NAcc [DA]$_e$ and cocaine concentrations from the same samples, and (2) demonstrating that response-dependent administration resulted in greater increases in NAcc [DA]$_e$ than observed with response-independent administration. Previous studies investigating [DA]$_e$ during cocaine self-administration may reflect the direct neurochemical consequences and not its reinforcing effects (Meil et al., 1995; Parsons et al., 1995; Pettit and Justice, 1989, 1991; Weiss et al., 1992). These data provide direct *in vivo* neurochemical evidence of NAcc dopaminergic involvement by demonstrating that the increases were related to the response-infusion contingency. In addition, these results contrast with an earlier study that demonstrated that response-dependent infusions of cocaine did not increase [DA]$_e$ in the NAcc, whereas response-independent infusions to drug-naive subjects resulted in a marked elevation (Hurd et al., 1989). While the reasons for these differences remain unclear, findings from the present study are consistent with experiments employing pharmacological manipulations that indicate a critical role for dopamine in cocaine self-administration.

Previous studies confirm the importance of contextual variables in the neurochemical correlates of cocaine self-administration. Dworkin et al. (1995) compared the effects of chronic cocaine exposure between rats self-administering cocaine (330 µg/infusion) and littermates receiving yoked infusions of cocaine or saline to determine changes in brain biogenic monoamine and amino acid neurotransmitter turnover rates as a consequence of cocaine withdrawal. Changes observed between self-administering rats that were not observed in rats receiving yoked-cocaine infusions (indirect or conditioned effects) included increased turnover rates of 5-HT in the pyriform cortex,

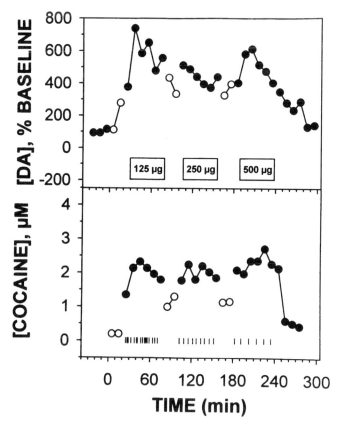

FIG. 5. Dialysate DA (*top panel)* and COC (*bottom panel)* concentrations during a self-administration session from a representative rat. Intravenous cocaine self-administration was maintained under an FR10 schedule of reinforcement using a multiple dosing procedure consisting of three 1-hr components (125, 250, and 500 µg/infusion). Microdialysis probes were located in the medial NAcc and samples were collected in 10-min intervals. $[DA]_e$ and [COC] were assayed from the same sample using microbore high-pressure liquid chromatography with electrochemical and ultraviolet detection, respectively, as reported previously (Hemby et al., 1995a,b). $[DA]_e$ is expressed as the percent change from baseline levels and as mean (± s.e.m.), whereas [COC] is expressed as µM. Baseline DA concentration was approximately 3.5 µM. Cocaine doses appear in boxes in the *top panel.* Tic marks in the *bottom panel* depict the time of infusions during each component. The first three *filled circles* in the top panel represent the baseline period prior to the beginning of the session and the last six *filled circles* represent samples obtained after the end of the self-administration session. *Open circles* represent the samples taken during 20-min blackout periods prior to each component.

norepinephrine in the caudate-putamen and GABA in the pyriform and motor-somatosensory cortices. Decreased 5-HT turnover rates were seen in the motor-somatosensory cortex and dentate gyrus in the rats receiving response-dependent infusions compared to the yoked-cocaine infused group. Perhaps the most interesting changes were those seen in the yoked-cocaine group that were reversed in the rats whose responding was maintained by cocaine. These included reversals of changes in the frontal and temporal-auditory cortices, NAcc, caudate-putamen, substantia nigra, and VTA. In general, these data indicate that chronic cocaine administration produces changes in brain neuronal activity that may represent rebound increases that could be related to the acute withdrawal responses seen after drug removal. Under similar experimental conditions, it has been demonstrated recently that dopamine turnover rates in the NAcc were increased by 46% in subjects self-administering cocaine compared with subjects receiving yoked response-independent infusions of cocaine (Smith et al., 1996). Increases in turnover rates were observed even though tissue concentrations of DA were not significantly different, as previously reported (Wilson et al., 1994).

Several studies have shown that opioid drugs or peptides can modulate mesolimbic DA function. In vivo microdialysis has shown that acute intraperitoneal or subcutaneous administration of μ or δ receptor agonists increase [DA]$_e$ in the NAcc (Di Chiara and Imperato, 1988b; Pothos et al., 1991; Rada et al., 1991; Spanagel et al., 1990a,b). As mentioned previously, there is a high density of opiate receptors as well as opioid peptides in the VTA and in several terminal fields including the NAcc (Mansour et al., 1987; Tempel and Zukin, 1987). This anatomical propinquity provides opportunity for an interaction between opiate receptors and mesolimbic DA neurons.

Recently, [DA]$_e$ during heroin self-administration sessions have been assessed using in vivo microdialysis and in vivo voltametry. Hemby et al. (1995b) demonstrated that acute

experimenter-administered heroin dose-dependently (5.4, 9, and 18 μg/infusion) increased [DA]$_e$ in the NAcc. However, self-administration of the same doses did not result in significant elevations during the self-administration sessions even though total heroin intake was dose-dependent. These results support data obtained from studies examining the effects of DA antagonists and DA lesions on heroin self-administration and suggest that heroin reinforcement is not directly mediated by DA in the NAcc. However, in contradiction, other investigators have reported moderate elevations in NAcc [DA]$_e$ as determined by high-speed chronoamperometry (Gratton and Wise, 1994; Kiyatkin et al., 1993) and in vivo microdialysis (Wise et al., 1995b). Differences between the results of these studies may be attributable to several factors, such differences in analytical techniques, heroin doses, and self-administration training procedures. As previously suggested, in vivo voltametry provides better temporal resolution in sampling than does microdialysis but this enhanced resolution is gained at the expense of chemical selectivity. Differences between the microdialysis results may be attributable to the range of heroin doses examined or the extent of self-administration history. In addition, studies reporting increases in NAcc [DA]$_e$ are incongruous with the results from several studies that have failed to demonstrate a significant role for NAcc DA in the self-administration of heroin (Ettenberg et al., 1982; Hemby et al., 1996a; Pettit et al., 1984; Van Ree and Ramsey, 1987). As with cocaine, several studies emphasize the importance of contextual variables in the neurochemical correlates of opiate self-administration. Most notably, DA turnover rates are increased in the striatum and decreased in the NAcc; acetylcholine turnover rates are increased in the NAcc. Additionally, opiate-dependent rats self-administering morphine showed effects comparable to rats receiving response-independent infusions, even though tissue concentrations were not significantly different between the groups (Smith et al., 1980, 1982, 1984a, 1984b).

Similar to cocaine self-administration studies, ethanol self-administration in nondependent rats is associated with an increase in NAcc $[DA]_e$, and this DA elevation is exaggerated in animals selectively bred for alcohol preference (i.e., P rats; Weiss et al., 1993). These data support evidence suggesting dopaminergic involvement in ethanol reinforcement.

To date only one study has examined the effects of drug self-administration on $[5-HT]_e$ in the NAcc. Parsons et al. (1995) demonstrated that NAcc $[5-HT]_e$ and $[DA]_e$ were elevated over 300% of baseline levels during 12-hour cocaine self-administration sessions. Following termination of the self-administration session, $[5-HT]_e$ decreased below baseline levels. These data have important implications for the involvement of 5-HT in the symptoms associated with cocaine withdrawal.

CONDITIONED PLACE PREFERENCE

CPP is a widely used paradigm for screening the abuse liability of abused drugs, including cocaine (Hemby et al., 1992a,b, 1994; Spyraki et al., 1982a), amphetamine (Carr and White, 1986; Hemby et al., 1992a; Spyraki et al., 1982b), opiates (Beach, 1957; Sherman et al., 1980), and ethanol (Reid et al., 1985). In general, most drugs that induce a place preference for the drug-paired environment also are self-administered and are abused by humans (Carr et al., 1989). However, nicotine-induced CPP has not been reliably demonstrated (Acquas et al., 1988; Carboni et al., 1989; Fudala and Iwamoto, 1986; Shoaib et al., 1994).

Pharmacology

With respect to most drugs investigated with this paradigm, evidence supports dopaminergic mediation of drug-induced place conditioning. For example, D_1 and D_2 dopamine receptor antagonism blocks amphetamine-induced CPP (Hoffman and Beninger, 1989; Mackey and van der Kooy, 1985). Cocaine and methylphenidate-induced CPP is blocked by DA antagonists when these drugs are administered intravenously

(Nomikos and Spyraki, 1988) but not when administered intraperitoneally (Mackey and Van der Kooy, 1985; Morency and Beninger, 1986; Spyraki et al., 1982a). These findings may be due to local anesthetic effects or preferential recruitment of nondopaminergic neurotransmitter systems. DA also appears to be involved in the opiate-induced CPP. DA antagonists attenuate the preference for the opiate-paired compartment, especially at high unit doses (Bozarth and Wise, 1981b; Leone and Di Chiara, 1987; Spyraki et al., 1983). Nicotine-induced CPP when established has been attenuated by D_1 receptor antagonists (Acquas et al., 1989). Also CPP to nicotine (0.6 mg/kg) is attenuated by the $5-HT_3$ antagonist, MDL 72222 (Carboni et al., 1988). There is evidence the $5-HT_3$ antagonists may play a role in opiate conditioning. In particular, $5-HT_3$ antagonists block CPP to morphine (Carboni et al., 1988). Interestingly, the benzodiazepine inverse agonist RO 15-4513 that reduced ethanol self-administration does not alter ethanol-induced CPP (Risinger et al., 1992).

Neurotoxic Lesions

Centrally, dopaminergic mediation of drug-induced CPP appears to be located in the NAcc since 6-OHDA lesions of this region attenuate CPP induced by amphetamine and heroin (Spyraki et al., 1982b, 1983). The 6-OHDA lesions of the NAcc or mPFC do not block cocaine-induced place conditioning (Hemby et al., 1992b; Mackey and van der Kooy, 1985; Spyraki et al., 1982a). Interestingly, 5,7-DHT lesions of the NAcc reduce morphine-induced CPP (Nomikos et al., 1986; Spyraki et al., 1988).

Intracranial Injections

Infusions of amphetamine directly into the NAcc induce a robust CPP for the drug-paired compartment (Carr and White, 1986; Hemby et al., 1992a), whereas intra-NAcc infusions of cocaine fail to induce CPP (Hemby et al.,

1992a). These latter findings, along with the report that systemic procaine injections also induce CPP (Hemby et al., 1994; Spyraki et al., 1982a), led to the suggestion of a two-component hypothesis of cocaine CPP (Morency and Beninger, 1986; Spyraki et al., 1982) wherein both the peripheral anesthetic effects and the central dopaminergic effects contribute to cocaine CPP. To test this hypothesis, Hemby et al. (1994) investigated the effects of systemically and centrally administered cocaine methiodide, a quaternary salt of cocaine, which does not cross the blood-brain barrier. Central, but not peripheral, administration of cocaine methiodide induced CPP demonstrating that cocaine CPP is mediated centrally.

The effects of dopamine receptor antagonism and selective neurotoxic lesions of the NAcc on cocaine and heroin-induced CPP stand in marked contrast to the effects of these manipulations observed in the self-administration paradigm. For example, 6-OHDA lesions of the NAcc attenuate cocaine but not heroin self-administration, whereas similar lesions block heroin but not cocaine CPP. Different results with similar pharmacologic manipulations obtained using self-administration and CPP may be due to several factors. First, drug administration in CPP is response-independent, whereas drug self-administration is response-dependent. As previously described, the context of drug administration has a significant influence on neurochemical events. Therefore, differences in effects obtained with pharmacologic or neurochemical manipulations between CPP and self-administration may reflect different underlying neurochemical events mediating response-independent versus response-dependent drug administration. Alternatively, CPP may be a measure of the conditioned stimulus effects and not the reinforcing effects of drugs, based on the operant definition of reinforcement. This is not to imply that the CPP does not provide important information in furthering the understanding of drug abuse, namely processes associated with conditioning. In contrast, self-administration is based on operant principles, and can also be used to study the conditioned stimulus effects

of abused drugs. Therefore, discrepancies in results obtained from these procedures may be attributable to differences in what these paradigms are measuring.

CRITERIA FOR ESTABLISHING NEUROTRANSMITTER INVOLVEMENT IN DRUG REINFORCEMENT

The previous review of the role of various neurotransmitters and their respective receptors in drug reinforcement is intended to be illustrative and not exhaustive. More likely, several neurotransmitters in various brain regions are probably involved in the complex phenomena of drug reinforcement. However, the relevance of studies investigating single neurotransmitter/single receptor types/single brain regions should not be minimized. Instead, the reader should keep in mind that a more complete understanding of drug reinforcement will require a multidimensional analysis of brain function. We propose the following set of criteria for establishing that a neurotransmitter is critical to reinforcing effects of drugs:

1. The neurotransmitter of interest, compounds that alter the availability of the neurotransmitter, or compounds that selectively activate respective neurotransmitter receptors should be self-administered directly into brain regions involved in drug reinforcement. Furthermore, these effects should be blocked by receptor specific antagonists.

2. Unspecified increases in neurotransmitter concentrations, locomotor activity or the induction of stereotypical behavior may not predict reinforcing effects. Furthermore, global effects on general performance or cognitive functioning may not be related to the reinforcing process.

3. The extracellular level of the neurotransmitter of interest should parallel the response-contingent behavior and this relationship should be a dose-dependent.

4. Selective neurotoxic lesions that alters the functional integrity of the neurotransmit-

ter pathway should alter the self-administration of the drug. The pattern of attenuated responding should be extinction-like if a complete blockade has been obtained.

5. The effects of neurotoxic lesions, central antagonist administration, and intracranial self-administration should be regionally specific. Gating the electrophysiologic response would be expected to have the same effect as pharmacologic or neuroanatomic blockade.

6. Selective breeding or genetic cloning to alter the availability of the neurotransmitter or neurotransmitter receptors should result in changes in response-contingent behavior compared to wild-type strains.

CONCLUSION

An essential facet of abused drugs is their ability to serve as reinforcers. It is clear that there is a biologic basis to reinforcement. While the last decade has witnessed a rapid expansion of research implicating the mesolimbic DA system as a critical substrate in drug reinforcement, it is becoming evident that the interaction between several neurotransmitters offers a more fundamental explanation. Interestingly, there have been few studies examining the effects of putative medications for drug abuse that have also explored the impact on natural reinforcers and the endogenous mechanisms that maintain them. Combinations, staging of medications, and an understanding of not only the effect of the neurobiologic process on behavior but the converse may be necessary. Clearly, integration of the biologic and psychosocial aspects of reinforcement will provide some potential solutions.

FUTURE DIRECTIONS

A greater integration of neuroscientific disciplines will play a strong role in the development of the field. Of note is the need to develop a better understanding of the internal principles that govern reinforcement itself, and how this accommodates biological and individual differences as well as the impact of contextual situations. Essential to this understanding is the use of appropriate behavioral models, namely procedures that rely on the response-dependent administration of drugs. Moreover, procedures to evaluate relative reinforcing efficacy and drug withdrawal/relapse need to be further developed. Of increasing importance is the need to apply what is learned from single drug studies to the more complex issue of multidrug use, the more frequently encountered human condition. Of equal importance is the need for the preclinical researcher to more closely approximate human drug intake patterns and drug usage. For instance, the use of drug combinations represents a growing trend in drug abuse but this trend is underrepresented in the preclinical literature.

SUMMARY

- An essential facet of abused drugs is their ability to function as reinforcers.
- DA remains the predominant neurotransmitter in our current understanding of the reinforcing effects for many abused drugs. However, non-DA mechanisms may predominate for opiates. It is evident that an improved understanding of neurotransmitter interactions in selective brain regions will lead to greater knowledge about the basic neurobiologic processes involved in drug reinforcement.
- The use of procedures employing response-dependent drug administration, instead of response-independent drug administration, is critical to furthering our understanding of the neurobiologic underpinnings of drug reinforcement.
- Few studies have addressed contemporaneously drug reinforced behavior and changes in neurotransmitter function. Thus, it has been difficult to predict the strength of the correlation between neuro-

transmitter concentrations and drug self-administration.

- Criteria have been established for determining whether or not a neurotransmitter is involved in the reinforcing effects of drugs.
- Integration of neuroscience and behavior offers the best hope for understanding drug reinforcement and developing effective pharmacotherapies for the treatment of drug abuse.

REFERENCES

Acquas, E., Carboni, E., Leone, P. and Di Chiara, G. (1988) 5-HT3 receptors antagonists block morphine- and nicotine- but not amphetamine-induced place-preference conditioning. *Pharmacol. Res. Commun.* 20: 1113–1114.

Audet, M.A., Descarries, L. and Doucet, G. (1989) Quantified regional and laminar distribution of the serotonin innervation in the anterior half of adult rat cerebral cortex. *J. Chem. Neuroanat.* 21: 29–44.

Bannon, M.J., Granneman, J.G. and Kapatos, G. (1995) The dopamine transporter: potential involvement in neuropsychiatric disorders. In: Bloom, F.E. and Kupfer, D.J. (eds.) *Psychopharmacology: the fourth generation of progress.* New York: Raven Press, pp. 179–188.

Barrett, R.J. and Appel, J.B. (1989). Effects of stimulation and blockade of dopamine receptor subtypes on the discriminative stimulus properties of cocaine. *Psychopharmacology* 99: 13–16.

Beach, H.D. (1957) Morphine addiction in rats. *Can. J. Psychol.* 11: 104–112.

Beardsley, P.M., Lopez, O.T., Gullikson, G. and Flynn, D. (1994) Serotonin 5-HT3 antagonists fail to affect ethanol self-administration in rats. *Alcohol* 11: 389–395.

Bergman, J., Madras, B.K., Johnson, S.E. and Spealman, R.D. (1989) Effects of cocaine and related drugs in non-human primates. III. Self-administration by squirrel monkeys. *J. Pharmacol. Exp. Ther.* 251: 150–155.

Bockaert, J., Sebben, M. and Dumuis, A. (1990) 5-hydroxytryptamine 4 (5-HT4) receptors positively coupled to adenylate cyclase in adult guinea pig hippocampal membranes: effect of substituted benzamide derivatives. *Mol. Pharmacol.* 37: 408–411.

Bormann, J. (1988) Electrophysiology of GABAA and GABAB receptor subtypes. *Trends Neurosci.* 11: 112–116.

Bozarth, M.A. and Wise, R.A. (1981a) Heroin reward is dependent on a dopaminergic substrate. *Life Sci.* 29: 1881–1886.

Bozarth, M.A. and Wise, R.A. (1981b) Intracranial self-administration of morphine into the ventral tegmental area of rats. *Life Sci.* 28: 551–555.

Caine, S.B., Heinrichs, S.C., Coffin, V.L. and Koob, G.F. (1995) Effects of the dopamine D-1 antagonist SCH 23390 microinjected into the accumbens, amygdala or striatum on cocaine self-administration in the rat. *Brain Res.* 692: 47–56.

Caine, S.B. and Koob, G.F. (1993) Modulation of cocaine self-administration in the rat through D3 dopamine receptors. *Science* 320: 1814–1816.

Caine, S.B. and Koob, G.F. (1994a) Effects of mesolimbic dopamine depletion on responding maintained by cocaine and food. *J. Exp. Anal. Behav.* 61: 213–221.

Caine, S.B. and Koob, G.F. (1994b) Effects of dopamine D-1 and D-2 antagonists on cocaine self-administration under different schedules of reinforcement in the rat. *J. Pharmacol. Exp. Ther.* 270: 209–218.

Caine, S.B. and Koob, G.F. (1995) Pretreatment with the dopamine agonist 7-OHDPAT shifts the cocaine self-administration dose-effect function to the left under different schedules in the rat. *Behav. Pharmacol.* 6: 333–347.

Carboni, E., Acquas, E., Leone, P., Perezzani, L. and Di Chiara, G. (1988) 5-HT3 receptor antagonists block morphine- and nicotine-induced place-preference conditioning. *Eur. J. Pharmacol.* 151: 159–160.

Carboni, E., Imperato, A., Perezzani, L., Di Chiara, G. (1989) Amphetamine, cocaine, phencyclidine and nomifensine increase extracellular dopamine concentrations preferentially in the nucleus accumbens of freely moving rats. *Neuroscience* 28:653–661.

Carr, G.D., Fibiger, H.C. and Phillips, A.G. (1989) Conditioned place preference as a measure of reward. In: Liebman, J.M and Cooper, S.J. (eds.) *The neuropharmacological basis of reward.* Oxford: Oxford University Press, pp. 264–319.

Carr, G.D. and White, N.M. (1986) Anatomical dissociation of amphetamine s rewarding and aversive effects: an intracranial microinjection study. *Psychopharmacology* 89: 340–346.

Carroll, F.I., Abraham, P., Lewin, A.H., Parham, K.A., Boja, J.W. and Kuhar, M.J. (1992b) Isopropyl and phenyl esters of 3β-(4-substituted phenyl)tropane-2β-carboxylic acids. Potent and selective compounds for the dopamine transporter. *J. Med. Chem.* 35: 2497–2500.

Carroll, F.I., Gao, Y., Abraham, P., Lewin, A.H., Lew, R., Patel, A., Boja, J.W. and Kuhar, M.J. (1992a) Probes for the cocaine receptor. Potentially irreversible ligands for the dopamine transporter. *J. Med. Chem.* 35: 1813–1817.

Carroll, M.E., Lac, S.T., Asencio, M. and Kragh, R. (1990) Fluoxetine reduces intravenous cocaine self-administration in rats. *Pharmacol. Biochem. Behav.* 35: 237–244.

Carroll, M.E., Lac, S.T., Walker, M.J., Kragh, R. and Newman, T. (1986) Effects of naltrexone on intravenous cocaine self-administration in rats during food satiation and deprivation. *J. Pharmacol. Exp. Ther.* 238: 1–7.

Childers, S.R. (1991) Opioid receptor-coupled second messenger systems. *Life Sci.* 48: 1991–2003.

Civelli, O. (1995) Molecular biology of the dopamine receptor subtypes. In: Bloom, F.E. and Kupfer, D.J. (eds.) *Psychopharmacology: the fourth generation of progress.* New York: Raven Press, pp. 155–161.

Clow, D.W. and Jhamandas, K. (1988) Effects of κ-receptor agonist, U-50,488H, on release of endogenous brain dopamine. *Can. J. Physiol. Pharmacol.* 66: 128–133.

Cooper, J.R., Bloom, F.E. and Roth, R.H. (1986) *The biochemical basis of neuropharmacology,* 5th ed. New York: Oxford University Press, pp. 259–314.

Cooper, S.J. (1991) Interactions between endogenous opioids and dopamine: implications for reward and aversion. In: Willner, P. and Scheel-Krüger, J. (eds.) *The mesolim-*

bic dopamine system: from motivation to action. Chichester, England: John Wiley, pp. 331–366.

Corrigall, W.A. (1987) Heroin self-administration: effects of antagonist treatment in lateral hypothalamus. *Pharmacol. Biochem. Behav.* 27: 693–700.

Corrigall, W.A. and Coen, K.M. (1991a) Cocaine self-administration is increased by both D1 and D2 dopamine antagonists. *Pharmacol. Biochem. Behav.* 39: 799–802.

Corrigall, W.A. and Coen, K.M. (1991b) Opiate antagonists reduce cocaine but not nicotine self-administration. *Psychopharmacology* 104: 167–170.

Corrigall, W.A. and Coen, K.M. (1991c) Selective dopamine antagonists reduce nicotine self-administration. *Psychopharmacology* 104: 171–176.

Corrigall, W.A. and Coen, K.M. (1994) Nicotine self-administration and locomotor activity are not modified by the 5-HT3 antagonists ICS 205-930 and MDL 72222. *Pharmacol. Biochem. Behav.* 49: 67–71.

Corrigall, W.A., Franklin, K.B., Coen, K.M. and Clarke, P.B. (1992) The mesolimbic dopaminergic system is implicated in the reinforcing effects of nicotine. *Psychopharmacology* 107: 285–289.

Corrigall, W.A. and Vaccarino, F.J. (1988) Antagonist treatment in nucleus accumbens or periaqueductal grey affects heroin self-administration. *Pharmacol. Biochem. Behav.* 30: 443–450.

Cunningham, C.L., Niehus, D.R., Marlott, D.H. and Prather, L.K. (1992). Genetic differences in the rewarding and activating effects of morphine and ethanol. *Psychopharmacology* 105: 84–92

Dahlström, A. and Fuxe, K. (1965) Evidence for the existence of monoamine-containing neurons in the central nervous system. I. Demonstration of monoamines in the cell bodies of brain stem neurons. *Acta Physiol. Scand. Suppl.* 62: 232: 1–55.

Damsma, G., Pfaus, J.G., Wenkstern, D., Phillips, A.G. and Fibiger, H.C. (1992) Sexual behavior increases dopamine transmission in the nucleus accumbens and striatum of male rats: comparison with novelty and locomotion. *Behav. Neurosci.* 106: 181–191.

Davies, H.M.L., Saikali, E., Huby, N.J.S., Gilliatt, V.J., Matasi, J.J., Sexton T. and Childers, S.R. (1994) Synthesis of 2β-acyl-3β-aryl-8-azabicyclo[3.2.1]octanes and their binding affinities at dopamine and serotonin transport sites in rat striatum and frontal cortex. *J. Med. Chem.* 37: 1262–1268.

Davies, H.M.L., Saikali, E., Sexton, T. and Childers, S.R. (1993) Novel 2-substituted cocaine analogues: binding properties at dopamine transport sites in the rat striatum. *Eur. J. Pharmacol.* 244: 93–97.

de Waele, J.P. and Gianoulakis, C. (1994) Enhanced activity of the brain beta-endorphin system by free choice ethanol drinking in C57BL/6 but not DBA/2 mice. *Eur. J. Pharmacol.* 258: 119–129.

de Wit, H. and Stewart, J. (1983) Drug reinstatement of heroin-reinforced responding in the rat. *Psychopharmacology* 79: 29–31.

de Wit, H. and Wise, R.A. (1977) Blockade of cocaine reinforcement in rats with the dopamine receptor blocker pimozide, but not with the noradrenergic blockers phentolamine and phenoxybenzamine. *Can. J. Psychol.* 31: 195–203.

Deutch, A.Y. and Bean, A.J. (1995) Colocalization in dopamine neurons. In: . Bloom, F.E. and Kupfer, D.J. (eds.)

Psychopharmacology: the fourth generation of progress. New York: Raven Press, pp. 197–206.

Devine, D.P., Leone, P., Pocock, D. and Wise, R.A. (1993) Differential involvement on ventral tegmental mu, delta and kappa opioid receptors in modulation of basal mesolimbic dopamine release: *in vivo* microdialysis studies. *J. Pharmacol. Exp. Ther.* 26: 1236–1246.

Devine, D.P. and Wise, R.A. (1994) Self-administration of morphine, DAMGO and DPDPE into the ventral tegmental area of rats. *J. Neurosci.* 14: 1978–1984.

DeWitte, P. (1984) Naloxone reduces alcohol intake in a free-choice procedure even when both drinking bottles contain saccharin sodium or quinine substances. *Neuropsychobiology* 12: 73–77.

Di Chiara, G. (1995). The role of dopamine in drug abuse veiwed from the perspective of its role in motivation. *Drug Alcohol Depend.* 38: 95–137.

Di Chiara, G. and Imperato, A. (1988a) Drugs abused by humans preferentially increase synaptic dopamine concentrations in the mesolimbic system of freely moving rats. *Proc. Natl. Acad. Sci. USA* 85:5274–5278.

Di Chiara, G. and Imperato, A. (1988b) Opposite effects of mu and kappa opiate agonists on dopamine release in the nucleus accumbens and in the dorsal caudate of freely moving rats. *J. Pharmacol. Exp. Ther.* 24: 1067–1080.

Dilts, R.P. and Kalivas, P.W. (1989) Autoradiographic localization of mu-opioid and neurotensin receptors within the mesolimbic dopamine system. *Brain Res.* 488: 311–327.

Doty P., Zachny J.P., de Wit, H. (1994) Effects of ondansetron pretreatment on acute responses to ethanol in social drinkers. *Behav. Pharmacol.* 54: 461–469

Dworkin, S.I., Co, C. and Smith, J.E. (1995) Rat brain neurotransmitter rates altered during withdrawal from chronic cocaine administration. *Brain Res.* 682:116–126.

Dworkin, S.I., Gleeson, S., Meloni, N., Koves, T.R. and Martin, T.J. (1995) Effects of ibogaine on responding maintained by food, cocaine and heroin reinforcement in rats. *Psychopharmacology* 117: 257–261.

Dworkin, S.I., Guerin, G.F., Co, C., Goeders, N.E. and Smith, J.E. (1988a) Lack of an effect of 6-hydroxydopamine lesions of the nucleus accumbens on intravenous morphine self-administration. *Pharmacol. Biochem. Behav.* 30: 1051–1057.

Dworkin, S.I., Guerin, G.F., Goeders, N.E. and Smith, J.E. (1988b) Kainic acid lesions of the nucleus accumbens selectively attenuate morphine self-administration. *Brain Res.* 646: 273–278.

Dworkin, S.I., Guerin, G.F., Co, C., Goeders, N.E. and Smith, J.E. (1988c) Effects of 5,7-dihydroxytryptamine lesions of the nucleus accumbens in rats responding on a concurrent schedule of food, water and intravenous morphine. In: *NIDA Research Monograph* No. 81. Washington, DC: U.S. Government Printing Office, pp. 149–155.

Elde, R., Schalling, M., Ceccatelli, S., Nakanishi, S. and Hokfelt, T. (1990) Localization of neuropeptide receptor mRNA in rat brain: initial observations using probes for neurotensin and substance P receptors. *Neurosci. Lett.* 120: 134–138.

Engel, J.A., Fahlke, C., Hulthe, P., Hard, E., Johannessen, K., Snape, B. and Svensson, L. (1988) Biochemical and behavioral evidence for an interaction between ethanol and calcium channel antagonists. *J. Neural Trans.* 74: 181–193.

Ettenberg, A., Pettit, H.O., Bloom, F.E. and Koob, G.F. (1982) Heroin and cocaine intravenous self-administration in rats: mediation by separate neural systems. *Psychopharmacology* 78:204–209.

Evans, C.J., Keith, D.E.J., Morrison, H., Magendzo, K. and Edwards, R.H. (1992) Cloning of a delta receptor by functional expression. *Science* 258: 1952–1955.

Fadda, F., Garau, B., Marchei, F., Colombo, G. and Gessa, G. (1991) MDL 72222, a selective 5-HT3 receptor antagonist, suppresses voluntary ethanol consumption in alcohol-preferring rats. *Alcohol* 26: 107–110.

Fibiger, H.C. and Phillips, A.G. (1986) Reward, motivation, and cognition: psychobiology of mesotelencephalic dopamine systems. In: *Handbook of physiology*. Baltimore: Williams and Wilkins, pp. 647–675.

Fiorino, D.F., Coury, A., Fibiger, H.C. and Phillips, A.G. (1993) Electrical stimulation of reward sites in the ventral tegmental area increases dopamine transmission in the nucleus accumbens of the rat. *Behav. Brain Res.* 55: 131–141.

Froelich, J.C., Harts, J., Lumeng, L., et al. (1990) Naloxone attenuates voluntary ethanol intake in rats selectively bred for high ethanol preference. *Pharmacol. Biochem. Behav.* 35: 385–390.

Fudala, P.J. and Iwamoto, E.T. (1986) Further studies on nicotine-induced conditioned place preference in the rat. *Pharmacol. Biochem. Behav.* 25: 1041–1049.

Gatto, G.J., McBride, W.J., Murphy, J.M., Lumeng, L. and Li, T.K. (1994) Ethanol self-infusion into the ventral tegmental area by alcohol preferring rats. *Alcohol* 11: 557–564.

Gerrits, M.A.F.M. and Van Ree, J.M. (1996) Effects of nucleus accumbens dopamine depletion on motivational aspects involved in initiation of cocaine and heroin self-administration in rats. *Brain Res.* 713: 114–124.

Gillan, M.G.C. and Kosterlitz, H.W. (1982) Spectrum of μ-, δ- and κ-binding sites in homogenates of rat brain. *Br. J. Pharmacol.* 77: 461–469.

Glick, S.D., Kuehne, M.E., Raucci, J., Wilson, T.E., Larson, D., Keller, R.W., Jr. and Carlson, J.N. (1994) Effects of iboga alkaloids on morphine and cocaine self-administration in rats: relationship to tremorigenic effects and to effects on dopamine release in nucleus accumbens and striatum. *Brain Res.* 657: 14–22.

Goeders, N.E., Dworkin, S.I. and Smith, J.E. (1986) Neuropharmacological assessment of cocaine self-administration into the medial prefrontal cortex. *Pharmacol. Biochem. Behav.* 24: 1429–1440.

Goeders, N.E., Lane, J.D. and Smith, J.E. (1984) Intracranial self-administration of methionine enkephalin into the nucleus accumbens. *Pharmacol. Biochem. Behav.* 20: 451–455.

Goeders, N.E. and Smith J.E. (1983) Cortical dopaminergic involvement in cocaine reinforcement. *Science* 221: 773–775.

Goeders, N.E. and Smith, J.E. (1986) Reinforcing properties of cocaine in the medial prefrontal cortex: primary action on presynaptic dopaminergic terminals. *Pharmacol. Biochem. Behav.* 25: 191–199.

Goldberg, .S.R., Kelleher, R.T. and Goldberg, D.M. (1981) Fixed ratio responding under second-order schedules of food presentation or cocaine injection. *J. Pharmacol. Exp. Ther.* 218: 271–281.

Goldberg, S.R., Morse, W.H. and Goldberg, D.M. (1976) Behaviour maintained under a second-order schedule by intramuscular injection of morphine or cocaine in rhesus monkeys. *J. Pharmacol. Exp. Ther.* 199: 278–286.

Goldberg, S.R. and Schuster, C.R. (1967) Conditioned suppression by a stimulus associated with nalorphine in morphine-depedent monkeys. *J. Exp. Anal. Behav.* 10: 232–242.

Goldberg, S.R. and Tang, A.H. (1977) Behavior maintained under second order schedules of intravenous morphine injection in squirrel and rhesus monkeys. *Psychopharmacology* 51: 235–242.

Goldberg, S.R., Woods, J.H. and Schuster, C.R. (1969) Morphine: conditioned increases in self-administration in rhesus monkeys. *Science* 166: 1306–1307.

Goldstein, A. and Naidu, A. (1989) Multiple opioid receptors: ligand selectivity profiles and binding site signatures. *Mol. Pharmacol.* 32: 265–272.

Gonon, F.G. (1988) Non-linear relationship between impulse flow and dopamine released by rat midbrain dopaminergic neurons as studied by *in vivo* electrochemistry. *Neuroscience* 24: 19–28.

Grant, K.A. and Barrett, J.E. (1991a) Blockade of the discriminative stimulus effects of ethanol with 5-HT3 receptor antagonists. *Psychopharmacology* 104: 451–456.

Grant, K.A. and Barrett, J.E. (1991b) Blockade of the discriminative stimulus effects and anxiolytic effects of ethanol with 5-HT3 receptor antagonists. In: Racagni, G., Brunello, N. and Fukada, T. *(eds.) Biological psychiatry: proceedings of the 5th World Congress*, vol. 2. Amsterdam: Elsevier, pp. 11–13.

Gratton, A. and Wise R.A. (1994) Drug- and behavior-associated changes in dopamine-related electrochemical signals during intravenous cocaine self-administration in rats. *J. Neurosci.* 14: 4130–4146.

Griffiths, R.R. and Balster, R.L. (1979) Opioids: similarity between evaluations of subjective effects and animal self-administration results. *Clin. Pharmacol. Ther.* 25: 611–617.

Griffiths, R.R., Bigelow, G.E. and Henningfield, J.E. (1980) Similarities in animal and human drug-taking behavior. In: Mello, N. (ed.) *Advances in substance abuse,* vol. 1. Greenwich, CT: JAI Press, pp. 1–90.

Gysling, K. and Wang, R.Y. (1983) Morphine-induced activation of A10 dopamine neurons in the rat. *Brain Res.* 415: 257–269.

Hahn, E.F., Carroll-Buati, M. and Pasternak, G.W. (1982) Irreversible agonists and antagonists: the 14-hydroxydihydromorphine azines. *J. Neurosci.* 2: 572–576.

Haraguchi, M., Samson, H.H. and Tolliver, G.A. (1990) Reduction in oral ethanol self-administration in the rat by the 5-HT uptake blocker fluoxetine. *Pharmacol. Biochem. Behav.* 35: 259–262.

Heijna, M.H., Padt, M., Hogenboom, F., Portoghese, P.S., Mulder, A.H. and Schoffelmeer, A.N.M. (1990) Opioid receptor mediated inhibition of dopamine and acetylcholine release from slices of rat nucleus accumbens, olfactory tubercle and frontal cortex. *Eur. J. Pharmacol.* 18: 267–278.

Hemby, S.E., Co, C., Dworkin, S.I. and Smith, J.E. (1996c) Synergistic effects of self-administered cocaine/heroin combinations on extracellular dopamine concentrations in the nucleus accumbens of rats. Submitted.

Hemby, S.E., Co, C., Reboussin, D., Davies, H.M.L., Dworkin, S.I. and Smith, J.E. (1995a) Comparison of a novel tropane analog, 2β-propanoyl-3β-(4-tolyl) tropane (PTT) with cocaine HCl in rats: nucleus accumbens extracellular dopamine and motor activity. *J. Pharmacol. Exp. Ther.* 273:656–666.

Hemby, S.E., Jones, G.H., Justice, J.B., Jr. and Neill, D.B. (1992a). Conditioned locomotor activity but not conditioned place preference following microinjections of cocaine into the nucleus accumbens. *Psychopharmacology* 106: 330–336.

Hemby, S.E., Jones, G.H., Neill, D.B. and Justice, J.B., Jr. (1992b). Six hydroxydopamine lesions of the medial prefrontal cortex fail to influence cocaine place conditioning. *Behav. Brain Res.* 49: 225–230.

Hemby, S.E., Jones, G.H., Neill, D.B. and Justice, J.B., Jr. (1994). Assessment of the relative contribution of peripheral and central components in cocaine place conditioning. *Pharmacol. Biochem. Behav.* 47: 973–979.

Hemby, S.E., Martin, T.J., Co, C., Dworkin, S.I. and Smith, J.E. (1995b) The effects of intravenous heroin administration on extracellular nucleus accumbens dopamine concentrations as determined by *in vivo* microdialysis. *J. Pharmacol. Exp. Ther.* 273:591–598.

Hemby, S.E., Smith, J.E. and Dworkin, S.I. (1996a) The effects of eticlopride and naltrexone on responding maintained by food, cocaine, heroin and cocaine/heroin combinations in rats. *J. Pharmacol. Exp. Ther.* 277: 1247–1258.

Hemby, S.E., Smith, J.E. and Dworkin, S.I. (1996b) Differences in extracellular dopamine concentrations in the nucleus accumbens during response-dependent and response-independent cocaine administration in the rat. Submitted.

Hervé, D., Pickel, V.M., Joh, T.H. and Beaudet, A. (1987). Serotoinin axon terminals in the ventral tegmental area of the rat: fine structure and synaptic input to dopaminergic neurons. *Brain Res.* 435: 71–83.

Higgins G.A., Tomkins, D.M., Fletcher, P.J., and Sellers, E.M. (1992) Effect of drugs influencing 5-HT function on ethanol drinking and feeding behavior in rats: studies using a drinkometer system. *Neurosci. Biobehav. Rev.* 16: 535–552

Hinson, R.E., Poulos, C.X., Thomas, W., and Cappell, H. (1986) Pavlovian conditioning and addictive behavior: relapse to oral self-administration of morphine. *Behav. Neurosci.* 100: 368–375.

Hiller, J.M., Angel, L.M. and Simon, E.J. (1981) Multiple opiate receptors: alcohol selectively inhibits binding to delta receptors. *Science* 214: 468–469.

Hodge, C.W., Samson, H.H., Lewis, R.S. and Erickson, H.L. (1993) Specific decreases in ethanol- but not water-reinforced responding produced by the 5-HT3 antagonist ICS 205-930. *Alcohol* 10: 191–196.

Hoebel, B.G., Monaco, A.P., Hernandez, L., Aulisi, E.F., Stanley, B.G. and Lenard, L. (1983) Self-injection of amphetamine directly into the brain. *Psychopharmacology* 81: 158–163.

Hoffman, D.C. and Beninger, R.J. (1989) The effects of selective dopamine D1 and D2 receptor antagonists on the establishment of agonist-induced place conditioning in rats. *Pharmacol. Biochem. Behav.* 33: 273–279.

Hubner, C.B. and Koob, G.F. (1987) Ventral pallidum plays a role in mediating cocaine and heroin self-administration in rats. *Brain Res.* 508: 20–29.

Hubner, C.B. and Moreton, J.E. (1991) Effects of selective D1 and D2 dopamine antagonists on cocaine self-administration in the rat. *Psychopharmacology* 105: 151–156.

Hurd, Y.L., Weiss, F., Koob, G.F. Andén N-A. and Ungerstedt, U. (1989) Cocaine reinforcement and extracellular dopamine overflow: an *in vivo* microdialysis study. *Brain Res.* 498: 199–203.

Hyytia, P. (1993) Involvement of mu-opioid receptors in alcohol drinking by alcohol-preferring AA rats. *Pharmacol. Biochem. Behav.* 45: 697–701.

Hyytia, P., and Koob, G.F. (1995) GABAA receptor antagonism in the extended amygdala decreases ethanol self-administration in rats. *Eur. J. Pharmacol.* 283: 151–159.

Hyytia, P., Sinclair, J.D. (1993) Responding for oral ethanol after naloxone treatment by alcohol-preferring AA rats. *Alcohol Clin. Exp. Res.* 17: 631–636.

Itzhak, Y. (1988) Multiple opioid binding sites. In: Pasternak, G.W., (ed.) *The opiate receptors.* Clifton, NJ: Humana Press, pp. 95–142.

Iverfeldt, K., Serfozo, P., Diaz Arnesto, L. and Bartfai, T. (1989) Differential release of coexisting neurotransmitters: frequency dependence of the efflux of substance P, thyrotropin releasing hormone and [3H] serotonin from tissue slices of rat ventral spinal cord. *Acta Physiol. Scand.* 137: 63–71.

Jacobson, I., Sandberg, M. and Hamberger, A. (1985) Mass transfer in brain dialysis devices—a new method for the estimation of extracellular amino acid concentrations. *J. Neurosci. Meth.* 15: 263–268.

Johnson, B.A., Campling, G.M., Griffiths, P. and Cowen, P.J. (1993) Some alcohol-induced mood changes and the desire to drink in humans are attenuated by 5-HT3 receptor blockade. *Psychopharmacology* 112: 142–145.

Johnson, B.A., Chen, Y.R., Swann, A.C., Lesser, J., Ruiz, P. (1996b) Ritanserin in the treatment of cocaine dependence. (In Press).

Johnson, B.A. and Cowen, P.J. (1993) Alcohol-induced reinforcement: dopamine and 5-HT3 receptor interactions in animals and humans. *Drug Dev. Res.* 30: 153–169.

Johnson, B.A., Jasinksi, D.R., Galloway, G.P., Kranzler, H., Weinreib, R., Anton, R., Mason, B., Bohn, M.J., Pettinati, H.M., Rawson, R. and Clyde, C. (1996a) Ritanserin in the treatment of alcohol dependence—a multi-center clinical trial. *Psychopharmacol.* 128: 206–215.

Johnson, S.W. and North, R.A. (1992) Opioids excite dopamine neurons by hyperpolarization of local interneurons. *J. Neurosci.* 12: 483–488.

June, H.L., Hughes, R.W., Spurlock, H.L. and Lewis, M.J. (1994) Ethanol self-administration in freely feeding and drinking rats: effects of RO 15-4513 alone and in combination with RO 15-1788 (flumazenil). *Psychopharmacology* 115: 332–339.

Kalivas, P.W. (1985) Sensitization to repeated enkephalin administration into the ventral tegmental area of the rat. II. Involvement of the mesolimbic dopamine system. *J. Pharmacol. Exp. Ther.* 235: 544–550.

Kalivas, P.W. and Duffy, P. (1990) Effect of acute and daily cocaine treatment on extracellular dopamine in the nucleus accumbens. *Synapse* 5: 48–58.

Katz, J.L. (1989) Drugs as reinforcers: Pharmacological and behavioural factors. In: Liebman, J.M. and Cooper, S.J. (eds.) *The neuropharmacological basis of reward.* Oxford: Clarendon Press, pp. 164–213.

Kebabian, J.W. and Calne, D.B. (1979) Multiple receptors for dopamine. *Nature* 277: 93–96.

Kieffer, B.L., Befort, K., Gaveriaux-Ruff, C. and Hirth, C.G. (1992) Isolation of a cDNA by expression cloning and pharmacological characterization. *Proc. Natl. Acad. Sci. USA* 89: 12048–12052.

Kiyatkin, E.A. and Stein, E.A. (1994) Biphasic changes in mesolimbic dopamine signal during cocaine self-administration. *Neuroreport* 5: 1005–1008.

Kiyatkin, E.A. and Stein, E.A. (1995) Fluctuations in nucleus accumbens dopamine during cocaine self-administration behavior: an *in vivo* electrochemical study. *Neuroscience* 64: 599–617.

Kiyatkin, E.A., Wise, R.A. and Gratton, A. (1993) Drug- and behavior-associated changes in dopamine-related electrochemical signals during intravenous heroin self-administration in rats. *Synapse* 14: 60–72.

Klitenick, M.A., Dewitte, P. and Kalivas, P.W. (1992) Regulation of somatodendritic dopamine release in the ventral tegmental area by opioids and GABA: an *in vivo* microdialysis study. *J. Neurosci.* 12: 2623–2632.

Knapp, D.J. and Pohorecky, L.A. (1992) Zacopride, a 5-HT3 receptor antagonist, reduces voluntary ethanol consumption in rats. *Pharmacol. Biochem. Behav.* 41: 847–850.

Koob, G.F. (1992) Drugs of abuse: anatomy, pharmacology and function of reward pathways. *Trends Pharmacol. Sci.* 13: 177–184.

Koob G.F. and Bloom, F.E. (1988) Cellular and molecular mechanisms of drug dependence. *Science* 242: 715–723.

Koob, G.F. and Goeders, N.E. (1989) Neuroanatomical substrates of drug self-administration. In: Liebman, J.M. and Cooper, S.J. (eds.) *The neuropharmacological basis of reward.* Oxford: Clarendon Press, pp. 214–263.

Koob, G.F., Pettit, H.O., Ettenberg, A. and Bloom, F.E (1984) Effects of opiate antagonists and their quaternary derivatives on heroin self-administration in the rat. *J. Pharmacol. Exp. Ther.* 229: 481–486.

Koob, G.F., Vaccarino, F.J., Amalric, M. and Bloom, F.E. (1987) Positive reinforcement properties of drugs: search for neural sbstrates. In: Engel, J. and Oreland, L. (eds.) *Brain reward systems and abuse.* New York: Raven Press, pp. 35–50.

Kuczenski, R., Segal, D.S. and Aizenstein, M.L. (1991) Amphetamine, cocaine, and fencamfamine: relationship between locomotor and stereotypy response profiles and caudate and accumbens dopamine dynamics. *J. Neurosci.* 11: 2703–2712.

Kuzmin, A., Zvartau, E., Gessa, G.L., Martellotta, M.C. and Fratta, W. (1992) Calcium antagonists isradipine and nimodipine suppress cocaine and morphine intravenous self-administration in drug-naive mice. *Pharmacol. Biochem. Behav.* 41: 497–500.

Lacosta, S. and Roberts, D.C.S. (1993) MDL 72222, kitanserin and methysergide pretreatments fail to alter breaking points on a progressive ratio schedule reinforced by intravenous cocaine. *Pharmacol. Biochem. Behav.* 44: 161–165.

Lane, J.D., Pickering, C.L., Hooper, M.L., Fagan, K., Tyers, M.B. and Emmett-Oglesby, M.W. (1992) Failure of ondansetron to block the discriminative stimulus effect of cocaine in the rat. *Drug Alcohol Depend.* 30: 151–162.

Lecesse, A.P. and Lyness, L. (1984) The effects of putative 5-hydroxytryptamine receptor active agents on d-amphetamine self-administration in controls and rats with 5,7-dihydroxytryptamine median forebrain bundle lesions. *Brain Res.* 303: 153–162.

Lecesse, A.P. and Lyness, L. (1987) Lesions of dopamine neurons in the medial prefrontal cortex: effects on self-administration of amphetamine and dopamine synthesis in the brain of the rat. *Neuropharmacology* 26: 1303–1308.

Leone, P. and Di Chiara, G. (1987) Blockade of D-1 receptors by SCH 23390 antagonizes morphine- and amphetamine-induced place preference conditioning. *Eur. J. Pharmacol.* 135: 251–254.

Leone, P., Pocock, D. and Wise, R.A. (1991) Morphine-dopamine interaction: ventral tegmental morphine increases nucleus accumbens dopamine release. *Pharmacol. Biochem. Behav.* 39: 469–472.

Lindvall, O. and Bjorklund, A. (1974) The organizing of the ascending catecholamine neuron system in the rat brain as revealed by the glyoxylic acid fluorescence method. *Acta Physiol. Scand.* 412(suppl): 1–48.

Lindvall, O. and Bjorklund, A. (1983) Dopamine- and norepinephrine- containing neuron systems: their anatomy in the rat brain. In: Emson, P.C. (ed). *Chemical neuroanatomy.* New York: Raven Press, pp. 229–255.

Loh, E.A., Fitch, T., Vickers, G. and Roberts, D.C.S. (1992) Clozapine increases breaking points on a progressive-ratio schedule reinforced by intravenous cocaine. *Pharmacol. Biochem. Behav.* 42: 559–562.

Loh, E.A. and Roberts, D.C.S. (1990) Break-points on a progressive ratio schedule reinforced by intravenous cocaine increase following depletion of forebrain serotonin. *Psychopharmacology* 101: 262–266.

Lönnroth, P., Jansson, P.A., Fredholm, B.B. and Smith, U. (1989) Microdialysis of intercellular adenosine concentration in subcutaneous tissue in humans. *Am. J. Physiol.* 256: E250–E255.

Lyness, W.H. (1983) Effect of l-tryptophan pretreatment on d-amphetamine self-administration. *Sub. Alcohol Actions/Misuse* 4: 305–312.

Lyness, W.H., Friedle, N.M. and Moore, K.E. (1979) Destruction of dopaminergic nerve terminals in the nucleus accumbens: effect on d-amphetamine self-administration. *Pharmacol. Biochem. Behav.* 11: 553–556.

Lyness, W.H., Friedle, N.M. and Moore, K.E. (1980) Increased self-administration of d-amphetamine after destruction of 5-hydroxytryptaminergic neurons. *Pharmacol. Biochem. Behav.* 12: 937–941.

Lyness, W.H. and Moore, K.E. (1983) Increased self-administration of d-amphetamine by rats pretreated with metergoline. *Pharmacol. Biochem. Behav.* 18: 721–724.

Mackey, W.B. and van der Kooy, D. (1985) Neuroleptics block the positive reinforcing effects of amphetamine but not of morphine as measured by place conditioning. *Pharmacol. Biochem. Behav.* 22: 101–105.

Maldanado, R., Robledo, P., Chover, A.J., Caine, S.B. and Koob, G.F. (1993) D-1 dopamine receptors in the nucleus accumbens modulate cocaine self-administration in the rat. *Pharmacol. Biochem. Behav.* 45: 239–242.

Mansour, A., Kachaturian, H., Lewis, M.E., Akil, H. and Watson, S.J. (1987) Autoradiographic differentiation of μ, δ, and κ opioid receptors in the rat forebrain and midbrain. *J. Neurosci.* 7: 2445–2464.

Mansour, A., Lewis, M.E., Khachaturian, H., Akil, H. and Watson, S.J. (1986) Pharmacological and anatomical evidence of selective mu, delta and kappa opioid receptor binding in rat brain. *Brain Res.* 399: 69–79.

Martellotta, M.C., Kuzmin, A, Zvartau, E., Cossu, G., Gessa, G.L. and Fratta, W. (1995) Isradipine inhibits nicotine intravenous self-administration in drug-naive mice. *Pharmacol. Biochem. Behav.* 52: 271–274.

Martin, T.J., Dworkin, S.I. and Smith, J.E. (1995) Alkylation of mu opioid receptors by β-funaltrexamine *in vivo*: comparison of the effects on in situ binding and heroin self-administration. *J. Pharmacol. Exp. Ther.* 272: 1135–1140.

Martin-Iverson, M.T., Szostak, C. and Fibiger H.C. (1986) 6-hydroxydopamine lesions of the medial prefrontal cortex fail to influence intravenous self-administration of cocaine. *Psychopharmacology* 88: 310–314.

Matthews, R.T. and German, D.C. (1984) Electrophysiological evidence for excitation of rat ventral tegmental area dopamine neurons by morphine. *Neuroscience* 11: 617–625.

McCullough, L.D., Cousins, M.S. and Salamone, J.D. (1993) The role of nucleus accumbens dopamine in responding on a continuous reinforcement operant schedule: a neurochemical and behavioral study. *Pharmacol. Biochem. Behav.* 46: 581–586.

McGregor, A., Baker, G. and Roberts, D.C.S. (1994) Effect of 6-hydroxydopamine lesions of the amygdala on intravenous cocaine self-administration under a progeressive ratio schedule of reinforcement. *Brain Res.* 646: 273–278.

McGregor, A., Lacosta, S. and Roberts, D.C.S. (1993) L-tryptophan decreases the breaking point under a progressive ratio schedule of intravenous cocaine reinforcement in the rat. *Pharmacol. Biochem. Behav.* 44: 651–655.

McGregor, A. and Roberts, D.C.S. (1993) Dopaminergic antagonism within the nucleus accumbens or the amygdala produces differential effects on intravenous cocaine self-administration under fixed and progressive ratio schedules of reinforcement. *Brain Res.* 624:245–252.

Meert, T.F. and Janssen, P.A.J. (1992) Ritanserin, a new therapeutic approach for drug abuse. Part 2: effects on cocaine. *Drug Dev. Res.* 25: 39–53.

Meil, W.M., Roll, J.M., Grimm, J.W., Lynch, A.M. and See, R.E. (1995) Tolerance-like attenuation to contingent and noncontingent cocaine-induced elevation of extracellular dopamine in the ventral striatum following 7 days of withdrawal from chronic treatment. *Psychopharmacology* 118: 338–346.

Moghaddam, B. and Bunney, B.S. (1989) Ionic composition of microdialysis perfusing solution alters the pharmacological responsiveness and basal outflow of striatal dopamine. *J. Neurochem.* 53: 652–654.

Molliver, M.E. (1987) Serotonergic neuronal systems: what their anatomic organization tells us about function. *J. of Clin. Psychopharm.* 7: 35-23S.

Morency, M.A. and Beninger, R.J. (1986) Dopaminergic substrates of cocaine-induced place conditioning. *Brain Res.* 399: 33–41.

Mulder, A.H., Warden, G., Hogenboom, F. and Frankhuyzen, A.L. (1989) Selectivity of various opioid peptides towards delta-, kappa- and mu-opioid receptors mediating presynaptic inhibition of neurotransmitter release in the brain. *Neuropeptides* 14: 99–104.

Mulder, A.H., Warden, G., Hogenboom, F. and Frankhuyzen, A.L. (1984) Kappa and delta-opioid receptor agonists differentially inhibit striatal dopamine and acetylcholine release. *Nature* 308: 278–280.

Murphy, J.M., Waller, M.B., Gatto, G.L., McBride, W.J., Lumeng, L. & Li, T.K. (1988) Effects of fluoxetine on the intragastric self-administration of ethanol in the alcohol preferring P line of rats. *Alcohol* 5: 283–286.

Myers, R.D. and Melchoir, C.L. (1975) Alcohol drinking in the rat after destruction of serotonergic and catecholaminergic neurons in the brain. *Res. Commun. Chem. Pathol. Pharmacol.* 10: 363–378.

Nedergaard, S., Hopkins, C. and Greenfield, S.A. (1988). Do nigro-striatal neurones possess a discrete dendritic modulatory mechanism? Electrophysiological evidence from the actions of amohetamine in brain slices. *Exp. Brain Res.* 69: 444–448.

Negus, S.S., Henriksen, S.J., Mattox, A., Pasternak, G.W., Portoghese, P.S., Takemori, A.E., Weinger, M.B. and Koob, G.F. (1993) Effects of antagonists selective of mu, delta and kappa opioid receptors on the reinforcing effects of heroin in rats. *J. Pharmacol. Exp. Ther.* 265: 1245–1252.

Nomikos, G.G. and Spyraki, C. (1988) Cocaine-induced place conditioning: importance of route of administration and other procedural variables. *Psychopharmacology* 94: 119–125.

Nomikos, G.G., Spyraki, C., Galanopoulou, P. and Papadopoulou, Z. (1986) Amphetamine and morphine induced place preference in rats with 5,7 dihydroxytryptamine lesions of the nucleus accumbens. *Psychopharmacology* 89: S26.

Oakley, N.R., Jones, B.J., Tyers, M.B., Costall, B. and Domeney, A.M. (1988). The effect of GR 38032F on alcohol consumption in the marmoset. *Br. J. Pharmacol.* 95: 870P.

O'Brien, C.P., Childress, A.R., McLellan, A.T. and Ehrman, R. (1992). Classical conditioning in drug dependent humans. In: Kalivas, P.W. and Samson, H.H. (eds.) *The neurobiology of drug and alcohol addiction*, vol. 654. New York: Ann. New York Acad. Sci. 654: 400–415.

Olds, M.E. (1982) Reinforcing effects of morphine in the nucleus accumbens. *Brain Res.* 237: 429–440.

O'Hearn, E., and Molliver, M.E. (1993) Degeneration of Purkinje cells in parasagittal zones of the cerebellar vermis after treatment with ibogaine or harmaline. *Neurosci.* 55: 303–310.

O'Malley, S.S., Jaffe, A.J., Chang, G., Schottenfeld, R.S., Meyer, R.E. and Rounsaville, B. (1992) Naltrexone and coping skills therapy for alcohol dependence. A controlled study. *Arch. Gen. Psychiatry* 49: 881–887.

Osborne, P.G., O'Connor, W.T. and Ungerstedt, U. (1991) Effect of varying the ionic concentration of a microdialysis perfusate on basal striatal dopamine levels in awake rats. *J. Neurochem.* 56: 452–456.

Pani, L., Carboni, S., Kuzmin, Gessa, G.L. and Rosetti, Z.L. (1990) Nimodipine inhibits cocaine-induced dopamine release and motor stimulation. *Eur. J. Pharmacol.* 176: 245–246.

Parsons, L.H., Caine, S.B., Sokoloff, P., Koob, G.F. and Weiss, F. (1996a) Neurochemical evidence that postsynaptic nucleus accumbens D3 receptor stimulation enhances cocaine reinforcement. *J. Neurochem.* in press.

Parsons, L.H., Koob, G.F. and Weiss, F. (1995) Serotonin dysfunction in the nucleus accumbens of rats during withdrawal after unlimited access to intravenous cocaine. *J. Pharmacol. Exp. Ther.* 274: 1182–1191.

Parsons, L.H., Weiss, F. and Koob, G.F. (1996b) Serotonin 1B receptor stimulation enhances dopamine-mediated reinforcement. *Psychopharmacology,* in press.

Pasternak, G.W. and Hahn, E.F. (1980) Long acting opiate agonists and antagonists: 14-hydroxydiphydromorphinone hydrazone. *J. Med. Chem.* 23: 674–676.

Paterson, S.J., Robson, L.E. and Kosterlitz, H.W. (1983) Classification of opioid receptors. *Br. Med. Bull.* 39: 31–36.

Peltier, P. and Schenk, S. (1991) GR38032F, a serotonin 5-HT3 antagonist, fails to alter cocaine self-administration in rats. *Pharmacol. Biochem. Behav.* 39: 133–136.

Peltier, P. and Schenk, S. (1993) Effects of serotonergic manipulations on cocaine self-administration in rats. *Psychopharmacology* 110: 390–394.

Pentney, R.J. and Gratton, A. (1991) Effects of local delta and mu opioid receptor activation of basal and stimulated dopamine release in striatum and nucleus accumbens of rat: an *in vivo* electrochemical study. *Neuroscience* 45: 95–102.

Pettit, H.O., Ettenberg, A., Bloom, F.E. and Koob, G.F. (1984) Destruction of dopamine in the nucleus accumbens selectively attenuates cocaine but not heroin self-administration in rats. *Psychopharmacology* 84:167–173.

Pettit, H.O. and Justice, J.B., Jr. (1989) Dopamine in the nucleus accumbens during cocaine self-administration as studied by *in vivo* microdialysis. *Pharmacol. Biochem. Behav.* 34:899–904.

Pettit, H.O. and Justice, J.B., Jr. (1991) Effect of dose on cocaine self-administration behavior and dopamine levels in the nucleus accumbens. *Brain Res.* 539:94–102.

Pfeffer, A.O. and Samson, H.H. (1985) Oral ethanol reinforcement: interactive effects of amphetamine, pimozide and food restriction. *Alcohol Drug Res.* 6: 37–48.

Phillips, G.D., Howes, S.R., Whitelaw, R.B., Robbins, T.W. and Everitt, B.J. (1994) Isolation rearing impairs the reinforcing efficacy of intravenous cocaine or intra-accumbens d-amphetamine: impaired response to intra-accumbens D1 and D2/D3 dopamine receptor antagonists. *Psychopharmacology* 115:419–429.

Piazza, P.V., Deminiere, J-M., Maccari, S., Le Moal, M., Mormede, P. and Simon, H. (1991). Individual vulnerability to drug self-administration: action of corticosterone on dopaminergic systems as a possible pathophysiological mechanism. In: Willner, P. and Scheel-Kruger, J. (eds.) *The mesolimbic dopamine system: from motivation to action.* Chichester: John Wiley, pp. 473–495.

Pickens, R. and Harris (1968) Self-administration of d-amphetamine by rats. *Psychopharmacologia* 12: 158–163.

Pickens, R., Meisch, R.A. and Thompson, T. (1978) Drug self-administration: an analysis of the reinforcing effects of drugs. In: Iversen, L.L., Iversen, S.D. and Snyder, S.H. (eds.) *Handbook of psychopharmacology,* vol. 12. New York: Plenum Press, pp. 1–37.

Pickens, R. and Thompson, T. (1968). Cocaine reinforced behavior in rats: effects of reinforcement magnitude and fixed ratio size. *J. Pharmacol. Exp. Ther.* 161: 122–129

Porrino, M.C., Ritz, M.C., Goodman, N.L., Sharpe, L.G., Kuhar, M.J. and Goldberg, S.R. (1989) Differential effects of the pharmacological manipulations of serotonin systems on cocaine and amphetamine self-administration in rats. *Life Sci.* 45: 1529–1535.

Pothos, E., Rada, P., Mark, G.P. and Hoebel, B.G. (1991) Dopamine microdialysis in the nucleus accumbens during acute and chronic morphine, naloxone-precipitated withdrawal and clonidine treatment. *Brain Res.* 566: 348–350.

Pucilowski, O., Overstreet, D.H., Rezvani, A.H. and Janowsky, D.S. (1992) Suppression of alcohol and saccharin preference in rats by a novel Ca^{2+} channel inhibitor, Goe 5438. *Psychopharmacology* 107: 447–452.

Pulvirenti, L., Maldanado-Lopez, R. and Koob, G.F. (1992) NMDA receptors in the nucleus accumbens modulate intravenous cocaine but not heroin self-administration in the rat. *Brain Res.* 594: 327–330.

Quarfordt, S.D., Kalmus, G.W. and Myers, R.D. (1991) Ethanol drinking following 6-OHDA lesions of nucleus accumbens and tuberculum olfactorium of the rat. *Alcohol* 8: 211–217.

Rada, P., Mark, G.P., Pothos, E. and Hoebel, B.G. (1991) Systemic morphine simultaneously decreases extracellular acetylcholine and increases dopamine in the nucleus accumbens of freely moving rats. *Neuropharmacology* 30: 1133–1136.

Ramsey, N.F. and Van Ree, J.M. (1991) Intracerebroventricular naltrexone treatment attenuates acquisition of intravenous cocaine self-administration in rats. *Pharmacol. Biochem. Behav.* 40: 807–810.

Rassnick, S., D Amico, E., Riley, E. and Koob, G.F. (1993a) GABA antagonist and benzodiazepine partial inverse agonist reduce motivated responding for ethanol. *Alcohol Clin. Exp. Res.* 17: 124–130.

Rassnick, S., D Amico, E., Riley, E., Pulvirenti, L., Zieglgänsberger, W. and Koob, G.F. (1992b) GABA and nucleus accumbens glutamate neurotransmission modulate ethanol self-administration in rats. *Ann. N.Y. Acad. Sci.* 654: 502–505.

Rassnick, S., Pulvirenti, L. and Koob, G.F. (1992a) Oral ethanol self-administration in rats is reduced by the administration of dopamine and glutamate receptor antagonists into the nucleus accumbens. *Psychopharmacology* 109: 92–98.

Rassnick, S., Stinus, L. and Koob, G.F. (1993b) The effects of 6-hydroxydopamine lesions of the nucleus accumbens and the mesolimbic dopamine system on oral self-administration of ethanol in the rat. *Brain Res.* 623: 16–24.

Reid, L.D., Hunter, G.A., Beaman, C.M. and Hubbell, C.L. (1985) Toward understanding ethanol s capacity to be reinforcing: a conditioned place preference following injections of ethanol. *Pharmacol. Biochem. Behav.* 22: 483–487.

Reith, M.E. (1990) 5-HT3 antagonists attenuate cocaine-induced locomotion in mice. *Eur. J. Pharmacol.* 186: 327–330.

Rezvani, A.H., Grady, D.R., and Janowsky, D.S. (1991) Effect of calcium-channel blockers on alcohol consumption in alcohol-drinking monkeys. *Alcohol-Alcoholism.* 26: 161–167.

Rezvani, A.H., Pucilowski, O., Grady, D.R., Janowsky, D. and O Brien, R.A. (1993) Reduction of spontaneous alcohol drinking and physical withdrawal by levemopamil, a novel Ca^{2+} channel antagonist, in rats. *Pharmacol. Biochem. Behav.* 46: 365–371.

Richardson, N.R., Piercey, M.F., Svennson, K., Collins, R.J., Myers, J.E. and Roberts, D.C.S. (1993) Antagonism of cocaine self-administration by the preferential dopamine autoreceptor antagonist, (+)-AJ 76. *Brain Res.* 619: 15–21.

Risinger, F.O., Malott, D.H., Riley, A.L. and Cunningham, C.L. (1992) Effect of RO 15-4513 on ethanol-induced conditioned place preference. *Pharmacol. Biochem. Behav.* 43: 97–102.

Ritz, M.C., Lamb, R.J., Goldberg, S.R. and Kuhar, M.J. (1987) Cocaine receptors on dopamine transporters are related to self-administration of cocaine. *Science* 237: 1219–1223.

Roberts, D.C.S., Corcoran, M.E. and Fibiger, H.C. (1977) On the role of ascending catecholaminergic systems in intravenous self-administration of cocaine. *Pharmacol. Biochem. Behav.* 6: 615–620.

Roberts, D.C.S. and Koob, G.F (1982) Disruption of cocaine self-administration following 6-hydroxydopamine lesions of the ventral tegmental area in rats. *Pharmacol. Biochem. Behav.* 17: 901–904.

Roberts, D.C.S., Koob, G.F., Klonoff, P. and Fibiger, H.C. (1980) Extinction and recovery of cocaine self-administration following 6-hydroxydopamine lesions of the nucleus accumbens. *Pharmacol. Biochem. Behav.* 12: 781–787.

Roberts, D.C.S., Loh, E.A., Baker, G.B. and Vickers, G. (1994) Lesions of central serotonin systems affect responding on a progressive ratio schedule reinforced either by intravenous cocaine or by food. *Pharmacol. Biochem. Behav.* 49: 177–182.

Roberts, D.C.S. and Vickers, G. (1984) Atypical neuroleptics increase self-administration of cocaine: an evaluation of a behavioural screen for antipsychotic activity. *Psychopharmacology* 82:135–139.

Rudnick, G. and Clark, J. (1993) From synapse to vesicle: the reuptake and storage of biogenic amine neurotransmitters. *Biochem. Biophys. Acta* 1144: 249–263.

Samson, H.H., Hodge, C.W., Tolliver, G.A. and Haraguchi, M. (1993) Effect of dopamine agonists and antagonists on ethanol-reinforced behavior: the involvement of the nucleus accumbens. *Brain Res. Bull.* 30: 133–141.

Schenk, S., Horger, B.A., Peltier, R. and Shelton, K. (1991) Supersensitivity to the reinforcing effects of cocaine following 6-hydroxydopamine lesions of the medial prefrontal cortex in rats. *Brain Res.* 543: 227–235.

Schoffelmeer, A.N.M., Rice, K.C., Jacobson, A.E., Van Gelderen, J.G., Hogenboom, F., Heijna, N.M. and Mulder, A.H. (1988) μ-, δ- and κ-opioid receptor-mediated inhibition of neurotransmitter release and adenylate cyclase activity in rat brain slices: studies with fentanyl isothiocyanate. *Eur. J. Pharmacol.* 154: 169–178.

Sellers, E.M., Tonetto, T., Romach, M.K., Somer, G.R., Sobell, L.C. and Sobell, M.B. (1994) Clinical efficacy of the 5-HT3 antagonist ondansetron in alcohol abuse and dependence. *Alcohol Clin. Exp. Res.* 18: 879–885.

Sepinwall J. and Cook, L. (1978). In: Iversen, L. L., Iversen, S.D. and Snyder, S.H. (eds.) *Handbook of psychopharmacology,* vol. 13. New York: Plenum Press, pp. 345–393.

Shaham, Y., Alvares, K., Nespor, S.M. and Grunberg, N.E. (1992) Effect of stress on oral morphine and fentanyl self-administration in rats. *Pharmacol. Biochem. Behav.* 41: 615–619.

Sherman, J.E., Pickman, C., Rice, A., Lidebskind, J.C. and Holman, E.W. (1980) Rewarding and aversive effects of morphine: temporal and pharmacological properties. *Pharmacol. Biochem. Behav.* 13: 501–505.

Shoaib, M., Stolerman, I.P. and Kumar, R.C. (1994) Nicotine-induced place preferences following prior nicotine exposure in rats. *Psychopharmacology* 113: 445–452.

Signs, S.A. and Schecter, M.D. (1988) The role of dopamine and serotonin receptors in the mediation of the ethanol interoceptive cue. *Pharmacol. Biochem. Behav.* 30:55–64.

Skinner, B.F. (1932) On the rate of formation of a conditioned reflex. *J. Gen. Psychol.* 7: 274–286.

Smith, A., Piercey, M. and Roberts, D.C.S. (1995) Effect of (-)-DS 121 and (+)-UH 232 on cocaine self-administration in rats. *Psychopharmacology* 120: 93–98.

Smith, J.E., Co, C. and Dworkin, S.I. (1996) Brain neurotransmitter turnover correlated with cocaine self-administration in rats. Submitted.

Smith, J.E., Co, C., Freeman, M.E. and Lane, J.D. (1982) Brain neurotransmitter turnover correlated with morphine-seeking behavior of rats. *Pharmacol. Biochem. Behav.* 16: 509–519.

Smith, J.E., Co, C., Freeman, M.E., Sands, M.P. and Lane, J.D. (1980) Neurotransmitter turnover in rat striatum is correlated with morphine self-administration. *Nature* 287: 152–154.

Smith, J.E., Co, C. and Lane, J.D. (1984a) Limbic acetylcholine turnover rates correlated with rat morphine-seeking behaviors. *Pharmacol. Biochem. Behav.* 20: 429–442.

Smith, J.E., Co, C. and Lane, J.D. (1984b) Limbic muscarinic cholinergic and benzodiazepine receptor changes with chronic intravenous morphine and self-administration. *Pharmacol. Biochem. Behav.* 20: 443–450.

Smith, J.E., Guerin, G.F., Co, C., Barr, T.S. and Lane, J.D. (1985) Effects of 6-OHDA lesions of the central medial nucleus accumbens on rat intravenous morphine self-administration. *Pharmacol. Biochem. Behav.* 23: 843–849.

Smith, J.E., Shultz, K., Co, C., Goeders, N.E. and Smith, J.E. (1987) Effects of 5,7-hidydroxytryptamine lesions of the nucleus accumbens on rat intravenous morphine self-administration. *Pharmacol. Biochem. Behav.* 26: 607–612.

Sokoloff, P., Giros, B., Martres, M.P., Bouthenet, M.L. and Schwartz, J.C. (1990) Molecular cloning and characterization of a novel dopamine receptor (D3) as a target for neuroleptics. *Nature* 347: 146–151.

Spanagel, R., Herz, A. and Shippenberg, T.S. (1990a) Identification of the opioid receptor types mediating β-endorphin-induced alterations in dopamine release in the nucleus accumbens. *Eur. J. Pharmacol.* 190: 177–184.

Spanagel, R., Herz, A. and Shippenberg, T.S. (1990b) The effects of opioid peptides on dopamine release in the nucleus accumbens: an *in vivo* microdialysis study. *J. Neurochem.* 55: 1734–1740.

Spanagel, R., Herz, A. and Shippenberg, T.S.(1992) Opposing tonically active endogenous opioid systems modulate the mesolimbic dopaminergic pathway. *Proc. Natl. Acad. Sci. USA* 89: 2046–2050.

Spyraki, C., Fibiger, H.C. and Phillips, A.G. (1982a) Cocaine-induced place preference conditioning: lack of effects of neuroleptics and 6-hydroxydopamine lesions. *Brain Res.* 253: 195–203.

Spyraki, C., Fibiger, H.C. and Phillips, A.G. (1982b) Dopaminergic substrates of amphetamine-induced place preference conditioning. *Brain Res.* 253: 185–193.

Spyraki, C., Fibiger, H.C. and Phillips, A.G. (1983) Attenuation of heroin reward in rats by disruption of the mesolimbic dopamine system. *Psychopharmacology* 79: 278–283.

Spyraki, C., Nomikos, G.G., Galanopoulou, P. and Daifotis, Z. (1988) Drug-induced place preference with 5,7-dihydroxytryptamine lesions of the nucleus accumbens. *Behav. Brain Res.* 29: 127–134.

Staley, J.K., Basile, M., Flynn, D.D. and Mash, D.C. (1994) Visualizing dopamine and serotonin transporters in the human brain with the potent cocaine analogue [^{125}I]RTI-55: in vitro binding and autoradiographic characterization. *J. Neurochem.* 62: 549–556.

Stolerman, I. (1992) Drugs of abuse: behavioural principles, methods and terms. *Trends Pharmacol. Sci.* 13: 170–176.

Suzdak, P.D., Glowa, J.R., Crawley, J.N., Schwartz, R.D., Skolnick, P. and Paul, S.M. (1986) A selective imidazobenzodiazepine antagonist of ethanol in the rat. *Science* 236: 1243–1247.

Svingos, A.L. and Hitzenmann, R. (1992) 5-HT3 antagonists block cocaine-induced locomotion in a PCPA-sensitive mechanism. *Pharmacol. Biochem. Behav.* 43: 871–879.

Swift, R.M., Davidson D., Whelihan W., Kuznetsov, O. (1996) Ondansetron alters human alcohol intoxication. *Biol Psychiatry* 40:514–521.

Tabakoff, B. and Hoffman, P.L. (1983) Alcohol interactions with brain opiate receptors. *Life Sci.* 32: 197–204.

Tempel, A. and Zukin, R.S. (1987) Neuroanatomical patterns of the μ, δ and κ opioid receptors of rat brain as determined by quantitative in vitro autoradiography. *Proc. Natl. Acad. Sci. USA* 84: 4308–4312.

Tiberi, M., Jarvie, K.R. and Sivia, C. (1991) Cloning, molecular characterization and chromosomal assignment of a gene encoding a second D1 dopamine receptor subtype: differential expression pattern in rat brain compared with the D1 receptor. *Proc. Natl. Acad. Sci. USA* 88: 7491–7495.

Ulm, R.R., Volpicelli, J.R. and Volpicelli, L. (1995) Opiates and alcohol self-administration in animals. *J. Clin. Psychiat.* 56: 5–14.

Ungerstedt, U. (1971) Stereotaxic mapping of the monoamine pathways in the rat brain. Acta Physiol. Scand. (Suppl.) pp. 1–48.

Vaccarino, F.J., Bloom, F.E. and Koob, G.F. (1985a) Blockade of nucleus accumbens opiate receptors attenuates intravenous heroin reward in the rat. *Psychopharmacology* 86: 37–42.

Vaccarino, F.J., Pettit, H.O., Bloom, F.E. and Koob, G.F. (1985b) Effects of intracerebroventricular administration of methyl naloxonium chloride on heroin self-administration in the rat. *Pharmacol. Biochem. Behav.* 23: 495–498.

Van Ree, J.M. and Ramsey, N. (1987) The dopamine hypothesis of opiate reward challenged. *Eur. J. Pharmacol.* 134: 239–243.

Volpicelli, J.R., Clay, K.L., Watson, N.T. and O Brien, C.P. (1995) Naltrexone in the treatment of alcoholism: predicting response to naltrexone. *J. Clin. Psychiat.* 56(Suppl 7): 39–44.

Volpicelli, J.R., Davis, M.A. and Olgin, J.E. (1986) Naltrexone blocks the post-shock increase in ethanol consumption. *Life Sci.* 38: 841–847.

Wagner, J.J. and Chavkin, C.I. (1995) Neuropharmacology of endogenous opioid peptides. In: Bloom, F.E. and Kupfer, D.J. (eds.) *Psychopharmacology: the fourth generation of progress.* New York: Raven Press, pp. 519–529.

Wang, J.B., Imai, Y., Eppler, C.M., Gregor, P., Spivak, C.E. and Uhl, G.R. (1993) μ opiate receptor: cDNA cloning and expression. *Proc. Natl. Acad. Sci. USA* 90: 10230–10234.

Weiss, F., Hurd, Y.L., Ungerstedt, U., Markou, A., Plotsky, P.M. and Koob, G.F. (1992) Neurochemical correlates of cocaine and ethanol self-administration. In: Kalivas, P.W. and Samson, H.H. (eds.) *The neurobiology of drug and alcohol addiction,* vol. 654. New York: Ann. New York Acad. Sci., pp. 220–241.

Weiss, F., Lorang, M.T., Bloom, F.E. and Koob, G.F. (1993) Oral alcohol self-administration stimulates dopamine release in the rat nucleus accumbens: genetic and motivational determinants. *J. Pharmacol. Exp. Ther.* 267: 250–258.

Welzl, H., Kuhn, G. and Huston, J.P. (1989) Self-administration of small amounts of morphine through glass micropipettes into the ventral tegmental area of the rat. *Neuropharmacology* 28: 1017–1023.

Wenkstern, D., Pfaus, J.G. and Fibiger, H.C. (1993) Dopamine transmission increases in the nucleus accumbens of male rats during their first exposure to sexually receptive female rats. *Brain Res.* 618: 41–46.

Westerink, B.H.C., Hofsteede, H.M., Damsma, G. and De Vries, J.B. (1988) The significance of extracellular calcium for the release of dopamine, acetylcholine and amino acids in conscious rats, evaluated by brain microdialysis. *Naunyn Schmiedebergs Arch. Pharmacol.* 337: 373–378.

Wilson, J.M., Nobrega, J.N., Corrigall, W.A., Coen, K.M., Shannak, K. and Kish, S.J. (1994) Amygdala dopamine levels are markedly elevated after self- but not passive-administration of cocaine. *Brain Res.* 668: 39–45.

Wilson, M.C., Hitomi, M. and Schuster, C.R. (1971). Psychomotor stimulant self-administration as a function of dosage per injection in the rhesus monkey. *Psychopharmacologia* 22, 271–281.

Wise, R.A. (1989) The brain and reward. In: Liebman, J.M. and Cooper, S.J. (eds.) *The neuropharmacological basis of reward.* Oxford: Clarendon Press, pp. 377–424.

Wise R.A. and Bozarth, M.A. (1987) A psychomotor stimulant theory of addiction. *Psych. Rev.* 94:469–492.

Wise, R.A., Leone, P., Rivest, R. and Leeb, K. (1995b) Elevations of nucleus accumbens dopamine and DOPAC levels during intravenous heroin self-administration. *Synapse* 21: 140–148.

Wise, R.A., Newton, P., Leeb, K., Burnette, B., Pocock, D. and Justice, J.B., Jr. (1995a) Fluctuations in nucleus accumbens dopamine concentration during intravenous cocaine self-administration in rats. *Psychopharmacology* 120: 10–20.

Wolfe, J. and Beaudet, A. (1992) Neurotensin terminals for synapses primarily with neurons lacking detectable tyrosine hydroxylase immunoreactivity in the rat substantia nigra and ventral tegmental area. *J. Comp. Neurol.* 321: 163–176.

Wolozin, B.L. and Pasternak, G.W. (1981) Classification of multiple morphine and enkephalin binding sites in the central nervous system. *Proc. Natl. Acad. Sci. USA* 78: 6181–6185.

Wood, P.L. (1983) Opioid regulation of CNS dopaminergic pathways: a review of methodology, receptor types, regional variations and species differences. *Peptides* 4: 595–601.

Yasuda, K., Raynor, K., Kong, H., Breder, C., Takeda, J., Reisine, T. and Bell, G.I. (1993) Cloning and functional comparison of κ and δ opioid receptors from mouse brain. *Proc. Natl. Acad. Sci. USA* 90: 6736–6740.

Yokel, R.A. and Pickens, R. (1973) Self-administration of optical isomers of amphetamine and methylamphetamine by rats. *J. Pharmacol. Exp. Ther.* 187: 27–33.

Yoshida, M., Yokoo, H., Tanaka, T., Mizoguchi, K., Emoto, H., Ishii, H. and Tanaka, M. (1993) Faciliatory modulation of mesolimbic dopamine neuronal activity by μ-opioid and nicotine as examined with *in vivo* microdialysis. *Brain Res.* 624: 277–280.

Zito, K.A., Vickers, G. and Roberts, D.C.S. (1985) Disruption of cocaine and heroin self-administration following kainic acid lesions of the nucleus accumbens. *Pharmacol. Biochem. Behav.* 23: 1029–1036.

Drug Addiction and its Treatment: Nexus of Neuroscience and Behavior, edited by Bankole A. Johnson and John D. Roache. Lippincott–Raven Publishers, Philadelphia, © 1997.

7

Neuropharmacological Basis for Tolerance and Dependence

David J. Nutt

Department of Mental Health, School of Medical Sciences, University of Bristol, University Walk, Bristol BS8 1TD United Kingdom

The use of most, or arguably all, drugs of abuse results in a degree of tolerance and dependence. Indeed, the concept of drug dependence is inextricably interlaced with those of tolerance and withdrawal, as characterized by the need of the addict to increase dose in a desperate attempt to regain the pleasures of the first hit (chasing the rush). Withdrawal is one of the major causes of maintenance of drug use as it brings with it physical distress and craving. The social and economic costs of drug abuse are inextricably bound up with tolerance development, and this might be the greatest issue with regard to the costs of drug abuse since the increased financial demands that tolerance brings leads directly to greater crime.

Moreover, as well as being major components of the dependence syndrome, the phenomena of tolerance and dependence offer insights into the nature of the addiction process. Studies on the mechanisms underlying these processes have focused on pharmacologic aspects of brain function and the functional neuroanatomy of the brain. Such studies, which have emanated from animal models, have raised hypotheses that now challenge the clinician to test these parameters in patients. Sadly, this opportunity has not yet been taken up with much enthusiasm, although the hope of contributors to the present volume is that by bringing together in an organized form the major advances of the neurobiology of addiction, interest will be raised, ideas sparked, and impetus given to accelerate clinical research efforts.

In addition, the observations from the preclinical side that a combination of behavioral and pharmacologic approaches is the best way for real progress to be made should encourage researchers from differing disciplines to work together toward a common goal.

LEVELS OF ADAPTATION

Adaptation is the process whereby the organism copes with the experience of an exogenous stimulus such as a drug. Adaptation to drugs in general takes one of two forms: the effects can either decrease—tolerance, or increase—sensitization. The most common is tolerance, a reduction in the activity of a given dose with repeated use. This can occur at many levels and by many different processes (Table 1). Sensitization is the opposite of tolerance, an increase in action on repeated administration of the drug. This latter process is seen mostly with stimulant drugs such as cocaine and amphetamines (Post and Kopanda, 1976; Segal and Kuczenski, 1992). The mechanisms of this increase in sensitivity have not yet been properly characterized. Brain microdialysis studies have shown increases in transmitter release to a standard dose of drug (Pettit and Pan, 1990).

TABLE 1. *Levels of tolerance*

Absorption: drug uptake may be slowed:
    Nasal scarring with cocaine
    Reduced alcohol absorption in alcoholics
Increased metabolism: drug is cleared faster on
chronic use
    Barbiturates induce own metabolism
    Increased microsomal alcohol oxidation
Reduced brain entry: altered cerebral blood flow or
blood-brain barrier
    Peripheral vasodilation following alcohol
Reduced tissue (brain) response
    Decreased euphoria with opiates
    Decreased sedation with benzodiazepines
    Neuronal death following ecstasy
Reduced neuronal response
    Decreased chloride flux with benzodiazepines
    Reduced K^+ channel opening with opiates
Reduced second messenger responses
    Less inhibition of cyclic AMP by opiates

Reasons for this may include downregulation of inhibitory presynaptic receptors, increased excitatory input, and, perhaps, increased brain entry of the drug. Other studies with cocaine and amphetamine have suggested increases in postsynaptic receptor or second messenger function (Hubner and Moreton, 1991). As is the case with tolerance, sensitization is a complex multisystem process that is relatively little studied. Its relevance to drug addiction is currently unclear, although it may contribute to adverse effects such as the development of paranoid psychosis with chronic stimulant use. As this is the topic of a separate discussion, the remainder of this chapter concentrates on the processes underlying tolerance and dependence.

TOLERANCE AND DEPENDENCE

Definitions

Simply stated, tolerance is the phenomenon whereby chronic drug administration results in a progressively reduced effect. It is not only found with drugs of abuse. Tolerance can be a major problem with other drugs, including those used in clinical therapeutics. For instance the anticonvulsant effects of benzodiazepines such as clobazam and clonazepam attenuate over time and an exacerbation of seizures is commonly found in their withdrawal. Tolerance and withdrawal rebound has also been reported from some antihypertensives, such as clonidine. More directly relevant to the field of drug addiction are the findings that the analgesic actions of opiates used for pain relief gradually decrease, resulting in breakthrough pain. This major clinical problem has spurred a great deal of work on the mechanisms of action of opiate tolerance, the findings of which are of great relevance to understanding the processes that might underlie opiate addiction.

The concept of dependence is more complicated. Traditionally it has been divided into two processes, psychological and physical, and the World Health Organization (WHO) 1964 definitions of these have become widely known. The WHO defined physical dependence in a straightforward way—the presence of signs of withdrawal when drug use stops. Such signs can vary from seizures (e.g., with alcohol and benzodiazepines) to tremor, shaking, and nausea (with opiates). Purely subjective experiences were categorized in the concept of psychological dependence, which therefore encompassed all other aspects of drug addiction such as craving, drug seeking behavior, and altered lifestyle. This distinction was always somewhat contentious since it is obvious that such psychological processes have their origins in the brain. Moreover, it tended to lead to psychological aspects being given less importance as goals for treatment. The naivete of this essentially dualistic approach to biologic phenomena has become more apparent over the intervening years with a growing understanding of the neural basis of psychology. Ongoing studies of the brain mechanisms of craving and reinforcement in humans using techniques such as positron emission tomography (PET), single-photon emission computed tomography (SPECT), and functional magnetic resonance imaging (MRI) should soon bridge the false divide between physical and psychological concepts in drug dependence. Nevertheless, it is clear that a full understanding of drug addiction must incorporate ideas and perspectives ranging from molecular and genetic mechanisms, through pharmacology and psychology, to social and political ones. Integrating these very disparate domains is one of the major hurdles that needs to be jumped so the field can progress with cooperation and understanding between the different disciplines rather than conflict and tension.

This chapter limits itself to the biologic basis of tolerance and physical dependence, touching on withdrawal where appropriate. Issues and explanations more directly in the province of experimental psychologists are covered elsewhere in this volume.

Mechanisms

Tolerance and/or dependence can occur in one of two ways. The effects of the drug can reduce, or counter (opponent) processes can develop. Another way of considering these is as intrinsic or extrinsic processes. Intrinsic ones relate to adaptations in processes that are directly affected by the drug, such as G-proteins by opiates or γ-aminobutyric acid-A (GABA-A) receptors by ethanol. Extrinsic processes are not directly related to drug effects but are activated as a secondary consequence; for example, increased 5-hydroxytryptamine (5-HT) activity on chronic benzodiazepine administration may lead to symptoms of overactivity on their withdrawal. The net result is the same, and for most drugs both processes probably occur and it may become almost a semantic differentiation.

One way of viewing tolerance and dependence is to consider as tolerance only those processes that directly attenuate the actions of the drug. Dependence can then be considered as the expression of drug-opponent processes in the absence of drug.

Levels of Tolerance and Dependence

The processes underlying tolerance and dependence involve alterations in the function of several different organ systems at various levels. For any single drug the relative importance of a given level will vary. The following sections look at the more important areas.

Absorption

The first line of defense for the body against the perturbation caused by an exogenous substance such as an abusable drug is to prevent its entry (i.e., reduce absorption). This is probably not of great importance, as the ability of the body to influence drug uptake is relatively limited, especially when the intravenous or inhalational routes are used. Perhaps for this reason alterations in absorption have not been greatly studied, but there is some evidence that this plays a role in alcoholics. At the simplest level, the mucosal damage that follows extensive alcohol or nasal cocaine abuse will tend to delay uptake into the bloodstream. A more subtle effect is that of reduced gastric blood flow in alcoholics, which serves the same purpose. This latter effect is almost certainly a conditioned response, and so can be considered an opponent process. However, recent studies in moderate drinkers have shown the opposite effect, namely a somewhat higher peak plasma concentration as compared with nondrinkers. The reasons for this are unclear and it is doubtful whether the size of the effect is of much clinical relevance. Whether similar processes are seen in the lungs of smokers of nicotine or other drugs is not yet established, and indeed may never have been studied.

Metabolism

Accelerating the rate at which the body metabolizes a drug can increase its rate of clearance. Most drugs of addiction are metabolized in the liver by enzymes of the cytochrome system, the P-450s. This series of enzymes is subject to genetic variation, with a small proportion of the population having an isoform that shows reduced activity—slow metabolizers. Such differences can be of importance with some drugs such as the antidepressants, where toxic plasma levels may result from dosing within the pharmacologic range. As yet, there have been no reports of similar problems with drugs of abuse, although the population of users is not one that is much in contact with clinical pharmacologists.

One important aspect of liver drug metabolism is that the enzymes involved in the metabolic processes are subject to genetic induction. This means that as the enzyme is activated to metabolize the compound, enzyme synthesis is turned on, more enzyme is manufactured, and subsequent metabolism is accelerated. This phenomenon of enzyme induction thus results in a reduced action of the drug: a form of tolerance called metabolic tolerance. The best examples of metabolic tolerance in the drug addiction field are the barbiturates and related drugs (e.g., meprobamate). A similar effect may be seen with alcohol but to a much lesser extent. High-dose alcohol users do have increased metabolism probably by the induction of extra pathways of metabolism (see Nutt and Peters, 1994). Other sedatives, in particular the benzodiazepines, do not show such metabolic tolerance; as will be seen later the main site of tolerance to them is in the end organ.

Other individual differences in metabolism can have a big impact on drug effects. The best recognized are the genetic variants in aldehyde dehydrogenase that result in delayed metabolism of acetaldehyde and the flushing reaction, like that produced by disulfiram or calcium carbide. This is most commonly found in Orientals and is thought to be the major factor behind the lower incidence of alcoholism in this ethnic group (see Ball and Murray, 1994). Individuals with the enzyme deficiency have a toxic reaction to drinking alcohol that includes flushing, nausea, headache, palpitations, and confusion. For most people this is aversive and so a conditioned avoidance of alcohol, or at least moderation of intake, results. Whether this genetic abnormality has any effect on the development of tolerance or withdrawal in those individuals that persist in drinking despite these adverse consequences is not known and would be hard

to study. However, it might be an interesting area to pursue as acetaldehyde itself has actions that could result in tolerance.

In theory, the body might adapt to a drug by reducing the rate it enters the brain from the bloodstream. I have speculated in Table 1 that the peripheral vasodilation seen following alcohol might reduce cerebral perfusion and so lessen brain alcohol entry. There has been no systematic study of the actions of abused drugs on the blood-brain barrier, although most of these are sufficiently lipophilic for minor changes to be of minimal importance. New techniques such as PET and SPECT imaging make a study of these issues more feasible, at least for drugs such as opiates and cocaine for which radiolabeled derivatives are now available.

One interesting aspect of metabolic tolerance is the effect alcohol has to deplete body stores of magnesium (Mg^{2+}). This ion sits in the cation channel of N-methyl-D-aspartate (NMDA) receptors, producing a voltage-dependent block. Alcohol, especially at high doses, also blocks these receptors (Lovinger et al., 1989). It is possible that the depletion of Mg^{2+} in alcoholics serves to increase brain excitability, which may help offset intoxication. However, the loss of Mg^{2+} in alcoholics has profound implications for withdrawal, since NMDA receptors are increased in number (i.e., upregulated, see below) and their natural inhibitor is reduced. The resultant state of hyperexcitability leads to many of the symptoms of withdrawal, which can be dramatically reduced with Mg^{2+} supplements (Wolfe and Victor, 1969).

End-Organ Tolerance

Alterations in brain function, an example of end-organ tolerance, is by far the most common mechanism by which the body adapts to drug misuse. This has many consequences. Perhaps the most obvious is that the toxic effects of drugs are diminished along with the pleasurable ones. In the case of opiates, this is manifested by a marked increase in the dose required to cause both euphoria and respiratory depression. Opiate addicts can therefore take doses of heroin or methadone that would cause fatal respiratory depression in normal subjects or in addicts who have been abstinent for a significant time. However, they need to do this in order to maintain their "high." This has two main consequences. First, if a purer form of heroin hits the street, then the usual hit becomes an inadvertent overdose that can kill by respiratory depression. Second, many opiate addicts experience tolerance to the high as well. To recapture this (chasing the rush), they seek out drugs with increased efficacy (see below). Such drugs, e.g., fentanyl and derivatives, which are used in anesthetic rather than analgesic practice, are highly potent and show greater efficacy than morphine or heroin in producing respiratory depression. This is not a great problem in the operating theatre as an anesthetist is on hand to take over ventilation. However, when these drugs hit the street they can cause fatal respiratory depression even in heroin addicts who have become tolerant to this action with heroin. The recent spate of deaths from street fentanyl in New York heroin addicts tragically illustrates this.

Differential Organ Tolerance

This is an important concept with significant health and human safety implications. If tolerance develops to a greater extent in the brain than in other target organs, problems of toxicity may emerge. This is most obvious with cocaine because the central effects—the high—wears off faster than the cardiovascular effects (tachycardia). As a consequence, when users take another shot to restore their high, plasma levels that are toxic to the cardiovascular system can be reached; this may be the reason for many cocaine-related deaths. Another facet of this problem is the combined use of cocaine and alcohol. This yields a new drug, cocoaethylene (Randall, 1992). Cocoaethylene has a similar pharmacology to cocaine, but may show greater cardiac effects and has a significantly longer half-life. It has

been suggested that these two factors play a role in cocaine-induced cardiac dysfunction. Similar processes may be obtained in the use of inhaled solvents where death from cardiac arrhythmias is also very common.

In a comparable way, tolerance to alcohol may develop faster in the brain compared with the liver; heavy drinking may thus continue with relatively few psychological sequelae, but leading to hepatic damage that can end in cirrhosis.

Neuronal Death as Tolerance

Another extreme example of differential tolerance is shown by the actions of the new generation of stimulants such as *Ecstasy*. These amphetamine derivatives appear to act by releasing the monoamines serotonin (5-HT) and noradrenaline. In animals, high doses result in the destruction of subtypes of 5-HT neurons, a loss that appears to be permanent (Green et al., 1995). Some data suggest the same may happen in humans; the 5-HT–mediated endocrine responses to the precursor L-tryptophan can be blunted in previous Ecstasy users (Price et al., 1989). It is possible to argue that alcohol shows a related but opposite pattern; heavy drinkers damage their brain and thereby reduce their ability to abstain, due to reduced frontal lobe function.

Processes of Neuronal Tolerance

Neuronal tolerance probably represents the major basis of tolerance to most drugs of abuse. It appears that there are both general and specific mechanisms (Table 2), and that different receptors may show various forms of tolerance, with differing durations.

For drugs that predominantly act at G-protein–coupled receptors (such as the opiates), alterations in the availability or activity of second messenger G-protein–linked systems seem to be a key mode of tolerance. For example, in the case of the opiates (which act through μ receptors to inhibit adenyl cyclase), some cells can compensate by increasing the amount of

TABLE 2. *Processes of neuronal tolerance*

Drug class	Form of tolerance
Opiate	Increase G-proteins/cAMP
	Reduced K$^+$ conductance
Alcohol	Reduced GABA-A receptor function
	Increased EAA receptor number/function
	Reduced inhibitory α$_2$-adrenoceptors
	Increased calcium channels
Benzodiazepines	Reduced receptor function
Nicotine	Reduced receptor function and 2nd messenger activation
Cocaine	Decreased monoamine turnover (sensitization also occurs)

the second messenger cyclic adenosine monophosphate (cAMP). This can occur through an increase in adenyl cyclase itself, in the G-protein subunits that stimulate the cyclase, or in related enzymes such as the protein kinases that mediate the effects of cyclase stimulation. In recent years, much attention has focused on the role of cAMP-dependent protein kinases in opiate tolerance (Nestler et al., 1993). For instance, opiate agonist-induced tolerance and receptor downregulation are associated with increased concentrations of protein kinase C (PKC) activity in the cytosol and can be accelerated by activation of this enzyme. Conversely, withdrawal signs can be attenuated by drugs that inhibit these enzymes such as H-7 and H-8 (Tokuyama et al., 1995), which may offer a new direction in the search for addiction treatments.

In addition, in noradrenergic neurons there is an increase in the synthetic enzyme tyrosine hydroxylase, thus increasing noradrenaline production and leading to an excess of the neurotransmitter in withdrawal. These changes all work to offset the depressant effects of opiates on cell firing and are the likely cause of the well-established noradrenergic overactivity seen in withdrawal.

Drugs that act through ion channel–linked receptors produce a very different form of tolerance. Here, alterations in receptor function or number seem to be the primary mode of adaptation to chronic administration. In the case of

the benzodiazepines, there generally appears to be no major change in receptor number but the functional coupling between the benzodiazepine receptor and the GABA-A receptor is disrupted. This is well demonstrated by the marked increase in the activity of benzodiazepine receptor inverse agonists in animals made tolerant to the actions of agonists.

This phenomenon is well illustrated by the increased propensity of the partial inverse agonists FG7142 and CGS8216 to cause seizures in mice pretreated with flurazepam (Little et al., 1988) (Figs. 1 and 2). In control mice these drugs are not convulsant; indeed, CGS8216 behaves like an antagonist in many models. However, in benzodiazepine-tolerant animals it causes seizures in a significant proportion and dramatically lowers body temperature. This effect is not due to withdrawal precipitated by the inverse agonist because brain levels of flurazepam have reduced to zero by the time of testing. We feel the most compelling explanation is that they are due to an alteration in the position of the benzodiazepine receptor spectrum so that the neutral or set point is shifted in the inverse agonist direction (Fig. 2). This would explain the reduction in agonist efficacy (tolerance), the increased inverse agonist efficacy, and the partial inverse properties of agents such as flumazenil that normally act as antagonists (see Little et al., 1987).

It appears that this shift occurs relatively early in the course of treatment with benzodiazepine agonists, and more prolonged exposure may subsequently downregulate GABA function directly (see Gallagher and Primus, 1993). The mechanisms underlying such changes in receptor sensitivity are not well understood, but probably involve altered expression of the messenger ribonucleic acid (mRNA) receptor subunit resulting in different functional characteristics.

One intriguing aspect of the alterations in benzodiazepine receptor function during tolerance is that it can be reversed in a rather dramatic fashion by treatment with the antagonist flumazenil. This was first demonstrated in electrophysiologic studies by Gallagher and colleagues (1986) and has since been

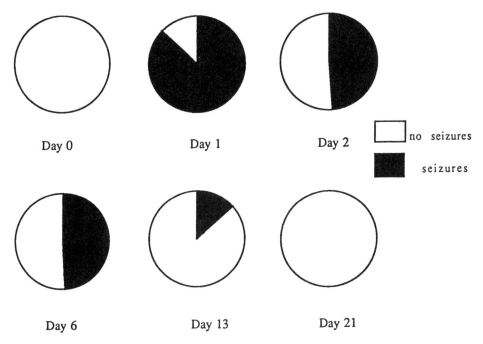

FIG. 1. Changes in sensitivity to inverse agonists after chronic flurazepam treatment.

shown in the whole animal (Nutt and Costello, 1987). There is also some suggestion of a similar effect in humans (Savic et al., 1991). These data suggest that tonic activation of the benzodiazepine receptor leads to allosteric alterations in the coupling of the GABA receptor to the chloride channel that can be reset by receptor occupation with a ligand that does not modulate GABA function.

A similar process of altered benzodiazepine-GABA receptor coupling in the inverse agonist direction appears to occur after chronic alcohol administration. Thus, the convulsant actions of inverse agonists are increased in alcohol withdrawal in the whole animal (Lister and Karanian, 1987) and in tissue samples (Buck et al., 1991a). As with the benzodiazepines, it is thought that this is

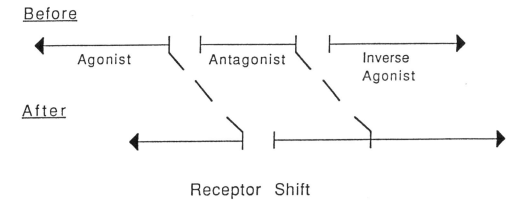

FIG. 2. Benzodiazepines—tolerance and withdrawal.

caused by differential effects of alcohol on GABA-A subunit expression, especially the α_1 subunit. However, this is unlikely to be the sole explanation, as it can also be demonstrated in isolated tissues and it begins to occur within a few hours, probably too fast for much new receptor synthesis. Perhaps direct membrane or receptor effects such as phosphorylation are involved. It is also fascinating that, as mentioned above with the benzodiazepines, this effect can be reversed by prior or cotreatment with flumazenil (Buck et al., 1991b). Perhaps such a reversal explains the ability of flumazenil to reduce alcohol consumption in rats (File et al., 1989). Unfortunately, a recent clinical study found no major therapeutic action for flumazenil in alcohol withdrawal (Potokar et al., 1995), which may suggest that other receptors are equally important in humans.

It should be noted that alcohol also acts at the NMDA and 5-HT$_3$ receptor-gated ion channels where it blocks or stimulates, respectively (Weight et al., 1993). On chronic dosing, a pronounced increase in NMDA receptor number is found, which can be construed as a compensatory mechanism to offset the sedative actions of the alcohol. When the alcohol is withdrawn there is a relative excess of NMDA receptor function that probably contributes to the hyperexcitability found in alcohol withdrawal and may, because of the consequent increase in intracellular calcium, contribute to neuronal death (see Nutt and Peters, 1994).

For nicotine, another drug that acts at ligand-gated ion channels, tolerance is well recognized and appears to reflect reduced receptor function rather than any change in number or affinity (Clarke, 1993). This is an intriguing aspect of the action of nicotine in that it appears to act as a sort of "partial agonist" at nicotinic receptors, producing desensitization but rather slowly. In contrast, another nicotinic agonist lobeline acts much more like a "full agonist" in that it produces very rapid desensitization. This then makes the receptor insensitive to nicotine so the effect of lobeline is effectively the same as that of antagonists such as mecamylamine. This action may underlie

the use of lobeline as a treatment for smoking dependence in the former Soviet Union.

EFFICACY AND TOLERANCE/DEPENDENCE

An interesting aspect of tolerance to opiates is its relation to drug efficacy. The more efficacious drugs maintain action longer than those of lower efficacy, such as partial agonists. This explains the attraction that highly efficacious agonists such as fentanyl and derivatives have for addicts, which is reflected in their street value (Fig. 3). In general, the same principle applies to all G-protein–coupled receptors. The reasons for this have been well characterized in the opiate receptor field. The more efficacious the agonist, the fewer receptors it has to activate in order to produce an effect on G-proteins (Nestler et al., 1993). Tolerance is manifest by a reduction of the ability of a drug-receptor interaction to couple to G-proteins. This effect can be mimicked by treating receptors with irreversible ligands, thus reducing their number. Such treatment mimics tolerance in that agonist actions reduce once receptor number is less than that needed for full actions. Take, for example, a tissue in which a full agonist needs to occupy only 20% of receptors to yield a maximal effect, whereas a partial agonist requires full occupation to produce the same. In this example, tolerance (the removal by desensitization of functional receptors) will immediately reduce the action of the partial agonist yet only impinge on the full agonist's activity once the percentage of functioning receptors (i.e., those able to couple to G-proteins) is less than 20% (Fig. 4).

It appears that a totally different situation applies in the case of drugs that act on ion channel–linked receptors. These receptors appear to desensitize to their endogenous neurotransmitters very rapidly. Similarly, tolerance develops to the effects of modulatory substances that act to enhance the actions of the natural transmitter. Thus, the actions of the benzodiazepine agonists reduce over time—tolerance. This occurs faster and to a greater degree to full rather than partial agonists. Thus, for the anticonvul-

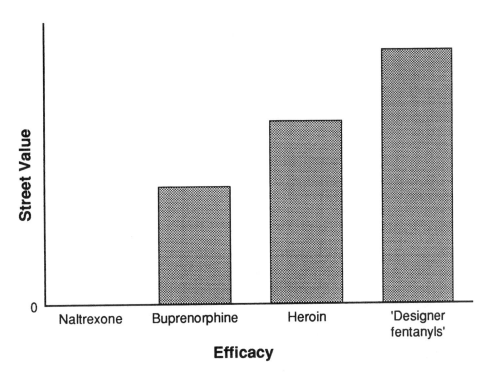

FIG. 3. Efficacy predicts street value of opioid ligands.

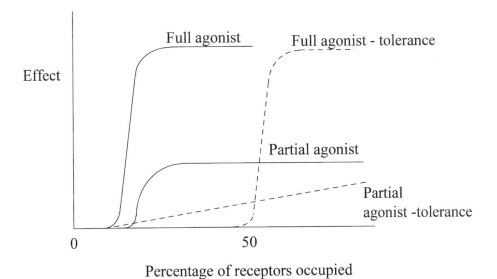

FIG. 4. Tolerance at G-protein–coupled receptors.

sant effects of the benzodiazepines (the best studied because they are the easiest to quantify), partial agonists show much less tolerance development than full agonists (Haigh and Feely, 1988a and 1988b). Moreover, there is growing evidence that physical dependence is not produced by partial agonists. This is well demonstrated by studies that precipitate withdrawal with either benzodiazepine receptor antagonists such as flumazenil, or with partial inverse agonists such as RO15-3505 (sarmazenil). When these are given to animals (rats, mice, or primates) that have received chronic benzodiazepine agonist, marked precipitated withdrawal is observed (Gallager et al., 1986). However, partial agonists such as bretazenil and abecarnil do not sensitize animals in this fashion. Given the increasing number of ligand-gated ion channels that have now been identified, it will be interesting to see if similar rules apply across the board.

OPPONENT PROCESSES

These can be considered of two sorts—whole body or system and cellular, with the latter driving the former. However, it will be a long time before the link is fully characterized, and in the interim it is most useful to consider them separately. The general principle of opponent processes are shown in Fig. 5 and Table 3.

Whole Animal

The classic whole body forms of opponent processing is that described by Macrae and colleagues (1987). Essentially, what appears to happen is that the body reacts to drugs (at least to depressant drugs) by initiating alerting processes. Thus, in response to drinking, alcoholics increase sympathetic arousal, presumably in an attempt to offset the sedative actions of the alcohol. The phenomenon of conditioned opponent processes is revealed by the use of placebo controls. If alcoholics are led to believe they will receive a drink yet are given placebo, these physiologic changes can be revealed. An increase in heart rate, blood pressure and skin conductance is seen, which indicates increased sympathetic tone (Newlin, 1986).

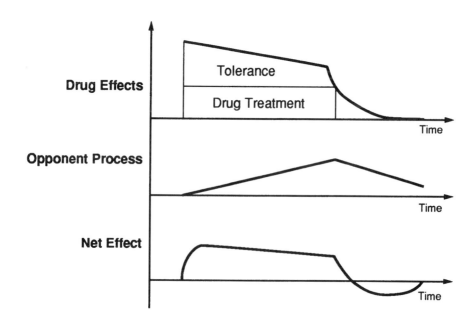

FIG. 5. Opponent processes.

TABLE 3. *Opponent processes*

Whole body
    Increased sympathetic arousal—opiates, alcohol
Cell
        Increased calcium channels and NMDA receptors
           with alcohol
        Increased cAMP with opiates

Subsequently, on repeated exposures the body begins to turn on the counter process in anticipation of drug intake; this arousal leads to anxiety and craving, which can accentuate drinking. Often, such opponent responses become conditioned to the places in which drug taking generally occurs. Thus, an alcoholic may begin to get activated or physiologically aroused going into a bar. Naturally, such arousal is itself aversive and will lead to increased urge to drink. Thus, conditioned opponent processes probably play a central role in craving as well.

Similar opponent processes have been demonstrated in opiate users also, with an increase in sympathetic arousal that minimizes the toxic actions of the opiate. In circumstances where opponent processes do not occur, the effects of the opiates will be unopposed and a relative overdose may result. This can occur in addicts in whom opiate use has become highly conditioned to a specific location. If they take their usual dose in different surroundings, they may experience enhanced effects. It has been suggested that many cases of accidental death from opiates are due to this phenomenon (Siegel, 1984).

What mechanisms might cause such whole body opponent processes? One possibility is that it is a form of conditioned autonomic reactivity, such as is found in other conditions, for example phobic states. Another is that there is the production of endocrine or chemical substances that produce these actions. One such substance has been suggested—tribulin. This is an as yet unidentified substance that is thought to act as a benzodiazepine receptor inverse agonist (i.e., it acts to raise anxiety and has proconvulsant properties). Increased excretion of tribulin is reported in states of withdrawal from sedative drugs such as benzodiazepines (Perturrson et al., 1982) and alcohol (Bhattacharya et al., 1982). It has been proposed that tribulin production is increased in an attempt to offset the sedative actions of these drugs, and anxiety results when its actions are met unopposed during withdrawal (Sandler, 1982).

Similar phenomena may underlay opiate tolerance. Some brain peptides such as FMFRamide and cholecystokinin have actions that oppose those of the exogenous opiates (i.e., they are antianalgesic and cause anxiety). Levels of these are increased on chronic dosing with the opiates, and again, relative overactivity may result once the opiate is washed out. These findings may offer new approaches to the treatment of withdrawal as antagonists of these substances could be expected to reduce withdrawal. Some evidence supports this concept in that a series of selective CCKB receptor antagonists has been synthesized in recent years, and a few have been shown to reduce opiate and other withdrawal states in animals (Costall et al., 1991). Human studies are now required to fully test the theory.

System Opposition

Examples of system opposition to drugs of dependence are relatively easy to find. Thus, the sedative effects of alcohol are in part due to its inhibitory effects on noradrenaline release and turnover. The brain appears to compensate for this by downregulating the normal processes that inhibit noradrenaline release, especially the presynaptic inhibitory α_2-adrenoceptors (Nutt et al., 1988). When alcohol levels fall, a state of relative disinhibition of the noradrenergic system results, brain and CSF noradrenaline levels rise, and this contributes significantly to withdrawal (Hawley et al., 1985).

A similar series of processes in the 5-HT system may contribute to benzodiazepine withdrawal. In normal volunteers, the acute administration of benzodiazepines reduces 5-HT turnover as shown by a blunting of the endocrine response to L-tryptophan (Nutt and Cowen, 1987). Tolerance appears to develop to this action over a couple of weeks, so it seems likely that during withdrawal there is a relative overactivity of 5-HT transmission. Indeed, recent in vitro data support this contention; brain slices taken from benzodiazepine-dependent rats were found to show increased potassium (K^+) stimulated 5-HT release (File and Andrews, 1993).

Recent animal data show that dopamine also appears to be important in withdrawal as well as in reinforcement. In rats made dependent on morphine, withdrawal can be precipitated by the injection of a dopamine D_2 receptor antagonist into the nucleus accumbens—the brain region in which the reinforcing actions of the opiates are mediated. These data support earlier work that revealed a reduction in dopamine function in opiate withdrawal, as shown by reduced release or an increase in self-stimulation thresholds (Di Chiara, 1995).

Cellular Opponent Processes

Cellular opponent processes are those alterations in function that do not directly alter the actions of the abused drug at its receptor or active site, but rather act downstream. Perhaps the best example is with the opiates. These drugs produce their reinforcing actions through an action at μ opiate receptors. As mentioned above, this action is mediated in part by the inhibition of adenyl cyclase and so reduces intracellular cAMP concentrations. Cells chronically exposed to opiates increase their intracellular concentrations of the second messenger cAMP, presumably in an attempt to compensate. As the opiates wash out of the body, the cells are left with an excess of cAMP, which renders them more excitable. There are two points to note about this phenomenon. First, it is more localized than might seem possible, with a general increase in intracellular second messenger lev-

els. Although μ opiate receptors and α_2-adrenoceptors are both inhibitory to adenyl cyclase, relatively little cross-tolerance seems to occur (Kennedy and Henderson, 1991). Moreover, these changes are not found in all cells. For instance, some elegant studies have revealed that the increased activity of noradrenergic neurons in opiate withdrawal, originally ascribed to changes in the locus coeruleus itself, is due not to an increase in the excitability of these cells but to increased excitatory glutamatergic input from other brain stem nuclei (Aghajanian and Wang, 1987).

Opiate/α_2-adrenoceptor interactions provide another fascinating observation of oppositional tolerance. Normally, noradrenaline acting through α_1-adrenoceptors increases GABA release from cortical interneurons. In morphine-tolerant guinea pigs, this action is inverted, and noradrenaline reduces GABA release via an action at α_2-adrenoceptors (Beani et al., 1991). However, the opposite action is found on acetylcholine release. The normal effect of noradrenaline is to decrease acethylcholine (ACh) release through α_2-adrenoceptors. In morphine-tolerant guinea pigs, the same procedures increases ACh release through an α_1-adrenoceptor mechanism (Tanganelli et al., 1989). Thus, it appears that unitary alterations in second messenger processes cannot fully explain opiate tolerance, and more complex system-change models that take account of regional variations in actions are required (see also Loh et al., 1988; Redmond and Krystal, 1984).

Adaptive changes in G-proteins underlie the tolerance found with other drugs that work through receptors coupled to this system. A good example is clonidine, an α_2-adrenoceptor agonist that lowers blood pressure. Tolerance develops to this action seemingly by a process of uncoupling the receptor from G-proteins (Schubert et al., 1993). This leads to a rebound of noradrenergic activity during withdrawal that results in hypertension. In the related β-adrenoceptor system, the nature of receptor tolerance has been fully elucidated and shown to occur in several stages. At first, the coupling of the receptor/agonist complex to G-proteins is blocked because an intracellular protein called β-adrenoceptor kinase (BARK) binds instead. This complex is then internalized and, depending on the ongoing degree of agonist/receptor occupation, is either recycled into the cell membrane or degraded in microsomes (Lefkowitz et al., 1990). Similar processes may underlie tolerance to opiates and other drugs of abuse that act through G-protein–linked receptors, although these have not been studied in as much detail.

Can Tolerance and Withdrawal be Separated?

There is a tendency for tolerance and withdrawal to be considered as similar, one being seen in the presence of the drug and the other when it is stopped. In many cases, this supposition is correct, but there is accumulating evidence that this is not necessarily so. The most detailed analysis of this issue has come in the field of alcohol. Early studies with drugs that deplete monoamine levels revealed that withdrawal could be attenuated but tolerance unaffected by depleting brain monoamines. Thus, reduction of either brain 5-HT concentrations with the selective neurotoxin 5,7-dihydroxytryptamine (Wood, 1980) or brain noradrenaline depletion with 6-hydroxy-dopamine (6-OH-DA) (Tabakoff and Ritzmann, 1977) reduced tolerance development but did not alter withdrawal.

More recently the group of Tabakoff and colleagues (Hoffman et al., 1983, 1990) have demonstrated conclusively that arginine vasopressin (AVP) is involved in alcohol tolerance but not withdrawal. Thus, AVP coadministered with alcohol prolongs tolerance via a noradrenaline-dependent mechanism, as this effect was abolished by selective depletion of this transmitter with 6-OH-DA. Further, by treating animals with selective AVP V1 receptor antagonists, they were able to block tolerance to the loss of the righting reflex effects of alcohol without affecting withdrawal.

These fascinating findings need to be extended for other drugs and perhaps also tested in the clinic.

THE DURATION OF TOLERANCE

Reinstatement

One of the great problems with drug addiction is the long-lasting risk of relapse. For some, this appears to be a lifetime risk, hence the encouragement of abstinence by many treatment agencies. An addict that does relapse often discovers that tolerance has been lost during the abstinent period. However, it is rapidly regained, often much faster than in the first or earlier bouts of drug taking. In addition, there is a more rapid decline in behavior such that the negative consequences of addiction emerge much more rapidly. This phenomenon of accelerated acquisition of tolerance and loss of control with repeated episodes of addiction is called reinstatement. It is best characterized with alcohol (Edwards, 1984), although it is also well recognized with other drugs, especially opiates.

The mechanisms of reinstatement have been little studied, but are thought to reflect the reacquisition of maladaptive patterns of behavior and function that were masked, but not eliminated, during abstinence. These occur in an individual with a prior predisposition to becoming addicted, and the combination of these two factors leads to relapse and reinstatement. Ongoing stress also makes it more likely that a lapse will turn into a relapse perhaps because cortisol levels directly influence drug intake (Piazza et al., 1993).

It is presumed that the processes and behavior patterns, including tolerance and dependence, are laid down in the early phases of addiction and these memories or skills can be rapidly regained. It seems likely that the extreme overlearning of some addictive behaviors, due to their multiple and repeated occurrences, contributes to the process. The breaking of such enduring patterns of brain malfunction presents a real difficulty for those treating addicts, and represents a new challenge in the search for therapies.

At the transmitter level it would seem likely that the processes responsible for reinstatement are similar to those that are important in other memory processes such as excitatory amino acids. The degree of tolerance to many drugs including opiates and alcohol can be attenuated by blocking the NMDA receptor with drugs such as dizocilpine (MK 801) (Trujillo and Akil, 1991). Although dizocilpine has too many unwanted actions to be of clinical use, other competitive and non-competitive modulators of this receptor complex with better adverse effects profiles are being developed. Perhaps this class of agent could be used to reduce tolerance in humans, and if so, they might also reduce the risk of reinstatement. Of particular interest is acamprosate, a drug currently marketed in France for the treatment of abstinent alcoholics on the basis of several multicenter-controlled trials that have shown it to reduce relapse. The mechanism of action is as yet unclear, but recent data suggest that excitatory amino acid receptors may be involved (Littleton, 1995), perhaps to reduce the learned or conditioned component of addiction to alcohol.

FUTURE DIRECTIONS

It is clearly established that the phenomena of tolerance and withdrawal are important aspects in relation to therapeutic drug use and illicit drug abuse. The emerging understanding of the mechanisms of these two states offers a new target for pharmaceutical invention. Important goals are findings drugs with less propensity for inducing adaptive changes, such as new partial agonists at ion channel–linked receptors. Alternative strategies might include drugs to prevent or reverse alterations in intracellular protein phosphorylation that contribute to desensitization to drugs that act through G-protein–linked receptors. Eventually, drugs targeting gene expression may prove viable

and effective means of controlling unwanted adaptive processes.

SUMMARY

- Drug tolerance and dependence are important aspects of drug use and abuse.
- They contribute to therapeutic failure with some drugs (e.g., benzodiazepine anticonvulsants, opioid analgesics).
- They lead to increased use of illicit drugs.
- Underlying processes are likely to be important in relapse and reinstatement.
- Mechanisms contributing to these phenomena include:
  whole body adaptations
  accelerated metabolism
  cellular adaptations
  receptor downregulation and uncoupling.

- Important differences exist between adaptations to drugs that act via G-protein–coupled receptors and those acting at ion channel-linked receptors.
- Ways to reduce or limit drug-induced adaptive changes should have benefits in the treatment and prevention of drug abuse as well as in prolonging the therapeutic value of CNS drug treatments.

REFERENCES

Aghajanian, G.K. and Wang, Y.Y. (1987) Common alpha 2- and opiate effector mechanisms in the locus coeruleus: intracellular studies in brain slices. *Neuropharmacology* 26: 793–799.
Ball, D.M. and Murray, R.M. (1994) Genetics of alcohol misuse. *Br. Med. Bull. Alcohol Probl.* 50(1): 18–35.
Beani, L., Bianchi, L., Morari, M., Simonato, G. and Tanganelli, S. (1991) a2-Adrenoceptor-mediated decrease in GABA outflow in cortical slices and synaptosomes during morphine tolerance. *J. Pharmacol. Exp. Ther.* 258:472–476.
Bhattacharya, S.K., Glover, V., Sandler, M., Clow, A., Topham, A., Bernadt, M. and Murray, R. (1982) Raised endogenous monoamine oxidase inhibitor output in post withdrawal alcoholics: effects of l-dopa and ethanol. *Biol. Psychiatry* 17: 687–694.
Buck, K.J., Heim, H. and Harris, R.A. (1991b) Reversal of alcohol dependence and tolerance by a single administration of flumazenil. *J. Pharmacol. Exp. Ther.* 257(3): 984–989.
Buck, K.J., McQuilkin, S.J. and Harris, R.A. (1991a) Modulation of gamma-aminobutyric acid receptor-operated chloride channels by benzodiazepine inverse agonists is

related to genetic differences in ethanol withdrawal seizure severity. *J. Neurochem.* 57: 2100–2105.

Clarke, P.B.S. (1993) Nicotine dependence— mechanisms and therapeutic strategies. In: Wonnacott, S., Lunt, G.G. (eds.) *Neurochemistry of drug dependence. Biochem. Soc. Symp.* 59: 83–95.

Costall, B., Domeney, A.M., Hughes, J., Kelly, M.E., Naylor, R.J. and Woodruff, G.N. (1991) Anxiolytic effects of CCK-B antagonists. *Neuropeptides* 19(suppl): 65–73.

Di Chiara, G. (1995) The role of dopamine in drug abuse viewed from the perspective of its role in motivation. *Drug Alcohol Depend.* 38: 95–137.

Edwards, G. (1984) Drinking in longitudinal perspective: career and natural history. *Br. J. Addict.* 79: 175–183.

File, S.E. and Andrews, N. (1993) Benzodiazepine withdrawal: behavioural pharmacology and neurochemical changes. In: Wonnacott, S., Lunt, G.G. (eds.) *Neurochemistry of drug dependence. Biochem. Soc. Symp.* 59: 97–106.

File, S.E., Baldwin, H.A. and Hitchcott, P.K. (1989) Flumazenil but not nitrendipine reverses the increased anxiety during ethanol withdrawal in the rat. *Psychopharmacology* 98: 262–264.

Gallagher, D.W., Heninger, K. and Heninger, G. (1986) Periodic benzodiazepine antagonist administration prevents benzodiazepine withdrawal symptoms in primates. *Eur. J. Pharmacol.* 132: 31–38.

Gallagher, D.W. and Primus, R.J. (1993) Benzodiazepine tolerance and dependence: GABA$_A$ receptor complex locus of change. In: Wonnacott, S., Lunt, G.G. *Neurochemistry of drug dependence.* Biochem. Soc. Symp. 59: 135–151.

Green, A.R., Cross, A.J. and Goodwin, G.M. (1995) Review of the pharmacology and clinical pharmacology of 3,4-methylenedioxymethamphetamine (MDMA or "Ecstasy"). *Psychopharmacology* 119: 247–260.

Haigh, J.R.M. and Feely, M. (1988a) Tolerance to the anticonvulsant effect of benzodiazepines. *Trends Pharmacol. Sci.* 9: 361–366.

Haigh, J.R.M. and Feely, M. (1988b) RO 16-6028, a benzodiazepine receptor partial agonist, does not exhibit anticonvulsant tolerance in mice. *Eur. J. Pharmacol.* 147: 283–285.

Hawley, R.J., Major, L.F., Schulman, E. and Linnoila, M. (1985) Cerebrospinal fluid 3-methoxy-4-hydroxyphenylglycol and norepinephrine levels in alcohol withdrawal. *Arch. Gen. Psychiatry* 42: 1056–1062.

Hoffman, P., Melchior, C.L. and Tabakoff, B. (1983) Vasopressin maintenance of ethanol tolerance requires intact brain noradrenergic systems. *Life Sci.* 32: 1065–1071.

Hoffman, P.L., Ishizawa, H.P., Gire, P.R., et al. (1990) The role of arginine vaspressin in alcohol tolerance. *Ann. Med.* 22: 269–274.

Hubner, C.B. and Moreton, J.E. (1991) Effects of selective D1 and D2 dopamine antagonists on cocaine self-administration in the rat. *Psychopharmacology* 105: 151–156.

Kennedy, C. and Henderson, G. (1991) M-opioid receptor inhibition of calcium current: development of homologous tolerance in single SH-SY5Y cells after chronic exposure to morphine in vitro. *Mol. Pharmacol.* 40: 1000–1005.

Lefkowitz, R.J., Hausdorff, W.P. and Caron, M.G.H. (1990) Role of phosphorylation in desensitization of the b-adrenoceptor. *TIPS* 11: 190–194.

Lister, R.G. and Karanian, J.W. (1987) RO 15-4513 induces seizures in DBA/2 mice undergoing alcohol withdrawal. *Alcohol* 4: 409–411.

Little, H.J., Gale, R., Sellars, N., Nutt, D.J. and Taylor, S.C. (1988) Chronic benzodiazepine treatment increases the effects of the inverse agonist FG 7142. *Neuropharmacology* 27: 383–389.

Little, H.J., Nutt, D.J. and Taylor, S.C. (1987) Kindling and withdrawal changes at the benzodiazepine receptor. *J. Psychopharmacol.* 1: 35–46.

Littleton, J. (1995) Acamprosate in alcohol dependence: how does it work? *Addiction* 90: 1179–1188.

Loh, H.H., Tao, P. and Smith, A.P. (1988) Role of receptor regulation in opiate tolerance mechanisms. *Synapse* 2: 457–462.

Lovinger, D.M., White, G. and Weight, F.F. (1989) Ethanol inhibits NMDA activated ion currents in hippocampal neurones. *Science* 243: 1721–1724.

Macrae, J.R., Scoles, M.T. and Siegel, S. (1987) The contribution of pavlovian conditioning to drug tolerance and dependence. *Br. J. Addict.* 82: 371–380.

Nestler, E.J., Hope, B.T. and Widnell, K.L. (1993) Drug addiction: a model for molecular basis of neural plasticity. *Neuron* 11: 995.

Newlin, D.B. (1986) Conditioned compensatory response to alcohol placebo in humans. *Psychopharmacology* 88: 247–251.

Nutt, D.J. and Costello, M. (1987) Flumazenil and benzodiazepine withdrawal. *Lancet* 2: 463.

Nutt, D.J. and Cowen, P.J. (1987) Diazepam alters brain 5-HT function in man: implications for the acute and chronic effects of benzodiazepines. *Psychol. Med.* 17: 601–607.

Nutt, D.J., Glue, P., Molyneux, S. and Clark, E. (1988) Alpha-2-adrenoceptor activity in alcohol withdrawal: a pilot study of the effects of i.v. clonidine in alcoholics and normals. *Alcohol Clin. Exp. Res.* 12: 14–18.

Nutt, D.J. and Peters, T.J. (1994) Alcohol: the drug. *Br. Med. Bull. Alcohol Probl.* 50(1): 5–17.

Perttursson, H., Bhattacharya, S.K., Glover, V., Sandler, M. and Lader, M.H. (1982) Urinary monoamine oxidase inhibitor and benzodiazepine withdrawal. *Br. J. Psychiatry* 140: 7–10.

Pettit, H.O. and Pan, H.T. (1990) Extracellular concentrations of cocaine and dopamine are enhanced during chronic administration. *J. Neurochem.* 55: 798–804.

Piazza, P.V., Deroche, V., Deminiere, J.M., Maccari, S., LeMoal, M. and Simon, H. (1993) Corticosterone in the range of stress induced levels possesses reinforcing properties: implication for sensation seeking behaviours. *Proc. Natl. Acad. Sci. USA* 90: 11738–11742.

Post, R.M. and Kopanda, R.T. (1976) Cocaine, kindling and psychosis. *Am. J. Psychiatry* 133: 627–634.

Potokar, J.P., Coupland, N.J., Malizia, A.L., Glue, P., Wilson, S.J., Bailey, J.E. and Nutt, D.J. (1995) Flumazenil in alcohol withdrawal. BAP summer meeting, Cambridge. *J. Psychopharmacol.* 9(3) (suppl A11): 41.

Price, L.P., Ricaurte, G.A., Krystal, J.H. and Heninger, G.R. (1989) Neuroendocrine and mood response to L-tryptophan in 3,4-methylenedioxymethamphetamine (MDMA) users. *Arch. Gen. Psychiatry* 46: 20–22.

Randall, T. (1992) Cocaine, alcohol mix in body to form even longer lasting, more lethal drug. JAMA 267(8): 1043–1044.

Redmond, D.E. and Krystal, J.H. (1984) Multiple mechanisms of withdrawal from opioid drugs. *Annu. Rev. Neurosci.* 7: 443–478.

Sandler, M. (1982) The emergence of tribulin. *TIPS* 3: 471–472.

Savic, I., Widen, L. and Stone-Elander, S. (1991) Feasibility of reversing benzodiazepine tolerance with flumazenil. *Lancet* 337: 133–137.

Schubert, T., Stoll, L., Fleckenstein, P., Riemann, D., Berger, M. and Mueller, W.E. (1993) Effects of single and repeated clonidine administration on the properties of central and peripheral a2-adrenoceptors in man. *Pharmacology* 46: 82–90.

Segal, D.S. and Kuczenski, R. (1992) Repeated cocaine administration induces behavioural sensitization and corresponding decreased extracellular dopamine responses in caudate and accumbens. *Brain Res.* 577: 351–355.

Siegel, S. (1984) Pavolvian conditioning and heroin overdose: reports by overdose victims. *Bull. Psychonomic. Soc.* 22: 428–430.

Tabakoff, B. and Ritzmann, R.F. (1977) The effects of 6OH-dopamine on tolerance to and dependence on alcohol. *J. Pharmacol. Exp. Ther.* 203: 319–332.

Tanganelli, S., Antonelli, T., Simonata, S., Spallatu, G., Tomasini, C., Bianchi, C. and Beani, L. (1989) a1-adreno-ceptor-mediated increase in ACh in brain slices during morphine tolerance. *J. Neurochem.* 53: 1072–1076.

Tokuyama, S., Feng, Y., Wakabayaski, H. and Ho, I.K. (1995) Possible involvement of protein kinases in physical dependence on opioids: studies using protein kinase inhibitors, H-7 and H-8. *Eur. J. Pharmacol.* 284: 101–107.

Trujillo, K.A. and Akil, H. (1991) Inhibition of morphine tolerance and dependence by the NMDA receptor antagonist MK-801. *Science* 251: 85–87.

Weight, F.F., Peoples, R.W., Wright, J.M., Lovinger, D.M. and White, G. (1993) Ethanol action on excitatory amino acid activated ion channels. In: Taberner, P.V. and Badawy, A.A.B. (eds.) *Advances in biochemical alcoholism research.* Oxford: Pergamon Press.

Wolfe, S.M. and Victor, M. (1969) The relationship of hypomagnesaemia and alkalosis to alcohol withdrawal symptoms. *Ann. N.Y. Acad. Sci.* 162: 973–984.

Wood, J.M. (1980) Effect of depletion of brain 5-HT by 5,7-dihydroxytryptamine on ethanol tolerance and dependence in the rat. *Psychopharmacology* 67: 67–72.

Drug Addiction and its Treatment: Nexus of Neuroscience and Behavior, edited by Bankole A. Johnson and John D. Roache. Lippincott–Raven Publishers, Philadelphia, © 1997.

8

The Behavioral Genetics of Addiction

Frank R. George

Amethyst Technologies, Inc., Scottsdale, Arizona 85257-3773

Individuals differ with respect to many traits, including responses to drugs. The study of these variations in behavior among individuals, their genetic and environmental bases, and their implications for society constitutes the field of *behavior genetics* (Plomin et al., 1990). A related field involving genetic factors related to drug effects is known as *pharmacogenetics*.

It is important to understand that finding genetic differences in susceptibility to drug abuse or addiction does not imply that there is an *addiction gene*. Rather, it is the complex interactions between an individual's genetic makeup, or *genotype*, and one's unique environment and history that determine one's eventual patterns of behavior and expression of specific traits, or *phenotypes*. In this way, risk for drug abuse may be viewed in a similar manner as risk for cancer or heart disease—people are born with varying degrees of genetic risk, but it is their life decisions that contribute greatly toward the development, or lack thereof, of these diseases. This chapter describes the current state of knowledge regarding genetic influences in susceptibility to drug abuse or addiction.

OVERVIEW OF BEHAVIORAL GENETICS

The beginnings of humankind's interest in the inheritance of various traits can be traced back in history for many centuries. For example, the breeding of domesticated animals such as dogs for specific characteristics and the development of farm animals for food can be traced back thousands of years. In addition, for centuries it has been accepted that personality traits and behavioral patterns, such as tendencies toward alcoholism, run in families, even though there has been little empirical evidence to support such attributions. Initial attempts to scientifically determine genetic contributions to human behavior began in the late 1800s. However, the emergence of behavioral genetics as a distinct academic discipline did not occur until around 1960, and investigations into the genetic basis of alcohol drinking began about the same time (Plomin et al., 1990). Today, behavioral genetics is an internationally active field, with investigators in this area using techniques ranging from surveys of human populations to molecular genetics.

Genes as Experimental Variables

A unifying concept in behavioral genetics is that genes may be utilized as independent variables. Thus, it can be asserted that when genotype is held constant within a population, any variability is due to environmental factors. In addition, it is possible to experimentally manipulate genes to develop a better understanding of their functional roles in determining biologic processes.

Most nonhuman pharmacogenetic and behavioral genetic studies employ one of two common genetic methods: inbreeding or selective breeding. Behavioral genetic methods can be complex but most nonhuman studies employ simple but elegant mating schemes based on principles outlined a century ago by Gregor Mendel. Much information concerning the extent of genetic contribution to a trait, its mode of transmission (e.g., dominant or recessive), and an estimate of the number of genes that mediate the trait can be ascertained within only a few generations of specified matings. Most human behavior genetic studies employ mathematical population models based on these same principles of inheritance.

NONHUMAN STUDIES

Studies with abused drugs such as ethanol, cocaine, and opiates have repeatedly demonstrated that genetic factors play an important role in regulating their effects (Broadhurst, 1979; Crabbe and Belknap, 1980; McClearn and Rodgers, 1959). One widely used measure in animal models of drug effects is locomotor activity. Genetic differences in locomotor response to ethanol, cocaine, and opiates, as well as xanthines and barbiturates have been found (Logan et al., 1986; Oliverio and Castellano, 1974; Ritz et al., 1981; Shuster et al., 1975; Suzuki et al., 1987).

Inbred Strains

Inbreeding reduces genetic variation within a population so that, over a number of generations, individuals become more alike. Inbreeding results from the mating of closely related individuals, such as brothers and sisters or first cousins. It requires some 20 generations of matings between siblings to produce offspring assumed to be genetically identical.

The real power of the inbred strain approach lies in the ability to observe effects across a large number of strains, and, as a result, form hypotheses based on strong and broadly based associations among measures.

In general, one must use several inbred strains in such a study to have sufficient confidence that any positive relationships may be causally related and not simply a coincidence resulting from random inbreeding.

In one of the first reports on genetics and cocaine using inbred strains, Schuster et al. (1977) showed that C57BL/6J mice were substantially more activated than A/J mice by 20 mg/kg cocaine. In the past few years several additional studies have confirmed and extended these initial findings. Ruth et al. (1988) showed significant genetic differences in Y-maze activity, rearing activity, and heart rate following cocaine. George (1989) has shown that cocaine is more potent in producing low-dose depressant effects in C57BL/6J relative to DBA/2J mice, while George and Ritz (1990) and de Fiebre et al. (1989) have shown that long sleep (LS) and short sleep (SS) mice differ substantially in their locomotor stimulant responses to cocaine. In addition, LS and SS mice differ in cocaine-induced seizures (de Fiebre et al., 1989; George, 1991c) but not lethality (George, 1991c), indicating that these two toxic responses to cocaine are mediated via distinct neuronal pathways. This research also showed that the incidence of seizures in F_1 and F_2 generation mice from hybrid matings of LS and SS parents was not consistent with a single-gene hypothesis, suggesting that multiple genes and receptors mediate seizurgenic responses to cocaine. Large genetic differences have been found in the locomotor stimulant effects of cocaine and amphetamine in rats from the ACI, F344, LEW, and NBR inbred strains (George et al., 1991b). Significant genetic differences were also found in cocaine-induced lethality in these animals, with a twofold difference in LD_{50} values seen between the most sensitive (NBR) and least sensitive (LEW) strains. Sensitivity to lethality was not correlated with sensitivity to stimulation (George, 1991b). This lack of association between stimulant and lethal effects of cocaine may be important in clinical manifestations of the cocaine sudden death syndrome. Certain individuals may experience stimulation and euphoria in response to cocaine at doses that are only slightly lower than lethal doses.

Several studies have shown that opiate-related physiologic and behavioral effects also are under a high degree of genetic influence (Belknap et al., 1989; Nichols and Hsiao, 1967; Oliverio et al., 1975). In addition, genotypic variance in response to opioids has been demonstrated across a number of species including mice (Belknap et al., 1982, 1989; Judson and Goldstein, 1978), rats (Dymshitz and Lieblich, 1987; Satinder, 1977), and monkeys (Ternes et al., 1983).

Selective Breeding

Selective breeding is a program of specific matings over a number of generations with the intention of changing particular traits. Selection is typically conducted in a bidirectional manner (Fig. 1) to produce maximally distinct populations, for example high alcohol drinking rats versus low alcohol drinking rats.

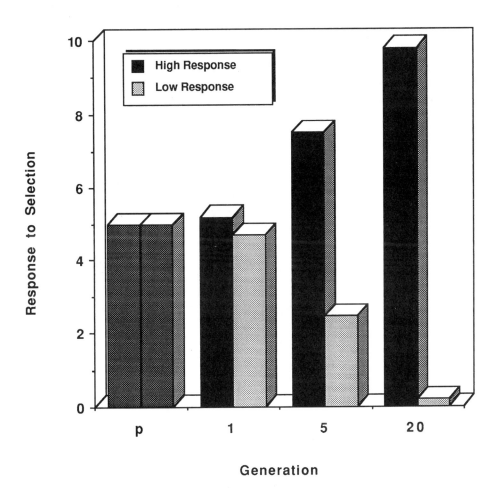

FIG. 1. A graphical representation of response to a theoretical selective breeding program. *P* represents the mean response of the original parental population. As the number of generations of selective breeding increases, the mean difference between the population bred for high response to the selection trait versus the mean response for the population bred for low response to the same trait increases, implying specific recombinations of the alleles for those genes contributing to the selection trait.

There are a number of reasons for conducting a selective breeding program. One is that if the selection is successful, this is a strong indication that genetic factors influence the trait being measured. Another reason is that once these different populations are created, they may be studied to help understand the genetic and biologic bases for the trait for which they were bred.

Much has been learned through selective breeding studies about ethanol and drug effects and the processes of addiction. The most well known of these selected lines of mice and rats are called the LS and SS lines. These are two lines of mice selectively bred respectively for long versus short duration of loss of the righting reflex following ethanol administration (Plomin et al., 1990). While they are not technically asleep, they have the appearance of sleeping, and measures of this response have come to be known as *sleep time*. The LS and SS mice currently differ in their neural sensitivity to ethanol by approximately 20-fold.

More recently, additional programs have been conducted in which mice have been selectively bred for other responses to ethanol. For example, a common symptom of ethanol withdrawal is a seizure. Based on this effect, mice have been bred to be either prone to having withdrawal seizures, the withdrawal seizure-prone mice (WSP) or resistant to withdrawal seizures, the withdrawal seizure-resistant (WSR) mice (Phillips et al., 1989).

Ethanol also disrupts the ability of mammals to regulate body temperature, and at temperate room or climatic temperatures typically produces a marked hypothermic effect. This effect is responsible for a number of deaths annually in colder climates when individuals consume ethanol in an attempt to stay warm. Another selective breeding study has produced mice known as the COLD and HOT lines. These lines of mice have been developed for differential sensitivity to the hypothermic effect of ethanol. COLD mice produce a pronounced hypothermic response to ethanol, whereas HOT mice show relatively little response (Phillips et al., 1989).

Studies measuring preference for ethanol have shown that rats and mice manifest large genetic differences in whether they prefer drinking an ethanol solution or water when given a choice between the two. This large genetic variability in ethanol *preference* as this choice test is called, has served as the basis for the establishment of selectively bred rodents that differ in their ethanol drinking and are relevant to the study of drug addiction.

These selectively bred rodent lines include the Alko alcohol (AA) and Alko nonalcohol (ANA) rats (Eriksson, 1968); alcohol preferring (P) and nonpreferring (NP) rats; and the high alcohol drinking (HAD) and low alcohol drinking (LAD) rats (Li et al., 1981). These rats were selectively bred based on their daily intake of an 8% ethanol solution. The success of these selection programs indicates that ethanol consumption is strongly influenced by genetic factors. The preferring lines characteristically drink most of their daily liquid intake in the form of ethanol solutions. In contrast, the nonpreferring animals drink very small amounts of ethanol daily. Ethanol intakes for these lines lie at the high and low extremes of intakes found in heterogeneous rats or across several inbred strains.

The original foundation, or parental, stock from which the selected lines are derived is an important consideration. The P and NP rats were selected from a foundation stock of randomly bred Wistar rats. The selection criterion for this pair of lines was based on daily intake of an 8% (w/v) ethanol solution defined as a consumption score (grams of ethanol per kilogram of body weight per day) (Fig. 2). The HAD and LAD rats were selected from the more heterogeneous and systematically outbred N/Nih stock, using a breeding design to minimize inbreeding. The selection criterion for this pair of lines was also based on daily intake of 8% (w/v) ethanol (g/kg/day). N/Nih rats, compared with Wistar rats, provide a possible advantage as a foundation population since N/Nih rats are less inbred and can be characterized as having potentially greater genetic diversity. These factors would tend to reduce false-negative

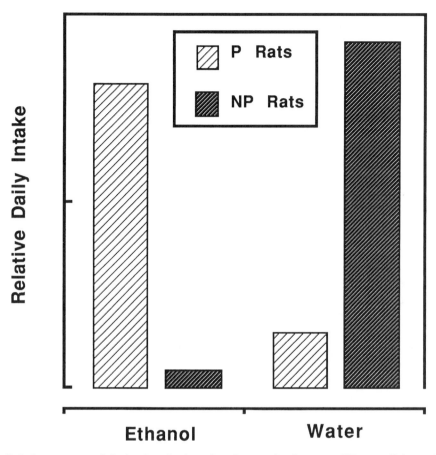

FIG. 2. Relative average daily intake of ethanol and water for P versus NP rats. (Adapted from Li et al., 1981.)

relationships and increase the strength of positive relationships among traits.

Genetic Correlations

Genetic correlational analysis may be applied to understanding mechanisms of action associated with drug effects. Whereas pharmacologic correlations involve the study of the relationship between the potencies of drugs in producing a response and their potencies at particular binding sites to determine sites of *pharmacologic initiation* of drug action, genetic correlations, in contrast, involve the determination of the relationship or correlation between biochemical and behavioral phenotypes across distinct genetic strains of animals to determine sites of *genetic variation* in drug action.

Genotypes that differ for a given trait can be used to test relationships between variables by determining correlations between traits hypothesized to be causally related. A lack of correlation is usually good evidence that the measures studied are not likely to be mechanistically related. A strong positive correlation, especially a perfect rank-order correlation across genotypes, enables one to hypothesize that the measures are causally related.

The use of genetic correlations has provided much information on the brain systems involved in mediating responses to drugs. If animals differ in a particular response to a drug, for example ethanol drinking, then one can examine various brain pathways and systems to determine whether there are differences in these systems that may account for the observed difference in drinking. Correlating biochemical differences with behavioral differences is a powerful approach in the attempt to determine the mechanisms of action of drugs, especially those effects that contribute to substance abuse disorders. Since it is apparent that alcohol and drug abuse are mediated through several genes, there are a number of neuronal systems that may be involved in mediating responses to drugs.

Studies using this approach have shown that serotonin (5-HT) neurotransmitter systems are involved in aspects of alcohol drinking. There has been a considerable amount of research attention focused on 5-HT and its relationship to ethanol drinking, with the first characterizations appearing almost three decades ago (Myers and Veale, 1968). Since that time, many studies have shown apparent influences of serotonergic neurotransmission on ethanol drinking.

A number of rodent stocks that differ in ethanol preference show correlated differences in various aspects of 5-HT function. Significant differences in measures of 5-HT release and turnover have been found between rodent stocks that self-administer ethanol versus those that do not, under either preference or reinforcement conditions. High alcohol preferring P and HAD rats exhibit lower levels of 5-HT in such brain regions as the frontal cortex, hypothalamus, and the nucleus accumbens compared with low alcohol preferring NP and LAD rats (Murphy et al., 1987).

Recently, McBride et al. (1990) showed that preferring P and HAD rats have significantly higher densities of 5-HT$_{1A}$ receptors, particularly in nucleus accumbens and frontal cortex, relative to nonpreferring NP and LAD rats. In our laboratory we have also begun a systematic investigation into the role of 5-HT systems in the reinforcing actions of ethanol. Initial evidence indicates that C57BL/6J and LS/Ibg mice, animals that self-administer ethanol (Elmer et al., 1986, 1988, 1990), ex-

hibit substantially lower densities of 5-HT$_2$ receptors labeled by ^{3}H-ketanserin in striatal, midbrain, and hippocampal brain regions, relative to nonreinforced SS/Ibg mice, for which ethanol does not appear to serve as a reinforcer (unpublished data from our laboratory). Differences found in this study were 200% to 300%, and represent robust differences in receptor densities. Taken together, these findings suggest that 5-HT receptor densities, but not neurotransmitter synthesis or turnover, may be associated with genetic differences in the reinforcing effects of ethanol. However, these results are far from conclusive, and other studies have failed to show differences in serotonergic functioning associated with alcohol consumption, for example, within the AA and ANA rat lines (Sinclair and Kiianmaa, 1989).

Other genetic studies have shown an involvement of the endogenous opioid system in alcoholism. The endogenous opioid system is one of the neuronal systems proposed to mediate some of the reinforcing effects of ethanol and other drugs. Differences in the brain endogenous opioid system between the AA and ANA rats have been shown. The content of brain endogenous opioids is significantly higher in AA rats. This difference may be important in controlling the differences in the voluntary ethanol consumption exhibited by these animals (Gianoulakis et al., 1992). Similar differences related to endogenous opioid functioning have been found between the P and NP rats (Froelich et al., 1987), and in another recent study ethanol-preferring C57BL/6 mice were shown to have a greater sensitivity of the endogenous opioid system to ethanol relative to ethanol-avoiding DBA/2 mice (De Waele et al., 1992).

Interestingly, while a substantial body of literature implicates brain dopaminergic pathways in the processing of rewarding events, including reinforcing effects of many drugs of abuse, few genetic studies using animal models have been conducted that show differential effects related to aspects of dopaminergic function associated with differences in drug-taking behavior. However, as discussed below, there are a number of human genetic studies related to dopaminergic neurotransmission and the rewarding effects of drugs.

Recombinant Inbred Strains

A behavioral genetic method gaining rapidly in popularity is the use of recombinant inbred strains. Recent advances in molecular biology are a large part of the reason for this interest. To understand this method, one need only look at its name. When using the recombinant inbred strain method, one simply mates members from two distinct inbred strains, which "recombines" them and produces new genetic strains. By "recombine" we mean that the two strains, and thus their genes, are cross-mated to produce new combinations, or recombinations, of genes. Following this initial recombination, the new animals that have been produced are then systematically inbred. An important feature of these new inbred strains is that they are all derived from the same two parent strains.

The use of recombinant inbred (RI) strains in genetic research can aid substantially in determining the genes involved in the expression of various traits. Individual differences in complex behavioral traits such as responses to drugs are likely to be influenced by many genes. Recombinant inbred strains are valuable not only for their originally developed purpose of detecting single or major gene effects, but also for identifying possible relationships between continuously distributed traits and multiple genes through the use of the quantitative trait loci (QTL) approach. This approach is becoming more widely used in drug abuse research, and recent findings hold promise for this technique in helping to determine the genes and biologic factors that contribute to alcohol and substance abuse disorders.

Quantitative Trait Loci Approach in Animal Models

Recent advances in molecular genetics have made it possible to analyze directly non-

human and human genes. The question may now be asked as to whether we can identify specific genes responsible for alcoholism and drug abuse disorders. The answer may lie in our growing understanding of whether the genes that may dispose certain individuals toward addiction are actually *abnormal* genes or *normal* and common versions of genes that, when combined in certain ways with other normal genes, result in stronger intoxicating or euphoric responses to ethanol and other drugs.

Some physiologic mechanisms are governed by a single gene. If different versions, or alleles, of this gene exist in a population, then there will likely be discrete, or qualitative, differences in expression of the trait determined by that gene. However, complex behavioral traits, such as taking drugs, presumably involve more than one gene or even many genes. The question arises as to how to study the individual contributions of each of these genes, when each single gene alone accounts for only a modest portion of the overall effect, and when individual gene effects are confounded by the collective effects of all of the contributing genes. One answer is through the combined use of recombinant inbred strains of mice plus genetic correlations within the QTL approach.

The QTL approach uses recombinant inbred strains within correlational analyses to detect genes that may be involved in particular traits. To do this, the trait of interest, for example alcohol drinking, is measured across a group of recombinant inbred strains. A typical finding would be that alcohol drinking was distributed across strains in such a manner as to suggest a continuous distribution mediated by several genes. Some strains might contain high alcohol drinkers, some might contain low drinkers, and several would likely contain animals whose drinking was at some intermediate level. This strain distribution pattern for alcohol drinking would then be correlated or compared with the frequency of several different genes and markers for genes on all of the mouse chromosomes. The finding of significant correlations between a chromosomal marker or site and the trait of alcohol drinking would suggest that a specific gene at or near the known chromosomal marker site was significantly contributing to propensity to drink alcohol. In this type of study, several of these correlated marker sites might be found, suggesting the existence of multiple genes contributing to alcohol drinking. Once these general marker sites are established, it is then possible to dissect the associated portions of the chromosome to attempt to identify the specific genes contributing to the trait.

This QTL approach is exciting and has been applied to several behavioral traits. Most of the behaviors showed strain distribution patterns suggestive of influence by more than one gene. Genetic correlations have identified potential gene locations for some of these behaviors, including avoidance and exploratory behavior (Neiderhiser et al., 1992). The QTL approach has also been applied recently to effects of amphetamine, ethanol, and morphine. Again, significant genetic correlations have been found with a number of potential gene locations (Gora-Maslak et al., 1991).

Overall, the production and use of genetically specified offspring is an important aspect of behavioral genetic methods; fortunately, however, it is not required of every investigator who wishes to take advantage of these designs. Many inbred and selectively bred animals currently exist, and large numbers of animals from well-studied inbred strains can be readily obtained from commercial suppliers.

Behavioral Genetic Studies of Drug Self-Administration

In addition to locomotor and other acute responses to drug challenge, genetic factors also appear to play a role in regulating drug-reinforced behavior. Numerous findings indicate that drug-reinforced behavior has a strong biologic basis (Griffiths et al., 1979; Meisch, 1984; Schuster and Thompson, 1969; Weeks, 1962). The use of inbred strains and selectively bred lines in studies on ethanol (Elmer et al., 1986; Eriksson, 1968; Eriksson and Rusi, 1981; George, 1987; Li et al., 1979; McClearn and Rodgers, 1961; Ritz et al., 1986; Rodgers and McClearn, 1962), has provided valuable information about the contribution of genetic factors to ethanol drinking.

Using operant models of drug discrimination and self-administration, researchers have attempted to study the influences of genetic factors on pharmacologic cues and the reinforcing effects of drugs. Several reports have shown significant genetic influences on the reinforcing effects of ethanol (Elmer et al., 1987; George, 1987, 1988; George and Goldberg, 1989; Ritz et al., 1986; Sinclair, 1974). The results obtained in these studies indicate that genetic analyses are important in studies related to the understanding of drug-reinforced behavior. Findings obtained with operant conditioning methods demonstrate that ethanol can serve as a positive reinforcer across a range of environmental conditions in certain inbred strains such as C57BL/6J mice and LEWIS rats. Conversely, ethanol does not appear to serve as a reinforcer for DBA/2J mice and BALB/cJ mice. These genetic differences, while typically substantial, are not necessarily always an all-or-none effect. F344 rats, for example, appear to be weakly but positively reinforced by ethanol (Suzuki, et al., 1988).

While ethanol can be readily established as a reinforcer in several rat and mouse genotypes, most of these animals appear to lack specific motivational factors that would facilitate continued responding under conditions requiring higher work loads. For example, high preferring HAD rats are modestly reinforced by ethanol, but show little persistence in responding for ethanol under conditions of high work loads. NP rats, on the other hand, while they are very low preferring, will show ethanol-reinforced responding for ethanol equivalent to that of the HAD rats when tested under low work loads, such as when only one lever press required to obtain a delivery of ethanol. Interestingly, NP rats also show a moderate level of persistence in responding when the work load, i.e., the number of required lever presses, is increased, and this persistence is much greater than that seen in HAD rats. The low preferring LAD rats are not reinforced by ethanol and show no significant persistence in responding for ethanol (Ritz et al., 1994). Conversely, of all the genotypes for which data exist, only P rats show the combination of high ethanol preference, high amounts of operant lever pressing to obtain ethanol, and persistence in lever press responding even under increasing work loads. Taken together, the results suggest that the propensity to consume ethanol involves the influence of multiple independent components, including (1) an intrinsic permissive factor contributing to ethanol preference, (2) direct rewarding effects, and (3) motivational factors. These findings are also important in that they indicate that ethanol drinking in a preference paradigm is not highly predictive of the reinforcing effects of ethanol.

Thus, genotype is an important variable in the reinforcing efficacy of ethanol. Even food deprivation, which has been shown to increase intake of ethanol and other drugs, fails to facilitate ethanol drinking in animals for which this drug does not serve as a reinforcer, such as BALB/cJ and DBA/2J mice. Food deprivation appears to enhance drug intake only in those animals predisposed genetically to accept a particular drug as a reinforcer (Elmer, et al., 1986, 1987, 1988).

Goudie et al. (1989) have described individual differences between rats in ability to discriminate cocaine in an operant paradigm. Furthermore, conditioned taste aversion tests of the same animals suggested that animals sensitive to the dysphoric effects of cocaine were less sensitive to its discriminative cues. Using a different approach, the recent integration of behavioral genetic research designs and animal models of drug self-administration has shown that the reinforcing effects of cocaine are mediated by at least some inherited traits. Recent operant studies have shown that cocaine, self-administered orally, serves as a strong reinforcer in Lewis rats, a marginal reinforcer in NBR rats, and does not

serve as a reinforcer in ACI and F344 rats (George and Goldberg, 1988, 1989). Another study utilizing a limited-access two-bottle choice procedure has also shown that cocaine serves as a positive reinforcer for Lewis rats, but not F344 rats (George and Goldberg, 1988, 1989).

While there exist fewer reports on intake of drugs other than ethanol using genetically specified subjects, the existing data, almost all of which involve home-cage drinking of opioid solutions, do suggest that large population differences may exist with regard to drug seeking behavior (Broadhurst, 1979; Crabbe and Belknap, 1980; Horowitz et al., 1977; Meade et al., 1973; Nichols and Hsiao, 1967).

In one operant study using etonitazene, a potent opioid agonist, Lewis rats made significantly more lever press responses when etonitazene was available than when the vehicle solution, water, was available as the reinforcer (Fig. 3). Conversely, F344 rats make fewer responses when etonitazene was available relative to water, suggestive of a genetically mediated avoidance of this drug (George and Goldberg, 1989; Suzuki et al., 1992).

In another series of studies, the operant response was entrance into the drug-appropriate arm of a Y maze to receive drug or vehicle injections. Y maze choice behavior was investigated in two outbred mice, ICR and Swiss-Webster, and in C57BL/6J and BALB/cJ (Eidelberg et al., 1975). Mice were first made dependent on morphine (40 mg/kg/day for 6 days) prior to establishing individual side preferences in a Y maze. Following the determination of side preferences, the mice were given saline when they entered their preferred side and morphine (40 mg/kg) when they entered the opposite side. This training protocol effectively reversed the original arm choice in every group except for the BALB/cJ strain. Interestingly, under similar Y-maze conditions, when BALB/cJ mice are implanted with a chronic indwelling cannula to the lateral hypothalamus without prior dependence induction, the rate of acquisition of the morphine-reinforced response showed a classical positively accelerating pattern that is often

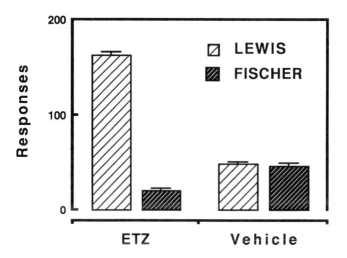

FIG. 3. Relative rates of operant lever pressing for etonitazine in two inbred rat strains. (From George and Goldberg, 1989.)

seen in learning studies. When saline was substituted for morphine the responding showed a pattern typically seen in behavioral studies during extinction, that is, when the behavioral response is no longer reinforced the rate of responding shows an orderly decline (Cazala et al., 1987).

Nichols and Hsiao (1967) selectively bred rats for high and low morphine consumption in a two bottle choice procedure. These experiments utilized a method that involved cycles of chronic morphine administration and preference testing. The protocol was based on the assumption that opiates have greater reinforcement efficacy if taken during opiate withdrawal and would take advantage of a repeated withdrawal periods to condition opiate reinforced drinking. Following the establishment of a population of Sprague-Dawley rats that were exposed to this procedure, rats displaying high opiate drinking were randomly inbred as were the low opiate drinking rats. Selectively breeding rats based on this protocol produced a bidirectional shift in opiate preference.

In 1971 Eriksson and Kiianmaa performed a genetic analysis of morphine preference in CBA/Ca, a nonpreferring strain, and C57BL/6J mice, a preferring strain, along with their F_1, F_2, and backcross generations using a similar cyclic-reinforcing technique to that of Nichols and Hsiao. Their

analysis of a 5-day preference measure between morphine in tap water and tap water following these techniques demonstrated high heritability and dominance in the direction of morphine preference.

The majority of subsequent studies investigating genotype-dependent opiate self-administration have incorporated saccharin in the morphine solution to enhance morphine intake (Eidelberg et al., 1975; Hadaway et al., 1979; Horowitz, 1976, 1981; Horowitz et al., 1977; Whitney and Horowitz, 1978). Consistently, C57BL/6J mice prefer morphine/saccharin (M/S) solutions to tap water and DBA/2J mice avoid M/S solutions. In a study that compared M/S versus water intake across nine inbred strains, DBA/2J, AKR/J, and SJL/J avoided the M/S solution, BALB/cJ mice showed no preference, and C3H mice showed a modest preference for the M/S solution. Three sublines of the C57BL mice (10J, 6J, and 6A) showed almost complete preference for the M/S solution. Interestingly, when the drug was presented unadulterated, C57BL/6J or 10J mice did not show a preference for morphine; only the C57BL/6A mice demonstrated a morphine preference. However, while saccharin-adulterated solutions may be a valid method for the induction of large opiate intake, unless the opposing choice solution is the vehicle used for morphine administration the results do not address the question of opiate-reinforced behavior. In studies of genetic differences in drug-reinforced behavior, the possibility of confounding drug × vehicle × genotype interactions must either be kept to a minimum or explored thoroughly.

Recently, Carney et al. (1991) have demonstrated clear opioid preference differences in C57BL/6J versus DBA/2J mice. Initially, saccharin was added to etonitazene in order to ensure adequate experience with the pharmacologic effects of the drug. When the saccharin concentration was gradually reduced to nil, only the C57BL/6J mice preferred etonitazene over vehicle. This study demonstrates a distinct difference between two inbred strains in their preference for etonitazene following adequate exposure to the pharmacologic effects of the drug and in the absence of confounding drug × vehicle interactions.

In a study by Forgie et al. (1988), the contribution of taste factors involved in morphine and etonitazine preference were investigated. Initial comparisons of morphine or etonitazine in water versus a presumed equally bitter solution of quinine in water demonstrated opiate preference in the C57 mice and not in the DBA mice. Interestingly, in a separate group of DBA and C57 mice, the C57 but not the DBA mice preferred saccharin to a saccharin/quinine solution. When a series of four comparisons were made sequentially, saccharin/morphine and saccharin/ etonitazine to saccharin/quinine and morphine, and etonitazine to quinine, C57 mice preferred only the morphine solutions and not the etonitazine solutions to the respective choice comparisons. DBA mice did not prefer either drug solution to vehicle. C57BL/6J mice spent significantly more time in the etonitazine-paired compartment following a single trial pairing, while DBA/2J mice spent an equivalent amount of time in both the saline and drug paired chambers. Interestingly, unlike the preference studies, conditioned place preference does not indicate a role for aversive stimulus properties in DBA/2J avoidance of opiates since a greater amount of time was not spent in the saline-paired chamber versus the drug-paired chamber.

Place Preference and Intracranial Self-Stimulation

Models of drug taking or *addiction* have been developed that do not involve actual self-administration of the drug under study by the test subject. One of these models, which has gained some popularity among researchers due to the relatively short time required to train animals and obtain data, is called *conditioned place preference*. The conditioned place preference paradigm pairs a specific environment with injections of a drug. Typically, this is done by making one side of the test apparatus dark and the other side light, and often combining this with one side having a smooth floor and the other having a rough floor. Subsequently, the animal is tested to see if it prefers the cocaine-related environment over another neutral environment. Preference for, or avoidance of, the place where the animal received the drug is presumed to be a measure of the reinforcing effects of that drug. Significant genetic differences have been found in conditioned place preference for cocaine between different inbred strains of mice. Studies in this area also indicate that substantial genetic differences can be found in place preference for amphetamine and opioids. Interestingly, the degree of response ranges from almost complete preference for, to strong avoidance of, the drug place (Seale and Carney, 1991). In addition, similar patterns of strain differences across eight inbred mouse genotypes for conditioned place preference associated with amphetamine, the potent dopamine inhibitor GBR 12909, and etonitazene were observed, suggesting that there may some common biochemical influences on the reinforcing effects of these compounds (Seale and Carney, 1991).

Here, however, is an area where the investigator must be aware of the interactions between genes and environments. It is also the case that significant genetic differences exist in the type of place preference environment alone that is preferred by mice of different strains. Thus, one must be careful to ensure that any differences in place preference response to a drug are not due simply to genetic differences in visual or tactile response to a lighter, darker, rougher or smoother testing environment.

Intracranial self-stimulation (ICSS) is another model for studying reinforcement processes. In this model, animals are trained to press a lever in order to transmit a mild electrical current through an electrode implanted in a region of the brain. When the electrode is placed in areas of the brain known to be associated with reinforcement, such as the nucleus accumbens, animals will readily learn the behavioral task required to turn on the current, and will respond at very high rates to obtain this brain stimulation.

While few studies have been conducted exploring the role of genetic factors in ICSS, the available data are interesting and suggest that inheritance plays an important role in determining an individual's reaction to environmental stress and the ability of stress to reduce responses to positive events. For example, responding for electrical stimulation in the nucleus accumbens has been studied in different mouse strains under conditions of imposed environmental stress. While all mice in this particular study learned to press a lever to obtain the stimulation reinforcer, DBA/2J mice showed a marked deterioration of self-stimulation responding under stress, while stress did not affect self-stimulation responding in C57BL/6J mice (Zacharko et al., 1987).

HUMAN STUDIES

Most human genetic studies on substance abuse can be divided into two groups based on methodology: twin studies and adoption studies. The best studies incorporate the use of both methods, using twins separated at an early age, adopted by different families, and, as a result, raised in different environments. There have been a number of studies conducted on genetic factors in alcohol drinking, but very few human genetic studies on opiates or psychostimulants. There are several reasons for the limited information in this area. Not only are twins and adoptees relatively rare, but

these individuals must also have substance abuse disorders. Information on substance use must also be available for both twins and for the adoptive as well as biologic parents.

Twin Studies

Identical, or *monozygotic* (MZ), twins share all of their genes. Thus, if a trait has significant genetic contributions toward its expression, the concordance rate among MZ twins should be high. *Concordance rate* is a measure of the extent to which one member of a twin pair will express a trait, such as alcoholism, if the other member of the twin pair expresses that trait. For example, if a trait is solely genetically determined, then the MZ twin concordance rate would theoretically equal 100%. Fraternal, or *dizygotic* (DZ), twins share, on average, one half of their genes. Thus, concordance rates for DZ twins should theoretically be about one half of the concordance rate for a given trait seen in MZ twins.

Twin studies have shown significant genetic contributions both for average weekly consumption of alcohol and for alcohol abuse. Genetic factors appear to account for some 50% of the variation in drinking among the individuals studied, and MZ twins are more concordant for alcoholism than DZ twins. The results from twin studies have been more robust for males than for females, consistent with a growing body of data suggesting that alcohol drinking disorders in males are under greater genetic control than in females.

The only other drug for which there exists a body of twin data is nicotine. Most of these studies have reported significant genetic contributions to smoking behavior among twins. If one member of a twin pair is a tobacco smoker, the probability that the co-twin will also be a smoker is significantly greater than what would be expected based on average population rates of smoking (Pickens and Svikis, 1991).

What little information exists on genetic predisposition to opiate or cocaine dependence in humans has been obtained as part of genetic studies on alcoholism where researchers also obtained data on the use of other drugs. These results suggest that alcohol problems appear to be associated with the abuse of a number of other drugs (Pickens and Svikis, 1991).

Adoption Studies

Adoption studies have the capability of providing the strongest evidence for genetic influences on complex human behaviors such as drug abuse. However, these studies can be difficult to conduct since they require (1) identification of adoptees with alcohol or drug problems who are willing to participate in a research study, (2) the consent and participation of the adoptive parents, and (3) the identification and participation of at least one and ideally both biologic parents.

Adoption studies can separate genetic and environmental influences by examining the distribution of traits among adopted individuals, their unrelated adoptive parents, and their related biologic parents. For example, if the adoptive parents have a history of alcohol abuse or alcoholism but the biologic parents do not, this would be consistent with environmental mediation of this disorder if the adopted individuals show the alcoholism trait. Conversely, if one or both biologic parents have a history of alcohol drinking disorders but the adoptive parents do not, alcoholism in the adopted away offspring would be consistent with genetic mediation of this disorder.

Several adoption studies have shown that adopted-away biologic sons of alcoholics have higher rates of alcoholism than do adopted-away biologic sons of nonalcoholics (Cadoret et al., 1994; Dinwiddie and Reich, 1993; Sigvardsson et al., 1985). Consistent with the data from twin studies, findings from studies with adopted females have been less robust, again suggesting that male alcoholism has a more robust genetic component than does alcoholism in females.

For example, in one study, 22% of adopted-away sons of alcoholic biologic fathers were themselves alcoholic. Since this rate of alcoholism is much higher than that seen in the population overall, this suggests a significant genetic contribution. Several other adoption studies are also consistent with genetic influences on alcoholism in males. However, it is important to note here that while 22% of these persons did develop alcoholism, 78% did not, even though they came from high-risk biologic families. Again, this illustrates the important interplay between genes and environments. Differences in the inheritance of specific biologic risk factors, as well as variations in environmental stressors or cultural values, could all be important in altering an individual's overall risk. For example, the genetic influence becomes stronger when the adopted-away sons are raised in lower-class adoptive families (Sigvardsson et al., 1985).

Genetic studies have led to the conclusion that at least two distinct subtypes of alcoholism exist. These subtypes can be distinguished in terms of personality traits, ages of onset, and the actual patterns of inheritance. *Type 1 alcoholism* is characterized by binge drinking primarily for sedative or antianxiety effects and rapid development of tolerance and dependence on the antianxiety effects of alcohol. This leads to loss of control and difficulty terminating drinking binges. *Type 2 alcoholism* is characterized by antisocial personality and persistent seeking of alcohol for its pleasurable effects. This leads to early onset of inability to abstain, a more continuous pattern of drinking, as well as fighting and arrests when drinking (Cloninger et al., 1988).

Results from other genetic studies suggest that the risk for substance abuse is associated with the risk for affective illnesses, such as depression. Both affective illness and substance abuse are more common in the biologic relatives of affectively ill adoptees than in relatives of healthy adoptees (Ingraham and Wender, 1992).

Thus, results from a number of twin and adoption studies strongly suggest that alcoholism has a substantial genetic component. Genetic contributions to abuse of other drugs are also evident, but more research is necessary to define accurately the extent and nature of these influences.

Allelic Polymorphisms in Humans

Following recent advances in molecular biology, a number of studies have been conducted in an attempt to define specific versions, or alleles, of genes that result in increased probabilities for the development of alcoholism or drug abuse disorders. To date, virtually all of the studies have involved alcohol. These studies, which are attempting to define allelic polymorphisms in human genes, have focused on the liver and the brain, two organs highly impacted by alcohol.

In the liver, the enzymes alcohol dehydrogenase (ADH) and aldehyde dehydrogenase (ALDH) are principally responsible for metabolizing ethanol. It has been shown that there are *polymorphisms*, or different versions of the alleles that make up the genes responsible for synthesizing these enzymes. Genetic variation in both ADH and ALDH may influence drinking behavior and the risk of alcoholism.

Some individuals exhibit a strong flushing response in the face following ingestion of ethanol. Ethanol and acetaldehyde are both vasodilators, and dilation of facial vasculature increases blood flow to this area and results in a reddening, or flushing, of the tissue. Alcohol-flush reactions occur commonly in Asians who inherit an ALDH gene that produces an inactive ALDH enzyme. Ethanol is converted to acetaldehyde by the ADH enzyme, and acetaldehyde is then broken down by ALDH. Without an appropriately active ALDH enzyme, high blood acetaldehyde levels build up, causing the unpleasant symptoms that follow drinking. Asians who have this particular ALDH gene, which results in an inactive form of ALDH, are more sensitive to ethanol, tend to be discouraged from drinking, and as a result typically show lower risk for alcohol-related disorders (Agarwal and Goedde, 1992).

Biologic factors related to brain function that mediate our bodies' responses to drugs form the other area of focus of human genetic

polymorphism studies. Recent findings suggest that alcoholics and nonalcoholics may differ in the allele they carry for the dopamine type 2, or D_2 receptor (Blum et al., 1990). This difference may make certain persons more responsive to the effects that certain drugs, such as ethanol, have on dopamine neurotransmitter systems. Since dopamine is believed to be critical in brain function related to reward and positive reinforcement, differences in the genetic regulation of this receptor could contribute to differences in propensity to find ethanol rewarding.

While this hypothesis is attractive, several other studies have failed to confirm this finding (Gelernter et al., 1991), so claims that the D_2 receptor gene plays a role in determining susceptibility toward alcoholism remain speculative and controversial.

COMMONALITIES AMONG DRUGS OF ABUSE

Another important question in substance abuse that can be effectively addressed using genetic methods is whether propensity to self-administer one drug, for example ethanol, shares common genetic control with the propensity to self-administer other drugs, such as cocaine or opiates. This *commonality* question can be addressed by measuring the extent to which animals from various inbred strains self-administer a variety of drugs.

There is growing evidence that drugs from several pharmacological classes will come to serve as reinforcers for animals of some genotypes, while these compounds are not reinforcers for other genotypically distinct animals. For example, C57BL/6J mice have shown consistently high preference and responding maintained by ethanol, opiates, and most recently cocaine (Broadhurst, 1979; Elmer et al., 1987; George, 1987; George and Goldberg, 1989; George et al., 1991a; Horowitz et al., 1977; McClearn and Rodgers, 1959). Results from these studies of drug self-administration across different drugs and strains suggest that genetic patterns of reinforcement from ethanol may correlate highly with patterns of reinforcement from cocaine and opiates, as summarized in Table 1 (George, 1991a).

In addition, similar patterns of conditioned place preference associated with cocaine, amphetamine, and opioids have been observed across several mouse inbred strains, suggesting that strains that show conditioned place preference for one of these drugs will tend to show the same place preference behavior for another drug (Seale and Carney, 1991). Thus, drug-seeking behaviors maintained by ethanol, cocaine, amphetamine, and opioids may have at least some common biologic determinants.

While propensity to take one drug, such as ethanol, may help to predict the likelihood of taking additional drugs, there are many other factors not related to drug responsivity per se that may also play important roles in determining risk for addiction. Factors such as personality traits and other mental disturbances, such as depression, also appear to be important indicators of risk for alcohol and drug abuse.

These comparisons can be used to determine the degree of common genetic control among these factors as well as to establish the extent to which one factor, such as neurosensitivity, covaries with another factor, such as self-administration. These and other issues, such as commonality of self-administration behavior across drugs, can be effectively addressed by using genetically defined animals within self-administration paradigms.

Table 1. *Commonality across drugs and genotypes for drug-reinforced behavior*

Genotype	Alcohol	Opiates	Cocaine
Rats			
LEW	+++	+++	++
F344	+−	−−−	−
Mice			
C57BL/6J	+++	+++	+++
DBA/2J	−−−	−−−	NA

Plus symbols indicate relative degree of positive reinforcement. Negative symbols indicate relative degree of nonreinforcement or avoidance. Three symbols is maximum response relative to all genotypes tested. NA = Data not available.
From George, 1991a.

FUTURE DIRECTIONS

Realizing that individuals may differ in addiction risk, as well as understanding the biologic factors related to vulnerability, can aid in the prevention and treatment of drug abuse. Resources for addiction intervention can be scarce. Thus, effective targeting of high-risk persons for the most intensive education and counseling programs is economically important. Early intervention in terms of education and counseling of high-risk groups has proven effective in other areas of medicine such as heart disease.

Genetic methods have great potential for increasing our understanding of addictions. Issues such as the biochemical sites of drug reinforcement, the relationship between drug preference and drug reinforcement, and the commonality of self-administration behavior across drugs can be effectively addressed using the behavior genetic approaches discussed in this chapter. The ability to define markers of substance abuse risk will greatly aid treatment and prevention efforts.

Although individual differences in human responses to particular alcoholism and drug abuse treatment regimens have been reported, these differences have not been studied systematically. In addition, since the problem of cocaine addiction has only recently increased to epidemic proportions, studies of genetic and environmental contributing factors in human cocaine abuse, and thus, effective treatment strategies, are still in their initial stages and require much further study.

It is unlikely that specific addiction genes exist. Rather, it seems more probable that biologic contributions to drug addiction result from interactions among several genes, each of which regulates a common and necessary biologic system. For example, since several neuronal pathways have been implicated in mediating the reinforcing effects of drugs, this immediately implicates the involvement of several distinct genetic mechanisms. However, in the case of persons who would be at high risk for drug abuse, the specific versions of these genes are present in a combination that is most conducive to making a drug an effective reinforcer. One important area of the brain in which several genes could act in concert to produce an organism highly responsive to drugs is the nucleus accumbens. Dopaminergic and other pathways interact here in ways important to the reinforcing effects of drugs. Indeed, it now appears that this brain region may represents a nexus where the determination of reinforcement is processed. Normal variations in receptors, metabolic enzymes, and other cellular components could, in high-risk individuals, be combined in a manner that maximizes drug effects related to reinforcement and euphoria.

Based on this information, treatment strategies for alcoholism and substance abuse disorders should therefore include a consideration of both positive and negative impacts on both the direct reinforcing effects of drugs, as well as motivational factors that can lead to sustained use and relapse. For example, if a treatment strategy is to remove access to a drug that is positively reinforcing, it would be prudent to provide an alternative positive reinforcer to take the place of the drug. This approach is found in community programs where alternative positive activities are provided, such as sports programs for adolescents. Hopefully, through an integrated approach to treatment combining pharmacotherapies, based on an understanding of the biologic and genetic contributors to substance abuse disorders, with psychosocial interventions, based on an understanding of both sociocultural and biologic risk factors, we may better treat the difficult biologic, behavioral, and social problems associated with alcoholism and substance abuse disorders.

SUMMARY

- The demonstration of genetic differences in response to abused drugs illustrates the importance of genetic control in experimental research.
- Behavioral genetic studies show that addiction is a complex process mediated by genetic and environmental factors, as well as critical interactions between the two.

- Drug-seeking behaviors maintained by ethanol, cocaine, and opiates may have at least some common biologic determinants.
- For alcoholism the evidence is strong that for certain persons addiction can develop early with minimal environmental contribution.
- Genetic differences among individuals in their ability to metabolize alcohol appear to contribute to the large individual and ethnic variations observed in alcohol drinking.
- Genetic approaches will ultimately aid in our overall understanding of the serious problems of alcohol and drug addiction.
- Findings from this area will likely provide useful information for developing effective drug abuse prevention and treatment programs.

REFERENCES

Agarwal, D.P. and Goedde, H.W. (1992) Pharmacogenetics of alcohol metabolism and alcoholism. *Pharmacogenetics* 2: 48–62.

Belknap, J.K., Haltli, N., Goebel, D. and Lame, M. (1982) Intercorrelations between levorphanol-induced antinociception, hypothermia, activity and constipation in a genetically heterogeneous mouse population, and the results of selective breeding for antinociception. *Proc. West. Pharmacol. Soc.* 25: 299–302.

Belknap, J.K., Noordewier, B. and Lame, M. (1989) Genetic dissociation of multiple morphine effects among C57BL/6J, DBA/2J and C3H/HeJ inbred mouse strain. *Physiol. Behav.* 46: 69–74.

Blum, K., Nobel, E.P., Sheridan, P.J., Montgomery, A., Richie, T., Jagadeeswaran, P., Nogami, H., Briggs, A.H. and Cohn, J.B. (1990) Allelic association of human dopamine D2 receptor gene in alcoholism. *JAMA* 263: 2055–2060.

Broadhurst, P. (1979) Drugs and the inheritance of behavior. New York: Plenum Press. pp. 20-6.

Cadoret, R., Troughton, E. and Woodworth G. (1994) Evidence of heterogeneity of genetic effect in Iowa adoption studies. *Ann. N. Y. Acad. Sci.* 708: 59–71.

Carney, J.M., Cheng, M.-S., Wu, C., and Seale, T.W. (1991) Issues surrounding the assessment of the genetic determinants of drugs as reinforcing stimuli. *Adv. Alcohol Subst. Abuse* 10: 163-178.

Cazala, P., Darracq, C. and Saint-Marc, M. (1987) Self-administration of morphine into the lateral hypothalamus in the mouse. *Brain Res.* 416: 283–288.

Cloninger, C.R., Sigvardsson, S., Gilligan, S.B., von Knorring, A.L., Reich, T. and Bohman, M. (1988) Genetic heterogeneity and the classification of alcoholism. *Adv. Alcohol Subst. Abuse* 7: 3–16.

Crabbe, J.C. and Belknap, J.K. (1980) Pharmocogenetic tools in the study of drug tolerance and dependence. Substance and Alcohol Actions/Misuse. 1: 305-413.

de Fiebre, C.M., Ruth, J.R. and Collins, A.C. (1989) Differential sensitivity to high doses of cocaine in long-sleep and short-sleep mice. *Pharmacol. Biochem. Behav.* 34: 887–893.

De Waele, J.P,. Papachristou, D.N. and Gianoulakis, C. (1992) The alcohol-preferring C57BL/6 mice present an enhanced sensitivity of the hypothalamic beta-endorphin system to ethanol than the alcohol-avoiding DBA/2 mice. *J. Pharmacol. Exp. Ther.* 261: 788–794.

Dinwiddie, S.H. and Reich, T. (1993) Genetic and family studies in psychiatric illness and alcohol and drug dependence. *J. Addict. Dis.* 12:17–27.

Dymshitz, J. and Lieblich, I. (1987) Opiate reinforcement and naloxone aversion, as revealed by place preference paradigm, in two strains of rats. *Psychopharmacology* 92: 473–477.

Eidelberg, E., Erspamer, R. Kreinick, C.J. and Harris J. (1975) Genetically determined differences in the effects of morphine on mice. *Eur. J. Pharmacol.* 32: 329–336.

Elmer, G.I., Meisch, R.A. and George, F.R. (1986) Oral ethanol reinforced behavior in inbred mice. *Pharmacol. Biochem. Behav.* 24: 1417–1421.

Elmer, G.I., Meisch, R.A. and George, F.R. (1987) Differential concentration-response curves for oral ethanol self-administration in C57BL/6J and BALB/cJ Mice. *Alcohol* 4: 63–68.

Elmer, G.I., Meisch, R.A., Goldberg, S.R. and George, F.R. (1988) A fixed ratio analysis of oral ethanol reinforced behavior in inbred mouse strains. *Psychopharmacology* 96: 431–436.

Elmer, G.I., Meisch, R.A., Goldberg, S.R. and George, F.R. (1990) Ethanol self-administration in long sleep and short sleep mice: evidence for genetic independence of neurosensitivity and reinforcement. *J. Pharmacol. Exp. Ther.* 254: 1054–1062.

Eriksson, K. (1968) Genetic selection for voluntary alcohol consumption in the albino rat. *Science* 159: 739–741.

Eriksson, K. and Kiianmaa, K. (1971) Genetic analysis of susceptibility to morphine addiction in inbred mice. *Ann. Med. Exp. Fenn.* 49: 73–78.

Eriksson, K. and Rusi, M. (1981) Finnish selection studies on alcohol-related behaviors: general outline. In: McClearn, G.E., Deitrich, R.A. and Erwin, V.G. (eds.) *Development of animal models as pharmacogenetic tools.* National Institute on Alcohol Abuse and Alcoholism, Research Monograph No. 6. Rockville, MD: DHHS, publication No. (ADM) 81-1133, pp. 87–117.

Forgie, M.L., Beyerstein, B.L. and Alexander, B.K. (1988) Contributions of taste factors and gender to opioid preference in C57BL and DBA mice. *Psychopharmacology* 95: 237–244.

Froelich, J.C., Harts, J., Lumeng, L. and Li, T.-K. (1987) Naloxone attenuation of voluntary alcohol consumption. *Alcohol Alcohol.* 1: 333–337.

Gelernter, J., O'Malley, S., Risch, N., Kranzler, H.R., Krystal, J., Merikangas, K., Kennedy, J.L. and Kidd, K.K. (1991) No association between an allele at the D2 dopamine receptor gene (DRD2) and alcoholism. *JAMA* 266: 1801–1807.

George, F.R. (1987) Genetic and environmental factors in ethanol self-administration. *Pharmacol. Biochem. Behav.* 27: 379–384.

George, F.R. (1988) The use of genetic tools in the study of substance abuse. *Alcoholism Clin. Exp. Res.* 12: 86–90.

George, F.R. (1989) Cocaine produces low dose locomotor depressant effects in mice. *Psychopharmacology* 99: 147–150.

George, F.R. (1991a) Is there a common genetic basis for reinforcement from alcohol and other drugs? *J. Addict. Dis.* 10: 127–139.

George, F.R. (1991b) Cocaine toxicity: genetic differences in cocaine-induced lethality in rats. *Pharmacol. Biochem. Behav.* 38: 893–895.

George, F.R. (1991c) Cocaine toxicity: Genetic evidence suggests different mechanisms for cocaine-induced seizures and lethality. *Psychopharmacology* 104: 307–311.

George, F.R. and Goldberg, S.R. (1988) Genetic factors in response to cocaine. In: Clouet, D., Asghar, K. and Brown, R. (eds.) *Mechanisms of cocaine abuse and toxicity.* Washington, DC: National Institute on Drug Abuse Monograph, 88: 239–249.

George, F.R. and Goldberg, S.R. (1989) Genetic approaches to the analysis of addiction processes. *Trends Pharmacol. Sci.* 10: 78–83.

George, F.R., Elmer, G.I., Meisch, R.A. and Goldberg, S.R. (1991a) Orally delivered cocaine functions as a positive reinforcer in C57BL/6J mice. *Pharmacol. Biochem. Behav.* 38: 897–903.

George, F.R., Porrino, L.J., Ritz, M.C. and Goldberg, S.R. (1991b) Inbred rat strain comparisons indicate different sites of action for cocaine and amphetamine locomotor stimulant effects. *Psychopharmacology* 104: 457–462.

George, F.R. and Ritz, M.C. (1990) Cocaine produces locomotor stimulation in SS but not LS mice: Relationship to dopaminergic function. *Psychopharmacology* 101: 18–24.

Gianoulakis, C., de Waele, J.P. and Kiianmaa, K. (1992) Differences in the brain and pituitary beta-endorphin system between the alcohol-preferring AA and alcohol-avoiding ANA rats. *Alcohol Clin. Exp. Res.* 16: 453–459.

Gora-Maslak, G., McClearn, G.E., Crabbe, J.C., Phillips, T.J., Belknap, J.K. and Plomin, R. (1991) Use of recombinant inbred strains to identify quantitative trait loci in psychopharmacology. *Psychopharmacology* 104: 413–424.

Goudie, A.J., Leathley, M., McNally, J. and West, C.R. (1989) Individual differences in cocaine discrimination. *Drug Devel. Res.* 16: 123–131.

Griffiths, R.R., Brady, J.V. and Bradford, L.D. (1979) Predicting the abuse liability of drugs with animal drug self-administration procedures: psychomotor stimulants and hallucinogens. In: Thompson, T. and Dews, P.B. (eds.) *Advances in behavioral pharmacology,* vol. 2. New York: Academic Press, pp. 163–208.

Hadaway, P.F., Alexander, B.K., Coambs, R.B. and Beyerstein, B. (1979) The effect of housing and gender on preference for morphine-sucrose solutions in rats. *Psychopharmacology* 66: 87–91.

Horowitz, G.P. (1976) Morphine self-administration by inbred mice: a preliminary report. *Behav. Gen.* 6: 109–110.

Horowitz, G.P. (1981) Pharmacogenetic models and behavioral responses to opiates. In: McClearn, G.E., Dietrich, R.A., Erwin, V.G. (eds.) *Development of animal models as pharmacogenetic tools,* NIAAA Res Monograph 6. Rockville, MD: U.S. Department of Health and Human Services, pp. 209–231.

Horowitz, G.P., Whitney, G., Smith, J.C. and Stephan, F.K. (1977) Morphine ingestion: genetic control in mice. *Psychopharmacology* 52: 119–122.

Ingraham, L.J. and Wender, P.H. (1992) Risk for affective disorder and alcohol and other drug abuse in the relatives of affectively ill adoptees. *J. Affect. Disord.* 26: 45–51.

Judson, B.A. and Goldstein, A. (1978) Genetic control of opiate-induced locomotor activity in mice. *J. Pharmacol. Exp. Ther.* 206: 56–60.

Li, T.-K., Lumeng, L., McBride, W.J. and Waller, M.B. (1979) Progress toward a voluntary oral consumption model of alcoholism. *Drug Alcohol Depend.* 4: 45–60.

Li, T.-K., Lumeng, L., McBride, W.J. and Waller, M.B. (1981) Indiana selection studies on alcohol-related behaviors. In: *Development of animal models as pharmacogenetic tools,* NIAAA Monograph 6. McClearn, G.E., Dietrich, R.A. and Erwin, V.G. (eds.) Rockville, MD: U.S. Department of Health and Human Services, pp. 171–191

Logan, L., Seale, T.W. and Carney, J.M. (1986) Inherent differences in sensitivity to methylxanthines among inbred mice. *Pharmacol. Biochem. Behav.* 24: 1281–1286.

McBride, W.J., Murphy, J.M., Lumeng, L. and T.-K. Li (1990) Serotonin, dopamine and GABA involvement in alcohol drinking of selectively bred rats. *Alcohol* 7: 199–205.

McClearn, G.E. and Rodgers, D.A. (1959) Differences in alcohol preference among inbred strains of mice. *Q. J. Stud. Alc.* 20: 691–695.

McClearn, G.E. and Rodgers, D.A. (1961) Genetic factors in alcohol preference of laboratory mice. *J. Comp. Physiol. Psych.* 54: 116–119.

Meade, R., Amit, Z., Pachter, W. and Corcoran, M.E. (1973) Differences in oral intake of morphine by two strains of rats. *Res. Commun. Chem. Pathol. Pharmacol.* 6: 1105–1108.

Meisch, R.A. (1984) Alcohol self-administration by experimental animals. In: Smart, R.G., Cappell, H.D., Glaser, F.B., Israel, Y., Kalant, H., Popham, R.E., Schmidt, W. and Sellers, E.M. (eds.) *Research advances in alcohol and drug problems,* vol. 8. New York: Plenum Press, pp. 23–45.

Murphy, J.M., McBride, W.J., Lumeng, L. and Li., T.-K. (1987) Contents of monoamines in forebrain regions of alcohol-preferring (P) and -non-preferring (NP) lines of rats. *Pharmacol. Biochem. Behav.* 26: 389–392.

Myers, R.D. and Veale, W.L. (1968) Alcohol preference in the rat: reduction following depletion of brain serotonin. *Science* 160: 1469–1471.

Neiderhiser, J.M., Plomin, R. and McClearn, G.E. (1992) The use of CXB recombinant inbred mice to detect quantitative trait loci in behavior. *Physiol. Behav.* 52: 429–439.

Nichols, J.R. and Hsiao, S. (1967) Addiction liability of albino rats: breeding for quantitative differences in morphine drinking. *Science* 157: 561–563.

Oliverio, A. and Castellano, C. (1974) Genotype-dependent sensitivity and tolerance to morphine and heroin: dissociation between opiate-induced running and analgesia in the mouse. *Psychopharmacology* 39: 13–22.

Oliverio, A., Castellano, C. and Eleftheriou, B.E. (1975) Morphine sensitivity and tolerance: A genetic investigation in the mouse. *Psychopharmacology* 42: 219–224.

Phillips, T.J., Feller, D.J. and Crabbe, J.C. (1989) Selected mouse lines, alcohol and behavior. *Experientia* 45: 805–827.

Pickens, R.W. and Svikis, D.S. (1991) Genetic influences in human substance abuse. *J. Addict. Dis.* 10: 205–214.

Plomin, R. DeFries, J.C. and McClearn, G.E. (1990) *Behavioral genetics: a primer,* 2nd ed. New York: W.H. Freeman.

Ritz, M.C., Garcia, J., Protz, D. and George, F.R. (1994) Operant ethanol-reinforced behavior in P, NP, HAD and LAD rats bred for high or low ethanol preference. Alcoholism: Clinical and Experimental Research. 18: 1406-1415.

Ritz, M.C., George, F.R. and Collins, A.C. (1981) Indomethacin antagonizes ethanol-induced but not pento-

barbital-induced behavioral activation. *Subst. Alc. Actions/Misuse* 2: 289–299.

Ritz, M.C., George, F.R., deFiebre, C. and Meisch, R.A. (1986) Genetic differences in the establishment of ethanol as a reinforcer. *Pharmacol. Biochem. Behav.* 24: 1089–1094.

Rodgers, D.A. and McClearn, G.E. (1962) Mouse strain differences in preference for various concentrations of alcohol. *Q. J. Stud. Alc.* 23: 26–33.

Ruth, J.A., Ullman, E.A. and Collins, A.C. (1988) An analysis of cocaine effects on locomotor activities and heart rate in four inbred strains. *Pharmacol. Biochem. Behav.* 29: 157–162.

Satinder, K.P. (1977) Oral intake of morphine in selectively bred rats. *Pharmacol. Biochem. Behav.* 7: 43–49.

Schuster, C.R. and T. Thompson (1969) Self-administration of and behavioral dependence on drugs. *Annu. Rev. Pharmacol.* 9: 483–502.

Schuster, L., Webster, G.W., Yu, G., and Eleftheriou, B.E. (1975) A genetic analysis of the response to morphine in mice: Analgesia and running. *Psychopharmacologia* 42: 249-254.

Schuster, L., Yu, G. and Bates, A. (1977) Sensitization to cocaine stimulation in mice. *Psychopharmacology* 52: 185–190.

Seale, T.W. and Carney, J.M. (1991) Genetic determinants of susceptibility to the rewarding and other behavioral actions of cocaine. *J. Addict. Dis.* 10: 141–162.

Sigvardsson,S., Cloninger, C.R. and Bohman, M. (1985) Prevention and treatment of alcohol abuse: uses and limitations of the high risk paradigm. *Soc. Biol.* 32: 185–194.

Sinclair, J.D. (1974) Rats learning to work for alcohol. *Nature* 249: 590–592.

Sinclair, J.D. and Kiianmaa, K. (1989) The AA and ANA rat lines, selected for differences in voluntary alcohol consumption. *Experienta* 45: 798–805.

Suzuki, T., George, F.R. and Meisch, R.A. (1988) Differential establishment and maintenance of oral ethanol reinforced behavior in Lewis and Fischer 344 inbred rat strains. *J. Pharmacol. Exp. Ther.* 245: 164–170.

Suzuki, T., George, F.R. and Meisch, R.A. (1992) Etonitazene delivered orally serves as a reinforcer for Lewis but not Fischer 344 rats. *Pharmacol. Biochem. Behav.* 42: 579–586.

Suzuki, T., Koike, Y., Yanaura, S., George, F.R. and Meisch, R.A. (1987) Genetic differences in the development of physical dependence on pentobarbital in four inbred strains of rats. *Jpn. J. Pharmacol.* 45: 479–486.

Ternes, J.W., Ehrman, R. and O'Brien, C. (1983) Cynomolgus monkeys do not develop tolerance to opioids. *Behav. Neurosci.* 97: 327–330.

Weeks, J.R. (1962) Experimental morphine addiction: method for automatic intravenous injections in unrestrained rats. *Science* 138: 143–144.

Whitney, G. and Horowitz, G.P. (1978) Morphine preference of alcohol-avoiding and alcohol-preferring C57BL mice. *Behav. Gen.* 8: 182–189.

Whitney, G., Horowitz, G.P. and Collins, R.L. (1977) Relationship between morphine self-administration and the effect of morphine across strains of mice. *Behav. Gen.* 7: 92–98.

Zacharko, R.M., Lalonde, G,T., Kasian, M. and Anisman, H. (1987) Strain-specific effects of inescapable shock on intracranial self-stimulation from the nucleus accumbens. *Brain Res.* 426: 164–168.

Drug Addiction and its Treatment: Nexus of Neuroscience and Behavior, edited by Bankole A. Johnson and John D. Roache. Lippincott–Raven Publishers, Philadelphia, © 1997.

9

Search for Biological Markers

Martin A. Javors, *John T. Pichot, †Thomas S. King, and ‡Raymond F. Anton

*Departments of Psychiatry and Pharmacology, The University of Texas Health Science Center,
San Antonio, Texas 78284; *Addiction Psychiatry Residency Program,
University of Texas Health Science Center; Substance Abuse Treatment Unit,
Audie Murphy Veteran's Administration Hospital, San Antonio, Texas 78284;
†Departments of Cellular and Structural Biology and Obstetrics and Gynecology,
University of Texas Health Science Center, San Antonio, Texas 78284;
‡Department of Psychiatry, and Behavioral Sciences,Medical University of South Carolina,
171 Ashley Avenue, Charleston, South Carolina 29425*

This chapter reviews biologic tests of substance abuse and addiction. The chapter is divided into two sections: the first is a discussion of tests for the detection of genetic susceptibility to the risk of developing a drug addiction (trait markers), and the second is a discussion of tests to measure the consumption or use of drugs of abuse (state markers). The bulk of the research in these areas has been devoted to the study of alcohol abuse and alcoholism, perhaps because these problems have been more persistent and have affected a much broader segment of our population. As a result, this chapter focuses on state and trait markers for alcoholism. Nevertheless, we intend to address the similarities between drugs of abuse for which information is available by communicating the state-of-the-art methods and conclusions coming from this line of research.

TERMINOLOGY

To compare the usefulness of tests for consumption or addiction, most investigators have determined the clinical sensitivity and specificity of the test. Clinical sensitivity is defined as the percentage of diseased persons with a positive test. Clinical specificity is de-fined as the percentage of nondiseased persons with a negative test. High values for sensitivity and specificity indicate an accurate and useful test. While the determination of sensitivity and specificity is useful for the evaluation of biologic tests, false-positive and false-negative results present some problems. A false-positive test is defined as a positive test in a person without the disease or condition. A false-negative test is defined as a negative test in a person with the disease or condition. False positives will usually be discovered with further testing, but false-negative tests may go undiscovered and produce greater problems subsequently. Diagnostic sensitivity and specificity are important determinants to establish the validity and utility of laboratory tests (Watson et al., 1986).

The values for positive and negative predictive value are often determined when evaluating biologic tests. Positive predictive value is defined as the percentage of true positive tests among true *and* false-positive tests. Negative predictive value is defined as the percentage of true negative tests among true *and* false-negative tests. Positive and negative predicative values are generally determined in a pure population of subjects, i.e., all of the subjects are known to have a given disease or condition. Use of these calculated values is somewhat limited when applied to clinical populations in which the prevalence of the condition may vary, e.g., clinical populations in an alcohol treatment clinic versus a family practice setting. Anton and colleagues have recently reviewed this topic (Allen et al., 1992). Nonetheless, these determinations provide further estimates of the validity of a biologic test.

These terms will be used frequently during this chapter in reporting the evaluations in the literature about the usefulness of these tests.

TESTS FOR GENETIC SUSCEPTIBILITY TO ADDICTION (TRAIT MARKERS)

Biologic markers of genetic susceptibility to addiction are generally conceptualized as inherited physical markers that are correlated with inherited alterations of the genetic code. Expression of the information contained in this altered genetic code changes physiologic functioning in a specific way. In combination with environmental factors, this significantly increases the statistical risk that the individual will manifest addictive behavior. This trait-marker–addiction paradigm is the basic concept driving the current research for biologic markers. The ultimate goal is to find markers that can be used in combination with clinical interventions to identify and prevent the onset, or reduce the severity, of addictive behavior.

It is essential to understand the distinction between trait and state markers. Accordingly, a biologic marker of a trait for addiction should be expressed in the individual in a detectable fashion prior to exposure, during active addiction, and during sustained full remissions. On the other hand, biologic markers of the state of active addictive behavior will be detected only with expression of the addicted state and will not be detectable either prior to expression of the addictive behavior or during full sustained remissions.

Reich's (1988) brief, but profound, editorial noted the importance of clearly demonstrating that enzyme abnormalities must meet three specific criteria to support the idea of genetic susceptibility to alcoholism. His criteria can be expanded to the broader scope of all proposed markers in stating that support for the trait-marker–addiction paradigm can be established only if (1) the biologic marker itself is proven to be highly heritable; (2) the biologic marker is present in as yet unaffected offspring of affecteds; and (3) there is an excess of affected individuals among relatives who also carry the biologic marker.

Most research in this area has focused on the addictive use of alcohol but increasingly other addictive behaviors are being studied. In actuality, there may be significant applicability of the biologic markers reviewed here to familial patterns of addiction to drugs and for addictive behaviors other than alcoholism, but this has yet to be demonstrated. Several factors have advanced biologic marker research in alcoholism ahead of marker research with other addictive drugs. These factors are summarized in Table 1.

Some progress has been made subtyping alcohol dependence. This subtyping has supported the study of biologic markers and is essential to the continued search for reliable markers. However, despite this apparent progress, Anthenelli et al. (1994) make a convincing argument that further refinement of our current categorizations of addictive behavior will be necessary to produce an accu-

TABLE 1. *Reasons marker research for drugs is less advanced than for alcohol*

Higher prevalence of alcohol use than use of any other single drug

Increased parallel use of multiple drug classes by individuals abusing drugs

Increased parallel use of multiple drug classes between current family members of individuals abusing drugs

Increased serial change over time in class of drug used by individuals abusing drugs

Increased serial change over time in class of drug used in families between generations

Increased complexity of defining distinct subgroups of drug users

Lack of a consistent data base that supports a genetically based inheritance pattern in nonalcohol drug abuse

rate understanding of the genetic contributions. Specifically, Anthenelli et al. reported that alcohol dependence and antisocial behavior may be separate behavior patterns that could be independently inherited. If this is accurate, then much of the past research with biologic markers utilizing the type I and type II subtyping concepts defined below may need to be replicated with study populations that separate out antisocial and addictive behaviors. Type I and II as initially reported by Cloninger et al. (1981, 1987) and summarized by Anthenelli et al. (1994) are outlined in Tables 2 and 3.

A different classification scheme that focuses on subtyping as either *primary alcoholism without antisocial personality disorder* or *primary antisocial personality disorder with secondary alcoholism*, is advocated by the research group lead by Schuckit in San Diego and is reviewed in Anthenelli et al. (1994). Primary antisocial personality disorder with secondary alcoholism is proposed as representative of the Type II subgroup and brings into question whether research that has been attributed to genetic traits for type II alcoholism may in fact be markers correlated with antisocial personality disorder. These subtypes are summarized in Table 4.

Starting in the early 1980s, Schuckit began to study children of alcoholics who were identified as family history positive (FHP). The subjects of the study cohort are continuing in follow-up with a nearly 100% follow-up rate for the last decade (Giller and Hall, 1983; Schuckit, 1980, 1981; Schuckit et al., 1988). Schuckit stated that the goal of this research effort was to compare the traits in the children of alcoholics (i.e., FHP subjects)

TABLE 3. *Type II alcoholism*

Occurs in male children with alcoholic biologic fathers; also known as male-limited

Environmental influence has little effect on the course of illness

Onset of alcoholism and antisocial behavior during adolescence or as young adults

Associated with significant criminal activity

and subjects with no family history of alcoholism (FHN). This research would take advantage of the threefold or higher increased risk of developing alcoholism in the sons of alcohol-dependent fathers. The research included the use of an alcohol challenge paradigm (ACP) that evaluated responses (both biologic and cognitive) after consumption of standardized doses of ethanol in groups of FHP and FHN subjects. The ACP has been described in detail (Giller and Hall, 1983; Schuckit, 1980, 1981). Schuckit notes that the results of his longitudinal follow-up studies must be interpreted in light of the composition of the study group, which consists of male, Caucasian, and non-Jewish subjects drawn from a group of functional blue-collar and white-collar individuals. To exclude the effects of fetal alcohol syndrome, attempts were made to exclude the sons of alcoholic mothers. Furthermore, subjects were excluded from the study if their fathers had a history of an additional psychiatric illness with onset before the onset of alcoholism. This exclusion criteria kept individuals with fathers with a history of antisocial personality disorder out of the study.

POTENTIAL CANDIDATES FOR BIOLOGIC MARKERS OF ADDICTION

Presently there are no definite markers yet identified for the trait-marker–addiction paradigm, although some proposed candidates look promising. There are a large number of proposed markers; protein alterations, electrophysiologic differences, and altered responses to alcohol are all examples of categories of proposed markers. This review

TABLE 2. *Type I alcoholism*

Occurs in both female and male offspring of alcoholic biologic mothers and fathers

Also known as milieu-limited because it is influenced by postnatal environment effects in the adoptive family

Onset of alcoholism during adulthood (usually ≥25 years of age)

Associated with minimal criminality

TABLE 4. *Classification of primary alcoholism and antisocial personality disorder*

Primary alcoholism without antisocial personality disorder	Alcohol dependence develops before onset of any other major psychiatric illness
Primary antisocial personality disorder with secondary alcoholism	Antisocial personality disorder, including conduct disorder criteria, displayed before onset of alcohol dependence

provides a list and a brief discussion of most of the currently proposed markers. A detailed discussion of each of the proposed markers is not possible in this chapter given space limitations; however, references for a more detailed review are provided. A summary list of proposed markers is provided in Table 5.

Adenosine

Adenosine is a purine neurotransmitter that serves primarily as a neuromodulator and appears to mediate some of the effects of ethanol in the brain. In addition to their presence in neuronal cell membranes, adenosine receptors are present on the membranes of the human lymphocyte. It has been reported that the inhibition of adenosine uptake by lymphocytes from nonalcoholics exposed to alcohol in vitro is absent in lymphocytes from alcoholics (Diamond and Gordon, 1994; Diamond et al., 1987).

TABLE 5. *Some proposed biologic trait markers of addiction*

Marker	Initial report
Adenosine	Diamond et al., 1987
Adenylyl cyclase	Tabakoff et al., 1988
Alcohol dehydrogenase	Thomasson et al., 1990
Aldehyde dehydrogenase	Mizoi et al., 1979
Body sway	Schuckit, 1980
CRH/ACTH/cortisol	Schuckit, 1984a
Dopamine receptor	Blum et al., 1990
Electroencephalography	Davis et al., 1941
Endorphins	Topel, 1988
Event-related potentials	Begleiter et al., 1984
Heart rate	Finn et al., 1987
Intoxication level	Schuckit, 1980
Monoamine oxidase	Takahashi et al., 1976
Prolactin	Lex et al., 1991
Serotonin—CSF	Linnoila, 1989
Serotonin—Platelet	Meltzer et al., 1988

Adenylyl Cyclase

Adenylyl cyclase is part of a complex of membrane-bound proteins that includes (1) an extracellular messenger-specific receptor; (2) a guanine nucleotide binding protein (G-protein); and (3) adenylyl cyclase, the enzyme that converts Mg–adenosine triphosphate (ATP) to cyclic adenosine monophosphate (cAMP). cAMP is a second messenger that communicates the action of receptor binding with the intracellular cascade that results in specific nucleic acid and/or protein production, alteration, or degradation through activation or inactivation of protein kinases. The induced stimulation of adenylyl cyclase activity in platelets exposed to fluoride in vitro is significantly decreased in the platelets from alcoholics compared with platelets obtained from nonalcoholics. It has been reported that this reduced response of adenylyl cyclase may be transmitted as a single major gene (Diamond et al., 1987; Hoffman and Tabakoff, 1990; Nagy et al., 1988; Tabakoff and Hoffman, 1988).

Alcohol Dehydrogenase

Individuals with a specific gene that encodes for the β_2 isozyme of alcohol dehydrogenase may have a reduced risk for developing alcoholism. Alcohol dehydrogenase, in combination with aldehyde dehydrogenase, accounts for about 90% of hepatic ethanol metabolism, and determines the rate of formation and elimination of acetaldehyde. The current research related to genetic variation of these enzymes is associated with changes that result in abnormally high levels of acetaldehyde. For alcohol dehydrogenase, this would mean increased activity with an associated increased rate of conversion of ethanol to and accumulation of acetaldehyde. Accumulation of acetaldehyde results in the alcohol-induced flushing (AIF) reaction.

The AIF was first discovered in Asian populations and is associated with elevated levels of acetaldehyde due to a known point mutation of an aldehyde dehydrogenase allele as discussed in the next section. The AIF is believed to be initiated by increased acetaldehyde levels leading to the release of histamine and kinins, which are the actual mediators of the adverse signs and symptoms. These adverse changes include rapid onset of skin vasodilatation involving the face, neck, and chest; skin flushing; tachycardia; headache; nausea; burning sensations in the stomach; hypotension; and drowsiness. The AIF reaction has also been clearly documented in non-Asian populations (Bosron and Li, 1986; Harada et al., 1982, 1983; Sherman et al., 1994; Suwaki and Ohara, 1985; Thomasson et al., 1993).

Aldehyde Dehydrogenase

Decreased levels of aldehyde dehydrogenase activity results in decreased conversion of acetaldehyde to acetic acid. This results in the accumulation of acetaldehyde and the development of the same AIF discussed in the previous section on alcohol dehydrogenase. Individuals with a specific gene that encodes for an isozyme of mitochondrial aldehyde dehydrogenase with a reduced activity (i.e., ALDH2) have the AIF on exposure to alcohol and, therefore, have a reduced risk of developing alcoholism. A recent paper by Novoradovsky et al.

(1995) discusses a newly discovered ALDH2 allele (i.e., ALDH2^3). The frequency of this allele in various ethnic populations is not known at this time; however, the authors hypothesize that there may be widespread distribution in North American Indians. It is also not clear at this time if there are changes in the functional properties of ALDH2 associated with this alteration of the protein subunit (Takeshita et al., 1994; Thomasson et al., 1990, 1993).

Body Sway

The alcohol challenge paradigm was utilized to assess the effects of the consumption of standardized doses of ethanol on the physical characteristic of body sway in FHP and FHN subjects. FHP subjects, both males and females, show significantly less body sway after ACS than do FHN subjects (Lex et al., 1988; Schuckit, 1980, 1981, 1985, 1994a).

Corticotropin-Releasing Hormone/Adrenocorticotropin Hormone/Cortisol

Compared to FHNs, FHPs exhibit significantly less change in the levels of both ACTH and cortisol after the alcohol challenge paradigm (Anthenelli and Schuckit, 1990; Schuckit, 1984b, 1988) (Fig. 1).

Dopamine Receptor

An association between the D2 dopamine receptor (D2DR) gene and alcoholism was reported in 1990 in a study seeking association

[Hypothalamus] → CRH*
      ↳ [Pituitary] → ACTH**
            ↳ [Adrenal] → Cortisol

*CRH = Corticotropin Releasing Hormone, **ACTH = Adrenocorticotrophin Hormone

FIG. 1. A scheme for the cascade of hormones which acccounts for the release of cortisol from the adrenal gland. ACTH, adrenocorticotropic hormone; CRH, corticotropin-releasing hormone.

between genetic markers and the disease state of severe alcohol dependence (Blum et al., 1990). Subsequent to that finding it was hypothesized that genotypic heterogeneity of the A1 allele at the D2DR gene may affect the progression to severe forms of alcoholism rather than represent the all-or-none precipitating cause of alcoholism. More recently it has been suggested that genotypic variance of the D2DR A1 allele is a marker of a larger category of compulsive disease that includes severe alcohol dependence. These theories are controversial and continue to be actively debated in the literature (Blum and Noble, 1994; Blum et al., 1990; Bolos et al., 1990; Comings et al., 1991; Gelernter et al., 1993; Goldman, 1993; Holden, 1994; Noble and Blum, 1993; Noble et al., 1991, 1993; Smith et al., 1991).

Electroencephalography

While baseline EEGs are similar, acute alcohol use appears to affect the EEG activity of FHP individuals differently than it does individuals who are FHN. After alcohol consumption there is an increase in slow alpha (7.5–10.0 Hz) activity in both FHP and FHN individuals, but the degree of this increase is significantly higher in the FHP individuals and can be used to discriminate between the two groups. FHP subjects have significantly increased slow alpha wave EEG activity during the ascent of the blood alcohol curve (BAC). Furthermore, during the descent of the BAC after a high dose of alcohol, FHP's slow alpha waves changes are decreasing at a time that FHN's slow alpha waves still increased (Cohen et al., 1991, 1993a, 1993b; Lukas et al., 1986, 1990; Propping, 1977; Schandler et al., 1988).

Endogenous Opioid Peptides

It has been demonstrated in animal models that the opioid receptor antagonist naltrexone dose-dependently reverses ethanol-induced increases in extracellular dopamine, which is thought to be an important neurotransmitter

in the mediation of substance-induced reinforcement or reward. Furthermore, clinical studies have demonstrated a significant decrease in alcohol consumption associated with the use of naltrexone. This suggests a significant role for an interaction between alcohol, the endogenous opioid system, and dopamine in brain areas associated with reward (Benjamin et al., 1993; Gianoulakis and de Waele, 1994; O'Malley et al., 1992; Tobel, 1988; Volpecelli et al., 1992).

Event-Related Potentials

Event-related potentials (ERPs) represent an enhanced form of detection and recording of the electrical activity of the brain. ERPs are used to correlate electrical activity changes with specific behaviors, such as auditory or visual stimuli, that are temporally associated with the recording. The P300 component wave appears to be a genetically determined wave that appears 300 milliseconds after an anticipated, but rare, stimulus given during the performance of cognitive tasks in normal individuals. It has been demonstrated that alcohol-naive sons of alcoholic biologic fathers display a reduced, or flattened, P300 component wave (Begleiter et al., 1984, 1987; Schuckit, 1986).

Heart Rate

In the late 1980s it was reported that the baseline heart rate increases significantly after ingestion of alcohol by FHP males. Furthermore, it has been demonstrated that drug-induced increases in heart rate have been linked with reward. FHP individuals may demonstrate (1) greater increases in heart rate than controls, when given ethanol without an additional stress-inducing paradigm; (2) greater increases in heart rate when exposed to a stress-inducing paradigm without ethanol; and (3) greater reductions in the physical effects a stress-inducing paradigm after ethanol consumption than are seen in controls (Finn and Pihl, 1988, 1990;

Finn et al., 1990; Fowles, 1983; Hill et al., 1980; Wise and Bozarth, 1987).

Intoxication Level

FHP individuals rate themselves as significantly less intoxicated than age-matched FHN controls at the same level of blood alcohol concentration. This decreased subjective feeling of intoxication, identified at 20 years of age, appears to be a strong predictor of the development of alcoholism by the age of 30. Interestingly, in this particular cohort, the decreased level of intoxication to alcohol did not predict an increased rate of other nonalcohol substance addiction or increased incidence of other psychiatric illness by age 30 (Anthenelli and Schuckit, 1990; Schuckit, 1984a, 1987, 1988, 1990, 1994a; Schuckit and Gold, 1988).

Monoamine Oxidase

Monoamine oxidases A and B (MAO-A and MAO-B) catalyze the metabolism of dopamine, epinephrine, and other biogenic amines. Both of these neurotransmitters have a role in the physiologic actions of alcohol in the central nervous system. A reduced level of MAO-B enzyme activity in platelets, but not a reduced MAO-B concentration in platelets, may be a biologic marker useful in subtyping genetic forms of alcoholism in humans. It has also been reported that low platelet MAO activity is heritable and cosegregates with alcoholism (Alexopoulos et al., 1983; Devor et al., 1993; Faraj et al., 1987; Lex et al., 1988; Major et al., 1981; Panday et al., 1988; Schuckit, 1981; Tabakoff et al., 1985, 1988; von Knorring et al., 1985; Wiberg et al., 1977). However, these data have been called into question recently because of the role that smoking appears to have on platelet function. It now appears from the Collaborative Study on the Genetics of Alcoholism (funded by the National Institute on Alcohol Abuse and Alcoholism) that smoking, and not alcohol, is the crucial variable in many of these findings. This points out that smoking, which is at a

high level in alcoholics, must be evaluated in data analysis of biologic marker studies.

Prolactin

FHP subjects have significantly less change in prolactin (PRL) levels, as compared with FHN controls, during alcohol challenge studies (ACS). Serum PRL levels rise significantly after breast stimulation in normal women subjects; however, this increase is strikingly blocked by ethanol consumption. The PRL response to breast stimulation was not changed by the treatment with naloxone alone. However, the ethanol-induced inhibition of the PRL response was blocked by naloxone (Garbutt et al., 1991; Schuckit et al., 1987; Volpi et al., 1994).

Serotonin and CSF 5HIAA

Several groups have reported a correlation between alcoholism and abnormal serotonin function in both animal and human studies. A lower concentration of the serotonin metabolite 5HIAA in the cerebrospinal fluid (CSF) has been reported in individuals with a high familial risk of alcoholism (Linnoila et al., 1983; Murphy et al., 1982; Tollefson, 1989). There is recent data from Linnoila and collaborators that suggest that reduced CSF 5HIAA occurs only in violent alcoholics (Linnoila et al., 1994; Mehlman et al., 1994; Virkkunen and Linnoila, 1993; Virkkunen et al., 1995).

Serotonin-Platelet Reuptake

The rate of serotonin uptake is influenced by genetic factors and may represent a specific biologic trait marker for alcoholism. The rate of serotonin uptake has been reported as higher in FHP individuals than in FHN controls. It has been suggested that the rate of uptake of serotonin by platelets is significantly higher in alcoholics than controls (Meltzer and Arora, 1988; Rausch et al., 1991; Simonsson et al., 1992).

Conclusion: Trait Markers

Schuckit (1994a,b) summarized future directions for the task of finding usable biologic markers of increased risk for the development of alcohol dependence. First, because there is genetic heterogeneity involved in the predisposition toward addictive behavior, the demonstration of a biologic marker among the family members of some addicted individuals could identify pedigrees that might share a similar biologic mechanism for their greater addiction risk. This step could simplify future genetic research by offering more homogeneous groups for study. Second, the biologic markers could be more sensitive than the symptoms of the addictive disorder itself in helping to identify which members of a pedigree have an enhanced risk because not everyone with the family predisposition will manifest the addictive behaviors. Third, the use of biologic markers has implications for prevention because family members of addicted individuals can not only be warned that they are genetically at increased risk, but can be taught about specific alcohol-induced phenomena associated with that risk. Finally, the use of these biologic markers might lead to the discovery of less cumbersome evaluation techniques that would make screening of family members and further clinical research more specific.

Clinical usefulness of biologic trait markers would have its greatest impact in primary prevention and aggressive intervention to prevent, or minimize, progression of the substance use disorder. Currently, physical and psychological damage as well as severe medical and social costs has often already taken place before the individual acknowledges that he or she has an addiction disorder and specific intervention has been undertaken.

The eventual success of the trait-marker–addiction paradigm has an associated risk. It is possible that the ability to clearly identify individuals at increased risk for the development of a substance use disorder may lead to their exclusion from social opportunities such as employment and health care coverage. This outcome may, ironically, increase the risk of progression of the addiction rather than lead to the development of preventive and therapeutic interventions.

TESTS FOR CONSUMPTION OR USE OF DRUGS OF ABUSE (STATE MARKERS)

These tests ascertain the use of substances during recovery, and are used for forensic applications, in work environments where sober employees are required due to safety issues, and in physician's practices to elucidate the etiology of certain health problems during patient evaluation.

The most direct, sensitive, and specific test for the use of any addictive substance is its measurement in urine, plasma, or serum. Highly sensitive tests are available for all of the drugs of abuse (Table 6). The usefulness of these tests is dependent on the sensitivity of the test and on the half-life of the drug and its metabolites. For example, the half-life of ethanol is relatively short, about 3 to 4 hours in most humans. Therefore, depending on the amount consumed, the presence of alcohol in blood or breath is not detectable for more than a few hours after the last drink. Despite the fact that acetaldehyde, the major metabolite of ethanol, may have a slightly longer half-life, its measurement in plasma is not useful for more than a few hours after the last drink either. Cocaine is only detectable for a few hours after administration because it has a short half-life ($t_{1/2} = 0.8$–1.5 hours); however, cocaine's major metabolite, benzoylecgonine ($t_{1/2} = 6$ hours), may be detectable for up to 7 days after the last dose.

Employment-related and forensic analysis for drugs of abuse has evolved into a two-stage process: (1) preliminary testing or screening followed by (2) confirmatory testing for the positives identified in preliminary testing. Preliminary testing is used to determine only the presence of a drug or class of drugs, usually in blood or urine samples. This provides a relatively economic means by

TABLE 6. *Analyses for drugs of abuse*

Drugs	Half-life (hrs)	EMIT[a] (ng/ml)	GC-MS[b] (ng/ml)	Detection after last use (days)
Amphetamines	10–15	300	100	1–2
Barbiturates				
Amobarbital	8–42	300	100	3–5
Secobarbital	22–29	300	100	6
Pentobarbital	20–30	300	100	6
Phenobarbital	80–120	300	100	16
Benzodiazepines				
Diazepam	20–35	300		
Nordiazepam	50–90	300	100	
Cocaine	0.8–1.5			
Benzoylecgonine	7.5	300	50	2–4
Opiates	2–4	300	100	1–2
Phencyclidine	7–16	75	10	2–8
Cannabinoids	10–40	20–100	10	2–8 (acute use) 14–42 (chronic use)

[a]Enzyme-multiplied immunoassay technique; cut-off values.
[b]Gas chromatography—mass spectroscopy; detection limits.

which to screen with reasonably high specificity large numbers of samples. Preliminary tests demonstrate the presence of drugs above an arbitrary threshold, the so-called concentration or cutoff threshold. Below this concentration of drug, a sample is said to be negative. Detection of drugs whose concentration is equal to or greater than the threshold concentration is considered a positive test. Preliminary testing or screening can include either chromatographic methods such as thin-layered chromatography (TLC) or various immunoassay techniques such as the enzyme-multiplied immunoassay technique (EMIT) (Fletcher, 1981). Initial screening can be followed by confirmation of drug detection. The confirmatory test is more specific for a particular drug analyte and may be used in addition to quantify the absolute levels of specific drug or drug metabolite in a particular sample. The sensitivity and specificity of the confirmatory test should be equal to or greater than that of the preliminary testing (Table 1).

A number of factors affect the pharmacokinetics of a particular drug including the pK_a (pH at which the drug is 50% ionized), lipid solubility, and protein binding. The elimination profile for a drug varies according to differences in drug metabolism rates related to factors such as genetics, age, and endocrine factors as well as to concurrent exposure to other drugs, dietary changes, and liver or renal disease. Often, the parent drug or compound has been metabolized or otherwise altered prior to collection of blood or urine specimens. As a result, analyses for drugs of abuse are not always measurements of the drug itself but one or more of the major metabolites of that drug. For that reason, it is very important to understand how these drugs are metabolized.

Central Nervous System (CNS) Stimulants

Substance abuse screens are used to evaluate urine samples for the presence of amphetamines and for cocaine. Preliminary drug screens also detect such over-the-counter substances as phenylpropanolamine, pseudoephedrine, and phenylephrine. Hence, it is necessary to know the limitations of the assay system being employed and, where necessary, confirm the presence of the drug of interest by additional testing using sensitive and specific assays.

Amphetamine has an elimination half-life ranging from 8 to 34 hours, depending, in part, on urinary pH (Rowland, 1969; Wan et al., 1978). The structurally related methamphetamine may be detected in urine samples as long as 40 to 48 hours after drug exposure (Beckett and Rowland, 1965). Methamphetamine is also slowly metabolized to form amphetamine (Caldwell et al., 1972; Beckett and Rowland, 1965). Amphetamine undergoes oxidative deamination to produce phenylacetone, which is inactive. The latter is oxidized to benzoic acid (Dring et al., 1970). To a lesser degree, amphetamine is also oxidized to norephedrine. Both amphetamine and the norephedrine metabolite can be hydroxylated to the pharmacologically active metabolites 4-hydroxynorephedrine and 4-hydroxyamphetamine. Amphetamine metabolites are eventually conjugated with glucuronide or glycine and eliminated by urinary excretion (Wan et al., 1978). Both unchanged methamphetamine and unchanged amphetamine can be detected in urine. If the urine is acidic, up to 80% of a dose of amphetamine, including 20% as unchanged drug, is excreted in urine. As the pH of urine increases, excretion of amphetamine is decreased significantly. Urinary excretion of a single dose of amphetamine is usually complete within several days.

Screening immunoassays for amphetamines vary in specificity: radioimmunoassay (RIA; Abuscreen, Roche Diagnostic) is specific for amphetamine; fluorescence polarization immunoassay (FPIA; Tdx System, Abbott Laboratories), for amphetamine and methamphetamine; EMIT (Syva, Palo Alto, CA), for amphetamine and methamphetamine as well as several other related phenethylamines. Urinalyses positive for amphetamines are further evaluated by confirmatory testing, primarily gas chromatography (GC), and GC with mass spectroscopy (GC-MS). Using microbore or fused silica capillary columns, underivatized amphetamines can be identified by retention time. Derivatization increases sensitivity and specificity.

Cocaine, another commonly abused stimulant, is available either in salt (cocaine HCl) or as free base (crack cocaine) form. Cocaine is very rapidly metabolized by hydrolysis of one or both ester bonds within the molecule (Ambre, 1985; Stewart et al., 1979). Nearly half of a dose of cocaine is hydrolyzed either enzymatically or nonenzymatically to form benzoylecgonine. Cocaine is also enzymatically hydrolyzed to form ecgonine methyl ester. Circulating butyrylcholinesterase activity catalyzes the rapid hydrolysis of cocaine. Considerable hydrolysis of cocaine may also occur following collection and during storage of biologic samples not properly stabilized (Baselt, 1983). Hydrolysis of cocaine in urine or blood samples can be retarded significantly by addition of sodium fluoride or cholinesterase inhibitors to the samples or by freezing the samples (Baselt, 1983).

Co-abuse of cocaine with other drugs is common, especially the simultaneous ingestion of ethanol (Grant and Harford, 1990). Trans-esterification of cocaine and ethanol, catalyzed by nonspecific carboxylesterases, results in the production of cocaethylene (benzoylecgonine ethyl ester, ethylcocaine). Significant levels of cocaethylene have been identified in urine, blood, and other samples obtained at autopsy from victims of apparent drug overdose (Hearn et al., 1991b). Cocaethylene demonstrates similar pharmacologic activity to that of cocaine (Hearn et al., 1991a). Thus, conversion of cocaine into the pharmacologically active cocaethylene, rather than the inactive metabolites benzoylecgonine or ecgonine methyl ester, could explain the increased toxicity when cocaine is used together with ethanol (Dean et al., 1991). Following appropriate sample preparation, cocaine and cocaethylene concentrations can be determined either by the methods of GC-MS or by high-performance liquid chromatography with ultraviolet detection (HPLC-UV) (Jatlow et al., 1991; Thompson and Dasgupta, 1995). Among 237 cases of cocaine-related deaths in Dade County, Florida, ethanol was frequently coidentified with cocaine in postmortem blood samples (Hearn et al., 1991a). In approximately 60% of those cases involving concurrent cocaine and ethanol use, blood screens for the presence of cocaethylene were also positive.

The elimination half-life for cocaine has been estimated to range from 0.8 to 1.5 hours

(Javaid et al., 1978, 1983; Jeffcoat et al., 1989; Wilkinson et al., 1980). Although the principal route of elimination is by metabolism, small amounts of unchanged cocaine may be detected in the urine. The percentage of unchanged cocaine excreted varies with urine pH. Benzoylecgonine and ecgonine methyl ester with average elimination half-lives of 7.5 and 3 hours, respectively, are excreted largely unchanged in urine (Ambre, 1985). With sensitive assays, these metabolites may be detectable in urine samples for several days or longer following cocaine use (Ambre, 1985). Ambre (1985) has suggested that an approximate time since drug ingestion can be estimated from the relative ratio among cocaine/benzoylecgonine/ecgonine methyl ester in urine samples.

Preliminary testing for cocaine relies on the detection of benzoylecgonine by RIA or other immunologically based detection systems such as EMIT (Syva, Palo Alto, CA). Neither immunoassay method exhibits appreciable cross-reactivity with either cocaine or ecgonine, although the RIA cross-reacts with cocaine. Cocaine can be confirmed by identification of the drug or its metabolites benzoylecgonine and ecgonine methyl ester by GC with a nitrogen detector (Ambre et al., 1988) or cocaine and benzoylecgonine by GC-MS (Evans and Morarity, 1980). Cocaine and benzoylecgonine, but not ecgonine methyl ester, can also be identified by HPLC-UV (Evans and Morarity, 1980; Masoud and Krupski, 1980).

Opiates

When injected intravenously, heroin is rapidly hydrolyzed to form morphine (Inturrisi et al., 1984). Acting as a so-called "prodrug," heroin is initially deacetylated to 6-monoacetylmorphine; this intermediary metabolite is then further deacetylated to morphine. Morphine and 6-acetylmorphine are considered equipotent as opioidergic agents. The circulating half-life of heroin is approximately 3 minutes.

The tissue distribution of morphine is very rapid with a volume of distribution of 1.0 to 6.2 L/kg (Sarve et al., 1981). Circulating levels of morphine decrease more slowly than those of either heroin or 6-acetylmorphine. The elimination half-life of morphine is approximately 177 minutes (Stanski et al., 1978). Morphine is then conjugated in the liver as well, to a lesser extent, within the intestinal wall. Less than 10% of the drug is excreted unchanged in urine. The remainder is excreted as water-soluble morphine-3-glucuronide and morphine-3-sulfate in a ratio of 4:1 (Yeh et al., 1976).

Orally ingested codeine is metabolized primarily by N-demethylation to form norcodeine, although as much as 10% is O-demethylated to form morphine (Posey and Kimble, 1984). Both codeine and its metabolites are conjugated as glucuronides and sulfates prior to urinary excretion. The presence of morphine, but no other opiates, in urine samples suggests illicit drug use. In the event that morphine and codeine are found concomitantly in a urine sample, additional investigation is necessary to ascertain whether the morphine is a derivative of legally prescribed codeine or a result of illicit morphine/heroin use. Codeine levels higher that those of morphine suggest that the latter were derived from codeine (Posey and Kimble, 1984). The presence of low concentrations of codeine and morphine in urine would not discriminate among prior ingestion of codeine, morphine, or heroin since street heroin contains acetylcodeine that is metabolized to codeine. In addition, consumption of baked goods with poppy seeds may result in detectable levels of morphine in the urine up to 60 hours following poppy seed ingestion (Fritschi and Prescott, 1985). It is possible, although not always easy, to distinguish heroin use from poppy seed ingestion by the presence of the heroin metabolite 6-monoacetylmorphine (Felin and Megges, 1985).

Opiates are commonly screened by immunoassays including EMIT (Fletcher, 1981), thin layer chromatography (TLC) (Budd et al., 1980), RIA (Cleeland et al., 1976), and other immunoassay-based procedures. These assays typically detect both free and conjugated morphine and codeine as well as a number of synthetic narcotics such as dihydrocodeine, oxycodone, hydromorphone, and hydrocodone. Since a majority of morphine or codeine is present in conjugated forms in urine samples, acid or enzyme hydrolysis is required prior to confirmatory testing using HPLC with electrochemical detection (Helper et al., 1979) or GC-MS (Paul et al., 1985).

Cannabinoids (Marijuana)

Delta[9]-tetrahydrocannnabinol (THC), the major active compound in marijuana, is rapidly converted into the pharmacologically active 11-hydroxy-delta[9]-THC (via the hepatic cytochrome P-450 system) followed by alcohol dehydrogenase-catalyzed oxidation to the pharmacologically inactive 11-nor-delta[9]-THC-9-carboxylic acid (11-carboxy-THC) (Wall et al., 1983). Up to two-thirds of the metabolites of THC are excreted in the feces, the remainder in urine (Wall and Perez-Reyes, 1981). Significant concentrations of THC are stored in tissues, providing a reservoir from which THC continues to reenter the general circulation (Jaffe and Schilling, 1991). This accounts for a relatively long elimination half-life, greater than 30 hours.

Within 72 hours of marijuana use, 70% of the THC is excreted either in the feces (40%) or in urine (30%). Unchanged THC is excreted only in trace amounts. 11-Carboxy-THC and other metabolites may be detected in urine samples for days or weeks following chronic marijuana use (Kanter and Hollister, 1977; Wall et al., 1983). Measurable levels of 11-carboxy-THC may also be present in urine or feces following passive inhalation of marijuana smoke (Morland et al., 1985).

Plasma THC is relatively stable in refrigerated or frozen samples kept in glass, but not plastic, containers for up to 4 to 6 months (Johnson et al., 1986). Preliminary screening for urinary cannabinoids is done by immunoassays, e.g., RIA and EMIT. These immunoassays detect the major urinary metabolite 11-carboxy-THC as well as numerous other THC metabolites. Confirmatory chromatographic techniques, including GC-MS (Baker et al., 1984) and HPLC with RIA (Law et al., 1984) or with electrochemical detection (Sutheimer et al., 1985), are commonly employed to measure 11-carboxy-THC.

Hallucinogens

Very little is known about tissue distribution, metabolism, or excretion of lysergic acid diethylamide (LSD) or other hallucinogens in humans. It is known that LSD is extensively metabolized (Nelson and Foltz, 1992b). In fact, less than 1% of a dose of LSD is excreted unchanged in urine (Lim et al., 1988). Known LSD metabolites in humans include *N*-demethyl-LSD, 13-hydroxy-LSD, and 14-hydroxy-LSD (Nelson and Foltz, 1992b). *N*-demethyl-LSD is usually present in the urine of LSD users; the hydroxylated metabolites are normally present in urine as glucuronide conjugates (Nelson and Foltz, 1992b). Numerous other metabolites of LSD may also be present.

Given the lower doses of 20 to 80 μg of LSD usually ingested and a plasma half-life of 3 to 5 hours (Nelson and Foltz, 1992b), detection of LSD in biologic samples requires sensitive analyses. Plasma and urine LSD concentrations will have declined to levels below 1 ng/ml within hours of drug ingestion (Lim et al., 1988). In addition, LSD is heat-sensitive and unstable in acidic solution (pH <4) (Paul et al., 1990). Several commercially available RIAs can be used to screen for the presence of LSD in blood or urine samples (e.g., Abuscreen, Roche Diagnostic Systems, Nutley, NJ; Coat-a-Count, Diagnostic Products, Los Angeles, CA). Confirmation of LSD in biologic samples is based on chromatographic separation and detection via fluorescence emission or by mass spectroscopy (Francom et al., 1988; McCarron et al., 1990; Nelson and Foltz, 1992a,b). LSD in subnanogram/ml concentrations becomes even more difficult to evaluate as a result of potentially significant adsorptive loss of drug during chromatographic analysis (Nelson and Foltz, 1992b).

Dissociative Anesthetics

Phencyclidine (1-1[phenylcyclohexyl]piperidine; PCP) is primarily metabolized by hydroxylation in the liver (Cook et al., 1982). Hydroxylated PCP metabolites (4-phenyl-4-piperidinocyclohexanol and 1-[1-phenylcyclohexyl]-4-hydroxypiperidine) is then conjugated with glucuronic acid and excreted in urine (Wong and Biemann, 1976). N-dealkylated as well as oxidized PCP metabolites have also been detected in urine. A small amount of PCP is excreted in urine as unchanged drug. As PCP is a weak base, lowering urinary pH below 5.0 will increase the excretion of unchanged PCP.

PCP can be detected in biologic samples by RIA with a sensitivity of 500 pg/ml (Owens et al., 1982) as well as chromatographically (GC-MS) with a sensitivity of 10 ng/ml (Cone et al., 1981). Due to significant sequestration and slow release from adipose and other lipid-rich tissues, PCP and metabolites are often detected in urine up to 10 days following ingestion of the drug (Bailey et al., 1978; Misra et al., 1979).

Benzodiazepines

Benzodiazepines are extensively metabolized, primarily within the liver. Many of the intermediary metabolites of benzodiazepines are pharmacologically active and remain in the body for prolonged periods of time. This also explains the similarities in pharmacologic activities among benzodiazepines. In addition, the ability to metabolize benzodiazepines may be impaired in patients with liver disease, leading to prolonged elevations in drug levels in these individuals (Klotz et al., 1975).

Benzodiazepines with 1- or 2-position substituents on the diazepine ring are initially metabolized by loss of the substituent. These metabolites are then usually N-desalkylated to form demoxepam, nordiazepam, or N-desalkylflurazepam. Demoxepam is converted into nordiazepam. The benzodiazepine clorazepate is metabolized by decarboxylation in the acidic environment of the stomach to form nordiazepam, which can then be absorbed completely (Harvey, 1985). Nordiazepam and N-desalkylflurazepam are then hydroxylated. Triazolam and alprazolam are directly hydroylated. All of the N-desalkyalted and hydroxylated metabolites are considered biologically active. The hydroxylated metabolites are finally conjugated with glucuronic acid and excreted. Less than 1% of a dose of benzodiazepine such as chordiazepoxide is excreted unchanged.

Chordiazepoxide is inherently unstable in biologic samples, forming desoxychlordiazepoxide (Entwhistle et al., 1986). Desoxychlordiazepoxide is then further degraded to form nordiazepam. Degradation of chlordiazepoxide in biologic samples makes accurate analysis of levels of this drug problematic. The high lipid solubility of these compounds results in long half-lives and long periods of detection.

Barbiturates

Barbiturates are primarily metabolized by oxidation of chemical groups attached at the C5 position (Harvey, 1985). The resulting ketones, alcohols, or acids are conjugated with glucuronide and excreted in urine. Elimination half-lives for this class of drugs are generally fairly long, many barbiturates being detectable in blood or urine samples for several days (Tang et al., 1975, 1977, 1979). The rate of barbiturate elimination is altered in pregnancy, infancy, older individuals, individuals with hepatic dysfunction, and individuals with repeated use of barbiturates (Harvey, 1985).

The majority of barbiturates undergo extensive metabolism. Their metabolism is catalyzed mainly by the hepatic microsomal enzyme system (Harvey, 1985). This enzyme system, which catalyzes the breakdown of many other types of drugs, is stimulated by barbiturates. Thus, barbiturates stimulate their own metabolism. Of the major classes of barbiturates, oxybarbiturates are metabolized only in the liver. However, thiobarbiturates are metabolized in the liver and, to a lesser extent, in brain, kidney, and other tissues (Harvey, 1985). Removal of sulfate from thiobarbiturates produces oxybarbiturates. Barbiturates may also undergo *N*-hydroxylation or opening of the barbiturate ring. Oxidation of the C5 position radical on the barbiturate ring results in inactivation of the drug.

Barbiturates can be identified in urine or blood samples using colorimetric and UV spectrophotometric methods of analysis. However, these tests are relatively nonspecific and only semiquantitative. There are also several commercially available RIAs and other immunoassay-based procedures that are routinely used to screen for barbiturates. Confirmatory testing generally involves GC with flame ionization detection.

Inhalants

Toluene is one of the more commonly abused inhalants due to its availability as a component of industrial products such as paint thinners, glues, and paints. Eighty percent of an inhaled dose of toluene is oxidized to benzoic acid, which is then conjugated with glucuronic acid or glycine and excreted in urine (Kapur et al., 1986; Pagnotto and Lieberman, 1967). A majority of the conjugated metabolites consists of the glycine conjugate, hippuric acid. Less than 1% of a dose of toluene is excreted unchanged in urine. Approximately 20% of an inhaled dose is eliminated as toluene through exhaled air.

Urine screens can be used to detect the presence of hippuric acid, the major metabolite of toluene. Toluene adsorbs easily onto plastics and rubber stoppers, undoubtedly accounting at least in part for the significant variations and low concentrations measured among samples known to contain toluene. Toluene can be detected in biologic samples by TLC and colorimetry (Ogata et al., 1969), direct colorimetry (Tomokuni and Ogata, 1972), or UV spectrophotometry (Pagnotto and Lieberman, 1967). Gas chromatography with flame ionization is often employed for toluene-specific confirmatory analysis (Garriott et al., 1981).

TESTS FOR CONSUMPTION OF ALCOHOL

As mentioned above, ethanol is unique in that its half-life is so short (3–4 hours) that it does not remain in the body for more than a few hours after drinking has ceased. Thus, there has been an intense search for indicators of consumption. Most of this effort has been directed toward initial identification and subsequent characterization of biochemical parameters that are altered by ethanol. These altered parameters are then studied in subject groups that vary in alcohol consumption. These studies have focused on the longer lasting effects of alcohol consumption, e.g., increased levels of proteins in serum (GGT, CDT), increased mean corpuscular volume, and others that will be briefly discussed in this chapter.

A number of tests for the consumption of alcohol have been developed and are used currently. Excellent recent reviews have described the studies evaluating the utility of the more established tests (Mihas and Tavassoli, 1992; Watson et al., 1986; Whelan, 1992). However, no single test has yet to provide an objective, accurate, biologically based indication of alcohol consumption with 100% sensitivity and specificity except for the direct measurement of ethanol in the blood.

We present here brief summaries of scientific studies that describe the markers and their normal physiologic function, the effects of ethanol on marker function, and the clinical usefulness and characteristics of the marker in detecting ethanol consumption.

Direct Measurement of Ethanol

The direct measurement of ethanol in the blood or other bodily fluid such as saliva, urine, or sweat is a specific means by which to detect consumption of the drug. Ethanol taken orally is absorbed very quickly from the stomach and the intestine and distributes in total body water. Approximately 80% of ingested ethanol is metabolized in the liver to acetaldehyde and the blood ethanol and acetaldehyde levels drop quite rapidly (Watson et al., 1986). The half-life of ethanol and acetaldehyde is about 3 to 4 hours. However, the elimination or clearance of ethanol is a function of the total elimination rate, which includes metabolism and excretion, as well as the blood ethanol level at the time when abstinence was begun. The maximal elimination rate is approximately 15 mg%/hr in the postabsorption phase of the blood alcohol curve. Therefore, a blood level of 100 mg%, which is the legal intoxication level in many states, would take about 6 hours to dissipate. Unless the patient is closely monitored or is in the hospital and daily tests for blood ethanol are made, the usefulness of these measurements is limited.

Obvious situations where direct measurement of blood ethanol concentration is helpful are (1) in the hospital emergency room to help in the treatment of a patient; (2) for forensic purposes, e.g., a driver might be suspected of being legally intoxicated; and (3) in recovering patients. For these purposes, devices have been developed to measure ethanol concentration in the breath. However, breath from alveolar air is required and this may present problems for some people such as the elderly (Watson et al., 1986). Furthermore, even actual measurements of blood ethanol concentrations by the more reliable methods such as gas chromatography are not foolproof in that significant variability in peak blood alcohol concentrations has been observed in different persons consuming the same amount of ethanol (O'Neill et al., 1983). Different metabolic rates among alcohol consumers is well known.

Ethanol can also be measured in urine, saliva, and sweat, but these measurements are less frequently used. Ethanol is present in the urine longer than in the blood, but the rela-

tionship between urine and blood levels is not always proportional. Blood ethanol levels can be determined by very sensitive laboratory tests that are readily available.

5-Hydroxytryptophol (Urinary 5HTOL/5HIAA)

The measurement of 5-hydroxytryptophol (5HTOL) in urine as a marker for ethanol consumption has only recently been proposed. 5-Hydroxytryptophol (5HTOL) is normally a minor metabolite of serotonin. Its formation accounts for only about 2% to 4% of the metabolism of serotonin. The major end product of serotonin metabolism is 5-hydroxyindoleacetic acid (5HIAA). It has been proposed that the consumption of ethanol changes the ratio of 5HTOL/5HIAA in urine for up to several hours after the disappearance of ethanol. Approximately 99% of urinary 5HTOL is in the conjugated form, either sulfate or glucuronide, apparently because of the lipid/water solubility of 5HTOL (Helander et al., 1995a).

Davis et al. (1967) showed that an acute dose of ethanol caused a significant increase in the production of 5HTOL and a corresponding decrease in 5HIAA production by measurements of the compounds in human urine. This shift in metabolism was probably due in part to an increase in the NADH/NAD$^+$ ratio (NADH is the reduced form of nicotinamide adenine dinucleotide and NAD$^+$ the oxidized form) by ethanol or the presence of acetaldehyde, both of which may play a role in the inhibition of aldehyde dehydrogenase, thereby blocking the formation of 5HIAA and forcing the aldehyde of serotonin into the reductive side of the metabolic pathway. Yoshimoto et al. (1992) demonstrated similar results in rat brain studies using brain microdialysis.

Helander et al. (1993) studied the time course of ethanol-induced changes in 5HT metabolism and reported that the increase of urinary 5HTOL correlated with blood ethanol curve; however, a considerable lag time was observed and urinary 5HTOL levels did not return to baseline until several hours after ethanol levels were undetectable. In this study, an ethanol dose of 0.5 g/kg produced an elevated urinary 5HTOL/5HIAA level. The half-life of the urinary 5HTOL/5HIAA ratio appeared to be about the same as that of ethanol.

Two recent clinical studies support the use of this marker as an indicator of recent ethanol consumption. Voltaire et al. (1992) reported that in a group of 69 subjects who were alcohol abstinent, the values of 5HTOL/5HIAA ratio varied between 4 and 17 pmol 5HTOL/nmol 5HIAA. They proposed that a ratio of 20 be used as the upper limit for a nonconsumer and that ratios >20 be used to indicate recent consumption. Using these criteria, the statistical probability for a false positive was calculated to be less than .001. Carlsson et al. (1993a) performed a study in 15 subjects attempting to abstain from alcohol over a 6-month period. They found that elevated urinary 5HTOL/5HIAA ratios and elevated CDT values correlated and suggested that the two measurements could be used in a complementary way for the detection of relapse in alcohol dependent patients.

Other drugs that inhibit aldehyde dehydrogenase may also increase the urinary 5HTOL/5HIAA ratio. For example, disulfiram, an aldehyde dehydrogenase inhibitor used for the treatment of alcoholism, has been shown to increase the 5HTOL/5HIAA ratio (Davis et al., 1967). However, in the study by Voltaire et al. (1992), several drugs and a variety of clinical conditions had no effect on urinary 5HTOL/5HIAA ratio. Ingestion of bananas, which are serotonin rich, or the presence of serotonin-producing carcinoid tumors caused higher rates of 5HTOL secretion, but the 5HTOL/5HIAA ratio did not differ in these subjects from controls (Helander et al., 1995a). High concentrations of serotonin are also present in tomato and pineapple (Udenfriend et al., 1955).

This marker has not yet been well tested and values for clinical sensitivity and specificity have not appeared in the literature. Nevertheless, this test has potential as an indicator of very recent alcohol use. Elevated levels of

5HTOL/5HIAA appear to remain for several hours after the disappearance of ethanol from the blood. Therefore, the probable utility of the urinary 5HTOL/5HIAA ratio will be as a prospective marker for relapse or in screening for very recent consumption. As an indicator of very recent ethanol use, this test might complement other tests in the assessment of alcohol consumption. Also, this test will have a place in forensic medicine to determine the postmortem formation, as opposed to premortem presence, of ethanol in urine (Helander et al., 1995b). The measurement of 5HTOL and 5HIAA in urine can be made using HPLC with electrochemical detection (Helander et al., 1992; Javors et al., 1984).

γ-Glutamyltransferase (GGT)

The measurement of GGT activity in serum has been used a marker for alcohol consumption for many years. γ-Glutamyltransferase (EC 2.3.2.2.), a glycoprotein, is an integral membrane enzyme that catalyzes the transfer of γ-glutamyl groups between γ-glutamyl peptides and small peptides or amino acids (Lilja et al., 1983). Normally, this enzyme plays an important role in the transport of amino acids across cell membranes, in peptide nitrogen storage, in protein synthesis, and in the regulation of tissue glutathione levels (Rosalki, 1975). GGT activity is normally highest in the kidney, but the pancreas, liver, and prostate also contain prominent amounts (Rosalki, 1975). Lower levels of the enzyme are also present in the spleen, lung, bowel, placenta, and thyroid. GGT levels in apparently healthy volunteers were found to be 50% higher in males than in females in one study (Rosalki, 1975), but Rosalki and Rau (1972) reported that males were only 20% higher.

The enzyme has a molecular weight of approximately 85,000 and consists of two subunits. The lighter subunit contains the catalytic site. Kottgen et al. (1976) showed that there are two forms of GGT in the adult liver, an adult form and a fetal form. Nishimura and Teschke (1983) reported that the ratio of adult/fetal GGT activity in serum of healthy controls was 3.1. In alcoholics with fatty liver, fibrosis, or cirrhosis, the ratios were 0.4, 0.6, and 1.8, respectively. These results and measurements of hepatic GGT suggest that ethanol selectively induces hepatic fetal GGT activity, which accounts for the increase in serum GGT after excessive alcohol use. Nishimura and Teschke (1983) proposed that increased serum GGT activity in the early stages of chronic alcohol intake was due primarily to hepatic enzyme induction rather than to hepatic injury. Moussavian et al. (1985) suggested that the increase in serum GGT was the result of enzyme induction and liver injury because GGT levels were much higher in alcoholics with liver disease. Both studies were done using subjects who were proven alcoholics and had demonstrated excessive intake of ethanol.

Hepatic microsomal injury may be one of the earliest effects of alcohol toxicity associated with high alcohol intake (Lieber and Rubin, 1968). Although the measurement of GGT in plasma or serum was first proposed as an marker for liver disease (Rosalki, 1975), it was recognized to have a potential use in alcoholism. Rollason et al. (1972) showed that serum GGT correlated with alcohol intake, but it took six drinks per day to raise the level of GGT above normal in 50% of the subjects, suggesting that the lower limit of sensitivity is a relatively high intake.

Nishimura and Teschke (1983) showed that the half-life of elevated serum GGT activity was between 2 and 3 weeks in patients with alcoholic liver disease after the beginning of abstinence.

For inpatient and outpatient alcoholics and outpatient heavy drinkers, Rosalki and Rau (1972) reported diagnostic sensitivities of 78%, 76.5%, and 75%, respectively. Diagnostic specificities were not reported in that study. Moussavian et al. (1985) reported sensitivities of 52% in alcoholic patients without liver disease and 100% in patients with alcoholic liver disease. In this study, however, patients with nonalcoholic liver disease all had elevated GGT levels (therefore, specificity =

0%); furthermore, serum GGT activity of patients with alcoholic liver disease did not decrease even after 8 weeks of abstinence. Also, it should be noted that other drugs such as phenobarbital and chlorpromazine can raise serum GGT (Nishimura and Teschke, 1983).

The measurement of GGT as a marker for ethanol consumption is well studied and well established. Serum GGT levels increase with prolonged excessive drinking and may remain elevated in a percentage of subjects for weeks. The lower limit of drinking required to raise serum GGT levels is approximately 150 g/day. However, reported diagnostic sensitivities for consumption range between 50% and 60% and diagnostic specificities are typically very low. False positives may be caused by other drugs and liver disease. Nevertheless, the measurement of GGT is currently useful as diagnostic confirmation in denying patients and for demonstrating the hepatic effects of excessive drinking habits to patients (Rosalki, 1975). It may also be helpful in monitoring excessive alcohol intake in recovering individuals.

Carbohydrate-Deficient Transferrin (CDT)

One of the recently developed and promising markers for ethanol consumption is the measurement of serum CDT. According to a large number of studies over the last 15 years, CDT appears to be a relatively sensitive and specific marker for alcohol consumption.

The physical properties and normal physiologic function of transferrin have been reviewed recently by Worwood (1989). Transferrin is a protein with a molecular weight of approximately 80,000 and a single polypeptide chain of 679 amino acids. There are two homologous domains within the molecule and each can bind one molecule of iron. The C-terminal half of transferrin, at amino acid numbers 413 and 611, contains two complex, oligosaccharide side chains. Up to eight sialic acid residues can be attached at the end of these two carbohydrate chains (de Jong and van Eijk, 1989). At least nine isoforms of transferrin are able to be separated on the basis of the number of sialic acid residues. Under normal conditions and in healthy controls, most transferrin molecules contain four sialic acid residues, two on each carbohydrate chain (Marz et al., 1982; Stibler, 1978). The physiologic function of transferrin is to bind and deliver iron to cells within various tissues.

The brief, but intense, history of the discovery of the effect of ethanol on transferrin was recently reviewed by Helena Stibler (1991), a Swedish scientist who made the initial observation and who has done much of the research since that time. The initial observation using isoelectric focusing revealed that the concentrations of isoforms of transferrin with higher pI values appeared in the serum of alcoholic patients (Stibler et al., 1978). Further studies showed that the reason these isoforms had higher pI values was that there were fewer sialic acid residues on their carbohydrate side chains, hence the term *carbohydrate deficient transferrin* (Stibler and Borg, 1981, 1986; Stibler et al., 1986). The major component of CDT that is increased in serum of alcoholics is disialotransferrin (Stibler, 1991).

The mechanism by which ethanol or its metabolite acetaldehyde causes fewer sialic acid residues to be attached to the transferrin is not completely understood at this time, but effects on glycosyltransferase activity have been observed in rat brain and liver and appear to be related to blood alcohol concentration and length of alcohol exposure (Stibler, 1991). Other components of the glycosylation process may also be involved.

As of 1991, a large number of clinical studies had been done that included at least 2,500 subjects (Stibler, 1991). These studies mostly involved distinct groups of subjects such as healthy controls and verified alcoholics and clinical sensitivities between 81% and 100% and clinical specificities between 97% to 100% reported for the CDT marker (Stibler, 1991). False positives occurred in only about 1% of the subjects in these studies due to severe hepatic insufficiency, a genetically rare

D-variant of transferrin, or carbohydrate-deficient glycoprotein (CDG) syndrome (Stibler et al., 1991b). A more recent study (Bell et al., 1994) of moderate drinkers (greater than 50 g/day for the past month) indicated a clinical sensitivity of 69% and specificity of 92% for CDT. Anton and Moak (1994) reported a sensitivity of 79% and a specificity of >90% for males who drank over 60 g/day in the month before admission. The sensitivity was only 44% among 18 female abusers.

A significant number of drugs have been studied and do not appear to interfere with the CDT test (Stibler et al., 1986). Serum CDT levels in healthy controls are slightly higher in women than men (Stibler et al., 1991a), but may not be as useful for more moderate forms of alcohol abuse in women as it is in men (Anton and Moak, 1994; Lof et al., 1994).

Salmela et al. (1994) reported that controlled drinking of 60 gm ethanol per day for two weeks in non-alcoholics raised CDT levels but questioned the clinical usefulness of the marker. The half-life of CDT after commencement of abstinence has been determined to be about 2 weeks (Stibler, 1991). This suggests that CDT measurements may be useful to identify heavy drinking as well as moderate drinking. CDT's ability to detect moderate drinking may be used to prevent the progression of alcoholism in some predisposed individuals. CDT measurements are useful in the treatment of recovering alcoholic (Anton et al., 1995; Carlsson et al., 1993b; Rosman et al., 1995).

Several different methods have been used for the determination of CDT in serum in the many studies that have been done (Bean and Peter, 1993; Stibler, 1991a; Xin et al., 1991, 1992). Currently, a double antibody RIA is available in kit form from Kabi Pharmacia (Piscataway, NJ). This technique has been used in more recent studies and seems to be adequate (Anton and Bean, 1994). Although it does not account for all of the carbohydrate deficient transferrin, it is adequately sensitive and takes less time to run than previous methods.

The CDT marker has been well-studied and appears to provide a useful tool for monitoring the consumption of alcohol. Serum levels of CDT increase after about 10 days of drinking at 50 to 80 g of ethanol per day. After beginning abstinence from heavy drinking, CDT remains remains elevated with a half-life of approximately 14 days. Reported clinical sensitivity for heavy drinking in alcoholics presenting for treatment is in the range of 80% to 100%, depending on the study. In population screening studies, the sensitivity for lower amounts or intensities of drinking is considerably lower. Clinical specificities have been reported to be 90% or higher, 100% in some studies. At this time, it appears that the excellent specificity of the CDT test will be its greatest value; that is, the percentage of false negatives is very low. There appear to be few interferences to this test. The use of this test will increase with time, especially if a more automated version becomes available.

Mean Corpuscular Volume (MCV)

The measurement of erythrocyte size in a Coulter counter is a straightforward, available, and inexpensive test that has been used as an indicator of excessive alcohol use. That macrocytosis was associated with cirrhosis was reported as long ago as 1884 (Gram, 1884). Since that time, several reports have appeared that relate the increased size of red cells with excessive alcohol use (reviewed in Herbert et al., 1963). In 1975 Wu et al. reported that 56 out of 63 men and women alcoholics (89%) who admitted to drinking more than 80 g/day had increased MCV when compared with 33 patients with nonalcoholic liver disease and 61 healthy members of the hospital staff. In this study, folate deficiency was ruled out as the cause of the enlarged RBCs. Other studies have verified that macrocytosis occurs in a significant percent of heavy abusers or alcoholics (Chick et al., 1981; Herbert et al., 1963; Wu et al., 1975). It should be noted that most of these studies were comparing groups of alcoholics or heavy drinkers against nondrinking controls. Therefore, the clinical sensitivities and specificities were optimized. Subsequent studies place the

sensitivity and specificity for this test in the 30% to 50% range.

The mechanism by which alcohol causes elevated MCV is not understood. In a more recent study by Wu et al. (1975) it was observed that the increased MCV in alcoholics (>80 g/day) was not necessarily associated with anemia or folate deficiency and it was concluded that "alcohol appears to produce a direct toxic action on the developing erythroblast leading to macrocytosis." Lindenbaum (1980) concluded that "macrocytosis, which is not related to folate deficiency or liver disease, occurs in the majority of alcoholics, often in the absence of anemia, and appears to be an unexplained effect of ethanol."

Several of the studies show that substances other than ethanol may interfere with the use of MCV as a marker for alcohol consumption. Chaput et al. (1979) suggested that cigarette smoking increased MCV as did drinking. Eschwege et al. (1978) cautioned that use of anticonvulsants and smoking could cause false-positive tests. Age might also affect MCV (Chick et al., 1981).

Increased MCV after heavy exposure to alcohol persists for several weeks after abstention (Chick et al., 1981; Lindenbaum, 1980) and may be related to the turnover rate of red blood cells. There is no study to date in which a correlation between amount of alcohol consumed and increased MCV was observed.

There is no question that MCV is increased in some patients after heavy alcohol use. However, the use of this marker should be limited to a complementary role with other markers such as CDT, GGT, and 5HTOL/5HIAA ratio, because heavy or alcoholic drinking is required to increase MCV and the sensitivity and specificity of this test are not sufficient for it to be used alone. Also, there are interferences as noted above.

Combination of Tests

The combination of tests for the identification of consumption generally produce higher sensitivities but lower specificities (Stibler,

1991). However, Anton and Moak (1994) showed that the combination of CDT and GGT produced higher sensitivity without lowering specificity.

The ultimate combination of tests was studied by Eckhardt, Rawlings, Ryback, and others when they applied quadratic discriminate analysis to the results of common laboratory tests to distinguish between alcoholics and nondrinking controls (Eckardt et al., 1984, 1986, 1988; Rawlings et al., 1982; Ryback et al., 1980, 1982a,b, 1983). Their results were very impressive in that once the control and alcoholic groups had been characterized at a given laboratory the clinical sensitivity and specificity for identifying alcoholics approached 100%. However, the complexity of establishing local values and evaluating the results appear to have prevented this approach from taking hold on a widespread basis.

Conclusion: State Markers

A summary of the utility of the state markers is presented in Table 7. With the advent of sophisticated technologies, increasingly interested investigators, and targeted research funding, the advance in knowledge of biologic markers of alcohol and other substance abuse is rapidly advancing. However, despite a number of remarkable discoveries, the overall utility of these markers is still quite restrained. This has not dampened the enthusiasm of the search and, undoubtedly, as even more advanced molecular techniques and enlightened investigators are drawn to the area, major breakthroughs are likely.

FUTURE DIRECTIONS

The future of this area of research is in the development of tests with higher combined levels of sensitivity and specificity. At this time, there is not a biologic trait marker or combination of markers to identify clear genetic sensitivity to alcoholism or drug abuse. Therefore, continued research to identify trait markers is important.

Substantial effort and progress has been made in the search for key biologic markers that will make the trait-marker–addiction paradigm a clinically useful tool. Progress is now being made in designing and implementing research that will seek correlation of specific biologic markers with more homogeneous diagnostic groups. It is essential that trait markers correlated with alcohol dependence are clearly distinguished from markers that are correlated with other behavioral syndromes such as antisocial personality disorder. Furthermore, it is important to continually emphasize the need to develop a full understanding of how success in correlating biologic markers with socially undesirable behaviors such as excessive drinking will be used by society in terms of the potential for both prevention and discrimination.

Tests that measure the presence of drugs of abuse in the blood or urine are readily available and useful as state markers. These tests are very sensitive and specific and are only limited by the half-lives of the drug and its metabolites and the length of abstinence. Other biologic measurements as state markers are based on biochemical or physiologic se-

TABLE 7. *Evaluation of tests for consumption of ethanol*

Test	Level of drinking for positive test	$t_{(1/2)}$ after abstention	Availability	Cost	Sensitivity	Specificity
Direct ethanol measure	Low	3–4 hours	Clinical lab	Low	100%	100%
MCV	High	2–4 months	Clinical lab	Low	~35%	~50%
GGT	High	2–3 weeks	Clinical lab	Low	40–60%	50–70%
CDT	Moderate	2 weeks	Specialty lab	High	80–100%[a]	90–100%
5HTOL	Low	Hours	Research lab	High	Not determined	Not determined

[a]Males only—about half the sensitivity is achieved in females at similar specificity.

quelae of drug use. There are no state markers of this type for drugs other than ethanol. Due to the short half-life of ethanol, it has been necessary to search for natural analytes whose normal metabolism is altered with ethanol abuse. Although much effort has been expended, we still do not have a single test or combination of tests that can clearly identify ethanol abuse. Once again, more research is required to alleviate this problem.

Several points can be made to help direct future research efforts. Our search for biologic markers of addiction must result in tests that provide greater combined sensitivity and specificity so that accurate clinical decisions can be made. Optimally, both sensitivity and specificity for a truly useful test should exceed 90%. Another important issue relates to the reporting of sensitivities for newly developed tests in scientific journals. That is, specificity should be kept above 90% in research studies so that sensitivities can be compared across research studies. Also, future research studies should include the measurement of state markers over time as opposed to a single measurement. This will provide a more valid assessment of the marker. Finally, Allen et al. (1982) have suggested design features that should be included in all research studies. The inclusion of these features will allow a more valid comparison among studies.

Finally, a meeting jointly sponsored by the National Institute on Alcohol Abuse and Alcoholism (NIAAA) and Pharmacia was held in Columbus, Ohio in January 1996. A group of prominent senior scientists discussed and developed guidelines for research on biologic state markers for ethanol consumption. A summary of the proceedings and recommendations from this meeting is being prepared and a publication is anticipated in the near future.

SUMMARY

Trait Markers

- Multiple family studies, adoption studies, and twin studies support the concept of a genetic influence in the increased risk of the addictive use of alcohol.

- A biologic marker of a genetic trait for addiction should be expressed in the individual in a detectable fashion prior to exposure, during active addiction, and during sustained full remissions.

- The trait-marker–addiction paradigm is the basic concept driving the current research for biologic markers. The ultimate goal is to find markers that can be used in combination with clinical interventions to identify and prevent the onset, or reduce the severity, of addictive behavior.

- Most research in this area has focused on the addictive use of alcohol, but increasingly other addictive behaviors are being studied. In actuality, there may be significant applicability of the biologic markers reviewed here to familial patterns of addiction to drugs and for addictive behaviors other than alcoholism, but this has yet to be demonstrated.

State Markers

- Many accurate and sensitive tests are available for the measurement of drugs of abuse other than ethanol. The usefulness of these measurements depends on the half-lives of the parent drugs and their metabolites. Their usefulness for medical and forensic purposes is well documented.

- Mean corpuscular volume (MCV) and serum γ-glutamyltransferase (GGT) determinations are commonly used to monitor consumption of ethanol. However, other factors than ethanol consumption may affect the levels of these analytes, thereby reducing the sensitivity and specificity of these tests. The measurement of MCV and GGT will continue to be useful in combination with other tests.

- The measurement of carbohydrate deficient transferrin (CDT) in serum is the most promising test developed to date for monitoring consumption of ethanol. The presence of ethanol produces an increase in one of the isoforms of transferrin and the increase correlates with consumption. The half-life of CDT is about 14 to 17 days and CDT appears to be elevated with moderate drinking over 2 weeks.

- All of the tests reviewed here have varied usefulness in the early detection of drug abuse, in the detection of drug abuse in the workplace, and in monitoring use or consumption of drugs of abuse during recovery.

REFERENCES

Alexopoulos, G.S., Lieberman, K.W. and Frances, R.J. (1983) Platelet MAO activity in alcoholic patients and their first-degree relatives. *Am. J. Psychiatry* 140: 1501–1504.

Allen, J.P., Litten, R.Z. and Anton, R.F. (1992) Measures of alcohol consumption in perspective. In: Litten, R.Z. and Allen, J.P. (eds.) *Measuring alcohol consumption:* psychosocial and biochemical methods. Totowa, NJ: Humana Press, pp. 205–226.

Ambre, J. (1985) The urinary excretion of cocaine and metabolites in humans: a kinetic analysis of published data. *J. Anal. Toxicol.* 9: 241–245.

Ambre, J., Ruo, T.I., Nelson, J. and Belknap, S. (1988) Urinary excretion of cocaine, benzoylecgonine, and ecgonine methyl ester in humans. *J. Anal. Toxicol.* 12: 301–306.

Anthenelli, R.M. and Schuckit, M.A. (1990) Genetic studies of alcoholism. *Int. J. Addict.* 25: 81–94.

Anthenelli, R.M., Smith, T.L., Irwin, M.R. and Schuckit, M.A. (1994) A comparative study of criteria for subgrouping alcoholics: the primary/secondary diagnostic scheme versus variations of the type 1/type 2 criteria. *Am. J. Psychiatry* 151: 1468–1474.

Anton, R.F. and Bean, P. (1994) Two methods for measuring CDT in inpatient alcoholics and healthy controls compared. *Clin. Chem.* 40: 364–368.

Anton, R. and Moak, D.H. (1994) CDT and GGT as markers of heavy alcohol consumption: gender differences. *Alcoholism Clin. Exp. Res.* 18: 747–754.

Anton, R.F., Moak, D.H. and Latham, P.K. (1995) CAD as a marker for relapse drinking in a pharmacologic treatment study of alcohol dependence. *Alcoholism Clin. Exp. Res. Suppl* 19: 43A

Bailey, D.N., Shaw, R.F. and Cuba, J.J. (1978) Phencyclidine abuse: plasma levels and clinical findings in casual users and in phencyclidine-related deaths. *J. Anal. Toxicol.* 2: 233–237.

Baker, T.S., Harry, J.V., Russell, J.W. and Myers, R.L. (1984) Urinary excretion of heroin and its metabolites. *J. Anal. Toxicol.* 8: 255–259.

Baselt, R.C. (1983) Stability of cocaine in biological fluids. *J. Chromatogr.* 268: 502–505.

Bean, P. and Peter, J.B. (1993) A new approach to quantitate CDT isoforms in alcohol abusers: partial iron saturation in isoelectric focusing/immunoblotting and laser densitometry. *Alcoholism Clin. Exp. Res.* 17: 1163–1170.

Beckett, A.H. and Rowland, M. (1965) Urinary excretion kinetics of methamphetamine in man. *J. Pharm. Pharmacol.* 17: 109S–114S.

Begleiter, H., Porjesz, B., Bihari, B. and Kissin, B. (1984) Event-related brain potentials in boys at risk for alcoholism. *Science* 225: 1493–1496.

Begleiter, H., Porjesz, B. and Bihari, B. (1987) Auditory brainstem potentials in sons of alcoholic fathers. *Alcoholism Clin. Exp. Res.* 11: 477–480.

Bell, H., Tallaksen, C.M.E., Try, K. and Hayg, E. (1994) CDT and other markers of high alcohol consumption: a study of 502 patients admitted consecutively to a medical department. *Alcoholism Clin. Exp. Res.* 18: 1103–1108.

Benjamin, D., Grant, E.R. and Pohorecky, L.A. (1993) Naltrexone reverses ethanol-induced dopamine release in the nucleus accumbens in awake, freely moving rats. *Brain Res.* 621: 137–140.

Blum, K. and Noble, E.P. (1994): The sobering D2 story [letter]. *Science* 265: 1346–1347.

Blum, K., Nobel, E.P., Sheridan, P.J., Montgomery, A., Ritchie, T., Jagadeeswaran, P., Nogami, H., Briggs, A.H. and Cohn, J.B. (1990) Allelic association of human dopamine D2 receptor gene in alcoholism. *JAMA* 264: 3156–3160.

Bolos, A.M., Dean, M., Lucas-Derse, S., Ramsburg, M., Brown, G.L. and Goldman, D. (1990) Population and pedigree studies reveal a lack of association between the dopamine D2 receptor and alcoholics. *JAMA* 264: 3156–3160.

Bosron, W.F. and Li, T.K. (1986) Genetic polymorphism of human liver alcohol and aldehyde dehydrogenase and their relationship to alcohol metabolism and alcoholism. *Hepatology* 6: 502–510.

Budd, R.J., Mathis, D.F. and Leung, W.J. (1980) Screening and confirmation of opiates by thin layer chromatography. *Clin. Toxicol.* 16: 61–66.

Caldwell, J., Dring, L.G. and Williams, R.T. (1972) Metabolism of [14C]-methamphetamine in man, the guinea pig, and the rat. *Biochem. J.* 129: 11–22.

Carlsson, A.V., Hiltunen, A.J., Beck, O., Stibler, H. and Borg, S. (1993a) Detection of relapses in alcohol-dependent patients: comparison of carbohydrate-deficient transferrin in serum, 5-hydroxytryptophol in urine, and self-reports. *Alcoholism Clin. Exp. Res.* 17: 703–708.

Carlsson, A.V., Hiltunen, A.J., Beck, O., Stibler, H. and Borg, S. (1993b) Detection of relapses in alcohol-dependent patients: comparison of carbohydrate-deficient transferrin in serum, 5-hydroxytryptophol in urine, and self-reports. *Alcoholism Clin. Exp. Res.* 17: 703–708.

Chaput, J.C., Lecomte, M.V., Poynard, T., Buffet, C., Labayle, D. and Etienne, J.P. (1979) [Relationship between mean corpuscular volume, alcohol consumption, smoking habits, and alcoholic liver disease in hospitalized patients (author's transl)]. *Gastroenterol. Clin. Biol.* 3: 221–226.

Chick, J., Kreitman, N. and Plant, M. (1981) Mean cell volume and gamma-glutamyl-transpeptidase as markers of drinking in working men. *Lancet* 1: 1249–1251.

Cleeland, R., Christenson, J., Usategui-Gomez, M., Heveran, J., Davis, R. and Greenberg, E. (1976) Detection of drugs of abuse by radioimmunoassay: a summary of published data and some new information. *Clin. Chem.* 22: 712–730.

Cloninger, C.R. (1987) Neurogenetic adaptive mechanisms in alcoholism. *Science* 236: 410–416.

Cloninger, C.R., Bohman, M. and Sigvardsson, S. (1981) Inheritance of alcohol abuse: cross-fostering analysis of adopted men. *Arch. Gen. Psychiatry* 38: 861–868.

Cohen, H.L., Porjesz, B. and Begleiter, H. (1991) EEG characteristics in males at risk for alcoholism. *Alcoholism Clin. Exp. Res.* 15: 858–861.

Cohen, H.L., Porjesz, B. and Begleiter, H. (1993a) The effects of ethanol on EEG activity in males at risk for alcoholism. *Electroencephalogr. Clin. Neurophysiol.* 86: 368–376.

Cohen, H.L., Porjesz, B. and Begleiter, H. (1993b) Ethanol-induced alterations in electroencephalographic activity in adult males. *Neuropsychopharmacology* 8: 365–370.

Comings, D.E., Comings, B.G., Muhleman, D., Dietz, G., Shahbahrami, B., Tast, D., Knell, E., Kocsis, P., Baumgarten, R. and Kovacs, B.W. (1991) The dopamine D2 receptor locus as a modifying gene in neuropsychiatric disorders [see comments]. *JAMA* 266: 1793–1800.

Cone, E.J., Buchwald, W. and Yousefnejad, D. (1981) Simultaneous determination of phencyclidine and monohydroxylated metabolites in urine of man by gas chromatography-mass fragmentography with methane chemical ionization. *J. Chromatogr.* 223: 331–339.

Cook, C.E., Brine, D.R. and Jeffcoat, A.R. (1982) Phencyclidine disposition after intravenous and oral doses. *Clin. Pharmacol. Ther.* 31: 625–634.

Davis, V.E., Brown, H., Huff, J.A. and Cashaw, J.L. (1967) The alteration of serotonin metabolism to 5-hydroxytryptophol by ethanol ingestion in man. *J. Lab. Clin. Med.* 69: 132–140.

de Jong, G. and van Eijk, H.G. (1989) Functional properties of the carbohydrate moiety of human transferrin. *Int. J. Biochem.* 21: 253–263.

Dean, R.A., Christian, C.D., Sample, R.H.B. and Bosron, W. (1991) Human liver cocaine esterases: ethanol-mediated formation of ethylcocaine. *FASEB J.* 5: 2735–2739.

Devor, E.J., Cloninger, C.R., Hoffman, P.L. and Tabakoff, B. (1993) Association of monoamine oxidase (MAO) activity with alcoholism and alcoholic subtypes. *Am. J. Med. Genet.* 48: 209–213.

Diamond, I. and Gordon, A.S. (1994) The role of adenosine in mediating cellular and molecular responses to ethanol. *EXS* 71: 175–183.

Diamond, I., Wrubel, B., Estrin, W. and Gordon, A. (1987) Basal and adenosine receptor-stimulated levels of cAMP are reduced in lymphocytes from alcoholic patients. *Proc. Natl. Acad. Sci. USA* 84: 1413–1416.

Dring, L.G., Smith, R.L. and Williams, R.T. (1970) The metabolic fate of amphetamine in man and other species. *Biochem. J.* 116: 425–435.

Eckardt, M.J., Rawlings, R.R., Graubard, B.I., Faden, V., Martin, P.R. and Gottschalk, L.A. (1988) Neuropsychological performance and treatment outcome in male alcoholics. *Alcoholism Clin. Exp. Res.* 12: 88–93.

Eckardt, M.J., Rawlings, R.R. and Martin, P.R. (1986) Biological correlates and detection of alcohol abuse and alcoholism. Prog. *Neuropsychopharmacol. Biol. Psychiatry* 10: 135–144.

Eckardt, M.J., Rawlings, R.R., Ryback, R.S., Martin, P.R. and Gottschald, L.A. (1984) Effects of abstinence on the ability of clinical laboratory tests to identify male alcoholics. *Am. J. Clin. Pathol.* 82: 305–310.

Entwhistle, N., Owen, P., Patterson, D.A., Jones, L.V. and Smith, J.A. (1986) The occurrence of chordiazepoxide degradation products in sudden deaths associated with chordiazepoxide overdosage. *J. Forensic Sci. Soc.* 26: 45–54.

Eschwege, E., Papoz, L., Lellouch, J., Claude, J.R., Cubeau, J., Pequignot, G., Richard, J.L. and Schwartz, D. (1978) Blood cells and alcohol consumption with special reference to smoking habits. *J. Clin. Pathol.* 31: 654–658.

Evans, M.A. and Morarity, T. (1980) Analysis of cocaine and cocaine metabolites by high pressure liquid chromatography. *J. Anal. Toxicol.* 4: 19–22.

Faraj, B.A., Lenton, J.D. and Kutner, M. (1987) Prevalence of low monamine oxidase function in alcoholism. *Alcoholism Clin. Exp. Res.* 11: 464–467.

Felin, J. and Megges, G. (1985) Detection of O-6-monoacetylmorphine in urine samples by GC/MS as evidence for heroin us. *J. Anal. Toxicol.* 9: 134–138.

Finn, P.R. and Pihl, R.O. (1988) Risks for alcoholism: a comparison between two different groups of sons of alcoholics on cardiovascular reactivity and sensitivity to alcohol. *Alcoholism Clin. Exp. Res.* 12: 742–747.

Finn, P.R. and Pihl, R.O. (1990) Men at high risk for alcoholism: the effects of alcohol on cardiovascular response to unavoidable shock. *J. Abnormal Psychol.* 99: 79–85.

Finn, P.R., Zeitouni, N.C. and Pihl, R.O. (1990) Effects of alcohol on psychophysiological hyperactivity to nonaversive and aversive stimuli in men at high risk for alcoholism. *J. Abnormal Psychol.* 99: 79–85.

Fletcher, S.M. (1981) Urine screening for drugs by EMIT. *J. Forensic Sci. Soc.* 21: 327–332.

Fowles, D.C. (1983) Motivational effects of heart rate and electrodermal activity: implications for research on personality and psychopathology. *J. Res. Personality* 17: 48–71.

Francom, P., Lim, H.K., Andrenyak, D., Jones, R.T. and Foltz, R.L. (1988) Determination of LSD in urine by capillary gas chromatography and electron impact mass spectrometry. *J. Anal. Toxicol.* 12: 1–8.

Fritschi, G. and Prescott, W.R. (1985) Morphine levels in urine subsequent to poppy seed consumption. *Forensic Sci. Int.* 27: 111–117.

Garbutt, J.C., Hicks, R.E., Clayton, C.J., Andrews, R.T. and Mason, G.A. (1991) Behavioral and endocrine interactions between thyrotropin-releasing hormone and ethanol in normal human subjects. *Alcoholism Clin. Exp. Res.* 15: 1045–1049.

Garriott, J.C., Foerster, E., Juarez, L., Garza, F., Mendiola, I. and Curoe, J. (1981) Measurement of toluene in blood and breath in cases of solvent abuse. *Clin. Toxicol.* 18: 471–479.

Gelernter, J., Goldman, D. and Risch, N. (1993) The A1 allele at the D2 dopamine receptor gene and alcoholism. A reappraisal [see comments]. *JAMA* 269: 1673–1677.

Gianoulakis, C. and de Waele, J.P. (1994) Genetics of alcoholism: role of the endogenous opioid system. *Metab. Brain Dis.* 9: 105–131.

Giller, E. and Hall, E. (1983) Platelet MAO activity in recovering alcoholics after long-term abstinence. *Am. J. Psychiatry* 140: 114–115.

Goldman, D. (1993) The DRD2 dopamine receptor and the candidate gene approach in alcoholism. *Alcohol Alcoholism Suppl* 2: 27–29.

Gram, C. (1884) Untersuchungen uber die grosse der roten blutkorperchen im normalzustande und bei verschiedenen krankheiten. *Fortschr. Med.* 2: 33

Grant, B.F. and Harford, T.C. (1990) Concurrent and simultaneous use of alcohol and cocaine: results of national survey. *Drug Alcohol Depend.* 25: 97–104.

Harada, S., Agarwal, D.P., Goedde, H.W. and Ishikawa, B. (1983) Aldehyde dehydrogenase isozyme variation and alcoholism in Japan. *Pharmacol. Biochem. Behav.* 18: 151–153.

Harada, S., Agarwal, D.P., Goedde, H.W., Tagaki, S. and Ishikawa, B. (1982) Possible protective role against alcoholism for aldehyde dehydrogenase isozyme deficiency in Japan [letter]. *Lancet* 2: 827.

Harvey, S.C. (1985) Hypnotics and sedatives. In: Gilman, A.G., Goodman, L.S., Rall, T.W. and Murad, F. (eds.) *The pharmacological basis of therapeutic.* New York: Macmillan, pp. 339–371.

Hearn, W.L., Flynn, D.D., Hime, G.W., Rose, S., Confino, J.C., Mantero-Atienza, E., Wetli, C.W. and Mash, D.C. (1991a) Cocaethylene: a unique cocaine metabolite displays high affinity for the dopaine transporter. *J. Neurochem.* 56: 698–701.

Hearn, W.L., Rose, S., Wagner, J., Ciareglio, A. and Mash, D.C. (1991b) Cocaethylene is more potent than cocaine in mediating lethality. *Pharmacol. Biochem. Behav.* 39: 531–533.

Helander, A., Beck, O. and Borg, S. (1992) Determination of urinary 5-hydroxytryptophol by high-performance liquid chromatography with electrochemical detection. *J. Chromatogr.* 579: 340–345.

Helander, A., Beck, O. and Boysen, L. (1995a) 5-Hydroxytryptophol conjugation in man: influence of alcohol consumption and altered serotonin turnover. *Life Sci.* 56: 1529–1534.

Helander, A., Beck, O., Jacobsson, G., Lowenmo, C. and Wikstrom, T. (1993) Time course of ethanol-induced changes in serotonin metabolism. *Life Sci.* 53: 847–855.

Helander, A., Beck, O. and Jones, A.W. (1995b) Distinguishing ingested ethanol from microbial formation by analysis of urinary 5-hydroxytryptophol and 5-hydroxyindoleacetic acid. *J. Forensic Sci.* 40: 95–98.

Helper, B.R., Sutheimer, C., Sunshine, I. and Sebrosky, G.F. (1979) Combined enzyme immunoassay-LCED method for the identification, confirmation, and quantitation of opiates in biological fluids. *Clin. Toxicol.* 14: 161–168.

Herbert, V., Zalusky, R. and Davidson, C.S. (1963) Correlation of folate deficiency with alcoholism and associated macrocytosis, anemia, and liver disease. *Ann. Intern. Med.* 58: 977–988.

Hill, S.Y., Goodwin, D.W., Cadoret, R., Osterland, C.K. and Doner, S.M. (1980) Association and linkage between alcoholism and eleven serological markers. *J. Stud. Alcohol.* 36: 981–989.

Hoffman, P.L. and Tabakoff, B. (1990) Ethanol and guanine nucleotide binding proteins: a selective interaction. *FASEB J.* 4: 2612–2622.

Holden, C. (1994) A cautionary tale: the sobering story of D2. *Science* 264: 1696–1697.

Inturrisi, C.E., Max, M.B., Foley, K.M., Schutz, M., Shin, S.J.J. and Houde, R.W. (1984) The pharmacokinetics of heroin in patients with chronic pain. *N. Engl. J. Med.* 310: 1213–1217.

Jaffe, J.P. and Schilling, R.F. (1991) Erythrocyte folate levels: a clinical study. *Am. J. Hematol.* 36: 116–121.

Jatlow, P., Elsworth, J.D., Bradberry, C.W., Winger, G., Taylor, J.R., Russell, R. and Roth, R.H. (1991) Cocaethylene: a neuropharmacologically active metabolite associated with concurrent cocaine-ethanol ingestion. *Life Sci.* 48:1787–1794.

Javaid, J.I., Fischman, M.W., Schuster, C.R., Dekirmenjian, H. and Davis, J.M. (1978) Cocaine plasma concentrations. Relation to physiological and subjective effects in humans. *Science* 202: 227–228.

Javaid, J.I., Mahmous, N.M., Fischman, M.W., Schuster, C.R. and Davis, J.M. (1983) Kinetics of cocaine in humans after intravenous and intranasal administration. *Biopharm. Drug Dispos.* 4: 9–18.

Javors, M.A., Bowden, C.L. and Maas, J.W. (1984) MHPG, 5HIAA, and HVA in human CSF: storage and measurement by reversed-phase HPLC and coulometric detection using MHPLA as an internal standard. *J. Chromatogr.* 336: 259–269.

Jeffcoat, A.R., Perez-Reyes, M., Hill, J.M., Sadler, B.M. and Cook, C.E. (1989) Cocaine disposition in humans after intravenous injection, nasal insufflation (snorting), or smoking. *Drug Metab.* Dispos. 17: 153–159.

Johnson, J.R., Jennison, T.A., Peat, M.A. and Foltz, R.L. (1986) Stability of delta^9-tetrahydrocannabinol (THC), 11-hydroxy-THC, and 11-nor-9-carboxy-THC in blood and plasma. *J. Anal. Toxicol.* 8: 202–204.

Kanter, S.L. and Hollister, L.E. (1977) Marihuana metabolites in urine of man. *Res. Commun. Chem. Pathol. Pharmacol.* 17: 421–431.

Kapur, B., Wong, E., Carlen, P.L. and Fornazzari, L. (1986) Biochemical changes and pharmacokinetics of toluene in inhalant abusers. *Clin. Chem.* 32: –1055.

Klotz, U., Avant, G.R., Hoyumpa, A., Schenker, S. and Wilkinson, G.R. (1975) The effects of age and liver disease on the disposition and elimination of diazepam in adult man. *J. Clin. Invest.* 55: 347–359.

Kottgen, E., Reutter, W. and Gerok, W. (1976) Two different gamma-glutamyl-transferases during development of liver and small intestine: a fetal (sialo-) and an adult (asialo-) glycoprotein. *Biochem. Biophys. Res. Commun.* 72: 61–66.

Law, B., Mason, P.A., Moffat, A.C. and King, C.V. (1984) Confirmation of cannabis use by the analysis of delta-9-tetrahydrocannabinol metabolites in blood and urine by combined HPLC and RIA. *J. Anal. Toxicol.* 8: 19–21.

Lex, B.W., Lukas, S.E., Greenwald, N.E. and Mendelson, J.H. (1988) Alcohol-induced changes in body sway in women at risk for alcoholism: a pilot study. *J. Stud. Alcohol* 49: 346–350.

Lieber, C.S. and Rubin, E. (1968) Alcoholic fatty liver in man on a high protein and low fat diet. *Am. J. Med.* 44: 200–206.

Lilja, H., Jeppsson, J. and Kristensson, H. (1983) Evaluation of serum gamma-glutamyltransferase by electrofocusing, and variations in isoform patterns. *Clin. Chem.* 29: 1034–1037.

Lim, H.K., Andrenyak, D., Francom, P., Foltz, R.L. and Jones, R.T. (1988) Quantification of LSD and N-demethyl-LSD in urine by gas chromatography/resonance electron capture ionization spectrometry. *Anal. Chem.* 60: 1420–1425.

Lindenbaum, J. (1980) Folate and vitamin B-12 deficiencies in alcoholism. *Semin. Hematol.* 17: 119–129.

Linnoila, M., Virkkunen, M., George, T., Eckardt, M., Higley, J.D., Nielsen, D. and Goldman, D. (1994) Serotonin, violent behavior and alcohol. *EXS* 71: 155–163.

Linnoila, M., Virkkunen, M., Scheinin, M., Nuutila, A., Rimon, R. and Goodwin, F.K. (1983) Low cerebrospinal fluid 5-hydroxyindoleacetic acid concentration differentiates impulsive from nonimpulsive violent behavior. *Life Sci.* 33: 2609–2614.

Lof, K., Seppa, K., Itala, L., Koivula, T., Turpeinen, U. and Sillanaukee, P. (1994) Carbohydrate-deficient transferrin as an alcohol marker among female heavy drinkers: a population-based study. *Alcoholism Clin. Exp. Res.* 18: 889–894.

Lukas, S.E., Mendelson, J.H., Benedikt, R.A. and Jones, B. (1986) EEG alpha activity increases during transient episodes of ethanol-induced euphoria. *Pharmacol. Biochem. Behav.* 25: 889–895.

Lukas, S.E., Mendelson, J.H., Kouri, E., Bolduc, M. and Amass, L. (1990) Ethanol-induced alterations in EEG alpha activity and apparent source of the auditory P300 evoked response potential. *Alcohol* 7: 471–477.

Major, L.F., Goyer, P.F. and Murphy, D.L. (1981) Changes in platelet monamine oxidase activity during abstinence. *J. Stud. Alcohol* 42: 1052–1057.

Marz, L., Hatton, M., Berry, L. and Regoeczi, E. (1982) The structural heterogeneity of the carbohydrate moiety of desialylated human transferrin. *Can. J. Biochem.* 60: 624–630.

Masoud, A.N. and Krupski, D.M. (1980) High-performance liquid chromatographic analysis of cocaine in human plasma. *J. Anal. Toxicol.* 4: 305–310.

McCarron, M.M., Walberg, C.B. and Baselt, R.C. (1990) Confirmation of LSD intoxication by analysis of serum and urine. *J. Anal. Toxicol.* 14: –165.

Mehlman, P.T., Higley, J.D., Faucher, I., Lilly, A.A., Taub, D.M., Vickers, J., Suomi, S.J. and Linnoila, M. (1994) Low CSF 5-HIAA concentrations and severe aggression and impaired impulse control in nonhuman primates. *Am. J. Psychiatry* 151: 1485–1491.

Meltzer, H.Y. and Arora, R.C. (1988) Genetic control of serotonin uptake in blood platelets: a twin study. *Psych. Res.* 24: 263–270.

Mihas, A.A. and Tavassoli, M. (1992) Laboratory markers of ethanol intake and abuse: a critical appraisal. *Am. J. Med. Sci.* 303: 415–428.

Misra, A.L., Pontani, R.B. and Bartolemo, J. (1979) Persistence of phencyclidine (PCP) and metabolites in brain and adipose tissue and implications for long-lasting behavioral effects. *Res. Commun. Chem. Pathol. Pharmacol.* 24: 431–445.

Morland, J., Bugge, A., Skuterud, B., Steen, A., Wethe, G.H. and Kjeldsen, T. (1985) Cannabinoids in blood and urine after passive inhalation of Cannabis smoke. *J. Forensic Sci.* 30: 997–1002.

Moussavian, S.N., Becker, R.C., Piepmeyer, J.L., Mezey, E. and Bozian, R.C. (1985) Serum gamma-glutamyl transpeptidase and chronic alcoholism. *Dig. Dis. Sci.* 30: 211–214.

Murphy, J.M., McBride, W.J., Lumeng, L. and Li, T.K. (1982) Regional brain levels of monoamines in alcohol preferring and non-preferring lines of rats. *Pharmacol. Biochem. Behav.* 16: 145–149.

Nagy, L.E., Diamond, I. and Gordon, A. (1988) Cultured lymphocytes from alcoholic subjects have altered cAMP signal transduction. *Proc. Natl. Acad. Sci. USA* 85: 6973–6976.

Nelson, C.C. and Foltz, R.L. (1992a) Determination of lysergic acid diethylamide (LSD), iso-LSD, and N-demethyl-LSD in body fluids by gas chromatography/tandem mass spectroscopy. *Anal. Chem.* 64: 1578–1585.

Nelson, C.C. and Foltz, R.L. (1992b) Chromatographic and mass spectrometric methods for determination of lysergic acid diethylamide (LSD) and metabolites in body fluids. *J. Chromatogr.* 580: 97–109.

Nishimura, M. and Teschke, R. (1983) Alcohol and gamma-glutamyltransferase. *Klin. Wochenschr.* 61: 265–275.

Noble, E.P. and Blum, K. (1993) Alcoholism and the D2 dopamine receptor gene [letter; comment]. *JAMA* 270: 1547–1548.

Noble, E.P., Blum, K., Khalsa, M.E., Ritchie, T., Montgomery, A., Wood, R.C., Fitch, R.J., Ozkaragoz, T., Sheridan, P.J. and Anglin, M.D. (1993) Allelic association of the D2 dopamine receptor gene with cocaine dependence [published erratum appears in Drug Alcohol Depend. 1993;34(1):83–84]. *Drug Alcohol Depend.* 33: 271–285.

Noble, E.P., Blum, K., Ritchie, T., Montgomery, A. and Sheridan, P.J. (1991) Allelic association of the D2 dopamine receptor gene with receptor-binding characteristics in alcoholism. *Arch. Gen. Psychiatry* 48: 648–654.

Novoradovsky, A., Tsai, S.L., Goldfarb, L., Peterson, R., Long, J.C. and Goldman, D. (1995) Mitochondrial aldehyde dehydrogenase polymorphism in Asian and American Indian populations: detection of new ALDH2 alleles. *Alcoholism Clin. Exp. Res.* 19: 1105–1110.

Ogata, M., Tomokuni, K. and Takatsuka, Y. (1969) Quantitative determination in urine of hippuric acid and m- or p-methylhippuric acid, metabolites of toluene, and m- or p-xylene. *Br. J. Indust. Med.* 26: 330–334.

O'Malley, S.S., Jaffe, A.J., Chang, G., Schottenfeld, R.S., Meyer, R.E. and Rounsaville, B. (1992) Naltrexone and coping skills therapy for alcohol dependence. *Arch. Gen. Psychiatry* 49: 881–887.

O'Neill, B., Williams, A.F. and Dubowski, K.M. (1983) Variability in blood alcohol concentrations: implications for estimating individual results. *J. Stud. Alcohol* 44: 222–230.

Owens, S.M., Woodworth, J. and Mayersohn, M. (1982) Radioimmunoassay for phencyclidine (PCP) in serum. *Clin. Chem.* 28: 1509–1513.

Pagnotto, L.D. and Lieberman, L.M. (1967) Urinary hippuric acid excretion as an index of toluene exposure. *Am. Indust. Hyg. Assoc. J.* 28: 129–134.

Panday, G.N., Fawcett, J., Gibbons, R., Clark, D.C. and Davis, J.M. (1988) Platelet monoamine oxidase in alcoholics. *Biol. Psychiatry* 24: 15–24.

Paul, B.D., Mell, J.L.D., Mitchell, J.M., Irving, J. and Novak, A.J. (1985) Simultaneous identification and quantitation of codeine and morphine in urine by gas chromatography and mass spectroscopy. *J. Anal. Toxicol.* 9: 222–226.

Paul, B.D., Mitchell, J.M., Burbage, R., Moy, M. and Sroka, M. (1990) Gas chromatographic-electron-impact mass fragmentometric determination of lysergic acid diethylamide in urine. *J. Chromatogr.* 529: 103–112.

Posey, B.L. and Kimble, S.N. (1984) High performance liquid chromatographic study of codeine, norcodeine, and morphine as indicator of codeine ingestion. *J. Anal. Toxicol.* 8: 68–73.

Propping, P. (1977) Genetic control of ethanol action on the central nervous system. An EEG study in twins. *Hum. Genet.* 35: 309–334.

Rausch, J.L., Monteiro, M.G. and Schuckit, M.A. (1991) Platelet serotonin uptake in men with family history of alcoholism. *Neuropsychopharmacology* 4: 83–86.

Rawlings, R.R., Rae, E.S., Graubard, B.I., Eckardt, M.J. and Ryback, R.S. (1982) A methodology for construction of a multivariate diagnostic instrument: an application to alcohol abuse screening. *Comput. Biomed. Res.* 15: 228–239.

Reich, T. (1988) Biologic marker studies in alcoholism. *N. Engl. J. Med.* 318: 180–182.

Rollason, J.G., Pincherle, D. and Robinson, D. (1972) Serum gamma-glutamyl transpeptidase in relation to alcohol consumption. *Clin. Chim. Acta* 39: 75–80.

Rosalki, S.B. (1975) Gamma-glutamyl transpeptidase. *Adv. Clin. Chem.* 17: 53–107.

Rosalki, S.B. and Rau, D. (1972) Serum gamma-glutamyl transpeptidase activity in alcoholism. *Clin. Chim. Acta* 39: 41–47.

Rosman, A.S., Basu, P., Galvin, K. and Lieber, C.S. (1995) Utility of CDT as a marker of relapse in alcoholic patients. *Alcoholism Clin. Exp. Res.* 19: 611–616.

Rowland, M. (1969) Amphetamine blood and urine levels in man. *J. Pharm. Sci.* 58: 508–509.

Ryback, R.S., Eckardt, M.J., Felsher, B. and Rawlings, R.R. (1982a) Biochemical and hematological correlates of alcoholism and liver disease. *JAMA* 248: 2261–2265.

Ryback, R.S., Eckardt, M.J., Negron, G.L. and Rawlings, R.R. (1983) The search for a biochemical marker in alcoholism. Substance *Alcohol Actions/Misuse* 4: 217–224.

Ryback, R.S., Eckardt, M.J. and Pautler, C.P. (1980) Biochemical and hematological correlates of alcoholism. *Res. Commun. Chem. Pathol. Pharmacol.* 27: 533–550.

Ryback, R.S., Eckardt, M.J., Rawlings, R.R. and Rosenthal, L.S. (1982b) Quadratic discriminant analysis as an aid to interpretive reporting of clinical laboratory tests. *JAMA* 248: 2342–2345.

Salmela, K.S., Laitinen, K., Nystrom, M. and Salaspuro, M. (1994) Carbohydrate-deficient transferrin during 3 weeks' heavy alcohol consumption. *Alcoholism Clin. Exp. Res.* 18: 228–230.

Sarve, J., Dahlstrom, B., Paalzow, L. and Rane, A. (1981) Pharmacokinetics of morphine in cancer patients. *Clin. Pharmacol. Ther.* 30: 629–635.

Schandler, S.L., Cohen, M.J. and McArthur, D.L. (1988) Event-related brain potentials in intoxicated and detoxified alcoholics during visuospatial learning. *Psychopharmacology* (*Berl*) 94: 275–283.

Schuckit, M.A. (1980) Self-rating alcohol intoxication by young men with and without family histories of alcoholism. *J. Stud. Alcohol* 41: 242–249.

Schuckit, M.A. (1981) Peak blood alcohol levels in men at high risk for the future development of alcoholism. *Alcoholism Clin. Exp. Res.* 5: 64–66.

Schuckit, M.A. (1984a) Subjective response to alcohol in sons of alcoholics and controls. *Arch. Gen. Psychiatry* 41: 879–884.

Schuckit, M.A. (1984b) Differences in plasma cortisol after ethanol in relatives of alcoholics and controls. *J. Clin. Psychiatry* 45: 374–379.

Schuckit, M.A. (1985) Ethanol-induced changes in body sway in men at high alcoholism risk. *Arch. Gen. Psychiatry* 42: 375–379.

Schuckit, M.A. (1986) Genetic aspects of alcoholism. *Ann. Emerg. Med.* 15: 991–996.

Schuckit, M.A. (1987) Biological vunerability to alcoholism. *J. Consult. Clin. Psychol.* 55: 301–309.

Schuckit, M.A. (1988) Reactions to alcohol in sons of alcoholics and controls. *Alcoholism Clin. Exp. Res.* 12:465–470.

Schuckit, M.A. (1994a) A clinical model of genetic influences in alcohol dependence. *J. Stud. Alcohol* 55: 5–17.

Schuckit, M.A. (1994b) Low level of response to alcohol as a predictor of future alcoholism. *Am. J. Psychiatry* 151: 184–189.

Schuckit, M.A., Butters, N., Lyn, L. and Irwin, M. (1987) Neuropsychologic deficits and the risk for alcoholism. *Neuropsychopharmacology* 1: 45–53.

Schuckit, M.A. and Gold, E. (1988) A simultaneous evaluation of multiple markers of ethanol/placebo challenges in sons of alcoholics and control. *Arch. Gen. Psychiatry* 45: 211–216.

Schuckit, M.A., Risch, S.C. and Gold, E.R. (1988) Alcohol consumption, ACTH level, and family history of alcoholism. *Am. J. Psychiatry* 145: 1391–1395.

Sherman, D.I., Ward, R.J., Yoshida, A. and Peters, T.J. (1994) Alcohol and acetaldehyde dehydrogenase gene polymorphism and alcoholism. *EXS* 71: 175–183.

Simonsson, P., Berglund, M., Oreland, L., Moberg, A.L. and Alling, C. (1992) Serotonin-stimulated phosphoinositide hydrolysis in platelets from post-withdrawal alcoholics. *Alcohol Alcoholism* 27: 607–612.

Smith, S.S., Gorelick, D.A., O'Hara, B.F. and Uhl, G.R. (1991) The dopamine D2 receptor gene and alcoholism. *JAMA* 265: 2667–2668.

Stanski, D.R., Greenblatt, D.J. and Lowenstein, E.D. (1978) Kinetics of intravenous and intramuscular morphine. *Clin. Pharmacol. Ther.* 24: 52–59.

Stewart, D.J., Inaba, T., Lucassen, M. and Kalow, W. (1979) Cocaine metabolism: Cocaine and norcocaine hydrolysis by liver and serum esterase. *Clin. Pharmacol. Ther.* 25: 464–468.

Stibler, H. (1978) The normal cerebrospinal fluid proteins identified by means of thin-layer isoelectric focusing and crossed immunelectrophoresis. *J. Neurol. Sci.* 36: 273–288.

Stibler, H. (1991) Carbohydrate-deficient transferrin in serum: a new marker of potentially harmful alcohol consumption reviewed. *Clin. Chem.* 37: 2029–2037.

Stibler, H., Allgulander, C., Borg, S. and Kjellin, K.G. (1978) Abnormal microheterogeneity of transferrin in serum and cerebrospinal fluid in alcoholism. *Acta Med. Scand.* 204: 49–56.

Stibler, H. and Borg, S. (1981) Evidence of a reduced sialic acid content in serum transferrin in male alcoholics. *Alcoholism Clin. Exp. Res.* 5: 545–549.

Stibler, H. and Borg, S. (1986) Carbohydrate composition of serum transferrin in alcoholic patients. *Alcoholism Clin. Exp. Res.* 10: 61–64.

Stibler, H., Borg, S. and Joustra, M. (1986) Micro anion exchange chromatography of carbohydrate-deficient transferrin in serum in relation to alcohol consumption (Swedish Patent 8400587-5). *Alcoholism Clin. Exp. Res.* 10: 535–544.

Stibler, H., Borg, S. and Joustra, M. (1991a) A modified method for the assay of CDT in serum. *Alcohol Alcoholism* 451–454.

Stibler, H., Jaeken, J. and Kristiansson, B. (1991b) Biochemical characteristics and diagnosis of the carbohydrate-deficient glycoprotein syndrome. *Acta Paediatr. Scand.* 375: 22–31.

Sutheimer, C.A., Yarborough, R., Helper, B.R. and Sunshine, I. (1985) Detection and confirmation of urinary cannabinoids. *J. Anal. Toxicol.* 9: 156–160.

Suwaki, J. and Ohara, H. (1985) Alcohol-induced facial flushing and drinking behavior in Japanese men. *J. Stud. Alcohol* 46: 196–198.

Tabakoff, B. and Hoffman, P.L. (1988) Genetics and biological markers of risk for alcoholism. *Public Health Rep.* 103: 690–698.

Tabakoff, B., Hoffman, P.L., Lee, J.M., Saito, T., Willard, B. and De Leon-Jones, F. (1988) Differences in platelet enzyme activity between alcoholics and nonalcoholics. *N. Engl. J. Med.* 318: 134–139.

Tabakoff, B., Lee, J.M., De Leon-Jones, F. and Hoffman, P.L. (1985) Ethanol inhibits the activity of the B form of monoamine oxidase in human platelet and brain tissue. *Psychopharmacology* (*Berl*) 87: 152–156.

Takeshita, T., Morimoto, K., Mao, X., Hashimoto, T. and Furuyama, J. (1994) Characterization of the three genotypes of low Km aldehyde dehydrogenase in a Japanese population. *Hum. Genet.* 94: 217–223.

Tang, B.K., Inaba, T. and Kalow, W. (1975) N-hydroxyamobarbital: The second major metabolite of amobarbital in man. *Drug Metab. Dispos.* 3: 479–486.

Tang, B.K., Inaba, T. and Kalow, W. (1977) N-hydroxylation of pentobarbital in man. *Drug Metab. Dispos.* 5: 71–74.

Tang, B.K., Kalow, W. and Grey, A.A. (1979) Metabolic fate of phenobarbital in man. *Drug Metab. Dispos.* 7: 315–318.

Thomasson, H.R., Crabb, D.W., Edenburg, H.J. and Ting-Kai, L. (1993) Alcohol and aldehyde dehydrogenase polymorphisms and alcoholism. *Behav. Genet.* 23: 131–136.

Thomasson, H.R., Li, T.K. and Crabb, D.W. (1990) Correlations between alcohol-induced flushing, genotypes for alcohol dehydrogenase and aldehyde dehydrogenase activities: implication in alcohol cirrhosis in white patients. *Hepatology* 15: 1017–1022.

Thompson, W.C. and Dasgupta, A. (1995) Confirmatory and quantitation of cocaine, benzoylecgonine, ecgonine methyl ester, and cocaethylene by gas chromatography/mass spectroscopy: use of microwave irradiation for rapid preparation of trimethylsilyl and t-butyldimethylsilyl derivatives. *Am. J. Clin. Pathol.* 104: 187–192.

Tobel, H. (1988) Beta-endorphin genetics in the etiology of alcoholism. *Alcohol* 5: 159–165.

Tollefson, G.D. (1989) Serotonin and alcohol: interrelationships. *Psychopathology* 22: 37–48.

Tomokuni, K. and Ogata, M. (1972) Direct colorimetric determination of hippuric acid in urine. *Clin. Chem.* 18: 349–351.

Udenfriend, S., Titus, E. and Weissbach, H. (1955) The identification of 5HIAA in normal urine and a method for its assay. *J. Biol. Chem.* 216: 499–505.

Virkkunen, M., Goldman, D., Nielsen, D.A. and Linnoila, M. (1995) Low brain serotonin turnover rate (low CSF 5-HIAA) and impulsive violence. *J. Psych. Neurosci.* 20: 271–275.

Virkkunen, M. and Linnoila, M. (1993) Brain serotonin, type II alcoholism and impulsive violence. *J. Stud. Alcohol Suppl.* 11: 163–169.

Volpecelli, J.R., Alterman, A.I., Hayashida, M. and O'Brien (1992) Naltrexone in the treatment of alcohol dependence. *Arch. Gen. Psychiatry* 49: 876–880.

Volpi, R., Chiodera, P., Gramellini, D., Cigarini, C., Papadia, C., Caffarri, G., Rossi, G. and Coiro, V. (1994) Endogenous opioid mediation of the inhibitory effect of ethanol on the prolactin response to breast stimulation in normal women. *Life Sci.* 54: 739–744.

Voltaire, A., Beck, O. and Borg, S. (1992) Urinary 5-hydroxytryptophol: a possible marker of recent alcohol consumption. *Alcoholism Clin. Exp. Res.* 16: 281–285.

von Knorring, A.L., Bohman, M., von Knorring, L. and Oreland, L. (1985) Platelet MAO activity as a biological marker in subgroups of alcoholism. *Acta Psychiatr. Scand.* 72: 51–58.

Wall, M.E. and Perez-Reyes, M. (1981) The metabolism of delta-9-tetrahydrocannabinol and related cannabinoids in man. *J. Clin. Pharmacol.* 21: 178S–189S.

Wall, M.E., Sadler, B.M., Brine, D., Taylor, H. and Perez-Reyes, M. (1983) Metabolism, disposition, and kinetics of delta-9-tetrahydrocannabinol in men and women. *Clin. Pharmacol. Ther.* 34: 352–363.

Wan, S.H., Matin, S.B. and Azarnoff, D.L. (1978) Kinetics, salivary excretion of amphetamine isomers, and effect of urinary pH. *Clin. Pharmacol. Ther.* 23: 585–590.

Watson, R.R., Mohs, M.E., Eskelson, C., Sampliner, R.E. and Hartmann, B. (1986) Identification of alcohol abuse and alcoholism with biological parameters. *Alcoholism Clin. Exp. Res.* 10: 364–385.

Whelan, G. (1992) Biological markers of alcoholism. *Aust. N.Z. J. Med.* 22: 209–213.

Wiberg, A., Gottfries, C.G. and Oreland, L. (1977) Low platelet monoamine oxidase activity in human alcoholics. *Med. Biol.* 55: 181–186.

Wilkinson, P., Van Dyke, C., Jatlow, P., Barash, P. and Byck, R. (1980) Intranasal and oral cocaine kinetics. *Clin. Pharmacol. Ther.* 27: 386–394.

Wise, R.A. and Bozarth, M.A. (1987) A psychomotor stimulant theory of addiction. *Psychol. Rev.* 94: 469–492.

Wong, L.K. and Biemann, K. (1976) Metabolites of phencyclidine. *Clin. Toxicol.* 9: 583–591.

Worwood, M. (1989) An overview of iron metabolism at a molecular level. *J. Intern. Med.* 226: 381–391.

Wu, A., Chanarin, I., Slavin, G. and Levi, A.J. (1975) Folate deficiency in the alcoholic—its relationship to clinical and haematological abnormalities, liver disease, and folate stores. *Br. J. Haematol.* 29: 469–478.

Xin, Y., Lasker, J.M., Rosman, A.S. and Lieber, C.S. (1991) Isoelectric focusing/western blotting: a novel and practical method for quantitation of carbohydrate-deficient transferrin in alcoholics. *Alcoholism Clin. Exp. Res.* 15: 814–821.

Xin, Y., Rosman, A.S., Lasker, J.M. and Lieber, C.S. (1992) Measurement of carbohydrate-deficient transferrin by isoelectric focusing/Western blotting and by micro anion-exchange chromatography/radioimmunoassay: comparison of diagnostic accuracy. *Alcohol Alcoholism* 27: 425–433.

Yeh, S.Y., Gorodetzky, C.W. and McQuinn, R.L. (1976) Urinary excretion of heroin and its metabolites. *J. Pharmacol. Exp. Ther.* 196: 249–256.

Yoshimoto, K., Komura, S. and Kawamura, K. (1992) Occurrence in vivo of 5-hydroxytryptophol in the brain of rats treated with ethanol. *Alcohol Alcoholism* 27: 131–136.

Drug Addiction and its Treatment: Nexus of Neuroscience and Behavior, edited by Bankole A. Johnson and John D. Roache. Lippincott–Raven Publishers, Philadelphia, © 1997.

10

Neurobehavioral Abnormalities Following Exposure to Drugs of Abuse During Development

Linda Patia Spear

Department of Psychology and Center for Developmental Psychobiology, Binghamton University, SUNY, Binghamton, New York 13902-6000

Drugs of abuse are used by a broad variety of individuals, including women who are pregnant. The vast majority of drugs cross the placenta and reach fetal tissue including brain (Spear et al., 1989a); thus, the fetuses of these women are also exposed to these drugs, albeit without a choice. Substantial interest has centered around determining the potential impact of such drug exposure early in life on later neurobehavioral functioning in the offspring. This chapter examines findings from animal models of such early exposure to drugs of abuse. Given that evolution of research in this field has endured a number of controversies regarding methodologic and control issues, consideration of these factors will be included as a background for the review of the animal literature in this field. It is important to first consider whether animal models are indeed of value in the field of developmental toxicology.

VALUE AND IMPORTANCE OF ANIMAL MODELS

The conduct of well-controlled clinical studies is an exceedingly difficult task. Among the more difficult challenges are the accurate detection of maternal use, and inclusion of an appropriate comparison group or other controls for confounding variables (for further discussion see Jacobson and Jacobson, 1990; Spear, 1994a). It is often difficult to derive an appropriate comparison group, as pregnant women who use drugs may differ on a number of fundamental dimensions and other risk factors from women of similar race and social class who are not drug users. These women rarely use but a single drug, thus making it difficult to ascribe adverse effects to a given drug. Statistical procedures designed to control for such potentially confounding variables require large sample sizes that are often impractical for clinical studies.

These and other difficulties associated with the conduct of interpretable clinical studies typically are not an issue when conducting research with laboratory animals. To the extent that animal models provide data relevant to humans, findings in animal studies can be used to confirm and extend clinical findings, and anticipate other potential consequences of early drug exposure. Importantly, the results of animal studies can offer insights into the mechanisms underlying observed behavioral effects as well as suggesting potential therapeutic approaches.

There is some evidence that animal models do provide clinically relevant data. In 1989 a workshop was held on *Qualitative and Quantitative Comparability of Human and Animal Developmental Neurotoxicity*, which was cosponsored by the Environmental Protection Agency and the National Institute on Drug Abuse (Kimmel et al., 1990). Data from humans, rodents, and nonhuman primates (when data were available) were compared regarding neurobehavioral consequences of exposure to toxicants early in life, using a list of toxicants for which there was a sufficiently large database in both human and animal studies to allow for cross-species comparisons. Toxicants subject to these cross-species comparisons included ethanol, the anticonvulsant phenytoin, and a number of environmental toxins such as methylmercury, lead, polychlorinated biphenyls, and ionizing radiation. Offspring outcomes were assessed across species within five categories of functional effects: sensory, motivation/arousal, cognitive, motor, and social. However, the specific tests used often varied markedly across species; for example, intelligence quotient (IQ) or language tests were typically used to assess cognitive function in humans, while classical or operant conditioning tasks were used to assess learning and retention in rodents. Examination of the cross-species similarity of findings with this large database revealed a remarkable degree of comparability. As stated in a summary report (Stanton and Spear, 1990, p. 265):

> At the level of functional category, close agreement was found across species for all the neurotoxic agents reviewed at this workshop. If a particular agent produced, for example, cognitive or motor deficits in humans, corresponding deficits were also evident in laboratory animals. This was true even when the specific endpoints used to assess these functions were often operationally quite different across species.

METHODOLOGIC CONSIDERATIONS

Many of the methodologic problems that complicate clinical studies of the developmental toxicology of abused drugs are not of concern in animal studies. Nevertheless, use of animal models mandates consideration of several critical methodologic issues, the more important of which are listed in Table 1. When

discussing these concerns, it should be recognized that there is no universal design that is appropriate for all animal research in neurobehavioral teratology. Careful consideration of both the compound under investigation as well as the questions to be addressed in the proposed work are necessary to determine to what extent particular methodologic concerns and controls are necessary for a given project. Unfortunately, a significant amount of the research examining the developmental toxicology of abused compounds has not considered certain of these methodologic and control issues. In large part, this may be because a significant portion of this research was conducted early in the evolution of research in developmental toxicology, prior to the resolution of many of these issues. Such methodologic shortcomings limit the nature and strength of the conclusions that can be drawn from this work. To provide a background for the subsequent review of research regarding the developmental toxicology of drugs of abuse, these methodologic issues in developmental toxicology will be reviewed first.

Choice of Animal Model

A variety of animal models of gestational drug exposure have been developed. The vast majority of the work to date has been conducted in mice and rats because of relatively low purchase and maintenance costs and the substantial available database with these species. Other animal models have been used occasionally. These include rabbits, chicks,

TABLE 1. *Critical methodological issues in animal studies of developmental toxicology*

Choice of animal model
Drug administration methods: route, dose, frequency, timing
Sampling issues: use of litter as unit of analysis; sample size determinations
Control of drug-induced nutritional insufficiencies: pair-feeding
Control of potential treatment-induced alterations in subsequent maternal behavior: surrogate fostering
Choice of dependent measures

sheep, and nonhuman primates. Certain animal models have particular advantages; for instance, use of the pregnant ewe has proved especially valuable in assessing the acute hemodynamic and cardiovascular effects of drugs on the fetus and pregnant female (Plessinger and Woods, 1991).

When conducting research with rodents, it is important to recognize that most rodents are born at a less mature stage than humans. With altricial rodents, drug exposure during the prenatal period typically models the first and second trimesters of human exposure. To model third trimester exposure, it is necessary for the drug to be administered during the early postnatal period (i.e., during the first 10 days postnatally in the rat) (Pierce and West, 1986).

While the vast majority of the animal models in behavioral teratology to date have focused on modeling maternal drug exposure, there is evidence that paternal exposure to a variety of different drugs such as ethanol (Abel, 1992) and cannabinoids (Dalterio et al., 1984) can also induce neurobehavioral teratogenicity. This chapter focuses on the consequences of maternal exposure, although it is recognized that investigation of male-mediated teratogenesis is an important area for further inquiry (Colie, 1993; Davis et al., 1992).

Administration Issues

Route of Administration

A fundamental decision for research in neurobehavioral teratology is what route of administration to use. Under ideal circumstances, the same route of exposure that is associated with human use/exposure should be used in animal work. However, this is not always possible. For instance, while free-base (crack) cocaine is smoked by humans, a procedure for administering cocaine free base to rats via inhalation has only recently been developed (Boni et al., 1991), and even this procedure does not appear to support sufficiently high maternal cocaine levels for use in devel-

opmental toxicology. Most typically, drugs are administered prenatally using intragastric, subcutaneous, and (more rarely) intravenous routes, and are sometimes placed in a liquid diet (particularly common in work conducted with prenatal ethanol exposure). Each of these routes has its strengths and weaknesses. For instance, absorption rates are typically quite variable for drugs administered orally; subcutaneous administration of numerous psychoactive drugs can produce skin necrosis; and intravenous routes typically produce very rapid rises and falls in drug levels. Although the intraperitoneal route is frequently used for drug administration in adulthood, in pregnant animals it is of questionable appropriateness as this route can produce fetal drug concentrations that are three or more times greater than those of the maternal circulation (DeVane et al., 1989), a clearly abnormal distribution pattern.

Dose

Dose considerations are also critical. In prenatal drug studies, the use of high doses that are toxic to the dams raises the possibility that neurotoxic effects observed in offspring may be merely an artifact of maternal toxicity. Hence, it has been recommended that the high dose used in dose-response analysis should be at or slightly below the threshold for the production of minimal maternal toxicity (Stanton and Spear, 1990).

In terms of cross-species comparisons, there is little evidence for comparability of effective administered doses across species. As can be seen in Table 2, typically much larger doses have to be administered to rodents to produce effects comparable to those observed in humans (Rees et al., 1990). However, as shown in Table 3, when dose equivalences are based on internal indices of drug levels reached in the organism, much closer cross-species comparability is evident (Rees et al., 1990). That is, due to species differences in pharmacokinetics, substantially larger administered doses are typically required in rodents

TABLE 2. Quantitative comparison of human and rodent data based on administered dose[a]

Agent	Administered dose	
	Human	Rodent
Phenytoin	Effective daily dose level	
	6–12 mg/kg	50–200 mg/kg
Methylmercury	Approximate LOAEL[b]	
	1–1.5 µg/kg/day	2.5 mg/kg/day
Polychlorinated biphenyls (PCBs)	Approximate NOAEL[c]	
	2.7×10^{-5} mg/kg/day	2×10^{-1} mg/kg/day

[a]Table derived from Rees et al. (1990).
[b]Lowest-observed adverse-effect level (lowest dose that produces an observable adverse effect).
[c]No observed adverse-effect level (highest dose shown to have no observable adverse effect).

to match blood levels produced by a given drug dose in humans (Rees et al., 1990). Thus, when determining relevant doses to be used in animal studies in developmental toxicology, it is important to consider comparability of internal dose levels rather than the administered doses themselves.

Frequency of Dosing

Frequency of drug administration is another factor of importance. For some drugs, the degree of teratogenicity is correlated with the peak concentrations of the drug reached, whereas for other drugs it is the area under the concentration-time curve (AUC) that correlates with the teratogenic response (Nau, 1986). For example, with alcohol exposure during the third trimester equivalent, central

nervous system (CNS) effects are more pronounced when the daily dose of alcohol is concentrated into a few exposure periods than when that same daily dose is distributed throughout the day (Pierce and West, 1986).

It is important to consider whether the chosen route and dosing parameters support a pattern of drug exposure consonant with that of human exposure. For instance, continuous drug exposure via minipumps may be appropriate for studies of substances where human use patterns typically result in fairly constant exposure to the drug, as with methadone in maintenance programs. In instances where exposure in humans is episodic, the use of minipumps in animal experimentation is of more questionable appropriateness. This issue may be particularly important when working with substances such as stimulants that may induce substantially different physiologic

TABLE 3. Quantitative comparison of human and rodent data based on internal dose[a]

Agent	Internal dose	
	Human	Rodent
	Measured blood levels	
Phenytoin	8–25 µg/ml	13–23 µg/ml
Lead	10–15 µg/dl	<20 µg/dl
	Estimated absorbed dose	
Ionizing radiation	0.1–1.0 Gy	0.1–1.0 Gy
	Estimated brain dose	
Methylmercury	0.3–1.0 ppm	≤2 ppm

[a]Table derived from Rees et al. (1990).

compensations (i.e., sensitization vs. tolerance) depending on whether drug exposure is episodic or continuous (for review see Post, 1980). Species differences in pharmacokinetic factors must also be considered when choosing appropriate administration patterns. For instance, the half-life of methadone is 25 hours in humans, but less than 2 hours in rats; thus, it has been argued that, although methadone is typically taken once daily in methadone maintenance treatment programs, the analogous (and commonly utilized) procedure of once daily methadone dosing in rats would result in daily withdrawal between doses, and hence is of limited clinical relevance (Sparber et al., 1986).

Timing of Administration

The nature of observed neurobehavioral teratogenic effects are dependent on when during development the drug is given. Even as little as a 1-day difference in drug exposure can result in a marked difference in behavioral outcome (Vorhees, 1987a). Vulnerability to CNS effects is protracted, with the period of greatest vulnerability for CNS structural injury occurring during early organogenesis, and for CNS functional injury during mid- to late organogenesis (Vorhees, 1987a). Some researchers interested specifically in neurobehavioral teratogenicity begin drug treatment at the time of neural tube closure and hence the beginnings of nervous system development (around embryonic day 8) (for discussion see Spear, 1994b). Other researchers argue that treatment should begin well before mating, as pregnant women abusing drugs rarely if ever initiate drug use during pregnancy. Exposure beginning prior to mating may be particularly critical for drugs that induce substantial tolerance (Sparber et al., 1986).

Exposure during the third trimester equivalent (which occurs postnatally in the rat) may produce effects different from, and sometimes opposite to, those observed from first and/or second trimester exposure (Akbari et al., 1992; Dow-Edwards et al., 1988, 1990); however,

these findings are sometimes difficult to interpret due to potential confounds in the amount of drug exposure across the treatment periods. That is, fetal exposure levels following a particular drug dose given prenatally may be quite different from offspring exposure levels to that same dose of drug given postnatally to the maternal female or via direct injection into the pups. In studies where the intent is to compare prenatal versus postnatal exposure effects, pharmacokinetic analyses seemingly would be necessary to derive equivalent drug doses at these different developmental stages. Interpretation of data derived from studies involving postnatal drug administration (e.g., during the third trimester equivalent in altricial rodents) is easier when the drug is administered directly to the offspring. Although drugs are often partitioned fairly effectively into milk, hence exposing suckling offspring (Atkinson and Begg, 1990), maternal drug exposure may result in alterations in maternal behavior (Matthews and Jamison, 1982) and in milk volume and/or availability (Hart and Grimble, 1990; Tyrey and Murphy, 1988). These possible disruptions in maternal/offspring interactions and offspring nutritional status associated with the maternal drug exposure would make it difficult to attribute observed effects to offspring drug exposure per se.

Sampling Issues

Much of the work in developmental toxicology has been conducted with rodents, which typically give birth to large litters. If multiple offspring from a given litter are considered as independent observations, large sample sizes can be achieved following testing of but a limited number of litters. The evidence is overwhelming that this approach is unacceptable. Animals within a litter are much less variable than animals across litters; analyses for litter effects typically yield large and significant findings not only for testing conducted during the preweaning period, but also in adulthood (Buelke-Sam et al., 1985; Holson and Pearce, 1992). Even inflating sample size by treating two pups per litter as independent observations nearly triples the likelihood of statistical significance in these experiments (Holson and Pearce, 1992).

Thus, it is essential that litter rather than individual pups should be considered the unit for analysis in developmental toxicology. When analyzing data (such as body weights at birth) that are routinely collected for all offspring in a litter, litter means (or the mean for each sex within the litter in the case of body weights) can be analyzed (Abbey and Howard, 1973). Another statistical approach that can be used when multiple pups from each litter are placed into a given assessment condition is to consider litter as a nested variable in analyses of variance of the data (Buelke-Sam et al., 1985). Alternatively, an often used and powerful approach is to assign only one animal per litter to each individual assessment measure. This procedure can sometimes prove to be logistically challenging if the different assessments involve sacrificing the offspring at different ages before weaning, given that any substantial reduction in litter size can influence nutritional status and maturational rate of the remaining preweanlings in the litter.

Appropriate consideration of sample size is another important issue. Sample sizes examined should be sufficiently large to detect a significant difference if a scientifically important treatment difference indeed exists. The use of sufficient sample sizes is critical not only when designing new experiments but also when interpreting negative findings in existing research. Power analyses provide an important tool in deriving appropriate sample sizes (Muller and Benignus, 1992; Vorhees, 1989a).

Finally, when sampling exposed offspring, gender may be an important independent variable. There are frequent reports of sex differences in the consequences of early drug exposure. For instance, Grimm and Frieder (1985) reviewed data derived from examination of a variety of drugs and concluded that prenatal insults often affect behavioral outcome predominantly in males, whereas early postnatal exposure affects both males and females.

Pair-Feeding

Some drugs of abuse (such as psychostimulants) are also anorexic agents. Such drug-induced reductions in maternal weight gain during pregnancy may contribute to observed offspring effects. Indeed, there is evidence from animal studies that the adverse effects of maternal drug exposure may be potentiated by risk factors such as inadequate nutrition (Charlebois and Fried, 1980; Fried, 1993). Conversely, nutritional adequacy (or enrichment) may protect against some adverse consequences of maternal drug exposure (Charlebois and Fried, 1980; Rao et al., 1988). For instance, when pregnant rats were exposed to marijuana smoke as well as a low protein diet, a marked increase in still births, litter destruction by the dams, as well as a reduction in activity in the pups were seen relative to the pregnancy outcomes of dams exposed to either marijuana smoke alone or only the restricted diet (Charlebois and Fried, 1980).

In instances where the drug under investigation produces maternal anorexia, nutritional controls are necessary to determine whether observed alterations in the offspring are related to the drug exposure itself, or merely to undernutrition associated with drug-induced anorexia in the pregnant dams. The usual control is a pair-fed group. Each animal in this nutritional control group is fed only the amount of food consumed on the corresponding day of pregnancy by the drug-exposed animal with which it has been paired. Typically, an ad libitum- fed group is also included to determine the impact, if any, of the reduction in maternal weight gain on the dependent measures of interest. That is, differences seen between the ad libitum group and both the pair-fed and drug-exposed groups are typically attributed to the nutritional consequences of the treatment, whereas differences evident between the drug-exposed group and both the ad libitum- and pair-fed control groups are presumably related to the drug exposure per se.

This procedure, however, is not without inherent limitations. It has been argued that pair-feeding is more of an experimental treatment than a control, as the deprivation associated with pair-feeding is a stressor that has behavioral, hormonal, and other physiologic consequences in the pregnant animal apart from the nutritional consequences of pair-feeding per se (see Spear and Heyser, 1993, for review). Yet, given the absence of viable alternatives, pair-feeding is still accepted as the best means currently available to assess the nutritional consequences associated with the administration of anorexia-producing drugs during gestation (Weinberg et al., 1992).

Different approaches must be taken to determine the nutritional contribution of drug treatments that are administered postnatally during the third trimester equivalent in altricial species such as rats and mice. Obviously, it is not possible to subject suckling offspring to a typical pair-feeding procedure. One type of approach that has been used is to match weight gain in nutritional control animals to that of the drug-treated animals through reducing milk access. Access to milk can be reduced either by rearing animals in larger than normal-sized litters, or by periodically placing litters of nutritional control offspring with nonlactating, caregiving "aunts". Unfortunately, there is evidence that these two methods of inducing offspring undernutrition have substantially different effects on brain parameters despite virtually identical effects on body weight (Tonkiss et al., 1988). Another type of approach that has been used extensively is to remove the mother from the situation entirely and artificially rear the pups during the treatment period by using intragastric cannulas to provide identical nutrition to drug-treated and control pups. Although this is a technically demanding procedure that markedly alters the social environment of the young pup, it has been used extensively and effectively in studies of the effects of alcohol exposure during the third trimester equivalent (Pierce and West, 1986).

Surrogate Fostering

Prenatal exposure of mammalian offspring to drugs essentially mandates concomitant maternal exposure. This prior maternal drug exposure may influence the behavior of the female following parturition when she is raising her young. Such drug-induced behavioral modifications in the dam could alter maternal-offspring interactions, with subsequent effects on offspring neurobehavioral maturation. Indeed, insults during pregnancy have been shown to alter a variety of postpartum maternal behaviors such as licking of the pups, nest building, and maternal aggression toward an intruder (Heyser et al., 1992a; Matthews and Jamison, 1982; Moore and Power, 1986). Moreover, physiologic and behavioral function of prenatally exposed offspring has been observed to vary depending on whether they are reared by their own dam or by a nontreated foster dam (Becker and Kowall, 1977; Birke and Sadler, 1987; Cierpial and McCarty, 1987; Goodwin et al., 1992; Moore and Power, 1986). For instance, being reared by an untreated foster mother rather than their own dam partially attenuates the retardation in motor development seen in prenatally stressed pups (Fride et al., 1985), and reduces deficits in acquisition of a classical conditioning task seen in offspring exposed prenatally to cocaine (Heyser et al., 1992a). These findings are not ubiquitous, however, and in some circumstances postnatal rearing conditions have been found to have few if any effects on later offspring neurobehavioral function (Vorhees, 1989b).

Given that potential drug-induced alterations in maternal behavior may have an impact on offspring neurobehavioral function apart from the direct effects of the drug on the developing organism, many developmental toxicologists have used surrogate fostering procedures. By fostering each litter of treated or control pups to an untreated maternal female shortly after birth, the experimenter avoids the possibility that neurobehavioral alterations observed in the offspring are merely related to insult-induced alterations in maternal behavior. The decision of whether to foster depends on the research questions being asked, along with the relative weighing of the additional costs associated with fostering versus the necessary ambiguity associated with the interpretation of data derived from studies where pups were reared by their own mothers. Certainly, if the offspring are not fostered, it cannot be concluded that observed effects in the offspring are necessarily related to their prenatal treatment per se.

Choice of Dependent Measures

When initially investigating the potential neurobehavioral teratogenicity of a substance, a test battery approach has often been used, where offspring behavioral functioning is broadly assessed across a number of different categories of function. For instance, a work group chaired by Geyer and Reiter (1985) recommended the following seven categories of functional effects for inclusion in initial test batteries: physical growth and maturation; reflexes; motor development/activity; sensory/attentional; affective; cognitive (learning/memory/performance); and reproductive behavior. However, if substantial information is already available on the neurobehavioral teratology of the drug or if the mechanisms of action of the test substance are known in the adult, this information can sometimes be used to guide the choice of more targeted behavioral tests.

Regardless of which dependent measures are chosen for assessment, it is important that these assessment tools be adequately reliable (replicable within and between laboratories), sensitive (able to detect dysfunction should it exist), and valid (measure what they are presumed to assess)—for discussion see Vorhees, 1987b. The evidence is also clear that using experimenter-blind procedures in all neurobehavioral assessments is of critical importance in developmental toxicology (Benignus, 1993).

After exposure to a developmental toxicant, there may be substantial reorganization following the exposure period. That is, primary neural alterations induced by exposure to a developmental toxicant may lead to secondary changes in the nervous system as it attempts to adapt and compensate for these initial effects. This has two important implications for neu-robehavioral assessment. First, assessments made early in ontogeny may be more likely to reveal primary deficits than testing later in life when further adaptations may have occurred. When attempting to develop principles about the types of neural alterations induced by specific classes of developmental toxicants, it may be important to focus initially on primary alterations rather than the full aggregate of subsequent reactions to the teratogen (Spear, 1990). Such early assessments are also cost effective, and may have greater cross-species comparability to available clinical data where most investigations are conducted in exposed infants and young children.

Second, although the nervous system may exhibit some degree of adaptation and recovery following exposure to a developmental toxicant, there may be a cost to such reorganization. That is, certain behavioral and physiologic functions may appear "normal" under basal testing conditions, but underlying deficits may become "unmasked" when subjected to challenges of various kinds. Among the challenges that may reveal such deficits are responsiveness to pharmacologic agents, complex cognitive tests, adaptability and reactivity to environmental or social demands and stressors, capacity to recover from subsequent brain damage, and ability to retain functions during the aging process (for further discussion see Spear, 1996). Thus, the ultimate cost of neural reorganization following developmental insults may be a decrease in adaptability and resilience. This point will be discussed in more detail later.

NEUROBEHAVIORAL TOXICOLOGY OF DRUGS OF ABUSE

Substantial research has examined the consequences of developmental exposure to drugs of abuse in animal models as well as in clinical populations. Numerous reviews are available that critique and summarize these research findings; however, these reviews have typically focused on a single drug and often are restricted to either clinical or laboratory animal findings. The intent of this presentation, in contrast, is to compare and contrast findings for a variety of standard end points across different drugs of abuse, with a particular focus on neurobehavioral assessments of alcohol, opiates (heroin, methadone), cocaine, and marijuana or component cannabinoids (typically, Δ-9-tetrahydrocannabinol, THC). Although this brief survey highlights findings using animal models, references to clinical studies are included where appropriate for purpose of comparison. Given that the neurobehavioral teratology of abused drugs has been examined in thousands of publications, this selective review necessarily is rather subjective in terms of the research chosen for discussion.

Much of the laboratory research in the area of the developmental toxicology of drugs of abuse was conducted beginning in the 1970s when the field of neurobehavioral teratology was just emerging. At that early time in the evolution of research in this area, consensus had not yet been reached on various control and methodologic issues such as those discussed earlier in this chapter. As a result, much of the initial research examining drugs of abuse such as opiates and THC has been strongly criticized (for discussion see Hutchings and Dow-Edwards, 1991; Lichtblau and Sparber, 1984). In contrast, awareness of, and control for, critical design and methodologic factors was higher in research examining early exposure to alcohol, presumably because the large number of researchers working in the area may have led to greater opportunities for consensus building. The more recent evolution of research regarding early cocaine exposure, although limited in terms of quantity, has had the advantage of hindsight from these earlier lessons learned.

Growth and Maturational Effects

Impairment in growth is a common consequence reported following developmental exposure to drugs of abuse. For instance, the administration of alcohol (Weinberg, 1985), THC (Hutchings et al., 1987), cocaine (Church et al., 1990), and opiates such as methadone or morphine (Hutchings et al., 1979) during fetal or early neonatal development have all been reported to reduce birth weight and hence presumably to impair offspring growth. Similar delays in reflex development, motor development, and the attainment of physical landmarks such as eye opening and incisor eruption have been also observed (methadone: Enters et al., 1991; ethanol: Driscoll et al., 1990; THC: Dalterio, 1986; cocaine: Spear, 1994b). However, before concluding that developmental exposure to these drugs impairs offspring growth and maturation, some cautions are in order. First, with some of these drugs, such as cocaine, alterations in reflex development are seen infrequently (Spear, 1994b), and reduced birth weight is only seen at relatively high exposure levels at which substantial maternal toxicity is also evident (Church et al., 1990). Thus, these reductions in birth weight may be a function of toxicity in the dam rather than a consequence of drug exposure to the fetus itself. Indeed, growth effects typically become evident at higher exposure levels than those necessary to induce neurobehavioral teratogenicity (Coles, 1993). In addition, these drugs generally decrease food intake and hence maternal weight gain during pregnancy. Yet, in some of the early research in this field, including much of the work with THC and methadone, pair-fed or weight-matched controls were not included. Hence, it is often not possible to determine whether the observed reductions in offspring body weights were simply a function of the reduction in maternal nutrient intake rather than a direct effect of the drug on growth processes (for discussion see Hutchings et al., 1989; Lichtblau and Sparber, 1984).

Despite these qualifiers, there are, however, some intriguing data to suggest that opiates may be involved in growth regulatory processes in the developing nervous system. Based on their work, Zagon and colleagues (1992) have suggested that the endogenous opioid peptide, [Met⁵]enkephalin, serves as an inhibitory growth factor regulating cell proliferation, and to some extent differentiation and survival, via stimulation of zeta receptors, a population of opiate receptors that is only evident early in life. Indeed, continuous blockade of opiate receptors via administration of high doses of opiate antagonists has been shown to increase body and brain weights, raise numbers of proliferating cells in the CNS, and accelerate dendritic arborization and spine formation (Hauser et al., 1989; Zagon and McLaughlin, 1987; Zagon et al., 1992). Conversely, the administration of exogenous opiates such as morphine or methadone would presumably increase the net opioid inhibitory influence on proliferative activities, impairing growth (Zagon and McLaughlin, 1987).

Neonatal Withdrawal

Withdrawal behavior has been characterized most clearly in neonates exposed prenatally to opiates such as heroin or methadone, with physical signs of abstinence being seen both clinically and in laboratory animals. The form of this withdrawal seen in neonates differs from that seen in adults; for example, neonatal rats do not show classical withdrawal signs such as tremors and diarrhea that are characteristic of withdrawal in adulthood (see for discussion Barr and Jones, 1994). In contrast, neonatal rats undergoing methadone withdrawal precipitated by naloxone exhibit symptoms such as oral behaviors, vocalizations, and hyperreactivity to touch (Enters et al., 1991). Clinically, opiate withdrawal symptoms in neonates include gastrointestinal dysfunction and feeding difficulties, sleep disturbances, hypertonicity and hyperreflexia, abnormal crying, restlessness, and irritability (Chiriboga, 1993). Due to the shorter half-life of heroin compared with methadone in clinical populations, the neonatal abstinence syndrome associated with heroin withdrawal develops sooner postpartum and dissipates more quickly than the methadone withdrawal syndrome (for discussion see Zuckerman and Bresnahan, 1991).

Some of the adverse consequences associated with prenatal opiate exposure may be indirectly a repercussion of the neonatal withdrawal process itself. For instance, Sparber and Lichtblau (1983) have shown that morbidity of rat neonates exposed prenatally to a long-lasting opiate agonist, levo-α-acetyl-methadol (LAAM), is increased by naloxone-precipitated withdrawal shortly after birth, and is reduced by continued neonatal exposure to LAAM. Clinically, neonates demonstrating symptoms of opiate withdrawal are often treated with pharmacologic agents such as paregoric (an opium tincture) or phenobarbital to manage withdrawal. The prognosis (at least in terms of weight gain) for infants so treated may be better than for symptomatic untreated neonates (Chiriboga, 1993).

Although abstinence following a period of chronic ethanol exposure produces a severe withdrawal syndrome in adulthood, only rarely has withdrawal been discussed as a characteristic of neonates exposed prenatally to ethanol (Chiriboga, 1993). Yet, ethanol-exposed neonates often exhibit acute behavioral signs that gradually dissipate and could reflect either withdrawal or transient CNS alterations that resolve with further development (Coles, 1993). For instance, feeding disturbances and disruptions in state regulation have been reported early in life in both clinical and laboratory animal offspring following fetal ethanol exposure (Driscoll et al., 1990).

With THC and cocaine, there is little clear evidence of an abstinence syndrome in exposed neonates, and there is likewise little indication of a well-characterized withdrawal syndrome in adults chronically exposed to these drugs (for discussion see Chiriboga, 1993; Spear, 1994b). Although some human neonates exposed prenatally to cocaine have been observed to exhibit abnormal neurobehavioral signs such as irritability, tremor, muscular rigidity, irregular sleep, poor feeding, and hyperactive reflexes, these behavioral alterations may represent signs of direct drug effects rather than withdrawal, as they are more likely to be seen in infants that still have cocaine in their systems (Cherukuri et al., 1988).

Alterations in Activity and Rest/Activity Cycles

Many kinds of nervous system disruptions alter locomotor activity. Hence it is not surprising that alterations in activity, typically in the form of hyperactivity, have been frequently reported in laboratory animal studies in offspring prenatally exposed to drugs of abuse, particularly ethanol and opiates. The findings are more mixed in studies with THC and cocaine. Reports of changes in locomotor activity are not ubiquitous and may depend on a number of factors including age at the time of testing. For instance, the frequently reported hyperactivity induced by fetal ethanol exposure is more evident in testing conducted during development (or in aged animals) than in adulthood (Driscoll et al., 1990). Similar transient hyperactivity early in life has also been reported following gestational cocaine exposure (Hutchings et al., 1989). Test situation may also be important. For example, cocaine-exposed offspring were found to be hyperactive when tested in a situation in which they received intermittent foot shocks, whereas they did not differ from controls in locomotor activity when examined in a similar, but relatively nonstressful test situation (Spear et al., 1989b).

Using a relatively long (8-hour) test period, Hutchings and colleagues (1993) examined rest-activity cycles in small groups of offspring and observed increased activity, poorer state regulation, and more state lability in 22-day-old offspring prenatally exposed to methadone (Hutchings et al., 1993) but not to THC (Hutchings et al., 1989). As pointed out by Hutchings et al. (1989), although prenatal THC exposure has been reported in a number of studies to induce hyperactivity, none of these experiments included pair-fed controls and surrogate fostering. In contrast, those studies that did include these controls found no changes in

activity (Hutchings et al., 1989). Thus, the induction of hyperactivity in THC-exposed offspring may be more related to prenatal nutritional insufficiencies and a possible inhibition of milk production/letdown than to the direct effects of THC exposure.

Cognitive Effects

Cognitive alterations are commonly seen in offspring following exposure to drugs of abuse. However, whether or not such deficits are evident in a given experiment may depend on factors such as the amount of training, test age, and the nature of the task and its complexity. Alterations in cognitive performance are rarely ubiquitous, however, and in some if not many test situations exposed offspring may exhibit cognitive performance indistinguishable from control animals. When pondering these data, it should be recognized that even mild disruptions obtained in simple tests of cognitive function in animal studies may be predictive of more severe cognitive dysfunctions in humans exposed to the same biologic insult. For instance, untreated phenylketonuria (PKU) produces clear mental retardation in humans, whereas studies using animal models of PKU have found relatively mild disruptions in cognitive performance, with these impairments predominantly being evident only in tasks involving the transfer of learning (Strupp et al., 1994).

To provide a context for the discussion of cognitive alterations, findings from prenatal alcohol exposure will first be reviewed, given the extensive literature available both in laboratory animals and clinically. Based on a number of criteria, including morphologic anomalies, growth retardation, and CNS dysfunction, some infants of mothers who drank heavily (consuming five or more standard drinks per occasion, and an average of two or more standard drinks per day) during pregnancy have been characterized as having fetal alcohol syndrome (FAS) (for discussion see Abel and Hannigan, 1995). These FAS offspring have been found to exhibit significant intellectual impairments that are evident not only during the early school-age years but also in adolescence and adulthood (Streissguth et al., 1991). These impairments result in an average intellectual level in the mildly retarded range, along with a lack of adaptive living skills necessary for survival outside of a structured environment (Streissguth, 1992). In animal studies, prenatal exposure to ethanol has been shown to result in classical conditioning deficits early in life that are not apparent later in life (Barron et al., 1988), and reversal deficits evident in adult testing (Riley et al., 1979). Alterations in performance are also seen in active and passive avoidance (Lochry and Riley, 1980). Given that active and passive avoidance tasks are markedly influenced by baseline levels of locomotor activity, and that increases in locomotor activity are commonly seen following prenatal alcohol exposure (reviewed in Riley, 1990), it is not clear whether the changes in performance on these tasks are associative in nature or related to alterations in response inhibition or activity. Various other conditioning deficits have been observed in these offspring such as impaired acquisition and performance in spatial tasks, including the Morris water maze (Blanchard et al., 1987).

Like offspring exposed prenatally to ethanol, prenatal cocaine exposure has also been reported to result in transient deficits in classical conditioning early in life (Heyser et al., 1990). Cognitive deficits are also evident in adulthood, particularly in terms of performance of reversal tasks (Heyser et al., 1992b). Deficits do not appear to be evident, however, in active/passive avoidance tasks (Riley and Foss, 1991), findings which may be related to the lack of consistent reports of hyperactivity in these offspring (Spear, 1994b).

Cognitive deficits have also been occasionally observed following prenatal exposure to methadone, with, for instance, impairments in active avoidance acquisition and discrimination learning reported in exposed offspring in adulthood (Zagon et al., 1979). However, negative findings are also evident (Hutchings et al., 1979). In general, the reports of cognitive deficits following prenatal methadone exposure were associated with studies that used a once daily injection procedure, an administration pattern that may result in daily withdrawal (see earlier discussion and Sparber et al., 1986). It is not clear whether evidence of conditioning deficits would be seen using an administration regimen that produces more sustained (and hence more clinically relevant) methadone levels. Similarly, although a variety of learning deficits have been reported in offspring exposed prenatally to THC (for review see Brown and Fishman, 1984), few if any of these studies included nutritional and fostering controls. As argued by Hutchings and Dow-Edwards (1991, p. 20), "Although these effects were assumed to represent primary effects of the compound, they were more likely secondary to maternal undernutrition or postnatally mediated by altered maternal behavior."

In summary, cognitive deficits have been more clearly characterized with ethanol where serious disruptions in intellectual performance lasting into adulthood are seen clinically, along with a variety of conditioning deficits in laboratory animals. From the limited amount of data in cocaine-exposed animals to date, it appears that the effects of prenatal cocaine exposure on conditioning may be somewhat less pronounced than those of prenatal ethanol exposure (for a discussion see Spear, 1995). Unfortunately, due to design and control insufficiencies in the current literature, it is difficult to draw conclusions regarding potential effects of prenatal exposure to opiates and THC on cognitive performance.

Alterations in Later Vulnerability to Stressors

One of the more intriguing but less investigated areas involves assessment of later stressor responsivity in offspring exposed to drugs of abuse early in life. In studies in developmental toxicology, behavioral testing of offspring is typically conducted in carefully controlled situations characterized by minimal environmental stressors and distractors. However, increasing the demands of the test situation through the use of environmental or other types of challenges may reveal (i.e., unmask) deficits that may not be evident under basal testing conditions.

The nervous system is a highly interactive and intrinsically self-regulating system that is usually homeostatically driven. Manipulating nervous system activity at any stage of life may lead to compensatory adaptations in other components of the nervous system, although the nature of those compensatory processes often varies with the type of the insult as well as age at the time of the insult. This remarkable capacity of the nervous system to reorganize and adapt to insults has been recognized as an important principle in the field of developmental toxicology for decades (Hughes and Sparber, 1978). Yet there may be a cost to such reorganization, with this cost being reflected by a decrease in adaptability. Certain behavioral and physiologic functions may appear "normal" under basal testing conditions, but underlying deficits may be revealed when the organism is subjected to challenges of various kinds (see earlier discussion and Hughes and Sparber, 1978).

Although the number of studies assessing stressor responsivity in offspring exposed gestationally to drugs of abuse is rather limited, the available research indicates that this type of challenge is a sensitive and robust indicator of long-lasting effects of early insults on offspring. These data are most convincing following prenatal exposure to ethanol. Offspring exposed to ethanol during gestation have been shown to exhibit consistent age-specific alterations in their pituitary-adrenal response to stressors, specifically, a blunted response in infancy and a hyperresponsive pituitary-adrenal stress response in adulthood (Taylor et al., 1986; Weinberg and Gallo, 1982). These hormonal effects are robust, particularly in female offspring, and have been replicated across laboratories (for review see Spear, 1996). Neurochemically, whereas no differences were observed between ethanol-exposed and control offspring examined under nonstressful conditions, effects of the prenatal exposure were evident following stressor exposure in terms of alterations in dopamine (DA) activity in amygdala (Kelly and Dillingham, 1994). Ethanol-exposed offspring also differ in their behavioral stress response in adulthood, as indexed by decreased immobility in swim tests (Bilitzke and Church, 1992; Nelson et al., 1984).

Altered responsivity to stressors also appears to be a robust and reliable finding in studies of prenatal cocaine exposure, although the focus to date has been on behavioral rather than hormonal assessments. Among the notable behavioral alterations observed are decreases in immobility (Bilitzke and Church, 1992; Molina et al., 1994) and increases in "frantic" (agitated, apparent escape-directed) behavior (Johns et al., 1992; McMillen et al., 1991) in response to acute stressors, as well as several longer-lasting behavioral changes following prior exposure to foot shock (Molina et al., 1994; Smith et al., 1989).

A few studies have evaluated responsivity to stressors in offspring exposed prenatally to other drugs of abuse. Adult mice prenatally exposed to morphine were observed to exhibit an enhanced responsiveness to restraint stress as indexed by stress-induced analgesia (Castellano and Ammassari-Teule, 1984), and following gestational methadone exposure were reported to be more influenced than controls by changes in their environment (Middaugh and Simpson, 1980). Offspring of rat dams treated with methadone during pregnancy were reported to be "hyperreactive to aversive stimuli" (Rech et al., 1980). Male mice exposed prenatally to THC were observed to exhibit abnormal responses to being housed with a female, weight loss and an elevation in basal corticosterone levels relative to control males (Dalterio, 1986).

Alterations in Later Drug Sensitivity

Another type of challenge that may unmask deficits in drug-exposed offspring is the use of pharmacologic tests. One approach (that will not be emphasized here) is to examine responsiveness to drugs affecting specific neurotransmitter systems, with the goal of assessing potential alterations in those neurotransmitter systems following prenatal drug exposure (see Bond 1986a,b, for examples of this approach following fetal alcohol exposure). Another strategy is to examine responsiveness to the same drug that was administered prenatally to determine whether the offspring exhibit decreased or increased sensitivity (i.e., tolerance or sensitization, respectively) to the previously exposed drug. A special case is with regard to subsequent drug self-administration: Does early exposure to a drug alter later self-administration of that substance?

As is often the case, most of the available data concern the effects of prenatal exposure to alcohol. The effects of early ethanol exposure on subsequent ethanol sensitivity depend on the response measure used (for a review see Spear, 1996). For instance, while there is general consensus that prenatal ethanol exposure does not alter the later hypnotic effects of ethanol as indexed by ethanol sleep times, early exposure typically results in tolerance to the later hypothermic effects of ethanol (Abel et al., 1981; Randall et al., 1983). In terms of ethanol intake, in most instances prenatal ethanol exposure has been reported to increase alcohol self-administration in adulthood (Randall et al., 1983). Yet it should be realized that most of these intake studies used two-bottle tests where ethanol intake is generally fairly modest and without notable pharmacologic consequences; such intake may be influenced by flavor factors and taste neophobia rather than the pharmacologic consequences of ethanol per se. Thus, although the data to date are consistent with the suggestion that early ethanol exposure generally increases later ethanol self-administration, these findings need to be confirmed using other procedures for initiating ethanol consumption and controlling for taste sensitivity/neophobia.

Assessment of responsiveness to later stimulant challenge following prenatal cocaine ex-posure has revealed a diversity of findings across (and even occasionally within) different response measures. In terms of stimulant-induced activity, for instance, decreases in sensitivity to stimulants has been reported in testing early in life (Sobrian et al., 1990), whereas increased sensitivity to stimulants (Peris et al., 1992) or no effect (Heyser et al., 1994) has been reported in adulthood. In general, when altered stimulant-induced activity effects have been observed in exposed offspring, they have been relatively modest (see Spear, 1996 for discussion). Cocaine-exposed offspring have been observed to be less sensitive to the discriminative stimulus effects of cocaine in the absence of any apparent alteration in the amount of cocaine reaching the brain in these animals (Heyser et al., 1994). These offspring have also been reported to demonstrate reduced sensitivity to the reinforcing properties of cocaine in adulthood as indexed by conditioned place preferences (CPP) (Heyser et al., 1992c). Manipulations that decrease CPP often (although not always) increase self-administration and vice versa, presumably because higher doses of the drug are necessary to compensate for the decreased rewarding efficacy of the drug (Le Moal and Simon, 1991). Consistent with this notion and the CPP data, a recent abstract has reported that cocaine-exposed offspring exhibit increased responding for intravenous cocaine self-administration in adulthood (Keller et al., 1994).

A number of studies have examined later sensitivity to opiate challenge after prenatal opiate exposure. Offspring prenatally exposed to methadone, while more sensitive to morphine analgesia as neonates, were observed to be tolerant to morphine analgesia by the age of weaning (21 days) (Enters et al., 1991). Similarly, offspring prenatally exposed to either methadone or morphine were observed to be tolerant to morphine's analgesic effects in adulthood (Hovious and Peters, 1984). Prenatal exposure to morphine has been reported to facilitate acquisition of intravenous morphine self-administration in adulthood (Glick et al., 1977), whereas prenatal exposure to morphine or methadone was found to increase oral self-administration of morphine (although not methadone) (Peters and Hovious, 1983). Given that morphine and methadone were administered orally in drinking fluids in the latter study, the concerns mentioned previously regarding taste/neophobia as contributing factors to observed alterations in ethanol intake are also relevant here. It should be noted that adult offspring exposed prenatally to methadone have also been reported to exhibit increased responding on a progressive ratio for food reward (Middaugh and Simpson, 1980), suggesting the possibility that increased drug self-administration seen in opiate-exposed offspring could potentially reflect a general increase in motivational factors.

Taken together, although the available data from offspring exposed prenatally to ethanol, cocaine, and opiates are still quite limited, they support the tentative suggestion that early chronic exposure to a drug of abuse may increase the propensity for later self-administration of that or related substances. More systematic research is needed to test this possibility and to determine whether increases are also evident in the later self-administration of other drugs, which would suggest an increased propensity for substance abuse more generally.

Social and Sexual Behaviors

A variety of other behaviors have also been examined as dependent measures in developmental toxicology. Among the potentially more significant are alterations in social or sexually dimorphic behavior. As systematically discussed in a recent review by Ward (1992), exposure during pregnancy to a wide range of drugs of abuse including ethanol, marijuana, and opiates suppresses testosterone levels in male fetuses. In general, functional rather than anatomical alterations were found to be the primary consequence of these suppressions in fetal testosterone, with these functional alterations typically not being detected until adolescence or adulthood.

Male rats exposed prenatally to ethanol exhibit feminized behavior patterns when indexed in terms of lordosis (Hård et al., 1984), saccharin intake (McGivern et al., 1987), and play patterns (Meyer and Riley, 1986). Adult male rats prenatally exposed to morphine exhibit feminized and incompletely masculinized copulatory behavior (Ward et al., 1983). Interestingly, young school-aged boys exposed prenatally to methadone were similarly found to exhibit subtle signs of gender-identity feminization along with an increased preference for stereotypically feminine play (Sandberg et al., 1990; Ward et al., 1989). Although less well investigated, prenatal and early postnatal exposure to THC has been reported to suppress male sexual behavior in adult rats (Dalterio, 1980), and prenatal exposure to cocaine has been reported to depress male-typical scent-marking behavior and copulatory behavior in adulthood (Raum et al., 1990). Thus, feminization and/or demasculinization appears to be a frequent outcome following prenatal exposure to drugs of abuse.

Social behaviors have been examined less often, although they also appear to be sensitive to the effects of prenatal insults with drugs of abuse. For instance, alterations in play behavior in adolescence and increased aggressive behavior in adulthood has been reported in adult rodents exposed to cocaine or ethanol during development (Elis and Krsiak, 1975; Johns et al., 1994; Meyer and Riley, 1986; Wood et al., 1995), with alterations in maternal behavior (Barron and Riley, 1985) and in active social interactions (Kelly and Dillingham, 1994) also being reported after prenatal alcohol exposure. These laboratory findings are reminiscent of clinical reports. For instance, infants and toddlers of drug-abusing mothers who were recruited on the basis of phencyclidine use (although the majority were also cocaine users) exhibited less representational play and were observed to be less securely attached to caregivers (Rodning et al., 1989, 1991). As adolescents and adults, offspring with fetal alcohol syndrome exhibited persistent deficits in socialization and were generally unresponsive to social cues (Streissguth et al., 1991). Thus, in both the laboratory animal and clinical literature, social interactions may pose a significant later challenge for offspring exposed to at least some drugs of abuse early in life.

Neural Alterations

The evidence is clear that exposure to drugs of abuse can alter nervous system functioning. However, most of the behavioral alterations discussed in the preceding sections have not yet been associated with specific neural alterations, which is not surprising in that the neural systems underlying most of these behaviors have not been clearly delineated to date. One exception is with regard to sexual dimorphism, where specific brain regions have been shown to reveal sexually dimorphic alterations following prenatal drug exposure in a manner reminiscent of observed dimorphisms in behavior. For instance, prenatal ethanol exposure results not only in feminization of behavior in males, but also in incomplete masculinization of the sexually dimorphic nucleus of the preoptic area (SDN-POA) in these animals (for review see Ward, 1992).

The literature regarding the neural consequences of developmental exposure to drugs of abuse is large and complex, and the observed alterations are often complicated and difficult to generalize. Nevertheless, from the literature available to date several principles seem to be emerging. These tentative generalizations are briefly discussed in this section, along with a few illustrative findings.

Although manipulating nervous system activity at any stage of life may lead to compensatory adaptations in other components of the nervous system, the nature of those compensatory processes occurring early in ontogeny are not necessarily analogous to those seen at maturity. Moving away from drugs of abuse for a dramatic example, consider the effects of chronic blockade of dopamine (DA) receptors via neuroleptic treatment. In adulthood

such treatment leads to an upregulation in DA receptor binding (Burt et al., 1977), whereas chronic blockade of these receptors early in development results in a decrease in DA receptor binding (Rosengarten and Friedhoff, 1979). Simplistically, it is as if chronic receptor blockade induces receptor upregulation in adulthood in an apparent attempt to maintain homeostatic equilibrium in the DA system, while, conversely, during development fewer receptors may be formed because fewer appear to be needed due to the chronic presence of the DA antagonist (see for discussion Spear and Scalzo, 1986). This ontogenetic reversal in compensatory processes is not necessarily evident with other neural systems. For instance, opiate agonists generally decrease (Tempel et al., 1988) and opiate antagonists increase (Bardo et al., 1983) opiate receptor numbers following treatment either during development or in adulthood. Such alterations are generally more transient following developmental drug exposure that exposure in adulthood, although the nervous system appears more sensitive to these effects during development than when it is mature (Kuhn et al., 1992).

The diversity of modifications associated with the effects of early drug exposure on a given neuronal system do not necessarily express themselves in parallel alterations in all affected components of that system to result in a simple up- or downregulation of synaptic functioning. For instance, although, as mentioned above, developmental exposure to opiate agonists generally increases opiate receptor number, levels of endogenous opiates themselves have varyingly been reported to be decreased or increased (for a review see Kuhn et al., 1992). Thus, while presynaptic mechanisms may also be affected by developmental exposure to opiate agonists, these presumed alterations in opiate synthesis, release, or degradation do not necessarily supplement the apparent synaptic upregulation evident in terms of opiate receptor binding. As another example, consider the complex pattern of alterations seen in the DA system following prenatal exposure to the DA uptake inhibitor, cocaine. Adult rats exposed prenatally to co-caine exhibit fewer spontaneous active DA neurons than control offspring (Minabe et al., 1992); these electrophysiologic data are consistent with behavioral and pharmacologic evidence of an attenuation in catecholamine [i.e., DA and/or norepinephrine (NE)] function in these offspring (for review see Spear, 1994b). Yet, DA levels and turnover per se do not appear to be altered in these offspring (Goodwin et al., 1995), and both increases and decreases in DA binding have been reported (Dow-Edwards et al., 1990; Henderson et al., 1991).

There are a multitude of components of a given neural system that could be influenced by developmental drug exposure. Some of these alterations may be induced by the drug exposure itself, whereas others may be compensatory to initial drug-induced modifications in the development of other portions of the system. For example, in the case of early cocaine exposure, although there may be an underlying deficit in DA functioning in exposed offspring as indexed by a decrease in the number of spontaneously active DA neurons (Minabe et al., 1992), compensatory processes may act to functionally counter this apparent attenuation in DA functioning under many baseline test conditions. Challenging the organism may reveal latent deficits in function that may not be evident in basal test situations, again emphasizing the value of testing animals under stressful or otherwise challenging circumstances.

Early exposure to a drug of abuse may affect a variety of neural structures in addition to the specific neuronal systems with which the exposed drug directly interacts. For instance, perinatal exposure to methadone influences development not only of the opiate system but also of nonopioid neurotransmitter systems, including the monoamine systems. As an example, Slotkin (1988) has shown that perinatal methadone exposure accelerates development of the peripheral sympathetic nervous system while conversely delaying ontogeny of central neurotransmitter systems including the catecholamine systems. Simi-larly, developmental exposure to cocaine alters not only the dopaminergic systems, but also other neural systems as well, including the serotonergic (Akbari et al., 1992), opiate (Clow et al., 1991), NE (Seidler and Slotkin, 1992), and cholinergic (Tyrala et al., 1992) systems. Numerous regionally specific alterations in brain glucose metabolism are also seen in these offspring (Dow-Edwards et al., 1990). Thus, to obtain an accurate profile of the neural alterations induced by drug exposure in early life, assessments should focus not only on functioning of the target neurotransmitter system(s) through which the exposed drug exerts its mechanism of action, but also on other neural systems as well.

FUTURE DIRECTIONS

Until recently, drug-exposed offspring have typically been examined under isolated test situations designed to minimize stress and distractions. Yet, these conditions may not be optimal for revealing potential deficits following developmental drug exposure. The nervous system may exhibit substantial reorganization after early insults in an attempt to compensate for the treatment-induced alterations in neural function. The cost of this neural reorganization following developmental insults may be associated with a decrease in adaptability that may not be evident under basal conditions, but rather only when the demands of the testing are increased. Indeed, the more recent literature suggests that tests particularly sensitive for revealing the effects of developmental toxicants may involve challenging the organism through exposure to stressors, pharmacologic tests, or via complex cognitive tasks (for discussion see Riley, 1990; Spear, 1995b). Indeed, although the data in some instances are rather limited, developmental exposure to each of the drugs of abuse examined in this chapter (ethanol, opiates, cocaine, THC) has been reported to alter behavioral, neurochemical, or hormonal responses to stressors. Yet, for none of these substances has a clear profile of the altered behavioral response strategies to stressors been delineated, nor have the neural and hormonal substrates of such altered behavioral responsivity been characterized. This would appear important for future inquiry. Such work will be challenging in that much remains to be understood about the neural/hormonal substrates underlying specific behavioral responses to stressors even in normal animals.

Another important area for further work revolves around the preliminary indications that developmental exposure to drugs of abuse may increase the later propensity for self-administration of those substances. Does prenatal drug exposure set up a "vicious circle" whereby individuals exposed gestationally to drugs have a greater propensity to use drugs of abuse in adulthood, hence increasing the probability that their own offspring will be exposed developmentally to drugs, and so on? More research is needed to extend and confirm these findings, and to determine whether the apparent alterations in self-administration are restricted to the previously exposed drug, or are seen across a broad range of self-administered compounds. As these findings are confirmed, it will become important to investigate the neural substrates underlying these apparent increases in drug abuse liability.

In addition to stressor and pharmacologic challenges, cognitive and social challenges would also appear to have promise as potentially sensitive indicators of the effects of developmental exposure to drugs of abuse. As with the examinations of responsivity to stressors, here, too, research needs to focus on determining a more complete profile of alterations in these response patterns, rather than relying on an isolated task or two. In tests of cognitive function, it is likely that tasks of greater complexity will provide more sensitive indicators of developmental exposure. Ultimately these behavioral findings need to be related to particular neural alterations.

Alterations in sexual differentiation, particularly in males, have been shown to be a surprisingly sensitive indicator of the effects of developmental exposure to drugs of abuse

(Ward, 1992). Why do males appear to be particularly susceptible? What are the commonalities and differences among different drugs of abuse in the altered patterns of differentiation observed, and what are the neural and hormonal substrates underlying these modifications? These questions would appear to be fruitful areas for further inquiry.

An important goal of research regarding the developmental toxicology of drugs of abuse is to derive appropriate intervention strategies for the treatment of exposed offspring. With the exception of research regarding fetal alcohol exposure (that has had the advantage of several continuous decades of concentrated research efforts), we are still far from seriously exploring potential interventions. For these other drugs of abuse, more research is needed to discern the precise profile of altered behavioral functions in exposed offspring, and the neural substrates underlying these altered response strategies. In this future work, it will be important to remember the lessons from the past, and to avoid the methodologic weaknesses that have beset some of the early research in this area.

SUMMARY

- Women using drugs of abuse during pregnancy also expose their fetuses to these drugs.
- The available evidence suggests that animal models of developmental toxicants provide data that are relevant clinically. Animal studies are useful in confirming and extending clinical findings, anticipating other consequences of early drug exposure, determining neural mechanisms underlying observed behavioral effects, and developing potential therapeutic approaches.
- There are a number of critical methodologic and control issues in animal studies of developmental toxicants. These include the route, dose, frequency, and timing of drug administration, use of litter as the unit of analysis, pair feeding, and surrogate fos-

tering. Unfortunately, some of these issues were not considered in early research assessing the developmental toxicity of abused drugs, limiting the conclusions that can be drawn.

- Of the drugs of abuse examined (ethanol, cocaine, marijuana, THC), neurobehavioral teratogenic effects appear most pronounced after early ethanol exposure (Table 4). These effects include hyperactivity, altered responsiveness to cognitive, stressful, and pharmacologic challenges, and altered sex-typical and social behaviors.

- Opiates have been shown to produce a variety of reliable neurobehavioral teratogenic effects. Notable findings include neonatal withdrawal, alterations in growth regulatory processes, hyperactivity, altered sensitivity to later opiate challenge, and changes in sex-typical behaviors in males.

- While the literature is less extensive with cocaine, cocaine does appear to be a neurobehavioral teratogen. Observed effects include altered responsiveness to cognitive, pharmacologic, and stress challenges, as well as preliminary indications of altered social behaviors and sex-typical behavior patterns in males.

- At present, the evidence is not strong that prenatal THC exposure per se perturbs offspring behavioral function due to the lack of nutritional and fostering controls in much of the early work in this area; the data for neurobehavioral effects are most convincing with respect to alterations in male sexual behavior.

- Neural adaptations in response to exposure to drugs of abuse during development are complex and not necessarily analogous to those adaptations seen after exposure in adulthood. Alterations may be seen in a variety of neural structures, and within a given neuronal system the observed changes may not be expressed as parallel alterations in all affected components of that system.

- There are a number of important directions for future research. These include neurobehavioral assessments of exposed offspring not only under baseline conditions, but also in response to various stressful, pharmacologic, or complex cognitive challenges that may unmask underlying deficits. Initial findings that exposure to drugs early in life may increase later drug self-administration have important implications, and need further confirmation and extension. As work in these areas proceeds, it will then be possible to address the critical issue of intervention strategies for offspring exposed to these drugs of abuse.

TABLE 4. *Summary of the behavioral teratogenic effects of drugs of abuse[a]*

	Alcohol	THC	Opiates	Cocaine
Impaired growth	++	+[b]	++	+[c]
Neonatal withdrawal	?	-	++	-
Activity alterations	++	+[b]	++	+[d]
Cognitive deficits	++	+[b]	+[e]	++
Increased stressor vulnerability	++	?	+	++
Increased drug self-administration	+	?	+	+
Impaired male sex-typical behaviors	++	+	++	+
Altered social behavior	++	?	?	+

[a]Effects noted as follows: ++ reliable effects replicated intra- or interlaboratory; + reported effects that need further confirmation; - no effect observed; ? insufficiently examined to draw conclusions. For discussion and references, see text.
[b]May be related to nutritional factors or alterations in maternal behavior.
[c]Seen at high exposure doses only.
[d]Inconsistent pattern of findings.
[e]May be related to daily withdrawal.

ACKNOWLEDGMENT

This work was supported in part by National Institute on Drug Abuse grants R01 DA04478 and K02 DA00140.

REFERENCES

Abbey, H. and Howard, E. (1973) Statistical procedure in developmental studies on species with multiple offspring. *Dev. Psychobiol.* 6: 329–335.

Abel, E.L. (1992) Paternal exposure to alcohol. In: Sonderegger, T.B. (ed.) *Perinatal substance abuse.* Baltimore: The Johns Hopkins University Press, pp. 132–160.

Abel, E.L., Bush, R. and Dintcheff, B.A. (1981) Exposure of rats to alcohol in utero alters drug sensitivity in adulthood. *Science* 212: 1531–1533.

Abel, E.L. and Hannigan, J.H. (1995) Maternal risk factors in fetal alcohol syndrome: provocative and permissive influences. *Neurotoxicol. Teratol.* 17: 445–462.

Akbari, H.M., Kramer, H.K., Whitaker-Azmitia, P.M., Spear, L.P. and Azmitia, E.C. (1992) Prenatal cocaine exposure disrupts the development of the serotonergic system. *Brain Res.* 572: 57–63.

Atkinson, H.C. and Begg, E.J. (1990) Prediction of drug distribution into human milk from physicochemical characteristics. *Clin. Pharmacokinet.* 18: 151–167.

Bardo, M.T., Bhatnagar, R.K. and Gebhart, G.F. (1983) Age-related differences in the effect of chronic administration of naloxone on opiate binding in rat brain. *Neuropharmacology* 22: 453–461.

Barr, G.A. and Jones, K. (1994) Opiate withdrawal in the infant. *Neurotoxicol. Teratol.* 16: 219–225.

Barron, S., Gagnon, W.A., Mattson, S.N., Kotch, L.E., Meyer, L.S. and Riley, E.P. (1988) The effects of prenatal alcohol exposure on odor associative learning in rats. *Neurotoxicol. Teratol.* 10: 333–339.

Barron, S. and Riley, E.P. (1985) Pup-induced maternal behavior in adult and juvenile rats exposed to alcohol prenatally. *Alcohol Clin. Exp. Res.* 9: 360–365.

Becker, G. and Kowall, M. (1977) Crucial role of the postnatal maternal environment in the expression of prenatal stress effects in the male rat. *J. Comp. Physiol. Psychol.* 91: 1432–1446.

Benignus, V.A. (1993) Importance of experimenter-blind procedure in neurotoxicology. *Neurotoxicol. Teratol.* 15: 45–49.

Bilitzke, P.J. and Church, M.W. (1992) Prenatal cocaine and alcohol exposures affect rat behavior in a stress test (the Porsolt Swim Test). *Neurotoxicol. Teratol.* 14: 359–364.

Birke, L.I. and Sadler, D. (1987) Differences in maternal behavior of rats and the sociosexual development of the offspring. *Dev. Psychobiol.* 20: 85–99.

Blanchard, B.A., Riley, E.P. and Hannigan, J.H. (1987) Deficits on a spatial navigation task following prenatal exposure to ethanol. *Neutoxicol. Teratol.* 9: 253–258.

Bond, N.W. (1986a) Prenatal alcohol exposure and offspring hyperactivity: effects of scopolamine and methylscopolamine. *Neurobehav. Toxicol. Teratol.* 8: 287–292.

Bond, N.W. (1986b) Prenatal alcohol exposure and offspring hyperactivity: effects of para-chlorophenylalanine and methysergide. *Neurobehav. Toxicol. Teratol.* 8: 667–673.

Boni, J.P., Barr, W.H. and Martin, B.R. (1991) Cocaine inhalation in the rat: pharmacokinetics and cardiovascular response. *J. Pharmacol. Exp. Ther.* 257: 307–315.

Brown, R.M. and Fishman, R.H.B. (1984) An overview and summary of the behavioral and neural consequences of perinatal exposure to psychotropic drugs. In: Yanai, J. (ed.) *Neurobehavioral teratology.* New York: Elsevier Science, pp. 3–54.

Buelke-Sam, J., Kimmel, C.A., Adams, J., Nelson, C.J., Vorhees, C.V., Wright, D.C., St. Omer, V., Korol, B., Butcher, R.E., Geyer, M.A., Holson, J.F., Kutscher, C. and Wayner, M.J. (1985) Collaborative behavioral teratology study: results. *Neurobehav. Toxicol. Teratol.* 7: 591–624.

Burt, D.R., Creese, I. and Snyder, S.H. (1977) Antischizophrenic drugs: chronic treatment elevates dopamine receptor binding in brain. *Science* 196: 326–327.

Castellano, C. and Ammassari-Teule, M. (1984) Prenatal exposure to morphine in mice: enhanced responsiveness to morphine and stress. *Pharmacol. Biochem. Behav.* 21: 103–108.

Charlebois, A.T. and Fried, P.A. (1980) Interactive effects of nutrition and cannabis upon rat perinatal development. *Dev. Psychobiol.* 13: 591–605.

Cherukuri, R., Minkoff, H., Feldman, J., Parekh, A. and Glass, L. (1988) A cohort study of alkaloidal cocaine ("crack") in pregnancy. *Obstet. Gynecol.* 72: 147–151.

Chiriboga, C.A. (1993) Fetal effects. *Neurol. Clin.* 11: 707–728.

Church, M.W., Overbeck, G.W. and Andrzejczak, A.L. (1990) Prenatal cocaine exposure in the Long-Evans rat: I. Dose-dependent effects on gestation, mortality, and postnatal maturation. *Neurotoxicol. Teratol.* 12: 327–334.

Cierpial, M.A. and McCarty, R. (1987) Hypertension in SHR rats: contribution of the maternal environment. *Am. J. Physiol.* 235: H980–H984.

Clow, D.W., Hammer, R.P., Jr., Kirstein, C.L. and Spear, L.P. (1991) Gestational cocaine exposure increases opiate receptor binding in weanling offspring. *Dev. Brain Res.* 59: 179–185.

Coles, C.D. (1993) Impact of prenatal alcohol exposure on the newborn and the child. *Clin. Obstet. Gynecol.* 36: 255–266.

Colie, C.F. (1993) Male mediated teratogenesis. *Reprod. Toxicol.* 7: 3–9.

Dalterio, S.L. (1980) Perinatal or adult exposure to cannabinoids alters male reproductive functions in mice. *Pharmacol. Biochem. Behav.* 12: 143–153.

Dalterio, S.L. (1986) Cannabinoid exposure: effects on development. *Neurobehav. Toxicol. Teratol.* 8: 345–352.

Dalterio, S., Steger, R.W. and Barke, A. (1984) Maternal or paternal exposure to cannabinoids affects central neurotransmitter levels and reproductive function in male offspring. In: Agurell, S., Dewey, W.L. and Willette, R.E. (eds.) *The cannabinoids: chemical, pharmacological and therapeutic aspects.* New York: Academic Press, pp. 411–425.

Davis, D.L., Friedler, G., Mattison, D. and Morris, R. (1992) Male-mediated teratogenesis and other reproductive effects: biologic and epidemiologic findings and a plea for clinical research. *Reprod. Toxicol.* 6: 289–292.

DeVane, C.L., Simpkins, J.W., Miller, R.L. and Braun, S.B. (1989) Tissue distribution of cocaine in the pregnant rat. *Life Sci.* 45: 1271–1276.

Dow-Edwards, D.L., Freed, L.A. and Fico, T.A. (1990) Structural and functional effects of prenatal cocaine exposure in adult rat brain. *Dev. Brain Res.* 57: 263–268.

Dow-Edwards, D.L., Freed, L.A. and Milhorat, T.H. (1988)

Stimulation of brain metabolism by perinatal cocaine exposure. *Dev. Brain Res.* 42: 137–141.

Driscoll, C.D., Streissguth, A.P. and Riley, E.P. (1990) Prenatal alcohol exposure: comparability of effects in humans and animals models. *Neurotoxicol. Teratol.* 12: 231–237.

Elis, J. and Krsiak M. (1975) Effect of alcohol administration during pregnancy on social behaviour of offsprings in mice. *Act. Nerv. Super.* 17: 281–282.

Enters, E.K., Guo, H., Pandey, U., Ko, D. and Robinson, S.E. (1991) The effect of prenatal methadone exposure on development and nociception during the early postnatal period of the rat. *Neurotoxicol. Teratol.* 13: 161–166.

Fride, E., Dan, Y., Gavish, M. and Weinstock, M. (1985) Prenatal stress impairs maternal behavior in a conflict situation and reduces hippocampal benzodiazepine receptors. *Life Sci.* 36: 2103–2109.

Fried, P.A. (1993) Prenatal exposure to tobacco and marijuana: effects during pregnancy, infancy, and early childhood. *Clin. Obstet. Gynecol.* 36: 319–337.

Geyer, M.A. and Reiter, L.W. (1985) Strategies for the selection of test methods. *Neurobehav. Toxicol. Teratol.* 7: 661–662.

Glick, S.D., Strumpf, A.J. and Zimmerberg, B. (1977) Effect of in utero administration of morphine on the subsequent development of self-administration behavior. *Brain Res.* 132: 194–196.

Goodwin, G.A., Heyser, C.J., Moody, C.A., Rajachandran, L., Molina, V.A., Arnold, H.M., McKinzie, D.L., Spear, N.E. and Spear, L.P. (1992) A fostering study of the effects of prenatal cocaine exposure: II. Offspring behavioral measures. *Neurotoxicol. Teratol.* 14: 423–432.

Goodwin, G.A., Rajachandran, L., Moody, C.A., Francis, R., Kuhn, C.M. and Spear, L.P. (1995) Effects of prenatal cocaine exposure on haloperidol-induced increases in prolactin release and dopamine turnover in weanling, periadolescent, and adult offspring. *Neurotoxicol. Teratol.* 17: 507–514.

Grimm, V.E. and Frieder, B. (1985) Differential vulnerability of male and female rats to the timing of various perinatal insults. *Int. J. Neurosci.* 27: 155–164.

Hård, E., Dahlgren, I.L., Engel, J., Larsson, K., Liljequist, S., Lindh, A.S. and Musi, B. (1984) Development of sexual behavior in prenatally ethanol-exposed rats. *Drug Alcohol Depend.* 14: 51–61.

Hart, A.D. and Grimble, R.F. (1990) The effect of methylxanthines on milk volume and composition, and growth of rat pups. *Br. J. Nutr.* 64: 339–350.

Hauser, K.F., McLaughlin, P.J. and Zagon, I.S. (1989) Endogenous opioid systems and the regulation of dendritic growth and spine formation. *J. Comp. Neurol.* 281: 13–22.

Henderson, M.G., McConnaughey, M.M. and McMillen, B.A. (1991) Long-term consequences of prenatal exposure to cocaine or related drugs: effects on rat brain monoaminergic receptors. *Brain Res. Bull.* 26: 941–945.

Heyser, C.J., Chen, W.J., Miller, J., Spear, N.E. and Spear, L.P. (1990) Prenatal cocaine exposure induces deficits in Pavlovian conditioning and sensory preconditioning among infant rat pups. *Behav. Neurosci.* 104: 955–963.

Heyser, C.J., Miller, J.S., Spear, N.E. and Spear, L.P. (1992c) Prenatal exposure to cocaine disrupts cocaine-induced conditioned place preference in rats. *Neurotoxicol. Teratol.* 14: 57–64.

Heyser, C.J., Molina, V.A. and Spear, L.P. (1992a) A fostering study of the effects of prenatal cocaine exposure: I. Maternal behaviors. *Neurotoxicol. Teratol.* 14: 415–421.

Heyser, C.J., Rajachandran, L., Spear, N.E. and Spear, L.P. (1994) Responsiveness to cocaine challenge in adult rats following prenatal exposure to cocaine. *Psychopharmacology* 116: 45–55.

Heyser, C.J., Spear, N.E. and Spear, L.P. (1992b) Effects of prenatal exposure to cocaine on conditional discrimination learning in adult rats. *Behav. Neurosci.* 106: 837–845.

Holson, R.R. and Pearce, B. (1992) Principles and pitfalls in the analysis of prenatal treatment effects in multiparous species. *Neurotoxicol. Teratol.* 14: 221–228.

Hovious, J.R. and Peters, M.A. (1984) Analgesic effect of opiates in offspring of opiate-treated female rats. *Pharmacol. Biochem. Behav.* 21: 555–559.

Hughes, J.A. and Sparber, S.B. (1978) d-Amphetamine unmasks postnatal consequences of exposure to methylmercury in utero: methods for studying behavioral teratogenesis. *Pharmacol. Biochem. Behav.* 8: 365–375.

Hutchings, D.E. and Dow-Edwards, D. (1991) Animal models of opiate, cocaine, and cannabis use. *Clin. Perinatol.* 18: 1–22.

Hutchings, D.E., Gamagaris, Z., Miller, N. and Fico, T.A. (1989) The effects of prenatal exposure to delta-9-tetrahydrocannabinol on the rest-activity cycle of the preweanling rat. *Neurotoxicol. Teratol.* 11: 353–356.

Hutchings, D.E., Morgan, B., Brake, S.C., Shi, T. and Lasalle, E. (1987) Delta-9-tetrahydrocannabinol during pregnancy in the rat: I. Differential effects on maternal nutrition, embryotoxicity, and growth in the offspring. *Neurotoxicol. Teratol.* 9: 39–43.

Hutchings, D.E., Towey, J.P., Gorinson, H.S. and Hunt, H.F. (1979) Methadone during pregnancy: assessment of behavioral effects in the rat offspring. *J. Pharmacol. Exp. Ther.* 208: 106–112.

Hutchings, D.E., Zmitrovich, A., Church, S. and Malowany, D. (1993) Methadone during pregnancy: the search for a valid animal model. *Ann. 1st. Super. Sanità* 29: 439–444.

Jacobson, J.L. and Jacobson, S.W. (1990) Methodological issues in human behavioral teratology. In: Rovee-Collier, C. and Lipsitt, L.P. (eds.) *Advances in infancy research*, vol. 6. Norwood, NJ: Ablex, pp. 111–148.

Johns, J.M., Means, M.J., Anderson, D.R., Means, L.W. and McMillen, B.A. (1992) Prenatal exposure to cocaine: II. Effects on open-field activity and cognitive behavior in Sprague-Dawley rats. *Neurotoxicol. Teratol.* 14: 343–349.

Johns, J.M., Means, M.J., Bass, E.W., Means, L.W., Zimmerman, L.I. and McMillen, B.A. (1994) Prenatal exposure to cocaine: effects on aggression in Sprague-Dawley rats. *Dev. Psychobiol.* 27: 227–239.

Keller, R.W., Jr., Raucci, J., LeFevre, R.G., Carlson, J.N. and Glick, S.D. (1994, November) Poster presentation at the 24th Annual Meeting of the Society for Neuroscience, Miami Beach, FL.

Kelly, S.J. and Dillingham, R.R. (1994) Sexually dimorphic effects of perinatal alcohol exposure on social interactions and amygdala DNA and DOPAC concentrations. *Neurotoxicol. Teratol.* 16: 377–384.

Kimmel, C.A., Rees, D.C. and Francis, E.Z. (eds.) (1990) Qualitative and quantitative comparability of human and animal developmental neurotoxicity (special issue). *Neurotoxicol. Teratol.* 12: 175–292.

Kuhn, C.M., Windh, R.T. and Little, P.J. (1992) Effects of perinatal opiate addiction on neurochemical development of the brain. In: Miller, M.W. (ed.) *Development of the central nervous system: effects of alcohol and opiates.* New York: Wiley-Liss, pp. 341–361.

Le Moal, M. and Simon, H. (1991) Mesocorticolimbic dopaminergic network: functional and regulatory roles. *Psychol. Rev.* 71: 155–234.

Lichtblau, L. and Sparber, S.B. (1984) Opioids and development: a perspective on experimental models and methods. *Neurobehav. Toxicol. Teratol.* 6: 3–8.

Lochry, E.A. and Riley, E.P. (1980) Retention of passive avoidance and T-maze escape in rats exposed to alcohol prenatally. *Neurobehav. Toxicol.* 2: 107–115.

Matthews, D. and Jamison, S. (1982) Effects of ethanol consumption on maternal behavior in the female rat. *Physiol. Behav.* 29: 595–597.

McGivern, R.F., Holcomb, C. and Poland, R.E. (1987) Effects of prenatal testosterone propionate treatment on saccharin preference of adult rats exposed to ethanol in utero. *Physiol. Behav.* 39: 241–246.

McMillen, B.A., Johns, J.M., Bass, E.W. and Means, L.W. (1991) Learning and behavior of adult rats exposed to cocaine throughout gestation. *Teratology* 43: 495.

Meyer, L.S. and Riley, E. P. (1986) Social play in juvenile rats prenatally exposed to alcohol. *Teratology* 34: 1–7.

Middaugh, L.D. and Simpson, L.W. (1980) Prenatal maternal methadone effects on pregnant C57BL/6 mice and their offspring. *Neurobehav. Toxicol.* 2: 307–313.

Minabe, Y., Ashby, C.R., Jr., Heyser, C., Spear, L.P. and Wang, R.Y. (1992) The effects of prenatal cocaine exposure on spontaneously active midbrain dopamine neurons in adult male offspring: an electrophysiological study. *Brain Res.* 586: 152–156.

Molina, V.A., Wagner, J.M. and Spear, L.P. (1994) The behavioral response to stress is altered in adult rats exposed prenatally to cocaine. *Physiol. Behav.* 55: 941–945.

Moore, C.L. and Power, K.L.L. (1986) Prenatal stress affects mother-infant interaction in Norway rats. *Dev. Psychobiol.* 19: 235–245.

Muller, K.E. and Benignus, V.A. (1992) Increasing scientific power with statistical power. *Neurotoxicol. Teratol.* 14: 211–219.

Nau, H. (1986) Species differences in pharmacokinetics and drug teratogenesis. *Environ. Health Perspect.* 70: 113–129.

Nelson, L.R., Taylor, A.N., Lewis, J.W., Branch, B.J. and Liebeskind, J.C. (1984) Prenatal exposure to ethanol alters responding in a "behavioral despair" paradigm. *Proc. West Pharmacol. Soc.* 27: 583–586.

Peris, J., Coleman-Hardee, M. and Millard, W.J. (1992). Cocaine in utero enhances the behavioral response to cocaine in adult rats. *Pharmacol. Biochem. Behav.* 42: 509–515.

Peters, M.A. and Hovious, J.R. (1983) Opiate self-administration in adult offspring of opiate-treated female rats. *Fed. Proc.* 42: 1363.

Pierce, D.R. and West, J.R. (1986) Blood alcohol concentration: a critical factor for producing fetal alcohol effects. *Alcohol* 3: 269–272.

Plessinger, M.A. and Woods, J.R., Jr. (1991) The cardiovascular effects of cocaine use in pregnancy. *Reprod. Toxicol.* 5: 99–113.

Post, R.M. (1980) Intermittent versus continuous stimulation: effect of time interval on the development of sensitization or tolerance. *Life Sci.* 26: 1275–1282.

Randall, C.L., Hughes, S.S., Williams, C.K. and Anton, R.F. (1983) Effect of prenatal alcohol exposure on consumption of alcohol and alcohol-induced sleep-time in mice. *Pharmacol. Biochem. Behav.* 18: 325–329.

Rao, G.A., Larkin, E.C. and Derr, R.F. (1988) Chronic alcohol consumption during pregnancy: alleviation of untoward effects by adequate nutrition. *Nutr. Res.* 8: 421–429.

Raum, W.J., McGivern, R.F., Peterson, M.A., Shryne, J.H. and Gorski, R.A. (1990) Prenatal inhibition of hypothalamic sex steroid uptake by cocaine: effects on neurobehavioral sexual differentiation in male rats. *Dev. Brain Res.* 53: 230–236.

Rech, R.H., Lomuscio, G. and Algeri, S. (1980) Methadone exposure in utero: effects on brain biogenic amines and behavior. *Neurobehav. Toxicol.* 2: 75–78.

Rees, D.C., Francis, E.Z. and Kimmel, C.A. (1990) Qualitative and quantitative comparability of human and animal developmental neurotoxicants: a workshop summary. *Neurotoxicology* 11: 257–270.

Riley, E.P. (1990) The long-term behavioral effects of prenatal alcohol exposure in rats. *Alcohol Clin. Exp. Res.* 14: 670–673.

Riley, E.P. and Foss, J.A. (1991) The acquisition of passive avoidance, active avoidance, and spatial navigation tasks by animals prenatally exposed to cocaine. *Neurotoxicol. Teratol.* 13: 559–564.

Riley, E.P., Lochry, E.A., Shapiro, N.R. and Baldwin, J. (1979) Response perseveration in rats exposed to alcohol prenatally. *Pharmacol. Biochem. Behav.* 10: 255–259.

Rodning, C., Beckwith, L. and Howard, J. (1989) Prenatal exposure to drugs: behavioral distortions reflecting CNS impairment? *Neurotoxicology* 10: 629–634.

Rodning, C., Beckwith, L. and Howard, J. (1991) Quality of attachment and home environments in children prenatally exposed to PCP and cocaine. *Dev. Psychopathol.* 3: 351–366.

Rosengarten, H. and Friedhoff, A. (1979) Enduring changes in dopamine receptor cells of pups from drug administration to pregnant and nursing rats. *Science* 203: 1133–1135.

Sandberg, D.E., Meyer-Bahlburg, H.F.L., Rosen, T.S. and Johnson, H.L. (1990) Effects of prenatal methadone exposure on sex-dimorphic behavior in early school-age children. *Psychoneuroendocrinology* 15: 77–82.

Seidler, F.J. and Slotkin, T.A. (1992) Fetal cocaine exposure causes persistent noradrenegic hyperactivity in rat brain regions: effects on neurotransmitter turnover and receptors. *J. Pharmacol. Exp. Ther.* 263: 413–421.

Slotkin, T.A. (1988) Perinatal exposure to methadone: How do early biochemical alterations cause neurofunctional disturbances? In: Boer, G.J., Feenstra, M.G.P., Mirmiran, M., Swaab, D.F. and Van Haaren, F. (eds.) *Progress in brain research*, vol 73. New York: Elsevier Science, pp. 265–279.

Smith, R.F., Mattran, K.M., Kurkjian, M.F. and Kurtz, S.L. (1989) Alterations in offspring behavior induced by chronic prenatal cocaine dosing. *Neurotoxicol. Teratol.* 11: 35–38.

Sobrian, S.K., Burton, L.E., Robinson, N.L., Ashe, W.K., James, H., Stokes, D.L. and Turner, L.M. (1990) Neurobehavioral and immunological effects of prenatal cocaine exposure in rat. *Pharmacol. Biochem. Behav.* 35: 617–629.

Sparber, S.B. and Lichtblau, L. (1983) Postnatal abstinence or acute toxicity can account for morbidity in developmental studies with opiates. *Life Sci.* 33: 1135–1140.

Sparber, S.B., Lichtblau, L. and Kuwahara, M.D. (1986) Experimental separation of direct and indirect effects of drugs on neurobehavioral development. In: Krasnegor, N.A., Gray, D.B. and Thompson, T. (eds.) *Developmental behavioral pharmacology*, vol 5. Hillsdale, NJ: Lawrence Erlbaum, pp. 225–263.

Spear, L.P. (1990) Neurobehavioral assessment during the

early postnatal period. *Neurotoxicol. Teratol.* 12: 489–495.

Spear, L.P. (1994a) Issues in developmental toxicology. In: Weiss, B. and O'Donoghue, J. (eds.) *Neurobehavioral toxicity: analysis and interpretation.* New York: Raven Press, pp. 59–69.

Spear, L.P. (1994b) Neurobehavioral consequences of gestational cocaine exposure: a comparative analysis. In: Rovee-Collier, C. and Lipsitt, L. (eds.) *Advances in infancy research*, vol 9. Norwood, NJ: Ablex, pp. 55–105.

Spear, L.P. (1995) Alterations in cognitive function following prenatal cocaine exposure: studies in an animal model. In: Lewis, M. and Bendersky, M. (eds.) *Mothers, babies and cocaine: the role of toxins in development.* Hillsdale, NJ: Lawrence Erlbaum, pp. 207–227.

Spear, L.P. (1996) Assessment of the effects of developmental toxicants: pharmacological and stress vulnerability of offspring. *NIDA Res. Monogr.* 164: 125–145.

Spear, L.P., Frambes, N.A. and Kirstein, C.L. (1989a) Fetal and maternal brain and plasma levels of cocaine and benzoylecgonine following chronic subcutaneous administration of cocaine during gestation in rats. *Psychopharmacology* 97: 427–431.

Spear, L.P. and Heyser, C.J. (1993) Is use of a cellulose-diluted diet a viable alternative to pair-feeding? *Neurotoxicol. Teratol.* 15: 85–89.

Spear, L.P., Kirstein, C.L., Bell, J., Yoottanasumpun, V., Greenbaum, R., O'Shea, J., Hoffmann, H. and Spear, N.E. (1989b) Effects of prenatal cocaine exposure on behavior during the early postnatal period. *Neurotoxicol. Teratol.* 11: 57–63.

Spear, L.P. and Scalzo, F.M. (1986) Behavioral, psychopharmacological, and neurochemical effects of chronic neuroleptic treatment during development. In: Riley, E.P. and Vorhees, C.V. (eds.) *Handbook of behavioral teratology.* New York: Plenum Press, pp. 173–184.

Stanton, M.E. and Spear, L.P. (1990) Workshop on the qualitative and quantitative comparability of human and animal developmental neurotoxicity, work group I report: Comparability of measures of developmental neurotoxicity in humans and laboratory animals. *Neurotoxicol. Teratol.* 12: 261–267.

Streissguth, A.P. (1992). Fetal alcohol syndrome: early and long-term consequences. *NIDA Res. Monogr.* 119: 126–130.

Streissguth, A.P., Aase, J.M., Clarren, S.K., Randels, S.P. LaDue, R.A. and Smith, D.F. (1991) Fetal alcohol syndrome in adolescents and adults. *JAMA* 265: 1961–1967.

Strupp, B.J., Bunsey, M., Levitsky, D.A. and Hamberger, K. (1994) Deficient cumulative learning: an animal model of retarded cognitive development. *Neurotoxicol. Teratol.* 16: 71–79.

Taylor, A.N., Branch, B.J., Nelson, L.R., Lane, L.A. and Poland, R.E. (1986) Prenatal ethanol and ontogeny of pituitary-adrenal responses to ethanol and morphine. *Alcohol* 3: 255–259.

Tempel, A., Habas, J., Paredes, W. and Barr, G. (1988) Morphine-induced down regulation of μ-opioid receptors in neonatal rat brain. *Dev. Brain Res.* 41: 129–133.

Tonkiss, J., Cohen, C.A. and Sparber, S.B. (1988) Different methods for producing neonatal undernutrition in rats cause different brain changes in the face of equivalent somatic growth parameters. *Dev. Neurosci.* 10: 141–151.

Tyrala, E.E., Mathews, S.V. and Rao, G.S. (1992) Effect of intrauterine exposure to cocaine on acetylcholinesterase in primary cultures of fetal mouse brain cells. *Neurotoxicol. Teratol.* 14: 229–233.

Tyrey, L. and Murphy, L.L. (1988) Inhibition of suckling-induced milk ejections in the lactating rat by Δ^9-tetrahydrocannabinol. *Endocrinology* 123: 469–472.

Vorhees, C.V. (1987a) Dependence on the stage of gestation: prenatal drugs and offspring behavior as influenced by different periods of exposure in rats. In: Fujii, T. and Adams, P.M. (eds.) *Functional teratogenesis.* Teikyo University Press, pp. 39–51.

Vorhees, C.V. (1987b) Reliability, sensitivity and validity of behavioral indices of neurotoxicity. *Neurotoxicol. Teratol.* 9: 445–464.

Vorhees, C.V. (1989a) Sample size determinations using examples drawn from the NCTR collaborative behavioral teratology study data. *Neurotoxicol. Teratol.* 11: 381–383.

Vorhees, C.V. (1989b) A fostering/crossfostering analysis of the effects of prenatal ethanol exposure in a liquid diet on offspring development and behavior in rats. *Neurotoxicol. Teratol.* 11: 115–120.

Ward, O.B. (1992) Fetal drug exposure and sexual differentiation of males. In: Gerall, A.A., Moltz, H. and Ward, I.L. (eds.) *Sexual differentiation, volume 11, Handbook of behavioral neurobiology.* New York: Plenum Press, pp. 181–219.

Ward, O.B., Kopertowski, D.M., Finnegan, L.P. and Sandberg, D.E. (1989) Gender-identity variation in boys prenatally exposed to opiates. In: Hutchings, D.E. (ed.) *Prenatal abuse of licit and illicit drugs: Annals of the New York Academy of Sciences,* Vol. 562. New York: New York Academy of Sciences, pp. 365–366.

Ward, O.B., Orth, J.M. and Weisz, J. (1983) A possible role of opiates in modifying sexual differentiation. In: Schlumpf, M. and Lichtensteiger, W. (eds.) *Monographs in neural sciences, vol. 9: drugs and hormones in brain development.* Basel: S. Karger, pp. 194–200.

Weinberg, J. (1985) Effects of ethanol and maternal nutritional status on fetal development. *Alcohol Clin. Exp. Res.* 9: 49–55.

Weinberg, J. and Gallo, P.V. (1982) Prenatal ethanol exposure: pituitary-adrenal activity in pregnant dams and offspring. *Neurobehav. Toxicol. Teratol.* 4: 515–520.

Weinberg, J., Sonderegger, T.B. and Chasnoff, I.J. (1992) Methodological issues: laboratory animal studies of perinatal exposure to alcohol or drugs and human studies of drug use during pregnancy. In: Sonderegger, T.B. (ed.) *Perinatal substance abuse.* Baltimore: The Johns Hopkins University Press, pp. 13–20.

Wood, R.D., Molina, V.A., Wagner, J.M. and Spear, L.P. (1995) Play behavior and stress responsivity in periadolescent offspring exposed prenatally to cocaine. *Pharmacol. Biochem. Behav.* 52: 367–374.

Zagon, I.S., Gibo, D.M. and McLaughlin, P.J. (1992) Ontogeny of zeta (ζ), the opioid growth factor receptor, in the rat brain. *Brain Res.* 596: 149–156.

Zagon, I.S. and McLaughlin, P.J. (1987) Endogenous opioid systems regulate cell proliferation in the developing rat brain. *Brain Res.* 412: 68–72.

Zagon, I.S., McLaughlin, P.J. and Thompson, C.I. (1979) Learning ability in adult female rats perinatally exposed to methadone. *Pharmacol. Biochem. Behav.* 10: 889–894.

Zuckerman, B. and Bresnahan, K. (1991) Developmental and behavioral consequences of prenatal drug and alcohol exposure. *Pediatr. Clin. North Am.* 38: 1387–1406.

PART III

New Horizons in Neuroscience

Drug Addiction and its Treatment: Nexus of Neuroscience and Behavior, edited by Bankole A. Johnson and John D. Roache. Lippincott–Raven Publishers, Philadelphia, © 1997.

11

Topographical Brain Mapping During Drug-Induced Behaviors

Scott E. Lukas

Department of Psychiatry (Pharmacology)/Harvard Medical School;
Clinical Neuropsychopharmacology Laboratory/Alcohol and Drug Abuse Research Center;
Sleep Disorders Center, McLean Hospital, Belmont, Massachusetts 02178

BACKGROUND

Direct correlations between specific behavioral states and changes in brain electrical activity have been difficult to identify. From a more general perspective, attempts to link specific behavioral traits such as introversion or extroversion with specific brainwave patterns have been somewhat successful once the inclusionary/exclusionary criteria for the behavioral state was clearly delineated (Eysenck, 1967; Gayle et al., 1971). The importance of taking subjective, emotional, or "mental" state information into account when analyzing electroencephalographic (EEG) activity was emphasized by Matejcek (1982) in his review of the psychological, physiologic, and pharmacologic components of vigilance and the waking EEG. Through an extensive list of experiments, Matejcek demonstrates that many factors must be taken into account when evaluating the correlates between brain electrical activity and a specific change in mood state. In particular, issues of activation, concentration, extroversion, motivation, memory, and biologic rhythms can effect the resultant recordings. Other reviews of the use of EEG techniques using both animal and human subjects have been published (Lukas, 1990, 1991b).

It is important to segregate any evaluation of brain electrical activity measures and behavior into trait and state categories. With respect to the former, many investigators have documented specific brainwave changes in individuals with chronic schizophrenia (Goldstein et al., 1963, 1965; Sugerman et al., 1964), depression (D'Elia and Perris, 1973; Goldstein, 1979; Von Knorring and Goldstein, 1982), neuroticism (Hoffman and Goldstein, 1981), hyperemotionality (Wiet, 1981), and anxiety (Koella, 1981). To some extent, these changes have been used diagnostically, but their utility in this regard (especially for a specific patient) is questionable. There is also the problem of identifying an organic source of the observed changes.

Changes in state have been studied electrophysiologically, but because of the very nature of such changes (i.e., rapidly changing, impossible to predict, difficult to quantify, etc.) conclusive findings have been difficult to obtain. Mental fatigue, menstrual tension, pain, sexual arousal, meditation, and drug-induced intoxication have all been quantified electrophysiologically. Of particular importance in this chapter are changes associated immediately after a reinforcing drug has been taken since it is presumed that the resultant mood state dictates to some extent whether the individual will take that particular drug again. In this regard, it is perhaps useful to think of pleasurable drug-induced behaviors such as feeling extremely good, high, or even "euphoric" to be on a continuum from other drug- or non–drug-related behaviors. Indeed, individuals have "cravings" for various foods (e.g., chocolate, candy, sweets) that appear to mimic at least qualitatively the cravings for certain drugs. The phenomenon known as the "runner's high" is another example of a positive mood state that can be generated without the benefit of an exogenous pharmacologic substance.

Regardless of the source of the change in state, measures of brain electrical activity are well suited for the task. For example, the EEG is available for measurement on a continual basis, i.e., the subject is not required to "do" anything. Thus, the measurements obtained are free of confound associated with techniques that require a response. This is in contrast to other neuroimaging techniques such as positron emission tomography (PET) and magnetic resonance imaging (MRI), which involve the injection of radioactive isotopes or submission to a confined, noisy environment, respectively. This chapter reviews some of these techniques and discusses their utility in studying drug-induced changes in behavioral state.

With the advent of high-speed computer technology, the methods for recording, quantifying, and displaying brain electrical activity have changed dramatically in the last decade. Because of this leap in technology, a brief review of current methods is given before the data on EEG and drug-induced behavioral states is presented.

METHOD DEVELOPMENT

Terminology

Spontaneous fluctuations in human brain electrical activity, as measured from the scalp, are typically quantified using two basic parameters: amplitude and frequency. The frequency of a biologic signal from the brain has been divided into four main bands, but additional smaller divisions have been added for special considerations. In 1929 Hans Berger (1931) discovered the first prominent wave-

form in scalp recordings: the alpha band. Waves in this band oscillate between 8 and 13 cycles per second or hertz (Hz). Typically, alpha activity is most prominent over the occipital and parietal areas of the human scalp and is highest in individuals who are awake but resting quietly. Alpha waves are immediately suppressed during any type of physical activity or when concentrating. Frequencies below 4 Hz are defined as "delta" activity; these waves are of usually large amplitude. Delta activity is considered pathologic if the subject is awake, but such slow wave activity is quite normal during various stages of deep sleep. The theta rhythm contains activity between 4 and 8 Hz and is typically not localized over any specific area of the scalp. Beta activity is defined as that above 13 Hz and does not have any specific topography. Beta activity has been further divided into β_1 and β_2 reflecting a more restricted frequency range.

Amplitude, measured in microvolts (μV) from the isoelectric point, provides a quantitative measure of the size of a specific waveform. The amplitude measures on the scalp EEG depend on the number of neurons firing synchronously, on the distance between these neurons and the recording electrode, and, to some extent, on the source of the activity being measured.

Experimental Setting and Procedure

Studies designed to measure changes in brain electrical activity and subjective mood states after acute drug administration are typically conducted within the framework of a multidisciplinary program as there are many different dependent variables that require nonoverlapping methods to measure them. In addition, the environment must be suitably shielded such that inappropriate artifact is not introduced by sound or electrical noise from the environment. Subjects also are typically required to sit relatively motionless in a comfortable chair while recordings are collected. This procedure minimizes the amount of artifact that would typically occur while collecting physiologic and behavioral data during the study. Thus, while these experiments do not simulate a naturalistic setting in which subjects are free to move about and engage in conversation with other subjects, they do provide a very well controlled environment such that the effects of the drug can be directly measured without confounds due to other variables present in the environment.

Once the subject has had the opportunity to acclimate to the environment, baseline data is collected and if blood sampling is to be done, an indwelling intravenous catheter is inserted. It is important to allow the subjects the opportunity to relax in the environment and to recover from any of the stresses associated with the application of the electrodes or the insertion of the intravenous catheter. Typically heart rate and blood pressure are measured during the course of drug-related studies. Once sufficient baseline data have been collected, the drug administration procedure can begin and EEG and other physiologic and subjective data can be collected on an almost continuous basis for the duration of the experiment.

EEG Recording/Power Spectral Analysis

Topographic brain mapping is an extension of traditional electroencephalography that monitors electrical activity from a number of individual electrode sites. The placement of the scalp electrodes has been standardized using the international 10–20 system reported by Jasper (1958). This method ensures that electrodes are placed not on the basis of an absolute measurement, but on a percentage of the distance from key external landmarks on the skull. This ensures that the electrodes will be placed over similar neuronal structures regardless of the subject's head size. Electrical activity from individual electrode sites is typically referenced to an area with little or no electrical activity of its own such as the earlobes, mastoids, or even the tip of the nose. More recently, some investigators have used Laplacian derivatives to reduce the influence of an active reference electrode (Nunez et al.,

1991). The first step in measuring brain electrical activity is to digitize the analog waveforms that are recorded from each electrode site. This is accomplished with a high-speed analog-to-digital converter typically embedded in the hardware of a computerized data acquisition system. The next step is to transpose the data from the time domain to the frequency domain. This is done by subjecting the digitized waveforms to a fast Fourier transformation (FFT). This mathematical algorithm fits the individual digitized data points to theoretical sine and cosine waves in order to determine the amount of activity located in specific frequency bands. A schematic of this process is shown in Fig. 1. Note that this figure simply shows the relationship of each waveform to the corresponding location in the final average power spectrum. As the amplitude is relatively small in beta waves, the amount of activity is correspondingly small in the average power spectrum.

Topographical Brain Mapping

Traditional methods of measuring the electrophysiologic effects of drugs have relied on visual inspection of up to 21 channels of brain electrical activity. While the human eye is very good at detecting subtle aberrations or asymmetries, the observed changes are impossible to quantify. Such tracings often provide too much information to be synthesized in a relatively short period. Nuwer (1988) comments on the utility of quantitative electroencephalography as a metric of CNS excitability. Topographic brain mapping is one such method that has been developed to provide a complete view of the distribution of brain electrical activity over the scalp.

Topographic brain mapping is essentially an extension of the data analysis procedure described in the previous section except that the amount of activity located *between* electrode sites is actually estimated using mathematical interpolation procedures. Essentially, a power spectrum is generated for the electrical activity that has been recorded at each of

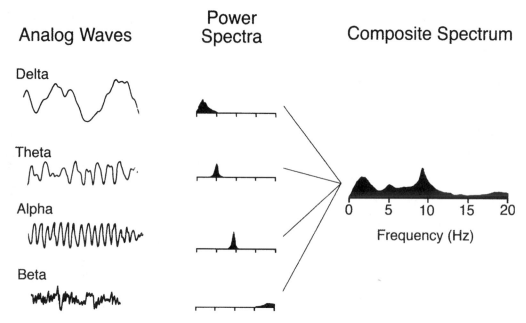

FIG. 1. Diagrammatic representation of the generation of power spectra from analog EEG waveforms.

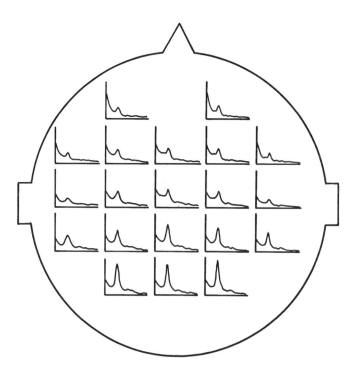

FIG. 2. Schematic diagram of the method employed in generating topographic brain maps. Power spectra are generated for electrical activity recorded in each of the individual 20 scalp electrodes.

the individual electrode sites (Fig. 2). The value of each data point located between electrode sites is a compilation of the amount of actually measured values from the electrode to which it is most closely located plus a percentage of the activity from surrounding electrodes. This is typically done using either a three- or four-point interpolation procedure. Once these intermediate values are calculated, topograms can be drawn by connecting the data points that have similar values. Examples of the resultant topographic brain map can be found later in this chapter (e.g., Figs. 3, 5, and 7). Values of similar amplitude or power can be color-coded to aid in the identification of patterns over the scalp. The selection of colors is often arbitrary and is typically used to illuminate the areas of interest rather than engendering any real physiologic significance to the range of colors observed.

Measuring Subjective Mood States

One of the biggest problems plaguing electrophysiologists who search for correlations between EEG activity and behavior has been the lack of a method to accurately identify specific mood changes using techniques that do not, in of themselves, alter the measured brain electrical activity. The use of questionnaires or verbal responding techniques would introduce movement artifact into the EEG recording, and, thus make it difficult to measure the brain activity that is associated with a specific change in mood state. To some extent, research comparing the correlation between brain electrical activity and various traits has not had similar problems since traits tend to be more stable over time while mood states frequently change during an experimental session. With respect to procedures for monitoring brain electrical activity changes during drug-induced behavioral states, one advantage is that the drug-taking event can be used as the focal point for initiating the recording procedure. Again, depending on the route of administration and the rate of onset of pharmacologic effects of the drug, the pro-

cedures can be optimized to accurately detect changes in brain electrical activity during the drug-induced behavioral states.

To accurately measure changes in brain wave activity during a specific mood state, the subject must be provided with a method of communicating to the researcher when such specific subjective changes have occurred. Some form of an instrumental joystick or switch closure device has been most frequently used by researchers in this field (Koukkou and Lehmann, 1976; Lukas and Mendelson, 1988; Lukas et al., 1986, 1990, 1995; McEachern et al., 1988; Volavka et al., 1973). The premise behind using an instrumental device is that the subject is not required to verbalize the response, which significantly reduces the potential for artifact in the EEG recordings. In addition, the instructional set can be kept very basic and simple such that only selective behaviors of interest are measured. One possible interrelationship between the joystick device, spontaneous brain electrical activity, and its mapping is shown in Fig. 3 (Lukas, 1993). Movement of the joystick device (lower right panel of figure) causes a corresponding deflection directly on the polygraph tracing. Thus, an immediate temporal relationship between changes in subjective mood state can be quantified along with corresponding changes in brain electrical activity. By keeping the response requirements as simple and as unobtrusive as possible, the amount of artifact on the resulting electroencephalogram is eliminated.

BRAIN MAPPING DURING ETHANOL-, COCAINE-, AND MARIJUANA-INDUCED INTOXICATION

Ethanol

Although topographic brain mapping of the EEG has been used in neurology for some time (e.g., Duffy, 1986), its utility in psychopharmacology has been limited to classifying various drugs on the basis of their phar-

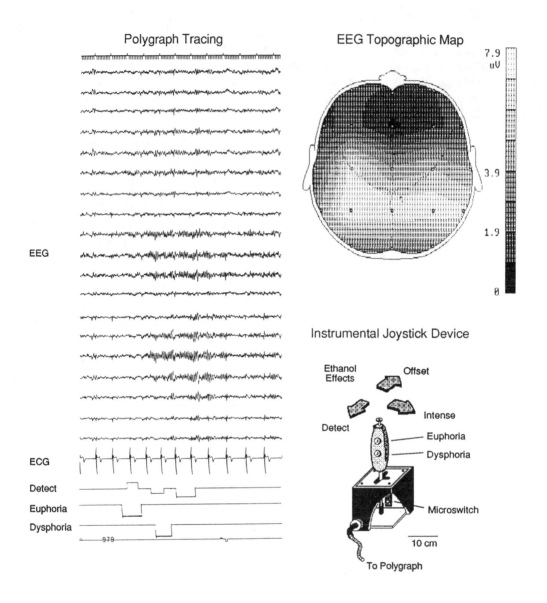

FIG. 3. Key elements of an electrophysiologic study in which subjective effects of a drug are correlated with specific brain wave patterns. The *left side* displays raw tracing from conventional EEG polygraphs. The *right side* shows a representative topographic brain map for a specific epic of EEG activity. An instrumental joystick device is depicted in the *bottom panel,* the output of which is directly recorded on the polygraph paper *(left side)* thus facilitating location of specific events. The position of the joystick conveys information relating to the detection of ethanol effects and whether the effects have become intense. (From London, 1993, with permission.)

macology. Only recently has this technique been exploited to its full potential with respect to assessment of changes in mood states after a psychoactive drug administration (Lukas 1993; Lukas et al., 1989). The acute behavioral effects of ethanol are well known (Begleiter and Platz, 1972; Davis et al., 1941; Doctor et al., 1966; Engel and Rosenbaum, 1945) and the acute effects on the EEG have been well described in the literature (Alha, 1951; Bjerver and Goldberg, 1950; Ekman et al., 1964; King, 1943). With the use of a continuous joystick device such as that described above, another behavioral profile emerged that was not expected. As is seen in Fig. 4, 0.7 g/kg of ethanol delivered over an 18-minute period produces not only observable intoxication and clear detection of ethanol effects, but paroxysmal bursts of intense well-being or "euphoria." Lower doses of ethanol and even placebo solutions will elicit a "detection" response but fail to elicit the intense well-being or euphoric response. When the individual episodes of euphoria are subjected to power spectral analysis a very characteristic pattern emerges. The spontaneous brain electrical activity associated with these periods of intense well-being

or euphoria are characterized by pronounced increases in alpha activity that predominated over the parietal and occipital areas of the scalp (Lukas et al., 1986, 1989). The use of topographic brain mapping techniques not only permits an evaluation of the acute effects of ethanol on human electroencephalogram, but also has revealed distinct differences in individuals with and without a family history of alcoholism (Lukas et al., 1989) and has documented differences in recovering alcoholics (Pollock et al., 1992). As can be seen in Fig. 5, EEG alpha activity predominates over the occipital/parietal areas of the scalp as indicated by the large amounts of brown and red colors (depicting larger amplitudes in μV) in the upper left hand panel of the figure. This is a typical topographic map of EEG alpha activity in an individual who has a negative family history of alcoholism. In contrast, the effects of 0.7 g/kg of ethanol are shown in the lower left panel in this individual. The increase in EEG alpha activity over the entire occipital area is clearly visible and increases in frontal alpha activity (reflected as an increase in voltage or in distribution) also appear. These abrupt changes in EEG alpha activity corresponded

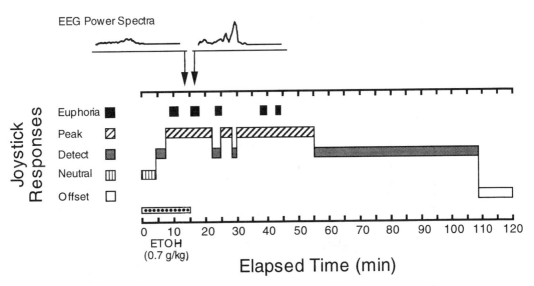

FIG. 4. Behavioral profile of a subject after receiving 0.7 g/kg of ethanol. Power spectra were generated for the EEG data that occurred just before and during one episode of euphoria or intense well-being.

with the subjective reports of intoxication and euphoria. Baseline EEG alpha activity in a representative individual who has a positive family history of alcoholism is shown in the upper right hand panel of this figure. It is also evident that there is more alpha activity during the baseline recording period in the family history positive (FHP) individual. Similar differences have been observed for both EEG activity (Bauer and Hesselbrock, 1993; Ehlers and Schuckit, 1991; Gabrielli et al., 1982; Lukas et al., 1989; Propping et al., 1981) and event-related potentials (Begleiter et al., 1984; O'Connor et al., 1987; Polich et al., 1994). The effects of ethanol in this individual are shown in the lower right panel and clearly demonstrate that there is even a slight reduction in the amount of spontaneous alpha activity after the same dose of ethanol. However, what is also different is that individuals with a positive family history of alcoholism do not report feeling intoxicated and certainly did not experience euphoria after this dose of ethanol (Lukas et al., 1989). These topographic maps

were taken during the same time as the family history negative subjects' data when plasma ethanol levels were approximately 70 mg/dl. Thus, while the time course in the plasma ethanol levels was exactly the same in these individuals, their EEG and subjective response to ethanol was very different. The group data (Fig. 6) demonstrates that individuals with a negative family history of alcoholism have a much larger increase in alpha activity than those who have a positive family history of alcoholism. This difference is not due to pharmacologic tolerance because the subjects have all had the same drinking history. That is, none has developed alcoholism. These differences in alpha activity may, however, reflect an "innate" tolerance that may be tied to the genetic predisposition of alcoholism. Full dose-response studies are necessary to determine if greater increases in alpha activity and intoxication are achieved in FHP subjects. However, the 0.7 g/kg ethanol dose is already quite high and it is unethical to give very high doses of ethanol to human subjects.

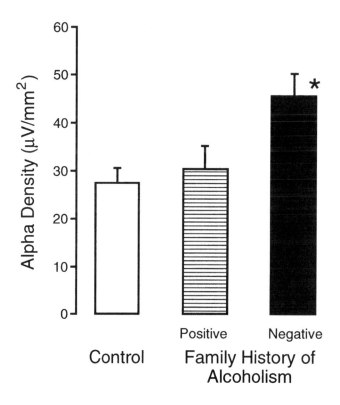

FIG. 6. Group data from male subjects with and without a positive family history of alcoholism who received an acute dose of ethanol (0.7 g/kg). The density of alpha activity was obtained by summing the amount of activity from the central/occipital scalp leads. (From London, 1993, with permission.)

Cocaine

As in the studies of ethanol-induced intoxication, a method for delivering cocaine had to be developed that did not induce a great deal of movement artifact so that EEG recordings could be made during the drug-taking procedure. An intranasal snort-stick device was developed that permitted a hands-free administration of cocaine via the intranasal route (Lukas, 1991a). With this device, the subject's dose of cocaine can be measured and placed in a test tube and mounted on a mechanical arm device much like a microphone stand. The subject simply places his/her nostril over the end of the test tube and inhales briskly to administer the dose.

As noted previously for ethanol, cocaine produced rapid increases in detection of cocaine's effects as well as the multiple episodes of intense well-being or euphoria. Using a similar procedure of identifying the euphoric events from the paper tracing and then subjecting the corresponding EEG activity to spectral analysis and topographic brain mapping techniques, very similar profiles were observed for cocaine-induced euphoria. Subjects experienced pronounced increases in EEG alpha activity that paralleled the subjective effects. In general, the alpha activity was localized to the occipital and parietal areas, but occasionally some subjects experienced increases in frontal alpha activity as well (Lukas, 1991a).

Berger (1931) reported a similar increase in alpha activity after cocaine administration. While Herning et al. (1985) replicated Berger's initial findings, he noted that the alpha increases do not persist for extended periods of time. However, it is quite possible that the reason for this rather modest alpha response is due to the fact that the subjects were required to perform a sequential subtraction test while activity was being recorded. It is well known that baseline EEG alpha activity is markedly reduced or even eliminated in individuals who are engaged in such performance tasks.

Marijuana/Cocaine Combination

In an extension of this study, some subjects were permitted to smoke a marijuana cigarette (2.64% Δ^9-THC) 30 minutes before the administration of 0.9 mg/kg intranasal cocaine. The results of this experiment are shown in Fig. 7. The control topographic map (upper left) reflects the typical distribution of alpha activity over the occipital area during a resting state with eyes closed. The first detection of cocaine's effects are shown in the lower left hand panel and full-blown intense well-being or euphoria are shown in the upper right hand panel. These are some of the largest increases in EEG alpha activity that we have observed in the laboratory. Occasionally individuals will feel anxious or report feeling nausea after some of these drug interaction studies. This is characterized by a complete blockade of the alpha rhythm and substitution of a desynchronized low-voltage EEG pattern. The lower right hand panel shows the distribution of electrical activity during drug-induced dysphoria.

Significance

Increases in EEG alpha activity are often associated with pleasurable, free-floating, and extremely relaxed states (Brown, 1970; Lindsley, 1952; Matejcek, 1982; Wallace, 1970). In addition, similar levels of increased alpha activity are seen in individuals who practice transcendental meditation (Wallace, 1970). The covariance between increased EEG alpha activity and subjective reports of euphoria after ethanol, cocaine, and marijuana suggests that this neurophysiologic response may be associated with the reinforcing effects of these drugs. Given the generality of alpha activity and its association with pleasurable mood states, it is plausible that increased EEG alpha activity may be associated with drug-induced reinforcement in general and may not be selective for a single drug class. This interpretation is consistent with the notion that drug-seeking behavior is a form of stimulus self-administration that produces a change (regardless of the direction) in subjective state (Mello, 1983).

LOCALIZATION OF BRAIN POTENTIALS USING MAGNETIC RESONANCE IMAGING

Spatial interpretation of EEG data is an important advance in neurology since many diagnoses are confirmed by various imaging techniques. Similarly, the changes in brain electrical activity observed during drug-induced behavioral states can more precisely be identified using such techniques. It would seem that the best solution to the problem is to combine the diverse array of information from various imaging technologies in order to obtain the best interpretation of the functional state of the CNS. However, this has remained a difficult task.

Improvements in spatial interpretation have been made via methods that estimate the position, orientation, and strength of the underlying generator of the EEG and magnetoencephalogram (Barth et al., 1989; De Munck, 1989, 1990; Salustri and Chapman, 1989). To date, we, along with others, have had good success in using an inverse solution algorithm to estimate the source of specific brain waves during ethanol intoxication (Lukas et al., 1990). However, a major deficiency of this technique is that the model assumes that the head is a perfect sphere and the apparent dipole sources are fit to this hypothetical model. Although this assumption helps keep the mathematical calculations manageable, the technique has numerous pitfalls. For example, a comparison of the source localization in one person is likely to lie at a different anatomic location in a second person, even thought the Cartesian coordinates of the sources are the same.

Thus, it is difficult to accurately visualize the precise location of the calculated dipole source. This problem was recognized by Torello et al. (1987) and van den Elsen et al. (1991), who matched brain electrical activity data with magnetic resonance images using external markers. We extended this technol-ogy by obtaining precise neuroanatomical information from subjects via MRI and then used this information to more precisely identify the source of the P300 waveform using three-dimensional reconstruction techniques.

P300 Waveforms

Event-related potentials (ERP) are those that are elicited from a specific stimulus in a subject's environment. The nature of the stimulus (e.g., auditory, visual) is of less importance than the relative significance of the stimulus to the subject in a particular experimental setting. Thus, auditory, visual, and somatosensory stimuli have all been used to elicit P300 waveforms. By definition, a P300 waveform is a positive wave occurring approximately 300 msec after the delivery of a specific stimulus. The resultant waveform is largest over the midline electrodes and is most prominent when the subject has been instructed to attend to a stimulus that occurs infrequently (Donchin et al., 1978). The P300 is particularly interesting because it reflects cognitive rather than sensory processes. Indeed, patients with psychiatric diseases associated with cognitive dysfunction such as dementia, depression, schizophrenia, and borderline personality disorder display altered P300 waveforms (Kutcher et al., 1987; Pfefferbaum et al., 1984; Polich et al., 1986). P300 activity also has been thought to reflect measures of familial predisposition to alcoholism. For example, Begleiter et al. (1984) demonstrated that P300 waveforms were markedly lower in young boys who had never been exposed to ethanol but whose fathers were alcoholic.

Because the magnitude of the P300 is greatest over the midline and central/parietal regions of the brain regardless of the stimulus used and its distribution is symmetrical and bilateral suggests that the P300 originates from a single site. The following study was designed to measure the changes in the apparent source of the P300 wave.

Adult male bodybuilders who had just finished a cycle of high-dose steroid use (6–7 weeks) provided informed consent to participate in this multidisciplinary study of the effects of ethanol on brain electrical activity, endocrine function, and behavior. Subjects were prepared with 21 scalp EEG electrodes using an electro-cap and sat in a darkened sound-attenuated electrically shielded chamber while P300 waveforms were generated using an auditory "oddball" paradigm. Tones were delivered via tubal insert headphones and subjects were instructed to sit quietly with their eyes closed and silently count the "rare" tones.

Binaural tones were presented at a rate of one every 2 seconds in a pseudorandom manner (i.e., no two rare tones occurred in succession). Rare tones constituted 25% of the total stimuli presented and a minimum of 25 artifact-free rare waveforms were collected and averaged together. Event-related potentials were recorded on a 21-channel polygraph and stored on a brain atlas (Bio-logic) signal averaging system. Stimulus characteristics were as follows: frequent tone—1.0 kHz at 70 dB SPL, rarefaction; rare tone—2.0 kHz at 70 dB SPL, rarefaction. Both stimuli were presented with a 9-msec rise/fall time and 10-msec plateau. Waveforms were collected at a 0.045- to 70-Hz bandpass.

MRI Recording Procedure

Immediately after the ERP procedure was completed, subjects were prepared for an MRI evaluation. The electro-cap was removed and vitamin E oil–filled capsules were attached to the scalp electrode sites using collodion (Torello et al., 1987). Subjects were then escorted to the Department of Neurology at McLean Hospital where MRIs were obtained using a GE 1.5 Tesla Signa magnetic resonance whole body imager. Subjects' heads were held fast to the table with tape to prevent image blurring. Images were constructed with T1 and T2 weighting (using multiecho sequences on the latter) and then viewed and interpreted for abnormalities by a neurologist. Standard recording parameters were followed to collect a total of 124 slices in the coronal

plane. A large number of very thin slices are needed to avoid slice artifact when visualizing the brain in planes other than that in which the scan was acquired (Tiede et al., 1990). Collecting so many slices increases scanning time, but the images were of better quality.

A volumetric representation of the MR data was built from contiguous slices of MR images. It consisted of a three-dimensional array of volume elements (or voxels) containing information about the density of tissue in the corresponding region of the MR scan. Each voxel has a unique position in three-dimensional space defined by its pixel location and slice number. Since we knew the size of voxels from the MR acquisition phase, voxel coordinates were converted to millimeter-unit coordinates by simple scaling transformation.

Dipole Construction

Estimates of the dipole sources were calculated via the "inverse" solution used in a commercially available software package (Bio-logic, Mundelein, IL). This strategy involves collecting topographic data from all electrode sites spanning a 20-msec window that includes the P waveform of interest. The source of the wave is then interpolated mathematically. We used a three-shell model, which takes into account the different electrical properties of the brain, skull and skin. This model has six parameters: X, Y, Z, ΔX, ΔY, and ΔZ. The first three coordinates (in millimeters) define the origin of the wave and the last three define the orientation. The inverse solution involves setting an initial "guess" of the source near the origin (i.e., 0, 0, 0 mm) and performing a series of iterations to determine the momentary solution of the waveform within the sample window. This process involved calculating the field distribution of voltages that would be predicted from the dipole solution. This field distribution was then compared to the measured field by determining whether the displacement (i.e., magnitude and direction) of the new guess from the previous guess was less than or greater than a preset level of error. If the displacement was less than this value, the search was terminated; if the displacement was greater than a preset margin of error, the search was continued with a new guess. The resultant data set provided an estimate of the location, direction, and magnitude of the P300 source. The dipole data were then converted to simple text or ASCII format, which presented the dipole data in two equivalent formats in millimeter units. A right-handed Cartesian coordinate system was used to define locations and dipole space.

To transform dipole data in the six-parameter format to a real anatomical location in the subject's brain, we established a common reference frame in both the EEG and the MRI data (Fig. 8). Considering the imaginary lines formed by the nasion/inion and preaurical points, the intersection of these lines form the

origin of the reference frame. Each line forms one axis of the reference frame and the third axis is perpendicular to the other two. To locate the reference frame in voxel space, we first studied the MR image slices and identified the locations most representative of the nasion/inion and preaurical points (e.g., Fpz, Oz, T3, and T4). These locations were then used to construct an orthonormal reference frame based midway between the lines found between Fpz and Oz and between T3 and T4 electrode sites. The Y axis of the reference frame is perpendicular to both Fpz/Oz and T3/T4, and the X and Z axes are approximately parallel to Fpz/Oz and T3/T4, respectively. Figure 9 shows the topographic mapping of P300 waveform before and 60 minutes after a subject consumed 0.7 g/kg of ethanol. The blood ethanol level at the time of the P300 determination was 97 mg/dl. The subject cor-

Dipole Transformation

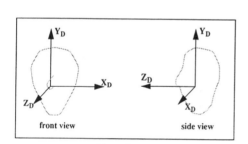

Dipole Space

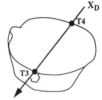

1. Assume X-axis of dipole space (X_D) goes through T3 and T4.

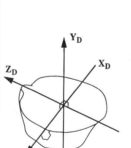

2. Place Z_D through nasion perpendicular to X_D.

3. Construct Y_D perpendicular to both X_D and Z_D.

FIG. 8. Reference frames for correlating EEG data with measured MR images.

rectly identified the number of rare tones in this trial but the P300 waveform was markedly displaced to the left parietal/occipital area. The electrically mediated dipole data and MR imaging scan are shown combined in Fig. 10. The dipole source of the peak of the P300 wave is located at the origin of the blue arrow projecting from the left temporal cortex in this subject. The projection of the arrow is to the top and rear of the scalp, which corresponds with the topographic maps of P300 waves (e.g., Fig. 9).

The results of this experiment are encouraging in that they demonstrate the feasibility of merging electrical and anatomical data from the same subject. The vitamin E capsules were easily applied and readily visible on the MR scans. The precision of their placement with respect to the electrodes sites was enhanced by applying them immediately

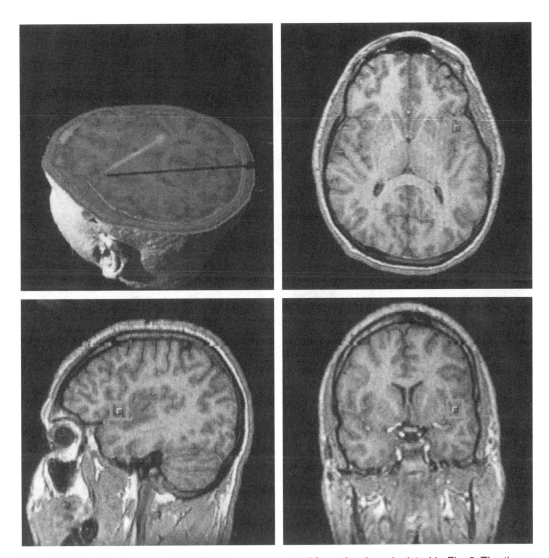

FIG. 10. Calculated source of the P300 wave generated from the data depicted in Fig. 9. The three-dimensional reconstruction of the MR data shown in the upper left panel is used to depict the origin and projection of the P300 waveform. The other three images identify the location of the origin using the appropriate MR slice.

after the P300 trial was completed. Alternatively, nonwashable ink pen could be used to mark the sites for later application. Although the clinical value of dipole calculations are just beginning to be realized, there are currently a few reports of their use in epilepsy (Ebersole and Wade, 1990; Wong, 1989). Once the accuracy of source estimations are improved, however, such use should have a larger impact in neurology.

There is good evidence that the P300 ERP is generated in allocortical structures such as the entorhinal cortex, amygdaloid body, and hippocampal formation (Halgren et al., 1982; Maurer et al., 1989; Okada et al., 1983). The fit of the dipole to the MR data would obviously be improved by using a more sophisticated model such as in the ellipse or by employing surface information of the head instead of a sphere (Meijs et al., 1987).

These studies are currently in the developmental stage as the individual techniques themselves are still being refined. Nevertheless, the integration of brain electrical activity mapping with direct visualization of sources using MR procedures has an inherent advantage in that the sources of drug-induced changes in brain electrical activity may help understand the mechanism by which these drugs are altering mood states. Collectively, studies of this type provide a unique profile of information that permits the integration of multiple modes of recording procedures.

FUTURE DIRECTIONS

The concept that drugs belonging to different pharmacologic classes share a common neurophysiologic response during drug-induced euphoria has numerous implications. First, from a basic science point of view, it paves the way for discovering the neuroanatomical sources of drug-related reinforcement. We are actively pursuing this area of research by increasing the precision with which we coregister the EEG and MRI data. We are now collecting both EEG and MRI data concurrently while the subject is in the magnet.

This technique will significantly improve our attempts to localize the waveform sources and, with the addition of MR, spectroscopy, and functional MRI (FMRI) techniques, this analysis can be extended to an even higher level. The second implication of the association between brain function and behavior is that a single therapy may be successful in treating dependence on two or more drugs at the same time. Such a finding would be of crucial clinical importance as the management of drug abusers is already a complex problem and any advancement that simplifies the treatment would be a welcome relief. We are currently exploring this area of research using novel pharmacotherapies.

As brain electrical activity is an excellent marker of ongoing CNS function, and its high temporal resolution allows it to be measured continuously along with ongoing behavior, we are now using EEG and P300 ERPs as indices of drug-seeking behavior and as measures of craving during exposure to drug-related cues. Brain wave patterns observed during active cocaine-seeking behavior are very similar to those observed when individuals are presented with visual, auditory, and tactile stimuli associated with cocaine. Although other investigators have clearly demonstrated that craving and physiologic responses such as skin temperature are affected by cue exposure, this area of research will help us determine if repeated cue exposure actually alters brain function during drug craving. Thus, this technique may become a useful adjunct to our current methods of treating drug abuse.

These future goals not only extend the prior years of research, but represent a new era of combining advanced neuroimaging techniques to study drug-induced behavior. Such ventures certainly have implications for advancing basic research, but, just as importantly, they provide a solid foundation for conducting applied research as well.

SUMMARY

• Brain electrical activity can be utilized to study various aspects of drug abuse.

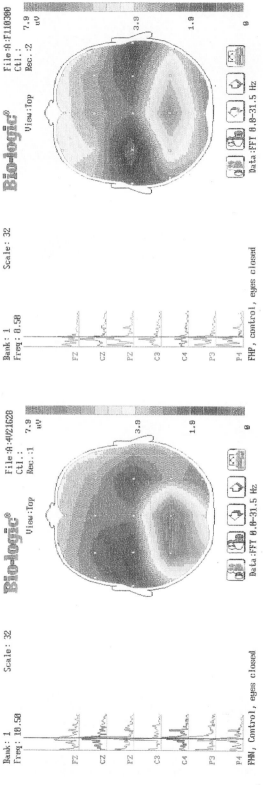

FIG. 5 A–D. Topographic brain maps of EEG alpha activity of two individuals having either a negative (**A,C**) or a positive (**B,D**) family history of alcoholism after both placebo (**A,B**) and 0.7 g/kg ethanol (**C,D**). The colors are scaled to represent a range of voltages in microvolts. Increased alpha activity is defined as an increase in the voltage (μV).

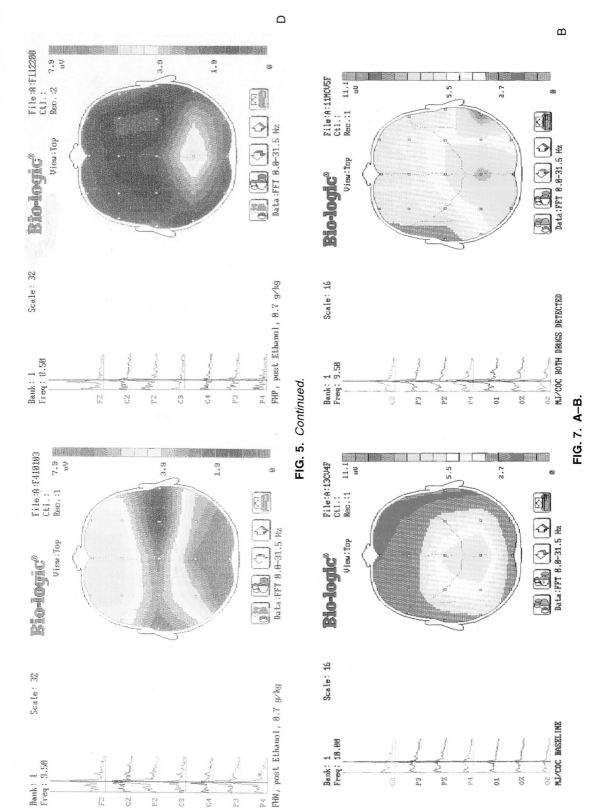

FIG. 5. *Continued.*

FIG. 7. A–B.

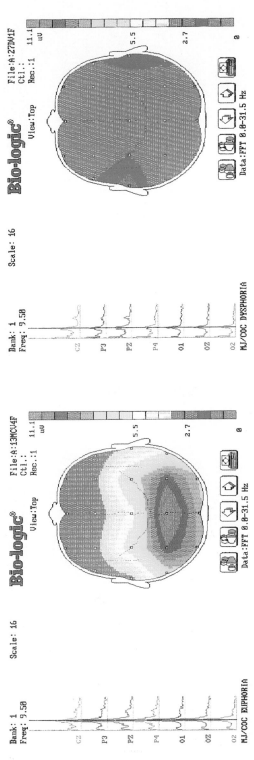

FIG. 7. C–D *Continued.* Topographic brain maps during **(A)** baseline control recording; **(B)** detection of acute effects of cocaine and marijuana; **(C)** intense euphoria or well-being after cocaine and marijuana; and **(D)** dysphoria after the drug combinations.

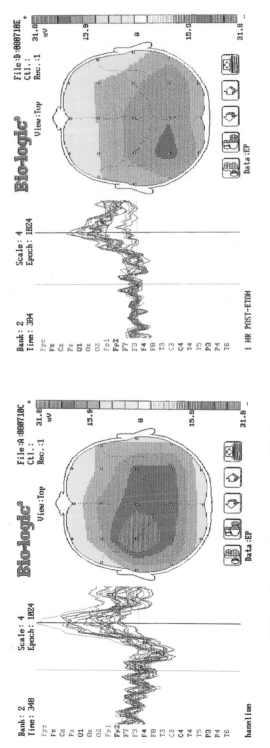

FIG. 9. Topographic brain map of P300 waves in an individual subject before (**A**) and after (**B**) an acute dose of ethanol. Note the pronounced shift to the left and a reduction in the distribution of the P300 wave after ethanol.

- To date, studies have focused on the acute effects of psychoactive drugs in an attempt to characterize or classify them into similar or dissimilar categories.
- The uniqueness of measuring brain electrical activity as compared to other measures of pharmacologic response resides in the fact that EEG is propagated on a continuous basis.
- The temporal relationship between brain wave activity and behavior permits the researcher to obtain correlations between EEG activity and many other physiologic behavioral responses.
- The use of an instrumental joystick device provides continuous recording of changes in mood state that can be directly correlated with rapidly changing patterns in brain electrical activity.
- Drugs belonging to different pharmacologic classes have similar behavioral effects such as producing intense good feelings or euphoria.
- Large increases in EEG alpha activity are temporally associated with positive mood states after various drugs, suggesting that this waveform may be tied to drug-related reinforcement.
- Measures of brain electrical activity can be combined with other neuroimaging techniques such as MRI to provide a unique and powerful tool to scientists who are studying the neurophysiologic and neuroanatomical basis of drug reinforcement. These two techniques capitalize on the superior temporal resolution afforded by the EEG measures and the excellent spatial resolution provided by the MR images.
- These studies may be useful in identifying biologic markers and indices of vulnerability to drug abuse.

REFERENCES

Alha, A. R. (1951) Blood alcohol and clinical inebriation in Finnish men. *Ann. Acad. Sci. Fenn.* 26: 1–92.

Barth, D. S., Baumgartner, C. and Sutherling, W. W. (1989) Neuromagnetic field modeling of multiple brain regions producing interictal spikes in human epilepsy. *Electroencephalogr. Clin. Neurophysiol.* 73: 389–402.

Bauer, L. O. and Hesselbrock, V. M. (1993) EEG, autonomic and subjective correlates of the risk for alcoholism. *J. Stud. Alcohol.* 54: 577–589.

Begleiter, H. and Platz, A. (1972) The effects of alcohol on the central nervous system in humans. In: Kissin, B. and Begleiter, H. (eds.) *The biology of alcoholism,* vol. 2. New York: Plenum Press, pp. 293–343.

Begleiter, H., Porjesz, B., Bihari, B. and Kissen, B. (1984) Event-related brain potentials in boys at risk for alcoholism. *Science* 225: 1493–1496.

Berger, H. (1931) Uber das Elektrenkephalogramm des Menschen. [On the electroencephalogram of man: third report]. *Arch. Psychiatr.* 94:16–60. Translated in: Berger, H. (1969) On the electroencephalogram of man. *Electroencephalogr. Clin. Neurophysiol. Suppl.* Gloor, P. (ed.) Amsterdam: Elsevier, pp. 95–132.

Bjerver, K. and Goldberg, L. (1950) Effects of alcohol ingestion on driving ability. *Q. J. Stud. Alcohol* 11: 1–30.

Brown, B. B. (1970) Recognition of aspects of consciousness through association with EEG alpha activity represented by a light signal. *Psychophysiology* 6: 442–452.

Davis, P. A., Gibbs, F. A., Davis, H., Jetter, W. W. and Trowbridge, L. S. (1941) The effects of alcohol upon the electroencephalogram (brain waves). *Q. J. Stud. Alcohol* 1: 626–637.

D'Elia, G. and Perris, C. (1973) Cerebral functional dominance and depression. *Acta Psychiatr. Scand.* 49: 191–197.

De Munck, J. C. (1989) A mathematical and physical interpretation of the electromagnetic field of the brain. Ph.D. thesis, University of Amsterdam.

De Munck, J. C. (1990) The estimation of time varying dipoles on the basis of evoked potentials. *Electroencephalogr. Clin. Neurophysiol.* 77: 156–160.

Doctor, R. F., Naitoh, P. and Smith, J. C. (1966) Electroencephalographic changes and vigilance behavior during experimentally induced intoxication with alcoholic subjects. *Psychosom. Med.* 28: 605–615.

Donchin, E., Ritter, W. and McCallum, W. C. (1978) Cognitive psychophysiology: the endogenous components of the ERP. In: Callaway, E., Tueting P. and Koslow S. (eds.) *Event-related brain potentials in man.* New York: Academic Press, pp. 349–411.

Duffy, F. H. (ed.) (1986) *Topographic mapping of brain electrical activity.* Boston: Butterworths.

Ebersole, J. S. and Wade, P. B. (1990) Spike voltage topography and equivalent dipole localization in complex partial epilepsy. *Brain Topogr.* 3: 21–34.

Ehlers, C. L. and Schuckit, M. A. (1991) Evaluation of EEG alpha activity in sons of alcoholics. *Neuropsychopharmacology* 4: 199–205.

Ekman, G., Frankenhaeuser, M., Goldberg, L., Hagdahl, R. and Myrsten, A.-L. (1964) Subjective and objective effects of alcohol as functions of dosage and time. *Psychopharmacologia* 6: 399–409.

Engel, G. L. and Rosenbaum, M. (1945) Delerium III. Electroencephalographic changes associated with acute alcohol intoxication. *Arch. Neurol. Psychiatry* 53: 44–50.

Eysenck, H. J. (1967) *The biological basis of personality.* Springfield, IL: Charles C. Thomas.

Gabrielli, W. F., Mednick, S. A., Volavka, J., Pollock, V. E., Schulsinger, F., Itil, T. M. (1982) Electroencephalograms in children of alcoholic fathers. *Psychophysiology* 19: 404–407.

Gayle, A., Coles, M., Kline, P. and Penfold, V. (1971) Extroversion/introversion, neuroticism and the EEG: basil and response measures during habituation of the orienting response. *Br. J. Psychol.* 62: 533–543.

Goldstein, L. (1979) Some relationships between quantitated hemispheric EEG and behavioral states in man. In: Gruzelier, J. and Flor-Henry, P. (eds.) *Hemispheric asymmetries of function and psychopathology.* New York: Elsevier, pp. 237–254.

Goldstein, L., Murphree, H. B., Sugerman, A. A., Pfeiffer, C. C. and Jenney, E. H. (1963) Quantitative electroencephalographic analysis of naturally occurring (schizophrenic) and drug-induced psychotic states in human males. *Clin. Pharmacol. Ther.* 4: 10–21.

Goldstein, L., Sugerman, A. A., Stolberg, H., Murphree, H. B. and Pfeiffer, C. C. (1965) Electrocerebral activity in schizophrenic and non-psychotic subjects: quantitative EEG amplitude analysis. *Electroencephalogr. Clin. Neurophysiol.* 19: 350–361.

Halgren, E., Squires, N. K., Wilson, C. L. and Crandall, P. H. (1982) Brain generators of evoked potential: the late endogenous components. *Bull. Los Angeles Neurol. Soc.* 47: 108–123.

Herning, R. I., Jones, R. T., Hooker, W. D., Mendelson, J. and Blackwell, L. (1985) Cocaine increases EEG beta: a replication and extension of Hans Berger's historic experiments. *Electroencephalogr. Clin. Neurophysiol.* 60: 470–477.

Hoffman, E. and Goldstein, L. (1981) Hemispheric quantitative EEG changes following emotional reactions in neurotic patients. *Acta Psychiatr. Scand.* 63: 153–164.

Jasper, H. H. (1958) The 10-20 electrode system of the International Federation. *Electroencephalogr. Clin. Neurophysiol.* 10: 371–375.

King, A. R. (1943) Tunnel vision. *Q. J. Stud. Alcohol* 4: 362–357.

Koella, W. P. (1981) Electroencephalographic signs of anxiety. *Prog. Neuropsychopharmacol.* 5: 187–192.

Koukkou, M. and Lehmann, D. (1976) Human EEG spectra before and during cannabis hallucinations. *Biol. Psychiatry* 11: 663–677.

Kutcher, S. P., Blackwood, H. R., St. Clair, D., Gaskell, D. F. and Muir, W. J. (1987) Auditory P300 in borderline personality disorder and schizophrenia. *Arch. Gen. Psychiatry* 44: 645–650.

Lindsley, D. B. (1952) Psychological phenomena and the electroencephalogram. *Electroencephalogr. Clin. Neurophysiol.* 4: 443–456.

London, E. (ed.) (1993) *Imaging drug action in the brain.* Boca Raton, FL: CRC Press.

Lukas, S. E. (1990) Drugs of abuse: in vivo measures of CNS excitability. In: Adler, M.W. and Cowan, A. (eds.) *Testing and evaluation of drugs of abuse, vol. 6 of modern methods in pharmacology.* New York: A. R. Liss, pp. 121–145.

Lukas, S. E. (1991a) Topographic brain mapping during cocaine-induced intoxication and self-administration. In: Racagni, G., Brunello, N. and Fukuda, T. (eds.) *Biological psychiatry,* vol. 2. New York: Excerpta Medica, pp. 25–29.

Lukas, S. E. (1991b) Brain electrical activity as a tool for studying drugs of abuse. In: Mello, N. K. (ed.) *Advances in substance abuse: behavioral and biological research,* vol. 4. London: Jessica Kingsley, pp. 1–88.

Lukas, S. E. (1993) Advanced electrophysiological imaging techniques for studying drug effects. In: London, E. D. (ed.) *Imaging drug action in the brain.* Boca Raton, FL: CRC Press, pp. 389–404.

Lukas, S. E., Benedikt, R. and Mendelson, J. H. (1995) Electroencephalographic correlates of marihuana-induced euphoria. *Drug Alcohol Depend.* 37: 131–140.

Lukas, S. E. and Mendelson, J. H. (1988) Electroencephalographic activity and plasma ACTH during ethanol-induced euphoria. *Biol. Psychiatry* 23: 141–148.

Lukas, S. E., Mendelson, J. H., Benedikt, R. A. and Jones, B. (1986) EEG alpha activity increases during transient episodes of ethanol-induced euphoria. *Pharmacol. Biochem. Behav.* 25: 889–895.

Lukas, S. E., Mendelson, J. H., Kouri, E., Bolduc, M. and Amass, L. (1990) Ethanol-induced alterations in EEG alpha activity and apparent source of the auditory P300 evoked response potential. *Alcohol* 7: 471–477.

Lukas, S. E., Mendelson, J. H., Woods, B. T., Mello, N. K. and Teoh, S. K. (1989) Topographic distribution of EEG alpha activity during ethanol-induced intoxication in women. *J. Stud. Alcohol* 50: 176–185.

Matejcek, M. (1982) Vigilance and the EEG: Psychological, physiological and pharmacological aspects. In: Herrmannd, W. M. (ed.) *EEG in drug research.* Stuttgart: Gustav Fischer, pp. 405–508.

Maurer, K., Dierks, T., Ihl, R. and Laux, G. (1989) Mapping of evoked potentials in normals and patients with psychiatric diseases. In: Maurer, K. (ed.) *Topographic brain mapping of EEG and evoked potentials.* Berlin: Springer-Verlag, pp. 458–473.

McEachern, J., Friedman, L., Bird, M., Lukas S.E., Orzack, M. H., Katz, D. L., Dessain, E. C., Beake, B. and Cole, J. O. (1988) Self-report versus an instrumental measure in the assessment of the subjective effects of d-amphetamine. *Psychopharmacol. Bull.* 24: 463–465.

Meijs, J. W. H., Bosch, F. G. C., Peters, M. J. and Lopes da Silva, F. H. (1987) On the magnetic field distribution generated by a dipole current source situated in a realistically shaped compartment model of the head. *Electroencephalogr. Clin. Neurophysiol.* 66: 286–298.

Mello, N. K. (1983) A behavioral analysis of the reinforcing properties of alcohol and other drugs in man. In: Kissin, B. and Begleiter, H. (eds.) *The pathogenesis of alcoholism, biological factors,* vol. 7. New York: Plenum Press, pp. 133–198.

Nunez, P. L., Pilgreen, K. L., Westdorp, A. F., Law, S. K. and Nelson, A. V. (1991) A visual study of surface potentials and Laplacians due to distributed neocortical sources: computer simulations and evoked potentials. *Brain Topogr.* 4: 151–168.

Nuwer, M. R. (1988) Quantitative EEG: II. Frequency analysis and topographic mapping in clinical settings. *J. Clin. Neurophysiol.* 5: 45–85.

O'Connor, S. Hesselbrock, V. M., Tasman, A. and DePalma, N. (1987) P3 amplitudes in two distinct tasks are decreased in young men with a history of paternal alcoholism. *Alcohol* 4: 323–330.

Okada, Y. C., Kaufman, L. and Williamson, S. J. (1983) The hippocampal formation as a source of the slow endogenous potentials. *Electroencephalogr. Clin. Neurophysiol.* 55: 417–426.

Pfefferbaum, A., Wenegrat, B. G., Ford, J. M., Roth, W. T. and Kopell, B. S. (1984) Clinical applications of the P3 component of event-related potentials. II. Dementia, depression and schizophrenia. *Electroencephalogr. Clin. Neurophysiol.* 59: 104–124.

Polich, J., Ehlers, C. L., Otis, S., Mandell, A. J. and Bloom, F. E. (1986) P300 latency reflects the degree of cognitive decline in dementing illness. *Electroencephalogr. Clin. Neurophysiol.* 63: 138–144.

Polich, J., Pollock, V. E. and Bloom, F. E. (1994) Meta-analysis of P300 amplitude from males at risk for alcoholism. *Psychol. Bull.* 115: 55–73.

Pollock, V. E., Schneider, L. S., Zemansky, M. F., Gleason, R. P. and Pawluczyk, S. (1992) Topographic quantitative EEG amplitude in recovered alcoholics. *Psychiatry Res.* 45: 25–32.

Propping, P., Kruger, J., Mark, N. (1981) Genetic disposition to alcoholism: an EEG study in alcoholics and their relatives. *Hum. Genet.* 59: 51–59.

Salustri, C. and Chapman, R. M. (1989) A simple method for 3-dimensional localization of epileptic activity recorded by simultaneous EEG and MEG. *Electroencephalogr. Clin. Neurophysiol.* 73: 473–478.

Sugerman, A. A., Goldstein, L., Murphree, H. G., Pfeiffer, C. C. and Jenney, E. H. (1964) EEG and behavioral changes in schizophrenia: a quantitative study. *Arch. Gen. Psychiatry* 10: 340–344.

Tiede, U., Hoehne, K., Bomans, M., Pommert, A., Riemer, M. and Wiebecke, G. (1990) Investigation of Medical 3D-rendering algorithms. *IEEE Computer Graphics & Applications.* 10(2): 41–53.

Torello, M. W., Phillips, T., Hunter, W. W. and Csuri, C. A. (1987) Combinational imaging: magnetic resonance imaging and EEG displayed simultaneously. *J. Clin. Neurophysiol.* 4: 274–275.

van den Elsen, P. A., Viergever, M. A., van Huffelen, A. C., van der Meij, W. and Wieneke, G. (1991) Accurate matching of electromagnetic dipole data with CT and MR images. *Brain Topogr.* 3: 425–432.

Volavka, J., Crown, P., Dornbush, R., Feldstein, S. and Fink, M. (1973) EEG, heart rate and mood changes ("high") after cannabis. *Psychopharmacologia* 32: 11–25.

Von Knorring, L. and Goldstein, L. (1982) Quantitative hemispheric EEG differences between healthy volunteers and depressed patients. *Res. Commun. Psychol. Psychiat. Behav.* 7: 57–67.

Wallace, R. K. (1970) Physiological effects of transcendental meditation. *Science* 167: 1751–1754.

Wiet, S. G. (1981) Some quantitative hemispheric EEG measures reflecting the affective profile of students differing in university academic success. *Biol. Psychiatry* 12: 25–42.

Wong, P. K. H. (1989) Stability of source estimates in Rolandic spikes. *Brain Topogr.* 2: 31–36.

Drug Addiction and its Treatment: Nexus of Neuroscience and Behavior, edited by Bankole A. Johnson and John D. Roache. Lippincott–Raven Publishers, Philadelphia, © 1997.

12

Structural and Functional Brain Imaging

David Lyons, Sharon R. Letchworth, James B. Daunais, and Linda J. Porrino

Department of Physiology and Pharmacology, Bowman Gray School of Medicine, North Carolina 27157

The brain is composed of many anatomical components with markedly different levels of organization and function. Other tissues such as the liver or pancreas are far more homogeneous than the brain. In these organs, cells function more similarly and more synchronously in response to a stimulus. The brain and the spinal cord, however, consist of a large number of different cell types integrated as networks and pathways, with only a subset of the cells operating in response to any given stimulus. Given the richness of the organization and function of the central nervous system, our knowledge of its operation requires an understanding of a multitude of processes, both in terms of precise localization of anatomical elements and the operation of these networks as functioning units.

Whether self-administered by an addict or given within the context of a therapeutic regimen, the administration of a psychoactive drug acts as a stimulus. The response is composed of a variety of pharmacologic actions that include both central and peripheral effects. The multiplicity of these effects depends on the variety of neurotransmitters affected, the characteristics of the receptor systems, as well as the number and sort of anatomical sites affected by the drug. Autoradiography, particularly quantitative autoradiography, has made it possible to identify and measure both structural and functional processes in the central nervous system. This advance has dramatically aided our quest to understand how the brain reacts to drugs of abuse, both on an acute and on a chronic basis.

This chapter provides an overview of autoradiographic imaging techniques in substance abuse research by highlighting three preclinical methods: receptor autoradiography, 2-deoxyglucose (2-DG) autoradiography, and *in situ* hybridization histochemistry (ISHH). These techniques are among the most useful, accessible, and commonly practiced research technologies available at present.

QUANTITATIVE AUTORADIOGRAPHY

The invention of autoradiography predates the discovery of radioactivity and can be attributed to Niepce De St. Victor in 1867, who explained the effect of uranium salts on photographic emulsion as a phenomenon of visible light (Kuhar, 1988). Much later, as an extension of biochemical methods of receptor binding in homogenized tissue begun in the 1970s, autoradiographic techniques were applied to resolve more fully the distribution of receptors in tissue. Like the rich literature on neuroanatomy that describes tissues using a variety of stains, quantitative receptor autoradiography with radiolabeled drugs has described the topography of drug binding sites, and thus, provides an important link between anatomy and pharmacology. Currently, autoradiography is used to examine the distribution of receptors, nucleic acids, sugars, and other molecules from the level of gross anatomy down to their intracellular distribution.

The primary advantage of autoradiography is the anatomical resolution it provides. It allows for the visualization not only of individual structures within the brain, but also of small subnuclei and even specific cell types within a given structure. It has been estimated that the increase in spatial resolution provided by autoradiography of tissue slices over liquid-phase homogenate experiments is about 1000-fold (Kuhar, 1988). In fact, proper technique for receptor autoradiography and ISHH can provide resolution even at the single-cell level. The predominant limiting factors result from the isotope used and diffusion and migration of the labeled compound in the tissue during freezing and cutting of the brain.

Another advantage of autoradiography and brain mapping in general is the ability to examine the entire central nervous system, allowing for a broad survey of possible effects at all levels of the brain that is not limited to investigations of loci in which effects are expected. If the whole brain is examined, effects of an experimental manipulation may be seen that would otherwise have gone unnoticed. Williams-Hemby and Porrino (1994), for example, mapped the effects of acute ethanol administration on rat brain and identified significant changes in rates of glucose utilization in 54 structures in a number of brain systems including sensory, motor, and limbic. This kind of an approach makes possible the assessment of effects in a number of systems without using multiple sets of animals.

It is a common misconception, however, that the ability to image the distribution of drug binding sites in the central nervous system, for example, is sufficient to characterize a pharmacologic or physiologic process in the brain. The behavioral/physiologic response to a drug depends on a number of factors including dose, route of administration, timing of drug administration, and the physiologic status of the organism. Most importantly, the distribution of binding sites or gene expression gives only structural or anatomical information, not information about the biochemical functions that result from the binding. Recent advances in the uses of quantitative autoradiography have allowed us to measure local concentrations of radiolabeled compounds *in vivo*. When applied in conjunction with specific procedures and

mathematical modeling, it is possible to measure local rates of a biochemical process such as energy use or protein synthesis. Particularly in view of the diversity of the neurochemical and behavioral effects that occur with administration of drugs of abuse, it is necessary to measure neural events in circuits and pathways throughout the brain from a functional perspective. The 2-[^{14}C]deoxyglucose (2-DG) method developed by Louis Sokoloff and his colleagues (1977) provides a means to investigate changes in functional activity, or energy use, that are related to various physiologic, pharmacologic, and behavioral states throughout the entire brain simultaneously.

Although cellular resolution is not possible at this time for glucose metabolism, it still provides a considerable degree of anatomical resolution. This is apparent in now-classic 2-DG studies of the visual system of primates in which occlusion of one eye resulted in a pattern of light and dark striations in the visual cortex (Kennedy et al., 1978). These columns correspond to ocular dominance columns identified electrophysiologically and anatomically. With many other neurochemical methods such as *in vivo* microdialysis or neurotransmitter turnover determinations, it is not possible to ascribe effects to particular divisions or subdivisions of brain regions simply because the method requires sampling from areas that are rather large.

GENERAL AUTORADIOGRAPHY METHODOLOGY

Autoradiographic techniques require the use of photosensitive emulsions to determine the radioactive content of tissue. Commercially available x-ray film is best suited for quantitative analysis of topography because the uniform distribution of emulsion affords accurate densitometry across the tissue. The tissue is placed in apposition to the x-ray film within a sealed cassette for a period of a few days to a few months, depending on the isotope, at which time the film is developed. The image on the film, known as an autoradiogram, is converted to a computer-generated digital image and regional optical density is determined with the aid of specially designed software. This can be accomplished with a video camera, a personal computer, and commercially available software.

The relationship between tissue radioactivity and optical density is not linear and is dependent on several factors, including exposure time. To characterize this relationship, radioactive standards are exposed along with tissue sections. The resultant standard curve is then used to estimate actual tissue activity. A basic assumption is made in tissue-slice autoradiography that the sections are of uniform thickness, yet small deviations are unavoidable. To control for this variability, determinations of optical density for a particular region must be made from several sections and averaged. Resolution at the single-cell level requires a slightly different approach. Film is limited by a relatively large grain size that may obscure resolution. Instead, slide-mounted tissue may be dipped directly into the emulsion or placed under dry emulsion-dipped coverslips. In this manner, the affected silver grains are evident on the tissue itself (Mantyh, 1988), and activity can be localized to particular cell types. In addition, the subcellular distribution of silver grains can be described using electron microscopy (Dykstra, 1992; Bozzola and Russell, 1992).

IN VITRO RECEPTOR BINDING AUTORADIOGRAPHY

Receptor binding involves the measurement of bound radiolabeled molecules in tissue. This is a critical step in understanding drug activity whereby potential sites of drug action can be identified. With regard to drug abuse research, the important advantage of this precise neuroanatomical localization is the linkage of our growing knowledge of normal levels and abuse-related changes in receptor distribution with our knowledge of the neural circuitry related to drug reinforcement and addiction. Receptor autoradiography follows the same basic principles of standard biochemical receptor binding methods. In general, liquid-phase studies incubate homogenized tissue with radiolabeled ligand. The quantity of membrane-bound

receptors is reflected in the amount of detectable membrane-bound radioactivity, which is generally obtained by centrifugation and filtration of tissue followed by liquid scintillation spectroscopy. Receptor autoradiography is accomplished in much the same way, except that tissue slices replace homogenates and film autoradiography replaces spectroscopy.

Specific binding, or the quantity of ligand bound to a specific site, is estimated by subtracting *nonspecific* binding from *total* binding; these latter two characteristics are determined empirically. Total binding is achieved by incubation of the tissue with radiolabeled drug and careful rinsing. Nonspecific binding is determined by incubating similar tissue with both the radiolabeled ligand and an excess of a selective blocker, a nonradiolabeled ligand that is known to bind only to the particular receptor(s) of interest. Thus, the remaining radiolabeled ligand is bound to sites other than those bound by the blocker.

As the number of specific binding sites are limited, specific binding is always saturable, approaching an asymptote with rising ligand concentration. Nonspecific binding, in contrast, generally shows a nonsaturable linear relationship with respect to ligand concentration. Specific binding is determined in autoradiograms by subtracting nonspecific from total binding. Since autoradiography has a spatial dimension, care must be taken to ensure that these values are obtained from the same region. With computer imaging it is now possible to superimpose the digital images of nonspecific and total binding and make the subtraction pixel by pixel. The resulting subtracted image can then be used to make regional assessments of radiolabeled drug binding.

Receptor autoradiography is a fully quantitative method, just like the biochemical methods from which it was derived. Several characteristics of the drug binding site can be determined using autoradiography by varying incubation times, ligand concentration, and blockers. These include the maximum number of binding sites (B_{max}), rate constants for coupling and uncoupling of the ligand and receptor (k_1 and k_2), the ligand dissociation constant (K_d), and inhibitor dissociation constants (K_i) (for a detailed discussion see Leslie and Altar, 1988; Yamamura et al., 1985). Although the methodology for these studies is relatively straightforward, a number of additional artifacts can arise based on ligand or tissue parameters that do require special attention (Bennett and Yamamura, 1985). Furthermore, (Kuhar, 1985; Kuhar and Unnerstall, 1985) has emphasized the advantages of *in vitro* binding studies over *ex vivo* and *in vivo* methods that involve systemic injection of the radiolabeled ligand into the intact subject. The tight control of the binding environment of *in vitro* studies allows for the optimization of binding conditions, the study of various chemical influences, and limited radioligand metabolism.

There are currently many highly selective compounds available for use in binding studies. New receptor subtypes, however, are being discovered regularly with the application of molecular biology. It is readily apparent, therefore, that even our current stock of ligands will soon be obsolete, because ligands once thought to be highly selective are now recognized to bind to several receptor subtypes. The need for highly selective compounds is recognized in the research community, and the pursuit of more useful compounds remains a high priority for academic researchers as well as pharmaceutical companies.

The most commonly used radiolabels for receptor autoradiography are ^3H or ^{125}I (Mantyh, 1988). Each has advantages and disadvantages. The spatial resolution of low-energy tritiated compounds is better than compounds labeled with ^{125}I, because low-energy particles travel shorter distances, affecting silver grains closer to the bound isotope. The emissions from ^3H are, however, differentially absorbed by tissues of varying densities, e.g., gray versus white matter. Defatting tissue can limit this type of artifact. The higher energy emissions of ^{125}I, in contrast, allow for much shorter exposure times but result in increased scatter of signal. A further difficulty with iodinated compounds results from the addition of the bulky iodine-containing group, which often changes the binding profile from that of the parent compound (Mantyh, 1988). This necessitates fur-

ther work characterizing the pharmacologic properties of the iodinated compound itself.

In general, the best results are obtained from unfixed fresh frozen tissue (Herkenham, 1988; Herkenham and Pert, 1982). Fixing tissue may alter cell membranes, in which most receptors reside, and adversely affect binding. Incubation media most often consists of an aqueous Tris-HCl buffer and radiolabeled drug, followed by various buffer, distilled water, and acetone washes. Optimization of binding conditions is determined empirically by varying several factors including temperature, incubation time, isotonicity, and the type of buffers and rinses.

Interpretation also has its pitfalls. First, receptor binding is a morphologic tool that identifies loci of ligand binding. This binding is not necessarily related to function. Since substance abuse involves the introduction of exogenous psychoactive compounds that bathe the brain *in vivo*, it is tempting to consider the anatomical distribution of bound radiolabeled compounds *in vitro* as representative of the array of active sites during abuse. The tracer concentrations used in autoradiography, however, may not correspond with the physiologically relevant concentrations achieved during abuse (Madras and Kaufman, 1994). Similarly, another common mistake is confusing high levels of binding for high levels of drug-receptor activity by failing to recall that drug-receptor efficacy varies. The strength, therefore, of receptor autoradiography lies in the ability to map the distribution of drug binding sites and the changes that occur in response to experimental treatment or abuse.

Example of Quantitative Receptor Autoradiography

Although the psychoactive component in marijuana *(Cannabis sativa)*, Δ^9-tetrahydrocannabinol (Δ^9-THC), is known (Gaoni and Mechoulam, 1964; Grunfeld and Edery, 1969), efforts to identify a selective binding site were pursued in vain for over two decades, presumably because the compounds used for binding were of low affinity and low specific activity (Devane et al., 1988; Herkenham et al., 1990, 1991). In the late 1980s, using a high-affinity synthetic cannabinoid (Johnson and Melvin, 1986), ^{3}H-CP55,940, a binding site was identified with enantioselectivity (Devane et al., 1988). Herkenham and coworkers (1990, 1991) then applied autoradiographic receptor binding techniques with ^{3}H-CP55,940 and mapped binding sites in rat, monkey, and human brain. Figure 1 illustrates the typical pattern of cannabinoid binding in the rat brain.

IN SITU HYBRIDIZATION HISTOCHEMISTRY

ISHH is a technique that is rapidly gaining popularity among substance abuse researchers. The term *in situ* is taken from Latin and means "at the original site." Briefly, this method involves the localization of endogenous nucleic acid sequences, usually messenger ribonucleic acid (mRNA), in tissue by their hybridization with detectable manufactured probes. As in the case of receptor-ligand binding studies, ISHH is a modification of liquid-phase biochemical techniques, and its particular utility derives from a dramatic gain in spatial resolution of probe targets in tissue.

This technique has proved itself as a reliable method for describing the spatial distribution of specific nucleic acids in tissue, such as the brain. Just as mapping proteins in the brain has advanced our understanding of the neural circuitry involved in drug action, ISHH extends our knowledge of drug-induced changes into the realm of gene expression. The effect of a drug, either acutely or after chronic administration, is the result of a perturbation of proteins (receptors, ion channels, or enzymes)

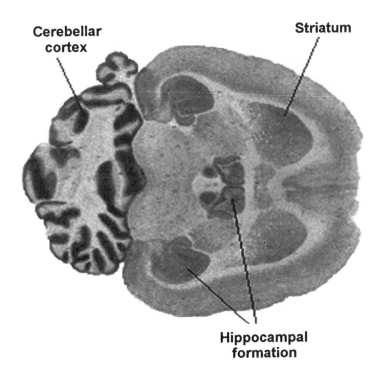

Cerebellar cortex

Striatum

Hippocampal formation

FIG. 1. Autoradiogram of a horizontal section of rat brain illustrating the localized distribution of cannabinoid binding sites using the tritiated ligand WIN-52-112-2. (From Sim, Porrino, Deadwyler and Childers, unpublished).

leading to modifications in gene expression of cellular proteins. Therefore, our understanding of drug effects on gene expression is essential to elucidate the full neurobiologic mechanism of drug response. In addition, since the magnitude of a drug effect is unequal throughout the brain, mapping these effects is necessary to identify regional changes.

Although the first studies of this kind examined deoxyribonucleic acid (DNA), more recently a considerable amount of research has been conducted to determine local levels of mRNA. Due to the fact that mRNA functions as the intermediary between gene expression and protein synthesis, its measurement provides a window into the synthesis of various proteins. Furthermore, since only a small percentage of DNA is actively expressed at any particular time, the quantity of specific mRNAs is a direct reflection of active transcription. Gene expression itself depends on many factors including cell type, environment, and the general needs of the cell. Many mRNAs, such as those that mediate the translation of proteins involved in basic cellular structure and maintenance, are common to most cells. Others are found only in specific cell types and under certain conditions. These mRNAs, which lend themselves to experimentation, function as useful indicators of dynamic intracellular events, from the induction of immediate early genes (IEG) that regulate transcription to the synthesis of cell-membrane proteins.

Generation of a nucleotide probe (either RNA or DNA) that has a complementary sequence to the nucleic acid of interest is the first critical step in ISHH. The choice of probe sequence is paramount and must be made carefully in order to impart a high degree of specificity, adequate penetration into the tissue, as well as hybrid stability. Probes can be manufactured by either recombinant techniques or by mechanical synthesis. Complementary DNA (cDNA) probes and RNA probes (riboprobes) produced by recombinant cloning require specific knowledge of molecular biologic techniques. An increasingly popular alternative is the automated generation of oligonucleotides with DNA synthesizers that

are becoming commonplace in research institutions. These facilities will often provide specific probes to investigators for a fee, making it possible for those with limited expertise in molecular biology to utilize this method. Polymerase chain reaction (PCR) technology is used to amplify (reproduce) the synthesized oligonucleotides producing usable quantities of single-stranded cDNA (ssDNA) probes directly. Unlike double-stranded probes, single-stranded probes cannot reanneal, so they provide a better signal than the same quantity of the double-stranded probes.

Different probes have their own advantages and disadvantages. In general, longer probes form a more stable hybrid, but shorter ones penetrate tissue better. Probes must be at least 15 bases long to ensure sequence specificity (Hélène, 1991), i.e., the probe will hybridize only to the site of interest. Riboprobes tend to form a stronger hybrid complex than DNA probes, and may be more sensitive for the detection of low levels of target. Riboprobes are, however, more difficult to use because they are extremely sensitive to ubiquitous RNases throughout the experimental process.

After the probe is made it must be labeled by chemical or radioactive means for purposes of visualization. Chemically labeled probes commonly use an avidin/biotin complex or similar method. Alternatively, specific antibodies can be raised to the probe itself. Common isotopes for radiolabeled probes are ^{3}H, ^{125}I, ^{35}S, and ^{32}P, although the most used isotope is ^{35}S. Autoradiography of radiolabeled probes provides the better resolution of the two general approaches and most importantly the ability to readily quantify the results. The chief advantages of chemically labeled probes comes in the form of decreased waste, increased safety, and increased speed of visualization (Hofler, 1990).

Arriving at the appropriate hybridization conditions depends on many factors (Chan and McGee, 1990; Chan et al., 1990). The length of the probe and the relative percentage of guanine-cytosine bases pairs, for example, influence hybrid stability. The base pairs coupled during hybridization are formed by temperature-sensitive noncovalent interactions. Given that the probe-target hybrid has a particular melting point, Tm (the temperature at which 50% of the hybrid is denatured), the temperature of the incubation media is designed to balance maximal hybridization of the probe to the target and minimal mismatch hybridization. In solution, it has been shown that hybridization to the target is optimal at 25°C below Tm. Other factors governing the stability of the hybrids formed are the ionic strength and/or formamide concentration of the incubation medium. The Tm of *in situ* hybrid preparations are similar to homogenate hybridization experiments with the added variable of tissue penetration. In this regard, careful pretreatment of slide-mounted sections is crucial for good results. The major concern in the treatment of tissue is effective fixation that permits good probe penetration while maintaining the integrity of the target as well as tissue morphology (Hofler, 1990). Further details of this method are covered comprehensively in several books (Chesselet, 1990; Uhl, 1986; Valentino, et al., 1987).

ISHH is a quantitative method (see Uhl, 1989). If the specific activity of the probe is known and radioactive standards are exposed along with the tissue, the amount of radiolabeled probe contained within tissue can be quantitatively determined. In addition, estimates of the maximum number of probe target molecules within a given region can also be assessed by saturation analyses, although this can present difficulties because the experiment often requires a large quantity of probe, a range of radioactive standards, and varied and prolonged exposure times. Perhaps the biggest hurdle to arriving at an absolute number of target molecules in tissue, though, is that the target mRNAs are contained within the cell and may be interacting with a number of intracellular components that prevent hybridization, thus diminishing the apparent number of mRNAs (Uhl, 1989).

Care must also be taken when interpreting changes in hybridization and what it means to the cell. First, mRNA is not the functional protein. Neither baseline levels nor treatment-induced changes in mRNA expression can be extrapolated to specific changes in the quantity of protein, e.g., enzymes or receptors. The functional protein, for example, may be located some distance from the site of the cell body where the mRNA is transcribed (Chesselet, 1990). Lack of correlation between mRNA and protein levels may also be due to great differences in the half-lives of mRNA and protein, e.g., the half-life of the glucose transporter (GLUT1) mRNA is on the order of 30 minutes to 1 hour, while that of the protein is 19 hours (Mountjoy and Flier, 1990; Sargeant and Paquet, 1990). Additionally, alterations in mRNA levels may be a factor of altered synthesis or increased stability of the message.

Example of *In Situ* Hybridization Histochemistry

Immediate early genes (IEGs), such as c-*fos* and *zif/268,* are rapidly and transiently induced in response to a variety of neuronal stimuli. Their proto-oncogene products Fos and Zif/268, respectively, are nuclear proteins that bind selective regulatory elements in the promoter regions of target DNA such as preprodynorphin (Douglass et al., 1989; McMurray et al., 1992; Naranjo et al., 1991) and preproenkephalin (Comb et al., 1992; Sonnenberg et al., 1989). They function as transcription regulatory factors by modulating the transcription rates of particular cellular genes (Draisci and Iadarola, 1989; Mochetti et al., 1989; Sonnenberg et al., 1989). The induction of expression of these IEGs by psychomotor stimulant administration has been well documented using ISHH. A single systemic dose of the indirect dopamine agonist, cocaine, induces c-*fos* and *zif/268* mRNAs in the striatum of the rat (Bhat et al., 1992a; Daunais and McGinty, 1994; Graybiel et al., 1990; Moratalla et al., 1992; Young et al., 1991). Likewise, acute exposure to cocaine has been shown to rapidly and transiently induce c-*fos* expression in cultured striatal neurons (Hope et al., 1992; Moratalla et al., 1992). In contrast, chronic administration of cocaine, whether self-adminis-tered (Daunais et al., 1993) or experimenter-administered (Bhat et al., 1992b; Daunais and McGinty, 1994; Hope et al., 1992; Steiner and Gerfen, 1993), results in a level of c-*fos* mRNA expression that is not quantitatively different from that of control levels. It appears that IEGs are expressed after a single injection but this expression is blunted or suppressed following prolonged exposure. Amphetamine, another indirect dopamine agonist, also elicits robust induction of c-*fos* and *zif/268* gene expression, but the dynamics and the topography of the re-sponse is different from that demonstrated for cocaine. A single injection of cocaine induces increased c-*fos* mRNA in the striosomes (patches) and matrix of the striatum, whereas amphetamine induces c-*fos* predominately in patches (Moratalla et al., 1992).

Figure 1A–D illustrates that a single injec-tion of cocaine elicits a dose-dependent in-crease in *zif/268* gene expression in the dorsal striatum and cortex of rat brain as compared to saline. Repeated administration of the same doses of cocaine also yields a dose-dependent increase in *zif/268,* but that response is muted as compared to the response elicited by a sin-gle injection of cocaine. Activation of IEG ex-pression may be one mechanism underlying the long-term adaptations resulting from pro-longed cocaine exposure. The advantage of ISHH over homogenate hybridization in this case was the ability to demonstrate increased *zif/268* expression within individual layers of sensory cortex. This isolation of changes re-quires quantitative autoradiography and cer-tainly would not be possible with homogenate methods. Since these sorts of changes are

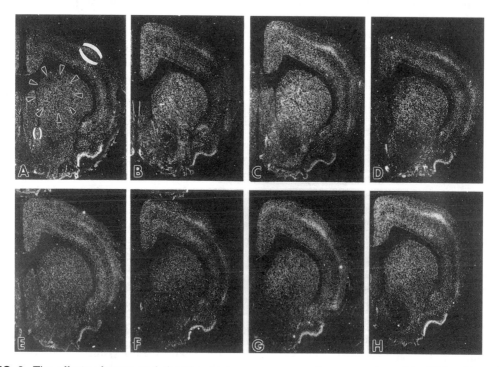

FIG. 2. The effects of acute and chronic cocaine exposure on the expression of the IEG, *zif/268,* in rat striatum are illustrated in this series of photomicrographs from emulsion-dipped slides. **A**: acute i.p. saline. **B**: 10 mg/kg cocaine i.p. x 1 day. **C**: 20 mg/kg cocaine i.p. x 1 day. **D**: 30 mg/kg cocaine i.p. x 1 day. **E**: saline i.p. x 10 days. **F**: 10 mg/kg cocaine i.p. x 10 days. **G**: 20 mg/kg cocaine i.p. x 10 days. **H**: 30 mg/kg cocaine i.p. x 10 days. The *arrowheads* indicate the area of the dorsal striatum that was measured. The *small* and *large parentheses* indicate the measured nucleus accumbens and cortex, respectively. (From Daunais and McGinty, 1994, with permission.)

more likely to occur in specific cells rather than homogeneously over large regions of the brain, the identification of spatially discrete changes within specific neural circuits is the reason these methods are so important for drug abuse research.

LOCAL CEREBRAL GLUCOSE UTILIZATION

The ability to image the sites at which a drug binds is only one step, a first step, in our understanding of the localization of drug action in the central nervous system. Identifying the substrates of drug response depends on an explicit knowledge of the dynamic neuro-chemical events that underlie drug binding, as well as the events that occur with chronic use. This requires a transition from the structural to the functional realm. The earliest work aimed at the development of methods to obtain functional information about the brain were based on cerebral blood flow (Kety and Schmidt, 1948) and provided information about the relationship between energy substrate delivery and use in the brain, but could not provide regional information about the exact localization and topography of responses to various stimuli.

To determine the neuroanatomical substrates of the effects of a drug, it is necessary to measure neural events in circuits and pathways throughout the entire brain. The 2-[^{14}C]deoxyglucose (2-DG) method developed by Sokoloff and colleagues (1977) provided a means to investigate changes in regional functional activity. This methodology has been used extensively in neuropharmacology to identify the neural circuits that mediate the effects of a wide variety of pharmacologic agents (for reviews see McCulloch, 1982; Porrino and Pontieri, 1993). The quantitative autoradiographic 2-DG method measures rates of local cerebral glucose utilization throughout all portions of the central nervous system. It is a biochemical method that determines the rate at which energy is consumed in neuroanatomically defined regions in the central

nervous system of conscious animals. The value of the measurement of rates of glucose utilization stems from the fact that in the brain, as in other tissues that do physicochemical work, the amount of energy used is correlated with the amount of work done in that tissue. Furthermore, glucose is virtually the exclusive substrate for energy metabolism in the brain. The basic rationale of the 2-DG method is that functional activity in any given brain region is directly related to energy metabolism in that region. It is possible, therefore, through the measurement of regional changes in rates of glucose utilization to identify brain regions in which functional activity is altered during various experimental manipulations.

Although there are a number of energy-requiring processes in the brain that contribute to basal rates of glucose utilization, e.g., transmitter synthesis, release and reuptake, and protein synthesis, it has been estimated that 80% of the energy generated in the brain is used to maintain and restore ionic gradients (Kurumaji et al., 1993). It is important to appreciate that the changes in rates of glucose utilization that are evoked by an experimental manipulation are thought to result mainly from increases or decreases in electrical activity or synaptic activity in the central nervous system.

The measurement of glucose utilization rates follows the basic principles for the measurement of rates of any reaction with radioactive tracers, and again was based on the methods used in homogenates. The amount of product formed over an interval of time is determined, related to the integrated specific activity (the ratio of the labeled precursor to the total precursor pool integrated over the time of measurement), and corrected for kinetic differences between the labeled and unlabeled compounds. Rates of local cerebral glucose utilization are measured with a radioactively labeled analogue of glucose, 2-[^{14}C]deoxyglucose. Like glucose, it is transported into cerebral tissue by the same carrier and phosphorylated by hexokinase. In contrast to 2-DG, glucose is not metabolized further and is, therefore, trapped within cells. It is this sequestration within cells that allows quantitative autoradiography to be used to measure actual rates of glucose utilization in individual brain regions.

The calculations of rates of glucose utilization with the 2-DG method (Fig. 3) are made from three measurements. The first is the concentration of radioactivity in the tissue measured autoradiographically, which is a measure of the product formed. The concentration of radioactivity in the tissue, however, is composed of both the product formed, 2-[^{14}C]deoxyglucose-6-phosphate, and the unmetabolized precursor, in this case 2-DG. The two cannot be distinguished autoradiographically. The percent of unmetabolized precursor must be subtracted from the total in order to measure the rate of the reaction accurately. This quantity is estimated from the measured amount of 2-[^{14}C]deoxyglucose remaining in blood at the end of the experimental period. The second and third measurements involved in the calculations of rates of glucose utilization are the levels of glucose and 2-DG in plasma determined during the experimental period. These variables are used to determine the integrated specific activity of the precursor in tissue. Levels in plasma are used because it is not possible to make direct tissue measurements. Corrections are made for the lag in tissue equilibration with plasma. The rate of glucose utilization is described mathematically by the operational equation of the method (Fig. 3). The details of the mathematical derivation of the 2-DG method and an extensive discussion of its theoretical basis are beyond the scope of this chapter (for review see Sokoloff, 1982; Sokoloff and Porrino, 1986; Sokoloff et al., 1977). In addition, the techniques used for the application of the 2-DG method have also been described in detail elsewhere (Porrino and Crane, 1990).

Although the original experiments with the 2-DG method were conducted in restrained or partially restrained animals, recent technical developments allow the use of the 2-DG method in freely moving, conscious animals (Crane and Porrino, 1989; Porrino and Crane, 1990). This approach allows the method to be applied to the study of behavior, permitting a more direct analysis of the neural substrates that are activated during the procedure. The 2-DG method has a number of limitations that should be considered particularly with regard to the interpretation of experimental results. First, the 2-DG method is unable to differentiate between direct and indirect effects of a given stimulus. An entire pathway or circuit may be metabolically activated even though the direct action of the stimulus may occur only at the origin of or at some point along the pathway. The 2-DG method, therefore, does not identify the sites at which a drug binds or the sites at which a drug initiates its actions. Although this lack of specificity may be a limitation in some instances, as in the case of determining the primary site of action of a drug, it is an advantage when the goal is to identify the neural circuits or pathways that mediate the effects of a drug that may have a broad range of nonspecific actions in the central nervous system.

Another limitation is the inability to distinguish between inhibitory and excitatory processes on the basis of increases or decreases in 2-DG uptake. Both excitation and inhibition at the neuronal level involve similar metabolic processes, in that maintenance and restoration of ionic gradients have similar energy requirements regardless of whether excitatory or inhibitory neurotransmitters are secreted at synaptic terminals. In an elegant study Ackermann and colleagues (1984) demonstrated that when either the fimbria-fornix or perforant paths were stimulated electrically, the resulting increases in 2-DG uptake within the hippocampus were a consequence of the long-lasting recurrent inhibitory processes rather than the brief excitatory potentials that also accompany the stimulation. The increased 2-DG uptake in this study resulted from the increased activity of afferents to the hippocampus. Excitation or inhibition was not the critical determinant of the direction of changes in rates of glucose utilization.

As constant or steady-state conditions are considered necessary for measurement of

General Equation for Measurement of Reaction Rates with Tracers:

$$\text{Rate of Reaction} = \frac{\text{Labeled Product Formed in Interval of Time, 0 to T}}{\left[\begin{array}{c}\text{Isotope Effect}\\ \text{Correction Factor}\end{array}\right]\left[\begin{array}{c}\text{Integrated Specific Activity}\\ \text{of Precursor}\end{array}\right]}$$

Operational Equation of $[^{14}C]$ Deoxyglucose Method:

Labeled Product Formed in Interval of Time, 0 to T

$$R_i = \frac{\overbrace{C_i^*(T)}^{\substack{\text{Total }^{14}\text{C in Tissue}\\ \text{at Time, T}}} - \overbrace{k_1^* e^{-(k_2^*+k_3^*)T}\int_0^T C_p^* e^{(k_2^*+k_3^*)t}\,dt}^{^{14}\text{C in Precursor Remaining in Tissue at Time, T}}}{\underbrace{\left[\frac{\lambda \cdot V_m^* \cdot K_m}{\phi \cdot V_m \cdot K_m^*}\right]}_{\substack{\text{"Isotope Effect"}\\ \text{Correction}\\ \text{Factor}}}\underbrace{\left[\underbrace{\int_0^T \left(\frac{C_p^*}{C_p}\right)dt}_{\substack{\text{Integrated Plasma}\\ \text{Specific Activity}}} - \underbrace{e^{-(k_2^*+k_3^*)T}\int_0^T \left(\frac{C_p^*}{C_p}\right)e^{(k_2^*+k_3^*)t}\,dt}_{\substack{\text{Correction for Lag in Tissue}\\ \text{Equilibration with Plasma}}}\right]}_{}}$$

Integrated Precursor Specific Activity in Tissue

FIG. 3. Operational equation of the radioactive deoxyglucose method and its functional anatomy. T, the time at the termination of the experimental period; C_i^*, the total ^{14}C concentration in brain tissue; C_p^* and C_p, the concentrations of ^{14}C and glucose in the arterial plasma, respectively. The constants k_1^*, k_2^*, and k_3^* represent the rate constants for carrier-mediated transport of $[^{14}C]$deoxyglucose from plasma to tissue, for carrier-mediated transport back from tissue to plasma, and for phosphorylation by hexokinase, respectively; λ, the ratio of the distribution space of deoxyglucose in the tissue to that of glucose; ϕ, the fraction of glucose that, once phosphorylated, continues down the glycolytic path; K_m^* and V_m^* and K_m and V_m represent the Michaelis-Menten kinetic constants of hexokinase for deoxyglucose and glucose, respectively. (From Sokoloff 1982).

rates of glucose utilization (Sokoloff et al., 1977), the long experimental time period can be a significant limitation in drug studies. Physiologic and behavioral responses to drug administration can vary significantly across the 45 minutes required for the application of the 2-DG method. Although the total experimental time is lengthy, the uptake and phosphorylation of 2-DG in the brain predominantly reflect its metabolism in the first 5 to 10 minutes of this period. This is because the tissue concentrations of free 2-DG available for metabolism are highest during the first 5 to 10 minutes after its injection (Sokoloff et al., 1977). If drug administration is timed so that the maximum drug response coincides with the time of maximum incorporation of 2-DG, the method can be very sensitive to changes in the effects of drugs across time.

Application of the 2-DG method to map the changes in functional activity associated with the administration of any drug can pose some unique problems. Significant changes in physiologic variables such as body temperature or respiratory status, both of which are frequently affected by pharmacologic agents, can confound the interpretation of the results of 2-DG experiments. Overall differences in uptake based on blood pressure or plasma glucose levels, for example, can sometimes obscure differences between groups that are actually the result of changes in functional activity. In large part, small changes in these variables are taken into account in the calculation of absolute rates of glucose utilization with the 2-DG method, but are not with non- or semi-quantitative modifications of the method. Valid comparisons can, therefore, still be made between groups, allowing both the identification of brain areas with altered functional activity and the magnitude of these changes, if the fully quantitative 2-DG method is used.

On the other hand, if the changes in physiologic status are large, the basic assumptions of the method may be violated and significant errors in the calculation of rates of glucose utilization may result. Moderate to high doses of ethanol, for example, can produce increases in plasma glucose levels that may be great enough to require the use of a different set of rate constants (Orzi et al., 1988) and a lumped constant for the calculation of glucose utilization rates. Furthermore, if plasma glucose concentrations change by more than 20% or 25% during the experimental period, a frequent occurrence with pharmacologic manipulations, a modified operational equation is required to compensate for the lack of constant or steady-state glucose levels (Savaki et al., 1980).

Example of Deoxyglucose Brain Mapping

One approach to the study of the neurobiologic actions of cocaine has been through the use of cocaine analogues. As many of the important behavioral and physiologic effects of cocaine have been attributed to its actions at dopaminergic synapses, tropane analogues that mimic cocaine can be useful tools. A variety of tropane analogues have been synthesized by a number of investigators to date (Abraham et al., 1992; Carroll et al., 1992a,b; Davies et al., 1991; Kozikowski et al., 1991; Lewin et al., 1992). One such compound (Davies et al., 1991, 1993), 2β-tropanoyl-3β-(tolyl) tropane (PTT), displayed a several hundred–fold greater potency for displacing [125I]RTI-55 binding than cocaine in rat striatal membrane preparations (Davies et al., 1993) and at least a 20-fold selectivity for binding to the dopamine transporter over other monoamine transporters. Like cocaine, PTT acted as a psychostimulant, but with a potency 10 to 30 times greater than cocaine for stimulating locomotor activity (Porrino et al., 1995). The entire spectrum of behavioral effects of PTT, however, did not coincide with those of cocaine when examined closely (Porrino et al., 1995). Animals treated with low doses of PTT, for example, exhibited little movement. These rats remained awake and alert but relatively motionless for long periods. Moderate doses increased locomotor activity in a manner very similar to cocaine. Higher doses, again like cocaine, elicited stereotypic behavior, but the intensity of the effect was greater after PTT. The differences in the behavioral effects elicited by cocaine and PTT support the view that their mechanism of action in the CNS differs.

Metabolic mapping with 2-DG was used (Porrino et al., 1995) to identify the effects of PTT on functional activity and to compare these effects to those of cocaine. Moderate and high doses of PTT lead to widespread increases in local cerebral glucose utilization (LCGU) in all portions of the nigrostriatal motor system, as well as throughout thalamus and cortex. These doses also elevated rates of cerebral metabolism in all portions of the mesocorticolimbic system, with the largest increases in the medial prefrontal cortex, olfactory tubercle, and nucleus accumbens. This distribution of LCGU changes closely parallels the dose-dependent metabolic changes observed following cocaine administration (Porrino et al., 1988). In contrast, low doses of PTT had little effect on LCGU in most brain regions, but significantly decreased metabolism in the mesocorticolimbic system (Fig. 4). The depression of metabolic activity in the nucleus accumbens, olfactory tubercle, and medial prefrontal cortex following PTT administration is clearly different from the pattern of changes produced by cocaine, which produces selective increases in metabolism in these same brain regions at low doses

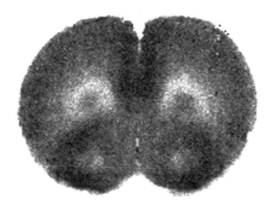

Vehicle

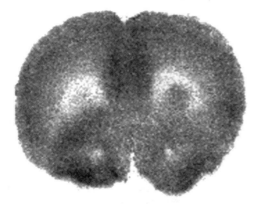

PTT 0.1 mg/kg

FIG. 4. Autoradiograms of coronal sections of rat brain in animals treated with a low dose of PTT, 0.1 mg/kg i.v., in which metabolism was depressed as compared to the vehicle treated control. This effect is consistent with the diminished locomotor activity also seen at this dose, and appears to be a unique property of PTT that is not shared with classical psychostimulants. Higher doses of PTT, which increased locomotor activity, produced an array of changes in glucose metabolism much more similar to the changes engendered by typical stimulants.

(Porrino et al., 1988). The decreases in metabolism observed following PTT administration are not seen following acute treatment with other psychostimulants (Porrino and Pontieri, 1993), nor other dopaminergic drugs, regardless of the dose range tested. PTT, then, is unique in its effects at low doses, although at higher doses its effects strongly resemble those of other psychostimulants. The significance of the 2-DG method for medication development, then, is that it can provide a powerful tool for investigating the nature, specificity, anatomical substrates, and potential neurotoxicity of abused drugs as well as agents developed for treatment of substance abuse or other diseases.

CONCLUSION

Quantitative autoradiographic methods have made it possible to visualize structural and functional changes in the central nervous system. The application of these techniques for the study of receptors, gene expression, and functional cerebral activity provide important new information regarding mechanisms of action underlying the acute and long-term effects of abused drugs, as well as the characterization of agents developed for the treatment of drug abuse. The advantage of autoradiography over homogenate techniques is the ability to localize effects to specific brain regions or even particular cells. This means that even small differences in one brain region can be identified with autoradiography. Furthermore, autoradiography provides a means to actually see differences that are only numbers with homogenate methods.

FUTURE DIRECTIONS

With regard to receptor binding and ISHH, new ligands and probes are constantly being developed in an effort to assess the myriad of newly discovered receptor subtypes and gene products. Autoradiographic imaging of brain structure and function has proved itself to be useful in the study of the neurobiology of abused drugs in rodents. Attention to the extension of this work in nonhuman primates will assuredly assist in our understanding the neurobiology of human drug abuse. Advances in technology will further drive imaging of human and nonhuman primates as the noninvasive imaging methodologies of positron emission tomography (PET), single-photon emission computed tomography (SPECT), and functional magnetic resonance imaging (fMRI) continue to improve. In addition, the increased computing power available to individual researchers in current microcomputers now allows for three-dimensional reconstruction of slice or volume data. Highly complex anatomical distributions of activity that were once difficult or impossible to reconstruct will soon be dramatically easier to describe and quantify.

SUMMARY

- Administration of a psychoactive drug acts as a stimulus that results in quantitative structural or functional changes in the brain.
- Quantitative autoradiography assesses these changes with perhaps as much as a 1000-fold improvement in spatial resolution over the strictly biochemical methods from which they were derived.
- The entire brain can be mapped in a single imaging experiment that often provides enough information for the emergence of spatial patterns of activity indicative of the participation of particular neural circuits.
- Receptor autoradiography is a structural imaging method that identifies the anatomical distribution of ligand binding sites.
- Receptor autoradiography is a fully quantitative method capable of discerning the maximum number of binding sites (B_{max}), rate constants for the coupling and uncoupling of the ligand-receptor complex (k_1 and k_2), the ligand dissociation constant (K_d), and the inhibitor dissociation constants (K_i).
- *In situ* hybridization histochemistry (ISHH) is a structural imaging method that identifies the anatomical distribution of the expression of particular genes.

- ISHH is also a quantitative method capable of describing the regional amount of labeled hybridized probe.

- With the increased availability of probes, either commercially or generated on site with an automated DNA synthesizer, investigators who are familiar with autoradiography but possess only minimal skill in molecular biology can now apply this technique.

- The 2-deoxyglucose (2-DG) method is a fully quantitative, functional imaging technique that identifies the anatomical distribution of energy use in tissue. It is considered a functional method because this energy usage is a reflection of cellular activity, in contrast to cellular structure.

- The 2-DG procedure works in the brain because (1) all cells must expend energy to do work, (2) neuronal firing places the greatest energy demand on brain cells, (3) glucose is virtually the only energy substrate in the brain under normal physiologic conditions, and (4) 2-DG is transported into cells like glucose but is trapped there. Thus, the regional accumulation of radiolabeled 2-DG demarcates areas of increased brain activity.

- Our understanding of the neurobiologic consequences of drug abuse will clearly improve as new ligands and probes become available for testing and advanced technology makes complex image analysis more accessible.

REFERENCES

Abraham, P., Pitner, J.B., Lewin, A.H., Boja, J.W., Kuhar, M.J. and Carroll, F.I. (1992) N-Modified analogues of cocaine. Synthesis and inhibition of binding to the cocaine receptor. *J. Med. Chem.* 35: 141–144.

Ackermann, R.F., Finch, D.M., Babb, T.L. and Engel, J. (1984) Increased glucose metabolism during long-duration recurrent inhibition of hippocampal pyramidal cells. *J. Neurosci.* 4: 251–264.

Bennett, J.P., and Yamamura, H.I. (1985) Neurotransmitter, hormone, or drug receptor binding. In: Yamamura, H.I., Enna, S.J. and Kuhar, M.J. (eds.) *Neurotransmitter receptor binding.* New York: Raven Press, pp. 61–90.

Bhat, R.V., Cole, A.J. and Baraban, J.M. (1992a) Role of monoamine systems in activation of zif/268 by cocaine. *J. Psychiatr. Neurosci.* 17: 94–102.

Bhat, R. V., Cole A.J. and Baraban, J.M. (1992b) Chronic cocaine treatment suppresses basal expression of zif/268 in rat forebrain: *in situ* hybridization studies. *J. Pharmacol. Exp. Ther.* 263: 343–349.

Bozzola, J.J. and Russell, L.D. (1992) Autoradiography/radioautography. In: *Electron microscopy.* Boston: Jones and Bartlett, pp. 262–277.

Carroll, F.I., Gao, Y., Abraham, P., Lewin, A.H., Parham, K.A., Boja, J.W. and Kuhar, M.J. (1992a) Isopropyl and phenyl esters of 3β-(4-substituted phenyl)tropane-2β-carboxylic acids: potent and selective compounds for the dopamine transporter. *J. Med. Chem.* 35: 1813–1817.

Carroll, F.I., Lewis, A.H., Boja, J.W. and Kuhar, M.J. (1992b) Cocaine receptor: biochemical characterization and structure-activity relationships of cocaine analogues at the dopamine transporter. *J. Med. Chem.* 35: 969–981.

Chan, V.T., Herrington, C.S. and McGee, J.O. (1990) Basic background of molecular biology. In: Polak, J.M. and McGee, J. O'D. (eds.) *In situ hybridization: principles and practice.* New York: Oxford University Press, pp. 1–14.

Chan, V.T. and McGee, J.O. (1990) Non-radioactive probes: preparation, characterization, and detection. In: Polak, J.M. and McGee, J. O'D. (eds.) *In situ hybridization: principles and practice.* New York: Oxford University Press, pp. 59–70.

Chesselet, M. (1990) *In situ hybridization histochemistry.* Boston: CRC Press.

Comb, M., Kobierski. L., Chu, H.M., Tan, Y., Borsook, D., Herrup, K. and Hyman, S.E. (1992) Regulation of opioid gene expression: a model to understand neural plasticity. *NIDA Res. Monogr.* 126: 98–111.

Crane, A.M. and Porrino, L.J. (1989) Adaptation of the quantitative 2-[14C]deoxyglucose method for use in freely-moving rats. *Brain Res.* 499: 87–92.

Daunais, J.B. and McGinty, J.F. (1994) Acute and chronic cocaine administration differentially alter striatal opioid and nuclear transcription factor mRNAs. *Synapse* 18: 35–45.

Daunais, J.B., Roberts, D.C.S. and McGinty, J.F. (1993) Cocaine self-administration increases preprodynorphin, but not c-*fos*, mRNA in rat striatum. *NeuroReport* 4: 543–546.

Davies, H.M.L., Saikali, E., Sexton, T. and Childers, S.R. (1993) Novel 2-substituted cocaine analogs: binding properties at dopamine transport sites in rat striatum. *Eur. J. Pharmacol.* 244: 93–97.

Davies, H.M.L., Saikali, E. and Young, W.B. (1991) Synthesis of (+)-ferruginine and (+)-anhydroecgonine methyl ester by a tandem cyclopropanation/Cope rearrangement. *J. Org. Chem.* 56: 5696–5703.

Devane, W.A., Dysarz, F.A.I., Johnson, M.R., Melvin, L.S. and Howlett, A.C. (1988) Determination and characterization of a cannabinoid receptor in rat brain. *Mol. Pharmacol.* 34: 605–613.

Douglass, J., McMurray, C.T., Garrett, J.E., Aldeman, J.P. and Calavetta, L. (1989) Characterization of the rat prodynorphin gene. *Mol. Endocrinol.* 3: 2070–2078.

Draisci, G. and Iadarola, M.J. (1989) Temporal analysis of increase of c-*fos,* preprodynorphin and preproenkephalin mRNAs in rat spinal cord. *Mol. Brain Res.* 6: 31–37.

Dykstra, M.J. (1992) Autoradiography. In: *Biological electron microscopy: theory, techniques and troubleshooting.* New York: Plenum Press, pp. 321–332.

Gaoni, Y. and Mechoulam, R. (1964) Isolation, structure, and partial synthesis of an active constituent of hashish. *J. Am. Chem. Soc.* 86: 1646.

Graybiel, A.M., Moratalla, R. and Robertson, H. (1990) Amphetamine and cocaine induce drug-specific activation of the c-*fos* gene in striosome-matrix compartments and limbic subdivisions of the striatum. *Proc. Natl. Acad. Sci. USA* 87: 6912–6916.

Grunfeld, Y. and Edery, H. (1969) Psychopharmacological activity of the active constituents of hashish and some related compounds. *Psychopharmacology (Berlin)* 14: 200–210.

Hélène, C. (1991) Rational design of sequence-specific oncogene inhibitors based on antisense and antigen oligonucleotides. *Eur. J. Cancer* 27: 1466–1471.

Herkenham, M. (1988) Receptor autoradiography: optimizing anatomical resolution. In: Leslie, F.M. and Altar, C.A. (eds.) *Receptor localization: ligand autoradiography.* New York: Alan R. Liss, pp. 37–48.

Herkenham, M., Lynn, A.B., Johnson, M.R., Melvin, L.S., de Costa, B.R. and Rice, K.C. (1991) Characterization and localization of cannabinoid receptors in rat brain: a quantitative *in vitro* autoradiographic study. *J. Neurosci.* 11: 563–583.

Herkenham, M., Lynn, A.B., Little, M.D., Johnson, M.R., Melvin, L.S., de Costa, B.R. and Rice, K.C. (1990) Cannabinoid receptor localization in brain. *Proc. Natl. Acad. Sci. USA* 87: 1932–1936.

Herkenham, M. and Pert, C.B. (1982) Light microscopic localization of brain opiate receptors: a general autoradiographic method which preserves tissue quality. *J. Neurosci.* 2: 1129–1149.

Hofler, H. (1990) Principles of in situ hybridization. In: Polak, J.M. and McGee, J.O D. (eds.) *In situ hybridization: principles and practice.* New York: Oxford University Press, pp. 15–30.

Hope, B., Kosofsky, B., Hyman, S.E. and Nestler, E.J. (1992) Regulation of immediate early gene expression and AP-1 binding in the rat nucleus accumbens by chronic cocaine. *Proc. Natl. Acad. Sci. USA* 89: 5764–5768.

Johnson, M.R. and Melvin, L.S. (1986) The discovery of nonclassical cannabinoid analgetics. In: Mechoulam, R. (ed.) *Cannabinoids as therapeutic agents.* Boca Raton, FL: CRC, pp. 121–145.

Kennedy, C., Sakurada, O., Shinohara, M., Jehle, M. and Sokoloff, L. (1978) Local cerebral glucose utilization in the normal conscious Macaque monkey. *J. Neurochem.* 4: 293–301.

Kety, S.S. and Schmidt, C.F. (1948) Nitrous oxide method for the quantitative determination of cerebral blood flow in man: theory, procedure, and normal values. *J. Clin. Invest.* 27: 475–483.

Kozikowski, A.P., Xiang, L., Tanaka, J., Bergmann, J.S. and Johnson, K.M. (1991) Use of nitrile oxide cycloaddition (NOC) chemistry in the synthesis of cocaine analogs; mazindol binding and dopamine uptake studies. *Med. Chem. Res.* 1: 312–318.

Kuhar, M.J. (1988) Overview. In: Leslie, F.M. and Altar, C.A. (eds.) *Receptor localization: ligand autoradiography.* New York: Alan R. Liss, pp. 1–7.

Kuhar, M.J. (1985) Receptor localization with the microscope. In: Yamamura, H.I., Enna, S.J. and Kuhar, M.J. (eds.) *Neurotransmitter receptor binding.* New York: Raven Press, pp. 153–176.

Kuhar, M.J. and Unnerstall, J.R. (1985) Quantitative receptor mapping by autoradiography: some current technical problems. *Brain Res.* 244: 178–181.

Kurumaji, A., Dewar, D. and McCulloch, J. (1993) Metabolic mapping with deoxyglucose autoradiography as an approach for assessing drug action in the central nervous system. In: London, E.D. (ed.) *Imaging drug action in the brain.* Boca Raton, FL: CRC Press, pp. 219–245.

Leslie, F.R. and Altar, C.A. (1988) *Receptor biochemistry and methodology: receptor localization.* New York: Alan R. Liss.

Lewin, A.H., Gao, Y., Abraham, J.W., Kuhar, M.J. and Carroll, F.I. (1992) 2β-Substituted analogues of cocaine. Synthesis and inhibition of binding to the cocaine receptor. *J. Med. Chem.* 35: 135–140.

Madras, B.K. and Kaufman, M.J. (1994) Cocaine accumulates in dopamine-rich regions of primate brain after i.v. administration: comparison with mazindol distribution. *Synapse* 18: 261–275.

Mantyh, P.W. (1988) Autoradiographic localization and characterization of receptor binding sites in the brain and peripheral tissues. In: Leslie, F.M. and Altar, C.A. (eds.) *Receptor localization: ligand autoradiography.* New York: Alan R. Liss, pp. 9–36.

McCulloch, J. (1982) Mapping functional alterations in the CNS with [14C]deoxyglucose. In: Iverson, L., Iverson, S. and Snyder, S. (eds.) *Handbook of psychopharmacology.* New York: Plenum, pp. 321–410.

McMurray, C.T., Pollock, K.M. and Douglass, J. (1992) Cellular and molecular analysis of opioid peptide gene expression. *NIDA Res. Monogr.* 126: 113–131.

Mochetti, I., De Bernardi, M.A., Szekely, A.M., Alho, H., Brooker, G. and Costa, E. (1989) Regulation of nerve growth factor biosynthesis by β-adrenergic receptor activation in astrocytoma cells: a potential role of c-*fos* protein. *Proc. Natl. Acad. Sci. USA* 86: 3891–3895.

Moratalla, R., Robertson, H.A. and Graybiel, A.M. (1992) Dynamic regulation of NGFI-A (zif/268, egr1) gene expression in the striatum. *J. Neurosci.* 12: 2609–2622.

Mountjoy, K.G. and Flier, J.S. (1990) Vanadate regulates glucose transporter (Glut-1) expression in NIH3T3 mouse fibroblasts. *Endocrinology* 127: 2025–2034.

Naranjo, J.R., Mellstrom, B., Achaval, M. and Sassone-Corsi, P. (1991) Molecular pathways of pain: Fos/Jun-mediated activation of a noncanonical AP-1 site in the prodynorphin gene. *Neuron* 6: 607–617.

Orzi, F., Lucignani, G., Dow-Edwards, D., Namba, H., Nehlig, A., Patlak, C.S., Pettigrew, K.D., Schuier, F. and Sokoloff, L. (1988) Local cerebral glucose utilization in controlled graded levels of hyperglycemia in the conscious rat. *J. Cereb. Blood Flow Metab.* 8: 346–356.

Porrino, L.J. and Crane, A.M. (1990) Metabolic mapping of the effects of drugs of abuse with the 2-[14C]deoxyglucose method. In: Adler, M.W. and Cowan, A. (eds.) *Modern methods in pharmacology: testing and evaluation of drugs of abuse.* New York: Alan R. Liss, pp. 147–164.

Porrino, L.J., Davies, H.M.L. and Childers, S.R. (1995) Behavioral and local cerebral metabolic effects of the novel tropane analog, 2β-propanoyl-3β-(4-toyl)-tropane. *J. Pharmacol. Exp. Ther.* 272: 901–910.

Porrino, L.J., Domer, F.R., Crane, A.M. and Sokoloff, L. (1988) Selective alterations in cerebral metabolism within the mesocorticolimbic dopaminergic system produced by acute cocaine administration in rats. *Neuropsychopharmacology* 1: 109–118.

Porrino, L.J. and Pontieri, F.E. (1993) Metabolic mapping of the effects of psychomotor stimulants in rats. In: London,

E.D. (ed.) *Imaging drug action in the brain*. Boca Raton, FL: CRC Press, pp. 247–263.

Sargeant, R.J. and Paquet, M.R. (1990) Effect of insulin on the rates of synthesis and degradation of GLUT1 and GLUT4 glucose transporters in 3T3-L1 adipocytes. *Biochem. J.* 290: 913–919.

Savaki, H.E., Davidsen, L., Smith, C. and Sokoloff, L. (1980) Measurement of free glucose turnover in brain. *J. Neurochem.* 35: 495–502.

Sokoloff, L. (1982) The radioactive deoxyglucose method: Theory, procedure, and applications for the measurement of local glucose utilization in the central nervous system.. In: Agranoff, B.W. and Aprison, M.H. (eds.) *Advances in neurochemistry*. New York: Plenum, pp. 7–36.

Sokoloff, L. and Porrino, L.J. (1986) Some fundamental considerations in the application of the deoxyglucose method to pharmacological studies. In: Kriegelstein, I. (ed.) *Pharmacology of cerebral ischemia*. Amsterdam: Elsevier, pp. 65–76.

Sokoloff, L., Reivich, M., Kennedy, C., DesRosiers, M.H., Patlak, C.S., Pettigrew, K.D., Sakurada, O. and Shinohara, M. (1977) The [^{14}C]deoxyglucose method for the measurement of local cerebral glucose utilization: theory, procedure and normal values in the conscious and anesthetized albino rat. *J. Neurochem.* 28: 897–916.

Sonnenberg, J.L., Rauscher, F.J. III, Morgan, J.I. and Curran, T. (1989) Regulation of proenkephalin by Fos and Jun. *Science* 246: 1622–1625.

Steiner, H. and Gerfen, C.R. (1993) Cocaine-induced c-*fos* messenger RNA is inversely related to dynorphin expression in striatum. *J. Neurosci.* 13: 5066–5081.

Uhl, G.R. (1986) *In situ hybridization in brain*. New York: Plenum Press.

Uhl, G.R. (1989) In situ hybridization: quantitation using radiolabeled hybridization probes. In: *Methods in enzymology,* vol. 168. New York: Academic Press, pp. 741–752.

Valentino, K.L., Eberwine, J.H. and Barchas, J.D. (1987) *In situ hybridization:* applications to neurobiology. New York: Oxford University Press.

Williams-Hemby, L. and Porrino, L.J. (1994) Low and moderate doses of ethanol produce distinct patterns of cerebral metabolic changes in rats. *Alcohol Clin. Exp. Res.* 18: 982–988.

Yamamura, H.I., Enna, S.J. and Kuhar, M.J. (1985) *Neurotransmitter receptor binding*. New York: Raven Press.

Young, S.T., Porrino, L.J., and Iadarola, M.J. (1991) Cocaine induces striatal c-fos-immunoreactive proteins via dopaminergic D$_1$ receptors. *Proc. Natl. Acad. Sci. USA* 88: 1291–1295.

Drug Addiction and its Treatment: Nexus of Neuroscience and Behavior, edited by Bankole A. Johnson and John D. Roache. Lippincott–Raven Publishers, Philadelphia, © 1997.

13

Molecular Cloning and Characterization of Receptors for Drugs of Abuse

Jia Bei Wang and Christopher K. Surratt

Molecular Neurobiology Section, Division of Intramural Research, National Institute on Drug Abuse, National Institutes of Health, Baltimore, Maryland 21224

The interaction between drugs of abuse and their receptors initiates the pathway leading to the physical and psychological dependencies associated with addiction. Several neurotransmitter transporter proteins and G protein–coupled receptors have been identified as receptors of abused drugs. Receptors relevant to drug addiction, including the dopamine transporter (cocaine receptor) and μ opiate (morphine) receptor, have been defined and extensively pursued via pharmacologic and functional studies (Horn, 1990; Pasternak, 1987).

The understanding of molecular aspects of drug receptors has been dramatically enhanced with the advent of recombinant DNA technology. Complementary DNAs (cDNAs) encoding key molecular targets of cocaine, amphetamine, heroin, morphine, and the cannabinoids have been cloned within the last 7 years. Because considerable structural and mechanistic information is suddenly at hand for these proteins, the cloned drug receptors that recognize this subset of the "high profile" drugs of abuse serve as the focus of this chapter. The role of cloned receptors in mediating the action of abused drugs, methodologies for the cloning of drug receptors, analyses of receptor structures predicted from the cDNAs, and structure/function inquiries via receptor mutagenesis will be addressed.

MECHANISMS OF ACTION OF DRUGS OF ABUSE

Cocaine and Amphetamine

One subfamily of the neurotransmitter transporter family, the monoamine transporters, is a primary target for cocaine and amphetamine, as well as the "tricyclic antidepressant" class of therapeutic drugs (Amara and Kuhar, 1993; Surratt et al., 1993a; Uhl, 1992). Plasma membrane transporters for dopamine, norepinephrine, serotonin, and the synaptic vesicle monoamine transporter (SVMT) constitute this subfamily (Blakeley et al., 1991; Erickson et al., 1992; Hoffman et al., 1991; Kilty et al., 1991; Liu et al., 1992; Pacholczyk et al., 1991; Shimada et al., 1991; Surratt et al., 1993b; Vandenbergh et al., 1992). The three plasma membrane transporters recognize cocaine, amphetamine, and their derivatives, as well as their cognate neurotransmitters, with affinities in the micromolar range. Cocaine is not recognized appreciably by the SVMT protein, while the affinity for d-amphetamine is within an order of magnitude of that for the monoamine neurotransmitter substrates (Gonzalez et al., 1993; Peter et al., 1994).

Several lines of evidence support the "dopamine hypothesis" in explaining the behavior-reinforcing properties of cocaine (Kuhar et al., 1991). Binding of cocaine by the dopamine transporter blocks dopamine re-uptake; the resultant flooding of the synapse with dopamine leads to an increase in postsynaptic receptor binding of the neurotransmitter and finally potentiation of the transduced signal that eventually effects reinforcement. Indeed, the postsynaptic dopamine D3 receptor has been recently linked with the reinforcing properties of cocaine (Caine and Koob, 1993, 1995). Pharmacologic and behavioral studies offer compelling support for the idea that the cocaine binding site responsible for the drug's reinforcing properties is within the dopamine transporter (Ritz et al., 1987; Spealman et al., 1989).

The mechanism of amphetamine action would appear to involve both the SVMT and at least one of the plasma membrane transporters. Clearly, amphetamine must cross the plasma membrane before exerting any effect on the synaptic vesicle, and indeed, the amphetamines are substrates for the plasma membrane monoamine transporters (Fischer and Cho, 1979; Liang and Rutledge, 1982; Rudnick and Wall, 1992). Once inside the cell, amphetamine is postulated to induce the efflux of large stores of dopamine from synaptic vesicles into the cytoplasm (Sulzer and Rayport, 1990). Such elevated levels of cytoplasmic dopamine and related monoamines may drive reverse transport of the neurotransmitter, returning the monoamine to the synapse (Rudnick and Wall, 1992; Sulzer et al., 1993). Amphetamine does indeed increase the synaptic concentration of dopamine (Carboni et al., 1989), and at this point the mechanisms for cocaine- and amphetamine-induced euphoria are presumably similar. The release of stored monoamines from the synaptic vesicle is mediated by amphetamine via the SVMT, as the amphetamine analogue methylenedioxymethamphetamine (MDMA) or, "ecstasy," has been observed to bind in stereospecific fashion to the SVMT (Rudnick and Wall, 1992). In addition to interfering with monoamine uptake, a second mechanism for the vesicular action of amphetamine is the "weak base" model (Sulzer and Rayport, 1990), in which the weak base amphetamine diffuses across the vesicular membrane, increasing the pH of the acidic vesicle lumen and triggering release of dopamine.

Morphine/Heroin and the Cannabinoids

The mechanisms of morphine, an active metabolite of heroin (diacetylmorphine), and cannabinoid action in the brain differ significantly from those of cocaine and amphetamine, a fact reflected by the difference in receptor types. As opposed to physically blocking or altering neurotransmitter transport, morphine and cannabinoids opportunistically bind to neuroreceptors wired to alleviate nociception, and in binding to their respective receptors, initiate a cascade of events culminating in both analgesia and euphoria. It should be noted here that the acetyl groups of heroin, which facilitate passage of the drug across the blood-brain barrier, are excised by an enzyme in the brain to yield morphine. In terms of the μ opiate receptor, morphine is therefore a key that turns the tumblers in a lock, driving a conformational change in the μ receptor that enables the receptor to associate with the inhibitory class of heterotrimeric G proteins in the plasma membrane (see Fig. 3B). This coupling triggers formation of a guanosine triphosphate (GTP)–G_α subunit complex that modifies the action of second messenger proteins including adenylate cyclase and phospholipase C (Blume et al., 1979; Sharma et al., 1975; Smart et al.,1994). The entire sequence of events, termed signal transduction, is employed by various neurotransmitters and hormones, utilizing one of several stimulatory or inhibitory G proteins (Strader et al., 1994). As with the μ receptor, the cannabinoid receptor is also coupled to an inhibitory G protein subunit (Felder et al., 1993; Howlett, 1985). Opiate receptors are reported to couple to stimulatory (G_s) proteins as well (Cruciani et al., 1993), the consequences of which remain poorly defined.

Agonist binding by a G protein–coupled receptor also stimulates the opening or closing of ion channels. Binding of opiate drugs and opioid peptides opens voltage-gated and inwardly-rectifying potassium channels and closes N-type calcium channels via direct G protein–coupling of the channel to the opiate receptor (Gross et al., 1990; North et al., 1987; Tallent et al., 1994; Wimpey and Chavkin, 1991). The opening of potassium channels is postulated to contribute significantly to the observed physiologic effects of systemically administered opiates (DiChiara and North, 1992).

CLONING OF DRUG RECEPTORS

Nomenclature

Before addressing the various methodologies employed in discovering and obtaining the receptors at which abused drugs act, it is necessary to define terminology that was once exclusively used by molecular biologists and is now recognized and used by scientists in many subdisciplines of biology, as well as the media. *Cloning* refers to the manipulation of a DNA fragment, which provides the means to generate an unlimited number of DNA copies of the sequence contained in the fragment. The process, for our purposes, involves preparing a DNA fragment, covalently linking the fragment to a bacterial *vector* (a small circular DNA that is replicated at high frequency in a bacterial cell), introducing the linked DNA fragment/vector into bacterial cells, isolating a single bacterial colony harboring the DNA fragment/vector, and amplifying the colony in culture media to produce large quantities of DNA of identical sequence to that of the fragment.

The terms *cDNA* and *gene* are often (unfortunately) used interchangeably, but hold quite different meanings with respect to cloning of drug receptors. To understand these terms requires an understanding of the flow of genetic information in a cell. A gene, comprised of double stranded DNA, is *transcribed* by the cell machinery in the nucleus to yield a heterogeneous nuclear RNA (hnRNA), an almost identical but short-lived, single-stranded version of the template DNA. The nascent hnRNA transcript is truncated and modified by a collection of processing enzymes to generate a "mature" messenger RNA (mRNA) molecule.

The mRNA is next exported to the cytoplasm and *translated* by the cell machinery, which assembles a polypeptide chain of amino acids (i.e., the receptor protein) by reading contiguous nucleotide triplets (*codons*) within the mRNA chain. In addition to using the mRNA as a template for protein synthesis (translation), it is also possible to run the transcription (DNA to mRNA) reaction in reverse; this ability is reserved for certain viruses, and is not observed *in vivo* for mammalian systems. The purified viral enzyme reverse transcriptase employs mRNA as a template *in vitro*, synthesizing a complementary DNA (cDNA) strand (that which forms Watson-Crick nucleoside base pairs with the template to form a double helix) to the mRNA. The resulting cDNA is considerably shorter than the original gene because its template was the mature mRNA. Nevertheless, an intact cDNA contains the information needed to direct synthesis of the entire receptor. For the 398 amino acid μ opiate receptor protein of the rat, 398 x 3 nucleotides (per codon) or 1194 nucleotides are minimally necessary to encode the receptor. The gene, in contrast, contains this 1194 nucleotide sequence plus the DNA regions (*introns*) encoding the jettisoned nascent mRNA fragments, plus DNA encoding the directions to regulate its own production: in total, the gene is a chain typically tens of thousands of nucleotides in length. Clearly, the cDNA is greatly preferred for cloning of drug receptors, and, happily, is far more accessible.

By isolating the total mRNA present in a given biologic tissue, reverse transcriptase can be employed to generate a *cDNA library*, i.e., a collection of cDNAs that encodes all mRNAs, and therefore all proteins, found in that tissue. If one is confident that a putative drug receptor is present in, for example, human brainstem tissue, a commercially available brainstem cDNA library is a powerful tool for isolating a novel cDNA encoding the receptor.

Cloning Strategies

Three distinct methodologies are generally utilized in the search for a novel receptor cDNA (Figs. 1 and 2). The first, most traditional, and most laborious method requires purification of the receptor and determination of at least a portion of its amino acid sequence (method 1; Fig. 1). Typically, the isolated receptor is digested with proteolytic enzymes, followed by purification and sequence determination of the fragments. Prior to the introduction of the cloning technology, the entire amino acid sequence of a protein was mapped in this fashion, requiring relatively huge amounts of purified protein and several months of work. Today, determination of a peptide sequence of only 15 to 25 consecutive amino acid residues enables *in vitro* synthesis of a DNA oligonucleotide that encodes the peptide. A radiolabeled version of the oligonucleotide can then be used as a probe to screen a cDNA library containing the full-length receptor cDNA. Different subsets of the constituent cDNAs that compose the library are immobilized on a nitrocellulose filter to form a grid-like array. By allowing the radiolabeled oligonucleotide to *hybridize* (engage in Watson-Crick base pairing to form a double helix) with the authentic receptor cDNA on the filter, the location of the receptor cDNA can be ascertained by observing which spots on the nitrocellulose grid are radioactive. After introducing the cDNAs contained in the radioactive spot into bacteria, a second or third round of hybridization should yield the novel drug receptor cDNA in unlimited quantities.

This method (Method 1; Fig. 1) was successfully employed to obtain the first drug receptor cDNAs, including those encoding the γ-aminobutyric acid subtype A (GABA$_A$; Schofield et al., 1987) and β-adrenergic (Dixon et al., 1986) receptors. Because a prerequisite for applying this method is a substantial source of the receptor tissue, not every receptor cDNA is accessible via Method 1. In addition, membrane proteins are among the most difficult to purify to homogeneity. Method 1 has fallen out of favor for these reasons, coupled with the relative ease of Methods 2 and 3, and, in fact, none of the drug receptors discussed in this chapter was cloned by this method.

A second approach for cloning a receptor cDNA (Method 2; Fig. 1) is not dependent on any information within the target receptor protein itself, but instead takes advantage of the sequence similarity between cDNAs encoding the target receptor and receptors within the same family (e.g., the neurotransmitter transporter family). Method 2 is easily the simplest and quickest method of the three for elucidation of a novel cDNA. This method is only useful, however, when the cDNA sequence of at least one of the family members is known. Isolation of a dopamine transporter cDNA (Shimada et al., 1991) was accomplished by first assuming that, because the substrate of the cloned and functionally related norepinephrine transporter is structurally very similar to dopamine, the amino acid sequences of the transporters must also be very similar. Indeed, 78% amino acid identity is observed between the two transporters (Giros et al., 1994). High amino acid sequence identity therefore indicates significant nucleotide sequence identity between the regions of the cDNAs that encode the transporter proteins. Because the highest amino acid identity between membrane-bound proteins is generally observed in the transmembrane domains, it is logical to design a cDNA screening probe that encodes some or all of these domains.

Preparation of a probe for cDNA library screening is achieved using the polymerase chain reaction (PCR) (Mullis and Faloona, 1987). Two DNA oligonucleotides of identical sequence to the cDNA encoding transmembrane regions of the norepinephrine transporter are first synthesized. One oligonucleotide is positioned at each end of the region of interest; typically, a stretch 500 to 1000 nucleotides in length separates the oligonucleotides. The PCR reaction then selectively amplifies only the 500 to 1000 nucleotide portion of the norepinephrine cDNA flanked by the oligonucleotides. This remarkable technology can afford the synthesis of greater than 1,000,000 copies of a receptor cDNA molecule for every molecule of template cDNA found in the library. The PCR-

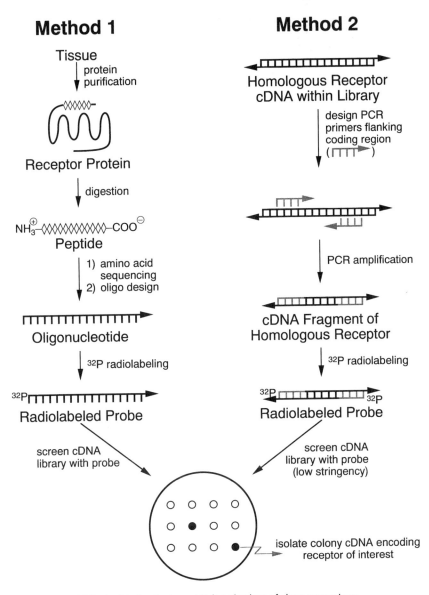

FIG. 1. Methods 1 and 2 for cloning of drug receptors.

generated 500 to 1000 nucleotide norepinephrine transporter cDNA fragment can be used, after radiolabeling, as a probe to screen a cDNA library for a novel dopamine transporter cDNA.

Because the norepinephrine and dopamine transporter cDNAs are nonidentical, the norepinephrine probe is allowed to hybridize with the dopamine transporter cDNA immobilized on the filter under conditions of low (mild) *stringency*. Stringency is determined by the temperature, ionic strength, and formamide concentration of the hybridization solution; mild conditions favor formation of double-stranded DNA hybrids with occasional mismatches between the strands (incorrect Watson-Crick base pairs). Each mismatch destabilizes the hybrid to some extent,

Method 3

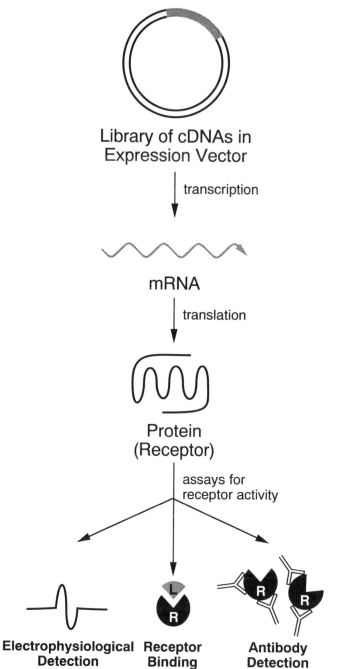

Library of cDNAs in
Expression Vector

transcription

mRNA

translation

Protein
(Receptor)

assays for
receptor activity

**Electrophysiological
Detection**

**Receptor
Binding**

**Antibody
Detection**

FIG. 2. Method 3 for cloning of
drug receptors.

such that conditions of higher stringency would disrupt the hybrid completely, and no radioactive spot would be detected on the filter grid. Low stringency conditions would therefore yield several radioactive spots on the grid, indicating the presence of dopamine transporter cDNA and any other cDNAs homologous to the norepinephrine transporter, as well as authentic norepinephrine transporter cDNA. Next subjecting the radioactive filter to conditions of high stringency would result in the disappearance of several radioactive spots. The remaining radioactive spots contain the authentic norepinephrine transporter cDNA and can be ignored. The transiently radioactive spots contain cDNAs with mismatches to the norepinephrine transporter cDNA probe, and are likely to encode the dopamine transporter or another closely related drug receptor cDNA.

A third method for cloning of drug receptor cDNAs, *expression* screening, involves a cDNA library in which every cDNA has been inserted into a circular, double-stranded DNA vector (Method 3; Fig. 2). The vector DNA (harbored by a mammalian cell) contains the information necessary to express the cDNA, meaning that a mRNA copy of the cDNA is transcribed and, if possible, the mRNA is translated to produce the receptor protein. The latter step is only possible if the mRNA possesses the initiation sequences required for translation; therefore, only cDNAs that encode enough of the receptor protein to synthesize a functional receptor will be detected by this screening method. Cells harboring a functional receptor are singled out using one or more standard assays for detection of the target receptor. Electrophysiologic detection, binding of radiolabeled agonists or antagonists, and antibody detection are three popular receptor assays; the cDNA can then be isolated from cells identified as containing the novel receptor. A clone selection strategy for drug resistance, an interesting version of expression cloning, yielded rat cDNAs encoding vesicular monoamine transporters (Liu et al., 1992). PC12 cells are far more resistant to the neurotoxin MPP$^+$ (*N*-methyl-4-phenylpyri-dinium) than CHO cells. Introduction of PC12 DNAs into CHO cells, followed by incubation of the CHO cells in the presence of 1 mM MPP$^+$, afforded a selected clone with resistance to the drug. A cDNA encoding the vesicular transporter was subsequently isolated from this clone and shown to be responsible for MPP$^+$ uptake—the transporter sequestered the neurotoxin, protecting the cell.

Regardless of the isolation method employed, it must be confirmed experimentally that the putative drug receptor cDNA encodes a functional receptor with the appropriate lig-and-binding specificity. This is achieved by *transfection* of a mammalian cell line (incorporation of the cDNA into the mammalian cell by one of several methods) and subsequent pharmacologic testing of the transfected cells for properties associated with the receptor encoded by the cDNA. As an example, transfection of mammalian COS or HeLa cells with candidate dopamine transporter cDNAs conferred in these cells a pharmacologic profile characteristic of the brain dopamine transporter; the cells acquired the ability to import dopamine in a fashion highly dependent on Na$^+$, Cl$^-$, and temperature, and uptake was effectively blocked by documented inhibitors of dopamine transport (cocaine and its analogue CFT, GBR-12909, mazindol, and the neurotoxin MPP$^+$). Transfection of a "control" cDNA containing all of the same DNA sequences except the transporter coding sequence did not confer the above properties on mammalian cells (Shimada et al., 1991).

A novel receptor cDNA may yield a tremendous amount of information about the encoded receptor; a great deal is known about the receptor before even initiating studies on the actual receptor protein itself. Analysis of the amino acid sequence of the receptor protein predicted from the cDNA can identify putative transmembrane (TM) domains, charged or otherwise uncommon TM domain residues that may form contacts with the drug of abuse, and consensus sites for posttranslational modification of the receptor, including those for glycosylation, palmitoylation, and phosphorylation. The predicted protein sequence can be compared with the sequences of all other proteins listed in worldwide computer databases, possibly revealing an otherwise undetectable connection with one or more fully characterized proteins that in turn may hint at unknown properties of the novel receptor.

Using the predicted amino acid sequences of recently cloned drug receptors, the molecular nature of the receptor and structure/function relationships that point to drug-protein contacts can be addressed.

PREDICTED MOLECULAR STRUCTURE OF DRUG RECEPTORS

The receptors at which amphetamine, cocaine, morphine, and the cannabinoids initiate both euphoria and the pathway to addiction can be assigned to one of two structural classes (Fig. 3). Amphetamine and cocaine interact with neurotransmitter transporter proteins (Fig. 3A), membrane proteins with 12 putative membrane-spanning domains, intracellular amino (NH_2) and carboxyl (COOH) termini, and a large extracellular loop containing consensus sites for glycosylation (addition of carbohydrate branches to specific asparagine amino acid residues). Morphine and the cannabinoids interact with specific seven-transmembrane domain, G protein–coupled receptor (GCR) proteins (Fig. 3B), which predict an extracellular amino terminus bearing glycosylation sites and an intracellular carboxyl terminus. For both drug receptor classes, several intracellular consensus sites for phosphorylation are present, which may include sites for protein kinase A, protein kinase C, or Ca^{2+}-calmodulin–dependent kinase II. It should be noted that the neurotransmitter transporters are not classical receptors, in the sense of directly coupling to intracellular "second messenger" effector molecules (signal transduction). We employ the phrase "drug receptor" here for a protein that serves as a principal site of action for an abused drug.

At first glance, each receptor's mechanism of recognizing and binding a specific drug of abuse would appear to vary widely. The ligands that interact with drug receptors are quite diverse in structure. Two functionally dissimilar classes of drug-binding proteins exist: one, the 12 TM domain, ion-dependent neurotransmitter transporters; and the other, the 7 TM domain G protein–coupled signal transducers. Nevertheless, commonalities are

---

FIG. 3. Schematic representation of the topology of drug receptor classes. The polypeptide backbone of the receptor protein is depicted as a *solid line.* The cell membrane is shown as a *horizontal rectangle;* extracellular regions of the receptor lie above the rectangle, with intracellular regions lying below. **A**: Neurotransmitter transporters, represented by the dopamine transporter. Hydrophobicity analysis suggests 12 membrane-spanning domains (transmembrane, or TM, domains). Intracellular amino (NH_2) and carboxyl (COOH) termini are predicted. The second extracellular loop (linking TM domains 3 and 4) is especially large, and contains sites for potential posttranslational modifications, including four consensus sites for glycosylation (indicated by *forks*) and a probable disulfide bond (*dashed line*) connecting cysteines 180 and 189. A TM 1 aspartic acid (Asp-79; circled D) is common to all of the reported monoamine transporters. TM 7 serine residues critical for efficient dopamine uptake (Ser-356 and Ser-359) are indicated (circled S's), while TM 4 and 5 tyrosine residues (Tyr-251 and Tyr-271) are important in cocaine binding (circled Y's). **B**: G protein–coupled receptors, represented by the μ opiate receptor. Seven TM domains and extracellular amino- and intracellular carboxyl-terminal tails are predicted. The amino terminus contains five glycosylation consensus sites. TM 2 and 3 aspartic acid residues and a possible disulfide linkage between extracellular cysteines are indicated, features common to the three major opiate receptor subtypes. Upon receptor activation of the heterotrimeric G protein (composed of α, β, and γ subunits), the α subunit modulates the activity of "second messenger" molecules including adenylate cyclase (AC).

present between the drug receptors with respect to protein structure, as well as the ligand pharmacophores recognized. Certain members of each drug receptor class possess overlapping but nonidentical binding sites for substrates and antagonists, and are postulated to form an ion pair with the incoming ligand.

Monoamine Neurotransmitter Transporters

In addition to the predicted topologic similarities, members of the neurotransmitter transporter family share varying degrees of amino acid sequence identity. This evolutionary *con-*

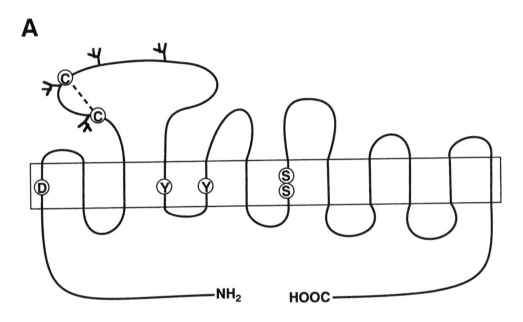

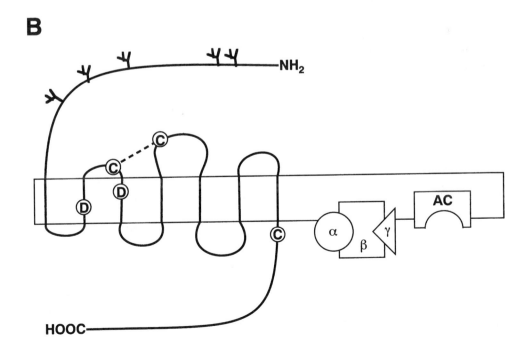

servation of sequence often indicates regions most critical for transporter function. The high degree of sequence conservation among the plasma membrane neurotransmitter transporters, especially at putative TM domains, has facilitated cloning of new members of the family. Based on the sequence information of previously cloned rat GABA and human norepinephrine transporter cDNAs (Guastella et al., 1990; Pacholczyk et al., 1991), rat dopamine and serotonin transporter cDNAs were cloned by several independent laboratories in 1991 (Blakely et al., 1991; Hoffman et al., 1991; Kilty et al., 1991; Shimada et al., 1991). Using these newly elucidated clones as templates, a second wave of transporter cDNAs was characterized, including transporters recognizing betaine (Yamauchi et al., 1992), taurine (Uchida et al., 1992), glycine (Smith et al., 1992), proline (Fremeau et al., 1992), and creatine (Guimbal and Kilimann, 1993). Human and bovine cDNA homologues of some of the above transporters have also been isolated (Giros et al., 1992; Usdin et al., 1991; Vandenbergh et al., 1992).

The degree of amino acid sequence identity between the rat dopamine transporter and rat cDNAs corresponding to the transporters mentioned above ranges from 45% to 67%, with considerably greater identity (80–90%) among TM domains. The sequence relatedness not only indicates the evolutionary pathway of a neurotransmitter gene, but also implies that the more highly conserved domains and individual amino acid residues may be required for transporter structure and function. It is likely that the TM domains are arrayed in essentially the same configuration for a transporter and its nearest evolutionary neighbors, and that the mechanism of neurotransmitter transport, including coupling of the downhill movement of Na^+ and Cl^- with the accumulation of neurotransmitter, is similar if not identical among such transporters; thus, one would expect highest sequence conservation among the TM domains. In the same vein, the regions of pronounced sequence divergence may be responsible for the features unique to that transporter, including substrate recognition.

The synaptic vesicle monoamine transporter (SVMT, VMAT), a site of amphetamine action, represents an interesting twist on the notion of sequence conservation as an indication of function. From the standpoint of predicted amino acid sequence identity, the SVMT is a distant relative of the plasma membrane monoamine transporters; cDNAs from chromaffin granules (Liu et al., 1992), rat brain (Erickson et al., 1992; Liu et al., 1992), and human brain (Peter et al., 1994; Surratt et al., 1993b) encoding this transporter predict no significant sequence similarity with the plasma membrane transporters. Still, SVMT cDNAs predict a topology similar to the aforementioned neurotransmitter transporters (Fig. 3A), with 12 TM domains, intracellular amino and carboxyl termini, and a large intralumenal loop with consensus sites for glycosylation. This intralumenal loop follows TM 1, as opposed to its extracellular counterpart following TM 3 in the plasma membrane monoamine transporters. More importantly, the SVMT serves as a dopamine, norepinephrine, and serotonin transporter, albeit at a level of efficiency 100 times lower than that of the plasma membrane counterparts. It would appear that the vesicular monoamine transporter sacrifices efficiency of neurotransmitter recognition and transport for its three-transporters-in-one versatility.

Despite the sequence dissimilarity between the vesicular and plasma membrane monoamine transporters, common threads must exist between the two that confer the ability to bind and transport the same substrates. Discrete amino acid residues common to the four monoamine transporters may serve as points of contact with the neurotransmitter, as each of the plasma membrane monoamine transporters also recognizes all three monoamines with some efficiency. The monoamine transporters share a negatively charged aspartic acid residue at the identical position in TM 1 (Asp-79, or D79, in the rat dopamine transporter; Fig. 3A). By hydrophobicity analysis, this residue is predicted to reside at the approximate midpoint of the lipid bilayer. An inherent importance is suggested for this

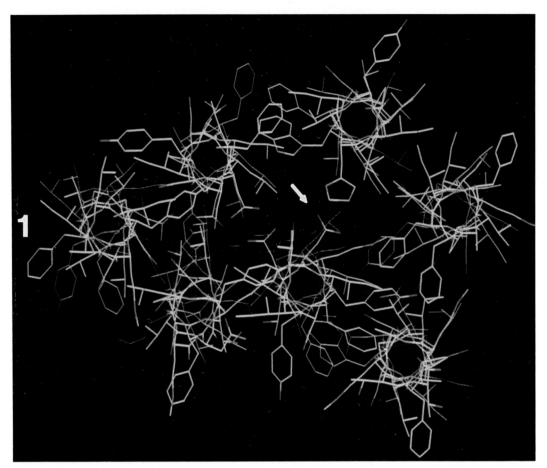

FIG. 4. Molecular modeling scenario of the μ opiate receptor. Right-handed α-helical representations of the seven receptor TM domains are shown from the extracellular perspective. The seven TM domains are arranged by superimposing each helix on the corresponding helix of rhodopsin (another G protein–coupled receptor; the rhodopsin helices were arrayed based on crystallographic data). Helices are arranged in counterclockwise fashion, starting with TM 1 (numbered), and presented as virtually perpendicular to the membrane lipid bilayer to facilitate viewing of amino acid side chains. The TM 3 aspartic acid (Asp-147) postulated to form an ion pair with the positive charge of morphine is located (*arrow*) in the central, putative binding site for ligands. Orientation of each TM helical face was assigned based on mutagenesis data, homology with other G protein–coupled receptors, and the presence of charged or polar residues.

residue. The TM 1 aspartic acid is one of only two negative charges located within the TM domains of the dopamine, norepinephrine, and serotonin transporters. Placing such a hydrophilic amino acid within the hydrophobic membrane bilayer is energetically unfavorable, and one would therefore expect an energetically compensatory interaction with this residue that is critical for transporter function. The aspartic acid side chain is very likely oriented toward a central, hydrophilic enclave, created by some or all of the 12 TM domains, that contains the substrate binding site. Still, a role for Asp-79 in maintaining the secondary structure of the transporter cannot be dismissed. The TM 1 aspartic acid residue may serve as the counterion for positively charged nitrogen atoms common to all ligands of the monoamine transporters. The monoamine neurotransmitters and amphetamines possess primary amine groups, while cocaine and its analogues feature a tropane nitrogen atom; each ligand is greater than 90% charged at physiologic pH. This postulated ionic interaction between transporter and ligand would constitute the single strongest bond linking the two, and possibly, the point of overlap between binding sites for neurotransmitter substrates and drugs of abuse. Mutagenesis of this aspartic acid residue in the dopamine and vesicular monoamine transporters severely curtailed uptake of monoamines (Kitayama et al., 1992; Merickel et al., 1995).

Serine residues common to the four monoamine transporters may provide a second tether to the monoamine substrates, anticipated to form hydrogen bonding interactions with the hydroxyl groups of the monoamine substrates. Several predicted serine residues in TM domains 7 and 8 are conserved among these transporters, all located at the approximate midpoint of the membrane bilayer. This motif, including the postulated aspartic acid–substrate primary amine ion pair, is suggested from studies of the β-adrenergic and dopamine D2 receptors (Strader et al., 1989; Tomic et al., 1993). The aromatic ring shared by the monoamines is a likely third pharmacophore of the substrate. Although a TM domain phenyl-alanine residue in the β-adrenergic receptor has been implicated in recognition of the aromatic ring (Dixon et al., 1988), no counterpart for this role for the monoamine transporters has been identified.

G Protein–Coupled Receptors: The Opiate and Cannabinoid Receptors

All three methods for the cloning of drug receptors discussed in this chapter have been employed by various laboratories in search of cDNAs encoding opiate receptors. An expression cloning strategy (Method 3) using a cDNA library constructed from the opiate receptor–rich NG108 cell line, coupled with a sensitive ligand-binding assay, led two independent laboratories in 1992 to the first opiate receptor cDNA, encoding a δ receptor (Evans et al., 1992; Kieffer et al., 1992). A milestone in opiate drug research, this advance quickly led to the cloning of μ and κ opiate receptor cDNAs (Chen et al., 1993; Fukuda et al., 1993; Knapp et al, 1994; Mansson et al., 1994; Wang et al., 1993, 1994a; Yasuda et al., 1993). The cloning of cDNAs encoding μ, δ, and κ receptor subtypes validated the premise of three unique opiate receptor proteins, the existence of which had been suggested based on pharmacologic studies alone (Martin et al., 1976). There are apparently subtypes of these subtypes; more than one version of the κ receptor has been postulated from pharmacologic evidence (Clark et al,. 1989), and new μ receptor sequences differing slightly at the carboxyl terminus from the first μ receptor have been recently reported (Bare et al., 1994, Zimprich et al., 1995). These μ receptors are apparently RNA splice variants derived from the same gene.

The cDNAs encoding the three opiate receptor subtypes predict an amino acid sequence identity of 60% to 70%. The predicted 7 TM topology (Fig. 3B) characteristic of the G protein–coupled receptor (GCR) family further affirmed previous work (Blume et al., 1979) indicating a functional link to G proteins for the opiate receptors. Of the cloned G protein–coupled receptors, only the somato-statin receptor (Li et al,. 1992) and the "noci-ceptin" (orphanin FQ) receptor (Meunier et al., 1995; Reinscheid et al., 1995) exhibit ho-mology to the μ, δ, and κ opiate receptors.

Prior to the cloning of a cannabinoid recep-tor, the lipophilic nature of the psychoactive cannabinoids found in marijuana suggested that these drugs might exert their effects on the central nervous system by diffusing across cell membranes, nonspecifically interfering with cell function. While this has not been eliminated as a pathway, a cannabinoid recep-tor cDNA has been cloned using an oligonu-cleotide probe derived from a bovine sub-stance K receptor sequence (Matsuda et al., 1990). The predicted topology was consistent with earlier indications (Howlett, 1985) that this drug receptor belongs to the GCR family; however, the predicted amino acid sequence displayed little homology to other GCR such that pharmacologic screening of many candi-date ligands was necessary to identify the re-ceptor (Matsuda et al., 1990).

Despite the aforementioned differences be-tween the neurotransmitter transporter and G protein–coupled receptor classes of drug re-ceptors, some of the discrete drug-protein contacts may be remarkably similar. As with the monoamine transporters, a TM aspartic acid residue conserved among the opiate re-ceptors may establish an ion pair with a posi-tively charged nitrogen atom, and again, this residue would be expected to extend into a central, hydrophilic ligand binding cavity (Fig. 4). In the case of the μ receptor, the pos-itively charged atom is a bridging nitrogen atom within morphine and other opiate alka-loids, and the N-terminal amine of the en-dogenous peptide agonist met-enkephalin. In-terestingly, this TM 3 residue (Asp-147 in the rat μ receptor) is conserved among GCRs that bind amine-containing ligands (Strader et al., 1988), including the three major opiate recep-tor subtypes. A cDNA encoding the cannabi-noid receptor (Matsuda et al., 1990) predicts a protein lacking this TM 3 aspartic acid, in keeping with the observation that neither the endogenous ligand anandamide (Devane et

al., 1992) nor the exogenous ligand and drug of abuse tetrahydrocannabinol (Δ^9-THC) pos-sesses a positively charged amine group. The opiate and cannabinoid receptors share a sec-ond negative charge within the transmem-brane domains, a TM 2 aspartic acid; in fact, this residue is present in a very large majority of the more than 200 members of the GCR su-perfamily. This extraordinary conservation combined with the significant structural di-versity of GCR ligands suggests a lesser role for the residue in ligand binding, and a more likely role in mediating the signal transduc-tion event.

Binding of agonists such as morphine or enkephalin to the μ opiate receptor is only an intermediate step in the mechanism of media-tion of addiction or analgesia; the signal must still be relayed through one of several intra-cellular G proteins to activate the biochemical pathway leading to a behavioral or physio-logic response. The μ receptor couples to members of the inhibitory G protein family; morphine therefore mediates inhibition of "second messenger" effector molecules. A large body of work has identified transmem-brane and intracellular regions of the GCR family directly or indirectly involved in G protein binding (reviewed by Strader et al., 1994). The second and third intracellular loops (connecting TM domains 3 and 4, and 5 and 6, respectively; Fig. 3B) and the carboxy-terminal tail of the receptor are especially in-volved in contacts with the G protein. These same regions for G protein contact are rich in potential phosphoacceptor sites. Virtually any intracellular serine or threonine residue may be utilized, as serine and threonine residues not belonging to an ostensible consensus site have been phosphorylated by the β-adrenergic and rhodopsin kinases (Dohlman et al., 1987; Onorato et al., 1991). Addition of phosphate groups to the intracellular aspects of the re-ceptor may regulate the receptor at the level of G protein coupling by either promoting or destabilizing its interaction with a given G protein. Receptor phosphorylation may also influence the sequestration (internalization) of the receptor in the presence of morphine or other agonists (Arden et al., 1995; Von Zastrow et al., 1994), an alternative regulatory mechanism.

STRUCTURE/FUNCTION STUDIES OF DRUG RECEPTORS

Cloned cDNAs encoding drug receptors have provided the wherewithal to explore the nature of the drug-receptor interaction, and for the G protein–coupled receptors, the mechanism of agonist-mediated activation. Methodologies involving PCR and site-directed mutagenesis permit the dissection, rearrangement, or alteration of both large polypeptide sections or individual amino acid residues at every position in the receptor. Examination of the consequences of such structural changes should yield insights concerning the mechanisms of action of drugs of abuse.

The plasma membrane dopamine transporter and the μ opiate receptor, representatives of each of the two described structural classes of drug receptors, have been the subject of intensive structure/function studies, and are the principal foci of this section.

The Dopamine Transporter

A collection of dopamine transporter mutants has been constructed that allows assessment of the contributions of putative TM domain residues and posttranslational modification sites in recognition of cocaine, dopamine, and analogues of both. The reversible binding of these ligands to the transporter may be mediated in part via an ionic interaction between the positively charged ligand and one of two negatively charged TM domain amino acid residues. Mutation of the TM 1 Asp-79 residue in the rat dopamine transporter (Kitayama et al., 1992) to alanine, glycine, or glutamic acid resulted in a pronounced loss of affinity for both dopamine and the cocaine analogue CFT. Alteration of the second predicted negatively charged TM domain residue, the TM 10 residue Glu-490, yielded a mutant not appreciably different in

function from the native transporter (Kitayama and Uhl, *personal communication*). The presence of a TM negative charge is not sufficient for high affinity binding of cocaine and dopamine, because the negatively charged glutamic acid did not serve as an effective substitute, implying that Asp-79 is at best only one putative point of contact for both cocaine and dopamine.

Serine residues predicted in TM 7, and possibly those in TM 8, are candidates for interaction with the catechol hydroxyl groups of dopamine. Of four TM 7 serine residues replaced with alanine, two of the residues (Ser-356 and Ser-359; Fig. 3A) on the same α-helical face of TM 7 were essential for dopamine uptake, but not binding of the cocaine analogue CFT (Kitayama et al., 1992). This finding indicates separate transporter contact points for cocaine and dopamine, echoing pharmacologic evidence that the transporter sites for cocaine and dopamine are overlapping but not identical (Berger et al., 1990; Javitch et al., 1984; Fig. 5).

Aside from the tropane nitrogen atom of cocaine, primary pharmacophores of the molecule are the 3′-phenyl moiety and, to some extent, the 2′-methyl ester (Carroll et al., 1992). Conceivably, the point of overlap between the cocaine and dopamine binding sites is the negative charge at Asp-79. In this model (Fig. 5), the 3′-phenyl moiety of cocaine would be expected to diverge from the path taken by the catechol group of dopamine (presumably in the direction of the TM 7 serine residues), and bind to the transporter in a way that facilitates an interaction with the π electrons of the 3′-phenyl group pharmacophore. Davis and colleagues (1994) have generated a transporter mutant that virtually eliminated cocaine binding without affecting dopamine uptake. Tyrosine-251 in TM 4 was replaced with alanine, serine, or phenylalanine; only the phenylalanine mutant restored high affinity binding of cocaine, suggesting that the π electrons of the Tyr-251 aromatic ring participate in an interaction. It is tempting to speculate that Tyr-251 directly engages the 3′-phenyl moiety of cocaine via a ring stacking

(π-π electron) interaction; still, it is entirely possible that the role of this residue lies in intrahelical contacts within the transporter that preserve the secondary and tertiary structure, preserving in turn the cocaine binding site. The Tyr-251 mutant represents the first reported dopamine transporter that transports dopamine in the presence of cocaine, an exciting advance in the search for a compound with dopamine-sparing cocaine antagonist properties.

A dopamine transporter that was intermediate between the wildtype and Tyr-251 mutant with respect to cocaine binding was obtained by mutation of a TM 5 tyrosine residue (Tyr-271; S. Davis, J.B. Wang, and G.R. Uhl, *unpublished results*). An intriguing observation is the fact that the TM 4 and 5 tyrosine residues are common to the three cocaine-binding, plasma membrane monoamine transporters; in contrast, the vesicular monoamine transporter, possessing no appreciable affinity for cocaine, contains no tyrosine residues in either TM domain. Further mapping of dopamine transporter-cocaine contacts may lead to development of therapeutic drugs that disrupt these contacts without interfering with dopamine uptake.

An alternative to site-directed mutagenesis for structure/function analysis of drug receptors is the construction of *chimeric* receptors, composed of elements from two or more discrete receptors. To elucidate specific regions necessary for cocaine or antidepressant binding and substrate transport, 14 dopamine/norepinephrine chimeric transporters were prepared by reducing both native transporters into four fragments each and interchanging corresponding pieces (Giros et al., 1994). This approach assigned the recognition of cocaine and the tricyclic antidepressants to TM domains 6 to 8, and substrate recognition to the carboxyl-terminal third of the transporters, starting with TM 9. Two of the chimeras, however, sustained approximately 30- to 80-fold losses in affinity for cocaine. This unexpected finding represents a caveat with chimeric receptor experiments, possibly indicating that the intrahelical TM domain

contacts have been subtly disrupted in a way that alters the cocaine binding site without seriously affecting other ligand binding sites.

Structural features of extracellular portions of the dopamine transporter may nonspecifically affect dopamine uptake and cocaine binding. Elimination of any one of five putative glycosylation sites yielded no effect on dopamine uptake or cocaine binding, while removal of two sites resulted in modest changes in both transporter activities (J.B. Wang, *unpublished data*). It is unclear mechanistically how the extent of glycosylation affects transporter function, although glycosylation was required for stabilization of the serotonin transporter (Tate and Blakely, 1994). Alanine substitution of four extracellular cysteines of the dopamine transporter revealed that two of the cysteine residues (Cys-180 and Cys-189) located in the large, putatively glycosylated loop were apparently necessary for correct folding and membrane insertion of the transporter protein (Wang et al., 1995). Immunocytochemical studies of COS cells transfected with mutants containing substitutions at either Cys-180 or Cys-189 revealed an irregular perinuclear staining pattern, indicating that these mutant proteins did not migrate to the cell surface efficiently. The cysteines may form a disulfide bond that, in part, preserves the structural integrity of the transporter.

G Protein–Coupled Receptors: Morphine and the μ Opiate Receptor

As with the dopamine transporter, the rat μ opiate receptor cDNA encodes two TM domain negative charges, one of which is proposed to form an ion pair with the positively charged nitrogen atom of its ligands. This role is most likely assumed by the TM 3 aspartic acid residue Asp-147, as a TM 3 aspartic acid is common to G protein–coupled receptors that bind amine-containing ligands (Strader et al., 1988). Mutagenesis analysis of both μ receptor TM domain aspartic acids (Surratt et al., 1994) corroborated this role for Asp-147, as high

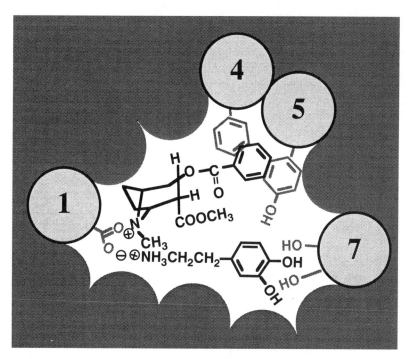

FIG. 5. Proposed points of contact between the dopamine transporter and cocaine or dopamine. In the schematic scenario, a cross-section of the TM domains of the transporter is pictured. As no high-resolution data concerning the three-dimensional structure of neurotransmitter transporters are currently available, the positioning of TM domains 1, 4, 5, and 7 is arbitrary. The side chains (gray atoms) of amino acid residues critical for recognition of cocaine, dopamine, or both are presented, attached to the corresponding TM domain. Positively charged nitrogen atoms of cocaine (above, *black*) and dopamine (below, *black*) are suggested to compete for the negatively charged TM 1 aspartic acid. TM 4 and 5 tyrosine residues may constitute selective contacts for cocaine and its structural analogues. It should be noted that phenylalanine is shown in place of the TM 4 tyrosine, as a mutant with this substitution bound cocaine at levels comparable to the native transporter. Two serine residues on the same α-helical face of TM 7 were essential for dopamine uptake, but relatively unimportant for cocaine binding. Due to lack of structural information, the scenario does not reflect transporter interactions with the aromatic ring of each ligand, the third major pharmacophore.

affinity binding of the agonists morphine and the met-enkephalin analogue DAMGO ([D-Ala²MePhe⁴Gly-ol⁵]enkephalin), as well as the antagonist naloxone, were lost upon substitution of Asp-147 with alanine, asparagine, or the negatively charged glutamic acid. Efficient binding of naloxone, but not morphine or DAMGO, was retained upon substitution of the TM 2 residue Asp-114 with asparagine or glutamic acid, confirming the existence of separate agonist and antagonist binding sites while casting doubt on an ionic interaction between μ antagonists and Asp-114. A theme common to the dopamine transporter, μ agonists and antagonists are proposed to compete for the TM

aspartic acid (Asp-147) to form an ion pair, although there are apparently more components to the respective ligand binding sites than simply a negatively charged residue. The TM 2 aspartic acid residue is a probable contributor in forming the agonist binding site, as high affinity agonist binding by the μ (Surratt et al., 1994) and δ (Kong et al., 1993) opiate receptors was lost upon substitution of this residue.

Extracellular regions of the opiate receptors also play a role in recognition of alkaloid drugs and opioid peptides. Conserved cysteine residues in extracellular loops 1 (connecting TM domains 2 and 3) and 2 (connecting TM domains 4 and 5) of the μ receptor may form a disulfide bond covalently linking the loops; extracellular cysteine residues of the β2-adrenergic receptor (Noda et al., 1994), rhodopsin (Karnik and Khorana, 1990), and other GCRs have been documented to form such a bond. The cysteines may therefore serve to stabilize the tertiary structure of the receptor as opposed to forming direct contacts with ligands (although the latter is still a possibility), as discussed above for the dopamine transporter. All five consensus sites for asparagine-linked glycosylation were dispensable with respect to the binding and G protein–coupling activities of the μ receptor (Wang et al., 1993).

The second extracellular loop of the κ opiate receptor is especially critical for binding of dynorphin and related larger opioid peptides. Comparing this loop with the corresponding loop of the μ and δ receptors, the κ loop is highly negatively charged, studded with aspartic and glutamic acid residues. Replacement of only extracellular loop 2 of the μ receptor with the κ loop 2 sequence yielded a μ/κ chimeric receptor with affinities for the κ-selective agonist dynorphin that rivaled that of the authentic κ receptor (Wang et al., 1994b). Other μ/κ and δ/κ chimeric receptors reflect an importance for the second κ loop in dynorphin binding (Kong et al., 1994; Meng et al., 1995; Xue et al., 1994). It would appear that the many positively charged amino acids of dynorphin form ionic contacts with the negative charges within the κ loop 2, a view supported by molecular modeling analysis (C.K. Surratt, *unpublished data*). The first and third extracellular loops of the opiate receptors are also reported to confer ligand selectivity (Fukuda et al., 1995; Minami et al., 1995; Onogi et al., 1995; Xue et al., 1995).

Relatively little has been elucidated regarding the specific regions of the μ receptor responsible for intrinsic activity. The negative charge of the highly GCR-conserved TM 2 aspartic acid residue would appear to be necessary for efficient G protein coupling; of three separate amino acid substitutions at this position, only the glutamic acid μ receptor mutant retained the ability to inhibit accumulation of the second messenger molecule cyclic AMP (Surratt et al., 1994). A charged residue was not required at this position for the δ receptor (Kong et al., 1993), as intrinsic activity was retained with an asparagine substitution. More interesting are mutant receptors that retain high affinity agonist binding but are decoupled from the G protein. For adrenergic receptors (Strader et al., 1987) and other GCRs, mutations of intracellular portions of the protein have compromised receptor activity without adversely affecting ligand binding. The third intracellular loop (connecting TM 5 and 6) and C-terminal sequences closest to TM 7 (and the membrane) are among the most conserved sequences within GCR subfamiles, and are thought to form direct contacts with the G protein.

ADDICTION AT THE LEVEL OF THE DRUG RECEPTOR

The various molecular and cellular modifications induced by chronic exposure to abused drugs, contributing to a state of biochemical addiction, are largely manifested "downstream" of the level of the drug receptor. Manipulation of intracellular levels of G proteins (Nestler et al., 1990), second messengers (Beitner et al., 1989), and mRNAs encoding regulatory proteins (Graybiel et al., 1990) by psychostimulants and opiates has been reviewed (Nestler et al., 1993), and an analysis of addiction at this level is beyond the scope of the chapter. It is conceivable, nevertheless, that phosphorylation (or dephosphorylation) of the drug receptor contributes to the biochemical pathway leading to addiction. Both structural classes of drug receptors possess intracellular serine and threonine residues, some of which may serve as sites for phosphorylation. These sites, not always marked by a consensus sequence, are predicted to regulate function of the drug receptor.

A growing body of evidence suggests that drug receptors are reversibly phosphorylated; receptor function is regulated to some extent by this posttranslational modification. Phorbol ester compounds, known activators of protein kinase C (PKC), an enzyme responsible for receptor phosphorylation, appear to downregulate the dopamine transporter, mediating a reduction in dopamine uptake (Kitayama et al., 1994), while upregulating glutamate transport in glial cells (Casado et al., 1991). Protein kinase C may also regulate serotonin transporter function (Myers et al., 1989). By controlling the kinetics of neurotransmitter uptake, this kinase may function much like cocaine to augment synaptic dopamine levels, and thus indirectly mediate addiction pathways.

The G protein–coupled receptor class may offer a more direct impact on addiction. The μ and δ opiate receptors are desensitized upon brief exposure to agonists (Harris and Williams, 1991; Law et al., 1983). Protein kinase A (PKA) and PKC may differentially regulate a G protein–mediated coupling between the μ receptor and a potassium channel (Chen and Yu, 1994); however, it is unclear whether the receptor, channel protein, or both, are phosphorylated. PKC-independent phosphorylation and desensitization of δ and μ opiate receptors were observed after acute agonist treatment, suggesting a causal relationship (Pei et al., 1995; Zhang et al., 1996). Desensitization of a μ receptor–coupled potassium channel has also been observed to be independent of phosphorylation (Kovoor et al., 1995). Desensitization to agonists has been effected by phosphorylation of the β-adrenergic receptor, effectively decoupling the receptor and G protein (Sibley and Lefkowitz; 1985). In the latter case, an intermediary facilitates the decoupling. Upon binding an agonist, the receptor is phosphorylated by β-adrenergic receptor kinase (βARK), presumably stimulating binding of β-arrestin to the phosphorylated receptor and precluding G protein binding (Lefkowitz, 1993). An intriguing concept recently advanced is the notion that chronic administration of an abused drug may constitutively activate its receptor (Z. Wang et al., 1994). Chronic morphine treatment is postulated to drive conversion of the μ opiate receptor toward constitutive activation (receptor activation in the absence of an agonist); the protein kinase inhibitor H7 suppressed this conversion, and reversed tolerance to morphine in mice.

At this point, there are few definitive answers regarding the connection between drug receptors and the molecular mechanism of addiction; still, the recent cloning of these receptors promises to galvanize this burgeoning area of research.

FUTURE DIRECTIONS

The cloning of cDNAs encoding drug receptors opens the door for a multifaceted approach in the study of drug addiction and its treatment. The cloned cDNAs are leading to the identification and isolation of genes encoding drug receptors. These genes will allow the development of transgenic mice "knockouts" that assess the role of a drug receptor in behavioral aspects of addiction. The information contained within drug receptor genes may identify regulatory elements that modulate the receptor, as well as polymorphic markers potentially useful in predicting an individual's predisposition toward addiction, or probable response to a given treatment. Antisense DNA or RNA molecules specifically targeted to drug receptor genes or other molecular intermediates in the addiction pathway may serve as therapeutics in the treatment of addiction.

Structure/function studies of the drug receptors coupled with structure/activity work with drugs of abuse may allow molecular biologists and medicinal chemists to identify the specific drug-receptor points of contact, and develop compounds that antagonize the drug of abuse while sparing native properties of the receptor (e.g., neurotransmitter uptake or mediation of analgesia). The cloning of drug receptors has offered for the first time the opportunity to study an individual receptor in a controlled system, free from the complications of heterogeneous populations of receptors and other components inherent with manipulation of biologic tissue. By cotransfecting drug receptor cDNAs in a cultured cell line with cDNAs encoding G proteins, G protein–activated ion channels, or other proteins directly or peripherally implicated in addiction, the various biochemical pathways of addiction may one day be mapped.

SUMMARY

- Receptors serving as the sites of action for abused drugs including cocaine, amphetamine, heroin, morphine, and the cannabinoids have been cloned using recombinant DNA methodologies in the last 7 years.
- Analysis and manipulation of elucidated cDNAs encoding these receptors are illuminating previously inaccessible areas of drug receptor research dealing with drug receptor mechanisms of action, molecular structure of drug receptors, and the correlation between receptor structure and function.
- Receptor mutagenesis may reveal specific points of contact with the drug of abuse, potentially leading to rational design of chemotherapies in the treatment of addiction.

REFERENCES

Amara, S. and Kuhar, M.J. (1993). Neurotransmitter transporters: recent progress. *Annu. Rev. Neurosci.* 16: 73–93.

Arden, J.R., Segredo, V., Wang, Z., Lameh, J. and Sadée, W. (1995). Phosphorylation and agonist-specific intracellular trafficking of an epitope-tagged μ-opioid receptor expressed in HEK 293 cells. *J. Neurochem.* 65: 1636–1645.

Bare, L.A., Mansson, E. and Yang, D. (1994). Expression of two variants of the human μ opioid receptor mRNA in SK-N-SH cells and brain. *FEBS Lett.* 354: 213–216.

Beitner, D., Duman, R.S. and Nestler, E.J. (1989). A novel action of morphine in the rat locus coeruleus: persistent decrease in adenylate cyclase. *Mol. Pharmacol.* 35: 559–564.

Berger, P., Elsworth, J.D., Reith, M.E.A., Tanen, D. and Roth, R.H. (1990). Complex interaction of cocaine with the dopamine uptake carrier. *Eur. J. Pharmacol.* 176: 251–252.

Blakely, R.D., Berson, H.E., Fremeau, R.T., Caron, M.G., Peek, M.M., Prince, H.K. and Bradley, C.C. (1991). Cloning and expression of a functional serotonin transporter from rat brain. *Nature* 354: 66–70.

Blume, A.J., Lichtshtein, D. and Boone, G. (1979). Coupling of opiate receptors to adenylate cyclase: requirement for Na⁺ and GTP. *Proc. Natl. Acad. Sci. USA* 76: 5626–5630.

Caine, S.B. and Koob, G.F. (1993). Modulation of cocaine self-administration in the rat through D-3 dopamine receptors. *Science* 260: 1814–1816.

Caine, S.B. and Koob, G.F. (1995). Pretreatment with the dopamine agonist 7-OH-DPAT shifts the cocaine self-administration dose-effect function to the left under different schedules in the rat. *Behav. Pharmacol.* 6: 333–347.

Carboni, E., Imperato, A., Perezzani, L. and DiChiara, G.D. (1989). Amphetamine, cocaine, phencyclidine and nomifensine increase extracellular dopamine concentrations preferentially in the nucleus accumbens of freely moving rats. *Neuroscience* 28: 653–661.

Carroll, F.I., Lewin, A.H., Boja, J.W. and Kuhar, M.J. (1992). Cocaine receptor: biochemical characterization and structure-activity relationships of cocaine analogues at the dopamine transporter. *J. Med. Chem.* 35: 969–981.

Casado, M., Zafra, F., Aragon, C. and Gimenez, C. (1991). Activation of high-affinity uptake of glutamate by phorbol esters in primary glial cell cultures. *J. Neurochem.* 57: 1185–1190.

Chen, Y., Mestek, A., Liu, J., Hurley, J.A. and Yu, L. (1993). Molecular cloning and functional expression of a μ-opioid receptor from rat brain. *Mol. Pharmacol.* 44: 8–12.

Chen, Y. and Yu, L. (1994). Differential regulation by cAMP-dependent protein kinase and protein kinase C of the μ opioid receptor coupling to a G protein-activated K⁺ channel. *J. Biol. Chem.* 269: 7839–7842.

Clark, J.A., Liu, L., Price, M., Hersh, B., Edelson, M. and Pasternak, G.W. (1989). Kappa opiate receptor multiplicity: evidence for two U50,488-sensitive κ₁ subtypes and a novel κ₃ subtype. *J. Pharmacol. Exp. Ther.* 251: 461–468.

Cruciani, R.A., Dvorkin, B., Morris, S.A., Crain, S.M. and Makman, M.H. (1993). Direct coupling of opioid receptors to both Gₛ and Gᵢ proteins in F-11 neuroblastoma X sensory neuron hybrid cells. *Proc. Natl. Acad. Sci. USA* 90: 3019–3023.

Davis, S.C., Wang, J.B. and Uhl, G.R. (1994). The phenyl ring of tyrosine-251 of the dopamine transporter is required for high-affinity binding of cocaine analogs. *Soc. Neurosci. Abs.* 20: 922.

Devane, W.A., Hanus, L., Breuer, A., Pertwee, R.G., Stevenson, L.A., Griffin, G., Gibson, D., Mandelbaum, A., Etinger, A. and Mechoulam, R. (1992). Isolation and structure of a brain constituent that binds to the cannabinoid receptor. *Science* 258: 1946–1949.

DiChiara, G. and North, R.A. (1992). Neurobiology of opiate abuse. *Trends Pharmacol. Sci.* 13: 185–193.

Dixon, R.A.F., Sigal, I.S. and Strader, C.D. (1988). Structure-function analysis of the beta-adrenergic receptor. *Cold Spring Harbor Symp. Quant. Biol.* 53: 487–597.

Dixon, R.A.F., Kobilka, B.K., Strader, D.J., Benovic, J.L., Dohlman, H.G., Frielle, T., Bolanowski, M.A., Bennett, C.D., Rands, E., Diehl, R.E., Mumford, R.A., Slater, E.E., Sigal, I.S., Caron, M.G., Lefkowitz, R.J. and Strader, C.D. (1986). Cloning of the gene and cDNA for mammalian β-adrenergic receptor and homology with rhodopsin. *Nature* 321: 75–79.

Dohlman, H.G., Bouvier, M., Benovic, J.L., Caron, M.G. and Lefkowitz, R.J. (1987). The multiple membrane-spanning topography of the beta2-adrenergic receptor: localization of the sites of binding, glycosylation, and regulatory phosphorylation by limited proteolysis. *J. Biol. Chem.* 262: 14282–14288.

Erickson, J.D., Eiden, L.E. and Hoffman, B.J. (1992). Expression cloning of a reserpine-sensitive vesicular monoamine transporter. *Proc. Natl. Acad. Sci. USA* 89: 10993–10997.

Evans, C.J., Keith, D.E., Morrison, H., Magendzo, K. and Edwards, R.H. (1992). Cloning of a delta opioid receptor by functional expression. *Science* 258: 1952–1955.

Felder, C.C., Briley, E.M., Axelrod, J., Simpson, J.T., Mackie, K. and Devane, W.A. (1993). Anandamide, an endogenous cannabimimetic eicosanoid, binds to the cloned human cannabinoid receptor and stimulates receptor-mediated signal transduction. *Proc. Natl. Acad. Sci. USA* 90: 7656–7660.

Fischer, J.F. and Cho, A.K. (1979). Chemical release of dopamine from striatal homogenates: evidence for an exchange diffusion model. *J. Pharmacol. Exp. Ther.* 208: 203–209.

Fremeau Jr., R.T., Caron, M.G. and Blakely, R.D. (1992). Molecular cloning and expression of a high affinity L-proline transporter expressed in putative glutamatergic pathways of rat brain. *Neuron* 8: 915–926.

Fukuda, K., Kato, S. and Mori, K. (1995). Location of regions of the opioid receptor involved in selective agonist binding. *J. Biol. Chem.* 270: 6702–6709.

Fukuda, K., Kato, S., Mori, K., Nishi, M. and Takeshima, H. (1993). Primary structures and expression from cDNAs of rat opioid receptor δ- and μ-subtypes. *FEBS Lett.* 327: 311–314.

Giros, B., Mestikawy, S.E., Godinot, N., Zheng, K., Han, H., Yang-Feng, T. and Caron, M.G. (1992). Cloning, pharmacological characterization, and chromosome assignment of the human dopamine transporter. *Mol. Pharmacol.* 42: 383–390.

Giros, B., Wang, Y., Suter, S., Mestikawy, S.E., Pifl, C. and Caron M.G. (1994). Delineation of discrete domains for substrate, cocaine, and tricyclic antidepressant interactions using chimeric dopamine-norepinephrine transporters. *J. Biol. Chem.* 269: 15985–15988.

Gonzalez, A.M., Walther, D., Pazos, A. and Uhl, G.R. (1993). Synaptic vesicular monoamine transporter expression: distribution and pharmacologic profile. *Mol. Brain Res.* 22: 219–226.

Graybiel, A.M., Moratalla, R. and Robertson, H.A. (1990). Amphetamine and cocaine induce drug-specific activation of the c-*fos* gene in striosome-matrix compartments and limbic subdivisions of the striatum. *Proc. Natl. Acad. Sci. USA* 87: 6912–6916.

Gross, R.A., Moises, H.C., Uhler, M.D. and Macdonald, R.L. (1990). Dynorphin A and cAMP-dependent protein kinase independently regulate neuronal calcium currents. *Proc. Natl. Acad. Sci. USA* 87: 7025–7029.

Guastella, J., Nelson, N., Nelson, H., Czyzyk, L., Keynan, S., Miedel, M.C., Davidson, N., Lester, H.A. and Kanner, B.I. (1990). Cloning and expression of a rat brain GABA transporter. *Science* 249: 1303–1306.

Guimbal, C. and Kilimann, M.W. (1993). A Na(+)-dependent creatine transporter in rabbit brain, muscle, heart, and kidney. cDNA cloning and functional expression. *J. Biol. Chem.* 268: 8418–8421.

Harris, G.C. and Williams, J.T. (1991). Transient homologous μ-opioid receptor desensitization in rat locus coeruleus neurons. *J. Neurosci.* 11: 2574–2581.

Hoffman, B.J., Mezey, E. and Brownstein, M.J. (1991). Cloning of a serotonin transporter affected by antidepressants. *Science* 254: 579–580.

Horn, A.S. (1990). Dopamine uptake: a review of progress in the last decade. *Prog. Neurobiol.* 34: 387–400.

Howlett, A.C. (1985). Cannabinoid inhibition of adenylate cyclase. *Mol. Pharmacol.* 27: 429–436.

Javitch, J.A., Blaustein, R.O. and Snyder, S.H. (1984). [^{3}H]Mazindol binding associated with neuronal dopamine and norepinephrine uptake sites. *Mol. Pharmacol.* 26: 35–44.

Karnik, S.S. and Khorana, H.G. (1990). Assembly of functional rhodopsin requires a disulfide bond between cysteine residues 110 and 187. *J. Biol. Chem.* 265: 17520–17524.

Kieffer, B.L., Befort, K., Gaveriaux-Ruff, C. and Hirth, C.G. (1992). The δ-opioid receptor: isolation of a cDNA by expression cloning and pharmacological characterization. *Proc. Natl. Acad. Sci. USA.* 89: 12048–12052.

Kilty, J.E., Lorang, D. and Amara S.G. (1991). Cloning and expression of a cocaine-sensitive rat dopamine transporter. *Science* 254: 578–579.

Kitayama, S., Dohi, T. and Uhl, G.R. (1994). Phorbol esters alter functions of the expressed dopamine transporter. *Eur. J. Pharmacol.* 268: 115–119.

Kitayama, S., Shimada, S., Xu, H., Markham, L., Donovan, D.M. and Uhl, G.R. (1992). Dopamine transporter site-directed mutations differentially alter substrate transport and cocaine binding. *Proc. Natl. Acad. Sci. USA* 89: 7782–7785.

Knapp, R.J., Malatynska, E., Fang, L., Li, X., Babin, E., Nguyen, M., Santoro, G., Varga, E.V., Hruby, V.J., Roeske, W.R. and Yamamura, H.I. (1994). Identification of a human delta opioid receptor: cloning and expression. *Life Sci.* 54: 463–469.

Kong, H., Raynor, K., Yano, H., Takeda, J., Bell, G.I. and Reisine, T. (1994). Agonists and antagonists bind to different domains of the cloned κ opioid receptor. *Proc. Natl. Acad. Sci. USA* 91: 8042–8046.

Kong, H., Raynor, K., Yasuda, K., Moe, S.T., Portoghese, P.S., Bell, G.I. and Reisine, T. (1993). A single residue, aspartic acid 95, in the δ opioid receptor specifies selective high affinity agonist binding. *J. Biol. Chem.* 268: 23055–230558.

Kovoor, A., Henry, D.J. and Chavkin, C. (1995). Agonist-induced desensitization of the mu opioid receptor-coupled potassium channel (GIRK1). *J. Biol. Chem.* 270: 589–595.

Kuhar, M.J., Ritz, C. and Boja, J.W. (1991). The dopamine hypothesis of the reinforcing properties of cocaine. *Trends Neurosci.* 14: 299–302.

Law, P.-Y., Hom, D.S. and Loh, H.H. (1983). Opiate receptor down-regulation and desensitization in neuroblastoma x glioma NG108-15 hybrid cells are two separate cellular adaptation processes. *Mol. Pharmacol.* 24: 413–424.

Lefkowitz, R.J. (1993). G protein-coupled receptor kinases. *Cell* 74: 409–412.

Li, X.J., Forte, M., North, R.A., Ross, C.A. and Snyder, S.H. (1992). Cloning and expression of a rat somatostatin receptor enriched in brain. *J. Biol. Chem.* 267: 21307–21312.

Liang, N.Y. and Rutledge, C.O. (1982). Comparison of the release of [^{3}H]dopamine from isolated corpus striatum by amphetamine, fenfluramine, and unlabeled dopamine. *Biochem. Pharmacol.* 31: 983–992.

Liu, Y., Peter, D., Roghani, A., Schuldiner, S., Prive, G.G., Eisenberg, D., Brecha, N. and Edwards, R.H. (1992). A cDNA that suppresses MPP$^+$ toxicity encodes a vesicular amine transporter. *Cell* 70: 539–551.

Mansson, E., Bare, L. and Yang D. (1994). Isolation of a human κ opioid receptor cDNA from placenta. *Biochem. Biophys. Res. Commun.* 202: 1431–1437.

Martin, W.R., Eades, C.G., Thompson, J.A., Huppler, R.E. and Gilbert, P.E. (1976). The effects of morphine and nalorphine-like drugs in the nondependent and morphine-dependent chronic spinal dog. *J. Pharmacol. Exp. Ther.* 197: 517–532.

Matsuda, L.A., Lolait, S.J., Brownstein, M.J., Young, A.C. and Bonner, T.I. (1990). Structure of a cannabinoid receptor and functional expression of the cloned cDNA. *Nature* 346: 561–564.

Meng, F., Hoversten, M.T., Thompson, R.C., Taylor, L., Watson, S.J. and Akil, H. (1995). A chimeric study of the molecular basis of affinity and selectivity of the kappa and the delta opioid receptor: potential role of extracellular domains. *J. Biol. Chem.* 270: 12730–12736.

Merickel, A., Rosandich, P., Peter, D. and Edwards, R.H. (1995). Identification of residues involved in substrate recognition by a vesicular monoamine transporter. *J. Biol. Chem.* 270: 25798–25804.

Meunier, J., Mollereau, C., Toll, L., Suaudeau, C., Molsand, C., Alvinerle, P., Butour, J., Gullemot, J., Ferrara, P., Monsarrat., B., Mazargull, H., Vassart, G., Parmentler, M. and Costentin, J. (1995). Isolation and structure of the endogenous agonist of opioid receptor-like ORL$_1$ receptor. *Nature* 377: 532–535.

Minami, M., Onogi, T., Nakagawa, T., Katao, Y., Aoki, Y., Katsumata, S. and Satoh, M. (1995). DAMGO, a mu-opioid receptor selective ligand, distinguishes between mu- and kappa-opioid receptors at a different region from that for the distinction between mu- and delta-opioid receptors. *FEBS Lett.* 364: 23–27.

Mullis, K.B. and Faloona, F.A. (1987). Specific synthesis of DNA *in vitro* via a polymerase-catalyzed chain reaction. *Methods Enzymol.* 155: 335–350.

Myers, C.L., Lazo, J.S. and Pitt, B.R. (1989). Translocation of protein kinase C is associated with inhibition of 5-HT uptake by cultured endothelial cells. *Am. J. Physiol.* 257: L253–258.

Nestler, E.J., Hope, B.T. and Widnell, K.L. (1993). Drug addiction: a model for the molecular basis of neural plasticity. *Neuron* 11: 995–1006.

Nestler, E.J., Terwilliger, R.Z., Walker, J.R., Sevarino, K.A. and Duman, R.S. (1990). Chronic cocaine treatment decreases levels of the G protein subunits $G_{i\alpha}$ and $G_{o\alpha}$ in discrete regions of rat brain. *J. Neurochem.* 55: 1079–1082.

Noda, K., Saad, Y., Graham, R.M. and Karnik, S.S. (1994). The high affinity state of the β_2-adrenergic receptor requires unique interaction between conserved and nonconserved extracellular loop cysteines. *J. Biol. Chem.* 269: 6743–6752.

North, R.A., Williams, J.T., Surprenant, A. and Christie, M.J. (1987). μ and δ receptors belong to a family of receptors that are coupled to potassium channels. *Proc. Natl. Acad. Sci. USA* 84: 5487–5491.

Onogi, T., Minami, M., Katao, Y., Nakagawa, T., Aoki, Y., Toya, T., Katsumata, S. and Satoh, M. (1995). DAMGO, a mu-opioid receptor selective agonist, distinguishes between mu- and delta-opioid receptors around their first extracellular loops. *FEBS Lett.* 357: 93–97.

Onorato, J.J., Palczewski, K., Regan, J.W., Caron, M.G., Lefkowitz, R.J. and Benovic, J.L. (1991). Role of acidic amino acids in peptide substrates of the beta-adrenergic receptor kinase and rhodopsin kinase. *Biochemistry* 30: 5118–5125.

Pacholczyk, T., Blakely, R.D. and Amara, S.G. (1991). Expression cloning of a cocaine- and antidepressant-sensitive human noradrenaline transporter. *Nature* 350: 350–354.

Pasternak, G.W. (1987). Opioid receptors. In: Meltzer, H.Y. (ed.) *Psychopharmacology:* the third generation of progress. New York: Raven Press, 29: 281–288.

Pei, G., Kieffer, B.L., Lefkowitz, R.J. and Freedman, N.J. (1995). Agonist-dependent phosphorylation of the mouse δ-opioid receptor: involvement of G protein-coupled receptor kinases but not protein kinase C. *Mol. Pharmacol.* 48: 173–177.

Peter, D., Jimenez, J., Liu, Y., Kim, J. and Edwards, R.H. (1994). The chromaffin granule and synaptic vesicle amine transporters differ in substrate recognition and sensitivity to inhibitors. *J. Biol. Chem.* 269: 7231–7237.

Reinscheid, R.K., Nothacker, H., Bourson, A., Ardati, A., Henningsen, R.A., Bunzow, J.R., Grandy, D.K., Langen, H., Monsma Jr., F.J. and Civelli, O. (1995). Orphanin FQ: a neuropeptide that activates an opioidlike G protein-coupled receptor. *Science* 270: 792–794.

Ritz, M.C., Lamb, R.J., Goldberg, S.R. and Kuhar M.J. (1987). Cocaine receptors on dopamine transporters are related to self-administration of cocaine. *Science* 237: 1219–1223.

Rudnick, G. and Wall, S.C. (1992). The molecular mechanism of "ecstasy" [3,4-methylenedioxymethamphetamine (MDMA)]: serotonin transporters are targets for MDMA-induced serotonin release. *Proc. Natl. Acad. Sci. USA* 89: 1817–1821.

Schofield, P.R., Darlison, M.G., Fujita, N., Burt, D.R., Stephenson, F.A., Rodriguez, H., Rhee, L.M., Ramachandran, J., Reale, V., Glencorse, T.A., Seeburg, P.H. and Barnard, E.A. (1987). Sequence and functional expression of the GABA$_A$ receptor shows a ligand-gated receptor super-family. *Nature* 328: 221–227.

Sharma, S.K., Nirenberg, M. and Klee, W.A. (1975). Morphine receptors as regulators of adenylate cyclase activity. *Proc. Natl. Acad. Sci. USA* 72: 590–594.

Shimada, S., Kitayama, S., Lin, C.L., Nanthakumar, E., Gregor, P., Patel, A., Kuhar, M.J. and Uhl, G.R. (1991). Cloning and expression of a cocaine-sensitive dopamine transporter. *Science* 254: 576–578.

Sibley, D.R. and Lefkowitz, R.J. (1985). Molecular mechanisms of receptor desensitization using the β-adrenergic receptor-coupled adenylate cyclase system as a model. *Nature* 317: 124–129.

Smart, D., Smith, G. and Lambert, D.G. (1994). μ-Opioid receptor stimulation of inositol (1,4,5) trisphosphate formation via a pertussis toxin-sensitive G protein. *J. Neurochem.* 62: 1009–1014.

Smith, K.E., Borden, L.A., Hartig, P.R., Branchek, T. and Weinshank, R.L. (1992). Cloning and expression of a glycine transporter reveal colocalization with NMDA receptors. *Neuron* 8: 927–935.

Spealman, R.D., Madras, B.K. and Bergman, J. (1989). Effects of cocaine and related drugs in nonhuman primates. II. Stimulant effects on schedule-controlled behavior. *J. Pharmacol. Exp. Ther.* 251: 142–149.

Strader, C.D., Candelore, M.R., Hill, W.S., Sigal, I.S. and Dixon, R.A.F. (1989). Identification of two serine residues involved in agonist activation of the beta-adrenergic receptor. *J. Biol. Chem.* 264: 13572–13578.

Strader, C.D., Dixon, R.A.F., Cheung, A.H., Candelore, M.R., Blake, A.D. and Sigal, I.S. (1987). Mutations that uncouple the β-adrenergic receptor from G$_s$ and increase agonist affinity. *J. Biol. Chem.* 262: 16439–16443.

Strader, C.D., Fong, T.M., Tota, M.R. and Underwood, D. (1994). Structure and function of G protein-coupled receptors. *Annu. Rev. Biochem.* 63: 101–132.

Strader, C.D., Sigal, I.S., Candelore, M.R., Rands, E., Hill, W.S. and Dixon, R.A.F. (1988). Conserved aspartic acid residues 79 and 113 of the β-adrenergic receptor have different roles in receptor function. *J. Biol. Chem.* 263: 10267–10271.

Sulzer, D., Maidment, N.T. and Rayport, S. (1993). Amphetamine and other weak bases act to promote reverse transport of dopamine in ventral midbrain neurons. *J. Neurochem.* 60: 527–535.

Sulzer, D. and Rayport, S. (1990). Amphetamine and other psychostimulants reduce pH gradients in midbrain dopaminergic neurons and chromaffin granules: a mechanism of action. *Neuron* 5: 797–808.

Surratt, C.K., Johnson, P.S., Moriwaki, A., Seidleck, B.K., Blaschak, C.J., Wang, J.B. and Uhl, G.R. (1994). µ Opiate receptor: charged transmembrane domain amino acids are critical for agonist recognition and intrinsic activity. *J. Biol. Chem.* 269: 20548–20553.

Surratt, C.K., Persico, A.M., Yang, X.D., Edgar, S.R., Bird, G.S., Hawkins, A.L., Griffin, C.A., Li, X., Jabs, E.W. and Uhl, G.R. (1993b). A human synaptic vesicle monoamine transporter cDNA predicts posttranslational modifications, reveals chromosome 10 gene localization and identifies TaqI RFLPs. *FEBS Lett.* 318: 325–330.

Surratt, C.K., Wang, J.B., Yuhasz, S., Amzel, M., Kwon, H.M., Handler, J.S. and Uhl, G.R. (1993a). Sodium- and chloride-dependent transporters in brain, kidney, and gut: lessons from cDNA cloning and structure-function studies. *Curr. Opin. Nephrol. Hypertension* 2: 744–760.

Tallent, M., Dichter, M.A., Bell, G.I. and Reisine, T. (1994). The cloned kappa opioid receptor couples to an N-type calcium current in undifferentiated PC-12 cells. *Neuroscience* 63: 1033–1040.

Tate, C.G. and Blakely, R. (1994). The effect of N-linked glycosylation on activity of the Na⁺- and Cl⁻-dependent serotonin transporter expressed using recombinant baculovirus in insect cells. *J. Biol. Chem.* 269: 26303–26310.

Tomic, M., Seeman, P., George, S.R. and O'Dowd, B.F. (1993). Dopamine D1 receptor mutagenesis: role of amino acids in agonist and antagonist binding. *Biochem. Biophys. Res. Commun.* 191: 1020–1027.

Uchida, S., Kwon, H.M., Yamauchi, A., Preston, A.S., Marumo, F. and Handler, J.S. (1992). Molecular cloning of the cDNA for a MDCK cell Na⁺-and Cl⁻-dependent taurine transporter that is regulated by hypertonicity. *Proc. Natl. Acad. Sci. USA* 89: 8230–8234.

Uhl, G.R. (1992). Neurotransmitter transporters (plus): a promising new gene family. *Trends Neurosci.* 15: 265–268.

Usdin, T.B., Mezey, E., Chen, C., Brownstein, M.J. and Hoffman B.J. (1991). Cloning of the cocaine-sensitive bovine dopamine transporter. *Proc. Natl. Acad. Sci. USA* 88: 11168–11171.

Vandenbergh, D.J., Persico, A.M. and Uhl, G.R. (1992). A human dopamine transporter cDNA predicts reduced glycosylation, displays a novel repetitive element and provides racially-dimorphic TaqI RFLP's. *Mol. Brain Res.* 15: 161–166.

Von Zastrow, M., Keith, D., Zaki, P. and Evans, C. (1994). Intracellular trafficking of epitope-tagged opioid receptors: different effects of morphine and enkephalin. *Regul. Pept.* 54: 315–316.

Wang, J.B., Imai,Y., Eppler, M.C., Gregor, P., Spivak, C. and Uhl, G.R. (1993). µ Opiate receptor: cDNA cloning and expression. *Proc. Natl. Acad. Sci. USA* 90: 10230–10234.

Wang, J.B., Johnson, P.S., Persico, A.M., Hawkins, A.L., Griffin, C.A. and Uhl, G.R. (1994a). Human µ opiate receptor: cDNA and genomic clones, pharmacological characterization and chromosomal assignment. *FEBS Lett.* 338: 217–222.

Wang, J.B., Johnson, P.S., Wu, J.M., Wang, W.F and Uhl, G.R. (1994b). Human κ opiate receptor second extracellular loop elevates dynorphin's affinity for human µ/κ chimeras. *J. Biol. Chem.* 269: 25966–25969.

Wang, J.B., Moriwaki, A. and Uhl, G.R. (1995). Dopamine transporter cysteine mutants: second extracellular loop cysteines are required for transporter expression. *J. Neurochem.* 64: 1416–1419.

Wang, Z., Bilsky, E.J., Porreca, F. and Sadee, W. (1994). Constitutive µ opioid receptor activation as a regulatory mechanism underlying narcotic tolerance and dependence. *Life Sci.* 54: 339–350.

Wimpey, T.L. and Chavkin, C. (1991). Opioids activate both an inward rectifier and a novel voltage-gated potassium conductance in the hippocampal formation. *Neuron* 6: 281–289.

Xue, J.-C., Chen, C., Zhu, J., Kunapuli, S., DeRiel, J.K., Yu, L. and Liu-Chen, L.-Y. (1994). Differential binding domains of peptide and non-peptide ligands in the cloned rat κ opioid receptor. *J. Biol. Chem.* 269: 30195–31199.

Xue, J.-C., Chen, C., Zhu, J., Kunapuli, S., DeRiel, J.K., Yu, L. and Liu-Chen, L.-Y. (1995). The third extracellular loop of the µ opioid receptor is important for agonist selectivity. *J. Biol. Chem.* 270: 12977–12979.

Yamauchi, A., Uchida, S., Kwon, H.M., Preston, A.S., Robey, R.B., Garcia-Perez, A., Burg, M.B. and Handler, J.S. (1992). Cloning of a Na⁺-and Cl⁻-dependent betaine transporter that is regulated by hypertonicity. *J. Biol. Chem.* 267: 649–652.

Yasuda, K., Raynor, K., Kong, H., Breder, C., Takeda, J., Reisine, T. and Bell, G.I. (1993). Cloning and functional comparison of κ and δ opioid receptors from mouse brain. *Proc. Natl. Acad. Sci. USA.* 90: 6736–6740.

Zhang, L., Yu, Y., Mackin, S., Weight, F., Uhl, G.R. and Wang, J.B. (1996). Differential µ opiate receptor phosphorylation induced by agonists and phorbol esters. *J. Biol. Chem.* 271: 11449–11454.

Zimprich, A., Simon, T. and Höllt, V. (1995). Cloning and expression of an isoform of the rat µ opioid receptor (rMOR1B) which differs in agonist induced desensitization from rMOR1. *FEBS Lett.* 359: 142–146.

Drug Addiction and its Treatment: Nexus of Neuroscience and Behavior, edited by Bankole A. Johnson and John D. Roache. Lippincott–Raven Publishers, Philadelphia, © 1997.

14

Substance Abuse and Gene Expression

Sheila L. Vrana and Kent E. Vrana

Department of Physiology and Pharmacology, The Bowman Gray School of Medicine, Winston-Salem, North Carolina 27157-1083

Altered CNS gene expression is a central aspect of substance abuse. The characterization of the involvement of gene expression has lagged, however, behind other indices of nervous system function such as neurochemistry, receptor binding, behavioral assessment, and brain imaging. This is due to the development of recombinant DNA technology (during the past 25 years) and the more recent isolation of genes that are relevant to substance abuse, e.g., cloning of the dopamine receptor, dopamine transporter, cannabinoid, γ-aminobutyric acid (GABA), and opiate receptor genes. A number of different approaches have been undertaken that clearly implicate gene expression in the predisposition of an individual or animal for drug-seeking behavior. Moreover, it is likely that long-term drug administration elicits changes in the pattern of CNS gene expression that contribute to issues such as physical dependence, tolerance, and addiction. It is particularly timely to assess the progress of this work and to evaluate future directions in this research arena. The central premise of this discussion is (a) inherited patterns of gene expression (inherited genotype) can predispose an organism to substance abuse, while (b) chronic drug administration can alter the normal pattern of gene expression (epigenetic imprinting) so as to contribute to the maintenance of drug-seeking behavior. Clearly, these two concepts are not mutually exclusive and may, taken together, generate synergistic interactions. In the course of this discussion, a general review of gene expression and its regulation will be presented, followed by a review of the current literature regarding epigenetic imprinting by drugs of abuse and genetic models of drug abuse. The chapter closes with an evaluation of future research directions with an emphasis on current technologies.

GENERAL REVIEW OF GENE EXPRESSION

We begin with the flow of genetic information within a cell (Fig. 1). Contrary to common misconception, evaluation of gene regulation involves more than just measuring steady-state levels of messenger RNA (mRNA). There are a number of processes in both the synthesis of RNA (transcription and processing) and the generation of mature protein product (translation and posttranslational processing) that are subject to regulation. The following discussion reviews the different experimental approaches used to characterize gene expression.

Genomic DNA

Nearly every cell in an organism, exclusive of haploid reproductive germ cells, contains the same genetic information (DNA). For a cell to develop, only those genes within the DNA that are necessary for making that particular cell will be expressed. This underlies several important points concerning substance abuse. First, if there is a gene (or a mutation within a gene) that is responsible for substance abuse, it could be transferred from generation

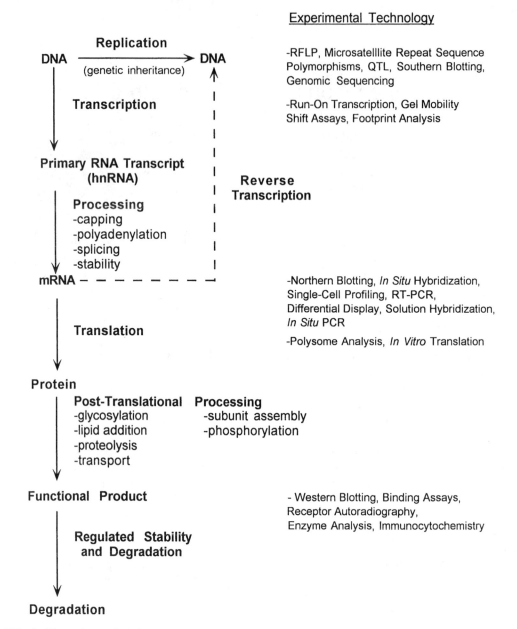

FIG. 1. Flow of genetic information. This figure provides a summary of the various steps involved in the conversion of the DNA sequences of a gene to its functional protein product. In addition, the experimental technologies that can be applied to the characterization of these processes are listed on the right. Relevant details of this figure are expanded within the text. hnRNA, heterogeneous nuclear RNA; mRNA, messenger RNA; PCR; polymerase chain reaction; RFLP, restriction length fragment polymorphism; QTL, quantitative trait loci; ESTs, expressed sequence tags; RT-PCR, reverse transcriptase-PCR.

to generation in an inherited manner. Although most investigators have given up on the concept of a single "addiction gene," there are a variety of studies that suggest that certain individuals carry a constellation of unknown genes that may predispose them to substance abuse. Second, if there is a pattern of gene expression that creates a normal neuron, it is entirely possible that changes in that pattern would produce a neuron whose sensitivity to drugs of abuse could contribute to addiction, tolerance, or physical dependence. It is therefore important to think of genetic information as being simultaneously stable (a constant heritable legacy) and maleable (a changing pattern of expression of the inherited information).

There are a number of powerful methods used to characterize genomic DNA and therefore the inherited potential of an organism. Unfortunately, techniques such as Southern blots and sequencing of genomic DNA are predicated on knowing information about specific genes of interest. For instance, if a gene has been isolated (cloned) and it is known to be linked to a disease state, then individuals can be tested for the defect using a Southern blot, polymerase chain reaction (PCR), or sequencing of the genomic DNA. The primary problem, therefore, is to identify the candidate genes involved in substance abuse and later characterize the genetic polymorphisms responsible for the altered behavior. There are a number of recombinant DNA techniques that are currently being utilized to study this problem—restriction fragment length polymorphism (RFLP) analysis and its more recent successor, microsatellite repeat polymorphism analysis, and characterization of quantitative trait loci (QTL). All of these approaches will be dramatically facilitated by the growing database of the Human Genome Sequencing Project and the construction of an extensive roadmap of the human genome using expressed sequence tags (ESTs).

Transcription

As stated earlier, while the information content within genomic DNA bears the poten-

tial of an individual, the subset of that information that is expressed (transcribed into RNA) determines the characteristics of an individual tissue or cell. In fact, alterations in the normal pattern of brain gene expression may underlie clinical issues such as addiction and withdrawal. The direct assessment of transcription and its regulation is accomplished using a number of different tools. These include runoff transcription (determining the number of active RNA polymerase molecules bound to a gene) as well as gel mobility shift assays and DNA footprint analysis (both of which assess specific DNA-binding protein activities under a given physiologic state). Again, this type of analysis requires significant prior information concerning the gene of interest. From the standpoint of substance abuse, these methods (specifically gel mobility shift assays) have proven valuable in the characterization of the pattern of gene expression following chronic drug administration. New levels of sensitivity in the study of gene expression are now being achieved through the use of in situ PCR. This combines the sensitivity of PCR with the anatomical resolution of in situ hybridization to provide unique information on tissue/cell-specific gene expression.

RNA Processing

There is a large black box between the initial transcription of a gene, creation of the primary transcript, and the formation of the mature mRNA product, termed RNA processing. During this maturation, the primary RNA transcript is capped by adding a unique 7-methyl guanosine on the 5′ terminus. This cap serves as a pivotal signal for translation initiation and possibly prevents premature degradation of message. Intron sequences, present within the gene, are removed from the transcript in a process termed splicing. In addition, a homopolymeric stretch of adenylate residues (the poly[A^+] tail) is added to the 3′ end of most, but not all, mRNA molecules. This latter modification increases the stability of the molecule and contributes to translation efficiency. Although the mechanisms of these processing steps are known, their regulation remains obscure. It seems likely, however, that the regulation of processing will prove to be very important for a number of different areas, including substance abuse.

As implied at the beginning of this discussion, the mention of gene expression to a majority of scientists will elicit thoughts of Northern blots and in situ hybridization, both of which measure mRNA levels. Whereas this is an important area of investigation, Northern blots and RNA dot blots only provide information concerning steady-state levels of mRNA. Similarly, although in situ hybridization can provide important anatomical resolution for the localization of changes in steady-state mRNA levels, the quantification of these signals requires meticulous attention to detail. New techniques in the realm of quantitative reverse transcriptase–polymerase chain reaction (RT-PCR) and solution hybridization (also known as the RNAse protection assay) are making it possible to examine changes in very rare message levels.

All of these approaches represent a static "snapshot" of mRNA levels, ignoring a wide variety of regulatory events that are responsible for observed changes in mRNA. That is, issues such as the regulation of transcription and RNA processing or altered RNA stability are not addressed. More importantly, mRNA levels that are not correlated with measurements of the functional product (in most cases mature protein or enzymatic activity) can be deceiving. Frequently, mRNA levels are presented as being indicative of protein levels when, in fact, this is not necessarily the case.

This discussion is not meant to trivialize the importance of measurement of mRNA levels. As we shall discuss, these approaches have proven to be pivotal in the initial characterization of the effects of drugs of abuse on gene expression. However, it is important to assess not only the mRNA, but also the functional end product that ultimately results from the gene expression.

Translation

There is growing evidence that the regulation of translation plays a major role in the expression of many disparate genes. Most of the characterization of translational control to date has been limited to systems involving large homogeneous tissues, such as liver (transferrin gene expression) or systems, like the pituitary gland, with well-characterized cell lines (e.g., POMC gene expression in AtT-20 cells). In fact, the available approaches limit this line of investigation in the CNS. Polysome analysis (i.e., analysis of mRNAs that are being actively translated by multiple ribosomes) and in vitro translation are difficult to perform in small tissue samples. There is, however, evidence for translational control of functional gene expression in the CNS.

Posttranslational Processing and Protein Stability

Finally, the modulation of posttranslational processing and the regulation of protein stability represent areas where a great deal of work has occurred in the substance abuse field. The pioneering work of Eric Nestler and colleagues (1993, 1994) has clearly established that second messenger transduction mechanisms and posttranslational phosphorylation play a central role in both the short- and long-term effects of substance abuse. In fact, it appears likely that alterations in the gene expression for some of these second messenger systems will be important in substance abuse. Another area of active investigation involves the potential for altering the coupling of receptors to second messenger systems or the post translational regulation of functional binding sites (receptor desensitization) in response to drugs of abuse. In this manner, there could be changes in the functional expression of receptor systems that are quite distinct from traditional assumptions concerning mRNA levels. These avenues of investigation on receptor coupling and desensitization make use of a variety of techniques that antecede the advent of recombinant DNA technology yet remain very important in the characterization of substance abuse (enzyme assays, receptor binding protocols, and immunochemical approaches). Subjects that need to be explored in this regard include glycosylation and the regulation of protein transit through the Golgi (e.g., membrane-bound receptors), control of proteolytic processing (e.g., the enkephalins and endogenous opioids), and lipid addition (e.g., the N-terminal regions of the G proteins). There is an entire vista of potential studies involving traditional biochemical and cell-biologic techniques. While reviewing the flow of genetic information, this section has illustrated the vast panoply of different experimental procedures that can be utilized. It is important to realize that changes in gene expression can occur anywhere in this genetic pathway. In characterizing the inherited and epigenetic phenomena associated with drug abuse, efforts must be made to view the entire process and not only one of the various steps.

INTRODUCTION TO DRUG ABUSE AND GENE EXPRESSION

Mesolimbic Dopamine Pathway

This section focuses primarily on the mesolimbic dopamine (DA) pathway. Originating in the ventral tegmental area (VTA; region A10), this pathway has been implicated in drug reinforcement (Koob, 1992) and is the subject of further detailed discussion in the chapters by Hemby et al., Lukas, and Lyons et al. Briefly, the cell bodies of the mesolimbic system project to a variety of forebrain structures including the nucleus accumbens (NAcc), olfactory tubercle, frontal cortex, amygdala, and septal region. This system is frequently referred to as a "brain reward pathway" due to its role in drug reinforcement and drug-seeking behaviors. Notably, a number of disparate studies have established that these neurons occupy a pivotal niche within the neural connections involved in the self-administration, conditioned

place preference, and drug discrimination responses for different drugs such as cocaine, opiates, and ethanol (DiChiara and North, 1992; Koob, 1992; Samson and Harris, 1992; Woolverton and Johnson, 1992). The mesolimbic DA pathway is of particular interest, in the present context, because the gene expression for a number of molecular components of the system have been characterized. Some of the principal players are reviewed in Fig. 2. The reader should keep in mind, however, that this is just one, well-characterized pathway in the complex brain network involved in substance abuse.

Molecular Components of the Mesolimbic Dopamine Neuron and Its Targets

A schematic model for a mesolimbic DA neuron is presented in Fig. 2. Gene expression for the A10 DA neuron itself commences in the nucleus of the cell body within the VTA. Messenger RNA molecules encoding critical cellular components such as tyrosine hydroxylase (TH), aromatic amino acid decarboxylase (AADC), DA receptors, neurofilament transport proteins (NF), G protein effector systems (G proteins), and the dopamine transporters (DAT) are transcribed and processed within the VTA and then transported to the NAcc. Although there is accumulating evidence for axonal and even terminal field protein synthesis, the vast majority of the protein translation for mesolimbic DA neurons occurs within the VTA. The proteins are then transported through the axon to the terminal fields. The role of this important chain of events (i.e., the final transport of functional protein product to the site of action) has only recently been addressed relative to problems of substance abuse.

Once the proteins reach the terminal fields, they are integrated into the complex processes involving neurotransmitter synthesis, packaging, release, receptor binding, and reuptake. These processes have been extensively reviewed in a variety of neurobiology texts. At this point, significant problems arise during the

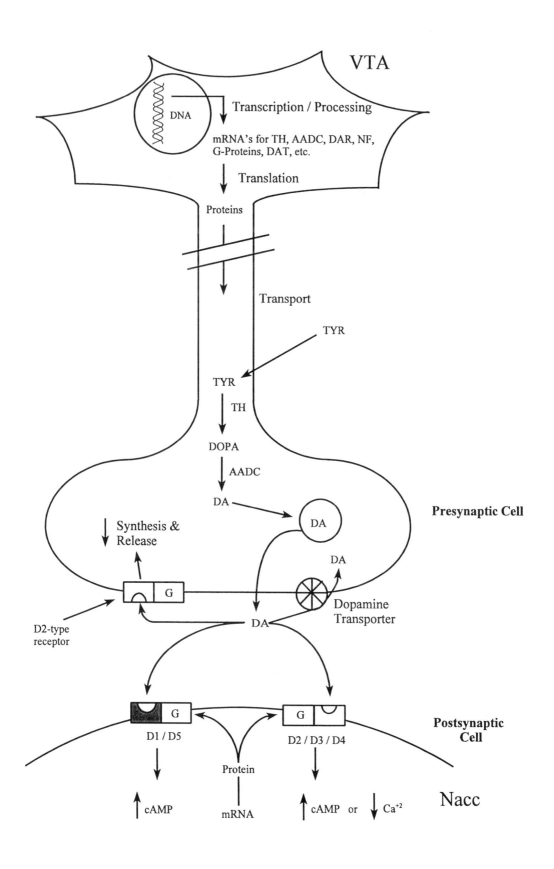

characterization of the end products of gene expression. This is perhaps best exemplified by examining the situation with DA receptors (Fig. 2). Imagine that one wished to examine changes in the expression of DA receptors in response to a drug such as cocaine. First, there are five different subtypes of the DA receptor (the situation is even more complex for GABA receptor subunits). This creates an experimental confound since there are currently no ligands that are selective for, and diagnostic of, each DA receptor subtype. It can be difficult to characterize DA receptor binding beyond the broad classification of D1 type (the D1 and D5 receptors) and D2 type (the D2, D3, and D4 receptors). Second, when evaluating receptor levels, one has to consider whether the signal is arising from the presynaptic or postsynaptic cell. Note that both locations express DA receptors. Therefore, it can be unclear whether a drug treatment is modulating gene expression in a target cell or the mesolimbic DA cell itself. This problem is obviated somewhat by examining the gene expression at the level of steady-state mRNA concentrations. Under these conditions, a change in NAcc levels of the DA receptor mRNA should reflect a change in the status of the postsynaptic cell (since gene expression for the presynaptic cell resides in the anatomically distant VTA). This approach suffers from the fact that there is significant homology between the DA receptor genes and so it can be difficult to selectively assess subtype-specific gene expression. However, the judicious use of subtype-specific oligonucleotides in RT-PCR applications or Northern hybridizations as well as sequence-specific solution hybridization studies (RNAse protection assays) will enable the acquisition of valuable information on gene expression.

In spite of these concerns, tremendous progress has been made. In particular, there is growing evidence that chronic drug administration can produce changes in the patterns of CNS gene expression for several of the molecular markers above. The drug produces an epigenetic imprint on the brain. In other words, an environmental factor (drug of abuse) generates a new pattern of gene expression (an imprint) that may place the organism at risk for further substance abuse. This is important for two reasons. First, several studies suggest that this imprint remains long after the cessation of drug administration. This provides a potential molecular basis for the clinical problem of relapse liability. Second, there is preliminary evidence that the mode of drug administration (i.e., investigator-initiated, response-independent, or self-administration) can alter the effects of a drug. These findings could explain how patterns of drug-seeking behavior could be established and maintained. Another important area of recent research involves the evidence that breeding can enhance selective drug-seeking behaviors and drug sensitivities. This genetic predisposition would have important implications in inherited substance abuse risk factors. We now discuss some of these issues in more detail.

FIG. 2. Mesolimbic dopamine neuron. This diagram illustrates some of the unique molecular biologic considerations inherent in analyzing neuronal gene expression. There is considerable evidence that the mesolimbic dopamine neuron, which projects from the ventral tegmental area (VTA) to the nucleus accumbens (NAcc) occupies an important niche in drug abuse. Genes, transcribed in the VTA, are translated and then transported to the axonal terminal. Important gene products include tyrosine hydroxylase (TH) and aromatic amino acid decarboxylase (AADC) (which synthesize dopamine), dopamine receptors (DAR), neurofilament proteins (NF), G proteins, adenylyl cyclase (AC), and dopamine transporters (DAT). Following transportation to the terminal fields, the proteins combine to establish the complex physiology that is characteristic of this neuronal system. Note that many of the same protein gene products are expressed by the postsynaptic neurons and extraneuronal cells. In this example, DAR and associated G proteins are expressed on the presynaptic mesolimbic dopamine neuron as well as on the postsynaptic target neurons. Therefore, analysis of ligand binding or G-protein activity within the NAcc will necessarily involve gene expression studies from disparate cells.

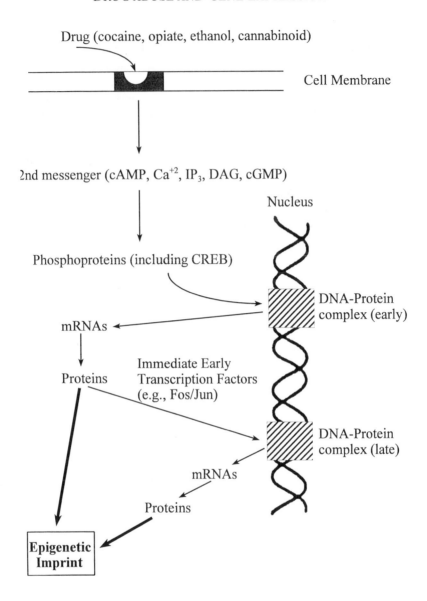

FIG. 3. Potential mechanisms for drug-induced changes in gene expression. Most, if not all, effects of drugs of abuse are initiated by interactions between the drug and cell surface receptors. This interaction triggers a cascade of processes that alter intracellular second messengers and activate a number of different protein kinases. The kinases phosphorylate a variety of intracellular proteins. Only a small fraction of these phosphoprotein targets are transcription factors. However, one important target is the cAMP response element binding protein (CREB). This transcription factor, once phosphorylated, acts as a "master switch" to increase the expression of a large number of different genes. Some of these induced genes, like *fos* and *jun,* produce proteins that are themselves transcription factors that return to the nucleus and induce the expression of additional genes. The end result of this complex interplay of factors following drug administration is a change in the pattern of gene expression—an alteration in the numbers and types of expressed proteins. One potentially important aspect of chronic drug abuse is that this change in gene expression could become stabilized, thus generating an "epigenetic imprint" or memory of drug abuse that could serve as a cellular/molecular correlate of physical dependence, tolerance, and addiction.

EPIGENETIC IMPRINTING AND SUBSTANCE ABUSE

One of the two major issues discussed below is the ability of drugs of abuse to alter the normal pattern of CNS gene expression. In so doing, chronic drug use could establish a new neuronal homeostatic set point that would place the individual at risk for continued abuse. In other words, altered gene expression (in response to chronic drug administration) almost certainly will contribute to physical dependence and may play a role in psychological addiction. A generalized schematic of the cellular flow of information from drug administration to altered gene expression is depicted in Fig. 3. In the ensuing discussion, documented examples of drug-induced changes in selected steps of this pathway are provided.

Receptor Interactions and Second Messengers

It is well established that virtually all of the effects of abused substances are mediated through their interaction with cell surface proteins and the subsequent modulation of second messenger levels. Cocaine is known to block the DA, serotonin, and norepinephrine transporter reuptake systems. As a result, both post- and presynaptic biogenic amine receptors will be hyperstimulated. Depending on the receptor subtype, this hyperstimulation can produce increases or decreases in cyclic adenosine monophosphate (cAMP) and may alter phosphatidylinositide metabolism (Schwartz et al., 1992). In contrast, opiate receptor stimulation by morphine or heroin and cannabinoid receptor stimulation will decrease cAMP. Finally, interaction of ethanol with the GABA receptor modulates chloride channel activity. Modulation of second messenger levels is clearly associated with changes in protein phosphorylation within the cell. These results are not reviewed here, except to highlight where such changes in phosphoproteins are directly related to gene expression.

Transcription Factor Gene Expression

If drugs of abuse are to exert an effect on gene expression at the level of mRNA, one would expect to see changes in the levels of transcription factors, their cognate mRNA levels, or their interaction with DNA. There is evidence, both direct and indirect, for all of these predicted outcomes. Fos and Jun represent members of a family of transcription factors that share a structural dimerization motif referred to as a leucine zipper. [Note that in commonly accepted nomenclature, *fos* and *jun* refer to the genes, while Fos and Jun refer to the protein products.] When associated as a heterodimer, Fos/Jun represents a functional DNA-binding complex called AP-1. This AP-1 complex binds to 5'-promoter elements of a wide variety of different genes leading to increased expression of those genes. In addition to their role as transcription factors/enhancers, Fos and Jun are often described as immediate early gene products because their own mRNA and peptide levels are rapidly induced (generally in less than an hour) by a wide variety of different stimuli (Sheng and Greenberg, 1990). It is very clear that a number of abused substances can act to increase levels of mRNA for the immediate early genes *fos* and *jun*. Early on in the molecular characterization of drug abuse, Ann Graybiel and coworkers (1990) observed that acute administration of cocaine or amphetamine could rapidly, and transiently, increase the levels of *fos/jun* mRNA as well as their corresponding protein products in selected areas of the brain. These findings illustrate the marked effects that these drugs can have on gene expression since the basal levels of Fos and Jun are largely undetectable and are then elevated following drug administration. Similarly, these increases in immunoreactive protein are correlated with (and probably mediated by) elevations in mRNA.

Stimulant-induced increases in immediate early gene expression are not limited to *fos* and *jun*. Other forms of these leucine zipper transcription factors are also modulated

(Hope et al., 1992; Nguyen et al., 1992; Young et al., 1991). Increases have been observed for the *jun-B* gene (a distinct gene that is related to *jun)*, a number of *fra* genes (*Fos-related antigens*), and *zif 268* (also known as NGFI-A, a leucine zipper-containing transcription factor). Recent studies suggest that CREB (*cAMP response element binding protein*) gene expression is affected both by cocaine and opiates (Guitart et al., 1992; Widnell et al., 1994). There appear to be changes in CREB mRNA levels, immunoreactive protein, and phosphorylation. This is particularly important given the central nature of CREB as a "master switch" in the response of cells to alterations in cAMP levels (Fig. 3). It is clear that administration of psychoactive stimulants has immediate and wide-ranging effects on early response transcription factors that can modulate the expression of other proteins (see below). It is not only psychoactive stimulants that induce immediate responses in transcription factor mRNAs and proteins; other abused substances appear to exhibit similar effects. For instance, morphine has been shown to regulate *fos* gene expression, and *fos, jun,* and *zif 268* gene expression are all elevated during alcohol withdrawal (Matsumoto et al., 1993).

To summarize, it may well be that most abused substances, by way of their receptor-stimulating nature, may elicit immediate (<1 hour) changes in transcription factor expression. This effect dominates changes in downstream gene expression that may represent epigenetic imprinting. The pharmacologic specificity will reside in the nature of the cells that are stimulated (i.e., those cells/brain regions expressing the relevant receptors) as well as the nature of downstream genes available for induction.

Downstream Effects

DNA-Protein Transcription Complexes

Changes in the levels of transcription factor mRNA and protein may not be sufficient to alter global cellular gene expression. More importantly, changes in transcription factor protein may be reflected as changes in functional DNA-protein transcription complexes. That is, the transcription factors must associate with their cognate genetic control elements (DNA sequences within or near the promoters of specific genes). Unfortunately, it is very difficult to directly assess transcription factor/DNA complexes within a cell, although there are a number of indirect measures of DNA binding activity. One of these methods, the DNA gel mobility shift assay (gel shift assay) has been applied to substance abuse and its related gene expression. In this procedure, small radioactive DNA fragments (probes) are synthesized that contain the sequence for transcription factor binding. For example, the DNA sequence, 5'-TGACTCA-3', is the Fos/Jun AP-1 binding site. When these probes (which have been radioactively labeled) are mixed with nuclear protein extracts from animals (or cells) that have been treated with drugs, and subjected to electrophoresis under nondenaturing conditions, the complex migrates as a discrete entity. The assumption is that the Fos/Jun dimer (or related dimers) present within the nuclear extract will associate with the DNA, and the DNA complex will migrate at a larger apparent molecular weight (gel mobility shift). Using this technique, it was established that acute administration of cocaine increases AP-1 binding activity in the NAcc, which correlated with changes observed in transcription factor (Fos/Jun) protein levels (Hope et al., 1992). This indicates increased immediate early transcription factor gene expression.

Delayed Gene Expression

Changes in transcription factor gene expression and function undoubtedly represent some of the earliest responses to drugs of abuse. Moreover, it is unlikely that these types of changes are restricted to drugs of abuse. For instance, the immediate early gene products are induced by a wide variety of stimuli (e.g., electroconvulsive shock). What is important is the effect that these immediate early transcription factors have on the expression of downstream genes that regulate the physiologic set point of cells. These downstream genes are expressed when immediate early transcription factor levels are altered (in this case, when they are increased).

A variety of experiments clearly establish that relevant systems of gene expression are perturbed by the administration of drugs of abuse. Turning again to the mesolimbic DA neuron model depicted in Fig. 2, a number of observations can be made. Tyrosine hydroxylase (TH) gene expression is increased following the administration of cocaine (Beitner-Johnson and Nestler, 1991; Vrana et al., 1993). Given the rate-limiting nature of TH within the biosynthetic pathway for the catecholamines, these changes can be expected to have a significant impact on the physiologic activity of the mesolimbic neuron. One interesting and perplexing finding was that statistically significant increases in TH mRNA, protein, and activity observed in the cell body regions (VTA) were not as pronounced (or were absent) in the terminal fields (NAcc). This finding was clarified with the observation that neurofilament mRNAs and proteins were also decreased by chronic cocaine administration (Beitner-Johnson et al., 1992). As a result, newly synthesized proteins are not efficiently transported to the terminal fields of the mesolimbic neuron. Characterization of the DA receptor in the terminal fields of the mesolimbic DA neuron suggests that cocaine produces dramatic changes in DA receptor binding and mRNA levels (Goeders and Kuhar, 1987; Kleven et al., 1990; Laurier et al., 1994). Unfortunately, given the different anatomical compartments present within the NAcc (pre- vs postsynaptic; core vs shell) as well as the different subtypes of DA receptor (D1 through D5), it is difficult to draw definitive conclusions from information that appears contradictory (e.g., conflicting views in relation to DA receptor function). Finally, mRNA levels for the DAT were decreased in the cell bodies of the nigrostriatal

pathway following cocaine administration (Cerruti et al., 1994), while ligand binding to the transporter is decreased in the NAcc following cocaine withdrawal (Pilotte et al, 1994). It is apparent from such data that cocaine is capable of altering the expression of proteins required for both the biosynthesis and synaptic detection of the catecholamines. The observation that axonal transport of DA neurons is impaired by the drug may have broader implications for the physiologic responsiveness of the cells. Moreover, cocaine also exerts effects on nonneuronal cells as evidenced by changes in glial fibrillary acidic protein (GFAP) following chronic treatment (Beitner-Johnson et al., 1993).

The types of observations discussed above are not limited to cocaine. Chronic ethanol is known to produce changes in DA receptor levels (Pecins-Thompson and Peris, 1993). Morphine has also been shown to produce an effect similar to cocaine on TH and neurofilament gene expression (Beitner-Johnson et al., 1992), and in a related area, both morphine and cocaine induce increases in preprodynorphin gene expression in the rat striatum. The same is true for substance P expression (but not proenkephalin expression) following cocaine. In contrast, morphine, by itself, does not affect preproenkephalin gene expression, although it will abrogate forskolin-induced increases in proenkephalin mRNA levels (Kluttz et al., 1995). A number of studies suggest that chronic administration of opiates upregulates many components of the cAMP system; this probably occurs as compensation for the inhibition of the adenylyl cyclase by opiates (Nestler et al., 1993). Nearly every component of this second messenger pathway is increased—adenyl cyclase, cAMP-dependent protein kinase, as well as the coupling G proteins, $G_{i\alpha}$ and $G_{0\alpha}$.

Acute vs Chronic Gene Expression

An issue central to the discussion of epigenetic imprinting involves differences between

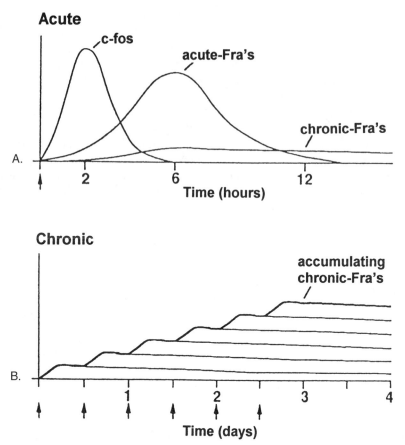

FIG. 4. Stable changes in transcription factor expression following chronic drug administration. This figure describes the hypothetical basis for the accumulation of long-lasting FRA (*fos*-related antigens) proteins following chronic drug abuse. **(A)** With each acute administration of drug (*arrow*), there is a large, transient induction of *fos* (which is rapidly degraded within several hours). There is also a large induction of acute FRA proteins with a slightly longer half-life. In addition, there is a small increase in a class of FRA proteins with a much longer lifetime. As a result, distinct combinations of FRA and Jun proteins form AP-1 binding complexes with potentially unique binding activities at different times in the process. **(B)** Following repeated chronic administration of the drug (*arrows*), the long-lasting chronic FRAs accumulate and provide for stable AP-1 complexes that could persist for weeks and perhaps months after the final dose of drug. (From Hope et al., 1994, with permission.)

acute and chronic gene expression. Notably, what types of changes in gene expression can be invoked to explain physical dependence and psychological addiction? Is there a molecular correlate to the behavioral observation that addicts remain at high risk for relapse long after cessation of drug administration? Although this is a very new field of endeavor, there is now evidence in support of the latter issue (Fig. 4) (Hope et al., 1995; Rosen et al., 1994). As

discussed previously, acute administration of cocaine or opiates produces a rapid and transient expression of *fos* and *jun*. This also corresponds to the appearance of AP-1 binding activity (presumably related to the Fos/Jun heterodimer). An important observation is that the chronic administration of cocaine produces AP-1 binding activity that is elevated *and* persistent. AP-1 complexes are formed that last for days, even weeks, following the last administration of drug. It appears that over the course of repeated drug administration, a class of delayed Fos-related antigens (chronic FRAs) are induced that form highly stable AP-1 complexes. These complexes then serve to "remember" the drug administration. This concept is represented graphically in Fig. 4. Of significant importance is the fact that AP-1 complexes, induced by acute or chronic electroconvulsive shock, exhibit differing affinities for the AP-1 DNA site. Therefore, acute and chronic stimulation produce transcription factor complexes with different stabilities and specificities. It is interesting to note that the induction of the chronic FRAs and chronic AP-1 complexes is accompanied by loss of the ability of cocaine to elicit transient increases in Jun. We now recognize that, at a very early stage in gene expression, mechanisms exist for the coordinated regulation/inhibition of transcription factor complexes of distinct stability and specificity. It remains to be seen how the data will apply to the regulation of delayed gene expression during chronic drug administration and withdrawal. These observations cannot account solely for the behavioral observations and, in fact, probably represent a minor portion of the explanation. However, it is encouraging to know that biochemical and molecular biologic correlates exist that may contribute to addiction.

Response-Dependent vs Response-Independent Gene Expression

Another important problem in substance abuse research focuses on the determination of neurochemical and physiologic differences associated with drug self-administration vs response-independent (investigator-initiated) administration. This problem is much more carefully and rigorously addressed in the chapter by Hemby et al. However, it is clear that the context of drug administration, that is, the ability of an animal to self-administer a drug by performing a task versus the lack of any such control, can have dramatic effects on neurochemical parameters, physiology, and

behavior. Gene expression studies are now being applied to this area of research. However, it appears that the motivation or activities associated with drug-seeking behaviors can modulate effects on gene expression (S. Vrana, K. Vrana, J. Smith, and S. Dworkin, *unpublished observations*). In these studies, the triad paradigm of self-administration was utilized in which an animal is trained to lever-press and receive an i.v. injection of cocaine. Coincident with this self-administration of drug, littermate animals receive response-independent administration of cocaine or saline. In other words, one animal has control over its drug intake while another has no control over the identical intake. The response-independent administration of cocaine produces an increase in TH mRNA within the VTA, an effect that has previously been documented (Vrana et al., 1993). The self-administration of the drug, however, failed to produce this increase in gene expression. This result was paralleled by changes in TH enzyme activity. These findings indicate that there are cognitive influences (i.e., effects of drug-seeking behavior) that can be superimposed on, and in this case obviate, the pharmacologic effects of drugs of abuse. Further work on this aspect of addiction is required. However, results to date strongly imply that aspects of drug-seeking behavior are associated with fundamental differences in expression of selected genes.

Antisense Oligonucleotide Perturbation of Drug-Seeking Behavior

Consideration of epigenetic imprinting will close with a discussion of a new approach to the characterization of drug-seeking behavior. Here, rather than characterize the effects of substance abuse on gene expression, an alternative philosophy is used whereby selected gene expression will be disrupted in an attempt to perturb drug-seeking behavior. This strategy has been utilized with great success in the *pharmacological* manipulation of drug-seeking behavior and is reviewed in the chapters by Carroll and Mattox, Hemby et al., and Nutt.

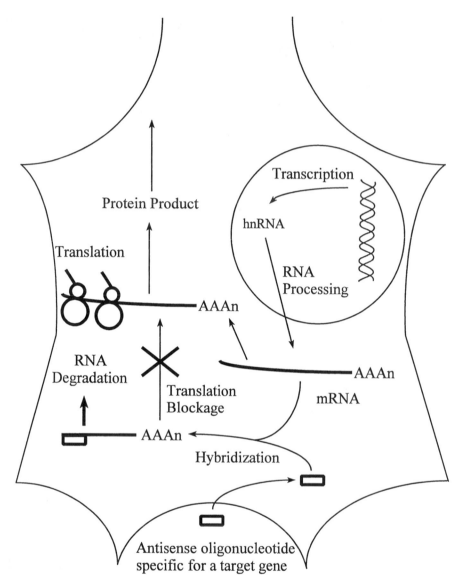

FIG. 5. Antisense oligonucleotide knockdown of gene expression. The investigator designs a DNA sequence (from 15 to 20 nucleotides) that will specifically hybridize to a single mRNA. Because the oligonucleotide is complementary to the mRNA, it is termed antisense. If this oligonucleotide is injected directly into brain tissue or a ventricle, it will be taken up by cells. It then seeks out and specifically binds to its cognate target, creating a short stretch of RNA/DNA duplex. This duplex is a substrate for a degradative enzyme called RNAse H. In addition, the duplex can serve as an impediment to translation elongation and initiation. The end result is that the expression of a specific gene can be blocked by the administration of an oligonucleotide.

Parallel systems are currently being developed whereby specific gene products are disrupted in an attempt to identify important genetic elements (Fig. 5). This technology uses synthetic oligodeoxynucleotides complementary to an RNA target and is termed antisense knockdown. It has recently been found that small oligodeoxynucleotides (15 to 20 nucleotides in length) can be directly injected into the brain and are taken up by cells. The sequences of these oligonucleotides can be carefully designed so that they will be uniquely complementary to a specific mRNA (e.g., complementary to the mRNA for a specific DA receptor subtype). The oligonucleotide will hybridize (or bind) to the mRNA leading to the targeted degradation of the message and/or the disruption of protein translation. These oligonucleotides are complementary to the sense protein-coding mRNA molecules and are termed antisense. Whatever the precise mechanism, the end result of antisense oligonucleotide administration is a reduction in the mRNA and protein product for a specific gene; gene expression is selectively "knocked-down." These antisense oligonucleotide molecules provide additional genetic tools for manipulating drug-seeking behavior. This approach has been successfully applied to the disruption of TH gene expression (with a concomitant reduction in food-reinforced behavior; Skutella et al., 1994) and to selectively disrupt D2-DA receptor subtype expression (Weiss et al., 1993; Zhang and Creese, 1993; Zhou et al., 1994). One example of the power of this experimental design is that it allows a level of selectivity that is currently lacking using other methods. Although there are DA ligands that differentiate the D1-type receptor from the D2-type, they poorly discriminate between the D1 and D5, and the D2, D3, and D4 genetic forms. Herein is a tool—the antisense oligonucleotide—that can provide the selectivity needed for evaluating DA receptor subtypes. Moreover, injection of an antisense oligonucleotide for the D2 receptor into the VTA will directly disrupt the expression of the presynaptic D2 receptors in the NAcc,

while sparing postsynaptic D2 receptors in the NAcc (Fig. 2).

GENETIC PREDISPOSITION AND SUBSTANCE ABUSE POTENTIAL

The discussion thus far has revolved around the effects of substance abuse on gene expression and how that might contribute to the problem of physical dependence and psychological addiction. However, there is a growing realization that genetics can play a role in one's predisposition to substance abuse. Studies are proceeding in a number of different directions to uncover those heritable traits that can increase the risk of substance abuse.

Selected Animal Models: Breeding for Substance Abuse Liability

While it is widely accepted that there are genetic factors that can predispose individuals to alcoholism and alcohol abuse, until recently it has not been possible to study these factors in experimental animals. Advances have been made in this area based on the finding that rats and mice display a wide variation in alcohol preference, and that selective breeding can be used to enrich a given preference within an inbred line. In this experimental paradigm, animals that display a higher preference for alcohol are mated with similar animals and their offspring assessed for the continued behavioral pattern. Repeating this process over time (20 to 30 generations) provides an inbred strain that prefers alcohol. Similarly, this breeding protocol can be applied to animals that do not prefer alcohol, animals that are more susceptible to the effects of alcohol, or animals that show a preference or unique response to any drug of abuse.

In the alcohol abuse field, selective breeding for alcohol preference has generated a variety of different inbred colonies (Crabbe et al., 1994). As an example, we will consider two sets of lines that originated in the research group of T.-K. Li at Indiana University (Li et al., 1993). Both the alcohol preferring/nonpreferring lines (P and NP lines) and the high alcohol drinking/low alcohol drinking (HAD and LAD lines) were selected for voluntary alcohol drinking behavior in the same way. Animals were given a free choice between 10% alcohol and water and their consumption of alcohol was monitored. Animals that consumed high amounts of alcohol were mated with similar behaving rats, while low alcohol–preferring animals were also selectively bred. These individual lines differ in the nature of their progenitor strains; the P/NP lines were created first from a genetically restricted strain, while the HAD/LAD lines were derived at a later time from a more diverse progenitor line and further precautions were taken to avoid sibling inbreeding. In both cases, however, the results are essentially the same. The alcohol-preferring animals (P and HAD) voluntarily consume 10 to 20 times the alcohol of the nonpreferring lines (NP and LAD). There appear to be common genetic CNS effects on the two sets of inbred lines. Notably, there are reductions in serotonin and DA function in the alcohol-preferring lines. In particular, the mesolimbic DA pathway appears to be an important component (see previous discussions). Further experiments will be required to determine the genetic basis for the abuse liability of this animal model of alcoholism. However, it should be obvious that this approach to genetically "fixing" the genes that contribute to alcohol-seeking behavior will prove valuable to future research efforts. In addition, experiments are now beginning to apply this approach to the characterization of other drugs of abuse.

Nonselected Inbred Animal Models

Additional information concerning the importance of genetics in substance abuse liability has come from characterizing different inbred strains of rats. In these examples, however, the breeding was not conducted with the intent of enriching drug-seeking behavior or preference. It was found, during the course of selection of animal strains for drug abuse experimentation, that the Lewis inbred strain self-administers drugs (cocaine, alcohol, and opiates) to a greater extent than the Fischer strain of rat. There are a variety of other parameters of substance abuse for which these two strains display different phenotypes. Given these behavioral differences, experiments have been undertaken to characterize biochemical indices that have previously been tested in animals following chronic drug administration. Interestingly, the Lewis and Fischer strains differ in their basal levels of cAMP-dependent protein kinase, adenylyl cyclase (AC), G protein, tyrosine hydroxylase (TH), GFAP, and neurofilaments. In fact, the overall picture of the Lewis rat (the drug-preferring animal) is that it most resembles the outbred Sprague-Dawley animal following chronic exposure to drugs of abuse. It seems possible that these two strains (the Fischer and Lewis strains) can be utilized to test the underlying genetics of their behavioral differences by gene linkage analysis (see below).

Quantitative Trait Loci (QTL)

The primary problem with identifying, isolating, and characterizing the genes responsible for substance abuse liability resides in the number of such genes and their relative contribution to the liability. In many genetic disorders, such as sickle cell anemia, Huntington's disease, and cystic fibrosis, a single gene mutation is the causative factor. However, it is generally accepted that this is not the case for complex behavioral disorders and therefore there will not be a single gene responsible for alcoholism and drug abuse. Instead, a number of different genes exist that each contribute quantitatively to some part of the overall behavior. The worst-case scenario (from an experimental standpoint) would be that a large number of genes would each contribute a very small amount to the liability. As one can imagine, this would present a nearly insurmountable task for characterization. However, current evidence suggests that there will not be an impossibly large number of genes responsible for substance abuse liability. It seems that a discrete number of genes of varying effect size will be involved. The analysis of these genes is termed quantitative trait loci (QTL) analysis.

QTL analysis relies on a combination of traditional genetic marker studies and selective breeding experiments. Basically, the approach uses classic reproductive genetics to sort through the gene sequences of an organism (in an unbiased way) to determine if a given segment of chromosome contributes to a behavior. QTL analysis then assigns a value to the amount that the sequence contributes toward the behavior. This analysis is best utilized in mouse models where selective breeding has been proceeding for some time and where extensive genetic maps are available. The central assumption is that completely inbred strains will be homozygous for all genes and homogeneous in their behavior. In other words, the researcher assumes that each of the animals will contain the same genes and will respond the same way to a drug of abuse. If *different* strains, with distinct behaviors (e.g., alcohol preference) are mated, the F_1 hybrid generation (the offspring) will have a gene copy from each parent. If the trait under study is polygenic—that is, if a number of different gene variants are responsible for the behavior—the offspring should behave uniformly and behave in a manner intermediate between the parent strains. If these F_1 individuals are now bred to each other, the various genes will begin to segregate so that some individuals within the F_2 generation will receive more of the quantitative trait(s) for a behavior than others. As a result, differing substrains can be developed (and then inbred) that have discrete behaviors as well as discrete genetic makeups. Without going into the details of the molecular biology and molecular genetics, commonly available genetic markers are then used to examine the association of individual chromosomal segments with the behavioral trait. [Genetic markers are recombinant DNA signposts for identifying various chromosomal locations.] In other words, if the inheritance of a certain segment of chromosome 1 from the alcohol-preferring progenitor strain (identified based on unique chromosome markers) is

statistically associated with alcohol preference in the F_2 generation, it becomes a candidate for a QTL for alcohol preference. Ongoing studies in the laboratories of Crabbe, Plomin, and McClearn indicate that there are as many as 75 candidate QTLs that contribute to a number of different behaviors associated with alcohol consumption. More importantly, many of these QTLs may also contribute to problems inherent in other drugs of abuse.

The Dopamine Receptor and Human Alcoholism

Considerable excitement was generated in 1990, when Blum and colleagues first reported that the D2 variant of the DA receptor (referred to as DRD2) was linked to human alcoholism (Blum et al., 1990). These investigators described a specific RFLP variant of the DRD2 locus (a TaqI restriction polymorphism near the DRD2 gene) was much more prevalent in alcoholics than normal controls. Following numerous attempts to confirm and extend these observations, diverse opinion now exists. Investigators agree that DRD2 does not cause alcoholism. One group, led by the original authors, maintain that while the DRD2 gene variant does not cause the disease it contributes significantly to the likelihood of succumbing to alcoholism as well as determining the severity of the disease. These investigators estimate that this genetic locus contributes upward of 27% of the alcoholism liability (Uhl et al., 1993). Furthermore, the same investigators suggest that this gene locus may contribute to cocaine dependence (Noble et al., 1993). On the other hand, other investigators believe that there is no strong association between the DRD2 genetic locus and human alcoholism (Gelernter et al., 1993). The discrepancy arises from the nature of the RFLP analysis and the difficulties in correlating variations in restriction endonuclease sites with complex behavioral diseases. In its simplest form, this type of RFLP analysis merely states that a specific restriction endonuclease pattern (around a given gene) is statistically associated with a disease. It does not prove that the gene causes the disease, just that something associated with that gene is genetically transmitted with the disease. Other factor(s) such as a defective regulatory element within the gene could be responsible. Combine this inherent "fuzziness" with the fact that there will surely be numerous genes and environmental factors that can contribute to substance abuse, and one can see the great difficulty in interpreting these kinds of genetic experiments.

Despite the controversy surrounding the role of the DRD2 locus as the genetic basis of alcoholism, most investigators agree that the receptor does play a part in the disease; defects in this receptor alone may not be the causative factor. Mounting evidence from animal studies makes it clear that the mesolimbic DA pathway will prove central to the neurobiologic basis of substance abuse (see previous discussions). At this time, however, it is not possible to target the D2 DA receptor subtype as the central component of the etiology of substance abuse liability.

FUTURE DIRECTIONS

Given this brief overview of current progress relating substance abuse to gene expression, there are several broad avenues of research that will prove valuable in the future. These predictions are based not only on recently developed techniques, but also on emerging technologies that may be applied to the problem.

Unbiased (Anonymous) Screening for Risk Factor Genes

To date, a great deal of our effort has revolved around genes that we suspect will be central to issues of drug abuse. Therefore, in light of the involvement of DA systems in substance abuse, much work has been conducted on the regulation of tyrosine hydroxylase, DA receptors, G proteins, catecholamine transporters, etc. In addition, since we suspect

that transcription factors will be important in drug-mediated epigenetic regulation of gene expression, experiments have examined the transcription factors *fos, jun, myc,* and CREB. Whereas these transcription factors and dopaminergic genes are logical targets, this approach necessarily limits our thinking to those gene products that have already been characterized. For instance, could there be a "cocaine-specific" transcription factor (or delayed-response gene product) that is as yet undefined but is central to the problem of drug abuse? Perhaps the greatest potential for a dramatic leap forward in our understanding of gene expression in substance abuse will be provided by techniques that are not limited to genes that have already been cloned, sequenced and characterized.

The prototypes for this approach are RFLP analysis (and the latest generation microsatellite repeat sequence polymorphism analysis) and QTL mapping approach. In these experimental paradigms, it is assumed that some anonymous genetic marker can be identified that will be associated with substance abuse liability. The fundamental idea is that the search will be driven in an unbiased way, not by what we know, but by what the existing genetics can tell us. These types of studies are quite labor-intensive and require a significant level of technical expertise. Moreover, the experiments are fraught with potential statistical artifacts (see the discussion of the D2 receptor above).

An alternative approach that is not limited by necessary prior information concerning a gene is subtraction cloning or differential display. In this technique, the mRNA molecules from normal and drug-treated animals are "subtracted" from one another to identify genes that are uniquely associated with substance abuse. Subtraction cloning has been utilized to determine that ezrin and osteonectin gene expression are enriched in the locus coeruleus (Bergson et al., 1993). A more recent development in this technique, termed differential display, uses polymerase chain reaction technology to rapidly identify genes whose expression is altered by physiologic or pharmacologic manipulations.

The use of subtraction cloning and differential display have been termed "fishing experiments" because no clear-cut hypothesis is tested, nor is a predicted outcome expected. Even when unique clones are identified, they still have to be characterized in terms of their physiologic/biochemical function. While all of these concerns are valid, the RFLP approach (similarly a blind screen) has been successfully utilized to identify a number of gene defects associated with inherited diseases. Moreover, the anonymous characterization of phosphorylated proteins in the laboratory of Paul Greengard was utilized to identify a number of important phosphoproteins like the synapsins. This type of analysis has tremendous potential, especially when combined with the genetic selection of substance liability behaviors.

All of these genetic approaches to studying substance abuse (polymorphism analyses, QTL, differential display, etc.) will be greatly facilitated by work associated with the human genome project. This ambitious effort has undertaken the complete sequencing and characterization of the human genetic material. In particular, the growing database of expressed sequence tags (ESTs) will provide signposts throughout the genome marking the positions of genes. ESTs are fragments of expressed genes (most of unknown function). Once a segment of chromosome has been linked to a disorder, expressed genes in the genetic neighborhood can be rapidly identified/characterized. Similarly, if differential display identifies a regulated gene, it can quickly be compared with known ESTs to identify its chromosomal location as well as previous studies on its expression.

Single-Cell Genetic Analysis

One of the problems associated with characterizing the role of CNS gene expression in substance abuse is the genetic complexity of many of the components. The DA receptors are now known to be encoded by five different genes that produce a number of splice variants. The story with GABA receptors is even more complicated. Added to this is the fact that a given brain region is composed of numerous neuronal subtypes or individual subtypes with diverse connections and influences. This provides a daunting amount of complexity to characterize. From a reductionist standpoint, recent technologies have provided tools for dramatically simplifying the situation. The laboratories of J. Eberwine and H. Yeh have developed procedures for amplifying RNA from single cells (Eberwine et al., 1992). In this technique, reverse transcriptase and oligo-dT–based primers are introduced (through a patch clamp pipette) to the interior of a given cell. This generates a collection of first-strand cDNAs that are converted to double-stranded DNA molecules (following aspiration of the cellular contents into a test tube) and amplified using in vitro transcription techniques. As a result, a single cell can be characterized electrophysiologically (including its response to a drug of abuse) and then its genetic makeup can be established post hoc. The use of selective PCR approaches can refine this technique further to concentrate on specific receptor subtypes or novel gene products. It is clear that simplified single-cell systems can be established to characterize the involvement of individual gene products in the cellular response to abused substances. Even within complex tissues, in situ PCR can be utilized to visualize expression of rare transcripts on the single-cell level.

Antisense Knockdowns and Genetic Knockouts

Clearly, the advent of antisense oligonucleotide knockdown technologies within the past several years has opened an entirely new vista of genetic and epigenetic studies. As the antisense oligonucleotide knockdown experiments (see previous discussions) are refined, more selective anatomical localization will be possible. One of the goals would be to precisely and selectively remove all of the mesolimbic presynaptic D2-type receptors of the nucleus accumbens (the mRNA for which originates in the VTA). This type of study cannot be performed using traditional pharmacologic methods (without killing the presynaptic cell) because ligand specificity for each DA subtype is inadequate. Moreover, one faces difficulties in targeting specific ultrastructural DA receptors (i.e., pre- vs postsynaptic). Near-term developments in this field will include the use of high-efficiency replication-deficient virus vectors. Work is rapidly progressing on the perfection of adenovirus and herpes simplex virus as potential vectors for gene replacement therapies (such as the introduction of tyrosine hydroxylase into the striatum of Parkinson's patients). It should be an easy matter to utilize these same vectors for the delivery of an antisense expression system. The high degree of neuronal infectivity as well as the overproduction of the antisense from the viral vector should provide a powerful tool for this type of intervention.

The extreme example of the knockdown experiment is the transgenic knockout of individual genes or the replacement of genes. Along these lines, it is not hard to imagine a situation where QTL analysis suggests that a given allele of a gene has been fixed in an inbred strain that has a high substance abuse potential. To establish that the gene in question was directly contributing to the behavior, that specific genetic unit could be destroyed by a transgenic knockout. Alternatively, the specific gene could be replaced with a different version. This idea is not at all farfetched given that these transgenic procedures currently exist. Using embryonic stem cells, homologous recombination is utilized to selectively replace one genetic sequence with an altered version (either a defective copy or a different allele). The stem cells are then grown up to adult organisms and tested. There are several problems associated with this type of approach. Homologous recombination studies are both time- and labor-intensive. Furthermore, these experiments cannot be performed until candidate genes are identified that are associated with drug abuse behaviors. However, as more information is gained concern-

ing the genes involved in substance abuse, this final proof will become de rigueur within the field. This fact is most powerfully demonstrated by the recent knockout analysis of the dopamine transporter that establishes its role in the physiologic response to cocaine and amphetamine (Giros et al., 1996).

CONCLUSION

The present discussion has focused on the current status of the role of CNS gene expression in substance abuse. While it is clear that drugs of abuse can alter the patterns and levels of gene expression in the brain (epigenetic imprinting), it is also apparent that inherited traits can influence (accentuate or decrease) drug-seeking behavior. Notably, new approaches need to be developed and/or perfected for the identification of those individual genes that, in combination, contribute to substance abuse liability and addiction. In addition, traditional molecular biologic techniques need to be combined with sophisticated aspects of behavior (drug self-administration models) and cell biology (single cell genetic profiling) to unravel the complex interplay of factors and genes that underlie this multivariate (genetic and environmental) problem.

SUMMARY

- Genetics and the regulation of gene expression clearly play a major role in substance abuse:
  1) Inherited constellations of genes can predispose an organism (or individual) to substance abuse.
  2) Chronic substance abuse can alter normal gene expression to create an epigenetic imprint. Such a stable genetic imprint could contribute to issues such as tolerance, physical dependence, and psychological addiction.
- It is unlikely that a single gene will be responsible for substance abuse liability. Rather, disparate genes (numbering from several to tens of individual genes) will each contribute a portion to the behavior.

- Future research efforts are required to identify those genes contributing to drug-seeking behavior and abuse liability using distinctive approaches:

  1) Inbreeding experiments coupled with genetic mapping (QTL analysis) to identify candidate genes.

  2) Use of single cell genetic analysis to illuminate the roles of individual receptor subtypes or subunits in substance abuse.

  3) Identification of genes whose expression is regulated by abused substances (subtraction cloning, differential display).

  4) Oligonucleotide knockdown and genetic knockout of candidate genes.

REFERENCES

Beitner-Johnson, D., Guitart, X. and Nestler, E.J. (1992) Neurofilament proteins and the mesolimbic dopamine system: common regulation by chronic morphine and chronic cocaine in the rat ventral tegmental area. *J. Neurosci.* 12: 2165–2176.

Beitner-Johnson, D., Guitart, X. and Nestler, E.J. (1993) Glial fibrillary acidic protein and the mesolimbic dopamine system: regulation by chronic morphine and Lewis-Fischer strain differences in the rat ventral tegmental area. *J. Neurochem.* 61: 1766–1773.

Beitner-Johnson, D. and Nestler, E.J. (1991) Morphine and cocaine exert common actions on tyrosine hydroxylase in dopaminergic brain reward regions. *J. Neurochem.* 57: 344–347.

Bergson, C., Zhao, H., Daijoh, K., Duman, R.S. and Nestler, E.J. (1993) Ezrin and osteonectin, two proteins associated with cell shape and growth, are enriched in the locus coeruleus. *Mol. Cell. Neurosci.* 4: 64–73.

Blum, K., Noble, E.P., Sheridan, P.J., Montgomery, A., Ritchie, T., Jagadeeswaran, P., Nagami, H., Briggs, A.H. and Cohn, J.B. (1990) Allelic association of human dopamine D_2 receptor gene in alcoholism. *JAMA* 263: 2055–2060.

Cerruti, C., Pilotte, N.S., Uhl, G. and Kuhar, M.J. (1994) Reduction of dopamine transporter mRNA after cessation of repeated cocaine administration. *Mol. Brain Res.* 22: 132–138.

Crabbe, J.C., Belknap, J.K. and Buck, K. (1994) Genetic animal models of alcohol and drug abuse. *Science* 264: 1715–1723.

DiChiara, G. and North, R.A. (1992) Neurobiology of opiate abuse. *TIPS* 13: 185–192.

Eberwine, J., Yeh, H., Miyashiro, K., Cao,Y., Nair, S., Finnell, R., Zettel, M. and Coleman, P. (1992) Analysis of gene expression in single line neurons. *Proc. Natl. Acad. Sci. USA* 89: 3010–3014.

Gelernter, J., Goldman, D., and Risch, N. (1993) The A1 allele at the D_2 dopamine receptor gene and alcoholism: a reappraisal. *JAMA* 269: 1673–1677.

Giros, B, Jaber, M., Jones, S.R., Wightman, R.M. and Caron, M.G. (1996) Hyperlocomotion and indifference to cocaine and amphetamine in mice lacking the dopamine transporter. *Nature* 379: 606–612.

Goeders, N.E. and Kuhar, M.J. (1987) Chronic cocaine administration induces opposite changes in dopamine receptors in the striatum and nucleus accumbens. *Alcohol Drug Res.* 7: 207–216.

Graybiel, A.M., Moratalla, R. and Robertson, H.A. (1990) Amphetamine and cocaine induce drug-specific activation of the c-fos gene in striosome-matrix compartments and limbic subdivisions of the striatum. *Proc. Natl. Acad. Sci. USA* 87: 6912–6916.

Guitart, X., Thompson, M.A., Mirante, C.K., Greenberg, M.E. and Nestler, E.J. (1992) Regulation of CREB phosphorylation by acute and chronic morphine in the rat locus coeruleus. *J. Neurochem.* 58: 1168–1171.

Hope, B.T., Kosofsky, B.E., Hyman, S.E. and Nestler, E.J. (1992) Regulation of IEG expression and AP-1 binding by chronic cocaine in the rat nucleus accumbens. *Proc. Natl. Acad. Sci. USA* 89: 5764–5768.

Hope, B.T., Nye, H.E., Kelz, M.B., Self, D.W., Iadarola, M.J., Nakabeppu, Y., Duman, R. and Nestler, E.J. (1994) Induction of a long-lasting AP-1 complex composed of altered Fos-like proteins in brain by chronic cocaine and other chronic treatments. *Neuron* 13: 1235–1244.

Kleven, M.S., Perry, B.D., Woolverton, W.L. and Seiden, L.S. (1990) Effects of repeated injections of cocaine on D1 and D2 dopamine receptors in rat brain. *Brain Res.* 532: 265–270.

Kluttz, B.W., Vrana, K.E., Dworkin, S. and Childers, S.R. (1995) Effects of morphine on forskolin-stimulated proenkephalin mRNA levels in rat striatum: a model for acute and chronic opioid actions in brain. *Mol. Brain Res.* 32: 313–320.

Koob, G.F. (1992) Drugs of abuse: anatomy, pharmacology and function of reward pathways. *TIPS* 13: 177–184.

Laurier, L., Corrigal, W. and George, S.R. (1994) Dopamine receptor density, sensitivity, and mRNA levels are altered following self-administration of cocaine in the rat. *Brain Res.* 634: 31–40.

Li, T.-K., Lumeng, L. and Doolittle, D.D. (1993) Selective breeding for alcohol preference and associated responses. *Behav. Genet.* 23: 163–170.

Matsumoto, I., Leah, J., Shanley, B. and Wilce, P. (1993) Immediate early gene expression in the rat brain during ethanol withdrawal. *Mol. Cell. Neurosci.* 4: 485–491.

Nestler, E.J. (1994) Molecular neurobiology of drug addiction. *Neuropsychopharmacology* 11: 77–87.

Nestler, E.J., Hope, B.T. and Widnell, K.L. (1993) Drug addiction: a model for the molecular basis of neural plasticity. *Neuron* 11: 995–1006.

Nguyen, T.V., Kosofsky, B.E., Birnbaum, R., Cohen, B.M. and Hyman, S.E. (1992) Differential expression of c-Fos and Zif268 in rat striatum after haloperidol, clozapine, and amphetamine. *Proc. Natl. Acad. Sci. USA* 89: 4270–4274.

Noble, E.P., Blum, K., Khala, M.E., Ritchie, T., Montgomery, A., Wood, R.C., Fitch, R.J., Ozkaragoz, T., Sheridan, P.J., Anglin, M.D., Paredes, A., Treiman, L.J. and Sparkes, R.S. (1993) Allelic association of the D_2 dopamine receptor gene with cocaine dependence. *Drug Alcohol Depend.* 33: 271–285 and published erratum 34: 83–84 (1993).

Pecins-Thompson, M. and Peris, J. (1993) Behavioral and neurochemical changes caused by repeated ethanol and cocaine administration. *Psychopharmacology* 110: 443–450.

Pilotte, N., Sharpe, L. and Kuhar, M.J. (1994) Withdrawal of repeated intravenous infusions of cocaine persistently reduces binding to dopamine transporters in the nucleus accumbens of Lewis rats. *J. Pharmacol. Exp. Ther.* 269: 963–969.

Rosen, J.B., Chuang, E. and Iadarola, M.J. (1994) Differential induction of Fos protein and a Fos-related antigen following acute and repeated cocaine administration. *Mol. Brain Res.* 25: 168–172.

Samson, H.H. and Harris, R.A. (1992) Neurobiology of alcohol abuse. *TIPS* 13: 206–211.

Schwartz, J.-C., Giros, B., Martres, M.-P. and Sokoloff, P. (1992) The dopamine receptor family: molecular biology and pharmacology. *Semin. Neurosci.* 4: 99–108.

Sheng, M. and Greenberg, M.E. (1990) The regulation and function of c-fos and other immediate early genes in the nervous system. *Neuron* 4: 477–485.

Skutella, T., Probst, J.C., Jirikowski, G., Holsboer, F. and Spanagel, R. (1994) Ventral tegmental area injections of tyrosine hydroxylase phosphorothioate antisense oligonucleotide suppress operant behavior in rats. *Neurosci. Lett.* 167: 55–58.

Uhl, G., Blum, K., Noble, E. and Smith, S. (1993) Substance abuse vulnerability and D_2 receptor genes. *TINS* 16: 83–88.

Vrana, S.L., Vrana, K.E., Koves, T.R., Smith, J.E. and Dworkin, S.I. (1993) Chronic cocaine administration increases CNS tyrosine hydroxylase enzyme activity and mRNA levels and tryptophan hydroxylase enzyme activity levels. *J. Neurochem.* 61: 2262–2268.

Weiss, B., Zhou, L.-W., Zhang, S.-P. and Qin, Z.-H. (1993) Antisense oligodeoxynucleotide inhibits D_2 messenger RNA. *Neuroscience* 55: 607–612.

Widnell, K.L., Russell, D.S. and Nestler, E.J. (1994) Regulation of cAMP response element binding protein (CREB) expression in the locus coeruleus in vivo and in a locus coeruleus-like cell line in vitro. *Proc. Natl. Acad. Sci. USA* 91: 10947–10951.

Woolverton, W.L. and Johnson, K.M. (1992) Neurobiology of cocaine abuse. *TIPS* 13: 193–200.

Young, S.T., Porrino, L.J. and Iadarola, M.J. (1991) Cocaine induces striatal c-Fos-immunoreactive proteins via dopaminergic D1 receptors. *Proc. Natl. Acad. Sci. USA* 88: 1291–1295.

Zhang, M. and Creese, I. (1993) Antisense oligodeoxynucleotide reduces brain dopamine D2 receptors: behavioral correlates. *Neurosci. Lett.* 166: 223–226.

Zhou, L.-W., Zhang, S.-P., Qin, Z.-H. and Weiss, B. (1994) In vivo administration of an oligodeoxynucleotide antisense to the D_2 dopamine receptor messenger RNA inhibits D_2 dopamine receptor-mediated behavior and the expression of D_2 dopamine receptors in mouse striatum. *J. Pharmacol. Exp. Ther.* 268: 1015–1023.

Drug Addiction and its Treatment: Nexus of Neuroscience and Behavior, edited by Bankole A. Johnson and John D. Roache. Lippincott–Raven Publishers, Philadelphia, © 1997.

15

Single and Ensemble Neuron Spike Train Analysis in Studies of Drugs of Abuse

Donald J. Woodward, *Barry D. Waterhouse, Jing-Yu Chang, Joseph M. Paris, *John Rutter, and *Errol Gould

Bowman Gray School of Medicine, Winston-Salem, North Carolina 27157;
*Medical College of Pennsylvania,Hahnemann University School of Medicine,
Allegheny University of the Health Sciences, Philadelphia, Pennsylvania 19102-1192

Substance abuse is a major problem for society in the United States and elsewhere because of the considerable medical and social liabilities associated with all abuse potential compounds. Due to their reinforcing effects, repeated administration of these agents leads to, and ultimately maintains, drug-seeking and drug-taking behaviors. Once established, these behaviors can become all-consuming for addicted individuals to the point where personal health, family relationships, and work activities are severely compromised.

A full accounting of the brain mechanisms that provide the basis for these social phenomena is a major challenge for neuroscience. The neurophysiologist who specializes in spike train analysis of neuronal activity has an important and unique role in clarifying the actions of drugs of abuse. Spike train neurophysiology provides an important link between the analysis of molecular and membrane mechanisms of drug action and studies of drug influences on neural circuit substrates of behavior.

Extensive behavioral studies involving humans and laboratory animals have defined the spectrum of sensory, cognitive, and motor effects observed after ingestion of abuse potential compounds. Thus, the impact of drugs of abuse on whole-organism behavior has been well characterized. Other in-depth studies have defined the pleasure centers, reward pathways, and neurotransmitter systems that are responsible for the potent reinforcing effects of compounds with abuse potential. In this regard, a preponderance of evidence (reviewed in Wise, 1984) favors involvement of dopaminergic mechanisms as a means for regulating drug-induced reinforcement mechanisms in the brain, thus lowering the threshold for evoking drug-taking behavior. Activation of this intrinsic reward system partially accounts for euphoria sometimes associated with drug self-administration. Further understanding of these effects requires a clarification of the patterns of neural activity within the brain circuits that directly mediate these behaviors.

Moreover, despite the considerable literature on drug-induced behaviors and mechanisms of reward and reinforcement, the physiologic bases of many other dimensions of drug dependence, such as the development of chronic patterns of substance abuse, are not well understood. These include such phenomena as drug craving, tolerance, sensitization, and withdrawal. A better understanding of the activity patterns and physiologic circuit mechanisms influenced by acute ingestion of recreational drugs as well as those that are altered by chronic patterns of substance abuse may lead to more rational and effective treatment of drug addiction.

Because of this belief and the generally accepted notion that individuals can be genetically predisposed to drug addictions, many molecular and membrane electrophysiologic strategies have been used to identify the intracellular targets and modes of action of abuse potential substances. Such reductionist approaches have yielded much new data and provided many new insights regarding possible cellular correlates of drug-seeking and drug-taking behaviors. Moreover, reduced preparations have identified many new potential targets for pharmacologic intervention and treatment of substance abuse. Nevertheless, this level of analysis leaves a considerable gap between the established molecular actions of drugs of abuse and their impact on behavior. Drug-associated states of craving (Markou et al., 1993), tolerance, sensitization, withdrawal, and reward develop over time and are the products of direct drug-induced changes and learned modifications within the sensory, motor, and associational circuits in the brain. *Sensitization,* a long-lasting change in the threshold for a physiologic or behavioral response to a single drug challenge induced by an initial repeated drug exposure, may result from long-lasting, learned adaptations, or more elementary physical changes in synapses or receptors. To better comprehend the physiologic bases of these aspects of drug abuse, studies are needed to determine the precise time course and outcome of drug influences on activity patterns, local circuit operations, and neural system interactions that directly mediate the whole organism responses to drug administration.

To provide information that is relevant to behavioral circumstances where all potential sites of drug action in the brain are accessed simultaneously via the bloodstream, drug effects on single neurons and local circuits must be evaluated in intact preparations. These circuit actions cannot be readily inferred from results of membrane or molecular studies. Studies of drug actions on neural activity in anesthetized animals are usually most effective when the design of research directly complements work on tissue slice or isolated cell

preparations. An end point, and an ideal experimental situation, is one in which the activity of multiple, single neurons can be monitored simultaneously in intact behaving animals as drug-induced changes occur. Such a preparation allows for examination of the time course of drug-induced modifications in single cell and neural circuit response properties under otherwise normal physiologic conditions. Cells or groups of cells can be recorded simultaneously from within a single region of the brain or across several functionally related circuits.

RATIONALE FOR SPIKE TRAIN ANALYSIS OF PSYCHOSTIMULANT EFFECTS ON CELLULAR AND CIRCUIT FUNCTIONS

There are numerous reasons why spike train analyses can provide answers for many of the open questions regarding actions of psychostimulants. Representative issues are described here along with examples of hypotheses to be tested.

Abuse Liability

Psychostimulants, such as cocaine and amphetamine, are particularly notorious for their abuse liability. These drugs are widely acknowledged as the most potent behavior reinforcing compounds known (Bozarth and Wise, 1985; Gawin, 1991; Gold, 1992; Gold et al., 1992; Johanson and Fischman, 1989). Although they are not physically addicting in the same sense as opiates, once the psychostimulant habit has been established, drug-seeking and drug-taking activities can become all-consuming for the addicted individual. Furthermore, the success rate for rehabilitating cocaine and amphetamine addicts even after detoxification and intensive drug counseling programs is extremely low (Gold, 1992; Gold et al., 1992; Johanson and Fischman, 1989; Lowenstein et al., 1987), and drug-free graduates of such rehabilitation programs report an overwhelming urge to restart cocaine self-administration after they have returned to their previous drug-taking environment or experience drug-taking cues that stimulate craving (Cohen, 1984; Gold, 1992; Gold et al., 1992; Post et al., 1992; Wise and Bozarth, 1987). These observations suggest the establishment of an irreversible, reciprocal, reinforcing link between sensory/behavioral stimuli and drug ingestion (Robinson and Berridge, 1993; Stewart et al., 1984). By analogy, it is like learning to ride a bicycle; once this motor task is established, it is difficult if not impossible to unlearn how to ride one.

An open question is whether the physical changes that occur with chronic drug use represent aberrant molecular, or structural changes caused by the drug, or a strongly reinforced normal form of learning. Recording of identified neurons (phenotype and connectivity) in well-defined anatomical areas will be needed in model animal systems (Markou et al., 1993) to establish how sensory cues can lead to enhanced drug-seeking and drug-taking activity. The concept of an overwhelming urge to ingest drug can be presumed to be encoded in patterns of neuronal activity across relevant brain circuits. It is reasonable that a search within the mesolimbic system or frontal cortical circuits would reveal the specific subsets of neurons that mediate enhanced triggering of drug taking. This neural substrate of substance abuse represents a distinct phenomenon in the virtual absence of the drug in the subject.

Neural Correlates of Subjective Sensations and Motor Activation

There will clearly be a long-term effort required to clarify the distributed patterns of neuronal activity responsible for many commonly reported drug-related phenomena. Individuals who self-administer psychostimulants report feelings of well-being and euphoria accompanied by arousal, enhanced sensory perception, hyperactivity, and increased capacity for mental and physical work (Byck and Van Dyke, 1977; Cohen, 1984; Fischman et al., 1977;

Freud, 1974; Gold, 1992; Gold et al., 1992). In laboratory animals, cocaine and amphetamine cause increased locomotion, arousal, and stereotyped behavior (Post and Rose, 1976; Post et al., 1992; Woods, 1977). Additionally, they produce increased sensitivity (as measured by motor responsiveness) to environmental changes including tactile stimuli (Scheel-Kruger et al., 1977; Wilson et al., 1976), electrical shock (Lal and Chessick, 1965) and temperature changes (Peterson and Hardinge, 1967). Changes in background activity of neurons or steady-state modulation of synaptic transmission in motivational, sensory, and motor regions are presumed to provide the physiologic substrate for these effects.

Many motor effects of drugs, such as hyperactivity or stereotypy, have not been the subject of intense neurophysiologic analysis. For example, a dose of 10 mg/kg cocaine causes a rat to move about a behavioral chamber continuously, whereas doses of 1 mg/kg during self-administration protocols induce stereotypy with head movements and chewing. Sensitization of the locomotor and stereotyped responses to cocaine can be seen for weeks (or much longer) after administration of sensitizing doses of cocaine or amphetamine (Post et al., 1992; White, 1990; White and Wolf, 1991). Changes in synaptic efficacy in the nucleus accumbens and in the ventral tegmental area (VTA) have been proposed to contribute to these effects (Henry and White, 1995). Expression of stereotypy occurs more readily in a familiar home cage, indicating that learned environmental cues have a major role in regulating the expression of this phenomenon (Post et al., 1992).

At present there is no clear idea as to which neural structures emit the signals that result in the enhanced locomotor output observed during sensitization. One hypothesis is that tonic activity decreases within the neurons of the substantia nigra reticulata and entopeduncular nucleus (globus pallidus, internal) due to excessive dopamine (DA). Disinhibition of thalamic nuclei (VL, ventral lateral; VA, ventral anterior; MD, medial dorsal) could then release normally suppressed default signals. Excess non–goal-directed locomotion and stereotypical movements may be suppressed in normal animals, but released when circuits are biased toward disinhibition with excess DA. In rats sensitized by chronic drug administration, an unfamiliar environment, different visual surround, or odorants may constitute novel sensory cues. These evoke attentional mechanisms that override expression of the array of abnormal movements. Recording and analysis of neuron spike trains within corticostriatal thalamic loops will be needed eventually to determine the origin and regulation of these postulated signals.

Circuit Actions of Monoamines

At the cellular level, cocaine blocks reuptake of the endogenous monoamine transmitters DA, norepinephrine (NE), and serotonin (5-HT). Amphetamine causes spontaneous release of central monoamines from storage sites in nerve terminals (Glowinski and Axelrod, 1965; Wallach and Gershun, 1971; Ross and Renyi, 1966; Koe, 1976; Hadfield et al., 1980). Regardless of the specific mechanism, the net effect of either of these actions is increased synaptic levels of NE, DA, and 5-HT in all central neuronal circuits where monoamine-containing fibers terminate. Thus, a predicted outcome of cocaine's neurochemical actions would be enhanced monoaminergic function in areas of the brain innervated by NE, DA, and 5-HT fibers. In this respect, the problem of clarifying cocaine action reduces to elucidation of mechanisms of drug-induced modulatory actions in monoaminergically innervated target circuits. The net effect of psychostimulants on a complex circuit such as the cerebellar cortex can be accurately assessed by recording spike train activity of neurons during monoaminergic modulation of transmission of physiologic signals (Moises et al., 1990; Woodward, 1992).

Drug Craving

A key issue that must be addressed in relation to psychostimulant abuse liability is the neurobiologic basis of drug-craving (Markou

et al., 1993). Acutely, cocaine and amphetamine produce a multitude of centrally mediated effects, some or all of which may contribute to a positive drug experience and the desire to repeat that experience. (Adams and Durell, 1984). Concerted efforts should be mounted to identify the neural activity patterns underlying cocaine and amphetamine's pleasurable effects and the processes linking them to establishment of drug craving. The concept of craving as it relates to physiologic mechanisms has been the subject of considerable debate (Markou et al., 1993). The discovery of specific neural responses precipitated by priming doses of drugs, by conditioned sensory cues, or during behavioral protocols designed to activate prolonged responding would have considerable value in establishing the physical reality of the concept (Markou et al., 1993).

Craving is postulated to be a type of "on state," which is triggered by condition sensory cues or internal chemical cues, and these can activate drug-seeking behavior. Is such a switch expressed as sustained neuronal activity, or is it to be found embedded in an altered synaptic efficacy seen only when probed with a test stimulus? One might hypothesize that internal and external cues reaching an area of the mesolimbic system, such as the medial prefrontal cortex, might recursively activate a short-term memory in the form of a "delay-period activity" (Fuster, 1989; Schultz et al., 1994). A sustained signal could arise through repeated activation of corticostriatal loops as the continually presented cues reactivate memories. In such a scheme the cortical projections into the medial caudate would enable a response selection process to activate a drug-seeking task sequence (Schultz et al., 1994). The recording of neuron ensembles throughout this process will provide a direct means of validating such a scenario.

The specificity of craving can be expected to correspond to a unique neural representation of activity within groups of neurons in mesolimbic and frontal cortex. The significance of tones, or visual or tactile stimuli, can readily be observed in spike train signals. An open question is how the selectivity of craving for food, drug, or other reinforcers is coded by patterns of spike train activity, and in what anatomical regions.

Reward Mechanisms

Many studies (Esposito et al., 1977; Kornetsky and Esposito, 1981; Kuhar et al., 1991; Risner and Jones, 1976; Roberts and Koob, 1982; Wise, 1984) have concentrated on identifying the reward pathways that mediate reinforcement of drug-seeking behavior. In general, the central monoaminergic pathways and their efferent targets have been the focus of this effort, and, in the case of cocaine and amphetamine, the preponderance of evidence (reviewed in Wise, 1984; Wise and Bozarth, 1987) favors involvement of dopaminergic modulatory mechanisms in conveying drug-induced stimulatory messages within appropriate reward centers of the brain. Activation of this intrinsic reinforcement system has been presumed to account for much of the euphoria associated with psychostimulant self-administration. Nevertheless, the specific dimensions of reward circuit function that are influenced by acute administration of psychostimulant drugs, as well as the physiologic processes that can be altered and ultimately changed to promote and support persistent drug-seeking behaviors, have not been identified.

Recent studies of neural activity changes in the rat nucleus accumbens during a simple lever press for cocaine have been initiated to explore the neurophysiology of the brain reward system (Chang et al., 1990, 1991, 1993, 1994a; Carelli and Deadwyler, 1994). Surprisingly, neuron firing in this region, which is a central component of the drug reward system, shows only a modest suppression of background activity during the intravenous administration of cocaine. However, precisely timed phasic excitation or inhibition of specific neurons is observed prior to the lever press and is found linked to the onset and termination of sequences of task-related movements leading from the resting state to the bar press for cocaine administration. The neu-

ronal activity patterns show the nucleus accumbens to behave much like the dorsal neostriatum in mediating signals linked to movement sequences toward a goal. The reinforcing action of the drug can be presumed to strengthen the association of contextual sensory cues to the triggering of behavioral responses. The long-term goal of neuron recording is to clarify the spatial-temporal patterns of drug-induced discharge throughout all the brain regions that mediate drug-seeking behavior.

Recreational Drugs and Neurophysiology

Related to this issue is the fact that the neurobiologic substrates underlying other major CNS effects of cocaine and amphetamine such as enhanced sensitivity to sensory stimuli have not yet been identified. These effects appear in regions not directly related to the reward system. Such an effect on perceptual processes may by itself be a recreationally desirable consequence of psychostimulant self-administration and as such may contribute to the overall pleasurable experience derived from these compounds. In previous reviews (Johanson et al., 1976; Johanson and Fischman, 1989; Wise, 1984) of cocaine's addictive potential, it has been noted that any positive features associated with cocaine ingestion may facilitate the reinforcing effects of the drug and thus add to its abuse liability. Furthermore, it has recently been suggested (Robinson and Berridge, 1993; Stewart et al., 1984) that psychostimulant-induced euphoria confers incentive salience to stimuli or events associated with drug taking. That is, over time drug-associated activities and environmental cues become salient, motivate movements to obtain the reinforcer, and contribute to drug craving. Despite these observations, a survey of the literature reveals a paucity of studies aimed at identifying the effects of cocaine or amphetamine on sensory information processing within the mammalian brain. In fact, up until the mid-1980s, there was little information available regarding the impact of drugs of abuse on electrophysiologic parameters of cell function in any circuit of the brain.

Cannabinoid Δ-g-tetrahydrocannabinol (THC), the activate constituent of cannabis, is a drug whose action is not clearly related to the DA receptors within the reward system. Deadwyler and his associates (Deadwyler et al., 1990; Heyser et al., 1993) have shown the selective inhibition of neural responses in hippocampus that normally appears immediately after the sample bar press in a delayed match to sample (DMTS) task with spatial information. Memory task performance is degraded by THC administration, an effect attributed in the rat to suppression of synaptic function in the hippocampus where THC receptors are abundant.

Chang et al. (1995) and Heyser et al. (1993) in preliminary studies have shown similar signals to be degraded in the medial prefrontal cortex of rats during the DMTS task even before the sample bar press and well before the signals reach the hippocampus. This effect has been attributed to distorted function of the corticostriatal loops activated during this cognitive task. Such a result can be anticipated in view of the high concentration of THC receptors in the globus pallidus and substantia nigra reticulata, the output regions targeted by striatal outflow. The receptors on terminals contacting DA neurons could influence reinforcement via a DA-dependent mechanism. A goal of neural recording studies should be to fully clarify the pattern of altered circuit function during cognitive tasks altered by cannabinoids. At some later point in the analysis, one might hope to discern an overall rationale for the recreational quality of the drug experience.

In summary, isolated whole cell or patch clamp procedures are clearly the methods of choice for questions regarding drug effects on membrane function or ion channel activity. However, spike train analysis involving individual cells or ensembles of neurons are required for investigating entirely different issues, such as the physiologic basis of drug-related behaviors. These are outside the realm of isolated preparations but rather can only be observed in intact animals.

METHODS OF SINGLE-UNIT STUDIES IN INTACT, ANESTHETIZED PREPARATIONS

Most traditional studies of the influence of abused drugs on spike train activity have employed anesthetized preparations with drugs administered systematically or via microiontophoresis. Extracellular activity from single or multiple neurons can be recorded from any region of the brain after induction of surgical anesthesia and fixation of the animal in a stereotaxic device. After removal of the skull and dura, recording electrodes (glass or metal) are driven to specific sites in the brain according to a standardized coordinate system referenced to a brain atlas and a stereotaxic device. Animals are respirated or allowed to breathe spontaneously over the course of the experiment while body temperature is maintained at 36°C to 37°C with a heating lamp or pad.

Under these laboratory conditions, viable preparations can be maintained for 8 hours or longer. Spike train activity from individual neurons can be electrically isolated and monitored for minutes to hours depending on the stability of the preparation. Spontaneous and stimulus evoked patterns of discharge can be characterized for individual neurons before, during, and after systemic or local (infusion, microiontophoretic) drug administration in order to identify drug-induced changes in cell or circuit function. Figure 1 shows the typical arrangement of instrumentation employed for iontophoretic drug application to neurons in anesthetized animals (Lee et al., 1995a,b).

There are three major advantages to using whole-animal preparations for assessing drug effects on brain circuits. First, cell activity is studied in intact neuronal networks that include all normal inputs and intrinsic neuronal and nonneuronal (glial) circuit elements. Second, cells are recorded in the presence of endogenous circulating hormones and other blood- or cerebrospinal fluid–borne factors that may influence their normal function. Third, with systemic administration there is the added advantage that behaviorally relevant doses of drugs can

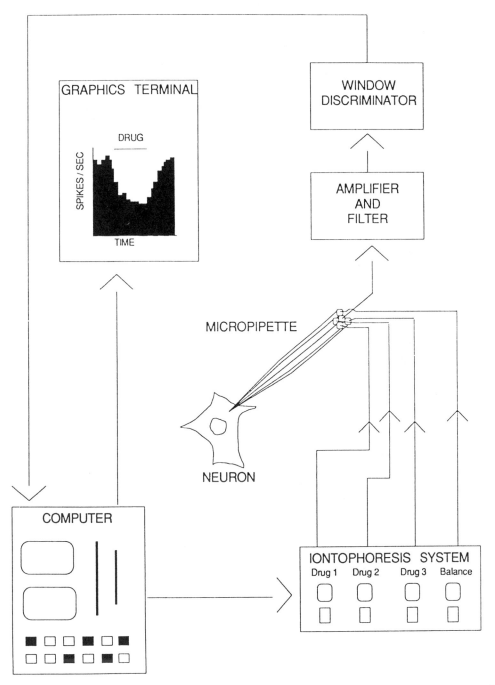

FIG. 1. Traditional instrumentation for study of influences of local circuit drug administration on spike train activity. Excitatory inhibitory or modulatory influences are inferred from altered firing rates. A single recording barrel of a multibarrel array is employed to examine impulse rate as indicated by a head-stage amplifier, filter, pulse window, and integrator. Data integrated by computer are displayed on a CRT or graphics plotter. Iontophoretic drug application is achieved by passing current through barrels containing agonist or antagonist drugs for various receptor systems. Drug physically leaves the barrel and reaches the neuron through a combination of iontophoresis, electro-osmosis, and diffusion. Uncharged drugs are dissolved in saline to allow electro-osmosis. Direct actions of electrical stimulation are minimized by use of a balance channel that provides local current opposite in polarity to the sum of current through the drug channels (Lee et al., 1995a). (With permission, Elsevier Pub.).

achieve access to the brain by normal physiologic channels and, likewise, can be inactivated by intact intrinsic mechanisms. Thus, all circuits in the brain are simultaneously exposed to drug for a period of time that is defined by the normal pharmacokinetics for that particular compound.

In addition to these general advantages of intact preparations for drug abuse studies, there are a number of more specific reasons for utilizing this approach. For example, throughout the course of an experimental protocol the brain is maintained at a constant, albeit anesthetized, state. This ensures that drug-induced alterations in motor activity or cognitive states that could occur in awake animals are not factors that could influence the dynamics of the cells or circuits being studied. The possibility that drug administration could alter the level of anesthesia and thus indirectly influence cell or circuit function can be ascertained by monitoring electroencephalograph (EEG) patterns throughout the experiment.

It is particularly important to point out that studies in anesthetized animals can provide important baseline information regarding drug effects on neuronal and network operations under controlled physiologic conditions. From this work it then becomes possible to make predictions about the effects of drugs on cells and circuits in awake animals as a function of changing behavioral contingencies. Changes in cell activity may be due to direct local actions on membranes or circuits, or a consequence of drug-induced changes in behavioral state. Interpretations of direct membrane actions require studies of reduced preparations employing isolated neurons or brain slices.

Intact preparations also allow for single neurons or functional ensembles of neurons to be activated by natural, electrical, or chemical stimulation of afferent pathways. Thus, drug effects can be measured within the context of the normal range of signal processing operations for the cell or circuit in question. Many initial electrophysiologic studies in intact preparations focus on whether a drug can increase or decrease the spontaneous firing rate of selected neurons. While this is a first step in demonstrating that a drug can act on a specific population of neurons, it does not fully define all of the parameters of neuronal function that can be influenced by drug actions. Additional studies must be conducted to determine how the cell or circuit receives and processes afferent information while the brain is under the influence of a systemically administered compound. A further specific advantage of the intact, anesthetized preparation is the ability to determine whether drug effects result from interactions with local circuit mechanisms or circuits that are afferent to, but remote from, the sites being examined. For example, cocaine blocks reuptake of synaptically released dopamine, norepinephrine, and serotonin and can therefore affect neuronal function by actions on monoamine-containing cells that project broadly throughout the central nervous system, or by influencing target cells in monoaminergic terminal fields (Fig. 2).

Parenteral drug administration provides the advantage of measuring the impact of system-wide drug actions on local electrophysiologic phenomena, whereas with local microiontophoretic drug application it is possible to isolate drug influences to the immediate vicinity of the cells or cell being recorded.

Once the spectrum of a drug's action on individual cells or circuits has been defined in a whole-animal preparation, numerous pharmacologic tools can be employed either through systemic or local administration to identify the transmitter-specific substrates of drug-induced effects. This is particularly useful since abuse potential substances not only have multiple potential anatomical loci of action but also can impact brain function through interactions with many different transmitter-receptor mechanisms.

Finally, intact anesthetized animal preparations allow for identification and characterization of multiple electrophysiologic measures of cell or circuit function following acute drug administration. Once these parameters of drug action are firmly established, it

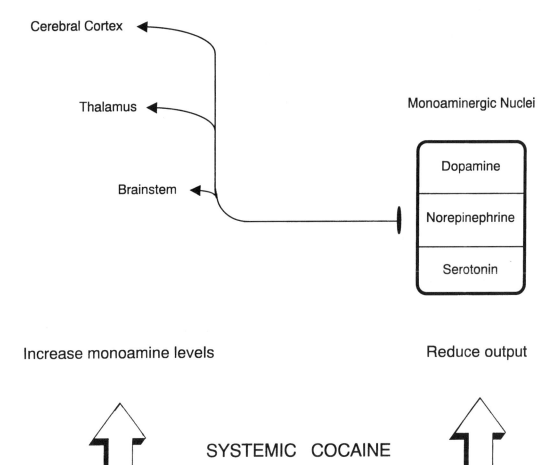

FIG. 2. Systemically administered cocaine can alter CNS function by blocking monoamine uptake at multiple sites throughout the brain. Blockade of reuptake at monoamine-containing cell bodies (*right*) can significantly alter the output of brain stem monoaminergic nuclei. Likewise, blockade of reuptake along axon terminals can elevate monoamine levels in efferent targets of the monoaminergic nuclei and thus, elicit monoamine-related physiologic actions in these areas (*left*). Each of these sites of action must be considered as a potential contributor to the net effect of systemic cocaine on brain function.

is then possible to look for changes in neuronal function before and after chronic drug treatments. Comparisons of cellular or neuronal circuit function in naive, chronically treated and drug-withdrawn animals can provide insights into the physiologic bases for the dependence, craving, tolerance, and sensitization phenomena that are observed with abuse potential compounds.

STUDIES OF MONOAMINE ACTIONS IN ANESTHETIZED PREPARATIONS

In recent years, much new information concerning the modulation of neural spike train patterns by central monoaminergic systems has emerged (reviewed in Aghajanian, 1981; Amaral and Sinnamon, 1977; Foote et al., 1983; Jacobs and Azmitia, 1992). In early studies, we demonstrated an enhancement of γ-aminobutyric acid (GABA) synaptic function in cerebellum and cortex by norepinephrine (Woodward et al., 1979, 1992). These *in vivo* studies have provided a new conceptual framework for evaluating the actions of agents that are known to interact with these systems. For example, based on numerous electrophysiologic studies employing single-unit extracellular recording and microiontophoretic drug application techniques in intact animal preparations, a low threshold, modulatory role for NE in complex neuronal network function has been proposed (Foote et al., 1975; McCormick, 1989; McCormick and Prince, 1988; Moises et al., 1979; Rogawski and Aghajanian, 1980; Sato and Kayama, 1983; Waterhouse et al., 1980; Waterhouse and Woodward, 1980). The NE-induced modulatory effects that have been observed are distinct from the classic high threshold, direct depressant action of this monoamine on spontaneous firing rate (Hoffer et al., 1971; Krnjevic, 1974; Nelson et al., 1973; Stone, 1973). Specifically, iontophoretically or synaptically released NE at doses subthreshold for producing direct suppression of spontaneous discharge can facilitate neuronal responses to both excitatory and inhibitory synaptic stimuli (Moises et al., 1979; Rogawski and Aghajanian, 1980; Sessler et al., 1988; Waterhouse and Woodward, 1980). Moreover, these effects exhibit pharmacologic specificity with respect to adrenergic receptor subtypes and putative neurotransmitters, particularly for the GABA system (Mouradian et al., 1991; Waterhouse et al., 1980, 1981, 1982). These findings in conjunction with additional data from anatomical and physiologic studies of the locus coeruleus (Aston-Jones and Bloom, 1981a,b; Berridge and Foote, 1991; Foote et al., 1983; Levitt and Moore, 1978; Morrison et al., 1978) have led to the view that a primary role of the central noradrenergic system may be to facilitate *non-monoamine* synaptic transmission in target neuronal circuits during periods of increased behavioral arousal and sustained attention.

A similar, but less extensive, series of studies focusing on the physiology of 5-HT in sensory neocortical circuits has revealed a net depressant action of this monoamine on unit responses to synaptic stimuli (Waterhouse et al., 1986). In addition, we (McLean et al., 1990; Waterhouse et al., 1990) and others (Kasamatsu and Heggelund, 1982; Kossl and Vater, 1989; Sato and Kayama, 1983) have determined that both 5-HT and NE can produce selective changes in the receptive field properties of individual somatosensory and visual cortical neurons. Thus, a reasonable working hypothesis at this time is that synaptically released NE and 5-HT may not only up- and downregulate the responsiveness of cortical cells to incoming sensory information, but also fine-tune the feature extraction properties of these sensory neurons through the modulatory actions on the amino acid transmitter systems.

It is important to note that in conjunction with the above-mentioned studies, a comprehensive set of electrophysiologic methodologies for evaluating single-neuron function when controlled sensory stimuli (visual, auditory, tactile), are presented to anesthetized or awake, behaving animals has been established. Many of these experimental strategies have already been employed in studies designed to identify the parameters of cell and neural network function that are altered by psychostimulant drug actions.

Once the acute effects of a drug of abuse on single-neuron response properties have been determined, additional studies can be conducted to measure cellular functions and neural circuit operations in animals that have been chronically maintained on drug or withdrawn from chronic drug treatment. Such investigations are crucial to understanding the physiologic bases for tolerance, sensitization, and persistence of drug-induced changes in neuronal function that accompany chronic drug self-administration.

Evidence of Neuromodulatory Actions in Anesthetized Preparations Provides a Rationale for Cellular/Molecular and Systems-Level Investigations

The results of single-unit studies in intact, anesthetized preparations have historically provided a conceptual framework for experiments utilizing more reductionist approaches, e.g. patch clamp and molecular biology, to study neuronal function. The point to be made here is that hypotheses regarding mechanisms underlying excitatory, inhibitory, or modulatory interactions in cells or circuits have come from carefully executed studies of drug actions on spike train activity. Details of mechanisms are worked out with use of intracellular or patch clamp analysis at a later stage.

For example, the demonstration in the late 1970s that microiontophoresis of NE (Moises et al., 1979) or stimulation of the noradrenergic pathway from locus coeruleus (Moises and Woodward, 1980) could augment GABA-induced suppression of Purkinje cell discharge in anesthetized rats led to a later series of whole-cell patch clamp studies in acutely dissociated Purkinje neurons (Cheun et al., 1993; Cheun and Yeh, 1992) that confirmed the effect. The analysis was extended by showing that such facilitating actions of NE on GABA responsiveness involved increased chloride conductance and were mediated by the catalytic subunit of protein kinase A following activation of the β-receptor–linked cyclic adenosine monophosphate (cAMP) second messenger system. The implication is that GABA-A receptor function in Purkinje cells is subject to regulation by NE through protein kinase A–mediated phosphorylation of the GABA receptor protein. Amphetamine-induced enhancement of Purkinje cell responsiveness to GABA (Fig. 3) could involve similar mechanisms, many of which could be subject to long-term modification under conditions of chronic drug administration.

The results obtained in single-unit studies in intact, anesthetized preparations also constitute the foundation for electrophysiologic investigations of drug actions in awake, behaving animals. Recently developed techniques involving microiontophoresis in awake animals (Michael et al., 1985; West and Woodward, 1984) and simultaneous recording of multiple single cells (Chang et al., 1994a) in awake, freely moving animals aim to provide basic insights into (1) the processes underlying the re-warding effects of drugs, (2) the anticipatory states of neurons and circuits prior to drug self-administration, and (3) the progression of changes in neural function that accompany chronic administration of an abuse potential compound. The many constraints and complexities of data interpretation that are related to normal and drug-induced changes in active behavioral states can be dealt with more readily if a base of information regarding drug effects on cell and circuit function in intact, stable preparations is available.

In summary, the general concepts of neuromodulation that can be applied to the study of drugs of abuse evolved primarily from determinations of monoamine effects on spontaneous and stimulus evoked firing rates of neurons using a variety of interactive drug administration protocols.

Investigations of the Physiologic Actions of Psychostimulants in Anesthetized Preparations

Because of their ability to elevate central synaptic levels of NE, 5-HT, and DA, and activate autoceptors on monoamine-containing cell bodies, cocaine and amphetamine have the potential to regulate the output of monoaminergic nuclei. In fact, studies by Cunningham and Lakoski (1988, 1990), Pitts and Marwah (1986, 1987), and Einhorn and colleagues (1988) have demonstrated depressant effects of low doses of cocaine on rat dorsal raphe (5 HT), locus coeruleus (NE), and ventral tegmental area (DA) neurons. Since NE-, DA-, and 5-HT–containing axons from these brain stem nuclei distribute widely throughout forebrain, brain stem, and spinal cord (Anden et al., 1971; Jacobs and Azmitia, 1992; Jones and Moore, 1977; Levitt and Moore, 1978; 1979; Lidov et al., 1978; Lindvall et al., 1974; Moore, 1981; Morrison and Foote, 1986; Morrison et al., 1978; Ungerstedt, 1971), any suppression of the tonic firing rate of these monoaminergic neurons could have a broad impact on neural circuit functions throughout the CNS.

A second potential site of psychostimulant action is within monoaminergic terminal field

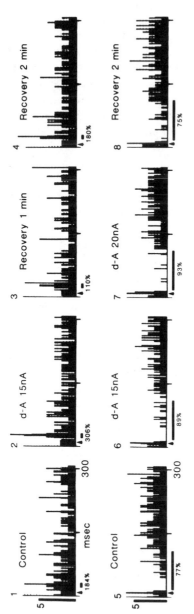

FIG. 3. d-Amphetamine enhances peripherally evoked responses to tactile stimulation in rat cerebellar Purkinje cells. Poststimulus histogram records show the responses of two cerebellar Purkinje neurons to electrical stimulation of the ipsilateral vibrissae before, during, and after d-A microiontophoresis. *Arrowheads* beneath each record mark the time at which the stimulus was presented. Responses of these cells to the applied stimulus (*solid bar* beneath histogram) were quantitated (number beneath bar) by comparison with spontaneous discharge. Each histogram sums unit activity during 50 stimulus presentations. The cell in the *upper horizontal panel* displayed an excitatory response (hist. 1) that was significantly augmented by 15nA d-A iontophoresis (hist. 2). Within 2 minutes of cessation of d-A iontophoresis the response returned to predrug levels (hist. 3, 4). The second cell depicted in the *lower horizontal panel* provided an inhibitory response (hist. 5). Application of 15nA d-A produced an augmentation in both magnitude and duration of the evoked response (hist. 6), and 20nA d-A administration (hist. 7) further potentiated this inhibition. Again, within 2 minutes of cessation of d-A iontophoresis the cell recovered predrug response patterns (hist. 8). Calibrations: horizontal, milliseconds; vertical, counts per bin.

regions themselves. Because of their ability to elevate central levels of NE, DA, and 5-HT, amphetamine or cocaine would be expected to produce monoamine-like modulatory actions in monoaminergically innervated circuits of the forebrain, brain stem, and spinal cord. It is also possible that elevated synaptic levels of NE, DA, or 5-HT could exert high-threshold direct depressant effects on spontaneous firing rate of target neurons in these areas (Hoffer et al., 1971, 1973; Nelson et al., 1973; Olpe, 1981; Parfitt et al., 1988; Stone, 1973). Figures 3 and 4 illustrate the results of experiments designed to test these possibilities.

Using poststimulus time histogram records, Fig. 3 illustrates the responses of two cerebellar Purkinje neurons to peripherally evoked synaptic inputs, before (Control), during (d-A 15 nA), and after (Recovery 1 and 2) local microiontophoretic administration of d-amphetamine at 15 nanoamp ejection current. Neurons were recorded from halothane-anesthetized rats. In the cell recording shown at the top, synaptically evoked excitation was enhanced above control levels during d-amphetamine application, whereas spontaneous firing rate was unchanged. In the cell shown at the bottom, stimulus-evoked inhibition was also augmented from control levels during d-amphetamine application, while spontaneous discharge was only minimally affected. Both of these examples indicate that locally applied d-amphetamine can enhance responsiveness of individual Purkinje neurons to excitatory and inhibitory synaptic inputs.

Several specific conclusions can be inferred from these results in conjunction with the formulation of additional testable hypotheses. First, although systemic effects of d-amphetamine on sites afferent to but remote from the cerebellum cannot be ruled out entirely as potential sites of drug action, it is clear that at least a component of d-amphetamine's actions are mediated by mechanisms within the immediate vicinity of the recorded neuron since drug administration was via localized microiontophoresis. Second, since DA is not prominent in cerebellum, the prediction is that the observed effects were either direct

actions of d-amphetamine on cell membranes or indirect via drug-induced release of NE or 5-HT. Third, the observed changes in neuronal responsiveness to synaptic inputs suggest either a pre- or postsynaptic site of action.

The experiment illustrated in Fig. 4 was conducted to test this latter possibility. In this case the responses of a single spontaneously firing cerebellar Purkinje neuron to regularly spaced, uniform iontophoretic pulses of the putative inhibitory transmitter GABA were monitored before, during, and after microiontophoresis of d-amphetamine. In essence, the iontophoretic delivery of GABA was substituted for synaptic release of GABA from axon terminals. As such, this experiment tested for a sole action of d-amphetamine on presynaptic mechanisms, and assessed drug interactions with a specific putative inhibitory transmitter. The results showed that d-amphetamine augmented GABA-induced suppression of Purkinje cell discharge. This effect occurred without any alteration in Purkinje cell spontaneous firing rate and persisted for several minutes after cessation of d-amphetamine ejection current. These findings (1) support the notion that d-amphetamine's modulatory effects occur as a result of actions within the local circuitry, (2) argue for a postsynaptic site of drug action in enhancing neuronal responses to synaptic inputs, and (3) suggest a specific facilitating interaction between d-amphetamine and GABA-mediated synaptic inhibition.

Overall, such drug-induced actions at synapses throughout the cerebellum could modify the operation of this circuit and, thus, perhaps provide a physiologic basis for the enhancement of motor activity observed with low doses of d-amphetamine. Furthermore, insofar as the cerebellum serves as a model system for testing the actions of neuropharmacologic agents (Bloom et al., 1972) these results may be extrapolated to other monoaminergic target regions of the brain where enhancement of synaptic efficacy would likewise have functional implications for neural circuit operations and behavioral responses.

To characterize further the physiologic actions of d-amphetamine on individual neurons

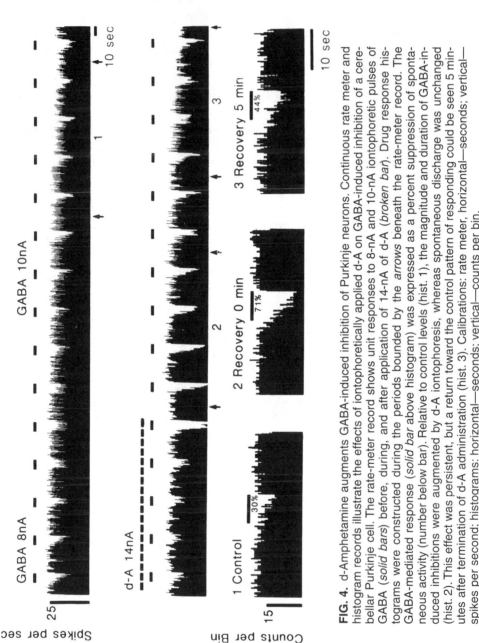

FIG. 4. d-Amphetamine augments GABA-induced inhibition of Purkinje neurons. Continuous rate meter and histogram records illustrate the effects of iontophoretically applied d-A on GABA-induced inhibition of a cerebellar Purkinje cell. The rate-meter record shows unit responses to 8-nA and 10-nA iontophoretic pulses of GABA (*solid bars*) before, during, and after application of 14-nA of d-A (*broken bar*). Drug response histograms were constructed during the periods bounded by the *arrows* beneath the rate-meter record. The GABA-mediated response (*solid bar* above histogram) was expressed as a percent suppression of spontaneous activity (*number below bar*). Relative to control levels (hist. 1), the magnitude and duration of GABA-induced inhibitions were augmented by d-A iontophoresis, whereas spontaneous discharge was unchanged (hist. 2). This effect was persistent, but a return toward the control pattern of responding could be seen 5 minutes after termination of d-A administration (hist. 3). Calibrations: rate meter, horizontal—seconds; vertical—spikes per second; histograms: horizontal—seconds; vertical—counts per bin.

in central circuits, several additional questions can be addressed using combinations of extracellular single-unit recording, microiontophoresis, and systemic drug administration. For example, are changes in neuronal responsiveness to synaptic inputs or putative amino acid transmitters evident with systemic administration of d-amphetamine at doses that elicit behavioral responses? What is the dose-response relationship and time course of such changes? Are the d-amphetamine actions observed thus far dependent on endogenous stores of DA, NE, or 5-HT or a unique combination of these monoamines? How does d-amphetamine influence response threshold and receptive field properties of individual neurons? Many of these issues have already been addressed with respect to cocaine's actions in cerebral cortex and cerebellum (Bekavac and Waterhouse, 1991; Jimenez-Rivera and Waterhouse, 1991; Waterhouse et al., 1981).

In summary, it is important to emphasize that concepts of monoamine neuromodulatory function as well as demonstrations of psychostimulant drug-induced changes in neuronal responsiveness to synaptic inputs have been derived solely from single-neuron spike train assays involving combinations of systemic or local iontophoretic drug application and presentation of physiologic stimuli.

ABUSED DRUGS STUDIED BY SPIKE TRAIN ANALYSIS IN AWAKE, BEHAVING RATS

The study of drugs of abuse through analysis of spike train activity serves different purposes in awake, behaving animals and anesthetized preparations. The activity levels and patterns of neuronal discharge observed in the anesthetized state following drug administration are more likely to reflect strictly pharmacologic influences on cells and local circuits. However, when the preparation is awake the entire brain adapts new response strategies that are reflected in sensory signal processing, motor activity patterns, and cognitive operations. There is little possibility in fact that drug-induced changes in activity will have a direct re-

lation to specific receptor activation. A mixture of direct cellular/membrane actions and indirect behavioral feedback can be expected.

A broader view that accounts for the complexity of the brain mechanisms being studied has to be taken in order to determine how influences of specific drug actions on neural circuits are expressed in the awake animal. A traditional paradigm for studying drugs of abuse is the operant behavior that requires an experimental animal to press a lever in order to obtain an intravenous injection of drug. After suitable training on a wide variety of schedules (fixed and variable intervals, numbers of lever presses), the rat or primate learns to press the lever with the expectation of obtaining a dose of drug (e.g., cocaine or heroin). After administration, the drug immediately induces stereotypy or a form of satiation in which further lever pressing is suppressed. When the drug effect attenuates, the animal is motivated to approach the lever and press it for a further drug reward. Even with this simplified task, numerous interacting neural circuits become engaged to activate the repetitive lever pressing sequence. Many questions remain regarding the levels and patterns of neural activity required to initiate and sustain this drug-induced behavior. For example, what brain regions are most critical for providing a triggering or go signal to initiate the lever press action? What regions of the brain respond to the rise and, later, fall in systemic blood levels of drug? How does the influence of falling drug level become translated into a neural signal that activates a behavioral sequence for drug acquisition? How does drug-dependent motivation become translated into specific motor command signals that orchestrate movement toward the lever?

Initial priming doses of drug must be detected by a neuronal mechanism capable of creating the motivation and incentive to achieve initial lever press. For a trained animal, different mechanisms must be engaged to initiate lever pressing. Environmental cues unique to the chamber, and memories of the effects of lever pressing and of the reinforcing qualities of the drug that have become ingrained as patterns of neuronal spike train activity, must guide the behavior under these circumstances. In accordance with this scenario, sensory stimuli that have become conditioned cues associated with reinforcement must gain access to a neural mechanism capable of providing an incentive to approach the lever and press it. Thus, in a conditioned animal, an aggregation of internal and external cues may activate a brain state, often conceptualized as craving (Markou et al., 1993), which corresponds to a sustained motivation to press a lever to obtain a reinforcing drug. All of the conditions mentioned above can be expected to correspond at some stage to neural representations, and coded spatial-temporal patterns of cell discharge within distributed neuronal networks.

Figure 5 illustrates the sequence of events conceptualized as establishing linkages between conditioned cues, craving, repeated drug-seeking behavior, and reinforcement or extinction. The internal neural logic of the linkage between cue processing and response initiation necessarily involves the parallel and sequential activation of many circuits. Schultz et al. (1994) have shown that neurons in the dorsal and ventral striatum exhibit a sequence of activation states during delayed response tasks, and that each neuron in these areas expresses a unique signature of spike train activity. Only a few percent of neurons in an area may express similar behavioral correlates in relation to temporal aspects of expectation, cue processing, delay period memory, or motor responding.

Different neurons generate activity related to expectation, cue information delay period activity, motor execution, or reward expectation. The fact that adjacent neurons behave quite differently suggests that different logical operations are nested coextensively (on top of the other) in space. One might assume that molecular mechanisms operate to specify connections cell by cell, and fiber by fiber. This degree of local heterogeneity also appears to be the case in rat nucleus accumbens (Chang et al., 1990, 1994a). Figure 6 schematically illustrates the diversity of information flow within the neostriatal component of the brain reward system.

It should be kept in mind that neural activity related to expectation corresponds to a representation generated from long-term memory to prepare an attentional state or motor preparation appropriate to the context. Different distributed patterns of activity may appear specific to the future concept of reward. The challenge in understanding the neurophysiology of drug abuse is to clarify the form by which logical information flows through each component of the brain reward system during each aspect of cue processing and drug-seeking behavior. Normal motivated behavior can be presumed to consist of a chain of events as depicted in Fig. 6. At each point in the task sequence, the subject acknowledges the context, remembers for a time what has happened, and develops expectations and motor preparations for what will happen next. The behavioral task also may be envisioned as a chain of task segments as illustrated in Fig. 5 for a single delayed response.

A segment of the brain reward system is illustrated in Fig. 7, which illustrates the diversity of input to the nucleus accumbens (NAC). This ventral striatal region receives convergent input from medial and lateral cortical areas and amygdala. Diverse conditioned cues, both external and internal, gain access to the NAC through these routes and then propagate an integrated signal to SN reticulata, VTA (ventral tegmental area), ventral pallidum, hypothalamus, and brain stem. The medial-dorsal nucleus of thalamus relays signals more widely to frontal cortex. Nested cortical striatal loops establish behavioral commands that eventually descend to brain stem and spinal cord.

Integrative functions of the NAC depend on an intact dopamine system (Salamone, 1992). The ability of cues to acquire and learn long-term incentive salience, and for the subject to generate long sequences of behaviors, evidently requires intact NAC-dopamine interactions to allow nested cortical-basal ganglia loops to function appropriately. For these reasons the NAC is often placed at the conceptual center of the brain reward system.

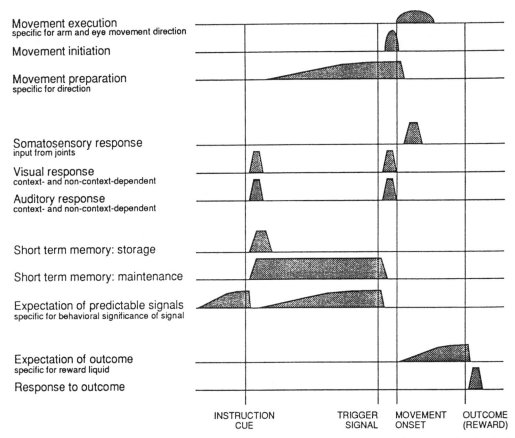

FIG. 5. Schematic overview of phasic spike train signals in neostriatum during sensorimotor tasks involving movements instruction cues, short-term memory, and reward. Phasic signals coincide with information cues, triggers, movements, or rewards. Activity also precedes each event suggestive of preparation of expectation. Activity follows each event suggestive of memory processing. Single striatal neurons usually participate in only one or two of the events. Normal complex behavioral events are presumed to be constructed from a chain of this type of neuronal logical signals. (After Schultz et al., 1994.)

It is clear that a major effort will need to be mounted to determine the detailed logical operations performed within each of the input and output neuroanatomical regions of the ventral striatum. The NAC region itself can be expected to exhibit most of the diversity of its information flow in the form of spatial-temporal patterns of spike train activity similar to that shown in Fig. 5. This overall scheme provides the major conceptual framework for ensemble neuron neurophysiology of the action of drugs of abuse and the brain reward system (Chang et al., 1994a).

Methods for Recording Many-Neuron Spike Trains for Drug Studies

Single-neuron spike trains have been recorded in behaving animals by methods developed in the 1970s. In the basic procedure, a sharpened tungsten electrode insulated except for the tip is driven into the brain region of interest to locate representative neurons. Recording sensors, amplifiers, filters, and spike detection devices relay the times of action potential or spike occurrences to a computer, which also records

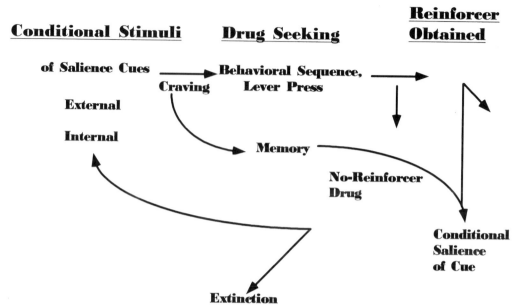

FIG. 6. Interactive sequence of activation in drug-seeking behavior. A combination of conditioned internal and external cues activates a sustained activation state termed *craving*. This enables execution of repeated behavioral sequences leading to reinforcer and enhancement of memory of cues and facilitated activation of behavioral sequences. Behavior in absence of reinforcer is subject to repeated activation by enhanced cue salience, but is subject to extinction if no reinforcer is obtained. Each phase of this sequence is presented to have a representation of ensemble spike brain activity in the brain reward system.

sensory or behavioral events in relation to neural times. Usually these are recorded on a trial-by-trial basis in relation to a single trigger pulse. Recording sites within a region are usually identified after the study by making lesions at the ends of electrode tracks and inferring recording locations by measuring distances between the brain surface and marked locations.

This experimental method, however, has received relatively limited use toward the goal of studying actions of drugs of abuse. Drug effects occur over many hours, and this makes it extremely costly, in terms of research resources, to acquire data related to an adequate population of neurons within any particular region of interest. For example, with great skill and discipline, repeated single electrode penetrations into the primate brain may typically yield recordings of up to 1500 neuron spike trains over a 6-month period (750 hours

of recording each of 30-minute duration). The 30-minute session allows for 200 repeated behavioral tasks of 10-second duration to be employed to examine a subset of sensory, motor, or cognitive variables. A nonsatiating water or juice drop reward is employed to motivate behavior during a session.

A major practical problem with traditional primate neuron recording technology for studies of substance abuse is that not enough repeated trials can be examined around the much less frequent doses of cocaine, ethanol, or other self-administered drugs to examine many statistical issues. Traditional single-neuron recordings are obtained under the assumption that the state of the brain of an animal be held stationary over repeated trials by design of experimental controls. In practice, this ideal is nearly impossible to obtain through any realistic design due to the gradual changes in blood levels during drug adminis-

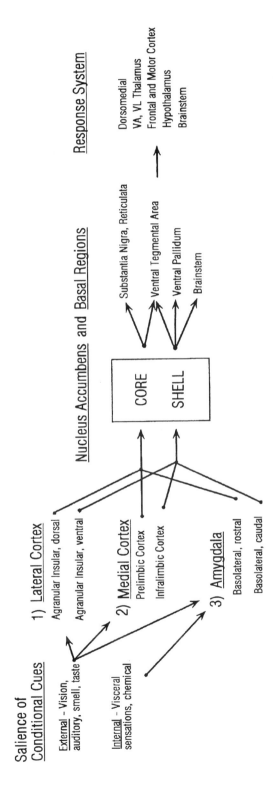

FIG. 7. Schematic role of the nucleus accumbens in the activation of drug-seeking behavior. Salient conditioned cues arrive at medial and lateral frontal cortex and amygdala and provide input to core and shell regions of the ventral neostriatum. Output of nucleus accumbens to the substantia nigra reticulata ventral tegmental area, ventral pallidum, and brain stem then reaches thalamus, frontal cortex, and other regions. These activate drug-seeking behaviors in the form of a chain of task sequences toward the reinforcement goal.

tration protocols and due to changes in attentional or motivational states and progressive learning. Given the long times, the subjects can be expected to learn and behaviorally adapt during the course of a single session, or even from trial to trial.

Single-neuron recording has been applied successfully to characterize the influence of ethanol on gating mechanisms that regulate sensory transmission to somatosensory I (SI) cortex in rat (Chapin and Woodward, 1983, 1989). Repetitive testing of the efficacy of sensory transmission to tactile input before, during, and after plateau of blood ethanol levels has demonstrated an ethanol-induced defective functioning of the gating mechanism for regulation of sensory input. Acute and chronic ethanol causes a condition in which the transmission gates are locked open, as though the rat loses the normal conscious control of an attentional mechanism. In those studies, rats received passive tactile information or active touch during treadmill locomotion that was carried out in the presence or absence of ethanol. For such studies, traditional single-neuron recordings proved adequate, but extremely tedious to conduct.

No two animals can be expected to repeat internal brain events in a precisely repeatable way since many neuronal states and conditions turn on or off by means of internally controlled training mechanisms. For these reasons, the single-neuron approach, no matter how intelligently applied, is limited in dealing with the majority of conceptual issues of interest in drug abuse research. A major advance in drug abuse research has been the introduction of modern chronic multichannel recording technology (Chang et al., 1990, 1994a; Nicolelis et al., 1993). Teflon-coated microwires (Fig. 8 can be implanted with reasonable accuracy in target locations. By passing current to deposit iron, the tip locations can be established within 50 μm by histologic reconstruction. Groups of 10 to 40 neurons can routinely be recorded throughout a drug administration protocol lasting often 1 to 3 hours. Recordings of the same neurons over 24 hours can even be acquired, and repeated recordings can be made over weeks. Newly devised multichannel amplifiers, spike sorters, computer workstations, and software (Biographics, Inc., Winston-Salem, North Carolina) make routine the tasks of recording, graphical display of histograms, and statistical analysis. Such new instrumentation makes feasible a new range of long-duration ensemble neuron recording studies on drug and hormone actions (Smith, 1995) in awake animals.

Future Studies of Distributed Patterns of Neuron Activity

A major hypothesis to be explored in the future of neural ensemble electrophysiology and drugs of abuse is that specific patterns of distributed activity may appear related to the expectation of receiving specific reinforcers. This may include either a drop of water or sweetened juice, cocaine, heroin, or other pharmacologic reinforcer. Unique patterns may appear concurrently with the motor behavior leading to a bar press for water or food or cocaine versus heroin. Moreover, in drug discrimination studies, an animal can be trained to make a decision based on evaluation of internal cues. Pressing a right versus left bar is done on the basis that one drug versus another has been administered and is acting to generate drug-specific interoceptive cues to guide the animal in making a decision. Such decisions can be presumed to correspond to unique distributed patterns of activity with the frontal cortex, striatum, and amygdala. Characteristic patterns of spike train activity should be detectable as information is being processed to encode behavioral choices corresponding to levers that indicate the perception of the drug to be administered. The symbolic representation of the reinforcer that motivates a behavioral sequence should correspond to patterns of activity within cortical regions of the brain reward system.

Multivariate statistics for detection of patterns of neuronal activity require use of such techniques as canonical variate and discriminant analysis, or more robust methods such as

LIGHTWEIGHT CABLING THAT CONNECTS TO COMMUTATOR

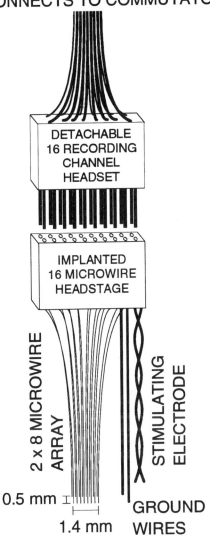

DETACHABLE 16 RECORDING CHANNEL HEADSET

IMPLANTED 16 MICROWIRE HEADSTAGE

2 x 8 MICROWIRE ARRAY

STIMULATING ELECTRODE

0.5 mm

1.4 mm

GROUND WIRES

FIG. 8. Multichannel probe array for obtaining simultaneous spike train recordings from an ensemble of neurons. Microwires and arrays are constructed from 50 μm diameter stainless steel wires coated with Teflon and arranged as rows of 2 x 8 or 4 x 4 in groups of 8 or 16. These are surgically implanted in selected regions of the brain reward system with the plug embedded in acrylic mounted on the animal's head. A plug headset with embedded FET sensors leads the multiple signals away to an amplifier spike sorting system and a computer for data storage and experimental control. Ensemble recording technology based on use of such probe arrays allows a search for patterns of activity within the brain reward system that encode the logical steps of drug-seeking behavior.

wavelet analysis. These and other means of classification are used to identify the patterns of responses across different trials or during different time epochs when ensemble neuronal vector responses are generated to drive behavior. Neuronal vectors are determined as the vector sum of spike events for each neuronal element during the time intervals in question. The goal of discriminant analysis is to compute the classification providing the best estimate of which category of ensemble activity patterns is coded by each neuronal vector sample. Canonical variate analysis involves determining a set of directions in n-dimensional space (n equals number of neurons) that optimize the ability to sort a sample into groups along the two to five variables that usually account for most of the variance, in the population vector samples (see Chang et al., 1994b; Deadwyler et al., 1996).

In practice, sometimes only a small fraction of neurons, 1% to 10% in cortex or neostriatum, may show a change in activity in a given context after presentation of a specific sensory stimulus. These highly specific neurons have been called grandmother cells, after the concept that some cells in higher levels of the visual system may become active selectively during the presentation of a unique visual stimulus (i.e., a face of an easily recognizable individual). In drug abuse research the equivalent task would be for a subject trained in drug discrimination to assess the concurrent presentation of multiple interoceptive cues stimulated by the administration of a mixture of drugs. Specific neurons, or patterns within groups of neurons, will become expressed corresponding to the judgment that the right or left lever press will lead to food reinforcement. The guiding principle of future drug research is that distributed patterns of activity in neuron ensembles can be expected to directly encode many of the brain states that regulate cognitive and motivational aspects of drug-seeking behavior.

SUMMARY

- Single- and many-neuron electrophysiologic spike train studies in anesthetized and awake, behaving animals provide a crucial link between cellular/molecular and behavioral studies of drugs of abuse.
- Traditional single-unit studies using either systemic or local iontophoretic drug administration strategies in anesthetized animals have played a significant initial role in identifying anatomical sites and modes of drug action as they pertain to specified sensory and reward circuits of the brain.
- The conceptual framework for each of these types of experiments was derived from earlier work designed to elucidate the neuromodulatory role of endogenous monoamine systems in brain function. In these studies, sophisticated in vivo protocols were developed for examining interactions between putative transmitter substances and neuronal responses to afferent synaptic inputs.
- Ensemble neuron spike train analysis in awake, behaving animals has begun to clarify the actions of drugs of abuse on computational and logic functions of local and distributed neural networks.
- In the context of abuse potential compounds, the major goal of single- and multi-neuron spike train analysis for the present and in future investigations will be to better comprehend the physiologic bases and time course of drug influences on single-neuron activity patterns, and their role in local circuit operations. The goal is to clarify neural system interactions during the sequences of behavioral tasks that characterize the drug-associated states of craving, tolerance, sensitization, withdrawal, and reward.

REFERENCES

Adams, E.H. and Durell, J. (1984) Cocaine: a growing public health problem. In: *NIDA Research Monograph #50.* Washington, DC: DHHS, pp. 1–14.

Aghajanian, G.K. (1981) The modulatory role of serotonin at multiple receptors in brain. In: Jacobs, B.L. and Gelperin, A. (eds.) *Serotonin neurotransmission and behavior.* Cambridge, MA: MIT Press, pp. 156–185.

Amaral, D.G. and Sinnamon, H.M. (1977) The locus coeruleus: neurobiology of a central noradrenergic nucleus. *Prog. Neurobiol.* 9: 147–196.

Anden, N.E., Dahlstrom, A., Fuxe, K., Larsson, K., Olson, L. and Ungerstedt, U. (1971) Ascending monoamine neurons to the telencephalon and diencephalon. *Acta. Physiol. Scand.* 67: 313–326.

Aston-Jones, G. and Bloom, F.E. (1981a) Activity of norepinephrine-containing locus coeruleus neurons in behaving rats anticipates fluctuations in the sleep-waking cycle. *J. Neurosci.* 1: 876–886.

Aston-Jones, G. and Bloom, F.E. (1981b) Norepinephrine-containing locus coeruleus neurons in behaving rat exhibit pronounced responses to non-noxious environmental stimuli. *J. Neurosci.* 1: 887–900.

Bekavac, I. and Waterhouse, B.D. (1995) Systemically administered cocaine selectively enhances long-latency responses of rat barrel field cortical neurons to vibrissae stimulation. *J. Pharmacol. Exp. Ther.* 272: 333–342.

Berridge, C.W. and Foote, S.L. (1991) Effects of locus coeruleus activation on electroencephalographic activity in neocortex and hippocampus. *J. Neurosci.* 11: 3135–3145.

Bloom, F.E., Hoffer, B.J. and Siggins, G.R. (1972) Norepinephrine mediated synapses: a model system for neuropharmacology. *Biol. Psychiatry* 4: 157–177.

Bozarth, M.A. and Wise, R.A. (1985) Toxicity associated with long term intravenous heroin and cocaine self-administration in the rat. *JAMA* 254: 81–83.

Byck, R. and Van Dyke, C: (1977) What are the effects of cocaine in man? In: Petersen, R.E. and Stillman, R.C. (eds.) *NIDA Research Monograph #13.* Washington, DC: U.S. Government Printing Office, pp. 97–118.

Carelli, R.M. and Deadwyler, S.A. (1994) A comparison of nucleus accumbens neuronal firing patterns during cocaine self-administration and water reinforcement in rats. *J. Neurosci.* 14(12): 7735–7746.

Chang, J.-Y., Laubach, M.G., Kirillov, A. and Woodward, D.J. (1994b) Neuronal activities in basal ganglia and frontal cortex during delayed match to sample task in freely moving rats. *Soc. Neurosci. Abstr.* 20(1): 718

Chang, J.-Y., Laubach, M.G. Kirillov, A.B. and Woodward, D.J. (1995) The effect of Δ^9-THC on neuronal activity in the frontal cortical-basal ganglia system during a delayed match to sample task in rats. *Soc. Neurosci. Abstr.* 758: 14.

Chang, J.-Y., Paris, J.M., Sawyer, S.F., Woodward, D.J. (1993) Ensemble recording in frontal cortex and nucleus accumbens in freely moving rats during cocaine self-administration. *Soc. Neurosci. Abstr.* 19(3): 1857.

Chang, J.-Y., Sawyer, S.F., Lee, R.-S., Maddux, B.N. and Woodward, D.J. (1990) Activity in nucleus accumbens during cocaine self-administration in freely moving rats. *Soc. Neurosci. Abstr.* 16: 252.

Chang, J.-Y., Sawyer, S.F., Lee, R.-S. and Woodward, D.J. (1991) Correlation between nucleus accumbens neuronal activity and cocaine self-administration behavior in rats. *Soc. Neurosci. Abstr.* 17: 679.

Chang, J.-Y., Sawyer, S.F., Lee, R-S. and Woodward, D.J. (1994a) Electrophysiological and pharmacological evidence for the role of the nucleus accumbens in cocaine self-administration in freely moving rats. *J. Neurosci.* 14: 1224–1244.

Chapin, J.K. and Woodward, D.J. (1983) Ethanol s effect on selective gathering of somatic sensory inputs to single cortical neurons. *Pharmacol. Biochem. Behav.* 18: 489–493.

Chapin, J.K. and Woodward, D.J. (1989) Ethanol withdrawal increases sensory responsiveness of single somatosensory cortical neurons in the awake behaving rat. *Alcohol Clin. Exp. Res.* 13: 8–14.

Cheun, J.E., Grigorenko, E.V. and Yeh, H.H. (1993) GABA-A receptor modulation by protein kinase-A (PKA) and beta-subunit expression in cerebellar Purkinje cells. *Soc. Neurosci. Abstr.* 19: 1183.

Cheun, J.E. and Yeh, H.H. (1992) Modulation of GABA-A receptor-activated current by norepinephrine in cerebellar Purkinje cells. *Neuroscience* 51: 951–960.

Cohen, S. (1984) Cocaine: acute medical and psychiatric complications. *Psychiatr. Ann.* 14: 747–749.

Cunningham, K.A. and Lakoski, J.M. (1988) Electrophysiological effects of cocaine and procaine on dorsal raphe serotonin neurons. *Eur. J. Pharmacol.* 148: 457–462.

Cunningham, K.A. and Lakoski, J.M. (1990) The interactions of cocaine with serotonin dorsal raphe neurons: single unit extracellular recording studies. *Neuropsychopharmacology* 3: 20–31.

Deadwyler, S.A., Bunn, T., and Hampson, R.E. (1996) Hippocampal ensemble activity during spatial delayed-non-match-to-sample performance in rats. *J. Neuroscience* 16: 354–372.

Deadwyler, S.A., Heyser, C.J., Michaelis, R.C. and Hampson, R.E. (1990) The effects of delta-9-THC on mechanisms of learning and memory. In: Erinoff, L. (ed.) *Neurobiology of drug abuse: learning and memory. NIDA Res. Monogr.* 97: 79–93.

Einhorn, L.C., Johansen, P.A. and White, F.J. (1988) Electrophysiological effects of cocaine in the mesoaccumbens dopamine system: studies in the ventral tegmental area. *J. Neurosci.* 8: 100–112.

Esposito, R.U., Motola, A.H.D. and Kornetsky, C. (1977) Cocaine: acute effects on reinforcement thresholds for self-stimulation behavior to the medial forebrain bundle. *Pharmacol. Biochem. Behav.* 8: 437–439.

Fischman, M.W., Schuster, C.R. and Krasnegor, N.A. (1977) Physiological and behavioral effects of intravenous cocaine in man. In: Ellinwood, E.H. and Kilbey, M.M. (eds.) *Cocaine and other stimulants.* New York: Plenum Press, pp. 647–664.

Foote, S.L., Bloom, F.E. and Aston-Jones, G. (1983) Nucleus locus coeruleus: new evidence of anatomical and physiological specificity. *Physiol. Rev.* 63: 844–914.

Foote, S.L., Freedman, R. and Oliver, A.P. (1975) Effects of putative neurotransmitters on neuronal activity in monkey auditory cortex. *Brain Res.* 86: 229–242.

Freud, S. (1974) Uber coca. In: Byck, R. (ed.) *Cocaine papers.* New York: Stonehill, pp. 47–74.

Fuster, J.M. (1989) *The prefrontal cortex.* Anatomy, physiology, and neuropsychology of the frontal lobe. New York, Raven Press.

Gawin, F.H. (1991) Cocaine addiction: psychology and neurophysiology. *Science* 251: 1580–1586.

Glowinski, J. and Axelrod, J. (1965) Effects of drugs on the uptake, release and metabolism of 3H-norepinephrine. *J. Pharmacol. Exp. Ther.* 149: 43–49.

Gold, M.S. (1992) Cocaine (and crack): clinical aspects. In: Lowinson, Ruiz, Millman and Langrod (eds.) *Substance abuse:* a comprehensive textbook. Baltimore: Williams and Wilkins, pp. 205–221.

Gold, M.S., Miller, N.S. and Jonas, J.M. (1992) Cocaine (and crack): neurobiology. In: Lowinson, Ruiz, Millman and Langrod (eds.) *Substance abuse:* a comprehensive textbook. Baltimore: Williams and Wilkins, pp. 222–235.

Hadfield, M.G., Mott, D.E.W. and Ismay, J.A. (1980) Cocaine: effects of in vivo administration on synaptosomal uptake of norepinephrine. *Biochem. Pharmacol.* 29: 1861–1886.

Henry, D.J. and White F.J. (1995) The persistence of behavioral sensitization to cocaine parallels enhanced inhibition of nucleus accumbens neurons. *J. Neurosci.* 15: 6287–6299.

Heyser, C.J., Hampson, R.E. and Deadwyler, S.A. (1993) Effects of Δ^9-tetrahydrocannabinol on delayed match to sample performance in rats: alteration in short-term memory associated with changes in task specific firing of hippocampas cells. *J. Pharmacol. Exp. Ther.* 264: 294–307.

Hoffer, B.J., Siggins, G.R. and Bloom, F.E. (1971) Studies on norepinephrine-containing afferents to Purkinje cells of rat cerebellum. II. Sensitivity of Purkinje cells to norepinephrine and related substances administered by microiontophoresis. *Brain Res.* 25: 522–534.

Hoffer, B.J., Siggins, G.R., Oliver, A.P. and Bloom, F.E. (1973) Activation of the pathway from locus coeruleus to rat cerebellar Purkinje neurons: pharmacological evidence of noradrenergic central inhibition. *J. Pharmacol. Exp. Ther.* 184: 553–569.

Jacobs, B.L. and Azmitia, E.C. (1992) Structure and function of the brain serotonin system. *Physiol. Rev.* 72: 165–229.

Jimenez-Rivera, C.A. and Waterhouse, B.D. (1991) Effects of systemically and locally applied cocaine on cerebrocortical neuron responsiveness to afferent synaptic inputs and glutamate. *Brain Res.* 546: 287–296.

Johanson, C.E., Balster, R.L. and Bonese, K. (1976) Self-administration of psychostimulant drugs: the effects of unlimited access. *Pharmacol. Biochem. Behav.* 4: 45–51.

Johanson, C.-E. and Fischman, M.W. (1989) The pharmacology of cocaine related to its abuse. *Pharmacol. Rev.* 41: 3–52.

Jones, B.E. and Moore, R.Y. (1977) Ascending projections of the locus coeruleus in the rat. II. Autoradiography study. *Brain Res.* 127: 23–53.

Kasamatsu, T. and Heggelund, P. (1982) Single cell responses in cat visual cortex to visual stimulation during iontophoresis of noradrenaline. *Exp. Brain Res.* 45: 317–327.

Koe, B.K. (1976) Molecular geometry of inhibition of the uptake of catecholamines and serotonin in synaptosomal preparations of rat brain. *J. Pharmacol. Exp. Ther.* 199: 649–661.

Kornetsky, C. and Esposito, R.U. (1981) Reward and detection thresholds for brain stimulation: dissociative effects of cocaine. *Brain Res.* 209: 496–500.

Kossl, M. and Vater, M. (1989) Noradrenaline enhances temporal auditory contrast and neuronal timing precision in the cochlear nucleus of the mustached bat. *J. Neurosci.* 9: 4169–4178.

Krnjevic, K. (1974) Vertebrate synaptic transmission. *Physiol. Rev.* 54: 418–540.

Kuhar, M.J., Ritz, M.C. and Boja, J.W. (1991) The dopamine hypothesis of the reinforcing properties of cocaine. *TINS* 14: 299–302.

Lal, H. and Chessick, R.D. (1965) Lethal effects of aggregation and electric shock in mice treated with cocaine. *Nature* 208: 295–296.

Lee, R.S., Smith, S.S., Chapin, J.K., Shimizu, N., Waterhouse, B.D., Maddux, B.N., and Woodward, D.J. (1995a) Effects of systemic and local ethanol on responses of rat cerebellar Purkinje neurons to iontophoretically applied norepinephrine and gamma-amino butyric acid. *Brain Res.* 687: 12–21.

Lee, R.S., Smith, S.S., Chapin, J.K., Waterhouse, B.D., Shimizu, N., Maddux, B.N., and Woodward, D.J. (1995b) Effects of systemic and local ethanol on responses of rat cerebellar Purkinje neurons to iontophoretically applied gamma-butyric acid. *Brain Res.* 687: 1–11.

Levitt, P. and Moore, R.Y. (1978) Noradrenaline neuron innervation of the neocortex in the rat. *Brain Res.* 139: 219–231.

Levitt, P. and Moore, R.Y. (1979) Origin and organization of brainstem catecholamine innervation in the rat. *J. Comp. Neurol.* 186: 525–528.

Lidov, H.G.W., Rice, F.L. and Molliver, M.E. (1978) The organization of brainstem catecholamine innervation tin the rat. *Brain Res.* 153: 577–584.

Lindvall, O., Bjorklund, A., Nobin, A. and Stenevi, U. (1974)The adrenergic innervation of the rat thalamus as revealed by the glyoxylic acid fluorescence method. *J. Comp. Neurol.* 154: 317–348.

Lowenstein, D.H., Massa, S.M., Rowbotham, M.C., Collins, S.D., McKinney, H.E. and Simon, R.P. (1987) Acute neurologic and psychiatric complications associated with cocaine abuse. *Am. J. Med.* 83: 841–845.

Markou, A., Weiss, F., Gold, L.H., Caine, S.B., Schulteis, G. and Koob, G.F. (1993) Animal models of drug craving. *Psychopharmacology* 112: 163–182.

McCormick, D.A. (1989) Cholinergic and noradrenergic modulation of thalamocortical processing. *TINS* 12: 215–221.

McCormick, D.A. and Prince, D.A. (1988) Noradrenergic modulation of firing pattern in guinea pig and cat thalamic neurons, in vitro. *J. Neurophysiol.* 59: 978–996.

McLean, J., Lin, C.-S. and Waterhouse, B.D. (1990) Effects of norepinephrine on velocity tuning and direction selectivity of cat visual cortical neurons. *Soc. Neurosci. Abstr.* 16: 1219.

Michael, A.J., West, M.O., Chapin, J.K., Waterhouse, B.D. and Woodward, D.J. (1985) Actions of d-amphetamine on cerebellar Purkinje cells in freely moving rats. *Soc. Neurosci. Abstr.* 11: 550.

Moises, H.C., and Woodward, D.J. (1980) Potentiation of GABA inhibitory action in cerebellum by locus coeruleus stimulation. *Brain Res.* 182: 327–344.

Moises, H.C., Burns, R.A., and Woodward, D.J. (1990) Modification of the visual response properties of cerebellar Purkinje neurons by norepinephrine. *Brain Res.* 514: 259–275.

Moises, H.C., Woodward, D.J., Hoffer, B.J. and Freedman, R. (1979) Interactions of norepinephrine with Purkinje cell responses to putative amino acid transmitters applied by microiontophoresis. *Exp. Neurol.* 64: 489–515.

Moore, R.Y. (1981) The anatomy of central serotonin neuron systems in the rat brain. In: Jacobs, B.L. and Gelperin, A. (eds.) *Serotonin neurotransmission and behavior.* Cambridge, MA: MIT Press, pp. 35–71.

Morrison, J.H. and Foote, S.L. (1986) Noradrenergic and serotonergic innervation of cortical, thalamic and tectal visual structures in old and new world monkeys. *J. Comp. Neurol.* 243: 117–138.

Morrison, J.H., Grzanna, R., Molliver, M.E. and Coyle, J.T. (1978) The distribution and orientation of noradrenergic fibers in neocortex of the rat: an immunofluorescence study. *J. Comp. Neurol.* 181: 17–40.

Mouradian, R.D., Sessler, F.M. and Waterhouse, B.D. (1991) Noradrenergic potentiation of excitatory transmitter action in cerebrocortical slices: evidence for mediation by an alpha-1 receptor-linked second messenger pathway. *Brain Res.* 546: 83–95.

Nelson, C.M., Hoffer, B.J., Chu, N.-S. and Bloom, F.E. (1973) Cytochemical and pharmacological studies on polysensory neurons in the primate frontal cortex. *Brain Res.* 62: 115–133.

Nicolelis, M.A.L., Lin, R.C.S., Woodward, D.J. and Chapin, J.K. (1993) Induction of immediate spatiotemporal changes in thalamic networks by peripheral block of ascending cutaneous information. *Nature* 361: 533–536.

Olpe, H.-R. (1981) The cortical projections of the dorsal raphe nucleus: some electrophysiological and pharmacological properties. *Brain Res.* 216: 61–71.

Parfitt, K.D., Freedman, R. and Bickford-Wimer, P.C. (1988) Electrophysiological effects of locally applied noradrenergic agents at cerebellar Purkinje neurons: receptor specificity. *Brain Res.* 462: 242–251.

Peterson, D. and Hardinge, J. (1967) The effect of various environmental factors on cocaine and ephedrine toxicity. *J. Pharmacol.* 19: 810–814.

Pitts, D.K. and Marwah, J. (1986) Electrophysiological effects of cocaine on central monoaminergic neurons. *Eur. J. Pharmacol.* 131: 95–98.

Pitts, D.K. and Marwah, J. (1987) Reciprocal pre- and postsynaptic actions of cocaine at a central noradrenergic synapse. *Exp. Neurol.* 98: 518–528.

Post, R.M. and Rose, H. (1976) Increasing effects of repetitive cocaine administration in the rat. *Nature* 260: 731–732.

Post, R.M., Weiss, S.R.B. and Pert, A. (1992) Sensitization and kindling effects of chronic cocaine administration. In: Lakoski, Galloway and White (eds.) *Cocaine:* pharmacology, *physiology and clinical strategies*. CRC Press, pp. 115–162.

Risner, M.E. and Jones, B.E. (1976) Role of noradrenergic and dopaminergic processes in amphetamine self-administration. *Pharmacol. Biochem. Behav.* 5: 477–482.

Roberts, D.C.S. and Koob, G.F. (1982) Description of cocaine self-administration following 6-hydroxydopamine lesions of the ventral tegmental area in rats. *Pharmacol. Biochem. Behav.* 17: 901–904.

Rogawski, M.A. and Aghajanian, G.K. (1980) Norepinephrine and serotonin: opposite effects on the activity of lateral geniculate neurons evoked by optic pathway stimulation. *Exp. Neurol.* 69: 678–684.

Ross, S.B. and Renyi, A.L. (1966) Uptake of some tritiated sympathomimetic amines by mouse brain cortex slices in vitro. *Acta Pharmacol. Toxicol.* 24: 56.

Salamone, J.D. (1992) Complex motor and sensorimotor functions of striatal and accumbens dopamine: involvement in instrumental behavior processes. *Psychopharmacology* 107: 160–174.

Sato, H. and Kayama, Y. (1983) Effects of noradrenaline applied iontophoretically on rat superior collicular neurons. *Brain Res. Bull.* 10: 453–457.

Scheel-Kruger, J., Braestrup, C. Nielsen, M., Golembiowski, R. and Mogilnicka, E. (1977) Cocaine: discussion of the role of dopamine in the biochemical mechanism of action. In: Ellinwood, E.H. and Kilbey, M.M. (eds.) *Cocaine and other stimulants*. New York: Plenum Press, pp. 373–407.

Schultz, W., Apicella, P., Romo, R. and Scarnati, E. (1994) Context-dependent activity in primate striatum reflecting past and future behavioral events. In: Houk, J.C.,David, J.L. and Beiser, D.G. (eds.) *Models of information processing in the basal ganglia*. Cambridge, MA: MIT Press,

Sessler, F.M., Cheng, J.-T. and Waterhouse, B.D. (1988) Electrophysiological actions of norepinephrine in rat lateral hypothalamus: I. norepinephrine-induced modulation of LH neuronal responsiveness to afferent synaptic inputs and putative neurotransmitters. *Brain Res.* 446: 77–89.

Smith, S.S. (1995) Sensor motor correlated discharge recorded from ensembles of cerebellar Purkinje cells varies across the estrous cycle of the rat. *J. Neurophysiol.* 74: 1095–1108.

Stewart, J., deWit, H. and Eikelboom, R. (1984) Role of unconditioned and conditioned drug effects in the self-administration of opiates and stimulants. *Psychol. Rev.* 91: 251–268.

Stone, T.W. (1973) Pharmacology of pyramidal tract cells in the cerebral cortex. *Naunyn Schmiedebergs*.

Ungerstedt, U. (1971) Stereotaxic mapping of the monoamine pathways in the rat brain. *Acta Physiol. Scand. Suppl.* 367: 1–48.

Wallach, M.B. and Gershon, S. (1971) A neuropsychopharmacological comparison of d-amphetamine, L-dopa and cocaine. *Neuropharmacology* 10: 743–752.

Waterhouse, B.D., Azizi, S.A., Burne, R.A. and Woodward, D.J. (1990) Modulation of rat cortical area 17 neuronal responses to moving visual stimuli during norepineph-

rine and serotonin microiontophoresis. *Brain Res.* 514: 276–292.

Waterhouse, B.D., Moises, H.C. and Woodward, D.J. (1980) Noradrenergic modulation of somatosensory cortical neuronal responses to iontophoretically applied putative neurotransmitters. *Exp. Neurol.* 69: 30–49.

Waterhouse, B.D., Moises, H.C. and Woodward, D.J. (1981) Alpha receptor mediated facilitation of somatosensory cortical neuronal responses to excitatory synaptic inputs and iontophoretically applied acetylcholine. *Neuropharmacology* 20: 907–920.

Waterhouse, B.D., Moises, H.C. and Woodward, D.J. (1986) Interaction of serotonin with somatosensory cortical neuronal responses to afferent synaptic inputs and putative transmitter substances. *Brain Res. Bull.* 17: 507–518.

Waterhouse, B.D., Moises, H.C., Yeh, H.H. and Woodward, D.J. (1982) Norepinephrine enhancement of inhibitory synaptic mechanisms in cerebellum and cerebral cortex: mediation by beta adrenergic receptors. *J. Pharmacol. Exp. Ther.* 221: 495–506.

Waterhouse, B.D., Stowe, Z.N., Jimenez-Rivera, C.A., Sessler, F.M. and Woodward, D.J. (1991) Cocaine actions in a central noradrenergic circuit: enhancement of cerebellar Purkinje neuron responses to iontophoretically applied GABA. *Brain Res.* 546: 297–309.

Waterhouse, B.D. and Woodward, D.J. (1980) Interaction of norepinephrine with cerebrocortical activity evoked by stimulation of somatosensory afferent pathways in the rat. *Exp. Neurol.* 67: 11–34.

West, M.D. and Woodward, D.J. (1984) A technique for microiontophoretic study of single neurons in the freely moving rat. *J. Neurosci. Methods* 11: 179–186.

White, F.J. (1990) Electrophysiological basis of the reinforcing effects of cocaine. *Behav. Pharmacol.* 1: 303–315.

White, F.J. and Wolf M.E. (1991) Psychomotor stimulants. In: Pratt, J.A. (ed.) *The biological bases of drug tolerance and dependence*. London: Academic, pp. 153–197.

Wilson, M.C., Bedford, J.A., Buelke, J. and Kibbe, A.H. (1976) Acute pharmacological activity of intravenous cocaine in the rhesus monkey. *Psychopharmacol. Comm.* 2: 251–262.

Wise, R.A. (1984) Neural mechanisms of the reinforcing actions of cocaine. In: *NIDA Research Monograph #50*. Washington, DC: DHHS, pp. 15–35.

Wise, R.A. and Bozarth, M.A. (1987. A psychomotor stimulant theory of addiction. *Psychol. Rev.* 94: 469–492.

Woods, J. (1977) Behavioral effects of cocaine in animals. In: *NIDA Research Monograph #13*. Washington, DC: DHHS, pp. 63– 96.

Woodward, D.J., Moises, H.C., Waterhouse, B.D., Hoffer, B.J. and Freedman, R. (1979) Modulatory actions of norepinephrine in the central nervous system. *Fed. Proc.* 38: 2109–2116.

Woodward, D.J., Moises, H.C., Waterhouse, B.D., Yeh, H.H. and Cheun, J.E. (1992) Modulatory actions of norepinephrine on neural circuits. In: Kito, S., Segawa, T. and Olsen, R.W. (eds.) *Neuroreceptor mechanisms in brain*. New York: Plenum Press, pp. 193–208.

PART IV

Treatment Applications

Drug Addiction and its Treatment: Nexus of Neuroscience and Behavior, edited by Bankole A. Johnson and John D. Roache. Lippincott–Raven Publishers, Philadelphia, © 1997.

16

Applying Learning and Conditioning Theory to the Treatment of Alcohol and Cocaine Abuse

Stephen T. Higgins

Departments of Psychiatry and Psychology, University of Vermont, Burlington, Vermont 05401

CONTEMPORARY APPROACHES TO DRUG ABUSE TREATMENT

Contemporary psychosocial treatments for drug abuse generally stem from two theoretically distinct orientations: the disease model and learning and conditioning models. The disease model assumes that drug abusers are predisposed, perhaps genetically, to seek out and use substances to excess once coming into contact with them. The disorder is deemed to be progressive, incurable, and ultimately fatal unless treated. Substance users and abusers are deemed to be qualitatively distinct. While the disease is considered incurable, it is considered manageable if the abuser ceases use of all mood altering substances. Hence, the fundamental goal of treatment is always total abstinence from all mood-altering substances, typically to be achieved and maintained through adherence to the 12 steps of recovery articulated by Alcoholics Anonymous (AA). Treatment can be obtained from professional counselors, who are often individuals in recovery from substance abuse themselves, or from participation in self-help programs like AA or Narcotics Anonymous (NA), in which substance abusers voluntarily assist each other with recovery efforts, or from some combination of the two.

The disease model is popular among clinicians and probably the most common approach to psychosocial treatment of drug abuse in the United States. Unfortunately, this approach has not been well researched and currently lacks strong empirical support (Miller et al., 1995).

Learning and conditioning models, which are the focus of this chapter, assume that drug use and abuse are learned response patterns that are governed by the same general principles of conditioning and learning as other behavior. Drug use and abuse are conceptualized as falling on a continuum ranging from patterns of little use and few problems to excessive use and many untoward effects including death, with the same principles of learning operating across the continuum. Treatment focuses on the systematic application of learning and conditioning principles to reduce or eliminate problematic substance use. Total abstinence or controlled use may be treatment goals depending on the characteristics and goals of the abuser. Treatment is professionally delivered, typically by individuals with postgraduate academic degrees. Learning and conditioning approaches are less popular among substance abuse clinicians and represent a minority approach to substance abuse treatment in the United States. In contrast to the disease model, learning and conditioning models have been relatively well researched and have extensive empirical support for their efficacy (Miller et al., 1995).

LEARNING AND CONDITIONING MODELS

Three areas of learning and conditioning theory have contributed significantly to contemporary treatments for substance abuse: operant conditioning, social learning theory, and respondent conditioning. Contributions from each of these areas to the treatment of alcohol and cocaine abuse are reviewed in this chapter. The treatment literature is more extensive for alcohol than cocaine abuse, but significant advances have been made in both areas. Learning-based treatments for abuse of opioids and nicotine are reviewed in Chapter 18 of this book. Before reviewing the literature on the efficacy of treatments derived from learning theory, brief descriptions of the conceptual framework of the operant, social learning theory, and respondent approaches to drug abuse are provided. These approaches should not be regarded as competing theoretical positions. Rather, they represent important scientific advances from specialized areas of basic behavioral research, each of which contributes to a comprehensive understanding of learning factors in the development, maintenance, and cessation of drug abuse. As is evident in the descriptions provided below, the influence of more than one conceptual approach is typically discernible in learning-based treatments. Also evident is the explicit emphasis of learning-based approaches on empiricism in both their conceptual foundations and in the evaluation of treatments emanating from them.

Operant Approach

An operant conditioning approach to drug abuse emphasizes the empirical observation that drugs of abuse function as reinforcers, that is, as stimulus events that when delivered closely following a response increase the probability that similar responses will be repeated in the future (Higgins and Morris, 1985). Interestingly, like food and sex, many drugs of abuse appear to be capable of func-

tioning as reinforcers with little or no training (i.e., unconditioned reinforcers). If drugs are reinforcers, then drug use represents an instance of operant behavior, i.e., behavior that is influenced by its environmental consequences. What is important about this observation is that it suggests that the extensive knowledge base that has been developed regarding other forms of operant behavior can be fruitfully applied to understanding and treating drug abuse.

Interestingly, most of the drugs that are abused by humans are also self-administered by laboratory animals (Griffiths et al., 1980). Neither a prior history of involuntary drug exposure nor physical dependence are necessary for these drugs to function as reinforcers and to maintain an ongoing pattern of drug self-administration. Effects of alterations in drug availability, drug dose, response requirement to obtain drug, and the effects of other environmental variables on drug ingestion are orderly and have generality across a variety of species, including humans, and across different types of drug dependence (Griffiths et al., 1980). Importantly, such commonalities across species and types of drug dependence support a theoretical position that the fundamental causes of drug use and abuse lie at the level of basic behavioral processes like reinforcement that are common across many species (Brady, 1981; Griffiths et al., 1980).

Like other reinforcers, the amount of behavioral control that drugs achieve depends on the environmental context in which they are available. Controlled laboratory studies conducted with nonhuman and human subjects have demonstrated, for example, that the availability of alternative, nondrug reinforcers can substantially reduce the acquisition and maintenance of drug use, especially when drug use reliably results in forfeiture of the nondrug reinforcer (Higgins, in press). That simple but important observation is the conceptual cornerstone for the operant clinical interventions described below. Systematically arranged aversive consequences can also suppress drug use (e.g., Grove and Schuster, 1974; Johanson, 1977). That observation can also be applied clinically, but use of aversive procedures may increase treatment dropout and hence has limitations in clinical settings (e.g., Stitzer et al., 1986). Reinforcing or aversive environmental consequences for drug use and abstinence can be arranged clinically through the use of arbitrary incentives (e.g., retail items, clinic privileges), by rearranging the environment to bring abusers into contact with naturalistic consequences (e.g., improved vocation and family/social relations), or a combination of those two strategies.

Social Learning Approach

Social learning theory emphasizes social factors involved in the acquisition and maintenance of drug use. Factors such as modeling, imitation, and various behavioral skills that are directly (e.g., controlled drinking) or indirectly (e.g., social skills) related to drug abuse are central components of this approach. A robust empirical literature exists supporting the influence of social factors on drug use, including cocaine and alcohol use (e.g., Babor, 1978; Caudill and Marlatt, 1975; Garlington and Dericco, 1977; Havassy et al., 1991; Higgins et al., 1994a). Drug abusers often report that they use substances to cope with unpleasant or stressful events, and such events have been reported to influence relapse (Marlatt, 1983). Hence, treatments based on this approach emphasize careful assessment and rearrangement of environmental factors, especially social factors, that affect the likelihood of drug use in conjunction with skills training to avoid or effectively manage those situations. This approach is more likely to emphasize the relation of thoughts and mood states to drug use than is an operant approach.

Respondent Approach

The respondent or Pavlovian model emphasizes the empirical observation that, in the same way that a neutral stimulus comes to elicit salivation in hungry dogs, neutral environmental events that predict the administration of a drug or the onset of drug withdrawal can acquire conditioned eliciting functions (Childress et al., 1992). These conditioned eliciting functions generally take two forms: First, they can take the form of the unconditioned response; that is, stimuli that predict drug administration or the onset of withdrawal can come to elicit conditioned responses that are similar to the unconditioned responses produced directly by the drug or induction of withdrawal. Second, they can take the form of drug-opposite compensatory responses; that is, stimuli that predict drug administration can come to elicit conditioned responses that are directly opposite to the unconditioned responses elicited by the drug. These two forms of conditioned drug and withdrawal effects have been demonstrated in nonhumans and humans in controlled experimental studies, and have been demonstrated with a variety of different abused drugs including alcohol and cocaine (e.g., Cooney et al., 1987; Ehrman et al, 1992; Goldberg and Schuster, 1970; O'Brien et al., 1977; Siegel, 1975). The most common effects of this type of conditioning in humans are conditioned psychophysiologic reactions, withdrawal signs and symptoms, and drug craving (Childress et al., 1992). Such conditioned responses are typically discussed as factors that may contribute to the high rates of relapse commonly observed in drug abuse treatment. Treatments based on this approach emphasize alteration of these conditioned relations via extinction procedures or by systematically teaching alternative responses to the drug-related stimuli (Childress, 1993; Childress et al., 1992).

LEARNING-BASED TREATMENTS FOR ALCOHOL ABUSE

A rather extensive empirical literature on learning-based treatments for problem drinking has developed over the past 25 years or more. *Problem drinking* is used here to refer to a continuum of alcohol-induced problems ranging from mild disruptions in functioning to severe dependence. An array of learning-based interventions has been developed. No empirical basis exists to assert that any one or combination of them is the superior intervention. Indeed, current thinking is that no one intervention should be expected to be effective with all problem drinkers. Hence, a more fruitful strategy might be to develop an empirical basis for systematically matching patient subgroups to optimal treatments (Miller and Hester, 1986). While matching is a plausible concept with some empirical support, its practical utility awaits thorough experimental evaluation. A multisite trial (Project MATCH, 1993) sponsored by the National Institute on Alcohol Abuse and Alcoholism is currently under way to examine the merits of this concept.

Only those interventions demonstrated to be efficacious in controlled clinical trials conducted with problem drinkers enrolled in treatment are reviewed in this chapter. Interested readers are referred to some promising learning-based primary and secondary prevention strategies for problem drinking that are not covered below as they fall outside the treatment focus of this chapter (e.g., Babor and Grant, 1991; Baer et al., 1992).

Community Reinforcement Approach (CRA)

CRA is a multicomponent treatment developed within an operant conceptual framework (Hunt and Azrin, 1973). CRA attempts to eliminate drinking by systematically altering naturalistic contingencies so that more reinforcement is available when the subject is abstinent and less during and immediately following drinking. Systematic interventions are used to improve marital/family relations, vocation, and social and recreational activities. The reason for including these different treatment components is to enrich the quality of the drinker's life when sober and to have him or her experience a loss of these presumably reinforcing circumstances when drinking recurs.

Three controlled studies have all supported the efficacy of this intervention. In the seminal study, 16 males admitted to a state hospital for alcoholism were divided into matched pairs and randomly assigned to receive CRA plus standard hospital care or the standard care alone (Hunt and Azrin, 1973). Following discharge from the hospital, CRA patients received a tapered schedule of counseling sessions beginning on a once weekly basis during the first month and then a once monthly basis across the next several months. During the 6-month follow-up period, patients who received CRA reported approximately 6- to 14-fold less time drinking, unemployed, away from their families, or institutionalized than control patients (Fig. 1).

With the goal of maintaining longer-term abstinence, CRA was subsequently refined to include disulfiram therapy that was monitored by a significant other, some additional crisis counseling after hospital discharge, and a "buddy" system wherein individuals in the alcoholic's neighborhood were available to give assistance with practical issues such as repairing cars (Azrin, 1976). Disulfiram is a medication that interferes with the breakdown of acetaldehyde (major metabolite of ethanol) (see Fuller, 1995). Hence, drinking while taking this medication causes a rapid accumulation of acetaldehyde, resulting in a very unpleasant reaction involving flushing, palpitations, dizziness, and nausea. This reaction is often sufficiently unpleasant to deter drinking, but maintaining compliance with the medication regimen can be difficult. That is the reason Azrin and colleagues developed procedures wherein significant others monitor and support medication compliance.

In a study examining the efficacy of this expanded CRA intervention, 20 matched pairs of alcoholic males were randomly assigned to receive CRA or the standard hospital program. During the 6 months after discharge, outcome in the CRA group was significantly better than controls replicating the earlier findings. During the 2 years following discharge, the CRA group spent 90% or more time abstinent; comparable data were not reported for controls. Compared to the prior CRA treatment package, this refined treatment involved less counseling time, and

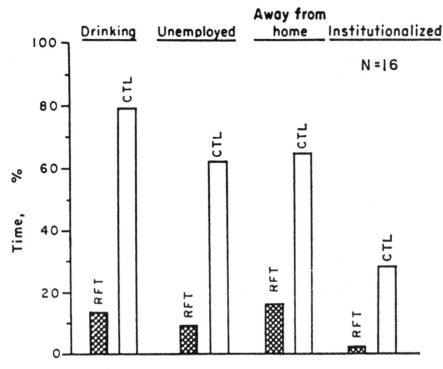

FIG. 1. A comparison of the dependent key measures for the reinforcement and control groups for the 6 months following hospital discharge: mean percentages of time spent drinking, unemployed, away from home, and institutionalized. (From Hunt and Azrin, 1973.)

longer-term abstinence appeared to be well maintained.

The third study was designed to dissociate the effects of monitored disulfiram therapy from the other aspects of CRA (Azrin et al., 1982). In a parallel-groups design, 43 alcoholic outpatients were randomly assigned to receive traditional treatment and traditional disulfiram therapy (no attempt to influence compliance), traditional therapy and disulfiram therapy involving significant others to monitor compliance, or CRA in combination with disulfiram therapy and significant-other monitoring. CRA in combination with disulfiram and compliance procedures produced the best outcome, disulfiram in combination with compliance procedures but without CRA produced intermediate results, and the poorest results were observed with the traditional treatment and disulfiram therapy. An interesting interaction was noted when the results were analyzed according to patients' marital status.

Married patients did equally well with the full CRA treatment package or disulfiram and compliance procedures alone. Only single subjects appeared to need the package of CRA treatment and monitored disulfiram to achieve abstinence, perhaps because they lacked the level of social support for abstinence that was available to married individuals.

Lastly, this same group examined the effects of adding a social club to a standard regimen of outpatient counseling for alcoholism (Mallams et al., 1982). The social club was designed to have the social atmosphere and presumably the social reinforcement associated with bars but without alcohol. Individuals had to be abstinent to attend. Forty alcoholics were randomly assigned to receive systematic encouragement to attend the social club or to a control group that was informed about the existence of the club but received no encouragement to attend. Efforts also were made to socially integrate the experimental subjects with other club members when they did attend. Similar efforts apparently were not made with controls. There were no significant differences between the treatment groups at baseline, but at 3-month follow-up only the experimental group showed significant improvements from intake on measures of quantity-frequency of drinking, behavioral impairment, and time spent in heavy-drinking situations.

The outcomes achieved with CRA in severely dependent alcoholics makes it an important addition to learning-based treatments for problem drinking. However, because all of the published studies supporting the efficacy of this approach were conducted by a single group of investigators and in a rural area of Illinois, questions remain about its generality to other settings and in the hands of other investigators. A replication effort with alcoholics is currently under way in Albuquerque, New Mexico, which should help to evaluate these questions. Also, as is described below, CRA in combination with an incentive program has been adapted as an effective outpatient treatment for cocaine dependence (Higgins et al., 1991, 1993, 1994b), although the efficacy of CRA independent of the contingency-management procedures has not yet been established in that research effort.

Behavioral Self-Control Training

Behavioral self-control training is based primarily on the social learning theory approach. The conceptual position is that drinking patterns are, at least in part, learned. Hence, individuals with problematic drinking patterns should be able to learn to abstain or develop a moderate, problem-free drinking style given the necessary skills and alterations in their drinking environment. That position has a great deal of empirical support, with the important qualification that controlled drinking is not an appropriate treatment goal in those with severe alcohol dependence (Foy et al., 1984; Miller et al., 1992).

This treatment teaches patients to systematically monitor their drinking, set limits on drinking frequency and quantity, use specific strategies to control drinking, reward successes in achieving goals, analyze and learn from failed efforts, and develop alternative means for obtaining some of the social and interpersonal benefits previously derived from drinking. It can be delivered in individual or group formats and by professional therapists or client-guided treatment manuals. Trials comparing these modes of treatment delivery have demonstrated significant clinical improvements with no significant differences related to the mode of treatment delivery (Miller and Baca, 1983; Miller and Taylor, 1980).

Among less-impaired individuals, outcome in behavioral self-control training does not appear to be influenced by whether the treatment goals are problem-free drinking or total abstinence. In a controlled trial examining this issue, subjects were randomly assigned to receive behavioral self-control training with treatment goals of moderate drinking or total abstinence (Sanchez-Craig et al., 1984). Approximately 75% of subjects in both treatment groups were problem-free drinkers or abstinent at 2-year follow-up with no significant differences in outcome resulting from the different treatment goals.

A series of experimental studies reported across a 10-year period suggest that approximately 20% to 70% of clinical samples can learn to drink moderately and that treatment gains can be maintained for up to 2 years after treatment termination (Miller and Baca, 1983; Sanchez-Craig et al., 1984; Vogler et al., 1975, 1977). Outcomes beyond 2 years appear more modest. Miller and colleagues (1992) conducted a follow-up study of 140 patients who received behavioral self-control treatment. Follow-ups conducted 3.5 to 8 years posttreatment with 99 of the originally treated patients revealed that 14% were asymptomatic drinkers (i.e., without clinical problems associated with drinking), 23% were totally abstinent, 22% were clinically improved but still impaired drinkers, 35% were unremitted problem drinkers, and 5% were deceased. Asymptomatic drinking was most likely to be achieved by those without severe alcohol dependence or a family history of alcoholism.

A limitation of this research literature is that few of the aforementioned studies have quantified the direct contribution of behavioral self-control training to the observed outcomes. That is, few of the clinical trials compared behavioral self-control training versus a no-treatment or standard-treatment control group. One such trial compared behavioral self-control training to drunk driver education or no-treatment control in a group of driving-while-intoxicated (DWI) offenders (Brown, 1980). The controlled drinking group showed a 52% reduction from pretreatment baseline in amount of drinking reported at 12-month follow-up compared with a 28% reduction and 14% increase in drinking in the standard education and untreated control groups, respectively, providing a clear, quantitative demonstration of the efficacy of this treatment intervention.

Behavioral self-control training is a well-researched and effective intervention for curtailing problem drinking. More thorough quantification of the contribution of the therapy to long-term outcomes is an important issue to address in future studies.

Skills Training

Researchers operating primarily from the social learning theory approach have examined whether training in social and problem-solving skills improves outcome in problem drinkers. The majority of trials in this area have examined skills training as an adjunct to inpatient treatment, and have focused on assertiveness and related social skills, as well as general problem-solving skills. Positive outcomes have been reported both when patients were specifically selected because they exhibited certain skill deficits (Ferrell and Galassi, 1981) and when training was done with general alcoholic samples (Eriksen et al., 1986).

In a seminal study on this topic, 40 inpatient, male alcoholics were randomly assigned to an eight-session skills-training group focused on drinking-related problem solving, or to a discussion control condition in which similar topics were discussed but no specific training was provided (Chaney et al., 1978). During a 1-year follow-up period, the skills group as compared with the combined control groups (which did not differ from each other) reported on average fourfold fewer drinks taken, sixfold fewer days drunk (11 versus 64 days during the 12-month follow-up), and a ninefold reduction in duration of drinking episodes (averaging 5 versus 44 days) (Table 1).

Assertiveness training can also improve outcome. An important study on this topic was conducted with 32 alcoholics residing in an inpatient program who had low baseline scores on an assertiveness scale (Oei and Jackson, 1982). Patients were matched on several relevant characteristics and assigned to one of four treatment groups: (1) skills training, (2) cognitive restructuring, (3) a combination of skills training and cognitive restructuring, or (4) a control group consisting of traditional supportive therapy. All of the experimental groups had better outcomes than the control group on measures of assertiveness and drinking during 1-year follow-up, but the combined group fared best. During the week preceding the 12-month follow-up, mean ethanol ingestion levels in the control, social skills, cognitive restructuring, and combined groups were 34 oz, 17 oz, 11 oz, and 5 oz, respectively.

One of the few negative trials on this topic compared problem-solving skills training to covert sensitization (i.e., pairing of imagined unpleasant scenes with imagery of drinking) and a discussion control in chronic alcoholics residing in a halfway house (Sanchez-Craig and Walker, 1982). No outcome differences were discerned across the three treatment groups at 6-, 12-, or 18-month follow-ups. Compared with levels observed during treatment, a marked deterioration was noted during follow-up in the ability of subjects assigned to the skills-training group to recall the problem-solving strategies they were taught. Whether those decrements in retention of the skills taught account for the failure to discern

TABLE 1. Posttreatment adjustment: 12–Month Outcome[a]

Measure	Group[b]	Mean	S.D.	df	t
Days of controlled drinking	1	4.9	17.8		
	2	1.2	2.6		
Days drunk	1	11.1	14.3		
	2	64.0	88.3	37	-2.21*
Total no. drinks	1	399.8	507.8		
	2	1,592.8	2,218.4	37	-2.01*
Average drinking period length	1	5.1	6.9		
	2	44.0	62.2	37	-2.32*
Days hospitalized	1	44.6	96.9		
	2	28.2	42.0	37	.74
Days abstinent	1	298.6	100.8		
	2	266.7	101.8	37	.94
Days employed[c]	1	204.0	132.0		
	2	178.7	124.5	32	.55
Weekly aftercare meetings	1	29.8	18.8		
	2	24.2	17.8	37	.93

[a]From Chaney, et al., 1978.
[b]Group 1 (n =14) subjects received skill training; group 2 (n = 25) subjects were in the discussion or non-addi-tional-treatment groups. One group 1 subject died after 5 months of an alcohol-aggravated illness following a 2-month period of sustained drinking.
[c]Five subjects were retired or pensioned (2 in group 1 and 3 in group 2).
*p <.05

positive effects at follow-up is unclear, but seems plausible.

A trial conducted by Kadden, Cooney, and colleagues suggests that particular subgroups of problem drinkers may respond differently to skills training (Cooney et al., 1991; Kadden et al., 1989). Ninety-six male and female problem drinkers who recently completed an inpatient treatment were randomly assigned to receive coping skills training or interactional therapy during aftercare. Interactional therapy examines interpersonal relations and pathology by exploring interactions and feelings that arise during group therapy sessions. Both treatment groups improved on measures of drinking and social stability, with no significant differences discernible between them. Interestingly, in a post-hoc examination of possible interactions between treatment groups and patient characteristics, coping skills therapy was significantly more effective than interactional therapy for patients higher in psychiatric severity (measured by the Addiction Severity Index Psychological Scale) and sociopathy (measured by the California Psychological Inventory Socialization Scale). Interactional therapy, on the other hand, was more effective than sills training for patients with lower psy-

chopathology as well as those who scored higher on neuropsychological impairment (derived from several scales). The same treatment-outcome interactions were still evident at a 2-year follow-up (Cooney et al., 1991). Prospective trials are needed to assess the reliability of these interesting observations.

In summary, skills training can produce significant and enduring improvements in drinking and social stability. More needs to be learned regarding the efficacy of different types of skills training on outcome and the merits of systematically matching skills-training interventions to particular skill deficits as well other patient characteristics.

Behavioral Marital Counseling

Three recent well-controlled studies have assessed the effects of behavioral marital therapy on treatment outcomes with problem drinkers. McCrady and colleagues (1986, 1991) randomly assigned 45 patients to one of three groups: (1) minimal spouse involvement, which consisted of individual counseling with the spouse present for support; (2) alcohol-focused spouse involvement, in which spouses learned specific therapeutic skills such as how to reinforce abstinence and decrease behaviors that might occasion drinking; and (3) alcohol behavioral marital therapy, which involved all of the above elements plus skills training on how to improve other aspects of the marriage. No significant differences emerged between the three groups in overall abstinence levels either during or after treatment. However, in time-trend analysis the percentage of days abstinent decreased steadily across 18 months in the minimal and alcohol-focused spouse involvement groups, but was reversed in the behavioral marital therapy group during the second half of the follow-up period. Those between-group differences were statistically significant, and based on graphic display appeared to represent approximately 10% to 15% more abstinent days in the behavioral marital therapy group during the second half of the follow-up period. Several measures of marital and personal adjustment also indicated better outcomes during follow-up with behavioral marital therapy.

A second trial on this topic (O'Farrell et al., 1985, 1992) involved 36 couples in which husbands had recently begun individual alcoholism treatment and received a prescription for disulfiram. Couples were randomly assigned to a no-marital-therapy control group, a behavioral couples group, or an interactional couples group. Couples in the behavioral group signed a contract regarding disulfiram compliance, and received counseling to increase positive family activities and improve communication. Couples in the interactional group primarily shared feelings about their relationship during therapy sessions. Behavioral couples therapy produced better outcomes on marital adjustment ratings than the other conditions, but there were no significant differences in abstinence among the three groups during treatment or follow-up.

A more recent study by O'Farrell and colleagues (1993) suggests that adding posttreatment relapse-prevention maintenance sessions to behavioral marriage counseling can improve outcomes in this treatment approach.

Relapse prevention is based on social learning theory and teaches patients skills to recognize high-risk situations for resuming drug use, to implement alternative coping strategies when confronted with high-risk events, and to apply strategies to prevent a full-blown relapse should an episode of drug use occur (Marlatt and Gordon, 1985). Fifty-nine couples, defined by the inclusion of an alcoholic husband, were randomly assigned to receive or not receive 15 maintenance sessions during a 12-month follow-up period. Assignment to the maintenance and no-maintenance groups occurred upon completion of 5 months of weekly behavioral marital therapy that included a contract for disulfiram compliance. Abstinence improved significantly from pretreatment levels in both groups, but couples who received the maintenance sessions reported significantly greater abstinence and greater use of the disulfiram contract during follow-up than those who did not receive the extra sessions. Improvements in marital adjustment outcomes during follow-up as compared with pretreatment also tended to favor the group that received extra sessions.

Two studies have examined the use of behavioral procedures involving spouses to increase disulfiram compliance, with one reporting positive (Azrin et al., 1982) and the other negative (Keane et al., 1984) outcomes. The studies differed along numerous dimensions, making it difficult to speculate on what might account for the different outcomes. However, the important potential practical benefits of this intervention, as illustrated by the Azrin et al. (1982) study (described in the CRA section above), make this an important area for further research.

In summary, the results obtained using behavioral marital therapy in the treatment of problem drinking provide reason for cautious optimism. The magnitude of improvements in during-treatment abstinence has not been impressive. However, behavioral marital therapy with and without the addition of relapse-prevention maintenance sessions may prevent relapse. Preventing relapse is of obvious and fundamental importance and those observations merit further study, as do the observations of Azrin et al. (1982) regarding the potential efficacy of spouse-assisted disulfiram compliance procedures.

Cue-Exposure Therapy

Cue-exposure therapy involves systematically exposing subjects to stimuli previously associated with drinking while preventing alcohol self-administration in an attempt to extinguish the drinking-related conditioned responses. In several studies conducted with alcoholics residing in controlled environments, exposure training in the form of holding a glass of the subject's favorite drink without consuming it (Rankin et al., 1983) or refraining from drinking after receiving a priming dose of alcohol (Laberg and Ellertsen, 1987) resulted in less desire to drink or difficulty turning down drinks in later sessions relative to control subjects. While these results suggest potential clinical applicability, to my knowledge no trials have been reported demonstrating the clinical efficacy of these procedures outside of controlled settings (Drummond et al., 1990).

LEARNING-BASED TREATMENTS FOR COCAINE ABUSE

While newer, and less extensively reported, than the interventions on problem drinking, effective learning-based interventions for cocaine abuse have been developed as well. These studies initially focused exclusively on treatment retention and during-treatment abstinence, but longer-term follow-up results have been reported more recently (Carroll et al., 1994a,b; Higgins et al., 1995). The treatments described below are those that have been demonstrated to be efficacious in controlled clinical trials.

Contingency Management

Contingency-management procedures are based on the operant approach and attempt to systematically apply environmental consequences to drug use and abstinence. Because drug use, especially illicit drug use, is often a clandestine activity, consequences are delivered contingent on an objective marker like urinalysis results rather than the drug-taking behavior itself. The efficacy of contingent reinforcing consequences for increasing cocaine abstinence when administered in combination with minimal or intensive counseling components has been demonstrated in a series of controlled trials.

Higgins and colleagues (1991, 1993, 1994b) have been investigating the efficacy of an outpatient treatment combining contingency-management procedures and CRA (described above). The primary contingency-management procedure used in this treatment is one in which patients earn vouchers exchangeable for retail items contingent on documentation via urinalysis testing that they have recently abstained from cocaine. The voucher system is in effect for weeks 1 to 12 of treatment, whereas a $1.00 state lottery ticket is awarded for each cocaine-negative urinalysis test during treatment weeks 13 to 24. The value of the vouchers increases with each consecutive cocaine-negative specimen delivered, and cocaine-positive specimens reset the value of vouchers back to their initial level. Those who are continuously abstinent (all cocaine negative urine tests) could earn the equivalent of $997.50 during weeks 1 to 12 and $24 during weeks 13 to 24. This translates to an average maximum earning of $6.08 per day for those who are continuously abstinent from cocaine; in practice, the average earning has been approximately $3.50 per day. As was noted in more detail above, CRA attempts to systematically alter the drug user's environment so that reinforcement density from nondrug sources is relatively high during sobriety and low during drug use.

Two trials examined the efficacy of this treatment by comparing it with standard outpatient drug counseling based on the disease-model approach to drug dependence and the 12 steps of recovery (Higgins et al., 1991, 1993). The first trial was 12 weeks in duration, while the second trial was 24 weeks. Both treatments were delivered by experts in the respective approaches during twice weekly sessions during weeks 1 to 12 of treatment and, in the randomized trial only, once weekly sessions during weeks 13 to 24. Patients were assigned to the two treatments as consecutive admissions in the first trial and randomly in the second trial. In both trials, the behavioral treatment retained patients significantly longer and documented significantly longer periods of continuous cocaine abstinence than standard counseling. For example, in the randomized trial, 58% of patients assigned to the behavioral treatment completed 24 weeks versus 11% of those assigned to standard counseling. Further, 68% and 42% of patients in the behavioral group achieved 8 and 16 weeks of documented, continuous cocaine abstinence versus 11% and 5% of those in the counseling group.

In a third trial conducted with this treatment, patients were randomly assigned to receive the behavioral treatment with or without the voucher program (Higgins et al., 1994b). Treatment was 24 weeks in duration and the voucher versus no-voucher difference was in effect during weeks 1 to 12 only. Both treatment groups were treated the same after week 12. This study was the first in a series of studies planned to dismantle this multicomponent treatment to determine which components actively contribute to outcome. Vouchers significantly improved treatment retention and cocaine abstinence; 75% of patients in the group with vouchers completed 24 weeks of treatment versus 40% in the group without vouchers, and the average duration of continuous cocaine abstinence documented was 11.7 ± 2.0 weeks in the former versus 6.0 ± 1.5 in the latter (Fig. 2). At the end of the 24-week treatment period, significant decreases from pretreatment scores were observed in both treatment groups on the Addiction Severity Index (ASI) family/social and alcohol scales, with no differences between the groups. Both groups also decreased on the ASI drug scale, but the magnitude of change was significantly greater in the voucher than the no-voucher group. Only the voucher

group showed a significant improvement on the ASI psychiatric scale.

Follow-up results at 6, 9, and 12 months after treatment entry were recently reported from the two randomized controlled trials comparing the CRA plus vouchers treatment to drug abuse counseling and to CRA without vouchers (Higgins et al., 1995). In the trial comparing CRA with vouchers to drug abuse counseling, significantly greater cocaine abstinence was documented via urinalysis at 9- and 12-month follow-ups in the former; both groups showed comparable and significant improvements on the ASI. In the trial comparing CRA with and without vouchers, there was a nonsignificant trend toward greater cocaine abstinence in urinalysis testing at the 12-month follow-up in the group with vouchers, the magnitude of improvement throughout follow-up on the ASI Composite Drug Scale was significantly larger in the voucher group, and only the voucher group showed significant improvement on the ASI Psychiatric Scale. Overall, comparisons during the trials and follow-up support the efficacy of the CRA with vouchers treatment throughout the year after treatment entry.

The studies by Higgins and colleagues were conducted in a clinic located in a small metropolitan area with almost exclusively Caucasian patients, raising important questions about the generality of these findings to inner-city and minority cocaine abusers. A recent, well-controlled study conducted with cocaine-abusing methadone-maintenance patients in a clinic located in Baltimore extended the generality of the voucher program to inner-city, intravenous cocaine abusers many of whom (49%) were African-American (Silverman et al., 1996). During a 12-week study, patients in the experimental group ($n = 19$) received vouchers exchangeable for retail items contingent on cocaine-negative urinalysis tests. A matched control group ($n = 18$) received the vouchers according to a schedule that was yoked (i.e., matched) to the experimental group but not contingent on urinalysis results. Both groups received a standard form of outpatient drug and alcohol abuse counseling. Cocaine use was substantially lower in

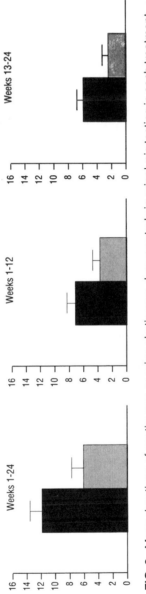

FIG. 2. Mean durations of continuous cocaine abstinence documented via urinalysis testing in each treatment group during weeks 1–24, 1–12, and 13–24 of treatment. *Solid bars* indicate the voucher group; *shaded bars,* the no-voucher group. Error bars represent ± S.E.M. (From Higgins et al., 1994b.)

the experimental than the control group. For example, 47% of patients in the contingent reinforcement group achieved 7 or more weeks of continuous cocaine abstinence versus none in the control group (Fig. 3). Among patients receiving vouchers for cocaine abstinence, those with less baseline cocaine use achieved greater abstinence during the intervention.

Additional promising results on the efficacy of this voucher program to inner-city populations come from a recent study conducted in methadone detoxification program in San Francisco (Tusel et al., 1995). One hundred subjects enrolled in a 180-day detox were randomly assigned to receive an adaptation of the voucher program described above or usual care. Up to $755 could be earned for abstinence from all illicit drugs and negative blood alcohol levels (BALs) in the voucher group. Significantly greater periods of sustained co-

caine abstinence were observed in the voucher group, for a mean cost of $145 per subject.

Another trial investigating the efficacy of contingency-management procedures for reducing cocaine abuse in methadone-maintenance patients assessed the reinforcing effects of methadone take-homes in 54 newly admitted maintenance patients randomly assigned to receive take-homes under contingent or noncontingent conditions (Stitzer et al., 1992). Medication take-home privileges involve dispensing an extra dose of methadone to patients so that they may ingest it at home on the following day rather than making the daily trip to the clinic. Take-homes were earned contingent on abstinence from supplemental drugs (cocaine and benzodiazepines) in the experimental group, while those in the control group received take homes noncontingently (i.e., independent of urinalysis results).

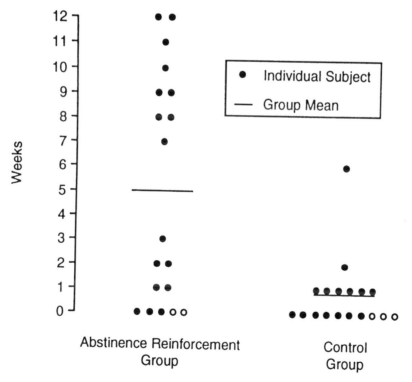

FIG. 3. Longest duration of sustained cocaine abstinence achieved during the 12-week voucher condition. Each point represents data for an individual subject and the lines represent group means. The 19 patients in the reinforcement condition are displayed in the left column and the 18 control patients in the right. *Open circles* represent patients who dropped out of the study early.

The conditional probability that a patient would improve on drug use was 2.5 times greater for the contingent as compared with the noncontingent study condition, whereas the probability of worsening on the drug use measure was twice as great for the noncontingent as for the contingent group. Overall, 32% of contingent patients achieved sustained periods of abstinence during the intervention (mean = 9.4 weeks; range = 5–15 weeks). The beneficial effect of contingent take-home delivery was replicated within the group of noncontingent patients who switched to the contingent intervention after their 6-month evaluation in the main study (partial crossover design). In this case, 28% improved substantially and achieved an average of 15.5 drug-free weeks. In both the main study and the partial crossover, lower rates of drug-positive urine specimens during baseline conditions (i.e., before intervention) predicted improvement under the contingent take-home program, and patients using cocaine or benzodiazepines were equally likely to improve.

A study by McLellan and colleagues (1993) illustrates how contingency-management procedures can be combined with other clinical services to reduce cocaine and illicit opiate use in methadone maintenance patients. Male veterans ($n = 92$) were randomly assigned to receive methadone with minimal, standard, or enhanced counseling services. The minimal counseling group received perfunctory contact with therapists focused on satisfying routine requests for information transfer to outside agencies, requests for methadone dose changes, and enforcement of program rules. These patients could receive medication take-homes based on employment but independent of urinalysis results. Standard and enhanced care patients met routinely with counselors to discuss their drug use and life adjustment issues. Treatment for these groups included contingencies targeted on drug use; that is, take-home medication privileges could be earned by employed clients who were also drug free. Further, the number of counseling sessions per week was increased for those submitting drug-positive urine specimens. A primary outcome examined during the 24-week study was the percent of patients meeting predetermined criteria for treatment failure. The criteria included unremitting illicit drug use and/or multiple emergency situations requiring immediate health care. Sixty-nine percent of patients receiving methadone with minimal counseling met these criteria and were transferred to standard care within the first 12 weeks of the study. In contrast, only 41% of the standard counseling patients and 19% of the enhanced counseling patients met treatment failure criteria during the course of the study. Further, 90% to 100% of patients in standard and enhanced care were able to sustain 8 or more weeks of abstinence from cocaine during the study as compared with only 30% of clients in the minimal services condition (Fig. 4). While the reductions in cocaine use in the enhanced and standard groups in this study cannot be attributed to the contingency-management intervention per se, they demonstrate the efficacy of a combination of contingency-management and other services in reducing cocaine use.

I am aware of one published report wherein contingent reinforcement did not reduce cocaine use in patients enrolled in methadone maintenance (Magura et al., 1988). In a within-subject (A-B-A) study design, 19 patients with cocaine-positive urinalysis results could earn a weekly medication take-home contingent on a week of verified abstinence. Four of the 19 (21%) patients reduced their cocaine use compared to the preintervention period while the others showed no change. Whether cocaine use during the postintervention period returned to preintervention levels in the four subjects who appeared to respond to treatment, which would have addressed whether those subjects were responders, was not reported. However, for the group as a whole, there were no significant differences between the preintervention, intervention, and postintervention conditions in rates of cocaine-positive urinalysis results.

Clearly, not all individuals decrease their cocaine use when provided the opportunity to earn incentives contingent on abstinence. Thus, it is important to identify reliable pre-

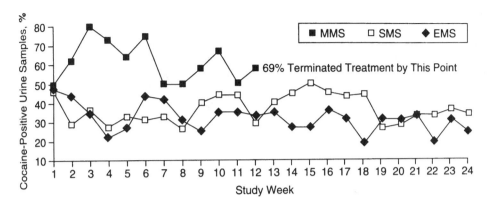

FIG. 4. Percentages of cocaine positive urine samples, per treatment group, by study week. The treatment groups are as follows: minimum methadone services (MMS), standard methadone services (SMS), and enhanced methadone services (EMS). (From McLellan et al., 1993.)

dictors of treatment response as well as conditions that might facilitate the efficacy of contingent incentives. Some progress has been made in that direction, although more is needed. Stitzer et al.'s (1992) and Silverman et al. (1996) results suggest that subjects with less baseline drug use are more likely to benefit from contingent incentives, and the relatively large response in the McLellan et al. (1993) study suggests that combining contingencies with more than just minimal counseling might increase the proportion of patients who respond.

Overall, seven controlled trials have been reported supporting the efficacy of treating cocaine abuse using contingency-management procedures in combination with minimal and intensive counseling, and there has been one negative report. Follow-up results have been reported only for use of contingency-management procedures in combination with CRA counseling, and those results were positive. At this time, this approach has solid empirical support as an effective clinical intervention for reducing cocaine abuse.

Skills Training

Skills training focused on relapse prevention (RP) has been demonstrated in controlled clin-

ical trials to be efficacious as an outpatient intervention for cocaine dependence (Carroll, 1991, 1994a,b). As was noted above, RP teaches patients to recognize high-risk situations for drug use, to implement alternative coping strategies when confronted with high-risk events, and to apply strategies to prevent a full-blown relapse should an episode of drug use occur (Marlatt and Gordon, 1985). The initial trial examined 42 cocaine-dependent patients who were randomly assigned to RP or interpersonal psychotherapy (IP), which teaches strategies for improving social and interpersonal problems. Both treatments were delivered by professional therapists during weekly sessions. Retention generally was better with RP than IP throughout treatment, but a statistically significant difference was observed only at week 4 of the 12-week trial, when 86% of RP patients remained in treatment versus 57% of IP patients. Nonsignificant trends were evident in the same direction for continuous cocaine abstinence, with 57% of those who received RP versus 33% of those who received IP achieving 3 or more weeks of continuous cocaine abstinence during the 12-week trial.

In the second trial reported by this group, RP and clinical management were compared in a two-by-two design in which patients also received either desipramine or placebo (Carroll et al., 1994a); 139 patients were randomized to one of four treatment groups (RP plus desipramine, RP plus placebo, clinical management plus desipramine, and case management plus placebo). Data analyses were based on 110 patients who received at least two sessions of their respective treatments. Clinical management was designed to provide a nonspecific therapeutic relationship and an opportunity for medical personnel to monitor patients' clinical status. Both treatments were delivered in weekly therapy sessions during the 12 weeks of treatment. All treatment groups improved from pretreatment to posttreatment on measures of cocaine use and the ASI drug, alcohol, family/social, and psychiatric scales; however, there were no significant main effects for psychosocial (RP versus clinical management) or drug treatment (desipramine versus placebo). An interesting retrospective analysis suggested outcome differences as a function of whether patients reported using high (>4.5 g) or low (1–2.5 g) amounts of cocaine per week at pretreatment. With RP, high-use patients were retained for a significantly greater mean number of sessions than low-use patients (8.6 versus 6.0). For clinical management, there was a nonsignificant trend in the opposite direction; that is, mean number of sessions with high-severity patients was less than with low-severity patients (6.1 versus 8.0). Comparable, nonsignificant trends in the same directions were noted when continuous cocaine abstinence in the two treatments was analyzed as a function of severity of cocaine use.

Interestingly, in a follow-up study conducted during the year after treatment termination, RP patients reported significantly higher levels of cocaine abstinence than patients who received clinical management (Carroll et al., 1994b). Those differences could not be confirmed by urinalysis testing, but certainly follow logically from the content of the RP treatment. This is a very interesting and promising finding that should be thoroughly explored in future trials.

One negative trial has been reported (Wells et al., 1994). One hundred ten cocaine abusers were alternately assigned to RP or twelve-step based counseling. No differences between the two groups were discerned in retention or cocaine use during the twenty-four week outpatient intervention or six-month follow-up.

In summary, RP offers promise as an effective outpatient treatment for cocaine dependence, although further studies will be needed to determine its reliability in producing positive during-treatment and longer-term outcomes. The initial trial by Carroll et al. (1991) supported its efficacy during treatment, but follow-up data were not reported. A subsequent trial (Carroll et al., 1994a,b) supported its efficacy at 1-year follow-up, but not during the treatment period. Finally, one trial failed to support its efficacy during treatment or follow-up (Wells et al., 1994).

Other Learning-Based Treatments

Three other learning-based treatment approaches appear promising based on preliminary results: active cue exposure (Childress, 1993), coping skills training (Rohsenow, 1993), and neurobehavioral treatment (Rawson, 1993). The first two treatments are designed to serve as adjuncts to more comprehensive treatments, while the third is a comprehensive treatment. Active cue exposure teaches patients to engage in coping behaviors (e.g., relaxation) when confronted with environmental stimuli that elicit a conditioned drug response (e.g., craving) or otherwise have previously set the occasion for drug use. Active cue exposure represents a departure from the passive extinction procedures that were tried earlier and shown to be ineffective in treating cocaine abuse (Childress, 1993; Childress et al., 1992). Coping skills training is similar to active cue exposure, but is designed to teach specific drug refusal and social skills deemed important for accessing alternatives to drug use and for coping with events that place the patient at high risk for drug use. As was noted above, this treatment emanates primarily from the social learning theory approach and has been demonstrated to be effective in treating alcohol abuse. The neurobehavioral treatment emphasizes many of the elements described above in relapse prevention and coping-skills training in an attempt to provide the user with the skills necessary to abstain from cocaine use and avoid relapse. As such, it falls within the social learning theory approach. The neuro- prefix is included to note special attention during the treatment process to difficulties that may arise as a function of neurobiologic changes that accompany initial and sustained abstinence from cocaine following chronic use.

Each of these treatments address important areas of concern or interest in the quest to develop empirically based and effective treatments for cocaine abuse. Additionally, each is currently being evaluated in one or more controlled clinical trials, with preliminary results suggesting they are effective.

Obviously, much remains to be learned about treatment of cocaine abuse, but, considered together, the learning-based treatments represent a promising start. That optimism is bolstered by the fact that most of the treatments that appear promising with cocaine abuse have been previously demonstrated to be efficacious in the treatment of other forms of substance abuse.

FUTURE DIRECTIONS

While significant progress has been made in the development of effective learning-based treatments for alcohol and cocaine abuse, they provide no magic bullets and many challenges remain. Drug abuse is a chronic relapsing disorder when treated with learning-based or other interventions. How to sustain abstinence or, more precisely, a lifestyle free of drug-related problems remains a primary challenge for all in the field. Learning-based treatments emphasizing systematic reinforcement of abstinence, prosocial lifestyle changes, relapse prevention, skills training, and involvement of significant others in treatment have shown efficacy for protecting alcohol and cocaine abusers from the insidious influence of factors that promote drug use, but there is room for improvements with all of these interventions. More research is also needed to parametrically assess which elements, duration, and intensity of learning-based treatments are necessary to

produce clinically significant outcomes. Such research is important for improving our scientific understanding of how to effectively treat alcohol and cocaine abuse as well as for the practical matter of curtailing costs. Finally, a persistent and fundamental challenge for this area is the development of effective strategies for the dissemination of research findings into everyday clinical practice. The use of learning-based treatments for alcohol, cocaine, and other forms of drug abuse in everyday clinical practice in the United States remains disproportionately low considering the relatively extensive empirical support for their efficacy.

SUMMARY

- Significant advances have been made in the development of effective treatments for alcohol and cocaine abuse via the application of psychological principles of learning and conditioning.

- Operant and social learning theory approaches have contributed to the majority of empirically supported psychosocial treatments for alcohol abuse and all of those for cocaine abuse. Less empirical support is available for the clinical applicability of the respondent approach, but recent advances are promising in that area as well.

- Sustaining long-term behavior change, parametric assessment of the necessary elements, duration, and intensity of treatment, and more effective dissemination into standard clinical practice remain important challenges for the learning-based approach to drug abuse treatment.

REFERENCES

Azrin, N.H. (1976) Improvements in the community-reinforcement approach to alcoholism. *Behav. Res. Ther.* 14: 339–348.

Azrin, N.H., Sisson, R.W., Meyers, R. and Godley, M. (1982) Alcoholism treatment by disulfiram and community reinforcement therapy. *J. Behav. Ther. Exp. Psychiatry* 13: 105–112.

Babor, T.F. (1978) Studying social reactions to drug self-administration. In: Krasnegor, N.A. (ed.) *Self-administration of abused substances:* methods for study. NIDA Research Monograph #20. DHEW publication (ADM) 78-727. Washington, DC: U.S. Government Printing Office, pp. 149–179.

Babor, T.F. and Grant, M. (1991) *Project on identification and management of alcohol-related problems. Report on Phase II: a randomized clinical trial or brief interventions in primary health care.* Geneva: World Health Organization.

Baer, J.S., Marlatt, G.A., Kivlahan, D.R., Fromme, K., Larimer, M.E and Williams E. (1992) An experimental test of three methods of alcohol risk reduction with young adults. *J. Consult. Clin. Psychol.* 60: 974–979.

Brady, J.V. (1981) Common mechanisms in substance abuse. In: Thompson, T. and Johanson, C.E. (eds.) *Behavioral pharmacology of human drug dependence.* NIDA Research Monograph 37. DHHS Publication No (ADM)81-1137. Washington, DC: U.S. Government Printing Office, pp. 11–20.

Brown, R.A. (1980) Conventional education and controlled drinking education courses with convicted drunken drivers. *Behav. Ther.* 11: 632–642.

Carroll, K.M., Rounsaville, B.J. and Gawin, F.H. (1991) Cocaine abusers: relapse prevention and interpersonal psychotherapy. *Am. J. Drug Alcohol Abuse.* 17: 229–247.

Carroll, K.M., Rounsaville, B.J., Gordon, L.T., Nich, C., Jatlow, P., Bisighinni, R.M. and Gawin, F.H. (1994a) Psychotherapy and pharmacotherapy for ambulatory cocaine abusers. *Arch. Gen. Psychiatry* 51: 177–187.

Carroll, K.M., Rounsaville, B.J., Nich, C., Gordon, L.T., Wirtz, P.W. and Gawin F.H. (1994b) One-year follow-up of psychotherapy and pharmacotherapy for cocaine dependence: delayed emergence of psychotherapy effects. *Arch. Gen. Psychiatry* 51: 989–997.

Caudill, B.D. and Marlatt, G.A. (1975) Modeling influences in social drinking: an experimental analogue. *J. Consult. Clin. Psychol.* 43: 405–415.

Chaney, E.F., O'Leary, M.R. and Marlatt, G.A. (1978). Skill training with alcoholics. *J. Consult. Clin. Psychol.* 46: 1092–1104.

Childress, A.R. (September, 1993) Using active strategies to cope with cocaine cue reactivity: preliminary treatment outcomes. Paper presented at the NIDA Technical Review Meeting on Outcomes for Treatment of Cocaine Dependence, Bethesda, MD.

Childress, A.R., Ehrman, R., Rohsenow, D.J., Robbins, S.J. and O'Brien CP. (1992) Classically conditioned factors in drug dependence. In: Lowinson, J.H.,Ruiz, P., Millman, R.B. and Langrod, J. (eds.) *Substance abuse:* a comprehensive textbook. Baltimore, MD: Williams & Wilkins, pp. 56–69.

Cooney, N.L., Gillespie, R.A., Baker, L.H. and Kaplan, R.F. (1987) Cognitive changes after alcohol cue exposure. *J. Consult. Clin. Psychol.* 55: 150–155.

Cooney, N.L., Kadden, R.M., Litt, M.D. and Getter, H. (1991) Matching alcoholics to coping skills or interactional therapies: two-year follow-up results. *J. Consult. Clin. Psychol.* 59: 598–601.

Drummond, D.C., Cooper, T. and Glautier, S.P. (1990) Conditioned learning in alcohol dependence: implications for cue-exposure treatment. *Br. J. Addict.* 85: 725–743.

Ehrman, R., Robbins, S., Childress, A.R. and O'Brien, C.P. (1992) Conditioned responses to cocaine-related stimuli in cocaine abuse patients. *Psychopharmacology* 106: 143–153.

Eriksen, L., Bjornstad, S. and Gotestam, K.G. (1986). Social skills training in groups for alcoholics: one-year treatment outcome for groups and individuals. *Addict. Behav.* 11: 309–329.

Ferrell, W.L. and Galassi, J.P. (1981) Assertion training and human relations training in the treatment of chronic alcoholics. *Int. J. Addict.* 16: 959–968.

Foy, D.W., Nunn, L.B. and Rychtarik, R.G. (1984) Broad-spectrum behavioral treatment for chronic alcoholics: effects of training controlled drinking skills. *J. Consult. Clin. Psychol.* 52: 218–230.

Fuller, R.K. (1995). Antidipsotropic medications. In: Hester, R.K. and Miller, W.R. (eds.) *Handbook of alcoholism treatment approaches:* effective alternatives, 2nd ed. Boston: Allyn and Bacon, pp. 123–133.

Garlington, W.K. and Dericco, D.A. (1977). The effect of modeling on drinking rate. *J. Appl. Behav. Anal.* 10: 207–211.

Goldberg, S.R. and Schuster C.R. (1970). Conditioned nalorphine-induced abstinence changes: persistence in post morphine dependent monkeys. *J. Exp. Anal. Behav.* 14: 33–46.

Griffiths, R.R., Bigelow, G.E. and Henningfield, J.E. (1980) Similarities in animal and human drug taking behavior. In: Mello, N.K. (ed.) *Advances in substance abuse: behavioral and biological research,* vol. 1. Greenwich, CT: JAI Press, pp. 1–90.

Grove, R.N. and Schuster, C.R. (1974). Suppression of cocaine self-administration by extinction and punishment. *Pharmacol. Biochem. Behav.* 2: 199–208.

Havassy, B.E., Hall, S.M. and Wasserman, D.A. (1991) Relapse to cocaine use following treatment: preliminary findings on the role of social support. In: Harris, L.S. (ed.) *Problems of Drug Dependence 1990, Proceedings of the 52nd Annual Meeting of the Committee on Problems of Drug Dependence.* NIDA Research Monograph #105. DHHS publication number (ADM) 91-1753. Washington, DC: U.S. Government Printing Office, pp. 502–504.

Higgins, S.T. (in press) The influence of alternative reinforcers on cocaine use and abuse: a brief review. *Pharmacol. Biochem. Behav.*

Higgins, S.T., Budney, A.J., Bickel, W.K. and Badger, G.J. (1994a). Participation of significant others in outpatient behavioral treatment predicts greater cocaine abstinence. *Am. J. Drug Alcohol Abuse* 20: 47–56.

Higgins, S.T., Budney, A.J., Bickel, W.K., Foerg, F.E., Donham, R., Badger, G.J. (1994b) Incentives improve treatment retention and cocaine abstinence in ambulatory cocaine-dependent patients. *Arch. Gen. Psychiatry* 51: 568–576.

Higgins, S.T., Budney, A.J., Bickel, W.K., Foerg, F.E., Ogden, D. and Badger, G.J. (1995) Outpatient behavioral treatment for cocaine dependence: one-year outcome. *Exp. Clin. Psychopharmacology* 3: 205–212.

Higgins, S.T., Budney, A.J., Bickel, W.K., Hughes, J.R., Foerg, F. and Badger, G. (1993). Achieving cocaine abstinence with a behavioral approach. *Am. J. Psychiatry* 150: 763–769.

Higgins, S.T., Delaney, D.D., Budney, A.J., et al. (1991). A behavioral approach to achieving initial cocaine abstinence. *Am. J. Psychiatry* 148: 1218–1224.

Higgins, S.T. and Morris, E.K. (1985). A comment on contemporary definitions of reinforcement as a behavioral process. *Psychol. Rec.* 35: 81–88.

Hunt, G.M. and Azrin, N.H. (1973). A community-reinforcement approach to alcoholism. *Behav. Res. Ther.* 11: 91–104.

Johanson, C.E. (1977). The effects of electric shock on responding maintained by cocaine injections in a choice procedure in the rhesus monkey. *Psychopharmacology* 53: 277–282.

Kadden, R.M., Cooney, N.L., Getter, H. and Litt, M.D. (1989) Matching alcoholics to coping skills or interactional therapies: posttreatment results. *J. Consult. Clin. Psychol.* 57: 698–704.

Keane, T.M., Foy, D.W., Nunn, B. and Rychtarik, R.G. (1984) Spouse contracting to increase Antabuse compliance in alcoholic veterans. *J. Clin. Psychol.* 40: 340–344.

Laberg, J.C. and Ellertsen, B. (1987) Psychophysiological indicators of craving in alcoholics: effects of cue exposure. *Br. J. Addict.* 82: 1341–1348.

Magura, S., Casriel, C., Goldsmith, D.S., Strug, D.L. and Lipton, D.S. (1988) Contingency contracting with polydrug-abusing methadone patients. *Addict. Behav.* 13: 113–118.

Mallams, J.H., Godley, M.D., Hall, G.M. and Meyers, R.J. (1982) A social-systems approach to resocializing alcoholics in the community. *J. Stud. Alcohol* 43: 1115–1123.

Marlatt, G.A. (1983) Stress as a determinant of excessive drinking and relapse. In: Pohorecky, L. and Brick, J. (eds.) *Stress and alcohol use.* New York: Elsevier, pp. 279–294.

Marlatt, G.A. and Gordon, J.R. (eds.) (1985) *Relapse prevention: maintenance strategies in the treatment of addictive behaviors.* New York: Guilford.

McCrady, B.S., Noel, N.E., Abrams, D.B., Stout, R.L., Nelson, H.F. and Hay, W.M. (1986) Comparative effectiveness of three types of spouse involvement in outpatient behavioral alcoholism treatment. *J. Stud. Alcohol* 47: 459–467.

McCrady, B.S., Stout, R., Noel, N., Abrams, D. and Nelson, H.F. (1991) Effectiveness of three types of spouse-involved behavioral alcoholism treatment. *Br. J. Addict.* 86: 1415–1424.

McLellan, A.T., Arndt, I.O., Metzger, D.S., Woody, G.E. and O'Brien, C.P. (1993) The effects of psychosocial services in substance abuse treatment. *JAMA* 269: 1953–1959.

Miller, W.R. and Baca, L.M. (1983) Two year follow-up of bibliotherapy and therapist-directed controlled drinking training for problem drinkers. *Behav. Ther.* 14: 441–448.

Miller, W.R., Brown, J.M., Simpson, T.L., Handmaker, N.S., Bien, T.H., Luckie, L.F., Montgomery, H.A., Hester, R.K. and Tonigan, J.S. (1995). What works? A methodological analysis of the alcohol treatment outcome literature. In: Hester, R.K. and Miller, W.R. (eds.) *Handbook of alcoholism treatment approaches: effective alternatives,* 2nd ed. Boston: Allyn and Bacon, pp. 12–44.

Miller, W.R. and Hester, R.K. (1986) Matching problem drinkers with optimal treatments. In: Miller, W.R. and Heather, N. (eds.) *Treating addictive behaviors: processes of change.* New York: Plenum, pp. 175–203.

Miller, W.R., Leckman, A.L., Delaney, H.D. and Tinkcom M. (1992) Long-term follow-up of behavioral self-control training. *J. Stud. Alcohol* 53: 249–261.

Miller, W.R. and Taylor, C.A. (1980) Relative effectiveness of bibliotherapy, individual and group self-control training in the treatment of problem drinkers. *Addict. Behav.* 5: 13–24.

O'Brien, C.P., Testa, T., O'Brien, T.J., Brady, J.P. and Wells, B. (1977). Conditioned narcotic withdrawal in humans. *Science* 195: 1000–1002.

Oei, T.P. and Jackson PR. (1982) Social skills and cognitive behavioral approaches to the treatment of problem drinking. *J. Stud. Alcohol* 43: 532–547.

O'Farrell, T.J., Choquette, K.A., Cutter, H.S.G., Brown, E.D. and McCourt, W.F. (1993) Behavioral marital therapy with and without additional couples relapse prevention sessions for alcoholics and their wives. *J. Stud. Alcohol* 54: 652–666.

O'Farrell, T.J., Cutter, H.S.G., Choquette, K.A., Floyd, F.J. and Bayog, R.D. (1992) Behavioral marital therapy for male alcoholics: marital and drinking adjustment during the two years after treatment. *Behav. Ther.* 23: 529–549.

O'Farrell, T.J., Cutter, H.S.G. and Floyd, F.J. (1985) Evaluating behavioral marital therapy for male alcoholics: effects on marital adjustment and communication from before to after therapy. *Behav. Ther.* 16: 147–167.

Project MATCH Research Group. (1993). Project MATCH: rationale and methods for a multisite clinical trial matching patients to alcoholism treatment. *Alcoholism Clin. Exp. Res.* 17: 1130–1145.

Rankin, H., Hodgson, R. and Stockwell, T. (1983) Cue exposure and response prevention with alcoholics: a controlled trial. *Behav. Res. Ther.* 21: 435–446.

Rawson, R.A. (September, 1993) The Matrix neurobehavioral approach: evidence of efficacy. Paper presented at the NIDA Technical Review Meeting on Outcomes for Treatment of Cocaine Dependence, Bethesda, MD.

Rohsenow D. (September, 1993) Social skills training for cocaine dependent individuals. Paper presented at the NIDA Technical Review Meeting on Outcomes for Treatment of Cocaine Dependence, Bethesda, MD.

Sanchez-Craig, M., Annis, H.M., Bornet, A.R. and MacDonald, K.R. (1984) Random assignment to abstinence and controlled drinking: evaluation of a cognitive-behavioral program for problem drinkers. *J. Consult. Clin. Psychol.* 52: 390–403.

Sanchez-Craig, M. and Walker, K. (1982) Teaching coping skills to chronic alcoholics in a coeducational halfway house: I. Assessment of programme effects. *Br. J. Addict.* 77: 35–50.

Siegel, S. (1975) Evidence from rats that morphine tolerance is a learned response. *J. Comp. Physiol. Psychol.* 89: 498–506.

Silverman, K., Higgins, S.T., Brooner, R.K., Montoya, I.D., Schuster, C.R. and Preston, K.L. (1996) Sustained cocaine abstinence in methadone maintenance patients through voucher-based reinforcement therapy. *Arch. Gen. Psychiatry* 53: 409–415.

Stitzer, M.L., Bickel, W.K., Bigelow, G.E. and Liebson, I.A. (1986). Effects of methadone dose contingencies on urinalysis test results of poly-abusing methadone-maintenance patients. *Drug Alcohol Depend.* 18: 341–348.

Stitzer, M.L., Iguchi, M.Y. and Felch, L.J. (1992) Contingent take-home incentive: effects on drug use of methadone maintenance patients. *J. Consult. Clin. Psychol.* 60: 927–934.

Tusel, D.J., Piotrowski, N.A., Sees, K.L., Reilly, P.M., Banys, P., Meek, P. and Hall, S.M. (1995) Contingency contracting for illicit drug use with opioid addicts in methadone treatment. In: Harris, L.S. (ed.) *Problems of drug dependence 1994: Proceedings of the 56th annual scientific meeting.* NIDA Research Monograph 153. Washington, DC: U.S. Government Printing Office, p. 155.

Vogler, R.E., Compton, J.V. and Weissbach, T.A. (1975) Integrated behavior change techniques for alcoholics. *J. Consult. Clin. Psychol.* 43: 233–243.

Vogler, R.E., Weissbach, T.A., Compton, J.V. and Martin, G.T. (1977) Integrated behavior change techniques for problem drinkers in the community. *J. Consult. Clin. Psychol.* 45: 267–279.

Wells, E.A., Peterson, P.L., Gainey, R.R., Hawkins, J.D. and Catalano, R.F. (1994) Outpatient treatment of cocaine abuse: A controlled comparison of relapse prevention and twelve-step approaches. *Am. J. Drug Alcohol Abuse* 20: 1–17.

Drug Addiction and its Treatment: Nexus of Neuroscience and Behavior, edited by Bankole A. Johnson and John D. Roache. Lippincott–Raven Publishers, Philadelphia, © 1997.

17

Clinical Efficacy of Pharmacotherapy

Ismene Petrakis and Thomas R. Kosten

Department of Psychiatry, Yale University School of Medicine, New Haven, Connecticut 06519

Current and evolving pharmacotherapies for opioid and cocaine dependence can be broadly categorized into two groups: (1) those for acute detoxification and initiation of abstinence, and (2) maintenance agents for prevention of relapse. This review chapter briefly covers some of the underlying neurobiology for opioids and cocaine that has led to the development of these pharmacotherapies, followed by a review of specific agents along with the relative strength of the existing databases for the efficacy of these agents. Several well-established agents exist for opioid detoxification and maintenance but cocaine pharmacotherapies remain experimental. Due to the relatively low severity of the cocaine withdrawal syndrome and the lack of major medical complications during cocaine withdrawal, no clear role for detoxification agents has evolved with cocaine. However, there is neurobiologic evidence for abnormalities after chronic cocaine use, suggesting that pharmacotherapy may have a role in initiating abstinence in order to reverse some of these brain abnormalities induced by cocaine. We will also discuss pharmacotherapies for nicotine and sedative dependence.

OPIOID PHARMACOTHERAPIES

Pharmacotherapies for intravenous heroin addicts have gained importance given the recent public health concern over the epidemic of acquired immunodeficiency syndrome (AIDS). The medications that have been developed for the treatment of opioid dependence are easily categorized into medications either for (1) the treatment of acute withdrawal or (2) chronic maintenance and the prevention of relapse.

Acute withdrawal from opioid dependence is a syndrome lasting about 2 weeks and includes a number of symptoms such as diarrhea, vomiting, muscle pains, and insomnia. While the syndrome can be quite uncomfortable, it is not associated with seizures or any life-threatening complications. It is clinically important, however, as these symptoms can lead to continued heroin use even when the addict no longer feels any euphoria from the drug but is using simply to avoid the discomfort of withdrawal. Protracted abstinence symptoms have also been described in addicts up to 9 months after discontinuation of drug use. This syndrome was first described by Himmelsbach in 1942 and includes symptoms of "abnormal" weight, sleep, basal metabolic rate, temperature, respiration, and blood pressure. Subsequent studies have described protracted abstinence with symptoms of elevated blood pressure, temperature, respiration rate, and an increase in pupillary dilation compared with baseline (Eisenman et al., 1969; Martin and Jasinski, 1968).

Animal models of protracted abstinence have been described with an attempt to identify the underlying psychopathology. Symptoms of decreased respiration, increased temperature, weight, metabolism, water intake, and wet-dog shakes were described in rats for up to 4 months after detoxification compared to saline-injected controls (Martin et al., 1963). Differences in response to morphine between treated rats and controls were observed as long as a year after abstinence (Cochin and Kornestsky, 1964). In monkeys, related work with the opioid antagonist nalorphine showed that an increased sensitivity to nalorphine persisted for over 3 months after detoxification from morphine (Goldberg and Schuster, 1969). While there was no effect with nalorphine in the controls, (non-opioid exposed animals) monkeys previously exposed to opioids exhibited emesis, excessive salivation, and hyperirritability to similar doses of nalorphine. Drug-seeking behavior is also seen months after detoxification (Wikler and Pescor, 1967). Studies have shown clear evidence for dopaminergic involvement in the protracted abstinence syndrome (Glick and Cox, 1977), which may have implications for treatment.

The clinical relevance of the protracted abstinence syndrome has been cited as a justification for methadone-maintenance treatment (Dole, 1988). Dole stated that relapse in addicts who are not in acute withdrawal is in part due to metabolic and conditioned factors, while psychological factors are seen as having a secondary role in addiction and as triggers for relapse. Pharmacotherapies for opioid dependence can be categorized as medications that target acute withdrawal and the associated symptoms or those that target protracted abstinence and the prevention of relapse.

Acute Withdrawal Pharmacotherapies

The standard approach to detoxification from opioid dependence is the substitution of the long-acting, orally active opioid methadone for heroin. The methadone dosage is then gradually tapered over 5 days to as long as several months in either an inpatient or outpatient setting (Kleber, 1981). This tapering of a long-acting substitution agent has the disadvantage of using a controlled substance that requires special licensing to administer. However, it has relatively few medical complications. A recent

extension of this substitution and tapering approach has used buprenorphine, a partial opioid agonist that can substitute for heroin and prevent the development of withdrawal symptoms. Buprenorphine also has a significantly less severe withdrawal syndrome than pure agonists such as heroin or methadone (Jasinski et al., 1978; Kosten and Kleber 1988b).

An alternative approach to detoxification has been the use of non-opioid compounds such as clonidine to reduce the severity of withdrawal (Gold et al., 1978; Kleber et al., 1985b). Clonidine is an α-adrenergic agonist that reduces the adrenergic hyperactivity that occurs during opiate withdrawal. This reduction is affected by feedback inhibition on the autoreceptors of noradrenergic neurons such as the locus ceruleus neurons. Inpatient studies with clonidine last about 5 to 6 days and involve escalating dosages of clonidine over the first couple of days followed by a tapering down of dosage. These studies have documented up to 90% success rates for detoxification (Gold, 1978). In an outpatient setting, success rates have been lower with only a 45% success rate reported by Kleber et al. (1985b) in a double-blind randomized clinical trial comparing clonidine to methadone tapering. In this 30-day study, there was no difference in success rates between clonidine and methadone tapering. However, patients who failed at clonidine detoxification dropped out within the first week, whereas patients failing methadone tapering generally did not fail until the last week of the protocol. Thus, overall costs per success were smaller with clonidine than with methadone tapering.

More recent improvements in the clonidine technique have involved the precipitation of opiate withdrawal using naltrexone, an opioid antagonist, while blocking the withdrawal symptoms using clonidine (Charney et al., 1982; Kleber et al., 1987; Vining et al., 1988). Using this ultra-rapid clonidine/naltrexone detoxification, patients can be completely drug free and maintained on the antagonist naltrexone within 3 days. This technique, therefore, can provide important cost savings because of the reduced duration of therapy and because the outpatient setting for cloni-dine detoxification can be a primary care medical clinic rather than a special metha-done program. Success rates with this tech-nique in a day hospital have been as high as 90%, and a recent comparison of clonidine alone to clonidine/naltrexone found greater success as well as lower costs with the cloni-dine/naltrexone technique (Shi et al., 1993).

This approach of using non-opioid agents to facilitate opioid detoxification has been successfully implemented with other medica-tions beyond adrenergic agents. While animal studies have suggested that both γ-aminobu-tyric acid (GABA) agents and excitatory amino acid antagonists would reduce opiate withdrawal, recent clinical studies have gen-erally been disappointing. A pilot study using baclofen, a GABA agonist, showed no superi-ority to placebo, and dextromethorphan, an excitatory amino acid antagonist, also showed no superiority to placebo (Krystal et al., 1992; Rosen et al., in review). While another study using γ-hydroxy butyric acid suggested effi-cacy for opioid withdrawal, a replication study failed to show its efficacy (Gallimberti et al., 1993; Rosen, *personal communication*). As better agents, particularly excitatory amino acid antagonists, become available, new treatments for opioid detoxification should evolve rapidly. Since the adrenergic and excitatory amino acid systems are com-plementary in their effects on opiate with-drawal, new treatment approaches that com-bine these agents to reduce adrenergic and excitatory amino acid activity may be partic-ularly effective in attenuating opiate with-drawal symptoms. Similarly, a combined ap-proach using the partial opioid agonist buprenorphine with clonidine and with other non-opioid agents can be very effective as treatment combinations to reduce withdrawal severity (Kosten et al., 1989).

Maintenance Pharmacotherapies

Three maintenance treatments are currently approved for use in the United States: metha-done, L-alpha acetylmethadol (LAAM), and naltrexone. Both methadone and LAAM are substitution agents that with once daily or less frequent dosing (LAAM) relieve opiate with-drawal symptoms in acutely dependent pa-tients and prevent continued illicit opiate use through cross-tolerance as well as sustained relief of withdrawal symptoms (Blaine et al., 1981). Naltrexone is an opioid antagonist that precipitates withdrawal in acutely dependent patients and, therefore, requires opiate detox-ification before being administered (Kosten and Kleber, 1984).

The efficacy of methadone maintenance has been examined for over 20 years with consistent findings of reduced heroin abuse, reduced arrests, and improved psychosocial functioning (Gerstein, 1992). The key factors ensuring optimal rehabilitation when using methadone include a minimum dosage of 60 to 65 mg/day, a minimum duration of treat-ment of about 2 years, and the availability of adjunctive psychosocial services. Critical problems in the use of methadone include poly-drug abuse, particularly of cocaine, ben-zodiazepines, and alcohol, as well as prob-lems with eventual detoxification from methadone and diversion of methadone when take-home medication is given. Poly-drug abuse has been addressed with both pharma-cological and nonpharmacological interven-tions and adjunctive medications such as anti-depressants may have a role in treating cocaine dependence in this population (Kosten, 1989). For alcoholism, disulfiram may have a role, particularly when given in conjunction with the daily methadone dosing. The issue of diversion of take-home methadone has recently been addressed by the introduction of LAAM, a long-acting form of methadone that needs to be given only three times per week (Blaine et al., 1981).

LAAM at dosages of approximately 100 mg/three times weekly has shown comparable efficacy to methadone at 65 mg daily (Ling et al., 1976). A clinical problem in the use of LAAM has been higher initial dropout from LAAM than comparable dosages of metha-done. This dropout appears to reflect the lower reinforcing properties of LAAM, perhaps because of its slower onset in reducing opioid withdrawal and in producing a buzz for patients. To address this problem, it has been suggested that patients be initially treated with methadone and then transferred to LAAM once stabilized at an adequate methadone dosage. As take-home medication is not usually prescribed with LAAM, its nonprescribed use is not an important problem. However, even if take-homes are allowed, its abuse potential appears to be lower than that of methadone, because of a very slow onset of action even when administered parenterally (Blaine et al., 1981; Ling et al., 1976).

The opioid antagonist naltrexone has been available since 1973 but is useful for a limited population of addicts. The major problem with naltrexone is compliance in taking the two to three times per week dosing (Kosten and Kleber, 1984). Various strategies have been developed to improve compliance such as working with family members, employers, and the legal probation system. While there are no serious medical complications of naltrexone use, there is a sustained elevation of corticosteroids and endorphins with naltrexone. This elevation has no clear clinical correlates. While some concern has also been raised about liver toxicity with naltrexone, the most carefully controlled studies suggest that liver functioning improves in opioid addicts treated with naltrexone due to their reduction in illicit heroin use (Morgan and Kosten, 1990). Additionally, the use of naltrexone in nonaddict subjects revealed dose-related increases in transaminase levels with dosages of 300 mg per day, which is six times the therapeutic dose (Maggio et al., 1985). As naltrexone is a pure opioid antagonist, when heroin addicts who are maintained on naltrexone abuse heroin, there is no effect at all—they do not get euphoria or any dysphoric symptoms from the heroin. Furthermore, tolerance to these effects of naltrexone do not occur even after months or years of treatment (Kleber et al., 1985a).

Another maintenance agent that has been carefully studied over the last few years is buprenorphine, a partial opioid agonist (Lewis, 1985). As a partial opioid agonist, this medication shares some of the properties of both methadone and naltrexone (Jasinski et al., 1978). At low dosages (2 to 4 mg per day sublingually), buprenorphine is primarily an agonist and will relieve opioid withdrawal in dependent patients. At higher dosages ($\geq$16 mg/day sublingually), buprenorphine exhibits antagonist properties such that it can precipitate withdrawal in opiate-dependent individuals (Jasinski et al., 1983). This antagonism increases the medical safety of buprenorphine, because overdose with it is very unlikely, as it will antagonize itself at high dosages. Two other benefits of buprenorphine are its relatively long-time action and moderate withdrawal syndrome, so that a single dose may last for 2 to 3 days (Fudala et al., 1990). When buprenorphine is discontinued abruptly, the withdrawal syndrome is only about two-thirds as severe as an equivalent dosage of a pure antagonist such as methadone (Kosten and Kleber, 1988b). Due to its antagonist activity at low to moderate dosages, buprenorphine also has high acceptability to heroin addicts and resembles methadone rather than naltrexone in its clinical utility. This acceptability also poses the risk of buprenorphine abuse (Quigley et al., 1984).

A number of large-scale randomized clinical trials have compared buprenorphine to methadone and found that buprenorphine at 8 to 16 mg/day has comparable efficacy to methadone at 65 mg/day (Johnson et al., 1992, Strain et al., 1994). The clinical efficacy of buprenorphine is clearly dose dependent, with larger dosages of buprenorphine more effective than 2 to 4 mg of buprenorphine in retaining patients in treatment and reducing heroin abuse (Kosten et al., 1993). Buprenorphine appears to reduce heroin use both through the relief of opiate withdrawal and blockade of heroin's effects. In a controlled study involving hydromorphine challenges in buprenorphine-stabilized individuals, buprenorphine at 12 mg/day appeared to block the effect of hydromorphine for up to 3 days (Rosen et al., 1994). In summary, buprenorphine appears to be an excellent additional medication for treating heroin dependence with equivalent efficacy to methadone and possibly greater safety.

Cocaine Pharmacotherapies

While a predictable sequence of symptoms has been described in patients who discontinue cocaine use, it is generally believed that these symptoms constitute at most a mild withdrawal syndrome that does not necessitate pharmacotherapy. These symptoms, which include depressed mood, fatigue, and sleep disturbance, and which typically occur after discontinuation of heavy cocaine use or binges (Siegal, 1982), have been further categorized into three phases, including the crash, withdrawal, and extinction phases (Gawin and Kleber, 1986b). While Gawin and Kleber (1986b) suggested that these phases have implications for treatment, others have suggested that the crash and withdrawal phases may be clinically indistinguishable from one another (Brower et al., 1988). For these reasons, pharmacotherapies for cocaine use do not easily lend themselves to categorization of medications for acute withdrawal and medications for maintenance. Nevertheless, a distinction between acute and chronic agents may be useful for the purposes of categorizing pharmacotherapies used in the treatment of cocaine abuse. Acute agents are pharmacotherapies that are used during the phase of initial abstinence, while chronic agents are those that target the prevention of relapse.

Cocaine has effects on multiple neurotransmitters including dopamine (DA), norepinephrine (NE), and serotonin (5-HT) (Koe, 1976). Catecholamine systems (i.e., NE and DA) have been the primary focus of research on the reinforcement and behavioral effects of cocaine (Johanson and Fischman, 1989; Kuhar et al., 1991). Cocaine blocks the dopamine and norepinephrine transporters and through this mechanism increases synaptic catecholamine levels in the brain regions implicated in reinforcement (Wise, 1987). Several studies have suggested the impor-

tance of dopamine in the reinforcing properties of cocaine. Dopamine but not norepinephrine receptor antagonists block cocaine self-administration in rats (De Wit and Wise, 1977; Schuster, 1974; Woolverton, 1987). The reinforcing effects of cocaine in rats are extinguished following lesions of the nucleus accumbens produced by the catecholamine neurotoxin 6-hydroxy dopamine (Koob, 1992; Roberts et al., 1977, 1980). Experimental data with in vivo brain microdialysis also suggests that mesolimbic dopamine is associated with cocaine reward (Fibiger et al., 1992). These and other studies have led to the dopamine depletion hypothesis, which states that during cocaine abstinence (the crash), a hypodopaminergic state leads to craving and subsequent drug use (Dackis and Gold, 1985; Gawin and Kleber, 1986a,b).

Cocaine is also a potent inhibitor of serotonin (5-HT) uptake (Ritz and Kuhar, 1989). In animal studies, the 5-HT reuptake inhibitor fluoxetine decreased cocaine self-administration (Carroll, et al., 1990). These and other studies have suggested that 5-HT may blunt the euphoria associated with cocaine use. Additionally, recent studies have suggested that chronic cocaine administration leads to a decrease in 5-HT neurotransmission.

The development of pharmacologic treatments of cocaine abuse is based on the premise that an altered neurochemical substrate underlies both the chronic and high intensity periods of abuse (binges) and the periods that follow after discontinuation of cocaine use (Kuhar, 1991). It is postulated that the neurochemical alterations induced by chronic cocaine use in animals also occur in humans and therefore may respond to agents that reduce receptor sensitivity, such as tricyclic antidepressants. Other studies based on the dopamine depletion model have evaluated the clinical utility of dopaminergic agents that may ameliorate the crash, block euphoria, or possess anti-craving properties. The evidence of serotonergic dysfunction in cocaine abuse has led to the evaluation of medications that affect central serotonergic regulation for the treatment of cocaine abuse.

Acute Pharmacotherapies

Acute pharmacotherapies are those medications used to treat patients during the initial stages of abstinence. These include pharmacotherapies that treat the symptoms that may occur immediately following discontinuation of cocaine use, as well as those that treat the symptoms of early withdrawal and anticraving agents (Table 1). Pharmacotherapies used to treat the symptoms that occur immediately following discontinuation of cocaine use are indicated primarily for severe symptom relief and will be mentioned only briefly. In severe cases, discontinuation of heavy cocaine use has been associated with significant paranoia and agitation and, in these instances, symptomatic treatment with neuroleptics and benzodiazepines may be initiated. Prior to initiating treatment, a thorough evaluation is indicated since cocaine overdose can present with similar symptoms of agitation and paranoia. Additionally, cocaine overdose has been associated with hyperthermia, and in this case, treatment with neuroleptics may actually worsen the

condition (Kosten and Kleber, 1988a). It is important to note that non-prescribed benzodiazepines are commonly used by cocaine abusers to counter symptoms of paranoia and agitation, and therefore an abuse potential exists (Woods et al., 1992). These agents should be used only in the context of a supervised setting such as an inpatient unit or an emergency room, or an agent with less abuse potential (Woods et al., 1992) should be considered.

Based on the dopamine depletion hypothesis, dopaminergic agents have been used to treat early withdrawal symptoms. Chronic cocaine use has been postulated to result in central dopamine depletion, and subsequent autoreceptor supersensitivity is hypothesized to be the mechanism underlying post-cocaine dysphoria, drug craving, and other withdrawal symptoms. Further, these symptoms may be alleviated by dopaminergic agents. Several studies have evaluated dopaminergic agents for the treatment of the symptoms of cocaine withdrawal, and these agents include amantadine, bromocriptine, and L-dopa. While these findings have not been replicated, it suggests that these agents may be useful in treating early withdrawal symptoms after cocaine binges because their onset of action has been within a day of initiating treatment (Gawin and Kleber, 1986b).

Amantadine in doses of 200 to 300 mg daily has been shown to reduce cocaine craving and cocaine use initially, but after 3 weeks of treatment was no more effective than placebo (Morgan et al., 1988; Tennant and Sagherian, 1987). While amantadine increases dopamine transmission, its mechanism of action is unclear and may be secondary to enhanced dopamine release, dopamine reuptake blockade, or through an effect on the dopamine receptors. It has been postulated that amantadine's early effects may be secondary to an early release of dopamine that then subsequently contributes to chronic dopamine depletion. This would suggest the role for amantadine during the initial phase of treatment of cocaine abuse may be limited.

Bromocriptine is a dopamine agonist with a high affinity for the D_2 receptor. Studies with

TABLE 1. *Pharmacotherapies for cocaine abuse*

Acute agents	Chronic agents
Early Severe Symptom Relief	Anticraving/Prevent Relapse
	Tricyclic antidepressants
Neuroleptics	Desipramine
Benzodiazepines	Serotonergic Agents
Withdrawal symptom relief	Fluoxetine
	Sertraline
Dopaminergic agents	
Amantadine	Gepirone
Bromocriptine	Dopaminergic Agents
L-Dopa	Bupropion
Tricyclic antidepressants	Block reinforcing properties
Desipramine	Dopamine antagonists
	Flupenthixol
Neurotransmitter precursors	Substitution medications
Tyrosine	Dopamine agonists
Tryptophan	Methylphenidate
	Mazindol
	Miscellaneous agents
	Carbamazepine
	Naltrexone
	Disulfiram

bromocriptine, including several open-label trials using dosages between 1.25 and 7.5 mg/day have been inconclusive and limited by a high dropout rate from side effects (Dackis et al., 1987; Giannini and Baumgartel, 1987; Tennant and Sagherian, 1987). These side effects include headaches, vertigo, and syncope. When bromocriptine was compared with amantadine, both drugs were found to be effective in decreasing cocaine withdrawal symptoms; however, because more patients completed treatment with amantadine, the authors concluded that amantadine was more effective than bromocriptine in treating cocaine withdrawal symptoms (Tennant and Sagherian, 1987).

Antidepressants have been evaluated both as acute and chronic agents and their efficacy in each category will be discussed. In evaluating pharmacotherapies for the early abstinence phase, it has been hypothesized that since the symptoms are similar to depressive symptoms, they may be amenable to treatment with antidepressant medication (Gawin and Kleber, 1986a). The tricyclic antidepressants, which reduce postsynaptic dopaminergic sensitivity, have been hypothesized to reverse cocaine-induced supersensitivity in the postsynaptic dopaminergic receptors. This effect, however, is seen only after approximately 2 weeks of initiating treatment, a distinct disadvantage in using these medications for the treatment of symptoms during the early abstinence phase. Clinically, desipramine therapy has been associated with decreased craving (Gawin et al., 1989a). Studies using desipramine at low doses (75 mg daily) have found it to be only minimally effective in the treatment of early cocaine withdrawal (10 days) (Tennant and Rawson, 1983). While use of desipramine at a higher dosage (200–250 mg daily) and for a longer period of time has been shown to be more effective, a dropout rate of 25% to 30% in the first 3 weeks of treatment is thought to be secondary to its delayed onset of action (Gawin et al., 1989a). These observations and studies suggest that (1) desipramine may not be effective in early cocaine withdrawal (its role in the prevention of relapse will be dis-

cussed below), or (2) there is an imperfect correlation between the pharmacologic and behavioral aspects of cocaine. Of note is a study by Giannini and Baumgartel (1987), in which the combination of desipramine and bromocriptine led to a significant improvement in cocaine withdrawal symptoms. This suggests that there may be a role in the use of combination treatments for the treatment of cocaine-abusing patients, and further studies would be indicated.

The symptoms of early abstinence have been linked not only to dopamine depletion, but to the depletion of other catecholamines such as norepinephrine and serotonin. For this reason, it has been hypothesized that neurotransmitter precursors, such as tyrosine and tryptophan would be helpful in relieving cocaine abstinence symptoms. This hypothesis has not adequately been tested in double-blind studies (Johanson and Fischman, 1989).

Overall, while dopaminergic agents, such as amantadine, bromocriptine, and L-dopa, have shown some promise in treating the early symptoms of cocaine abstinence, the use of these medications has been limited by the side effect profile (bromocriptine), the high dropout rates, and the lack of confirmation of efficacy in controlled trials. Other agents, such as desipramine, have had less success as acute agents. While preclinical research suggests the use of agents such as the neurotransmitter precursors, these have yet to be tested in controlled trials. In general, it is important to remember that the symptoms that occur in the early abstinence phase are self-limited and will resolve even without treatment. For these reasons, it may be more useful to focus treatment for cocaine-abusing patients on decreasing the cocaine-taking behavior, and specifically on pharmacotherapies that are used to prevent relapse.

Maintenance Pharmacotherapies

The agents referred to as chronic pharmacotherapies are those that focus on the prevention of relapse to cocaine use in cocaine-abstinent patients. The agents that focus on the prevention of relapse may be pharmacotherapies that act as anti-craving agents, either by blocking the reinforcing effects of cocaine or by acting as substitution agents. These include the tricyclic antidepressants such as desipramine, serotonergic agents such as fluoxetine, sertraline, and gepirone, the dopaminergic agent bupropion, dopaminergic antagonists such as flupenthixol, dopaminergic agonists such as methylphenidate and mazindol, and some miscellaneous agents such as carbamazepine, naltrexone, and disulfiram. While there have been a number of promising agents from open-label studies, in general double-blind trials have not confirmed their efficacy.

The tricyclic antidepressants are one of the most studied medications in the treatment of cocaine abuse. The advantages to their use include their potential in reversing cocaine-induced dopaminergic supersensitivity, their relatively benign side effect profile, and lack of abuse potential. Their delayed onset of action of approximately 2 weeks after the initiation of treatment suggests that they would be more suited as agents to prevent relapse than as a treatment for cocaine withdrawal symptoms. Of the tricyclic antidepressants, desipramine is the medication studied most extensively.

While several studies, including both open-label and double-blind trials, have suggested that desipramine is effective and leads to decreases in cocaine craving and in cocaine use (Gawin and Kleber, 1986a; Gawin et al., 1989a), other studies have shown no difference in cocaine abuse in patients who were treated with desipramine compared to those who were not (Kosten et al., 1992; Tennant and Rawson, 1983). It is difficult to compare the results of these studies as (1) the dosages used were not comparable (range from 75 to 250 mg daily); (2) the duration of treatment ranged from 10 days (Tennant and Rawson, 1983) to at least 4 weeks (Gawin et al., 1989a); and (3) while most studies were conducted in "pure" (i.e., not polydrug) cocaine abusers, at least one study (Kosten et al., 1992a) has evaluated desipramine in patients

who were methadone-maintained opioid-dependent cocaine abusers. Additionally, it has been reported that desipramine can be associated with an "early tricyclic jitteriness syndrome" in some cocaine abusing patients who were having cocaine cravings. The symptoms included anxiety, insomnia, and stimulation, and were reminiscent of the patient's cocaine use. These symptoms led to cocaine craving and subsequent cocaine use (Weiss, 1988).

Currently the use of desipramine for cocaine use is not an established treatment. For future research, some clinical considerations are important. Clinical trials suggest that adequate dosages (200–250 mg daily), for longer periods of time (4–6 weeks) may be necessary for a treatment response, but serum desipramine levels greater than 200 mg/ml have been associated with a greater likelihood of relapse to cocaine use (Weiss, 1988). These points underlie the importance of treatment in the context of close clinical monitoring, including the monitoring of serum desipramine concentration. It has been suggested that desipramine therapy may simply provide a window of opportunity (Gawin et al., 1989a) approximately 3 to 8 weeks after the initiation of treatment, during which time behavioral treatments may take effect.

Based on evidence that cocaine is a potent serotonergic (5-HT) reuptake blocker, that 5-HT may blunt the euphoria associated with cocaine use, and that chronic cocaine administration leads to a decrease in 5-HT neurotransmission, several studies have evaluated medications that affect central serotonergic regulation for the treatment of cocaine abuse. The most studied of these agents is the antidepressant fluoxetine, which is a potent serotonergic uptake inhibitor. There have been number of both open-label and controlled studies evaluating fluoxetine in the treatment of cocaine abuse and they have been conducted in both primary cocaine abusers and in methadone-maintained opioid-dependent cocaine abusers. These studies have had inconsistent results, and while some have shown that fluoxetine significantly reduces cocaine use (Batki et al., 1993; Pollack and Rosenbaum, 1991), others have shown that patients treated with fluoxetine have no better outcome than those treated with placebo (Grabowski et al., 1995; Petrakis, 1994). These studies have been difficult to compare because different outcome measures were used including qualitative urine toxicology results, quantitative urine toxicology results, self-reported cocaine use, and treatment retention. While fluoxetine is well tolerated, with a benign side effect profile and a low risk of overdose, its efficacy in cocaine abuse is still being debated.

Other serotonergic agents that have been evaluated include sertraline and gepirone. In an open trial of 11 cocaine abusers treated with sertraline, five subjects had reduced cocaine craving and at least 3 weeks of abstinence (Kosten TA et al., 1992). These results have not been confirmed in controlled trials. In a pilot study of gepirone, there was no evidence of efficacy of gepirone compared to placebo in the treatment of cocaine abuse (Jenkins et al., 1992).

Bupropion, a second-generation antidepressant, is a dopaminergic agent that has little effect on noradrenergic or serotonergic neurotransmission. An open pilot study with bupropion in methadone-maintained cocaine abusers suggested that bupropion, at dosages of 100 mg three times daily, may be effective in treating cocaine abuse (Margolin et al., 1991). The study is limited by its small sample size (six subjects) and because it was an open-label pilot study. The results have recently been tested in a multisite controlled trial of cocaine-abusing methadone patients and no overall efficacy was determined for bupropion, although a subgroup of depressed patients did respond (Margolin, *personal communication,* June 1994).

It has been hypothesized that because of the role of dopamine in the reinforcing properties of cocaine, agents that block dopamine receptors, such as neuroleptics, may block this effect and therefore may be useful in the treatment of cocaine abuse. This hypothesis is supported by evidence that haloperidol blunted cue-induced craving for cocaine in humans (Berger et al., 1993). An open study

with flupenthixol, a thioxanthene neuroleptic used in Europe as an antipsychotic and antidepressant, at dosages of either 10 or 20 mg, led to decreased cocaine craving and cocaine use within 3 days of treatment (Gawin et al., 1989b). Again, these results have not been confirmed in controlled trials.

In evaluating pharmacotherapies for cocaine abuse, it has been hypothesized that the use of dopamine agonists may be effective as substitution agents, in the model of methadone as a treatment for heroin addiction. Two such agents that have been evaluated are methylphenidate and mazindol. Methylphenidate is a stimulant with less abuse potential than cocaine or amphetamine, a rapid onset of action, and a longer duration of action than cocaine. In an open trial of methylphenidate (Gawin et al., 1985), subjects had a rapid decrease in cocaine craving and cocaine use. However, continued maintenance doses of methylphenidate resulted in tolerance, which required increased doses. After 2 weeks of the study, patients reported increased stimulation, an increased desire for cocaine, and increased cocaine use, necessitating the discontinuation of the trial.

Mazindol, which was originally developed as an appetite suppressant, is a more promising agent, as it has not been associated with the development of tolerance and dependence or with euphoria. However, after some promising results in an open trial, a brief crossover study showed no improvement in cocaine craving or cocaine use (Kosten et al., 1993). Mazindol's potential as a pharmacotherapy for cocaine use has yet to be determined.

Several miscellaneous agents have been evaluated in the treatment of cocaine abuse. These include carbamazepine, naltrexone, and disulfiram. Carbamazepine, an anticonvulsant medication also used in the treatment of mania, has been hypothesized to reverse cocaine-induced kindling and dopamine-receptor supersensitivity. While an open study has suggested that carbamazepine may have some efficacy in treating cocaine abuse (Halikas et al., 1989), human laboratory work evaluating cocaine administration in the presence of carbamazepine, has not supported these findings (Gorelick et al., 1993). Additionally, there may be problems with cardiovascular toxicity (Hatsukami et al., 1991).

The opioid antagonist naltrexone has been examined as a potential treatment for cocaine abuse, possibly as an agent that blocks the reinforcing properties of cocaine. A laboratory study evaluated the effect of cocaine administration in several doses (0, 0.125. 0.25, and 0.50 mg/kg) after 10 days of naltrexone or placebo treatment (50 mg daily) in non–treatment-seeking cocaine abusers. Naltrexone augmented cocaine-induced increases in peak heart rate, but did not affect blood pressure. Subjects also reported on dollar value of cocaine and unpleasant feelings with cocaine administration; both of these self-reports were blunted with naltrexone compared to placebo treatment (Kosten et al., 1992b). Naltrexone has not yet been evaluated in clinical trials.

There is a high incidence of concurrent alcohol abuse in cocaine abusers. A recent study suggests that, in patients with concurrent alcohol and cocaine abuse, disulfiram may reduce cocaine use (Carroll et al., 1993). It is not clear whether this effect on cocaine use was an an indirect effect of disulfiram's effect on alcohol use, which led to a decrease in subsequent cocaine use. There is some evidence that disulfiram may have a more direct mechanism of action. A recent study of cocaine and disulfiram administration was conducted in humans. Subjects received either disulfiram (250 mg) or placebo 60 minutes prior to cocaine or placebo (2 mg/kg) administration. There were no significant physiologic effects of the disulfiram/cocaine administration compared to cocaine administration alone. While subjects reported no effect on the cocaine high with disulfiram, they did report decreased cocaine craving and several subjects reported significant dysphoria during cocaine/disulfiram administration. These results suggest that further research on the use of disulfiram in cocaine abuse is warranted.

Overall, a number of agents have been evaluated in the treatment of cocaine abusers. Several open-label pilot studies have suggested efficacy for a number of agents in the treatment of cocaine abuse. In contrast, however, controlled trials have usually found no effect. While some of these discrepancies may be due to the use of different or more rigorous outcome variables, the results emphasize the importance of only concluding efficacy for medications that have been proven in double-blind clinical trials. It has been suggested that the most efficacious strategy in treating cocaine abusers may be to use a combination treatment of an acute agent such as a dopaminergic agonist with a medication that may prevent relapse such as desipramine. Additionally, treatments with a pharmacotherapy may provide only a window of opportunity, during which behavioral interventions can have their maximum effect.

Nicotine Dependence

The treatment of nicotine dependence and withdrawal has benefited from the use of nicotine substitution and from various symptomatic treatments such as clonidine. At least four types of nicotine substitution systems have been tested: policrilex gum, transdermal, nasal spray, and inhaler. Three of these systems lead to relatively rapid increases in blood levels of nicotine, while the transdermal route leads to a rather slow rise in blood levels (Russell et al., 1983; Srivastava et al., 1991). The slow steady-state administration of transdermal nicotine is designed to produce gradual and better tolerated withdrawal. The transbuccal gum, which was introduced almost 20 years ago, proved to be useful in clinical trials, but successful outcomes at 6 months were not sustained at 1-year follow-up (Fagerstrom, 1982; Schneider et al., 1983). Despite this success in research triangles, the gum was not successful in clinical practice because of underdosing and incorrect usage. Patients need to chew the gum very precisely for adequate and sustained nicotine absorption (Schneider et al., 1983). Transdermal nicotine systems were developed to address this compliance problem and initially had difficulties with local skin reactions (Eichelberg et al.,

1989). In comparison to placebo these patches have twice the success rates in producing abstinence (Daughton et al., 1991), but are limited by a long time (4–6 hours) for nicotine blood levels to rise and by inflexible dosing. The nicotine nasal spray and inhalers allow excellent control of blood levels by self-administration, but questions have arisen about whether relief of withdrawal symptoms is better than with slower onset systems, or if craving may be stimulated by this administration of a priming dose of nicotine.

Symptomatic treatments for nicotine withdrawal include clonidine, anxiolytics (benzodiazepines), and antidepressants, as well as antagonists such as mecamylamine and either propranolol or naltrexone. Clonidine, an α_2-adrenergic agonist, may act by decreasing the release of norepinephrine, thereby reducing nicotine withdrawal symptoms. In a 3 to 6 month trial Glassman and colleagues (1988) reported that smoking cessation was enhanced in females but not males. Later trials including those with clonidine patches rather than tablets have had mixed results, and a large multisite trial showed some reduction in anxiety, but no superiority of clonidine for smoking cessation (Covey et al., 1991; Franks et al., 1989; Prochazka et al., 1990). Anxiolytics such as benzodiazepines and buspirone have mostly been evaluated in pilot studies or as controls in clonidine trials, although one controlled trial found twice the cessation rates with buspirone over placebo (Wei and Young, 1988; West R., in press). Antidepressants have not shown efficacy in controlled trials (Naranjo et al., 1990). The nicotine agonist mecamylamine has been reported to increase rather than decrease smoking (Rose et al., 1984; Stolerman et al., 1973). Propranolol has not had controlled trials and naloxone may decrease craving for tobacco, but the effect is quite modest (Karras and Kane, 1980; Nemeth-Costlett and Griffiths, 1989).

Sedative Dependence

Treatment of barbiturate and benzodiazepine dependence primarily involves detoxification using a long-acting agent that is gradually tapered, although pilot studies have suggested that carbamazepine may be useful for these withdrawal symptoms (Malcolm et al., 1989; Smith and Wesson, 1970, 1971). The substitution of a long-acting agent such as phenobarbital or chlordiazepoxide and gradually tapering it avoids the problem of abrupt discontinuation, which can result in life-threatening seizures (Fraser, 1952). Lethal doses of phenobarbital are also many times higher than toxic doses and signs of toxicity are easy to observe. These signs include sustained nystagmus, slurred speech, and ataxia. Stabilization on this barbiturate begins with asking the patient what dose they are taking on the street, because the patient may exaggerate his/her use, but the amount then given will lead to easily observed intoxication. This intoxication is then easily managed by omitting one or more doses of medication. In the worst case of overdose, flumazenil can be given to reverse partially the barbiturate effects. Flumazenil is a benzodiazepine antagonist, but it acts on the same receptors as barbiturates only at a different site (Hunkeler et al., 1981). Thus, it can counteract some of the effects of barbiturates. For benzodiazepine substitution this antagonist is quite specific and within minutes will reverse any benzodiazepine overdose. The only risk is the short-time action of flumazenil, necessitating repeated dosing or intravenous drip administration.

FUTURE DIRECTIONS

Joint behavioral and pharmacologic treatments hold promise for development of medications for substance dependence. Pharmacologic treatments may, therefore, either act synergistically with psychosocial programs, or simply provide time for dependent individuals to engage in social rehabilitation. Largely, the logical development of anti-craving medications that alter directly the major neurotransmitters (e.g., dopamine and serotonin) associated with the important behavioral effects of cocaine has not yielded efficacious compounds. Hence, the key to effective development of these anticraving agents may require more complex strategies. This may include sequencing of medications to address behavioral issues at different stages of recovery from addiction, combinations of pharmacotherapies, and the consideration of indirect neuromodulators of neurotransmitter function. Better animal models are needed that are predictive of the efficacy of anti-craving pharmacotherapies for substance dependence. Technological advances in neuroscience, especially genetics and immunology, are rapidly improving our understanding of the basic underlying process that governs substance dependence, and in the future may offer new vistas for treatment.

SUMMARY

- Typical withdrawal syndromes are well established for alcohol, nicotine, and benzodiazepine dependence but not for cocaine dependence.

- The demonstration for efficacious pharmacotherapies for substance dependence have been most fruitful in establishing the effective use of anti-withdrawal agents.

- The standard for an antiwithdrawal strategy has been the use of the long-acting opioid methadone as a substitution for heroin, which is a shorter-acting agent. Recently, however, the use of the nicotine patch as an effective adjuctive pharmacologic agent to a smoking cessation program has been demonstrated.

- Maintenance therapies with agents such as methadone and LAAM have been most successful for harm reduction and avoidance of high-risk (e.g., for communicable diseases such as human immunodeficiency virus infection) drug use in the treatment of opiate addiction.

- While open-label studies have suggested the utility of a variety of anti-craving agents (e.g., bromocriptine and amantadine) for the treatment of cocaine depen-

dence, these results have not been confirmed in double-blind clinical trials.

REFERENCES

Batki, S.L., Manfredi, L.B., Jacob, P. III, Jones, R.T. (1993) Fluoxetine for cocaine dependence in methadone maintenance: quantitative plasma and urine cocaine/benzoylecognine concentration. *J. Clin. Psychopharmacol.* 13: 243–250.

Berger, S.P., Crawford, C.A., Hall, S.E. (1993) *Effects of haloperidol on conditioned cocaine cue reactivity.* Honolulu, HI: American College of Neuropsychopharmacology.

Blaine, J.D., Thomas, D.B., Barnett, G., et al. (1981) Levo-alpha-acetylmethadol (LAAM): clinical utility and pharmaceutical development. In: Lowinson, J.H. and Ruiz, P. (eds.) *Substance abuse:* clinical problems and perspectives. Baltimore: Williams and Wilkins, pp. 360–388.

Brower, K.J., Maddahian, E., Blow, F.C., Beresford, T.P. (1988) A comparison of self-reported symptoms and DSM-IIIR criteria for cocaine withdrawal. *Am. J. Drug Alcohol Abuse* 14: 347–356.

Carroll, K., Ziedonis, D., O'Malley, S., McCance-Katz, E., Gordon, L., Rounsaville, B. (1993) Pharmacologic interventions for abusers of alcohol and cocaine: disulfiram versus naltrexone. *Am. J. Addict.* 2: 77–79.

Carroll, M.E., Lac, S.T., Asencio, M., Kraugh, R. (1990) Floxetine reduces intravenous cocaine self administration in rats. *Pharmacol. Biochem. Behav.* 35: 237–244.

Charney, D.S., Riordan, C.E., Kleber, H.D., et al. (1982) Clonidine and naltrexone: a safe, effective and rapid treatment of abrupt withdrawal from methadone therapy. *Arch. Gen. Psychiatry* 39: 1327–1332.

Cochin, J., Kornetsky, C. (1964) Development and loss of tolerance to morphine in the rat after single and multiple injections. *J. Pharmacol. Exp. Ther.* 145: 1–10.

Covey, L.S., Glassman, A.H. (1991) A meta-analysis of double-blind placebo controlled trials of clonidine for smoking cessation. *Br. J. Addict.* 86: 991–998.

Dackis, C.A. and Gold, M.S. (1985) New concepts in cocaine addiction: the dopamine depletion hypothesis. *Neurosci. Biobehav. Rev.* 9: 469–477.

Dackis, C.A., Gold, M.S., Sweeney, D.R., Byron, J.P., Clinko, R. (1987) Single-dose bromocriptine reverses cocaine craving. *Psychiatry Res.* 20: 261–264.

Daughton, D.M., Heatly, S.A., Predergrast, J.J., et al. (1991) Effect of transdermal nicotine delivery as an adjunct to low-intervention smoking cessation therapy. A randomized, placebo-controlled, double-blind study. *Arch. Intern. Med.* 151: 749–752.

De Witt, H. and Wise, R.A. (1977) Blockade of cocaine reinforcement in rats with the dopamine receptor blockade pimozide but not with the noradrenergic blockers phentolamine or phenoxybenzamide. *Can. J. Psychol.* 31: 195–203.

Dole, V.P. (1988) Implications of methadone maintenance for theories of narcotic addiction. *JAMA* 260: 3025–3029.

Eichelberg, D., Stolze, P., Block, M., Buchkremer, G. (1989) Contact allergies induced by TTS-treatment. *Methods Find Exp. Clin. Pharmacol.* 11(3): 223–225.

Eisenman, A.J., Sloan, J.W., Martin, W.R., et al. (1969) Catecholamine and 17-hydroxycorticosteroid excretion during a cycle of morphine dependence in man. *J. Psychiatr. Res.* 7: 19–28.

Fagerstrom, K. (1982) A comparison of psychological and pharmacological treatment in smoking cessation. *J. Behav. Med.* 5: 343–351.

Fibiger, H.C., Phillips, G.A., Brown, E.E. (1992) The neurobiology of cocaine-induced reinforcement. *Ciba Found. Symp.* 166: 96–124.

Franks, P., Harp J., Bell, B. (1989) Randomized, controlled trial of clonidine for smoking cessation in a primary care setting. *JAMA* 262: 3011–3013.

Fraser, H.F., Shaver, M.R., Maxwell, E.S., Isbell, H., Wikler, A. (1952) Fetal termination of barbiturate abstinence syndrome in man. *J. Pharmacol. Exp. Ther.* 106: 387.

Fudala, P.J., Jaffe, J.H., Dax, E.M., Johnson, R.E. (1990) Use of buprenorphine in the treatment of opioid addiction. II. Physiological and behavioral effects of daily and alternate day administration and abrupt withdrawal. *Clin. Pharmacol. Ther.* 47: 525–534.

Gallimberti, L., Cibin, M., Pagnin, P., Sabbion, R., Pani, P.P., Pirastu, R., Ferrara, S.D., Gessa, G.L. (1993) Gamma-hydroxybutyric acid for treatment of opiate withdrawal syndrome. *Neuropsychopharmacology* 9: 77–81.

Gawin, F.H., Allen, D., Humblestone, B. (1989b) Outpatient treatment of 'crack' cocaine smoking with flupenthixol decanoate. *Arch. Gen. Psychiatry* 46: 322–325.

Gawin, F.H., Kleber, H.D. (1986a) Pharmacological treatment of cocaine abuse. *Psychiatr. Clin. North Am.* 9: 573–583.

Gawin, F.H., Kleber, H.D. (1986b) Abstinence symptomatology and psychiatric diagnosis in chronic cocaine abusers. *Arch. Gen. Psychiatry* 43: 107–113.

Gawin, F.H., Kleber, H.D., Byck, R., Rounsaville, B.J., Kosten, T.R., Jatlow, P.I., Morgan, C. (1989a) Desipramine facilitation of initial cocaine abstinence. *Arch. Gen. Psychiatry* 46: 117–121.

Gawin, F.H., Riordan, C.A., Kleber, H.D. (1985) Methylphenidate use in non-ADD cocaine abusers—a negative study. *Am. J. Drug Alcohol Abuse* 11: 193–197.

Gerstein, D.R. (1992) The effectiveness of drug treatment. In: O'Brien, C.P. and Jaffe, J.H. (eds.) *Addictive states.* New York: Raven Press, pp. 253–282.

Giannini, A.J., Baumgartel, P., DiMarzio, L.R. (1987) Bromocriptine therapy in cocaine withdrawal. *J. Clin. Pharmacol.* 27: 267–270.

Glassman, A.H., Stetner, F., Walsh, T.B., et al. (1988) Heavy smokers, smokers cessation and clonidine. *JAMA* 19: 2863–2866.

Glick, S., Cox, R.D. (1977) Changes in sensitivity to operant effects of dopaminergic and cholinergic agents following morphine withdrawal in rats. *Eur J. Pharmacol.* 42: 303–306.

Gold, M.S., Redmond, D.E., Kleber, H.D. (1978) Clonidine for opiate withdrawal. *Lancet* 1: 929–930.

Goldberg, S.R., Schuster, C.R. (1969) Nalorphine: increased sensitivity of monkeys formerly dependent on morphine. *Science* 166: 1548–1549.

Gorelick, D.A., Weinhold, L.L., Henningfield, J.E. (1993) Carbamazepine (CBZ) does not alter cocaine self-administration in human cocaine addicts. *CPDD 1993 Annual Scientific Meeting Abstracts.*

Grabowski, J., Rhoades, H., Elk, R., Schmitz, J., Davis, C., Creson, D., Kirby, K. (1995) Fluoxetine is in effective for treatment of cocaine dependence or concurrent opiate and cocaine dependence: two placebo-controlled, double-blind trials. *J. Clin. Psychopharmacol.* 15: 163–174.

Halikas, J., Kemp, K., Kuhn, K., Carlson, G., Crea, F. (1989) Carbamazepine for cocaine addiction? *Lancet* 1: 623–624.

Hatsukami, D., Keenan, R., Halikas, J., Pentel, P.R., Brauer, L.H. (1991) Effects of carbamazepine on acute responses to smoked cocaine-base in human cocaine users. *Psychopharmacology* 104: 120–124.

Himmelsbach, C.K. (1942) Clinical studies of drug addiction. *Arch. Gen. Intern. Med.* 69: 766–772.

Hunkeler, W., Mohler, H., Pieri, L., et al. (1981) Selective antagonists of benzodiazepines. *Nature* 290: 514–516.

Jasinski, D.R., Henningfield, J.E., Hickey, J.E., Johnson, R.E. (1983) Progress report of the NIDA Addiction Research Center, Baltimore MD, 1982. In: Harris, L.S. (ed.) *Problems of drug dependence 1982.* NIDA research monographs no.43. Rockville MD: NIDA, pp. 92– 98.

Jasinski, D.R., Pevnick, J.S., Griffith, J.D. (1978) Human pharmacology and abuse potential of the analgesic buprenorphine. *Arch. Gen. Psychiatry* 35(4): 501–516.

Jenkins, S.W., Warfield, N.A., Blaine, J.D., Cornish, J., Ling, W., Rosen, M.I., Urschel, H., Wesson, D., Ziedonis, D. (1992) A pilot trial of gepirone vs. placebo in the treatment of cocaine dependency. *Psychopharmacol. Bull.* 28: 21–26.

Johanson, C.E., and Fischman, M.W. (1989) The pharmacology of cocaine related to its abuse. *Pharmacol. Rev.* 41 (1): 3–52.

Johnson, R.E., Fudala, P.J., Jaffe, J.H. (1992) A controlled trial of buprenorphine for opioid dependence. *JAMA* 267: 2750–2755.

Karras, A. and Kane, J. (1980) Naloxone reduces cigarette smoking. *Life Sci.* 27: 1541–1545.

Kleber, H.D. (1981) Detoxification from narcotics. In: Lowinson, J.H. and Ruiz, P. (eds.) *Substance abuse:* clinical problems and perspectives. Baltimore: William and Wilkins, pp. 317–338.

Kleber, H.D., Kosten, T.R., Gaspari, J., Topazian, M. (1985) Non-tolerance to the opioid antagonism of naltrexone. *Biol. Psychiatry* 20: 66–72.

Kleber, H.D., Topazian, M., Gaspari, J., et al. (1987) Clonidine and naltrexone in the outpatient treatment of heroin withdrawal. *Am. J. Drug Alcohol Abuse* 13: 1–18.

Koe, B.K. (1976) Molecular geometry of inhibitors of the uptake of catecholamines and serotonin in synaptosomal preparations of rat brain. *J. Pharmacol. Exp. Ther.* 199: 649–661.

Koob, G.F. (1992) Neural mechanisms of drug reinforcement. *Ann. NY Acad. Sci.* 654: 171–191.

Kosten, T.R. (1989) Pharmacotherapeutic interventions for cocaine abuse: matching patients to treatments. *J. Nerv. Ment. Dis.* 177: 379–389.

Kosten, T.R., Kleber, H.D. (1984) Strategies to improve compliance with narcotic antagonists. *Am. J. Drug Alcohol Abuse* 10(2): 249–266.

Kosten, T.R., Kleber, H.D. (1988a) Rapid death during cocaine abuse: variant of the neuroleptic malignant syndrome? *Am. J. Drug Alcohol Abuse* 14(3): 335–346.

Kosten, T.R., Kleber, H.D. (1988b) Buprenorphine detoxification from opioid dependence: a pilot study. *Life Sci.* 42: 635–641.

Kosten, T.A., Kosten, T.R., Gawin, F.H., Gordon, L.T., Hogan, I., Kleber, H.D. (1992) An open trial of sertraline for cocaine abuse. *Am. J. Addict.* 1: 349–353.

Kosten, T.R., Morgan, C.M., Falcioni, J., and Schottenfeld,

R.S. (1992a) Pharmacotherapy for cocaine-abusing methadone-maintained patients using amantadine or desipramine. *Arch. Gen. Psychiatry* 49: 894–899.

Kosten, T.R., Morgan, C., Krystal, J.H., Price, L.H., Charney, D.S., Kleber, H.D. (1989) Rapid detoxification procedure using buprenorphine and naloxone. (letter). *Am. J. Psychiatry* 147: 1349.

Kosten, T.R., Schottenfeld, R.S., Ziedonis, D., et al. (1993) Buprenorphine vs. methadone maintenance for opioid dependence. *J. Nerv. Ment. Dis.* 181: 358–364.

Kosten, T.R., Silverman, D.G., Fleming, J., Kosten, T.A., Gawin, F.H., Compton, M., Jatlow, P., Byck, R. (1992b) Intravenous cocaine challenges during naltrexone maintenance: a preliminary study. *Biol. Psychiatry* 32: 543–548.

Krystal, J.H., McDougle, C.J., Kosten, T.R., Price, L.H., Aghajanian, G.K., Charney, D.S. (1992) Baclofen assisted detoxification from opiates: a pilot study. *J. Subst. Abuse Treat.* 9: 139–142.

Kuhar, M.J., Ritz, M.C., Boja, J.W. (1991) The dopamine hypothesis of the reinforcing properties of cocaine. *Trends in Neurosci.* 14(7): 299–302.

Lewis, J.W. (1985) Buprenorphine. *Drug Alcohol Depend.* 14: 363–372.

Ling, W., Charuvastra, V.C., Kain, S.C., et al. (1976) Methadyl acetate and methadone as maintenance treatment for heroin addicts. *Arch. Gen. Psychiatry* 33: 709–712.

Maggio, C.A., Presta, E., Bracco, E.F., et al. (1985) Naltrexone and human eating behavior; a dose-ranging inpatient trial in moderately obese men. *Brain Res. Bull.* 14: 657–661.

Malcolm, R., Ballenger, J.C., Sturgis, E.T., et al. (1989) Double-blind controlled trial comparing carbamazepine to oxazepam treatment of alcohol withdrawal. *Am. J. Psychiatry* 146: 617–621.

Margolin, A., Kosten, T., Petrakis, I., Avants, S.K., Kosten, T. (1991) Bupropion reduces cocaine abuse in methadone-maintained patients. *Arch. Gen. Psychiatry* 48: 87.

Martin, W.R., Jasinski, D.R. (1968) Physiological parameters of morphine dependence in man—tolerance, early abstinence, protracted abstinence. *J. Psychiatr. Res.* 7: 9–17.

Martin, W.R., Wikler, A., Eades, C.G., et al. (1963) Tolerance to and physical dependence on morphine in rats. *Psychopharmacologia* 4: 247–260.

Morgan, C., Kosten, T.R. (1990) Potential toxicity of high dose naltrexone in patients with appetitive disorders. In: Reid, L. (ed.) *Opioids, bulimia, and alcohol abuse and alcoholism.* New York: Springer-Verlag, pp. 261–274.

Morgan, C.H., Kosten, T.R., Gawin, F.H., Kleber, H.D. (1988) A pilot trial of amantadine for cocaine abuse. *NIDA Res. Monogr. Ser.* 81: 81–85.

Naranjo, C.A., Kadlee, K.E., Sanhueza, P., Woodley-Remus, D., Sellers, E.M. (1990) Fluoxetine differentially alters alcohol intake and other consummatory behaviors in problem drinkers. *Clin. Pharmacol. Ther.* 47(4): 490–498.

Nemeth-Coslett, R., Griffiths, R.R. (1986) Naloxone does not affect cigarette smoking. *Psychopharmacology* 89: 261–264.

Petrakis, I., Gordon, L., Carroll, K., Rounsaville, B.J. (1994) Fluoxetine treatment for dually diagnosed methadone maintained opiod addicts: a pilot study. *J addict. Dis.* 13 (3): 25–32.

Pollack, M.H., Rosenbaum, J.F. (1991) Fluoxetine treatment of cocaine abuse in heroin addicts. *J. Clin. Psychiatry* 52: 31–33.

Prochazka, A., Petty, T.L., Nett, L.M., et al. (1990) Catapres-TTS in smoking cessation. *Chest* 92: 68S.

Quigley, A.J., Bredemeyer, D.E., Seow, S.S. (1984) A case of buprenorphine abuse. *Med. J. Aust.* 142: 425–426.

Ritz, M.C., Kuhar, M.J. (1989) Relationship between self-administration of amphetamine and monoamine receptors in brain: comparison with cocaine. *J. Pharmacol. Exp. Ther.* 248: 1010–1017.

Rose, J.E., Jarvik, M.E., Rose, K.D. (1984) Transdermal administration of nicotine. *Drug Alcohol Depend.* 13: 209–213.

Rosen, M.I., McMahon, T.J., Pearsall, H.R., Woods, S.W., Kosten, T.R. The effect of dextromethorphan on naloxone precipitated opiate withdrawal (under review).

Rosen, M.I., Wallace, E.A., McMahon, T.J., Pearsall, H.R., Woods, S.W., Price, L.H., Kosten, T.R. (1994) Buprenorphine: duration of blockade of effects of intramuscular hydromorphone. *Drug Alcohol Depend.* 35: 141–150.

Russell, M.A., Jarvis, M.J., Feyerabend, C., Ferno, O. (1983) Nasal nicotine solution: a potential aid to giving up smoking? *British Med J. Clin. Reasearch Ed.* 286(6366): 683–684.

Schneider, N.G., Jarvik, M.E., Forsythe, A.B., Read, L.L., Elliot, M.E., Schweiger, A. (1983) Nicotine gum in smoking cessation: a placebo-controlled, double-blind trial. *Addict. Behav.* 8: 256–261.

Schuster, C.R., Grove, R.N. (1974) Suppression of cocaine self-administration by extinction and punishment. *Pharmacology, Biochem and Behav.* 2(2): 199–208.

Shi, J.M., O'Connor, P.G., Constantino, J.A., et al. (1993) Three methods of ambulatory opiate detoxification: preliminary results of a randomized clinical trial. National Institute on Drug Abuse Research Monograph #132 (NIH Publ No 93-3505). Washington, DC: U.S. Government Printing Office, p. 309.

Siegal, R.K. (1982) Cocaine smoking. *J. Psychoactive Drugs* 14: 271–355.

Smith, D.E., Wesson, D.R. (1970) A new method for treatment of barbiturate dependence. *JAMA* 231: 294.

Smith, D.E., Wesson, D.R. (1971) A phenobarbital technique for withdrawal of barbiturate abuse. *Arch. Gen. Psychiatry* 24: 56.

Srivastava, E.D., Russell, M.A.H., Feyerabend, C., Masterson, J.G., Rohdes, J. (1991) Sensitivity and tolerance to nicotine in smokers and nonsmokers. *Psychopharmacology* 105: 63–68.

Stolerman, I.P., Goldfarb, T., Fink, R., Jarvik, M. (1973) Influencing cigarette smoking with nicotine antagonists. *Psychopharmacology* 28: 247–259.

Strain, E.C., Stitzer, M.L., Liebson, I.A., Bigelow, G.E. (1994) Comparison of buprenorphine and methadone in the treatment of opioid dependence. *Am. J. Psychiatry* 151: 1025–1030.

Tennant, F.S., Rawson, R.A. (1983) Cocaine and amphetamine dependence treated with desipramine. *NIDA Res. Monogr. Ser.* 43: 351–355.

Tennant, F.S., Sagherian, A.A. (1987) Double-blind comparison of amantadine and bromocriptine for ambulatory withdrawal from cocaine dependence. *Arch. Intern. Med.* 147: 109–112.

Vining, E., Kosten, T.R., Kleber, H.D. (1988) Clinical utility of rapid clonidine naltrexone detoxification for opioid abusers. *Br. J. Addict.* 83: 567–575.

Wei, H., Young, D. (1988) Effect of clonidine on cigarette cessation and in the alleviation of withdrawal symptoms. *Br. J. Addict.* 83: 1221–1226.

Weiss, R.D. (1988) Relapse to cocaine abuse after initiating desipramine treatment. *JAMA* 260: 2545–2546.

West, R., Hakjek, P., McNeill, A. (In press) Effect of buspirone on cigarette withdrawal symptoms and short-term abstinence rates in a smokers clinic. *Psychopharmacology*

Wikler, A., Pescor, F.T. (1967) Classical conditioning of a morphine abstinence phenomenon, reinforcement of opioid-drinking behavior and "relapse" in morphine-addicted rats. *Psychopharmacologia* 10: 255–284.

Wise, R. (1987) The role of reward pathways in the development of drug dependence. *Pharmacol. Ther.* 35: 227–263.

Woods, J.H., Katz, J.L., Winger, G. (1992) Benzodiazepines: use, abuse and consequences. *Pharmacol. Rev.* 44: 151–347.

Woolverton, W.L. (1987) Evaluation of the role of norepinephrine in the reinforcing effects of psychomotor stimulants in rhesus monkeys *Pharmacol. Biochem. Behav.* 26: 835–839.

Drug Addiction and its Treatment: Nexus of Neuroscience and Behavior, edited by Bankole A. Johnson and John D. Roache. Lippincott–Raven Publishers, Philadelphia, © 1997.

18

Integrating Behavioral and Pharmacological Treatments

Kimberly C. Kirby, *Joy M. Schmitz, and †Maxine L. Stitzer

Medical College of Pennsylvania and Hahnemann University,
Allegheny University of the Health Sciences, Philadelphia, Pennsylvania 19102-1192;
*University of Texas Medical School, Houston, Texas 77030;
†Division of Psychiatry, Johns Hopkins University School of Medicine, Baltimore, Maryland 21224

Approximately 50 years ago, a new approach to the problem of drug addiction began to emerge that blended the ideas and methods of experimental psychology, with those of medical/pharmacological approaches to disease. Traditionally, pharmacological approaches to drug addiction emphasized physiological changes produced by abused drugs, particularly the development of tolerance and withdrawal. Prevention of unpleasant withdrawal symptoms was seen as a major motive for continuing drug use, while activation of brain reward mechanisms later became a dominant theme in the explanation of drug-seeking behaviors (Wise, 1987). In contrast, traditional psychological approaches searched for a psychological or personality defect within the individual to explain persistent drug use, rather than focusing on effects of the drug itself. A common theme was that people with certain personality characteristics were prone to the use of drugs to reduce stress, anxiety, or tension and "escape from reality" (Stolerman and Goldberg, 1986, p.2). Both approaches had limitations. For example, the traditional pharmacological approach had difficulty explaining why drugs with no clear withdrawal reaction were abused. The traditional psychological approach was challenged by research showing that laboratory animals could come to self-administer drugs persistently without any evidence of a preexisting abnormal psychology or conditions of stress (Griffiths et al., 1980). Despite these limitations, research in pharmacology and psychology made significant contributions by laying the foundation for the emergence of a new approach to the problem of drug dependence and a new scientific discipline associated with that approach. That discipline was behavioral pharmacology.

An important development facilitating the blending of pharmacology and psychology came from significant developments within the field of psychology itself. Since about the turn of the century, psychology had been struggling with the introduction and development of an experimental approach that turned the focus of investigation from thoughts, feelings, and other factors inside the individual to observable behaviors and environmental factors more easily accessible to experimentation. During the 1930s significant conceptual and methodological developments clearly emerged from experimental psychology, and classical and operant conditioning were born (Konorski and Miller, 1928, 1937; Skinner, 1931, 1935a,b, 1937, 1938). The emergence of a conceptual approach more in keeping with natural science and the promise of its associated methodology provided an essential foundation for the integration of psychology and pharmacology.

The natural science approach of operant and classical conditioning has many parallels with pharmacological approaches to discovering lawful relationships between organisms and their internal or external environments. In the first part of this chapter, we outline some components of behavioral and pharmacological approaches. In the second part, we review a wide variety of drug abuse treatments that have successfully combined behavioral and pharmacological treatment components. Finally, in the section on future directions, we suggest a conceptual model for improving integration of the approaches by viewing the functions of pharmacotherapies within a behavioral framework, and then discuss practical aspects of treatment development needing more research.

COMPONENTS OF BEHAVIORAL AND PHARMACOLOGICAL APPROACHES

Psychology: The Analysis of Behavior

The analysis of behavior focuses on delineating interactions between the organism and the environment relative to a specific behavior, and measuring the effects of those interactions on that behavior. Conceptually, behavior analysis divides events into three categories to examine these interactions. The three categories are: the antecedent events, or events that precede the behavior of interest; the behavior itself; and consequent events, or events that follow the behavior of interest. In behavioral treatments of drug addiction, drug dependence is conceptualized as a disorder of operant behavior in which drug reinforcement has produced persistent and high rates of drug seeking and administration, displacing other more productive operant behaviors. Antecedents and consequences of behavior are removed, introduced, or altered, and the effects of these manipulations on the behaviors of interest are monitored. Behavioral interventions aim to (1) eliminate or reduce the antecedents that elicit or set the occasion for drug taking; (2) arrange reinforcement for more desirable alternative behaviors to drug taking, while eliminating

consequences that reduce the probability of abstinence from the drug; and (3) change the environmental consequences of drug taking in a way that alters the characteristic effect of those consequences on drug taking.

Antecedent Interventions

Several behavioral approaches have been developed to address the antecedents of drug taking. One approach, based on respondent conditioning models, provides repeated exposure to the antecedent stimuli in an environment in which these stimuli will not be followed by drug taking (Childress et al., 1986). Disrupting the pairing of the stimuli and the drug effects disrupts or extinguishes the eliciting function of the stimuli, and they no longer function as antecedents for drug taking. This procedure is known as *respondent extinction*. Another intervention, known as *relapse prevention*, is closely tied to operant conditioning models (Marlatt, 1985). This intervention involves teaching the drug user to identify stimuli and events that set the occasion for drug use, and to execute responses to avoid drug taking. Other procedures involving these principles make use of *instructions* to provide new or modulate existing antecedent events that occasion behaviors related to drug taking or abstinence.

Increasing Alternative Behaviors

Another type of behavioral intervention focuses on increasing desirable behaviors that will effectively compete with the drug taking. This is accomplished by identifying a behavior incompatible with drug self-administration. Once a competing behavior is identified, steps are taken to ensure that performing the behavior results in consequences that increase the frequency of the behavior. This procedure is known as *positive reinforcement*. If a number of desirable competing behaviors are positively reinforced and occurring at a fairly high rate, less time is available for the undesirable behavior of drug taking. This behavioral strategy has been incorporated into an intervention known as the community reinforcement approach (CRA), a comprehensive treatment that has been successfully used to treat both alcoholism (Azrin 1976; Hunt and Azrin, 1973) and cocaine addiction (Higgins et al., 1991, 1993). By arranging positive reinforcement of competing behaviors, CRA interventions also alter some of the consequences of abstinence from drinking or drug taking. The initial phases of abstinence can involve losing not only the reinforcement provided by the drug, but also other reinforcers associated with drinking or drug taking, such as those associated with specific activities and friends. Some of the competing behaviors incorporated into this approach provide drug-free environments for socializing, and therefore replace the former sources of reinforcement.

Changing the Consequences of Drug Taking

In addition to increasing positive reinforcement of competing behaviors, *operant extinction* methods have been used to change or eliminate the positive consequences of drinking or drug taking. For example, in CRA, family or friends are trained to eliminate positive social consequences following drinking or drug taking by ignoring the individual or no longer providing special comforts (e.g., letting a drinker stay passed out on the floor, rather than cleaning him up and putting him to bed).

Another method of changing the consequences of drug taking involves *punishment* procedures. Instead of eliminating the positive reinforcers of drug taking, these procedures arrange for the provision of an aversive consequence that will result in a reduction of drug-taking behavior. For example, an early intervention for cocaine-addicted professionals involved a time-limited agreement in which the patient wrote a letter confessing to drug use, then gave the letter to a therapist (Anker and Crowley, 1982; Crowley, 1984). The therapist would then send the letter to the licensing agency if the individual failed to provide a cocaine-free urine. Under this arrangement, the undesirable behavior of cocaine use would be followed immediately by the consequence of professional license loss rather than leaving this possible consequence to the vagaries of the social and institutional environment in which the drug abuser operates. This arrangement was successful in reducing cocaine use while the agreement was in effect. Other behavioral interventions have used *response-cost* procedures in which access to positive reinforcers is blocked or eliminated contingent on drug taking. For example, Higgins et al. (1991, 1993) used a positive reinforcement procedure in which vouchers of increasing values could be earned for cocaine abstinence. Provision of a cocaine-positive urine sample resulted in resetting voucher values to their initial low levels. This constituted a response cost, whereby positive reinforcers were lost as a consequence of drug taking.

Thus, strategies for behavioral therapies have included (1) altering antecedents of the behavior by removing them, extinguishing their function, or introducing new antecedents; (2) increasing alternative responses through reinforcement procedures; and (3) altering the consequences of drug use by removing the collateral reinforcement or introducing aversive consequences contingent on drug use.

Pharmacology: The Analysis of Drug Action

Pharmacological treatments are generally considered within a medical disease model in which the drug produces beneficial effects on symptoms by alleviating some physiologic or neurochemical imbalance of the organism. In this model, a pharmacological therapy interacts with the internal environment of the organism rather than the external environment and any benefits to behavior of the organism are achieved passively as a result of physiological alterations or corrections. The objectives of an analysis of drug action are to identify the site of drug action, to delineate the chemical or physical interactions between drug and cell, and to characterize the resulting physiological effects (Ross, 1990). The effects of most drugs result from their interaction with macromolecular components of the organism known as receptors. Any functional macromolecular component of the organism can operate as a drug receptor, but a group of proteins that normally serve as receptors for endogenous regulatory ligands such as hormones or neurotransmitters are particularly important. Many drugs act on these receptors. Those that mimic the effect of the endogenous regulatory compound are called *agonists*. Other drugs may bind to the receptor, interfering with the effect of the endogenous compound, but otherwise having no regulatory activity. Drugs that have no intrinsic regulatory activity but cause effects by inhibiting the action of an endogenous compound are called *antagonists* (Ross, 1990).

Pharmacological treatments of drug abuse usually focus on altering the action of abused drugs, rather than those of endogenous compounds. Many pharmacological treatments of drug abuse involve the administration of a medication that functions as a substitute for the abused drug at receptors (agonist), or as a blockade for the abused drug at receptors (antagonist).

Agonist Interventions

At sufficient doses, agonist medications bind to available receptors where they prevent the abused drug from binding, while at the same time activating the receptors and causing direct effects of their own. This may create *cross-tolerance* and result in marked attenuation of the drug effects. Thus, administration of the abused drug may have little or no effect during agonist replacement treatment. Agonist medications have direct actions that are similar to the abused drug and therefore can prevent or reduce withdrawal symptoms. As such, these medications *replace* the abuse drug by providing a more desirable alternative to it. For example, the opiate agonist methadone is an accepted pharmacological treatment for heroin addiction. This medication is believed to bind to the same receptors as heroin. Under these circumstances, heroin is prevented from binding to receptors and cross-tolerance develops so that typical doses of heroin have less effect. Finally, methadone has pharmacological properties that are sufficiently similar to those of heroin to provide replacement therapy and suppress the withdrawal syndrome associated with cessation of chronic heroin use. It provides a more desirable alternative to intravenous heroin administration because it is effective by the oral route, has a slower onset of action and an extended duration of action, and effectively reduces the injections associated with higher risk of HIV and other infections (cf. Jaffe and Martin, 1990, pp. 508–509). Methadone replacement has been most effective when used continuously, as in methadone maintenance treatment, but has also been used temporarily, as in methadone detoxification treatments designed to transition the patient to a drug-free state (Jaffe and Kleber, 1989).

Antagonist Interventions

While antagonist medications also bind to available receptors, preventing the abused drug from binding, they do not produce cross-tolerance or effects that are similar to the abused drug. As such, they are ineffective in preventing withdrawal (and can actually induce withdrawal symptoms by displacing agonist drug from the receptor if agonist is present prior to administration of the antagonist). Therefore, in pharmacological treatments of drug dependence, the sole mechanism of action for antagonist medications is through a *blockade* that prevents discernible effects when the drug of abuse is administered.

Drug Metabolism Interventions

Although many pharmacological treatments of drug abuse involve administering either an agonist, partial agonist, or antagonist for the abused drug, there are medications that work via alternative mechanisms. For example, disulfiram, a pharmacological agent used in the treatment of alcoholism, works through *alteration of the intermediary metabolism* of alcohol (Rall, 1990, p. 378). Disulfiram interferes with the action of the enzyme aldehyde dehydrogenase, which is the primary agent responsible for oxidizing the acetaldehyde produced by ethanol consumption. As such, levels of acetaldehyde accumulate in tissue and produce unpleasant signs and symptoms including flushing, headache, nausea, vomiting, chest pain, thirst, and vertigo. The possibility of experiencing aversive effects is generally sufficient to motivate avoidance of alcohol ingestion during disulfiram therapy.

Symptomatic Treatment Interventions

Another example of pharmacological treatments that use neither agonists nor antagonists for the abused drug is the use of antidepressants in the treatment of chronically depressed alcoholics or cocaine addicts. Antidepressant medications do not alter the effect of the abused drug, but rather treat an underlying psychiatric disorder that has been suggested to be part of the cause of the drug abuse (i.e., in cases in which drug use is believed to be motivated by escape from chronic depression). As such, administering the antidepressant may *medicate the antecedent symptoms* that occasion the drug use.

Thus, traditional strategies for pharmacotherapies have included (1) providing replacement therapy, or a more desirable alternative to the abused drug that also alleviates withdrawal symptoms; (2) eliminating or reducing effects of the abused drug through blockade or cross-tolerance; (3) altering the intermediary metabolism of the abused drug in a way that changes its characteristic effect; and (4) treating the antecedent symptoms that were believed to occasion the drug use.

INTEGRATING APPROACHES

When behavioral and pharmacological treatments are integrated, the combination usually produces better outcomes than either therapy given individually. Additive integra-

tions of behavioral and pharmacological interventions may reduce use of the primary drug more than either therapy given individually. Alternately, behavioral interventions may be combined with a pharmacological treatment to address secondary drug abuse or other concurrent behavioral problems that the pharmacological intervention is not designed or intended to address. Another important integration is one in which behavioral interventions are added to increase compliance with a pharmacological intervention that is otherwise associated with poor compliance and treatment retention. A fourth additive integration involves combining behavior therapies with pharmacotherapy to address patterns of multiple drug use in which drug interactions may lead to relapse. Finally, we should note that sometimes the effects of combining behavioral and pharmacological treatments are not additive. In some instances, one intervention may modulate the effects of the other. In the following sections we review a wide variety of drug abuse treatments that have successfully combined behavioral and pharmacological approaches according to the four additive integrations described above, and we provide an example of a way that one intervention can modulate the effects of another.

Combining Interventions to More Effectively Address Primary Drug Abuse

The effectiveness of many drug abuse treatments can be enhanced by combining pharmacotherapy and behavior therapy. In these applications, the two interventions that target the same behavior produce a combined therapeutic effect greater than either independent effect. One reason for this may be that pharmacological and behavioral interventions address different aspects of the dependence process (e.g., physiological versus environmental factors). Nicotine replacement therapy, for example, effectively reduces tobacco withdrawal symptoms, but is relatively less effective in increasing alternative responses in the presence of smoking-related cues. Thus, a combined treatment that addresses the pharmacological and behavioral aspects of smoking cessation may be indicated.

Example: Pharmacological and Behavioral Treatments for Tobacco Dependence

The most developed group of medications for smoking cessation are replacement therapies using nicotine-delivery products such as nicotine polacrilex (gum) and transdermal nicotine (patch). The primary mechanism of action for nicotine replacement is via suppression of many of the acute tobacco-withdrawal symptoms. This pharmacological effect has been reliably demonstrated in studies examining nicotine gum (Henningfield and Jasinski, 1988; Hughes and Hatsukami, 1985; Hughes et al., 1984; Russell, 1988; Schneider and Jarvik, 1984; West et al., 1984) and transdermal nicotine (Fagerstrom et al., 1992; Hughes and Glaser, 1993; Palmer and Faulds, 1992).

Results from numerous studies suggest that adding nicotine gum to behavioral treatment increases quit rates among smokers (Hughes, 1991). Killen et al. (1984) conducted one of the first tests of combining nicotine gum and behavior therapy. Following a 7-week behavioral smoking cessation program, 64 subjects were randomly assigned to one of three maintenance therapies: nicotine gum alone, skills training alone, or combined nicotine gum plus skills training. As predicted, the combined maintenance therapy improved outcome over both single treatments. Similar findings were reported by Hall et al. (1985), in an early study comparing behavior therapy with or without gum or a low-contact therapy with gum. Although additive effects of the combined therapy are not universally reported (Hall et al., 1987), a recent meta-analysis reviewed more than a decade of treatment outcome research and concluded that nicotine gum consistently improves the efficacy of smoking cessation treatment under a variety of conditions, but particularly when combined with intensive behavioral counseling (Cepeda-Benito, 1993). When used in the context of intensive therapy, the effect size for nicotine gum over placebo was statistically significant at the end of treatment and at long-term follow-up intervals (12 months after treatment). When used without the intensive therapy, nicotine gum was better than placebo and no-gum controls at short-term but not at long-term follow-up.

Recent studies have also evaluated nicotine patch therapy with and without behavioral interventions. As with gum, active patch therapy is effective as compared with placebo patch when delivered in a variety of behavioral support contexts. A recent meta-analysis by Fiore and colleagues (1994a) of placebo controlled studies concluded that the patch produces a two- to threefold increase in smoking cessation rates. The interaction between behavioral and pharmacological therapies is nicely illustrated in a recent set of patch studies by Fiore and colleagues (1994b). Six-month abstinence rates were 34% versus 21% for active versus placebo patch subjects who had been treated with intensive (1 hour per week) behavior therapy. In contrast, abstinence rates were only 18% versus 7% for active versus placebo patch subjects who had been treated with a minimal (15 minutes per week) behavioral intervention. In both cases, active patch produced significantly better outcomes than placebo patch, but absolute quit rates were much better for the intensive therapy groups.

In the case of tobacco dependence treatment, both behavioral and pharmacological interventions have independent efficacy, but best results are achieved when the two types of therapy are combined. Presumably, this is because nicotine replacement addresses physiological factors in dependence by suppressing withdrawal, while behavior therapy addresses environmental and behavioral aspects of dependence by teaching relapse prevention techniques.

Example: Pharmacological and Behavioral Treatments for Alcohol Dependence

Recent evidence suggests that naltrexone, an opioid antagonist, is an effective pharmacological agent in the treatment of alcohol dependence (Volpicelli, 1992). The extent to which naltrexone enhances abstinence rates may depend on the type of concurrent behavior therapy provided. O'Malley and colleagues (1992) studied this medication-therapy interaction by randomly assigning 97 alcohol-dependent patients to receive either naltrexone or placebo and either behaviorally based relapse prevention or a supportive therapy. The behavior therapy was designed to foster acquisition of coping skills. Subjects were trained to monitor their drinking behavior and urges to drink, while learning alternative "coping" responses for handling antecedent stimuli or situations associated with drinking. In the event of a lapse to drinking, subjects were taught specific responses designed to alter the consequences of the lapse so as to prevent a full relapse. For example, subjects were encouraged to regulate their negative thoughts, leave the situation, or call a friend. In contrast, subjects receiving supportive therapy were not taught specific coping skills and total abstinence was strongly recommended. As expected, naltrexone was superior to placebo, producing higher overall rates of abstinence independent of the behavior therapy delivered. However, there was an important interaction observed between naltrexone and the type of behavior therapy delivered. Among the naltrexone-treated subjects, those receiving behavior therapy were actually more likely to sample alcohol following treatment compared with those receiving supportive therapy. However, relapse rates among naltrexone-treated subjects who sampled alcohol were considerably lower for those receiving behavior therapy than for those receiving supportive therapy. In other words, subjects who learned coping skills to prevent a lapse from becoming a relapse were less likely to return to heavy drinking compared with subjects who did not receive relapse prevention training, but naltrexone appeared important in helping them prevent the lapse from turning into a relapse. Patients who received behavior therapy without the pharmacological support of naltrexone showed no better relapse rates than those receiving supportive therapy with placebo. This study supports the combined efficacy of medication plus behavior therapy for the treatment of alcohol dependence, although the mechanism for naltrexone's beneficial effects in preventing relapse is not presently understood.

Combining Interventions to Address Secondary Behavioral Problems

In the treatment of drug addiction, the primary behavior of interest is usually drug taking, but other aspects of physical health and psychosocial functioning (e.g., employment, social interaction, legal involvement, depression) are important secondary clinical concerns. Since the effects of pharmacotherapies tend to be specific to self-administration of a particular drug of abuse, these interventions tend to focus primarily on the drug-taking problem. For example, while methadone treatment is well established as an effective treatment for reducing opiate abuse, it is not a panacea. Patients rarely report to treatment with the isolated problem of opiate addiction. Usually additional nonopiate drugs are secondary problems of abuse (Condelli et al., 1991; Dunteman et al., 1992; Iguchi et al., 1993; Kosten et al., 1987; Stitzer et al., 1981) and multiple psychosocial and/or medical problems are present (Dunteman et al., 1992). Methadone alone will not address these additional problems; however, the addition of behavioral interventions may help these secondary clinical concerns.

Example: Methadone Maintenance and Contingency Management

Numerous studies have documented the effectiveness of adding behavioral contingencies to address use of a nonopiate drug or polysubstance abuse problems during treatment (Dolan et al., 1985; Glosser, 1983; Iguchi et al., 1988; Magura et al., 1988; Milby et al., 1978; Saxon et al., 1992; Stitzer et al., 1982a,b, 1986, 1992). A variety of contingencies have been employed, including positive-reinforcement procedures in which goods and/or privileges are given contingent upon provision of urine samples free of illicit drugs, and treatment termination procedures in which methadone or other treatment components are removed contingent upon provision of drug-positive samples. Results from studies using treatment termination procedures have shown decreases in illicit substance use approximately equal to the results obtained in studies employing positive-reinforcement procedures. Stitzer et al. (1986) conducted a systematic comparison of treatment termination and positive-reinforcement contingencies. Study participants were 20 opiate-dependent patients who were maintained on an average daily methadone dose of 51.8 mg and who tested illicit drug-positive (predominantly for benzodiazepines) on half or more of their urine samples. Subjects were randomly assigned to two groups: one received a methadone dose-increase contingency and the other received a dose-decrease contingency. For both groups of subjects, each urine sample that contained detectable quantities of any drug besides methadone resulted in a 5-mg dose decrease, while each sample free of all supplemental drugs resulted in a 5-mg dose increase. Patients on the dose-increase contingency were able to increase their dose to 160% of its original value by providing drug-free urines. Dose increases were lost if drug-positive specimens were provided, but the dose could not drop below its original value. Patients on the dose-decrease contingency could have their dose reduced to 40% of its original value if drug-positive urines were provided. The dose could be restored back to its original value by providing a sufficient number of drug-free specimens, but it could not increase above its original level. About half of the subjects in each condition showed substantial improvement with no difference in extent of supplemental drug use reduction between the two groups. However, one important qualitative difference in outcomes for study failures was noted between groups. Almost half of the subjects in the dose-decrease condition dropped out of treatment, while no subjects assigned to the dose-increase contingency left treatment. This

suggests that while the contingencies were equally effective in reducing illicit drug use, their effect on collateral behaviors (i.e., treatment retention) showed important differences.

Several studies have focused contingency management in methadone treatment on non-drug behaviors. Stitzer and Bigelow (1984) showed that methadone dose take-home privileges or a program fee rebate could be applied contingently to increase timely fee payment in methadone programs. Milby et al. (1978) reported that a combined contingency on illicit drug use and "productivity" (e.g., employment) not only decreased illicit drug use, but also led to increases in productive activity. Similarly, Magura et al. (1988) reported that behavioral contracts that provided take-home privileges contingent upon performance of behaviors other than drug abstinence were initially successful. A direct examination of the effects of behavioral contracting for drug use versus behaviors other than drug use was conducted by Iguchi et al. (1996). They randomly assigned subjects to earn vouchers either for provision of urine free of unauthorized substances (UA group) or for the completion of objectively defined treatment plan–related tasks (TP group). The value of the vouchers that could be earned weekly was the same in both groups. The authors found that subjects in the TP group performed significantly better with respect to abstinence from illicit substances than did subjects in the UA group.

Example: Methadone Maintenance and Psychosocial Treatment

The addition of psychosocial treatment to pharmacological treatment is based on the rationale that most medications, even effective agents such as methadone, are unlikely to influence other problem domains, such as family and social functioning, and legal and employment problems. Researchers at the Penn-VA Center have systematically evaluated whether increasing the amount of psychosocial treatment services for methadone patients leads to improved clinical outcomes. In a recent study

(McLellan et al., 1993), 92 intravenous opiate users, maintained on a therapeutic dose of methadone (60–90 mg/d), were randomly assigned to one of three treatment groups for a 6-month clinical trial. Subjects assigned to the minimum methadone services (MMS) received methadone alone, without counseling, contingency management, or psychosocial services. The standard methadone services (SMS) group offered methadone plus regular counseling sessions involving the application of rewarding and punishing contingencies to achieve positive behavioral change. The enhanced methadone services (EMS) condition provided the highest level of intensity by offering regular counseling, contingency management, and extended on-site medical/psychiatric, employment, and family therapy services. Results clearly favored the enhanced methadone services group in terms of overall clinical improvement. The EMS condition produced significantly more improvements than did the SMS and MMS in the problem areas of employment, alcohol use, criminal activity, and psychiatric status. Subjects receiving methadone only showed more cocaine and opiate use than did the other two groups, with 69% of MMS patients requiring "protective transfer" or termination because of unremitting illicit drug use, compared with 41% and 19% in the SMS and EMS intervention, respectively. Interestingly, those MMS patients who were transferred to standard care showed significant reductions in opiate and cocaine use within 4 weeks after the transfer, and at approximately the same dose of methadone.

Combining Interventions to Increase Medication Compliance

In some cases, the medication employed in substance abuse treatment can itself function as a reinforcer when administered in a treatment context. For example, methadone is readily self-administered by the opiate-dependent clients for whom it is prescribed (Spiga et al., 1996; Thompson et al., 1993) and it is chosen over other reinforcers (Stitzer et al., 1979,

1983). On the other hand, nicotine replacement therapy less readily functions as a positive reinforcer. In pharmacotherapies in which the treatment agent does not readily function as a reinforcer, compliance with the intervention and treatment retention often become issues. These problems are most apparent with nonagonist medications such as disulfiram and opiate antagonists, which not only fail to function as a reinforcers themselves but also prevent the reinforcing effects of the abused drug. Behavioral interventions have been useful in addressing compliance and retention problems in pharmacotherapies that involve medications that do not function as reinforcers.

Example: Behavioral Interventions and Disulfiram Treatment

Several studies have documented the difficulties of compliance associated with disulfiram treatment, indicating that fewer than 10% of patients continue to administer disulfiram regularly (Guerrein et al., 1973; Lubetkin et al., 1971; Ludwig et al., 1970). However, when strict contingencies are placed on disulfiram ingestion, favorable results have been obtained (Bickel et al., 1989; Bigelow et al., 1976; Bourne et al., 1966; Haynes, 1973; Liebson and Bigelow, 1972; Liebson et al., 1973).

Liebson et al. (1978) examined the effectiveness of adding a contingency for disulfiram ingestion in reducing alcohol consumption among alcoholic methadone patients. For one group of randomly assigned patients in this study, access to the daily methadone dose was contingent upon first ingesting a dose of disulfiram. The other group of patients were given their disulfiram and instructed to ingest it at home. The investigators found a significant reduction in days drinking for the group of patients ingesting disulfiram contingently and concluded that the addition of a contingency for disulfiram ingestion was quite effective in reducing alcohol consumption among alcoholic methadone patients in comparison to a usual care disulfiram prescription procedure.

A systematic comparison of disulfiram alone, disulfiram with contingencies for ingestion (disulfiram assurance procedure), and disulfiram assurance plus behavior therapy was conducted by Azrin et al. (1982). Forty-three outpatients from an alcoholism treatment clinic were randomly assigned to one of the three groups. Clients in all three groups were requested to bring in a significant other (spouse, relative, close friend) and were scheduled to receive five weekly counseling sessions, followed by a monthly contact thereafter. They all received educational materials and were encouraged to stay totally abstinent from alcohol. Clients in the traditional group were instructed that disulfiram administration was their responsibility and told to take it daily as prescribed. The disulfiram assurance group received specific training in adhering to the disulfiram regimen in which they were trained to take the medication at a set time, place, and in the company of the significant other. In addition, the client and significant other were trained in communication skills to assist in handling situations in which the client did not want to take the disulfiram. Clients in the third group received disulfiram assurance and also received behavior training specified by the community reinforcement program. This included training in relaxation, drink refusal, social skills training, advice on recreation, job-finding counseling, and reciprocity counseling with the significant other. The results clearly showed the traditional treatment was least successful, disulfiram assurance was more effective, and the comprehensive behavior therapy was the most effective in terms of compliance with the disulfiram regimen and in terms of days of abstinence. Not only did adding behavioral contingency contracting increase the effectiveness of the pharmacotherapy, but the more comprehensive the behavioral intervention, the better the results.

Example: Behavioral Interventions and Opiate Antagonist Treatment

Opiate antagonists, which have no dependence potential, have been suggested as alternatives to methadone treatment for opiate ad-

diction. Like disulfiram, opiate antagonist medications have been associated with poor treatment compliance when administered alone; however, some data suggest they may be applied more successfully when combined with behavioral interventions. Grabowski et al. (1979) provided payments to opiate-dependent patients receiving naloxone according to several different schedules of reinforcement. For the first week after entering the study, subjects received payments on a continuous reinforcement schedule (CRF) in which they received $3.35 each day they attended the clinic and ingested their naloxone. After the first week, patients were assigned to receive payments on one of four schedules: CRF, fixed ratio (FR), variable ratio (VR), or fixed interval (FI). The total possible payments per month ($40.20) was constant across all schedules with CRF payments continuing at $3.35 each, and FR, VR, and FI payments being $10.05 each. Results showed that response-based schedules (i.e., CRF, FR, and VR) produced 88.0% attendance and naloxone ingestion compared with only 72.8% for the time-based schedule (FI). This difference was statistically significant ($p < .001$). Unfortunately, the study only compared different reinforcement schedules; it did not include a systematic comparison of naloxone with and without contingency management. The authors reported that overall clinic retention at 1 month improved from 60% prior to introducing the payment schedules to 89% when the payment schedules were in effect; however, this was not a controlled comparison and, as the authors noted, increased duration of treatment alone does not assure development of the regular pattern of naloxone ingestion that is necessary to maintain the opiate blockade.

Callahan et al. (1980) compared an intervention involving naltrexone alone with a combined treatment of naltrexone and behavior therapy. The behavioral therapy used was nonspecific, placing emphasis on skills training and behavioral contracts to enhance general aspects of program function, rather than focusing on increasing naltrexone administration or program attendance. Despite this nonspecificity, they found that the combined intervention initially produced significantly better compliance with naloxone administration than the intervention involving naloxone alone. However, differences between groups diminished after 7 months of treatment, with the naltrexone-only group increasing in compliance to levels comparable to the combined group. These results are difficult to interpret, since the specifics of the behavioral contingency contracting were not reported, the duration of the behavioral intervention was not clear, and treatment of missing data was not specified. Nonetheless, the study does support the conclusion that a combined behavioral/pharmacological intervention can produce better initial results than pharmacotherapy alone and suggests that Azrin et al.'s (1982) results may extend to other pharmacotherapies that involve nonreinforcing treatment agents.

Combining Interventions to Address Multiple Drug Use Increasing Relapse Risk

Some combinations of drugs can have important implications for treatment because they interact in such a way that a secondary drug sets the occasion for use of the primary drug that is identified as the problem. While understanding that a particular situation is a relapse risk is generally considered a behavioral treatment approach, in some cases pharmacological interventions can be used to address these specific relapse risk factors.

Example: Alcohol and Cigarette Smoking

Studies demonstrate a reliable relationship between alcohol and cigarette smoking such that drinking alcohol under a variety of conditions reliably increases cigarette smoking (Griffiths et al., 1976; Mello and Mendelson, 1972; Mello et al., 1980). These findings are consistent with a study of relapse following smoking cessation in which alcohol consumption was cited as an antecedent for nearly one-

fifth of the subjects (Shiffman, 1982). Clearly awareness and understanding of the relationship between cigarette smoking and alcohol consumption could be helpful in planning relapse prevention strategies for individuals who have quit smoking. A logical extension of these observations is that there might be benefits to treating certain smokers with disulfiram as a relapse-prevention strategy during an attempt to quit smoking.

Example: Alcohol and Cocaine

Both clinical and epidemiological studies suggest the prevalence of concurrent use of alcohol and cocaine and the comorbidity of alcoholism and cocaine addiction are greater than would be expected by chance occurrence of two independent conditions (Gorelick, 1992). These findings are consistent with a study of cocaine use among methadone maintenance clients in which 50% of the subjects interviewed identified alcohol consumption as an activity that occasioned their cocaine use (Kirby et al., 1995). Furthermore, of all the activities identified, drinking alcohol was most frequently endorsed as a "high-impact" situation, a situation that was likely to lead to cocaine use when it occurred, even if it occurred infrequently. These observations suggest that interventions to stop alcohol drinking might be helpful to individuals trying to abstain from cocaine.

Recently, Higgins et al. (1993) reported a combined behavioral and pharmacological intervention designed specifically for patients abusing both cocaine and alcohol. Sixteen patients who entered a behavioral therapy program received disulfiram therapy during a portion of the study. Patients reported less drinking while on disulfiram than when off and the percentage of cocaine-positive urine specimens was significantly lower when patients were taking disulfiram than it was when they were not taking it. Supervised disulfiram therapy was therefore associated with significant decreases in both alcohol and cocaine use. There is little pharmacological reason to assume that disulfiram would be an effective pharmacotherapy for cocaine addiction. It is likely, therefore, that the effectiveness of disulfiram in reducing cocaine use was modulated through behavioral factors. For example, if cocaine use most often occurs in the context of alcohol use, reducing alcohol use can in turn lead to reduced cocaine use. Similar findings have been suggested in the treatment of concurrent cocaine and opiate use (Kosten et al., 1989).

Modulating the Effects of One Intervention by Combining with Another

The additive integrations described above involved combining behavioral and pharmacological treatments that may be effective individually, but are more effective when combined. Interventions in which one component modulates the effects of the other might be considered a more subtle method of integrating behavioral and pharmacological treatments. This type of integration involves understanding the relationships between components and the ways in which the function of one component can change in the context of the other.

Example: The Effect of Instructions on Methadone Detoxification Treatment

Providing patients with information and instructions is generally recognized as ineffective when it is the primary strategy in behavioral treatments of drug abuse. However, in the context of a moderately effective pharmacotherapy, providing patients with information can modulate the effects of the pharmacotherapy. For example, Green and Gossop (1988) randomly assigned 30 patients entering methadone detoxification treatment to informed or uninformed groups. Prior to beginning the pharmacotherapy, the informed group was provided with specific information about the dosing regimen and about the length and intensity of the symptoms they might experience. The uninformed group was not provided with specific information a priori. The

informed group showed reduced withdrawal symptoms and better treatment retention compared with the uninformed group.

Example: The Effect of Instructions on Nicotine Gum for Smoking Cessation

The ability of instructions to modulate the effects of a pharmacotherapy was systematically examined by Hughes et al. (1989). They assigned 77 smokers who quit smoking to one of six groups composing a 3 x 2 double-blind design contrasting instruction and receipt of nicotine gum. Subjects were given one of three instructions: (1) they would receive nicotine gum, (2) they would receive placebo gum, or (3) they would not know whether the gum they received was active or placebo. Within each of these three groups, half of the subjects actually received nicotine gum (2 mg) and half received placebo. At weekly postcessation meetings several measures of smoking behavior, withdrawal symptoms, and side effects were monitored. Receiving active nicotine gum or being told that one received nicotine gum increased measures of abstinence and decreased number of days smoking. However, the effects of the two components differed on other measures. With respect to withdrawal, receiving active nicotine gum reduced symptoms, but being told that one received active gum did not. Measures of craving were decreased, and gum self-administration and reported helpfulness of the gum were increased by being told the gum was active; however, the type of gum actually received did not influence these measures. Finally, the effects of instructions and nicotine interacted. For example, receiving nicotine gum increased abstinence more if subjects were told they received placebo gum or if they were blind to the gum received, than if they were told they received active gum. The results of this study suggested that the effects of instructions and nicotine are not mutually exclusive, vary across dependent variables, and interact such that instructions modify the therapeutic and subjective effects of nicotine. Thus, in combining behavioral and pharmacological interventions, it is important to understand that one intervention can modulate the other such that the effectiveness of each is influenced by the context provided by the other.

FUTURE DIRECTIONS: MODELS OF INTEGRATED TREATMENT

This chapter describes some of the many ways in which behavioral and pharmacological interventions have been used together in the treatment of substance dependence. As illustrated by the examples reviewed above, the effects of integrated approaches can be modulating, but are usually additive. Indeed, an integrated approach appears to be optimal for addressing the broadest range of drug-dependence issues and treatment needs. Beyond this general framework, it has been difficult to identify the specific mechanisms of action to explain the positive effect of behavioral-pharmacological treatments. This may be due in part to the lack of a conceptual model for integrating the two types of interventions. Such a model should provide guidelines for developing, evaluating, and understanding combined treatments.

One way to conceptually integrate behavioral and pharmacological interventions is to view pharmacotherapies from a behavioral rather than a medical perspective and identify the functions of pharmacological manipulations according to current concepts of behavioral analysis. Table 1 provides this perspective and shows that this reconceptualization of pharmacological therapies can be readily accomplished. Table 1 lists behavioral strategies in the first column and provides example procedures in the second column. The third column lists traditional pharmacological strategies that we believe function similarly to the behavioral strategy, with example drug treatments provided in the last column. Thus, the impact of pharmacological interventions are described in terms of whether the pharmacological agent functions to remove, introduce, or alter the behavior, its antecedents, or its consequences. Table 1 shows that some phar-

macological strategies fulfill only one function, while others fulfill multiple functions. For example, the use of antidepressants in the treatment of chronically depressed cocaine addicts or alcoholics may fulfill only one behavioral function: removing the antecedents of drug use by medicating the depression that may occasion its use. In contrast, replacement therapies such as methadone can fulfill multiple functions: (1) altering potential antecedents of drug use by eliminating withdrawal symptoms, (2) increasing alternative responses by providing a safer treatment medication that can be taken instead of the drug, and (3) altering the consequences of drug taking by removing some of the subjective effects of drug administration (e.g., "drug high"). Not all replacement therapies fulfill all three functions. For example, while nicotine replacement can effectively alter potential antecedents of smoking by eliminating withdrawal symptoms, it does not readily produce positive reinforcement due to slow onset and steady blood levels relative to inhaled nicotine. Further, its ability to produce cross-tolerance to the effects of inhaled nicotine may be limited (Benowitz and Jacob, 1990; Pickworth et al., 1994).

By understanding the differences in behavioral functions of pharmacotherapies, we may be able to predict which treatments will be more effective in reducing the targeted drug use when applied as an isolated pharmacotherapy. We would expect that medications that fulfill multiple functions would be more likely to reduce the targeted drug use than those that address only one function. This type of analysis not only provides a basis for predicting the differential effectiveness of pharmacotherapies, it also may suggest specific behavioral interventions that would be best combined with a particular pharmacotherapy. After considering the behavioral functions fulfilled by the pharmacotherapy, one could choose environmental manipulations that address functions missed by the pharmacotherapy.

While conceptually integrating behavioral and pharmacological interventions may pro-

TABLE 1. *A model for integrating behavioral and pharmacological strategies according to functional similarities*

Behavioral strategies		Pharmacological strategies	
Description	Example	Description	Example
1) ALTER ANTECEDENTS		**1) ALTER ANTECEDENTS**	
Remove (e.g., avoid, eliminate, reduce)	Relapse prevention training	**Remove** (e.g., Withdrawal suppression via replacement therapy or symptomatic treatment)	Methadone Maintenance Nicotine Gum/Patch Antidepressants
Extinguish (e.g., expose to stimuli in absence of drug effect)	Respondent extinction	**Extinguish** Blockade medication	Naltrexone (for opiate abuse)
Provide new antecedents (e.g., provide new stimulus control or modulate stimulus control)	Instructions		
2) INCREASE ALTERNATIVE RESPONSES		**2) INCREASE ALTERNATIVE RESPONSES**	
Provide reinforcement for alternative behaviors (e.g., reward specific prosocial activity or nonspecific evidence of abstinence)	Voucher/take-home incentives Community reinforcement approach	**Provide reinforcement for alternative behaviors** Provide alternative therapeutic medications	Methadone maintenance nicotine gum/patch
3) ALTER CONSEQUENCES		**3) ALTER CONSEQUENCES**	
Remove (e.g., remove direct or concurrent reinforcers of drug use)	Operant extinction	**Remove** Blockade or replacement therapy	Naltrexone Methadone maintenance
Punish (e.g., apply aversive consequences or remove on drug use)	Punishment Response-cost	**Punish** Alter intermediary metabolism	Disulfiram

vide a framework for developing and understanding new combinations of interventions, other more practical questions concerning treatment delivery need attention. For example, little is known about sequencing or timing of interventions. For some applications is it best to start with a behavioral treatment, then add medication, or vice versa? Related to timing is the question of treatment durability. Are there differences in the durability of effects of behavior therapy relative to pharmacotherapy? This question seems particularly pertinent in the case of smoking treatment in which nicotine replacement therapy has an immediate, short-term effect of decreasing

nicotine withdrawal symptoms during initial cessation, while behavioral interventions theoretically effect later, long-term stages of cessation associated with relapse prevention and lifestyle modifications. Finally, more research is needed to determine whether the effects of two treatments combined differ across individuals. One might expect that patients with certain characteristics might benefit more from pharmacological treatment, whereas behavioral interventions may be better suited for another type of patient. As new data about patient-treatment matching become available, specific recommendations for clinical practice can be confidently made.

Despite the frequent and successful combination of behavioral and pharmacological interventions, our understanding of them is limited. Conceptualizing pharmacological manipulations into current concepts of behavior analysis may provide some guidelines for developing, evaluating, and understanding combined treatments. A recent trend in behavioral treatments of drug abuse has been toward more comprehensive approaches that go beyond providing simple clinic-based incentives for change to addressing multiple aspects of the client's life. Incorporating pharmacological interventions into these comprehensive approaches should prove promising and further improve the efficacy of behavioral and pharmacologic treatments for drug dependence.

SUMMARY

- Behavior pharmacology grew out of contributions from (1) behavior analysis, which examines the interactions between the organism and environment, and (2) traditional pharmacology, which examines the chemical or physical interactions between drug and cell.

- Behavioral and pharmacological interventions have been combined to (1) enhance the outcomes achieved by either treatment applied independently, (2) address secondary problems, (3) increase medication compliance, and (4) address the relapse risks attributable to multiple drug use.

- Conceptualizing pharmacological manipulations in current concepts of behavior analysis may provide some guidelines for developing, evaluating, and understanding combined treatments.

- Future research needs to address practical issues regarding the sequencing and optimal duration of interventions and the optimal combination of interventions for different individuals.

- Treatments of drug abuse recently have tended to employ comprehensive approaches addressing multiple aspects of the client's life. Incorporating pharmaco-

logical interventions into these comprehensive approaches should prove promising and further improve the efficacy of behavioral and pharmacological treatments for drug dependence.

REFERENCES

Anker, A.A. and Crowley, T.J. (1982) Use of contingency contracts in specialty clinics for cocaine abuse. In: Harris, L.S. (ed.) *Problems of drug dependence 1981.* NIDA Research Monograph No. 41. Washington, DC: U.S. Government Printing Office, pp. 452–459.

Azrin, N.H. (1976) Improvements in the community-reinforcement approach to alcoholism. *Behav. Res. Ther.* 14: 339–348.

Azrin, N.H., Sisson, R.W., Meyers, R. and Godley, M. (1982) Alcoholism treatment by disulfiram and community reinforcement therapy. *J. Behav. Ther. Exp. Psychiatry* 13: 105–112.

Benowitz, N.L. and Jacob, P. (1990) Intravenous nicotine replacement suppresses nicotine intake from cigarette smoking. *J. Pharmacol. Exp. Ther.* 264: 1000–1008.

Bickel, W.K., Rizzuto, P., Zielony, R.D., Klobas, J., Pangiosonlis, P., Mernit, R. and Knight, W.F. (1989) Combined behavioral and pharmacological treatment of alcoholic methadone patients. *J. Subst. Abuse* 1: 161–171.

Bigelow, G., Strickler, D., Liebson, I. and Griffiths, R. (1976) Maintaining disulfiram ingestion among outpatient alcoholics: a security-deposit contingency contracting procedure. *Behav. Res. Ther.* 14: 378–381.

Bourne, P.G., Alford, J.A. and Bowcock, J.Z. (1966) Treatment of skid-row alcoholics with disulfiram. *Q. J. Stud. Alcohol* 27: 42–48.

Callahan, E.J., Rawson, R.A., McCleave, B., Arais, R., Glazer, M. and Liberman, R.P. (1980) *Int. J. Addict.* 15: 795–807.

Cepeda-Benito, A. (1993) Meta-analytical review of the efficacy of nicotine chewing gum in smoking treatment programs. *J. Consult. Clin. Psychol.* 61: 822–830.

Childress, A.R., McLellan, A.T. and O'Brien, C.P. (1986) Abstinent opiate abusers exhibit conditioned craving, conditioned withdrawal and reductions in both through extinction. *Br. J. Addict.* 81: 655–660.

Condelli, W.S., Fairbank, J.A., Dennis, M.L. and Rachal, J.V. (1991) Cocaine use by clients in methadone programs: Significance, scope, and behavioral interventions. *J. Subst. Abuse. Treat.* 8: 203–212.

Crowley, T. (1984) Contingency contracting treatment of drug-abusing physicians, nurses, and dentists. In: Grabowski, J., Stitzer, M. and Henningfield, J. (eds.) *Behavioral interventions in drug abuse treatment.* NIDA Research Monograph No. 46. Washington, DC: U.S. Government Printing Office, pp. 131–146.

Dolan, M.P., Black, J.L., Penk, W.E., Robinowitz, R. and DeFord, H.A. (1985) Contracting for treatment termination to reduce illicit drug use among methadone maintenance treatment failures. *J. Consult. Clin. Psychol.* 53: 549–551.

Dunteman, G.H., Condelli, W.S. and Fairbank, J.A. (1992) Predicting cocaine use among methadone patients: analysis of findings from a national study. *Hosp Community Psychiatry* 43: 608–611.

Fagerstrom, K.-O., Hurt, R.D., Sawe, U. and Tonnesen, P. (1992) Therapeutic use of nicotine patches: efficacy and safety. *J. Smoking Rel. Dis.* 3: 247–261.

Fiore, M.C., Kenford, S.L., Jorenby, D.E., Wetter, D.W., Smith, S.S. and Baker, T.B. (1994b) Two studies of the clinical effectiveness of the nicotine patch with different counseling treatments. *Chest* 105: 534–533.

Fiore, M.C., Smith, S.S., Jorenby, D.E. and Baker, T.B. (1994a) The effectiveness of the nicotine patch for smoking cessation. *JAMA* 271: 1940–1947.

Glosser, D.S. (1983) The use of a token economy to reduce illicit drug use among methadone maintenance clients. *Addict. Behav.* 8: 93–104.

Gorelick, D.A. (1992) Alcohol and cocaine: clinical and pharmacological interactions. *Recent Dev. Alcohol* 10: 37–56.

Grabowski, J., O'Brien, C.P., Greenstein, R., Ternes, J., Long, M. and Steinberg-Donato, S. (1979) Effects of contingent payment on compliance with a naltrexone regimen. *Am J. Drug Alcohol Abuse* 6: 355–365.

Green, L. and Gossop, M. (1988) Effects of information on the opiate withdrawal syndrome. *Br. J. Addict.* 83: 305–309.

Griffiths, R.R., Bigelow, G.E. and Henningfield, J.E. (1980) Similarities in animal and human drug-taking behavior. In: Mello, N.K. (ed.) *Advances in substance abuse*, vol. 1. Greenwich, CT: JAI Press, pp. 1–90.

Griffiths, R.R., Bigelow, G.E. and Liebson, I. (1976) Facilitation of human tobacco self-administration by ethanol: a behavioral analysis. *J. Exp. Anal. Behav.* 25: 279–292.

Guerrein, J., Rosenberg, C.M. and Manohar, V. (1973) Disulfiram maintenance in outpatient treatment of alcoholism. *Arch. Gen. Psychiatry* 28: 798–802.

Hall, S.M., Tunstall, C.D., Ginsberg, D., Benowitz, N.L. and Jones, R.T. (1987) Nicotine gum and behavioral treatment: a placebo controlled trial. *J. Consult. Clin. Psychol.* 55: 603–605.

Hall, S.M., Tunstall, C.D., Rugg, D., Jones, R.T. and Benowitz, N. (1985) Nicotine gum and behavioral treatment in smoking cessation. *J. Consult. Clin. Psychol.* 53: 256–258.

Haynes, S.N. (1973) Contingency management in a municipally administered Antabuse program for alcoholics. *J. Behav. Ther. Exp. Psychiatry* 4: 31–32.

Henningfield, J.E. and Jasinski, D.R. (1988) Pharmacologic basis for nicotine replacement. In: Pomerleau, O.F. and Pomerleau, C.S. (eds.) *Progress in clinical and biological research: Vol. 261. Nicotine replacement: a critical evaluation.* New York: Alan R. Liss, pp. 35–62.

Higgins, S.T., Budney, A.J., Bickel, W.K., Hughes, J.R. and Foerg, F. (1993) Disulfiram therapy in patients abusing cocaine and alcohol. *Am. J. Psychiatry* 150: 675–676.

Higgins, S.T., Delaney, D.D., Budney, A.J., Bickel, W.K., Hughes, J.R., Foerg, F. and Fenwick, J.W., (1991) A behavioral approach to achieving initial cocaine abstinence. *Am. J. Psychiatry* 148: 1218–1224.

Hughes, J.R. (1991) Combined psychological and nicotine gum treatment for smoking: a critical review. *J. Subst. Abuse* 3: 337–350.

Hughes, J.R. and Glaser, M. (1993) Transdermal nicotine for smoking cessation. *Health Values* 17: 24–31.

Hughes, J.R., Gulliver, S.B., Amori, G., Mireault, G.C. and Fenwick, J.F. (1989) Effect of instructions and nicotine on smoking cessation, withdrawal symptoms and self-administration of nicotine gum. *Psychopharmacology* 99: 486–491.

Hughes, J.R. and Hatsukami, D. (1985) Short-term effects of nicotine gum. In: Grabowski, J. and Hall, S.M. (eds.) *Pharmacological adjuncts in smoking cessation.* NIDA Research Monograph No. 53. Rockville, MD: National Institute on Drug Abuse, pp. 68–82.

Hughes, J.R., Hatsukami, D.K., Pickens, R.W., Krahn, D., Malin, S. and Lukmic, A. (1984) Effect of nicotine on the tobacco withdrawal syndrome. *Psychopharmacology* 83: 82–87.

Hunt, G.M. and Azrin, N.H. (1973) A community reinforcement approach to alcoholism. *Behav. Res. Ther.* 11: 91–104.

Iguchi, M.Y., Handelsman, L., Bickel, W.K. and Griffiths, R.R. (1993) Benzodiazepine and sedative use/abuse by methadone maintenance clients. *Drug Alcohol Depend.* 32: 257–266.

Iguchi, M.Y., Lamb, R.J., Belding, M.A., Platt, J.J., Husband S.D., and Morral, A.R. (1996). Contingent reinforcement of group participation versus abstinance in a methadone maintenance program. *Exp. Clin. Psychopharm.* 4(3): 315–321.

Iguchi, M.Y., Stitzer, M.L., Bigelow, G.E. and Liebson, I.A. (1988) Contingency management in methadone maintenance: effects of reinforcing and aversive consequences on illicit polydrug use. *Drug Alcohol Depend.* 22: 1–7.

Jaffe, J.H. and Kleber, H.D. (1989) Opioids: general issues and detoxification. In: Karasu, T.B. (ed.) *Treatments of psychiatric disorders. Vol.2. A task force report of the American Psychiatric Association.* Washington, DC: American Psychiatric Association, pp. 1309–1332.

Jaffe, J.H. and Martin, W.R. (1990) Opioid analgesics and antagonists. In: Goodman, G.A., Rall, T.W., Nies, A.S. and Taylor, P. (eds.) *The pharmacological basis of therapeutics,* 8th ed. New York: Pergamon Press, pp. 485–521.

Killen, J.D., Maccoby, N. and Taylor, C.B. (1984) Nicotine gum and self-regulation training in smoking relapse prevention. *Behav. Ther.* 15: 234–248.

Kirby, K.C., Lamb, R.J., Iguchi, M.Y., Husband, S.D. and Platt, J.J. (1995) Situations occasioning cocaine use and cocaine abstinence strategies. *Addiction* 90: 1241–1252.

Konorski, J. and Miller, S. (1928) Sur une forme particuliere des reflexes conditionnels (On a particular form of conditioned reflex). Les Comptes Rendus des Seances de la Societe de biologie. Societe Polonaise de Biologie 99: 1155. (Reprinted in *J. Exp. Anal. Behav.* 12: 187–189.)

Konorski, J. and Miller, S. (1937) On two types of conditioned reflex. *J. Gen. Psychol.* 16: 264–272.

Kosten, T.R., Kleber, H.D. and Morgan, C. (1989) Role of opioid antagonists in treating intravenous cocaine abuse. *Life Sci.* 44: 887–892.

Kosten, T.R., Roundaville, B.J. and Kleber, H.D. (1987) A 2.5 year follow-up of cocaine use among treated opiate addicts. *Arch. Gen. Psychiatry* 44: 281–284.

Liebson, I. and Bigelow, G. (1972) A behavioral-pharmacological treatment of dually addicted patients. *Behav. Res. Ther.* 10: 403–405.

Liebson, I., Bigelow, G. and Flamer, R. (1973) Alcoholism among methadone patients: a specific treatment method. *Am. J. Psychiatry* 130: 483–485.

Liebson, I., Tommasello, A. and Bigelow, G. (1978) A behavioral treatment of alcoholic methadone patients. *Ann. Intern. Med.* 89: 342–344.

Lubetkin, B.S., Rivers, P.C. and Rosenberg, C.M. (1971) Difficulties of disulfiram therapy with alcoholics. *Q. J. Stud. Alcohol* 32: 118–171.

Ludwig, A.M., Levine, J. and Stark, L.H. (1970) *LSD and alcoholism.* Springfield, IL: Charles C. Thomas.

Magura, S., Casriel, C., Goldsmith, D.S., Strug, D.L. and Lipton, D.S. (1988) Contingency contracting with poly-drug abusing methadone patients. *Addict. Behav.* 13: 113–118.

Marlatt, G.A. (1985) Relapse prevention: theoretical rationale and overview of the model. In: Marlatt, G.A. and Gordon, J.R. (eds.) *Relapse prevention: maintenance strategies in the treatment of addictive behaviors.* New York: Guilford Press, pp. 3–70.

McLellan, A.T., Arndt, I.O., Metzger, D.S., Woody, G.E. and O'Brien, C.P. (1993) The effects of psychosocial services in substance abuse treatment. *J. Consult. Clin. Psychol.* 269: 1953–1959.

Mello, N.K. and Mendelson, J.H. (1972) Drinking patterns during work contingent and non-contingent alcohol acquisition. *Psychosomatic Med.* 34: 139–164.

Mello, N.K., Mendelson, J.H., Sellers, M.L. and Kuehnle, J.C. (1980) Effect of alcohol and marijuana on tobacco smoking. *Clin. Pharmacol. Ther.* 27: 202–209.

Milby, J.B., Garrett, C., English, C., Fritschi, O. and Clarke, C. (1978) Take-home methadone: Contingency effects on drug-seeking and productivity of narcotic addicts. *Addict. Behav.* 3: 215–220.

O'Malley, S.S., Jaffe, A.J., Chang, G., Schottenfeld, R.S., Meyer, R.E. and Rounsaville, B. (1992) Naltrexone and coping skills therapy for alcohol dependence: a controlled study. *Arch. Gen. Psychiatry* 49: 881–887.

Palmer, K.J. and Faulds, D. (1992) Transdermal nicotine: a review of its pharmacodynamic and pharmacokinetic properties, and therapeutic use as an aid to smoking cessation. *Drugs* 44: 498–529.

Pickworth, W.B., Bunker, E.B. and Henningfield, J.E. (1994) Transdermal nicotine: reduction of smoking with minimal abuse liability. *Psychopharmacology* 115: 9–14.

Rall, T.W. (1990) Hypnotics and sedatives; ethanol. In: Gilman, A.G., Rall, T.W., Nies, A.S. and Taylor, P. (eds.) *The pharmacological basis of therapeutics*, 8th ed. New York: Pergamon Press, pp. 345–382.

Ross, E.M. (1990) Pharmacodynamics: mechanisms of drug action and the relationship between drug concentration and effect. In: Gilman, A.G., Rall, T.W., Nies, A.S. and Taylor, P. (Eds.) *The pharmacological basis of therapeutics*, 8th ed. New York: Pergamon Press, pp. 33–48.

Russell, M.A.H. (1988) Nicotine replacement: the role of blood nicotine levels, their rate of change and nicotine tolerance. In: Pomerleau, O.F. and Pomerleau, C.S. (eds.) *Progress in clinical and biological research: Vol. 261. Nicotine replacement: a critical evaluation.* New York: Alan R. Liss, pp. 63–94.

Saxon, A.J., Calsyn, D.A., Kivlahan, D.R. and Roszell, D.K. (1992) Outcome of contingency contracting for illicit drug use in a methadone maintenance program. *Drug Alcohol Depend.* 31: 205–214.

Schneider, N.G. and Jarvik, M.E. (1984) Time course of smoking withdrawal symptoms as a function of nicotine replacement. *Psychopharmacology* 82: 143–144.

Shiffman, S. (1982) Relapse following smoking cessation: A situational analysis. *J. Consult. Clin. Psychol.* 50: 71–86.

Skinner, B.F. (1931) The concept of the reflex in the description of behavior. *J. Gen. Psychol.* 5: 427–458.

Skinner, B.F. (1935a) The generic nature of the concepts of stimulus and response. *J. Gen. Psychol.* 12: 40–65.

Skinner, B.F. (1935b) Two types of conditioned reflex and a pseudo-type. *J. Gen. Psychol.* 12: 66–77.

Skinner, B.F. (1937) Two types of conditioned reflex: A reply to Konorski and Miller. *J. Gen. Psychol.* 16: 272–279.

Skinner, B.F. (1938) *The behavior of organisms.* Princeton, New Jersey: Prentice-Hall.

Spiga, R., Grabowski, J., Silverman, P.B. and Meisch, R.A. (1996) Human methadone self-administration: effects of dose and ratio requirement. *Behav. Pharmacol.* 7: 130–137.

Stitzer, M.I., Bickel, W.K., Bigelow, G.E. and Liebson, I.A. (1986) Effect of methadone dose contingencies on urinalysis test results of poly-drug abusing methadone-maintenance patients. *Drug Alcohol Depend.* 18: 341–348.

Stitzer, M.L. and Bigelow, G.E. (1984) Contingent methadone take-home privileges: effects on compliance with fee payment schedules. *Drug Alcohol Depend.* 13: 395–399.

Stitzer, M., Bigelow, G. and Liebson, I. (1979) Reducing benzodiazepine self-administration with contingent reinforcement. *Addict. Behav.* 4: 245–252.

Stitzer, M., Bigelow, G. and Liebson, I. (1982a) Contingent reinforcement of benzodiazepine-free urines from methadone maintenance patients. In: Harris, L.S. (ed.) *Problems of drug dependence, 1981: Proceedings of the 43rd annual scientific meeting of the Committee on Problems of Drug Dependence.* NIDA Research Monograph No. 41. Washington, DC: DHHS, pp. 282–287.

Stitzer, M.L., Bigelow, G.E., Liebson, I.A. and Hawthorne, J.W. (1982b) Contingent reinforcement for benzodiazepine-free urines: evaluation of a drug abuse treatment intervention. *J. Appl. Behav. Anal.* 15: 493–503.

Stitzer, M.L., Griffiths, R., McLellan, A.T., Grabowski, J. and Hawthorne, J.W. (1981) Diazepam use among methadone maintenance patients: patterns and dosages. *Drug Alcohol Depend.* 8: 189–194.

Stitzer, M.L., Iguchi, M.Y. and Felch, L.J. (1992) Contingent take-home incentive: effects on drug use of methadone maintenance patients. *J. Consult. Clin. Psychol.* 60: 927–934.

Stitzer, M.L., McCaul, M.E., Bigelow, G.E. and Liebson, I.A. (1983) Oral methadone self-administration: effects of dose and alternative reinforcers. *Clin. Pharmacol. Ther.* 34: 29–35.

Stolerman, I.P. and Goldberg, S.R. (1986) Introduction: brief history and scope of behavioral approaches to dependence. In: Goldberg, S.R. and Stolerman, I.P. (eds.) *Behavioral analysis of drug dependence.* Orlando, FL: Academic Press, pp. 1–8.

Thompson, W., Spiga, R., Grabowski, J., Silverman, P.B. and Meisch, R.A. (1993) Studies in human drug self-administration: methadone. In: Harris, L.S. (ed.) *Problems in drug dependence 1993: Proceedings of the 55th annual scientific meeting of the College on Problems of Drug Dependence.* National Institute on Drug Abuse Research Monograph. Washington, DC: U.S. Government Printing Office.

Volpicelli, J.R., Alterman, A.I., Hayashida, M. and O'Brien, C.P. (1992) Naltrexone in the treatment of alcohol dependence. *Arch. Gen. Psychiatry* 49: 876–880.

West, R.J., Jarvis, M.J., Russell, M.A.H., Carruthers, M.E. and Feyerabend, C. (1984) Effect of nicotine replacement on the cigarette withdrawal syndrome. *Br. J. Addict.* 79: 215–219.

Wise, R.A. (1987) The role of reward pathways in the development of drug dependence. *Pharmacol. Ther.* 35: 227–263.

Drug Addiction and its Treatment: Nexus of Neuroscience and Behavior, edited by Bankole A. Johnson and John D. Roache. Lippincott–Raven Publishers, Philadelphia, © 1997.

19

Medicational Aids to Treat Alcohol Problems

Raye Z. Litten and John P. Allen

Treatment Research Branch, National Institute on Alcohol Abuse and Alcoholism, Bethesda, Maryland 20892-7003

Alcoholism is a devastating disease that affects over 15 million Americans and costs this society $100 billion a year (National Institute on Alcohol Abuse and Alcoholism, 1993). Fortunately, over the last decade, alcohol-related research has intensified. Particular attention has been focused on establishing effective treatment strategies (Allen and Mattson, 1993). Development of medications represents one of the most promising strategies.

In this chapter we review recent clinical findings on medications to alleviate acute alcohol withdrawal, pharmacological agents to reduce drinking, and antidepressive and anxiolytic medications to assist alcoholics suffering collateral psychiatric problems. In conclusion, clinical issues and future research directions of pharmacotherapy for each of these medicational classes are posed.

PHARMACOLOGICAL AGENTS TO ALLEVIATE ACUTE ALCOHOL WITHDRAWAL

Acute alcohol withdrawal can occur in alcohol-dependent patients from abrupt cessation of drinking, resulting in a variety of symptoms. These may range from relatively mild symptoms such as sweating, tachycardia, hypertension, tremors, and anxiety, to more serious consequences, including seizures and delirium tremens, a condition characterized by disorientation, hallucinations, and severe autonomic nervous system overactivity (Litten and Allen, 1991). Mild symptoms and seizures usually occur within 48 hours after the last drink, while delirium tremens can occur 24 to 150 hours after the last drink (Naranjo and Sellers, 1986).

Medications to relieve acute alcohol withdrawal symptoms have been more successfully clinically applied than agents developed for any other purpose in alcoholism treatment. Over the past 25 years benzodiazepines have been widely used to treat symptoms of acute alcohol withdrawal and have consistently shown efficacy and safety for this purpose (Institute of Medicine, 1989; Liskow and Goodwin, 1987; Litten and Allen, 1991). Benzodiazepines have been shown to be effective in suppressing symptoms of withdrawal and reducing risk of withdrawal seizures and delirium tremens (Fuller and Gordis, 1994; Litten and Allen, 1991; Nutt et al., 1989).

Both long-acting and short-acting benzodiazepines may be used to manage withdrawal. Diazepam and chlordiazepoxide are the most frequently used long-acting agents. Short-acting agents include lorazepam and oxazepam. Short-acting benzodiazepines may be preferable for managing alcoholics with cirrhosis or other liver disease, since their metabolism is less dependent on the hepatic oxidizing system.

Standard fixed benzodiazepine dosing regimens are typically employed, although variability across patients in need of medication and attempts to minimize use of benzodiazepines have suggested other strategies. For example, Sellers et al. (1983) argued for a "loading dose" approach in which 20 mg diazepam or placebo are given every 2 hours to inpatients in moderate to severe withdrawal until they become asymptomatic. All subjects also receive supportive care. A similar strategy was formally evaluated by Sullivan et al. (1991) and Wartenberg et al. (1990). Each of these latter projects found that monitoring severity of withdrawal symptoms with the Clinical Institute Withdrawal Assessment (CIWA-A) and hourly dosing with chlordiazepoxide or diazepam while symptoms presented at a moderate to severe level prevented over- as well as undermedicating patients. Subsequently, Saltz et al. (1994) found that subjects randomly assigned to symptom-prompted administration of chlordiazepoxide required fewer hours of medication (9 hours vs 68 hours) and less total medication (100 mg vs 425 mg) than those administered chlordiazepoxide on a fixed 6-hour schedule.

While benzodiazepines have proven to be effective and safe in treating acute alcohol withdrawal, certain undesirable side effects, are associated with their use. These include memory loss, incoordination, drowsiness, lethargy, and possible drug dependency (Litten and Allen, 1991). Further, the depressive action of benzodiazepines on the central nervous system is synergistic with that caused by alcohol.

α_2-Adrenergic agonists and β-adrenergic antagonists have also been employed. Unfortunately, these agents do not appear as beneficial overall as the benzodiazepines (Litten and Allen, 1991, 1994). These classes of drugs attenuate symptoms caused by the acute withdrawal activation of the sympathetic nervous system, such as tremor, tachycardia, and hypertension, while producing little effect on other symptoms, including anxiety, seizures, delirium tremens (Litten and Allen, 1991).

Newer medications are now being investigated in the hope of having at least the same efficacy as benzodiazepines with fewer side effects. Currently, the most promising alternative to benzodiazepines is the anticonvulsant carbamazepine. Several studies have shown it effective in reducing severity of symptoms during acute alcohol withdrawal without the side effects observed with benzodiazepines (Butler and Messiha, 1986; Gallant, 1992; Litten and Allen, 1994). In a double-blind trial with alcohol-dependent patients, Malcolm et al. (1989) reported carbamazepine to be as successful as oxazepam in reducing symptoms of severe acute withdrawal. Importantly as well, dropout rates due to side effects for carbamazepine were low. Stuppaeck et al. (1992) also contrasted carbamazepine with oxazepam in patients suffering major acute withdrawal and found efficacy for the two medications equivalent. Carbamazepine appears to hold several advantages over the benzodiazepines, including less sedation, absence of drug abuse potential, and no interaction with alcohol (Litten and Allen, 1994). Nevertheless, aplastic anemia and agranulocytosis (severe reduction in the number of leukocytes) have been associated with carbamazepine. However, incidence of such problems is quite low and the duration of treatment is short.

Several other medications to relieve acute alcohol withdrawal are in earlier stages of research. Flumazenil is promising in this regard (File et al., 1992; Gerra et al., 1991; Nutt et al., 1993). N-methyl-D-aspartate (NMDA) antagonists have also demonstrated effectiveness in reducing alcohol withdrawal seizures in rats (Grant et al., 1990). Tiapride, a dopamine-2 antagonist, proposed as a possible agent to reduce drinking, may also alleviate symptoms of withdrawal with the exception of seizures (Peters and Faulds, 1994). Other potential agents include gangliosides, a family of naturally occurring sialoglycosphingolipids that are constituents of neuronal membranes. Exogenous gangliosides may have neuroprotective potential against the toxic effects of alcohol (Hungund and Mahadik, 1993). Medications that interact with the hypothalamic-pituitary-adrenal axis may also be beneficial. This system seems to be activated during acute alcohol withdrawal and may contribute to the symptoms observed. Since high doses of glucocorticoids have been shown to cause brain damage in animals

(Sapolsky, 1993), it has been postulated that repeated alcohol withdrawal episodes may lead to neuronal damage (Adinoff et al., 1988; Gallant and Pena, 1992). Recently, Rassnick et al. (1993a) showed that microinjection of a corticotropin-releasing factor antagonist into the amygdala of rats reduced the anxiogenic effect of alcohol withdrawal.

PHARMACOLOGICAL AGENTS TO REDUCE THE DESIRE TO DRINK

Progress in understanding biological bases of alcohol drinking behavior has led to development of a broad range of agents that seem to directly reduce the desire to drink, perhaps by attenuating alcohol craving and/or blocking the euphoric effect derived from drinking alcohol. Those that alter functional activity of several neurotransmitter systems appear to reduce alcohol intake in various animal models and, for some, in humans as well (Litten and Allen, 1993). Potentially useful agents include opioid antagonists, serotonin reuptake inhibitors, $5\text{-}HT_2$ antagonists, $5\text{-}HT_3$ antagonists, dopamine agonists and antagonists, and γ-aminobutyric acid (GABA) agonists.

Opioid Antagonists

To date, the opioid antagonists seem most promising to reduce drinking in alcohol-dependent subjects. In particular, naltrexone has demonstrated efficacy and safety and has recently been approved by the Food and Drug Administration (FDA) as an adjunct treatment of alcoholism, the first medication approved in over 50 years. Effectiveness of opioid antagonists naloxone, naltrexone, and nalmefene was first demonstrated in animal models. Significant reduction in alcohol intake was observed in rats as well as monkeys (Litten and Allen, 1993). Two well-designed 12-week trials (O'Malley et al., 1992; Volpicelli et al., 1992) have now found strikingly similar positive effects of naltrexone with alcohol-dependent human subjects in treatment. Volpicelli et al. reported that only 23% of patients treated

with 50 mg of naltrexone per day relapsed to heavy drinking compared with 54% of those receiving placebo. Naltrexone-treated patients also experienced lower craving for alcohol and fewer days drinking than the placebo group. Interestingly, those naltrexone subjects who did "sample" alcohol were less likely to persist in drinking than patients receiving placebo. Ninety-five percent of the latter group who tried alcohol suffered severe relapses, contrasted with only 50% of those treated with naltrexone. Importantly, naltrexone was well tolerated with few side effects, a finding further confirmed by Dupont-Merck (Croop, 1995).

In the project by O'Malley et al. (1992) 97 patients were administered either 50 mg of naltrexone or placebo in addition to one of two types of psychosocial therapy, supportive counseling or coping skills/relapse prevention therapy. As in the Volpicelli et al. study, subjects treated with naltrexone reported fewer days drinking and fewer major relapses. Type of psychosocial treatment also interacted with naltrexone. Individuals receiving naltrexone/supportive therapy enjoyed a higher rate of abstinence (61%) than those administered naltrexone and coping skills/relapse prevention therapy (28%), placebo/supportive therapy (19%), and placebo and coping skills/relapse prevention therapy (21%). Nevertheless, when alcohol was sampled, subjects receiving naltrexone and coping skills/relapse prevention were less likely to experience severe relapse than the other three groups.

Other projects have been completed on the use of naltrexone in alcoholism treatment. Volpicelli et al. (1994) observed that patients compliant with naltrexone and attending scheduled follow-up evaluations drank on fewer days and were less likely to relapse than placebo-treated patients. Not surprisingly, however, those who were less compliant realized minimal effects on their drinking.

Bohn et al. (1994) has completed a 6-week open trial of naltrexone with nondependent heavy drinkers, i.e., for males, 28 drinks or more per week, and for females, 18 drinks or more per week, or both have a current *Diag-*

nostic and Statistical Manual (DSM-III-R) diagnosis of alcohol abuse. Subjects received daily doses of either 25 or 50 mg naltrexone as well as brief counseling therapy. Both dose levels of naltrexone were effective in lowering frequency and amount of alcohol consumption as well as serum levels of γ-glutamyl transpeptidase (GGT), a biochemical marker associated with heavy alcohol usage. These changes endured for the 1-month postmedication follow-up. A double-blind, placebo-controlled study is currently under way to confirm these findings.

Still other lines of research are exploring physiologic mechanisms that may underlie naltrexone's effects on alcohol consumption. Volpicelli et al. (1995) assessed alcoholics during the original naltrexone trial who had "slipped," having had at least one drink. They were asked to rate subjective effects including drinking intoxication, coordination, "high," memory loss, craving, and anger. While those treated with naltrexone reported less "high" than did relapsers who had received placebo, use of naltrexone was not associated with the other drinking effects. In that the naltrexone-treated subjects also drank less than the placebo-treated patients, it is unclear if diminished euphoria resulted from the direct effect of naltrexone on alcohol intake or from its indirect effect of decreasing alcohol reinforcement value. The latter explanation receives some support from Swift et al. (1994), who found that naltrexone-treated social drinkers reported less euphoria after drinking than did placebo subjects.

Several clinical trials are currently under way to resolve a range of clinical issues and questions surrounding use of naltrexone. These include dosage and duration of treatment, specification of subpopulations of drinkers particularly responsive to naltrexone, and selection of psychosocial therapies to be used in conjunction with naltrexone.

Finally, Mason and coworkers (1994) are evaluating nalmefene, a relatively new opioid antagonist, for treatment of alcoholism. Nalmefene appears to offer several pharmacologic advantages over naltrexone, including less liver toxicity, longer half-life, and greater affinity for opioid receptors. In a 12-week pilot study contrasting daily doses of 10 mg nalmefene, 40 mg nalmefene, or placebo, the higher dose of nalmefene was demonstrated as more effective for alcohol-dependent subjects in reducing relapse ($p \leq 0.05$) and increasing number of days abstinent ($p \leq 0.09$) than 10 mg dose or placebo. Both doses of nalmefene, however, exceeded placebo in reducing drinks per drinking day. The medication was well tolerated with no serious adverse effect. A large scale study of nalmefene is ongoing.

Serotonin Reuptake Inhibitors

Serotonin reuptake inhibitors are most commonly used to treat depression, although they also seem helpful in relieving certain types of anxiety disorders (Michels and Marzuk, 1993). Further, they may attenuate alcohol consumption. Several studies in animals have shown that they may suppress intake by up to 60% to 80% (Gorelick, 1989). In human studies, a decrease in alcohol drinking has also been observed, although far less dramatic. Naranjo and his colleagues (1984, 1987, 1989, 1990, 1992) conducted research on several of these agents with early problem drinkers receiving no other treatment. Fluoxetine and viqualine appeared to reduce amount of alcohol consumed per drinking occasion, while viqualine and zimelidine were more effective in decreasing frequency of drinking episodes (Naranjo et al., 1989, 1990, 1992).

In a 4-week trial with alcohol-dependent patients, Gorelick and Paredes (1992) found that alcohol consumption decreased by 15% following use of fluoxetine for a week. No such reduction occurred in placebo treatment subjects. Unfortunately, subsequent drinking levels of the fluoxetine group ultimately returned to baseline levels.

Gerra et al. (1992) contrasted the effect of fluoxetine with acamprosate (see below) on alcoholics with and without familial history of alcoholism. In addition to their positive history, familial alcoholics evidenced more social problems, learning disabilities, conduct disorders, and symptoms of hyperactivity. After 1 month of treatment fluoxetine reduced alcohol consumption by 53% in family history positive subjects and by 25% in those without familial history of alcoholism. This patient-pharmacological treatment interaction may be related to differences in serotonergic function between the groups since it has been postulated that alcoholics with early-onset drinking are deficient in serotonin (Buydens-Branchey et al., 1989; Linnoila and Virkkunen, 1992; Linnoila et al., 1989). Although age of onset of heavy drinking was not reported by Gerra et al., in general alcoholics with positive family history begin problematic drinking earlier than do their nonfamilial peers and are more likely to suffer collateral cognitive and emotional problems. Further studies are needed to explore the apparent differential effect of fluoxetine on family history positive alcoholics.

Kranzler et al. (1995) have recently concluded a 12-week trial in which alcoholic patients in relapse prevention therapy received either fluoxetine (maximum 60 mg daily) or placebo. Although no differences in outcome between them were apparent, both groups substantially decreased frequency and intensity of consumption. The potent effect of psychosocial therapy, high levels of compliance, and treatment retention in each of the groups may have overwhelmed potential effects of fluoxetine.

Finally, in a 5-week crossover study of heavy drinkers (mean daily intake of 111 g of alcohol), Balldin et al. (1994) failed to find differences between citalopram- and placebo-treated subjects in number of days abstinent or amount of alcohol consumed. Nevertheless, secondary analysis suggested that citalopram may have produced some advantage with subjects drinking less at admission.

In summary, serotonin reuptake inhibitors may decrease drinking in certain types of alcoholics, such as those with positive family history or those drinking at lower levels. Research to be described below also suggests that they may assist alcoholics suffering severe depression. These agents are generally tolerated quite well by patients, although some serotonin reuptake inhibitors produce adverse ef-

fects (Kranzler et al., 1993; Litten and Allen, 1993). Further studies are needed to identify optimal dosage and duration as well as to specify type and intensity of the psychosocial intervention to accompany their use.

5-HT₃ Antagonists

Several 5-HT₃ antagonists have also demonstrated efficacy in reducing alcohol intake in various animal models (Hodge et al., 1993; Johnson and Cowen, 1993). These include ondansetron, zacopride, MDL 7222, and ICS 205-930. It has been postulated that these compounds block 5-HT₃ stimulation of release of dopamine, especially in dopamine neurons originating from the ventral tegmental area, thereby diminishing the reinforcement value of alcohol (Johnson and Cowen, 1993). To further investigate this possibility, Johnson and his coworkers (Johnson and Cowen, 1993; Johnson et al., 1993) administered ondansetron to healthy male volunteers. Following ingestion of alcohol, a range of pleasurable subjective effects was assessed. Ondansetron significantly reduced several effects of alcohol, including cheerfulness, confidence, optimism, contentment, and desire to drink.

In a 6-week trial of daily doses of 0.50 mg of ondansetron, 4.0 mg of ondansetron, or placebo, Sellers et al. (1994) found that alcohol-dependent patients receiving the lower dose of ondansetron reduced alcohol intake more than did the 4.0-mg or placebo groups. Interestingly, when the subjects were further subdivided into light and heavy baseline drinkers, the former group responded significantly to the 0.05-mg dose, while the consumption of the heavy baseline drinkers were not affected by either dose of ondansetron. The investigators concluded that ondansetron treatment is most effective with patients having lower baseline drinking levels and more education.

5-HT₂ Antagonists

Similarly to 5-HT₃ antagonists, 5-HT₂ antagonists may also reduce drinking, although the evidence is clearly of a more preliminary nature. Several studies have shown that 5-HT$_2$ antagonists ritanserin, amperozide, and risperidone reduce alcohol consumption in rats (Lin and Hubbard, 1994; Meert and Janssen, 1991; Myers et al., 1993; Panocka and Massi, 1992; Panocka et al., 1993). A single-blind study of ritanserin in five chronic alcoholics also indicated that ritanserin decreased intake and diminished symptoms of depression and anxiety (Monti and Alterwain, 1991). However, an 11-site trial of ritanserin in alcohol-dependent patients has failed to show any significant difference from placebo (Johnson et al., 1996).

GABAergic Agents

The GABAergic system has also been implicated in mediating alcohol consumption (Korpi 1994; Litten and Allen, 1993). In humans acamprosate (calcium acetylhomotaurinate), a synthetic derivative of homotaurine and a structural analogue of GABA, has shown potential to reduce drinking. Interestingly, the precise mechanism through which it exerts effects remains unknown, although acamprosate has been shown to interact with excitatory amino acid receptors such as glutamate (Zeise et al., 1993). Lhuintre et al. (1985) first showed acamprosate as effective in reducing relapse in chronic alcoholics. In a subsequent 3-month study (Lhuintre et al., 1990) it was found to lower serum levels of GGT in alcohol-dependent patients. Finally, Gerra et al. (1992) found that acamprosate reduced drinking by 60% in nonfamilial alcoholic patients but produced little effect with familial alcoholic subjects. Twelve independent multisite trials on acamprosate are ongoing or have recently been completed in Europe. Results of the studies should be forthcoming soon.

γ-Hydroxybutyric acid (GHB), a metabolite believed to enhance the GABAergic system, is also being investigated. In a 3-month study with alcohol-dependent subjects, Gallimberti et al. (1992) found that GHB reduced frequency and level of drinking. Percentages of days abstinent were 26% for the GHB-treated group versus 8% for placebo group. The active treatment group had an average 4.7 drinks per day, while subjects receiving placebo averaged 9.3. Further, craving for alcohol was also reduced in patients taking GHB.

Dopamine Agonists and Antagonists

The mesocorticolimbic dopamine pathways are believed responsible, at least in part, for the reinforcing effects of alcohol (Koob, 1996). Curiously, both dopamine agonists and antagonists reduce reinforcement value and intake of alcohol in rats (Dyr et al., 1993; Hodge et al., 1992; Pfeffer and Samson, 1988; Rassnick et al., 1992, 1993b), although the two classes of drugs may produce different types of changes in subsequent drinking pattern (Dyr et al., 1993; Pfeffer and Samson, 1988).

While the dopamine agonist bromocriptine was initially reported to reduce craving and improve social functioning and mood levels in chronic alcoholics (Borg, 1993), a later 8-week study with outpatient alcoholics found no differences that could be ascribed to bromocriptine in frequency and amount of drinking (Dongier et al., 1991).

Tiapride, a selective dopamine D$_2$-receptor antagonist, may assist in alleviating alcohol dependence. In a 6-month placebo-controlled study with 32 alcohol-dependent patients suffering collateral anxiety or depression, Shaw et al. (1987) reported that tiapride reduced average daily intake of alcohol by 43% and increased total days abstinent by 79%. In addition, those administered tiapride displayed less prominent symptoms of depression and anxiety and improved their self-esteem and satisfaction with life. This research team has very recently completed a further study of tiapride with alcoholics immediately after detoxification (Shaw et al., 1994). Both frequency and amount of drinking were reduced following use of tiapride for 1 to 3 months. Daily intake of alcohol was lowered by 60% and number of days of abstinence increased by 53% when compared with placebo. As in their previous study, improvements in self-esteem and satisfaction with life were also observed.

Both of Shaw et al.'s studies indicate that tiapride is efficacious in treating alcoholism. It appears to be well tolerated and does not seem to produce major adverse effects. As an atypical neuroleptic agent, use of tiapride should be monitored closely. Further studies are clearly warranted. Currently, a multisite 6-month trial on tiapride is being conducted in Germany (Gastpar et al., 1994).

AVERSIVE AGENTS

In addition to naltrexone, disulfiram (Antabuse) has been approved by the FDA to treat alcoholism. Although available for almost 50 years, the efficacy of disulfiram has been questioned. To date only a few well-designed studies have been conducted. In a multisite Veterans Administration trial, Fuller et al. (1986) found no significant differences between disulfiram and placebo groups in total abstinence, time to first drink, employment, or social stability. Despite this, a few positive findings emerged. Among patients who did drink and who had completed all assessment interviews, those on disulfiram reported fewer days drinking than their counterparts receiving placebo. Also, individuals who were older and had longer residential stability responded positively to disulfiram.

Several studies have suggested that strategies such as incentives, contracts, or monitoring to enhance compliance with disulfiram improve treatment outcome (Allen and Litten, 1992). Most recently in a 6-month, single-blind, trial, Chick et al. (1992) found that patients taking disulfiram under observed conditions increased total days abstinent by 33% and reduced alcohol intake by 35% over those receiving supervised administration of vitamin C. Decrease in drinking was objectively confirmed by reduction in serum GGT levels in the disulfiram group while elevation occurred in the placebo condition.

A few studies have suggested that disulfiram and other aversive agents when used with psychosocial therapies may particularly improve outcome for certain subtypes of alcoholics. For example, Annis and Peachey (1992) found that integrating calcium carbimide, another aversive agent, with a relapse prevention therapy was effective in reducing alcohol consumption in alcoholic subjects. Also, Azrin et al. (1982) found that combining disulfiram with the community reinforcement approach to treatment was particularly helpful for unmarried male alcoholics. Finally, some investigators (e.g., Carroll et al., 1993; Higgins et al., 1993) have observed that administration of disulfiram to alcoholics with collateral cocaine dependence diminishes both alcohol and cocaine intake.

ANTIDEPRESSANTS AND ANXIOLYTICS

Alcoholics in treatment often suffer collateral depression and anxiety. Despite the prevalence and adverse consequences of comorbidity, only a few well-designed pharmacologic studies to address this issue have so far been conducted (Litten and Allen, 1995).

Preliminary results by Mason and Kocsis (1991) indicate that desipramine reduces severity of depression in alcoholics. This is significant since most efficacy trials on antidepressants have excluded alcoholics. Subjects treated with desipramine also tended to better avoid drinking than did those receiving placebo. Additional patients are currently being recruited in this study.

Nunes et al. (1993) conducted a 12-week open trial of the tricyclic antidepressant imipramine among alcoholics with comorbid major depression or dysthymia. Forty-five percent of the patients responded favorably to imipramine, improving mood and drinking behavior. An additional 13% improved with further increase in dosage of imipramine or treatment with disulfiram. Patients who responded positively were subsequently randomized to a 6-month, placebo-controlled study of imipramine. They were found less vulnerable to relapse than were placebo-treated patients.

Several studies of the serotonin reuptake inhibitors fluoxetine and sertraline with depressed alcoholics are in progress. While, as noted earlier, serotonin reuptake inhibitors appear to reduce consumption in nondepressed alcoholics, they may be particularly helpful with alcoholics who are depressed. Preliminary results suggest that fluoxetine enhances mood and diminishes intake in suicidal patients dually diagnosed for major depression and alcohol dependence (Cornelius et al., 1993).

Several trials have also been conducted with alcoholics suffering from collateral anxiety disorders using the anxiolytic agent buspirone. Buspirone, a partial 5-HT_{1A} agonist, produces fewer adverse effects than benzodiazepines, including lack of cognitive and psychomotor impairment, no liability for drug dependence, and no synergistic reaction with alcohol (Litten and Allen, 1995). In an a 8-week study of alcoholics with mild to moderate symptoms of anxiety, Bruno (1989) found that buspirone reduced craving for alcohol, depression, and anxiety. Further, patients receiving buspirone remained in treatment longer than did those administered placebo.

Tollefson et al. (1992) confirmed the beneficial effects of buspirone. In alcoholics with concurrent generalized anxiety disorder, buspirone proved superior to placebo in reducing craving, anxiety, and risk of leaving treatment prematurely.

Kranzler et al. (1994) also recently completed a randomized, 12-week, placebo-controlled trial of buspirone with anxious alcoholics. Buspirone led to greater reduction in anxiety symptoms, slower return to heavy drinking, and better treatment retention than placebo. Six-month posttreatment assessment also revealed that buspirone-treated subjects spent fewer days drinking than did those on placebo.

Contrasting with these positive findings, Malcolm et al. (1992) failed to discover any advantage of buspirone over placebo in a 6-month trial with dually diagnosed alcoholic and anxious patients. Lack of effect may reflect the nature of the sample. Patients in Mal-

colm's study may have been less stable and, perhaps, may have been at a more advanced stage of illness (Malcolm et al., 1992).

FUTURE DIRECTIONS

Advances in pharmacotherapy, both at basic neuroscience and at clinical levels, have suggested important directions for further research.

Pharmacotherapy for acute alcohol withdrawal has proven generally effective. Several issues, however, require further research. For example, does a patient undergoing detoxification require medication, or can he or she be safely withdrawn using nonpharmacological support alone? While classic studies suggest that many patients can be detoxified without medication in a quiet, nonthreatening, reassuring setting (Naranjo et al., 1983; Whitfield et al., 1978), acute alcohol withdrawal syndrome is now known to induce profound changes in the autonomic and hormonal systems, thereby rendering risk of possible damage to the nervous system and increased sensitization for seizures, the so-called kindling effect (Adinoff et al., 1988; Booth and Blow, 1993; Brown et al., 1988; Gallant and Pena, 1992). Future studies should address this clinical concern and identify patients at risk for such effects if they are withdrawn without medicational support. Finally, while recent studies have suggested using the CIWA to monitor severity of withdrawal symptoms as a basis for specifying dosing regime, it is not without shortcomings. Most specifically, since the CIWA gauges autonomic disturbances and subjective symptoms, it is possible that other illnesses as well as withdrawal from other drugs might inappropriately influence CIWA scores.

Multiple neurotransmitter systems seem to alter alcohol consummatory behavior, and further investigation is needed to clearly identify these neural pathways and explore how neurotransmitters influence their functional activity. It is also important to determine how psychological states and social/environmental factors modify activity of these systems. New technologies, such as noninvasive brain imaging (Zakhari and Witt, 1992), may provide important new information on sites, types of neurotransmitter, and altered neural activities associated with chronic drinking behavior. In addition, research is needed to identify how other neural cellular events relate to alcohol-seeking behavior. Such activities include those prompted by G proteins, second messenger systems, ion channels, gene expression, and translational and posttranslational process systems, many of which appear to be affected by drinking (Alling et al., 1993). Continued research on these topics will likely lead to development of new types of medications for reducing drinking.

Despite FDA approval of naltrexone, important clinical concerns yet remain on naltrexone and other agents that may reduce the urge to drank. For example, it is important to identify subtypes of alcoholics most responsive to medication. Current literature on "matching" alcoholic subtypes to alternative psychosocial interventions is quite encouraging (Mattson et al., 1994). The type and intensity of psychosocial therapy most effectively combined with medication also needs to be specified. Further, techniques to maximize compliance with medicational intervention need to be devised and evaluated. As noted above, patient compliance has proven problematic with disulfiram (Allen and Litten, 1992) and may also be of concern for naltrexone (Volpicelli et al., 1994).

Development of medications to treat alcoholics with comorbid psychiatric disorders remains in the early stages. Several fundamental research questions need to be addressed (Litten and Allen, 1995). For example, research should determine if alcoholics with psychiatric comorbidity respond differently to medications than do non-comorbid alcoholics. Also, it would be useful to explore how successful treatment of either alcoholism or psychiatric disorder relates to outcome for the other problem. Finally, it is important to develop algorithms to quickly and accurately identify psychiatric syndromes in alcoholics that do not abate simply with abstention from alcohol.

CONCLUSION

Significant advances have been made in the development of medications to treat alcoholism. Over the past two decades benzodiazepines have proven quite useful for managing acute alcohol withdrawal. Recent studies have indicated that more efficient dosing is possible by administering the medication hourly during the period of moderate to severe levels of withdrawal. Research continues to be needed on new medications that may be more effective than benzodiazepines and produce fewer side effects. Carbamazepine is currently the most promising medication in this regard.

Pharmacologic agents that reduce desire or craving to drink seem particularly promising. Recent FDA approval of the opioid antagonist naltrexone tangibly evidences this potential. Research continues to evaluate the efficacy and limitations of naltrexone and other opioid antagonists. Studies are also ongoing to investigate the therapeutic potential of several pharmacologic agents that interact with serotonergic, GABAergic, and dopaminergic systems.

Although disulfiram has been available for four decades, few well-designed trials have evaluated its efficacy. Recent studies have suggested that disulfiram can improve treatment outcome in certain types of alcoholics, particularly if techniques to enhance compliance are used. However, more research is needed on disulfiram, its metabolites (Hart and Faiman, 1994), and related aversive agents.

Alcoholics entering treatment often suffer comorbid psychiatric problems. A few studies have demonstrated buspirone to be helpful for reducing symptoms of anxiety, increasing treatment retention, and decreasing drinking in alcoholics with anxiety disorders. Also potentially useful are antidepressant serotonin reuptake inhibitors for depressed alcoholics. Development of successful medicational-psychosocial treatment regimen is also needed.

Pharmacotherapy has progressed remarkably during the past decade. Future research should elucidate further therapeutic potential of medications and advance understanding of how drugs can be incorporated into psychosocial therapies to further enhance treatment of alcoholism.

SUMMARY

- Over the past two decades benzodiazepines have proven effective in treating symptoms of acute alcohol withdrawal. Newer medications are being investigated including carbamazepine.

- The opioid antagonist naltrexone was recently approved by the FDA as an adjunct treatment of alcoholism to help reduce drinking and prevent relapse. Research is ongoing to further evaluate the efficacy and limitations of naltrexone as well as other opioid antagonists. Pharmacologic agents that interact with the serotonergic, GABAergic, and dopaminergic systems are also being investigated.

- Although only a few well-designed studies have been conducted over the past several decades dealing with efficacy of disulfiram, they nevertheless suggest that disulfiram may enhance treatment outcome in certain subtypes of alcoholics, particularly if used in conjunction with techniques to enhance compliance.

- Little research has been conducted on developing an effective pharmacological-behavioral therapy for alcoholics evidencing comorbid psychopathology. A few studies have indicated that buspirone may help reduce anxiety and increase treatment retention in alcoholics with comorbid anxiety disorder. In depressed alcoholics preliminary studies suggest that antidepressants are useful in not only decreasing depression, but also improving drinking outcome.

REFERENCES

Adinoff, B., Bone, G.H.A. and Linnoila, M. (1988) Acute ethanol poisoning and the ethanol withdrawal syndrome. *Med. Toxicol.* 3: 172–196.

Allen, J.P. and Litten, R.Z. (1992) Techniques to enhance compliance with disulfiram. *Alcohol Clin. Exp. Res.* 16: 1035–1041.

Allen, J.P. and Mattson, M.E. (1993) Strategies for the treatment of alcoholism. In: Giles, T.R. (ed.) *Handbook of effective psychotherapy.* New York: Plenum Press, pp. 379–406.

Alling, C., Diamond, I., Leslie, S.W., Sun, G.Y. and Wood, W.G. (1993) *Alcohol, cell membranes, and signal transduction in brain.* New York: Plenum Press.

Annis, H.M. and Peachey, J.E. (1992) The use of calcium carbimide in relapse prevention counselling: results of a randomized controlled trial. *Br. J. Addict.* 87: 63–72.

Azrin, N.H., Sisson, R.W., Meyers, R. & Godley, M. (1982) Alcoholism treatment by disulfiram and community-reinforcement therapy. *J. Behav. Ther. Exp. Psychiatry* 13: 105–112.

Balldin, J., Berggren, U., Engel, J., Eriksson, M., Hard, E. and Soderpalm B. (1994) Effect of citalopram on alcohol intake in heavy drinkers. *Alcohol Clin. Exp. Res.* 18: 1133–1136.

Bohn, M.J., Kranzler, H.R., Beazoglou, D. and Staehler, B.A. (1994) Naltrexone and brief counseling to reduce heavy drinking. *Am. J. Addict.* 3: 91–99.

Booth, B.M. and Blow, F.C. (1993) The kindling hypothesis: further evidence from a U.S. national study of alcoholic men. *Alcohol Alcohol.* 28: 593–598.

Borg, V. (1983) Bromocriptine in the prevention of alcohol abuse. *Acta Psychiatr. Scand.* 68: 100–110.

Brown, M.E., Anton, R.F., Malcolm, R. and Ballenger, J.C. (1988) Alcohol detoxification and withdrawal seizures: clinical support for a kindling hypothesis. *Biol. Psychiatry* 23: 507–514.

Bruno, F. (1989) Buspirone in the treatment of alcoholic patients. *Psychopathology* 22(suppl 1): 49–59.

Butler, D. and Messiha, F.S. (1986) Alcohol withdrawal and carbamazepine. *Alcohol* 3: 113–129.

Buydens-Branchey, L., Branchey, M.H., Noumair, D. and Lieber, C.S. (1989) Age of alcoholism onset: II. Relationship to susceptibility to serotonin precursor availability. *Arch. Gen. Psychiatry* 46: 231–236.

Carroll, K., Ziedonis, D., O'Malley, S., McCance-Katz, E., Gordon, L. and Rounsaville, B. (1993) Pharmacologic interventions for alcohol-and cocaine-abusing individuals. *Am. J. Addict.* 2: 77–79

Chick, J., Gough, K., Falkowski, W., Kershaw, P., Hore, B., Mehta, B., Ritson, B., Ropner, R. and Torley, D. (1992) Disulfiram treatment of alcoholism. *Br. J. Psychiatry* 161: 84–89.

Cornelius, J.R., Salloum, I.M., Cornelius, M.D., Perel, J.M., Thase, M.E., Ehler, J.G. and Mann, J.J. (1993) Fluoxetine trial in suicidal depressed alcoholics. *Psychopharmacol. Bull.* 29: 195–199.

Croop, R.S. (1995) An open label usage study of naltrexone as adjunctive pharmacotherapy for individuals with alcoholism. Presented at Research Society on Alcoholism Annual Scientific Meeting, Steamboat Springs, Colorado, June, 1995.

Dongier, M., Vachon, L. and Schwartz, G. (1991) Bromocriptine in the treatment of alcohol dependence. *Alcohol Clin. Exp. Res.* 15: 970–977.

Dyr, W., McBride, W.J., Lumeng, L., Li, T.K. and Murphy J.M. (1993) Effects of D_1 and D_2 dopamine receptor agents on ethanol consumption in the high-alcohol-drinking (HAD) line of rats. *Alcohol* 10: 207–212.

File, S.E., Zharkovsky, A. and Hitchcott, P.K. (1992) Effects of nitrendipine, chlordiazepoxide, flumazenil, and baclofen on the increased anxiety resulting from alcohol withdrawal. *Prog. Neuropsychopharmacol. Biol. Psychiatr.* 16: 87–93.

Fuller, R.K., Branchey, L., Brightwell, D.R., Derman, R. M. Emrick, C.D., Iber, F.L., James, K.E., Lacoursiere, R.B., Lee, K.K., Lowenstam, I., Maany, I., Neiderhiser, D., Nocks, J.J. and Shaw, S. (1986) Disulfiram treatment of alcoholism: A Veterans Administration cooperative study. *JAMA* 256: 1449–1455.

Fuller, R.K. and Gordis, E. (1994) Refining the treatment of alcohol withdrawal. *JAMA* 272: 557–558.

Gallant, D.M. (1992) One more look at carbamazepine in the treatment of alcohol withdrawal. *Alcohol Clin. Exp. Res.* 16: 1174–1175.

Gallant, D.M. and Pena, J.M. (1992) Plasma cortisol concentrations during ethanol withdrawal. *Alcohol Clin. Exp. Res.* 16: 139–140.

Gallimberti, L., Ferri, M., Ferrara, S.D., Fadda, F. and Gessa, G.L. (1992) Gamma-hydroxybutyric acid in the treatment of alcohol dependence: a double-blind study. *Alcohol Clin. Exp. Res.* 16: 673–676.

Gastpar, M., Rosinger, M. and Bender, C.S. (1994) A German multi-centre study with tiapride in the long-term management of alcoholics. *Neuropsychopharmacology* 10(3S/part 2): 72S.

Gerra, G., Caccavari, R., Delsignore, R., Bocchi, R., Fertonani, G. and Passeri, M. (1992) Effects of fluoxetine and Ca-acetyl-homotaurinate on alcohol intake in familial and nonfamilial alcoholic patients. *Curr. Ther. Res.* 52: 291–295.

Gerra, G., Caccavari, R., Volpi, R., Maninetti, L., Delsignore, R. and Coiro, V. (1991) Effectiveness of flumazenil in the treatment of ethanol withdrawal. *Curr. Ther. Res.* 50: 62–66.

Gorelick, D.A. (1989) Serotonin uptake blockers and the treatment of alcoholism. In: Galanter, M. (ed.) *Recent developments in alcoholism, vol 7: treatment research.* New York: Plenum Press, pp. 267–281.

Gorelick, D.A. and Paredes, A. (1992) Effect of fluoxetine on alcohol consumption in male alcoholics. *Alcohol Clin. Exp. Res.* 16: 261–265.

Grant, K.A., Valverius, P., Hudspith, M. and Tabakoff, B. (1990) Ethanol withdrawal seizures and the NMDA receptor complex. *Eur. J. Pharmacol.* 176: 289–296.

Hart, B.W. and Faiman, M.D. (1994) In vivo pharmacodynamic studies of the disulfiram metabolite S-methyl N,N-diethylthiolcarbamate sulfoxide: inhibition of liver aldehyde dehydrogenase. *Alcohol Clin. Exp. Res.* 18: 340–345.

Higgins, S.T., Budney, A.J., Bickel, W.K., Hughes, J.R. and Foreg, F. (1993) Disulfiram therapy in patients abusing cocaine and alcohol. *Am. J. Psychiatry* 150: 675–676.

Hodge, C.W., Samson, H.H. and Haraguchi, M. (1992) Microinjections of dopamine agonists in the nucleus accumbens increase ethanol-reinforced responding. *Pharmacol. Biochem. Behav.* 43: 249–254.

Hodge, C.W., Samson, H.H., Lewis, R.S. and Erickson, H.L. (1993) Specific decreases in ethanol- but not water-reinforced responding produced by the 5-HT$_3$ antagonist ICS 205-930. *Alcohol* 10: 191–196.

Hungund, B.L. and Mahadik, S.P. (1993) Role of gangliosides in behavioral and biochemical actions of alcohol: cell membrane structure and function. *Alcohol Clin. Exp. Res.* 17: 329–339.

Institute of Medicine (1989) *Prevention and treatment of alcohol problems: research opportunities.* Washington, DC: National Academy Press.

Johnson, B.A., Campling, G.M., Griffths, P. and Cowen, P.J. (1993) Attenuation of some alcohol-induced mood changes and the desire to drink by 5-HT$_3$ receptor blockade: a preliminary study in healthy male volunteers. *Psychopharmacology* 112: 142–144.

Johnson, B.A. and Cowen, P.J. (1993) Alcohol-induced reinforcement: dopamine and 5-HT$_3$ receptor interactions in animals and humans. *Drug Dev. Res.* 30: 153–169.

Johnson, B.A., Jasinski, D.R., Galloway, G.P., Kanzler, H., Weinreib, R., Anton, R., Mason, B., Bohn, M.J., Pettinati, H.M., Rawson, R., Clyde C. (1996) Ritanserin in the treatment of alcohol dependence—a multi-center clinical trial. *Psychopharmacology.* 128:206–215.

Koob, G.F. (1996) Drug addiction: The yin and yang of hedonic homeostasis. *Neuron* 16: 893–896.

Korpi, E.R. (1994) Role of GABA$_A$ receptors in the actions of alcohol and in alcoholism: recent advances. *Alcohol Alcohol.* 29: 115–129.

Kranzler, H.R., Burleson, J.A., Del Boca, F.K., Babor, T.F., Korner, P., Brown, J. and Bohn, M. (1994) Buspirone treatment of anxious alcoholics: a placebo-controlled trial. *Arch. Gen. Psychiatry* 51: 720–731.

Kranzler, H.R., Burleson, J.A., Korner, P., Del Boca, F.K., Bohn, M.J., Brown, J. and Liebowitz, N. (1995) Placebo-controlled trial of fluoxetine as an adjunct to relapse prevention in alcoholics. *Am. J. Psychiatry* 152: 391–397.

Kranzler, H.R., Del Boca, F., Korner, P. and Brown, J. (1993) Adverse effects limit the usefulness of fluvoxamine for the treatment of alcoholism. *J. Subst. Abuse Treat.* 10: 283–287.

Lhuintre, J.P., Daoust, M., Moore, N.D., Chretien, P., Saligaut, C., Tran, G., Boismare, F. and Hillemand, B. (1985) Ability of calcium bis acetyl homotaurine, a GABA agonist, to prevent relapse in weaned alcoholics. *Lancet* 1: 1014–1016.

Lhuintre, J.P., Moore, N., Tran, G., Steru, L., Langrenon, S., Daoust, M., Parot, Ph., Ladure, Ph., Libert, C., Boismare, F. and Hillemand, B. (1990) Acamprosate appears to decrease alcohol intake in weaned alcoholics. *Alcohol Alcohol.* 25: 613–622.

Lin, N. and Hubbard, J.I. (1994) The increased ethanol preference in rats induced by choice, darkness, or drugs is reduced by ritanserin. *Brain Res. Bull.* 33: 633–638.

Linnoila, M., DeJong, J. and Virkkunen, M. (1989) Family history of alcoholism in violent offenders and impulsive fire setters. *Arch. Gen. Psychiatry* 46: 613–616.

Linnoila, M.I. and Virkkunen, M. (1992) Aggression, suicidality and serotonin. *J. Clin. Psychiatry* 53(suppl): 46–51.

Liskow, B.I. and Goodwin, D.W. (1987) Pharmacological treatment of alcohol intoxication, withdrawal and dependence: a critical review. *J. Stud. Alcohol* 48: 356–370

Litten, R.Z. and Allen, J.P. (1991) Pharmacotherapies for alcoholism: promising agents and clinical issues. *Alcohol Clin. Exp.* Res. 15: 620–633.

Litten, R.Z. and Allen, J.P. (1993) Reducing the desire to drink: pharmacology and neurobiology. In: Galanter, M. (ed.) *Recent developments in alcoholism, vol. 11: ten years of progress.* New York: Plenum Press, pp. 325–344.

Litten, R.Z. and Allen, J.P. (1994) Pharmacological therapies of alcohol addiction. In: Miller, N.S. and Gold, M.S.

(eds.) *Pharmacological therapies in drug and alcohol disorders*. New York: Marcel Dekker, pp. 127–141.

Litten, R.Z. and Allen, J.P. (1995) Pharmacotherapy for alcoholics with collateral depression or anxiety: An update of research findings. *Exp. Clin. Psychopharmacol.* 3: 87–93.

Malcolm, R., Anton, R.F., Randall, C.L., Johnston, A., Brady, K. and Thevos, A. (1992) A placebo-controlled trial of buspirone in anxious inpatient alcoholics. *Alcohol Clin. Exp. Res.* 16: 1007–1013.

Malcolm, R., Ballenger, J.C., Sturgis, E.T. and Anton, R. (1989) Double-blind controlled trial comparing carbamazepine to oxazepam treatment of alcohol withdrawal. *Am. J. Psychiatry* 146: 617–621.

Mason, B.J. and Kocsis, M.D. (1991) Desipramine treatment of alcoholism. *Psychopharmacol. Bull.* 27: 155–161.

Mason, B.J., Ritvo, E.C., Morgan R.O., Salvato, F.R., Goldberg, G., Welch, B. and Mantero-Atienza, E. (1994) A double-blind, placebo-controlled pilot study to evaluate the efficacy and safety of oral nalmefene HCl for alcohol dependence. *Alcohol Clin. Exp. Res.* 18: 1162–1167.

Mattson, M.E., Allen, J.P., Longabaugh, R., Nickless, C.J., Connors, G. and Kadden, R. (1994) A chronological review of empirical studies matching alcoholic clients to treatment. *J. Stud. Alcohol Suppl.* 12: 16–29.

Meert, T.F. and Janssen, P.A.J. (1991) Ritanserin, a new therapeutic approach for drug abuse. Part 1: effects on alcohol. *Drug Dev. Res.* 24: 235–249.

Michels, R. and Marzuk, P.M. (1993) Progress in psychiatry (second of two parts). *N. Engl. J. Med.* 329: 628–638.

Monti, J.M. and Alterwain, P. (1991) Ritanserin decreases alcohol intake in chronic alcoholics. *Lancet* 337: 60.

Myers, R.D., Lankford, M.F. and Bjork, A. (1993) 5-HT$_2$ receptor blockade by amperozide suppresses ethanol drinking in genetically preferring rats. *Pharmacol. Biochem. Behav.* 45: 741–747.

Naranjo, C.A., Kadlec, K.E., Sanhueza, P., Woodley-Remus, D. and Sellers, E.M. (1990) Fluoxetine differentially alters alcohol intake and other consummatory behaviors in problem drinkers. *Clin. Pharmacol. Ther.* 47: 490–498.

Naranjo, C.A., Poulos, C.X., Bremner, K.E. and Lanctot, K.L. (1992) Citalopram decreases desirability, liking, and consumption of alcohol in alcohol-dependent drinkers. *Clin. Pharmacol. Ther.* 51: 729–739.

Naranjo, C.A. and Sellers, E.M. (1986) Clinical assessment and pharmacotherapy of the alcohol withdrawal syndrome. In: Galanter, M. (ed.) *Recent developments in alcoholism*, vol 4. New York: Plenum Press, pp. 265–281.

Naranjo, C.A., Sellers, E.M., Chater, K., Iversen, P., Roach, C. and Sykora, K. (1983) Nonpharmacologic intervention in acute alcohol withdrawal. *Clin. Pharmacol. Ther.* 34: 214–219.

Naranjo, C.A., Sellers, E.M., Roach, C.A., Woodley, D.V., Sanchez-Craig, M. and Sykora, K. (1984) Zimelidine-induced variations in alcohol intake by nondepressed heavy drinkers. *Clin. Pharmacol. Ther.* 35: 374–381.

Naranjo, C.A., Sellers, E.M., Sullivan, J.T., Woodley, D.V., Kadlec, K. and Sykora, K. (1987) The serotonin uptake inhibitor citalopram attenuate ethanol intake. *Clin. Pharmacol. Ther.* 41: 266–274.

Naranjo, C.A., Sullivan, J.T., Kadlec, K.E., Woodley-Remus, D.V., Kennedy, G. and Sellers, E.M. (1989) Differential effects of viqualine on alcohol intake and other consumatory behaviors. *Clin. Pharmacol. Ther.* 46: 301–309.

National Institute on Alcohol Abuse and Alcoholism (1993) *Eighth special report to the U.S. Congress on alcohol and*

health. Rockville, MD: U.S. Department of Health and Human Services.

Nunes, E.V., McGrath, P.J., Quitkin, F.M., Stewart, J.P., Harrison, W., Tricamo, E. and Ocepek-Welikson, K. (1993) Imipramine treatment of alcoholism with comorbid depression. *Am. J. Psychiatry* 150: 963–965.

Nutt, D., Adinoff, B. and Linnoilia, M. (1989) Benzodiazepines in the treatment of alcoholism. In: Galanter, M. (ed.) *Recent developments in alcoholism, vol 7: treatment research*. New York: Plenum Press, pp. 283–313.

Nutt, D., Flue, P., Wilson, S., Groves, S., Coupland N. and Bailey, J. (1993) Flumazenil in alcohol withdrawal. *Alcohol Alcohol. Suppl.* 2: 337–341.

O'Malley, S.S., Jaffe, A.J., Chang, G., Schottenfeld, R.S., Meyer, R.E. and Rounsaville, B. (1992) Naltrexone and coping skills therapy for alcohol dependence. *Arch. Gen. Psychiatry* 49: 881–887.

Panocka, I. and Massi, M. (1992) Long-lasting suppression of alcohol preference in rats following serotonin receptor blockade by ritanserin. *Brain Res. Bull.* 28: 493–499.

Panocka, I., Pompei, P. and Massi, M. (1993) Suppression of alcohol preference in rats induced by risperidone, a serotonin 5-HT$_2$ and dopamine D$_2$ receptor antagonist. *Brain Res. Bull.* 31: 595–599.

Peters, D.H. and Faulds, D. (1994) Tiapride: a review of its pharmacology and therapeutic potential in the management of alcohol dependence syndrome. *Drugs* 47: 1010–1032.

Pfeffer, A.O. and Samson, H.H. (1988) Haloperidol and apomorphine effects on ethanol reinforcement in free feeding rats. *Pharmacol. Biochem. Behav.* 29: 343–350.

Rassnick, S., Heinrichs, S.C., Britton, K.T. and Koob, G.F. (1993a) Microinjection of a corticotropin-releasing factor antagonist into the central nucleus of the amygdala reverses anxiogenic-like effects of ethanol withdrawal. *Brain Res.* 605: 25–32.

Rassnick, S., Pulvirenti, L. and Koob, G.F. (1992) Oral ethanol self-administration in rats is reduced by the administration of dopamine and glutamate receptor antagonists into the nucleus accumbens. *Psychopharmacology* 109: 92–98.

Rassnick, S., Pulvirenti, L. and Koob, G.F. (1993b) SDZ-205,152 a novel dopamine receptor agonist, reduces oral ethanol self-administration in rats. *Alcohol* 10: 127–132.

Saitz, R., Mayo-Smith, M.F., Roberts, M.S., Redmond, H.A., Bernard, D.R. and Calkins, D.R. (1994) Individualized treatment for alcohol withdrawal: a randomized double-blind controlled trial. *JAMA* 272: 519–523.

Sapolsky, R.M. (1993) Glucocorticoid neurotoxicity: Is this effect relevant to alcoholic neurotoxicity? In: Zakhari, S. (ed.) *Alcohol and the endocrine system*. NIAAA Research Monograph No. 23. Washington, DC: U.S. Government Printing Office, pp. 271–280.

Sellers, E.M., Naranjo, C.A., Harrison, M., Devenyi, P., Roach, C. and Sykora, K. (1983) Diazepam loading: simplified treatment of alcohol withdrawal. *Clin. Pharmacol. Ther.* 34: 822–826.

Sellers, E.M., Toneatto, T., Romach, M.K., Somer, G.R., Sobell, L.C. and Sobell, M.B. (1994) Clinical efficacy of the 5-HT$_3$ antagonist ondansetron in alcohol abuse and dependence. *Alcohol Clin. Exp. Res.* 18: 879–885.

Shaw, G.K., Majumdar, S.K., Waller, S., MacGarvie, J. and Dunn, G. (1987) Tiapride in the long-term management of alcoholics of anxious or depressive temperament. *Br. J. Psychiatry* 150: 164–168.

Shaw, G.K., Waller, S., Majumdar, S.K., Alberts, J.L., Latham, C.J. and Dunn, G. (1994) Tiapride in the prevention of relapse in recently detoxified alcoholics. *Br. J. Psychiatry* 165: 515–523.

Stuppaeck, C.H., Pycha, R., Miller, C., Whitworth, A.B., Oberbauer, H. and Fleischhacker, W.W. (1992) Carbamazepine versus oxazepam in the treatment of alcohol withdrawal: a double-blind study. *Alcohol Alcohol.* 27: 153–158.

Sullivan, J.T., Swift, R.M. and Lewis, D.C. (1991) Benzodiazepine requirements during alcohol withdrawal syndrome: clinical implications of using a standardized withdrawal scale. *J. Clin. Psychopharmacol.* 11: 291–295.

Swift, R.M., Whelihan W., Kuznetsov, O., Buongiorno, G. and Hsuing, H. (1994) Naltrexone-induced alterations in human ethanol intoxication. *Am. J. Psychiatry* 151: 1463–1467.

Tollefson, G.D., Montague-Clouse, J. and Tollefson, S.L. (1992) Treatment of comorbid generalized anxiety in a recently detoxified alcoholic population with a selective serotonergic drug (buspirone). *J. Clin. Psychopharmacol.* 12: 19–26.

Volpicelli, J.R., Alterman, A.I., Hayashida, M. and O'Brien, C.P. (1992) Naltrexone in the treatment of alcohol dependence. *Arch. Gen. Psychiatry* 49: 876–880.

Volpicelli, J.R., O'Brien, C.P. and Watson, N.T. (1994) Naltrexone therapy for alcoholism: recent findings. Presented at American Psychiatric Association Annual Meeting, Philadelphia, Pennsylvania.

Volpicelli, J.R., Watson, N.T., King, A.C., Sherman, C.E. and O'Brien, C.P. (1995) Effect of naltrexone on alcohol "high" in alcoholics. *Am. J. Psychiatry* 152: 613–615.

Wartenberg, A.A., Nirenberg, T.D., Liepman, M.R., Silvia, L.Y., Begin, A.M. and Monti, P.M. (1990) Detoxification of alcoholics: improving care by symptom-triggered sedation. *Alcohol Clin. Exp. Res.* 14: 71–75.

Whitfield, C.L., Thompson, G., Lamb, A., Spencer, V., Pfeifer, M. and Browning-Ferrando, M. (1978) Detoxification of 1,024 alcoholic patients without psychoactive drugs. *JAMA* 239: 1409–1410.

Zakhari, S. and Witt, E. (1992) *Imaging in alcohol research.* DHHS Publication No. (ADM)92-1890. Rockville, MD: DHHS.

Zeise, M.L., Kasparov, S., Capogna, M. and Zieglgansberger, W. (1993) Acamprosate (calcium acetylhomotaurinate) decreases postsynaptic potentials in the rat neocortex: possible involvement of excitatory amino acid receptors. *Eur. J. Pharmacol.* 231: 47–52.

Subject Index

drug reinforcement and, 141–144
GABA, 144
opioids, 143–144
serotonin, 142–143
Neurotransmitters
drug reinforcement and, 159–160
Nicotine dependence. *See also* Tobacco
dependence
pharmacotherapy and, 396–397
Nondrug reinforcement
drug reinforcement and, 26–27
Nutritional insufficiences
drug-induced, 234, 238–239

O

Operant behavior
assumptions of, 41–44
definition, 39, 40
discriminative stimuli and, 40
drug-taking and, 39–41
experimental analysis of behavior and, 40
principles of, 41–44
strategies of investigation, 41–44
Operant extinction
integrated treatments and, 405
Opiate receptor antagonists
drug self-administration and, 145–146, 148, 149
Opiate receptors, 305–307, 308–310
Opiates
analysis methods, 213
reinforcing efficacy summary, 104
state markers and, 215–216
typical response profile, 103
Opioid antagonists
alcohol abuse and, 423–424
Opioid peptides
as addiction biological markers, 210
Opioid pharmacotherapies, 387–401. *See also*
Pharmacotherapy
Opioids
acute withdrawal form, 387
drug reinforcement and, 143–144, 145–146, 148–149
Opponent processes
cellular, 181, 182–183
general principles of, 180, 181
system opposition, 181–182
tolerance and, 180–183. *See also* Tolerance
whole animal, 180–181
Oral drug reinforcement, 7–10
concurrent access method, 9
drug access, 9
drug-admixed food, 9–10
fading method, 9

food-induced drinking, 8–9
schedule-induced polydypsia, 8
substitution method, 9
Organismic variables
drug reinforcement and, 24–25
Own-price elasticity of demand
behavioral economics and, 74–75, 76

P

P300 waveforms
brain mapping and, 268–269, 271
Pair feeding
drug studies and, 234, 238–239
Pattern of responding
drug reinforcement and, 4–5
Pavlovian conditioning
addiction and, 116. *See also* Classical
conditioning
Persistent drug-taking behavior, 39–71. *See also*
Human drug self-administration
Pharmacogenetics
behavioral genetics and, 187. *See also*
Behavioral genetics
Pharmacotherapy. *See also* Integrated treatments;
Medicational aids
acute, 393–393
acute withdrawal, 388–389
agonist interventions, 406
AIDS and, 387
antagonist interventions, 406
blockade and, 406
clinical efficacy of, 387–401
cocaine, 391
components of, 404–407
cross-tolerance and, 406
drug action analysis and, 405–407
drug metabolism interventions, 406–407
future directions, 397–398
maintenance, 389–391, 393–396, 398
nicotine dependence and, 396–397
opioid, 387–401
sedative dependence and, 397
summary points, 398
symptomatic treatment interventions, 407
Pharmacotherapy development
interoceptive stimulus effects, 107–108
Phencyclidine
analysis methods, 213
Placebo
human drug self-administration studies and, 57–58
Polydypsia
schedule-induced, 8
Polymorphisms
allelic, 200. *See also* Behavioral genetics